Darrell Young

Mastering the
Nikon Z6

rockynook

NikoniansPress

Mastering the Nikon Z6
Darrell Young (a.k.a. Digital Darrell)
www.PictureAndPen.com

Editor: Jocelyn Howell
Project manager: Lisa Brazieal
Marketing coordinator: Mercedes Murray
Layout and type: Petra Strauch
Cover design: Helmut Kraus, www.exclam.de
Indexer: Darrell Young
Back Cover Photo: © Jacques Grilli (grillij)

ISBN: 978-1-68198-480-3
1st Edition (1st printing, November 2019)
© 2020 Darrell Young
All images © Darrell Young unless otherwise noted

Rocky Nook, Inc.
1010 B Street, Suite 350
San Rafael, CA 94901
USA

www.rockynook.com

Distributed in the U.S. by Ingram Publisher Services
Distributed in the UK and Europe by Publishers Group UK

Library of Congress Control Number: 2019942801

This book is printed on acid-free paper.
Printed in China

This book is dedicated to:

My wonderful wife of many years, Brenda, the love of my life and best friend…

*My children, Autumn, David, Emily, Hannah, and Ethan,
five priceless gifts…*

*My dear mother and late father, Barbara and Vaughn, who brought me into this world
and quided my early life, teaching me sound principles to live by…*

*My friends J. Ramón Palacios and Bo Stahlbrandt, who make it possible to belong to
Nikonians.org, the world's best Nikon Users' Community …*

*The staff of Rocky Nook, including Scott Cowlin, Ted Waitt, Jocelyn Howell,
Maggie Yates, Mercedes Murray, and Lisa Brazieal…*

And, finally, to Nikon, who makes the world's best cameras and lenses.

Special thanks to:

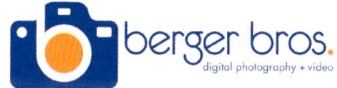

Brad Berger of **www.Berger-Bros.com** (800-542-8811) for helping me obtain a Nikon Z6 early in the camera's release cycle so that I could write this book. For 11 years now, I have purchased my camera equipment from Brad Berger. I highly recommend Berger-Bros.com for your cameras, lenses, and accessories. Berger-Bros offers the best customer service I have ever experienced, fast shipping, and they even have classes for your photographic educational needs!

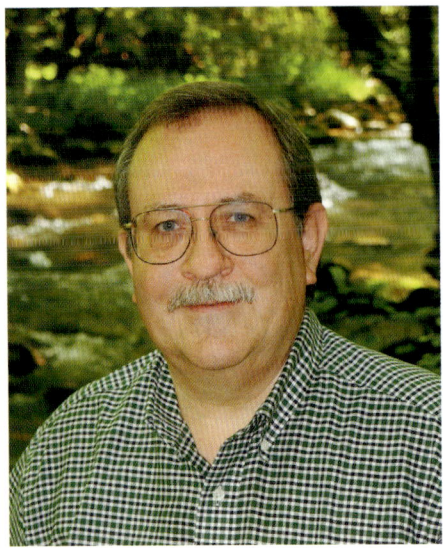

Darrell Young (*DigitalDarrell*) is a full-time author and professional photographer, with a background in information technology engineering. He has been an avid photographer since 1968 when his mother gave him a Brownie Hawkeye camera.

Darrell has used Nikon cameras and Nikkor lenses since 1980. He has an incurable case of Nikon Acquisition Syndrome (NAS) and delights in working with Nikon's newest digital cameras. Living near Great Smoky Mountains National Park, Blue Ridge Parkway, and Cherohala Skyway has given him a real concern for the natural environment and a deep interest in nature photography. You'll often find him standing behind a tripod in the beautiful mountains of Tennessee and North Carolina, USA.

Darrell loves to write, as you can see in the Resources area of the Nikonians Online community (**Nikonians.org**) and on his blog, *Master Your Nikon* (**MasterYourNikon.com**). He joined the Nikonians community in 2000, and his literary contributions led to an invitation to become the founding member of the Nikonians Writers Guild.

Table of Contents

Foreword

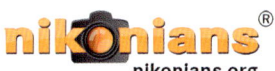
nikonians.org

This is the 19th Anniversary of the Nikonians® community and this is the 20th book of the Mastering the Nikon DSLR and Z series books, authored by Nikonian Darrell Young (known to us as *DigitalDarrell*). This joint venture between Nikonians Press and Rocky Nook has developed a strong following in the "camera instruction" genre and Darrell's fastidious attention to detail has been the key ingredient in that trend.

The Nikon Z6 is Nikon's answer to the major paradigm shift that mirrorless photography has become. With its big, luxurious 24.5 MP backlit FX imaging sensor (CMOS BSI) and the new more powerful EXPEED 6 microprocessor, it has expanded dynamic range and image quality like few other mirrorless cameras today. The Z6 is an advanced digital single-lens mirrorless (DSLM) camera, with a lightweight, weather-sealed, magnesium-alloy body, excellent in-body image stabilization, 273-point autofocus system, live histogram, exposure preview of images, up to 12-fps image capture, 4K 10-bit N-log 4:2:2 HDMI video output, and the ability to use not only the amazing new Nikkor Z lenses, but also our dependable F-mount Nikkor lenses via the FTZ adapter. The Nikon Z6 is faster and more feature rich than even some of the world's most expensive cameras. Its external control system has been refined so that all controls are within easy reach for various hand sizes, plus it has the new fingertip touch, pinch, and swipe control interface for smartphone-like handling of camera menus and internal settings.

We fully agree with Darrell's statement: "*Because of the multi-genre focus of the Nikon Z6, it can be successfully used for anything from unhurried landscapes to natural history photography. It can easily handle portraiture, along with family and event photography and video. The Nikon Z6 gives a strong edge to advanced amateur, enthusiast, and professional photographers and videographers. If you want to carry just one comparatively lightweight camera with you for all styles of photography and excellent video capture, the new Nikon Z6 will do the job.*"

We are proud to include Darrell's body of work in our ever-growing and never-ending resources for our community, such as the Nikonians forums, The Nikonian eZine, Nikonians Academy Workshops, Nikonians News Blog, our Wiki, Galleries, Members' Portfolios, eBooks, and newsletters. Our community continues to grow as we now surpass 575,000 members on record.

Nikonians has earned a reputation as a friendly, reliable, informative, and passionate Nikon® user's community, thanks in great measure to members like our own Digital Darrell, who have taken the time to share the results of their experiences with Nikon imaging equipment.

Enjoy this book, the Nikonians community, and your Nikons.

J. Ramón Palacios (jrp) and Bo Stahlbrandt (bgs)
Nikonians Founders **www.nikonians.org**

Camera Body Reference

Following are the locations and names of all the controls mentioned in this book. You may want to place a bookmark here so you can refer back to this control location reference list when an unfamiliar control name is mentioned in the book. This list covers 53 separate external camera controls, showing their locations and Nikon-supplied names.

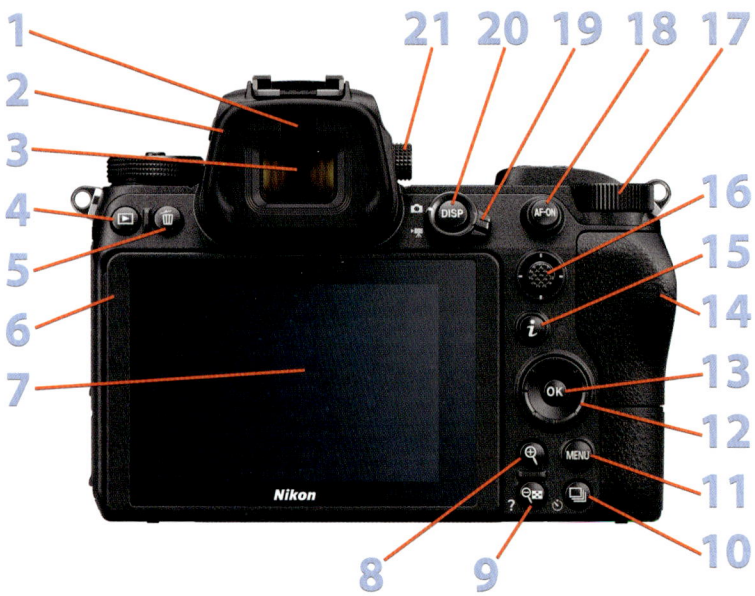

Figure 1: Back of camera

Back of Camera (figure 1)

1. Eye sensor
2. Viewfinder (EVF) eyepiece (removable rubber attachment)
3. Viewfinder (EVF)
4. Playback button
5. Delete button
6. Tilting monitor frame
7. Monitor
8. Zoom in button
9. Zoom out/Help button
10. Release mode/Self-timer button
11. MENU button
12. Multi selector pad
13. OK button
14. Memory card slot cover/Thumb rest
15. *i* button (for *i* Menu)
16. Sub-selector joystick
17. Main command dial
18. AF-ON button (back-button focus)
19. Photo/movie selector lever
20. DISP button
21. Diopter adjustment control

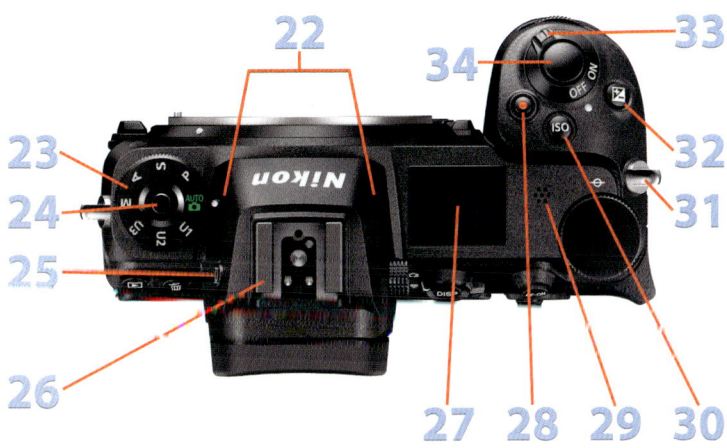

Figure 2: Top of camera

Top of Camera (figure 2)

22. Stereo microphone (left and right)
23. Mode dial
24. Mode dial lock release button
25. Monitor mode button
26. Accessory shoe (hotshoe)
27. Control panel
28. Movie-record button
29. Speaker (sound output)
30. ISO button
31. Strap eyelet post (pair on either side of camera)
32. +/− Exposure compensation button
33. Power switch (ON/OFF)
34. Shutter-release button

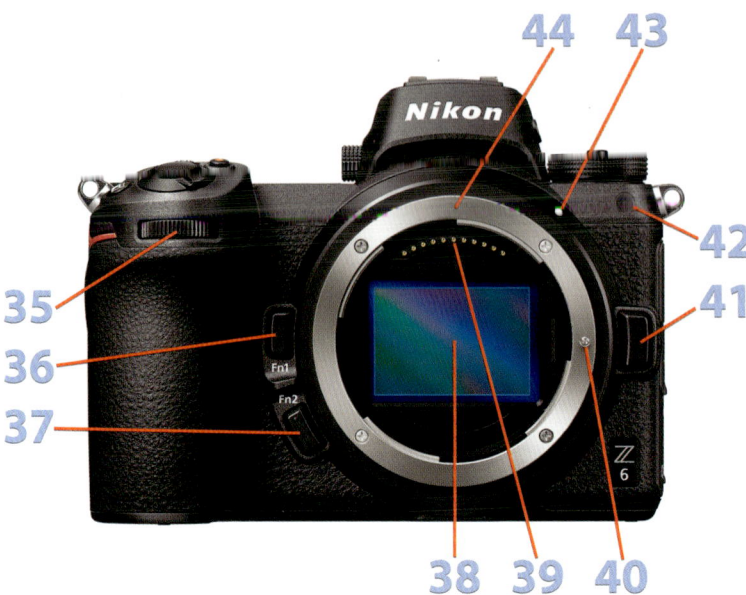

Figure 3: Front of camera

Front of Camera (figure 3)

35. Sub-command dial
36. Fn1 button
37. Fn2 button
38. Image sensor
39. CPU contacts (lens electronic connections)
40. Lens lock pin (retracted with Lens release button #41)
41. Lens release button
42. AF-assist illuminator/Red-eye reduction lamp/Self-timer lamp
43. Lens mounting mark (align with dot on lens)
44. Lens mount (Z-mount)

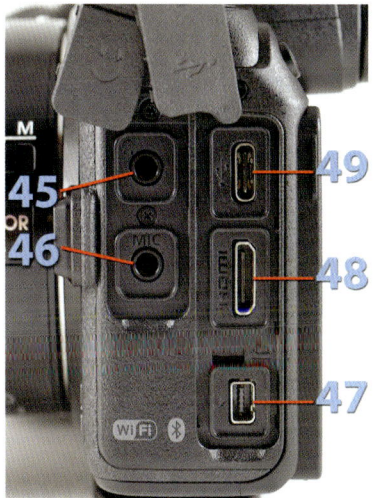

Figure 4: Camera connectors under the rubber Connector cover

External Connectors (figure 4)

45. Headphone connector
46. Microphone connector
47. Accessory terminal
48. HDMI connector (mini C)
49. USB connector (USB C)

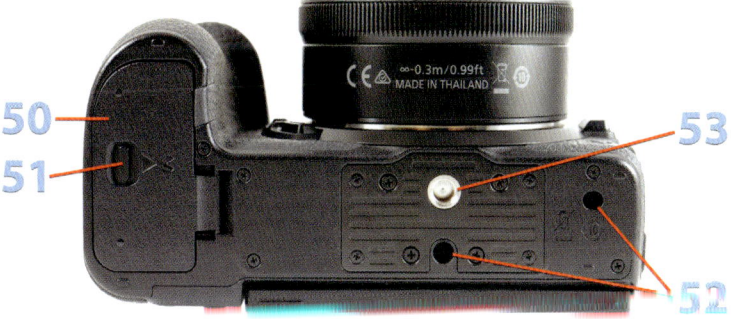

Figure 5: Bottom of camera

Bottom of Camera (figure 5)

50. Battery-chamber cover
51. Battery-chamber cover latch
52. Alignment sockets for optional battery pack
53. Tripod socket

Colors and Wording Legend

Throughout the book, you'll notice that in the numbered, step-by-step instructions there are colored terms as well as terms that are displayed in italic font.

1. Blue is used to refer to the camera's physical features.
2. Green is for functions and settings displayed on the camera's LCD screens.
3. Purple is for physical camera controls that also have touchscreen counterparts when a choice of control is involved. You can choose to touch the control with your fingertip on the camera's Monitor, or you can press a physical camera button. A good example is the physical OK button and the OK selection on the camera's touch screens.
4. *Italic* is for textual prompts seen on the camera's LCD screens.
5. *Italic* or ***bold italic*** is also used on select occasions for special emphasis.

Here is a sample paragraph with the colors and italic font in use:

Press the MENU button, select the Setup Menu, and then choose the Format memory card option by pressing the down arrow on the Multi selector pad, or by tapping the option with your fingertip. You will see the following message: *All images on Memory card will be deleted. OK?* Select Yes and then press or touch the OK control. ***Please make sure you've transferred all your images first!***

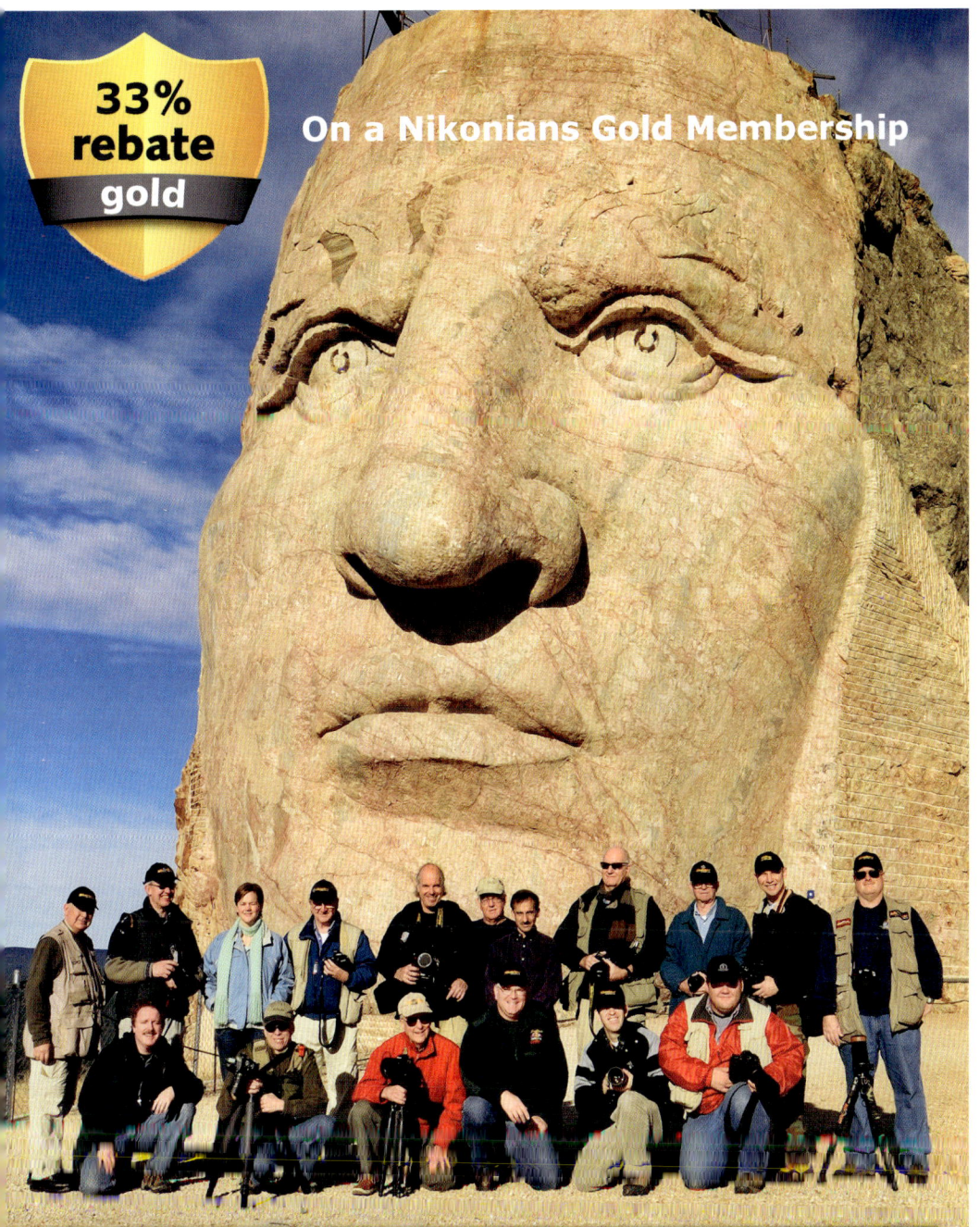

1 Introduction and Initial Camera Setup

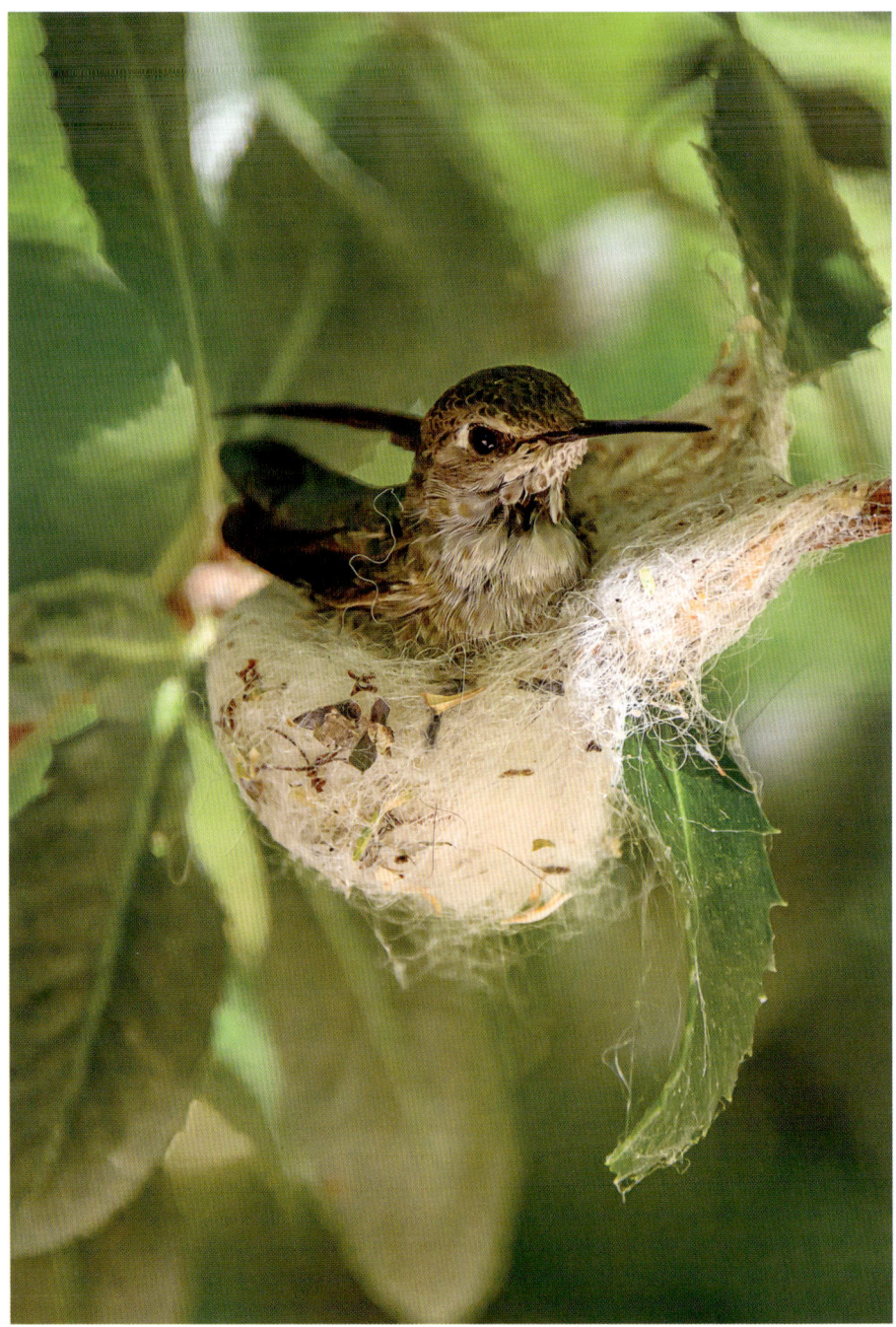

Ready for Her Chicks © 2019 Fred Crowden (*freqflyerfred*)

Congratulations on your purchase of a Nikon Z6 camera, one of the most exciting new Nikons released in several years! The Z6 is a full-frame (FX), mirrorless interchangeable lens camera (MILC) in Nikon's professional line of digital cameras.

The Z6 has a radio-frequency control system built in, including Wi-Fi and low-energy Bluetooth, so it can communicate directly with your smart device (smartphone and tablet) using the Nikon SnapBridge app. You can manually or automatically send pictures and videos to your smart device (2 megapixel or full-size), embed Global Positioning Satellite (GPS) location data into your images, and even use your smart device to control the camera remotely.

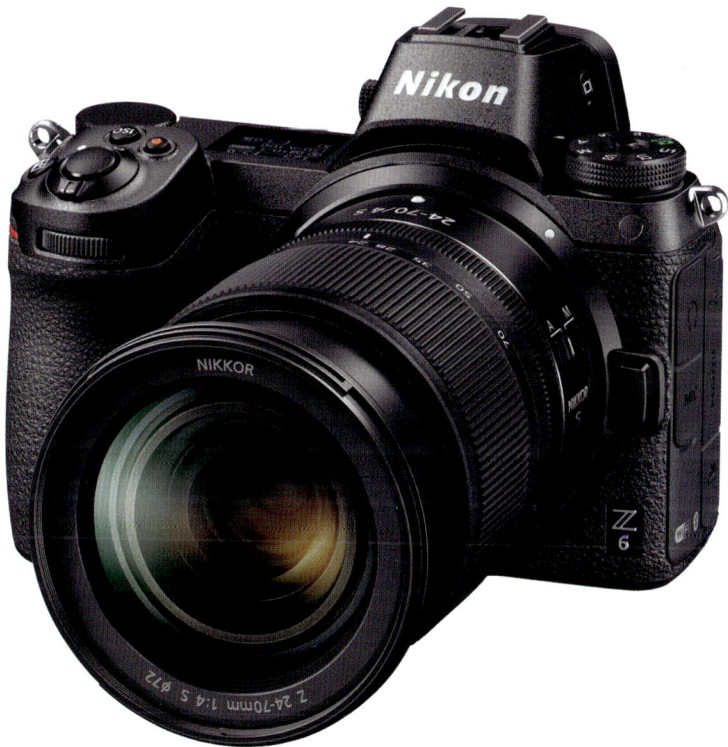

Additionally, with the purchase of a Nikon WR-10 Wireless Remote Controller set, you can use the Z6 to control other Nikon cameras in a master/slave relationship, or multiple banks of Speedlight flash units. The cool thing is that you are using radio-frequency control to do all these things, including flash control (with compatible flash units).

The Z6 simply has everything a professional or enthusiast photographer needs to bring home incredibly good images. The high resolution of the 24.5 MP sensor, for superb still images and clean, broadcast-quality video makes the Z6 one of the world's best hybrid-digital, mirrorless cameras. The video subsystem provides Full HD (1080p) and UHD 4K (2160p), with 8-bit H.264 internal video to the XQD card, or 10-bit N-Log video to an external recorder.

The Z6 has a compact BSI (backlit) CMOS full-frame sensor, a 200,000-frame shutter, a tilting screen, robust magnesium alloy construction, extensive weather sealing, 273 auto-focus points, and a massive new Z-mount for some of the sharpest lenses Nikon has ever made, just to mention a few of the camera's features!

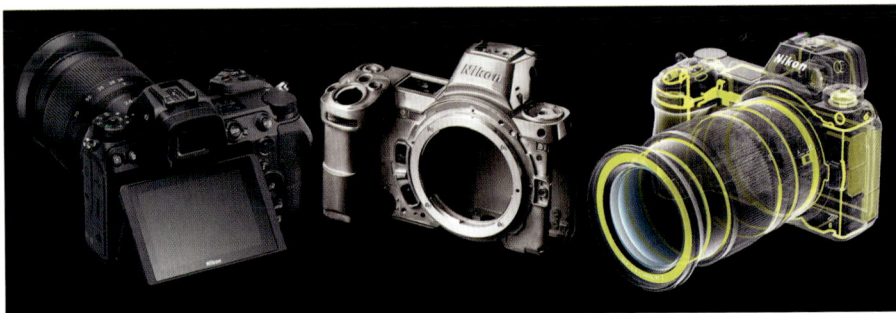

The camera has a compact, yet robust, 20.7 ounce (585 gram) body designed to last. Instead of buying a new mirrorless every couple of years, you can invest in new Nikkor Z lenses instead.

The Z6 has implemented a complete touchscreen system that allows you to adjust most of the camera's functions and features without using the Multi selector. You can select camera menus and submenus, and make adjustments, by tapping on the LCD Monitor. You can pinch and stretch with your fingers to zoom out and in on an image, and you can swipe to change to a different image, just like you do on your smartphone.

You can use the Z6's electronic viewfinder (EVF) to display and adjust menu settings, change camera settings, preview images, and examine pictures and videos after the fact. If you want, you can turn off the rear LCD monitor and use the EVF instead for virtually all camera functions.

As mentioned, the EVF allows you to preview an image before you take it. When you make adjustments to exposure and color balance, without taking your eye away from the viewfinder, you will instantly see the result.

You can use a live histogram in the EVF, too, to achieve the most accurate exposures possible. The Z6's EVF is so sharp, fast, and crystal clear that you might forget you are using an electronic viewfinder.

You can use Nikon's new Z-mount lenses, or with the optional Nikon FTZ adapter, you can use your favorite F-mount Nikkor lenses. Nikon claims that more than 350 different F-mount Nikkor lenses can be mounted on the FTZ adapter. This gives you a wide choice of existing lenses to use while Nikon develops new Z-mount Nikkor S lenses. The S lenses are decidedly sharper edge-to-edge, even wide open, due to the short 16mm flange distance (from rear of lens to front of sensor) and large rear lens elements. The Nikkor S-lens's large rear elements and specialized internal design allows more light to pass through, and the light rays hit the sensor at a more direct angle, which drastically reduces chromatic and other aberrations.

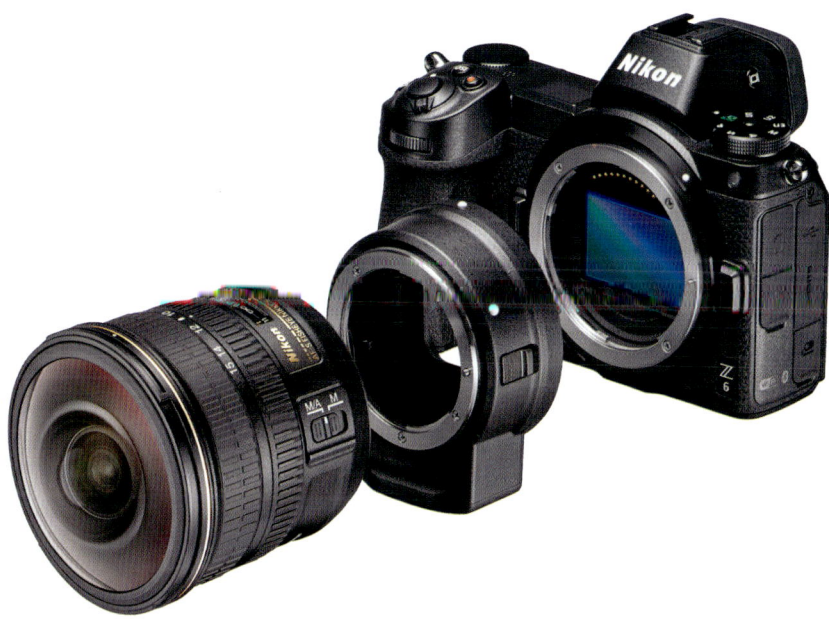

The camera has in-body 5-axis image stabilization (page 267) with Z-mount lenses, and in-body 3-axis image stabilization for F-mount lenses on the FTZ adapter. Since the stabilization is built into the camera body, all lenses—even older manual focus lenses—mounted on the camera or adapter have VR (vibration reduction). Imagine using your older Nikkors that do not have VR and being able to handhold them at slower shutter speeds (up to five stops). In-body VR—aka IBIS (in body image stabilization)—really makes a difference for those who like to handhold the camera.

Mirrorless has finally arrived for Nikon users! We have waited a long time for this fine new camera. Let's continue in our quest to master the Nikon Z6.

Use This Book with Camera in Hand

Having written books for most of the enthusiast and professional small-bodied Nikon camera models that have been released since 2007, I have seen the complexity of Nikon mirrorless cameras grow with each new generation. In my experience, the Nikon Z6 is one of the most complex and feature-rich Nikons I have ever used.

This camera is extremely customizable. It has multiple programmable buttons and dials that allow you to use it for virtually any style of photography. To get the best results out of the camera, it is important to spend time with this book with your camera in hand.

Use *Mastering the Nikon Z6* to carefully examine each of the features built into the camera so that you will be prepared to use it for better photography later. Prepare to experiment so that you can wrap your mind around some of the new, powerful features. There are many of them!

Without further ado, let's learn how to configure and use your new Z6.

What Is the Purpose of This Book?

Mastering the Nikon Z6 is not so much a book about general photography principles as it is a book about understanding the workings of the Nikon Z6. Photographic principles are discussed, but only in relation to how a certain control or setting will affect the execution of that principle.

In other words, this book does not directly teach you how to become a better photographer, but instead shows how the Z6 works so that you can use it expertly to make great pictures. There are many, many books out there that will help you become a better photographer with any camera. This book gives you a deep understanding of the Nikon Z6 so that you can use it to its maximum potential.

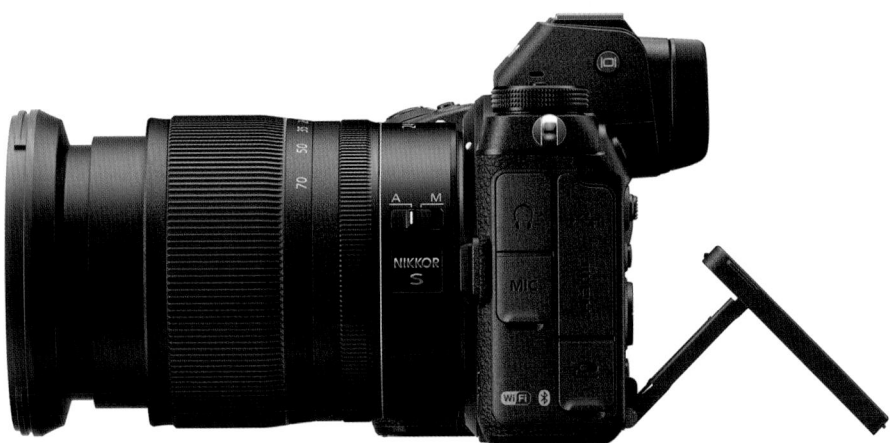

In this book, I have attempted to balance the needs of a new mirrorless user with the needs of an enthusiast or professional photographer. I cover the entire camera in great detail, with easy-to-understand terms, tips, and suggestions, so that you will have a complete understanding of its many settings.

There are literally hundreds of things that may be configured on this advanced mirrorless camera. In this chapter, I'll give a new Z6 user a place to start. Later, as you progress through this book, we'll look at all the buttons, switches, dials, and menu settings in detail, which will allow you to fully master the operation of your Nikon Z6.

Each menu in the camera has its own chapter or section. Plus, there is additional information on how to put it all together in chapters like **Camera Control Screens**; **Metering, Exposure Modes, and Histogram**; **White Balance**; and **Focus, AF-Area, and Release Modes**.

Things to Know When Reading This Book

Here are a couple of things you'll need to remember as you read this book:

- I use Nikon-assigned names for the controls on the camera, as found in the Nikon Z6 User's Manual (and Reference Manual). For instance, I may say something like "press the Zoom out button" to show you how to execute some function, and you'll need to know where this button is located. Use the **Camera Body Reference** in the front of the book to memorize the locations of the camera controls.
- I list a few page numbers from the Nikon User and Reference Manuals for things like big reference charts that are not included in this book. Nikon replaced their older User and Reference manuals when they released firmware version C2.00, taking their individual Z7 and Z6 User and Reference Manuals and creating combined Z7/Z6 User and Reference Manuals. You may want to download these new combined manuals if you have updated your camera to firmware C2.00. Here is a link for both:
  https://downloadcenter.nikonimglib.com/en/products/493/Z_6.html

Accessing the Camera Menus

To access the various menus for configuring the Z6, you'll use the MENU button and the *i* button on the back of the camera (figure 1.0A). Please remember the locations of these two buttons—they will be mentioned often in this book.

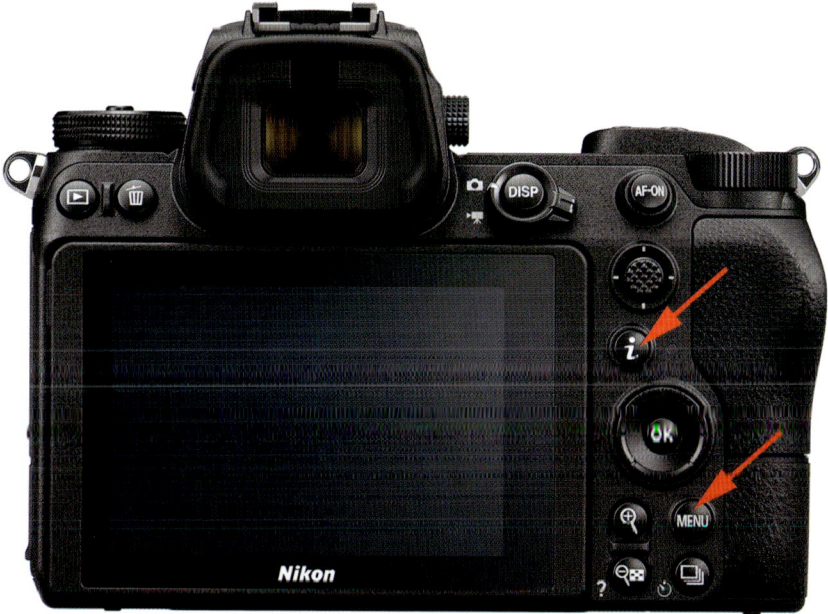

Figure 1.0A: Press the MENU button to open the main camera menus and the *i* button to open the context-sensitive shortcut menus.

There are seven primary menu systems in the camera, which work for both Viewfinder photography and Live view photography and videos. They are listed as follows:

- Playback Menu
- Photo Shooting Menu
- Movie Shooting Menu
- Custom Setting Menu
- Setup Menu
- Retouch Menu
- My Menu or Recent Settings

Additionally, there are several *i* button shortcut "Quick" menus available for image play-back, photography, and movies (along with the normal main menus listed previously). This book has a chapter devoted to each of the main menus and fully discusses the *i* button shortcut menus in appropriate places.

Let's take a brief look at the opening screens of the seven main menus, shown in figure 1.0B, images 1–7. You get to these seven menus by pressing the MENU button and scrolling up or down with the Multi selector. A selector bar with tiny icons will appear on the left side of the Monitor when you press the MENU button. You can see the selector bar at the left of each menu in figure 1.0B, images 1–7.

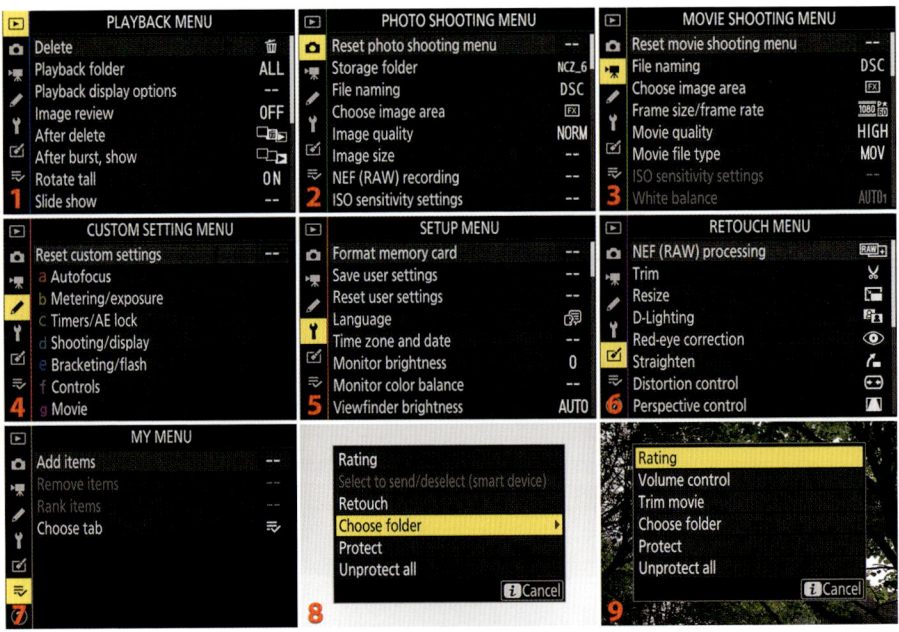

Figure 1.0B: Seven primary camera menus, photo quick menu, and movie quick menu

As you scroll up or down in the selector bar, you'll see each menu appear on the Monitor, with its icon highlighted in yellow on the left side of the screen, and the menu on the right. The name of the menu you are currently using will be displayed at the top of the screen—except when you are accessing the *i* Menus (figure 1.0B, images 8 and 9).

There are four *i* button shortcut menus. Figure 1.0B, image 8, displays an example of the *i* button photo shortcut menu for working with still photography. Figure 1.0B, image 9, displays the *i* button movie shortcut menu for working with video.

Again, we will discuss each of these menus and their functions and settings in great detail as we go through this book.

Note: My Menu (figure 1.0B, image 7) can be toggled with an alternate menu called Recent Settings by using the Choose tab setting at the bottom of My Menu. These two menus—My Menu and Recent Settings—can't be active at the same time, so only one of them is shown in figure 1.0B (image 7). My Menu is much more functional for most people. The chapter titled **My Menu and Recent Settings** covers both of these options in detail so you can choose which one you want to appear most of the time on your camera. My Menu allows you to add the most-used menu items from any of the other menus to create your own personal menu, and Recent Settings shows you the last 20 menu items you've changed.

Touch-Sensitive Monitor

A welcome addition to the new Nikon Z6 is the touch-sensitive monitor. Try pressing the MENU button and then selecting menu items with your fingertip. Scroll up and down in the menu by swiping up and down on the Monitor.

Press the Playback button to display a picture, and then you can pinch and stretch with your fingers to zoom out and in on the picture, or use a finger swipe to change to a new picture.

You will find that the touch-sensitive monitor acts more like your smartphone. This new feature makes the Z6 easier and more intuitive to use for those of us who are familiar with using smartphones.

We will cover the touchscreen system in detail in the chapter titled **Camera Control Screens** (page 19).

Now, let's start with the initial configuration of a brand-new Nikon Z6. There are five specific steps you should complete when you first turn on the camera.

Five Steps for First-Time Camera Configuration

This section is devoted to first-time configuration of the camera. There are certain settings (covered in this section) that should be set up right away, and others that should be configured before you use the camera extensively (covered in a later section, **Camera Functions for Initial Configuration,** on page 14).

I won't go into detail on all possible settings in this chapter. Those details are reserved for the individual chapters that cover the various menus and functions.

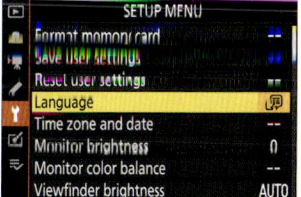

Figure 1.1A: Use the Setup Menu to configure the first five camera settings.

Instead, I'll walk you through five steps for first-time configuration of the camera. We will start with the Setup Menu (figure 1.1A).

Then, in the **Camera Functions for Initial Configuration** section, I'll refer you to the page numbers that provide the screens and menus for each function that should be configured *before* you use your camera for the first time. The later chapters will cover virtually all camera settings.

Setting the Language: Step 1

The Z6 is multilingual and multinational. As partially shown in figure 1.1B, the menus can be displayed in one of four languages (with firmware C 1.00). The number of languages will likely increase with later firmware updates since previous Nikon DSLRs (e.g., D850, D750) come with 36 languages available. More than likely, the camera will already be configured to the language spoken in your area since various world distributors have the camera somewhat preconfigured.

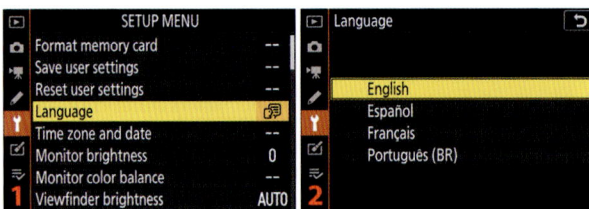

Figure 1.1B: Setting the camera's language

If you want to change the language for the menus and screens, use the following steps to select your preferred language:

1. Tap on the wrench icon on the left of the screen to select the Setup Menu (figure 1.1B, image 1). (***Note:*** In the chapter called **Camera Control Screens** (page 19) we will discuss how to use the touchscreen system with its touch-sensitive controls.)
2. Choose Language from the Setup Menu with your fingertip (figure 1.1B, image 1).
3. Tap on the Language of your choice (e.g., English) (figure 1.1B, image 2).

Next we will consider the Time zone screen.

Setting the Time Zone: Step 2

This is an easy screen to use as long as you can recognize the area of the world in which you live. Use the map shown in figure 1.1C, image 3, to find your area, and then select it.

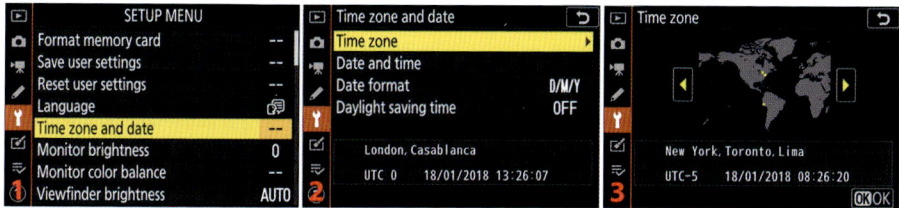

Figure 1.1C: Setting the Time zone

Here are the steps to select the correct Time zone for your location:

1. Follow the Setup Menu screen flow shown in figure 1.1C, images 1 and 2 (*Time zone and date > Time zone*), until you arrive at the third screen in the series.
2. Use the little yellow arrows to scroll to the left and right until your world location is selected (figure 1.1C, image 3). You will see tiny yellow dots marking the locations of major cities (e.g., New York, Toronto, Lima) in the selected time zone, and the names of the cities will appear above the Coordinated Universal Time number (e.g., UTC-5). At the bottom of the screen you will see the currently selected Time zone. Mine is set to New York, Toronto, Lima, as shown in figure 1.1C, image 3. Select the OK control (either tap OK on the screen or press the OK button) to lock in your Time zone.

Next in the series are the Date and time settings.

Setting the Date and Time: Step 3

This screen allows you to enter the current date and time. It is in year, month, day (Y, M, D) and hour, minute, second (H, M, S) format.

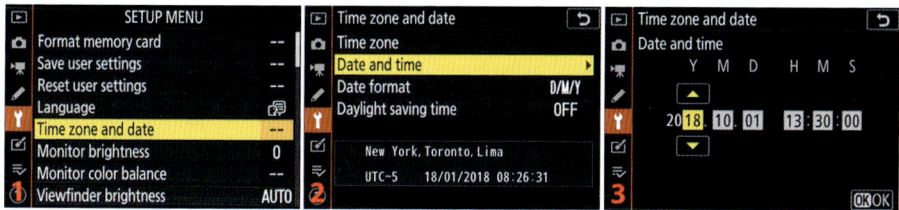

Figure 1.1D: Setting the Date and time

Here are the steps to set the Date and time:

1. Follow the Setup Menu screen flow shown in figure 1.1D, images 1 and 2 (*Time zone and date > Date and time*), until you arrive at the third screen in the series.
2. Select the various date and time sections, such as the year section shown in figure 1.1D, image 3 (18). Tap on the tiny yellow up or down arrows to set the values for each field (Y—year, M—month, D=day, H=hour, M—minute, S=second). The time values (H, M, S) use a 24-hour clock, or military time. Press or touch the OK control once you have entered the Date and time.

Next let's configure the Date format.

Setting the Date Format: Step 4

Various date formats are used around the world, and the Nikon Z6 allows you to choose from the most common ones. Here are the three date formats you can select from (figure 1.1E):

- Y/M/D: Year/Month/Day (2018/12/31)
- M/D/Y: Month/Day/Year (12/31/2018)
- D/M/Y: Day/Month/Year (31/12/2018)

United States residents usually select the M/D/Y format. However, you may prefer a different format.

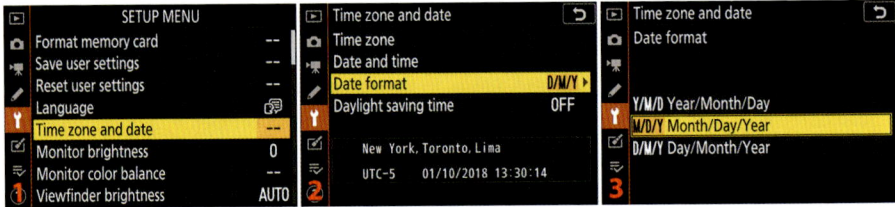

Figure 1.1E: Setting the Date format

Here are the steps to select the Date format you like best:

1. Follow the Setup Menu screen flow shown in figure 1.1E, images 1 and 2 (*Time zone and date > Date format*), until you arrive at the third screen in the series.
2. Tap on the date format you prefer (figure 1.1E, image 3).

Finally, let's configure Daylight saving time.

Setting Daylight Saving Time: Step 5

Many areas of the United States observe daylight saving time. In the springtime, most U.S. residents set their clocks forward by one hour on a specified day each year. Then in the fall they set their clocks back, leading to the clever saying, "spring forward and fall back."

You can use the Daylight saving time setting to adjust the time on your Z6's clock forward or back by one hour, according to whether daylight saving time is currently in effect in your area.

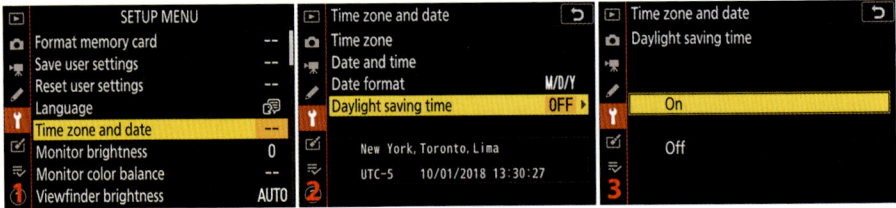

Figure 1.1F: Setting Daylight saving time

To choose an initial Daylight saving time setting, follow these steps:

1. Follow the Setup Menu screen flow shown in figure 1.1F, images 1 and 2 (*Time zone and date* > *Daylight saving time*), until you arrive at the third screen in the series.
2. Tap on the setting you want to use (On or Off). If daylight saving time is currently in effect in your area (spring and summer in most areas of the United States), select On. When daylight saving time ends, you will need to change this setting to Off (via the Setup Menu) to adjust the clock back by one hour.

Settings Recommendation: If you live in an area that observes daylight saving time, it's a good idea to adjust this setting whenever daylight saving time begins and ends. This is *not* an automatic setting, so you will need to adjust it twice per year. When you set the time forward or back on your clocks, you should adjust it on your camera, too. If you don't, your images will have internal metadata reflecting a time that is off by one hour for half the year.

Using the Camera's Help System

The Z6 is complex enough that it needs a help system. Fortunately, Nikon provides one. Many functions in the menus allow you to press the Zoom out/Help button (figure 1.2, image 2) and a help screen will appear for that function. You must press the button again to turn off the help screen.

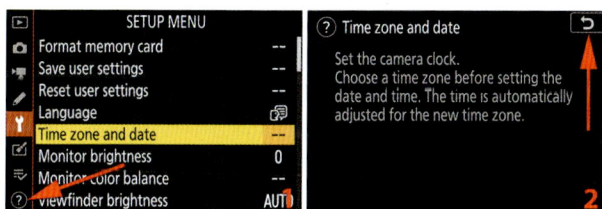

Figure 1.2: Using the Help touch control to understand functions

Use the following steps to access the help system:

1. Highlight a function (e.g., Time zone and date) for which there is a small question mark in a gray circle at the bottom of the menu selection column (figure 1.2, image 1, red arrow). If the question mark does not appear, help is not available for that function (e.g., Language does not have a help menu, therefore the question mark will not appear). Tap the little help control (question mark in a circle) to access a help screen for the highlighted function.
2. A help screen will open that shows a brief description of what the selected function does (figure 1.2, image 2). When you have finished reading the help screen, tap the back control (image 2, red arrow) to close the help screen and return to the previous screen (go back).

Check out the useful help screens. They are excellent for when you could use a quick reminder of exactly what a function does. They are available for many of the menu items, but not all of them.

Now let's examine a group of functions that should be configured before you shoot a lot of pictures with your new Z6.

Camera Functions for Initial Configuration

The following is a list of functions that you may want to configure before you take many pictures or capture a lot of video. These set up the basic parameters for camera usage. Each function is covered in great detail on the page number shown, so I did not repeat the information in this chapter. Please turn to the indicated page and fully configure the function, then return here and move on to the next function. When you are done, your camera will be ready for use.

Playback Menu
- Playback folder: Page 141
- Playback display options: Page 142
- Image review: Page 150
- Rotate tall: Page 154

Photo Shooting Menu
- Image quality: Page 175
- Image size: Page 180
- NEF (RAW) recording: Page 182
- ISO sensitivity settings: Page 186
- White balance: Page 197
- Set Picture Control: Page 200
- Color space: Page 221
- Active D-Lighting: Page 223
- Long exposure NR: Page 226
- High ISO NR: Page 227
- Vignette control: Page 230
- Diffraction compensation: Page 231
- Metering: Page 235
- Focus mode: Page 261
- AF-area mode: Page 264
- Vibration reduction: Page 267

Movie Shooting Menu
- Choose Image area: Page 315
- Frame size/frame rate: Page 316
- Movie quality: Page 318
- Movie file type: Page 320
- ISO sensitivity settings: Page 321
- White balance: Page 324
- Set Picture Control: Page 326
- Active D-Lighting: Page 337
- High ISO NR: Page 338
- Vignette control: Page 339
- Diffraction compensation: Page 340
- Metering: Page 343
- Focus mode: Page 344
- AF-area mode: Page 345
- Vibration reduction: Page 347
- Microphone sensitivity: Page 350

Custom Setting Menu
- a1 AF-C priority selection: Page 365
- a2 AF-S priority selection: Page 366
- a3 Focus tracking with lock-on: Page 367
- a4 Auto-area AF face detection: Page 369
- a5 Focus points used: Page 370
- a6 Store points by orientation: Page 371
- a7 AF activation: Page 373 (if you want to use back-button focus)

- a8 Limit AF-area mode selection: Page 375
- a10 Focus point options: Page 377
- a11 Low-light AF: Page 380
- a12 Built-in AF-assist illuminator: Page 381
- c3 Power off delay: Page 394
- d5 Shutter type: Page 403
- d7 File number sequence: Page 405
- d9 Framing grid display: Page 408
- d10 Peaking highlights: Page 409
- f1 Customize *i* menu: Page 422 (for still photography)
- f2 Custom control assignment: Page 423 (for still photography)

- f3 OK button: Page 436 (for still photography)
- f7 Reverse indicators: Page 450 (if you are coming from an older Nikon)
- g1 Customize *i* menu: Page 452 (for video capture)
- g2 Custom control assignment: Page 453 (for video capture)
- g3 OK button: Page 461 (for video capture)
- g4 AF speed: Page 463
- g5 AF tracking sensitivity: Page 464
- g6 Highlight display (zebra stripes): Page 465

Setup Menu

- Format memory card: Page 472
- Image comment: Page 501
- Copyright information: Page 503
- Beep options: Page 505

- Touch controls: Page 507
- Connect to smart device: Page 528
- Connect to PC: Page 542

Of course, there are hundreds more functions to configure, and you may find one function more important than another; however, these are the functions you ought to at least give a once-over before you use the camera extensively.

Camera Settings Recommendations

All through the book I offer my personal recommendations for settings and how to use them. Look for the **Settings Recommendation** paragraph at the end of most sections. These suggestions are based on my experience with Nikon cameras in various types of shooting situations. You may eventually decide to configure things differently, according to your own needs and style. However, these recommendations are good starting points while you become familiar with your new Z6.

Downloadable Resources Website

To keep this book small enough to carry as a reference in your camera bag, I have provided some less-used information in downloadable documents on the following website:

http://www.rockynook.com/NikonZ6

I will refer to these documents throughout the book when they apply to the material being discussed.

Author's Conclusion

Keep this book in your camera bag for reference, or purchase an electronic copy for use on your smartphone or tablet. You can purchase electronic copies of this book directly from the publisher's website (**rockynook.com**), which includes three eBook formats: PDF, ePub, and Mobi (Kindle Reader). Use the coupon code YOUNGRN40 to receive a 40% discount at checkout (for readers of my books).

Let's get started on our examination of this powerful and highly programmable mirrorless camera system. There are many individual functions and many settings within these functions. We will consider each of them so that you can use your camera to the fullest extent of its potential and improve your photography in the process.

Again, it is best if you have your camera in hand so that you can make adjustments and experiment with each setting as you go. Then, after you have read through the book, you will have discovered the functions that are most important to you, where they are located, and how to adjust them.

Are you ready? Let's master your new mirrorless camera!

2 Camera Control Screens

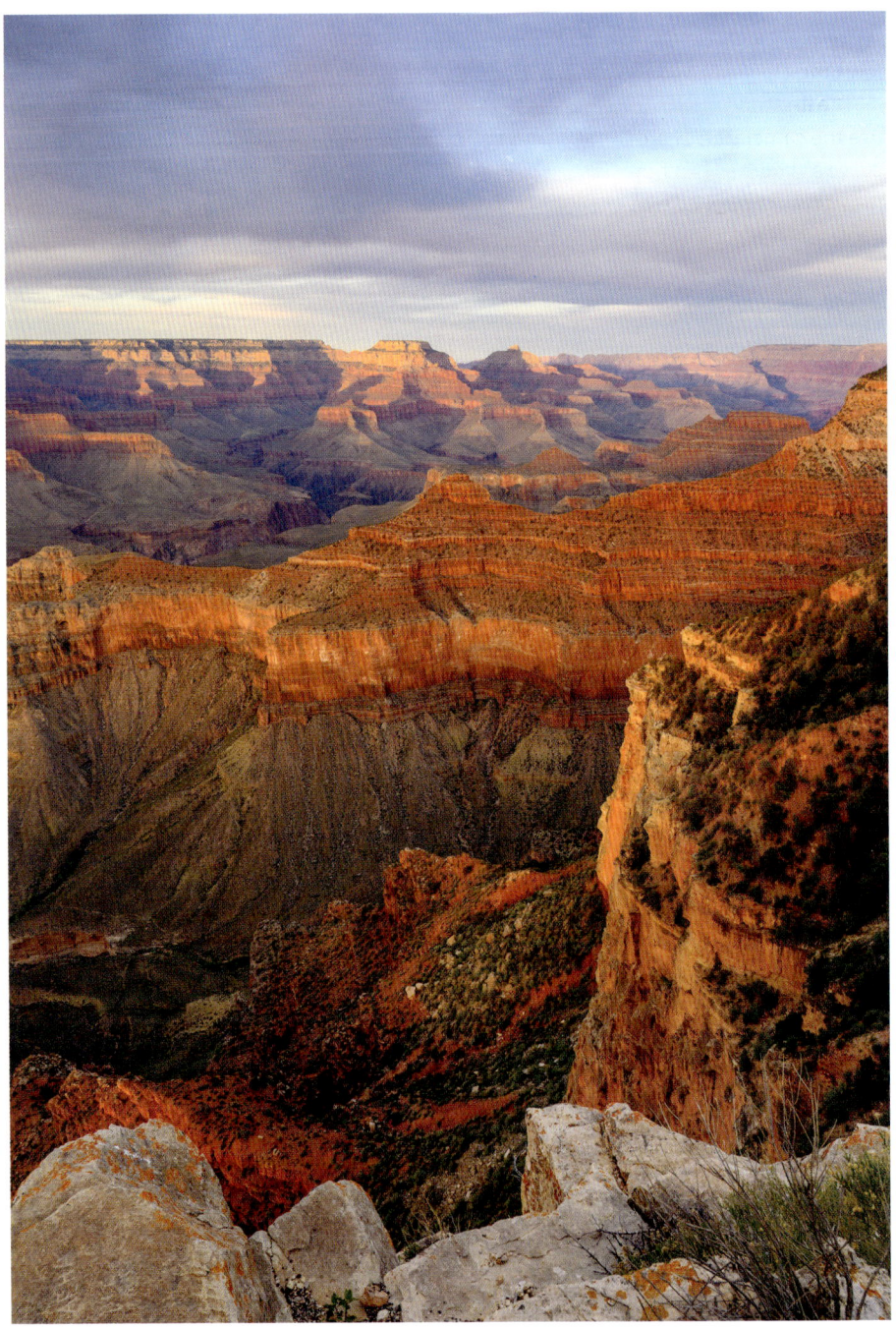

Grand Canyon at Sunset © 2019 Francine Dollinger (*Francine*)

The Nikon Z6 digital single-lens mirrorless (DSLM) camera has some significant differences when compared to your Nikon DSLRs. Along with physical changes (e.g., fewer buttons), there are additional camera control screens. These control screens allow you a lot of flexibility in how you make setting changes. While the camera may feel a little different the first few times you use it, you will quickly come to enjoy the new mirrorless way of doing things.

The first time I took my Z6 out for a shoot, I had no serious problems figuring out how to use the camera, and I brought home great pictures. However, there was an initial learning curve as I figured out how to access and configure the various camera settings that were previously controlled by buttons on my Nikon DSLRs. Once I got used to the new camera control screens in the Z6, I felt right at home with my new camera. As you read over this chapter—with your camera in hand, of course—your learning curve won't be quite as steep, and you'll become familiar with the camera much more quickly.

Mirrorless Is Different, Yet the Same

When you are using a mirrorless Nikon, you do not have an optical viewfinder (OVF), like you do in a DSLR camera. The Z6 camera is in Live view mode all the time, using either the electronic viewfinder (EVF) or the rear LCD monitor to display your subject, adjust the exposure, and capture the image or video. Your view of the subject is always based on what the sensor detects after the light has traveled through the lens. In other words, you are seeing a live electronic view directly off the camera's sensor.

Interestingly, Nikon seems to be moving away from the term "Live view" in relation to the use of a mirrorless Nikon. What is the point of saying the camera is in Live view—compared to OVF view—when, by default, it's always in Live view?

Therefore, unlike with your Nikon DSLR, you will see no references to *Live view photography* mode or *Movie live view* mode in the user's manual. Instead, Nikon now uses the terms "Photo mode" and "Movie mode." Again, both of those modes always give you a live view of what the sensor sees, so the camera is perpetually in what used to be called Live view mode.

You have likely been a DSLR user for many years. If you have not used a mirrorless camera before your new Z6, there are some adjustments to make. In this chapter, we will consider the various control screens, special menus, and new touchscreen methods you may use to change camera settings, in both Photo mode and Movie mode.

All the old menus are there, just where you expect them to be, with few changes from your DSLR days. However, with the control screens in your Z6, Nikon is attempting to make it easier for you to make changes in camera settings without burrowing down into menus as often. We will consider the camera's main menu system in later chapters.

Technical TFT-LCD Monitor Information

As mentioned previously, the Z6 has a tilting, 3.2-inch (8 cm), 170-degree wide-viewing angle, TFT-LCD, touch-sensitive rear Monitor with enough resolution, size, and viewing angle to allow you to easily take pictures, make settings adjustments, and play back images and videos (figure 2.0A).

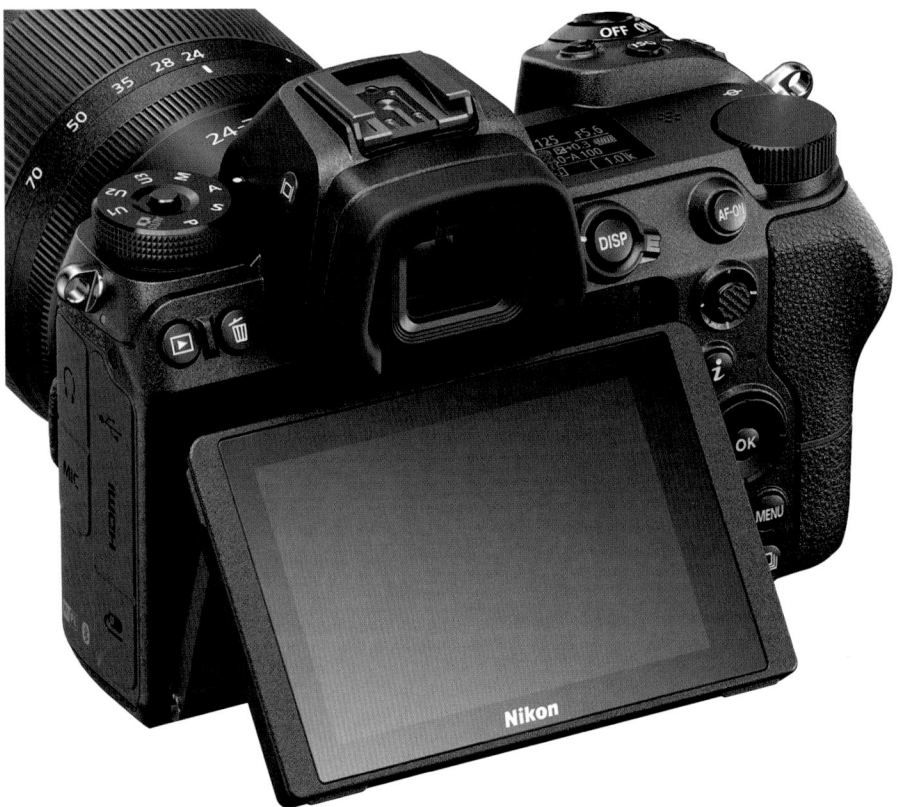

Figure 2.0A: The Z6 Monitor

The Monitor screen has excellent clarity for your image previewing needs, allowing you to zoom in to pixel-peeping levels. The Monitor also offers 11 levels of brightness.

   Technical geek stuff: The Monitor is based on a 2.1-million dot, thin-film transistor (TFT), liquid-crystal display (LCD) panel. It has 2.1-million *dots* of resolution, not *pixels*. Technically, an individual pixel on your Z6's Monitor is a combination of three colored dots: red, green, and blue (RGB). The three dots are blended together to provide shades of color and are equal to one pixel. This means the Monitor is limited to one-third of 2,100,000 dots, or approximately 700,000 pixels of real image resolution. This is very close to the XGA standard (786,432 pixels) and is significantly higher than many of the Z6 predecessors' 307,200-pixel VGA resolution monitors.

Technical EVF Information

The Z6 has an excellent electronic viewfinder (EVF), with more resolution than other cameras in its class (figure 2.0B). It is widely praised as one of the best EVFs available, with sufficient resolution and magnification to almost make you feel as though you are using an optical viewfinder.

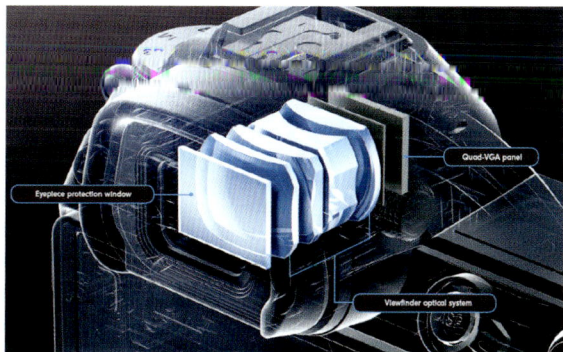

Figure 2.0B: The Z6 electronic viewfinder (EVF)

However, by using an EVF, you're gaining a live view of your subject that will immediately reflect any changes in exposure, color saturation, and focus. This live image preview is a WYSIWYG (what you see is what you get) display. You are viewing the image that will be saved to the memory card when you press the Shutter-release button. Live image preview!

As the picture in figure 2.0B reflects, the QVGA panel is viewed though a superior optical system and uses powerful image-processing technology to give you a clear view of your subject and WYSIWYG preview of your upcoming picture.

Technical geek stuff: The EVF uses a 0.5-inch (1.27 cm), approximately 3.69-million dot, Quad-VGA, OLED panel, with 100% frame coverage, 0.8x magnification, 37-degree diagonal viewing angle, and 11 levels of manual brightness adjustment.

The EVF has a 60Hz refresh rate, which means that the EVF screen refreshes itself 60 times per second, adding to the lifelike view in the Viewfinder, with no flicker.

Additionally, Nikon has applied a fluorine coating to the rear Eyepiece protection window glass. This coating repels dust while reducing flare, allowing you a comfortable, high-clarity view of your subject (similar to an OVF).

Next, let's consider the first of the camera control screens we will discuss in this chapter, the *i* Menu.

The *i* Menu: A Shortcut to Critical Camera Functions

The Nikon Z6 camera—being a significantly smaller mirrorless style—works a little differently than a Nikon DSLR. The first thing you will notice is that there are fewer physical controls on the camera body. Some of the functions that are controlled by buttons on a

Nikon DSLR are instead controlled by an easily accessible menu system called the *i* Menu. Additionally, several other Quick menu screens are available. Each of these screens is attached to various camera functions, which we will consider in this and later chapters.

This chapter is primarily concerned with showing you the location and functionality of the camera's various control screens, and not so much with how each item on the control screens works. The individual functions on each control screen will be considered in detail as we proceed through the book, and often, page number references will be provided to make it a bit easier to find specific information on how a certain function works. Let's start by examining the *i* Menu system.

Since there are fewer buttons on the Z6 (compared to a DSLR), the *i* Menu is designed to put the most critical camera functions in one place. This special menu is accessed by pressing the *i* button (figure 2.0C, image 1) on the back of the camera.

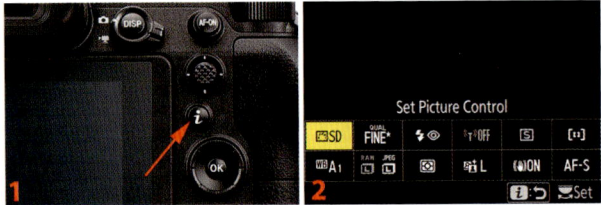

Figure 2.0C: Press the *i* button (1) to open the *i* Menu (2).

The *i* Menu (figure 2.0C, image 2) is programmable, which means you can select from a large number of camera control functions which ones you want to feature on it. Nikon has made good choices in assigning functionality to the *i* Menu. The default items are some of the most important camera controls you will use on a regular basis. However, if you don't like a certain assignment and would like to substitute another, you can easily do so.

The *i* Menu can be displayed either on the camera's rear Monitor or in the electronic viewfinder (EVF). The camera will switch between the Monitor and EVF according to whether your eye is positioned at the Viewfinder. The benefit of using the rear Monitor is that you can touch *i* Menu items with your fingertip to change and select settings. When you are using the *i* Menu from within the EVF, you will need to use external camera controls to change and select settings.

In this chapter, we'll discuss the default features of the *i* Menu and how to use them. Later in the book we'll discuss how to assign different items to the *i* Menu (page 422). First, let's examine the two *i* Menu modes.

Two *i* Menu Modes

Your Nikon Z6 is a pro-level *still-photography* camera (Photo mode) and a powerful *video* camera (Movie mode). The Z6 provides you with an *i* Menu for each mode.

Each *i* Menu is a shortcut menu system that substitutes for the same functions found in the camera's main menu system (e.g., Photo and Movie Shooting Menus). The items found on the *i* Menu are mostly concerned with selecting a certain setting, not making deeper adjustments to those settings. To fully understand the functionality behind the *i* Menu items, it is best to consider the same functions in the camera's main menu system. There-fore, page numbers to the appropriate material in this book are listed for each *i* Menu item.

Let's examine how to select the individual settings on the two *i* Menu types and how the *i* Menu choices differ for each mode.

Note: In my presentation of the *i* Menu and its various settings, I captured screenshots with a lens cap on so that you can see each *i* Menu setting with no distractions. Normally, you will see your subject through the lens, overlaid with the *i* Menu.

Photo Mode *i* Menu

First, let's examine the *i* Menu that is available when the camera is in Photo mode. The items on this version of the *i* Menu are specific to taking pictures only.

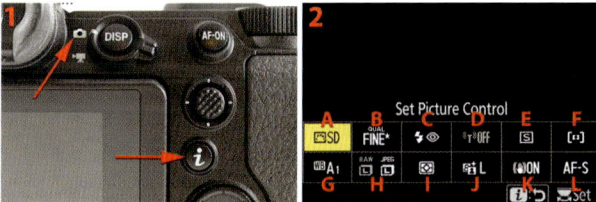

Figure 2.1A: Accessing the Photo mode *i* Menu

To access the Photo mode, switch the Photo/movie selector lever to the top position (fig-ure 2.1A, image 1, top red arrow). Then press the *i* button (figure 2.1A, image 1, bottom arrow) to open the *i* Menu on the rear Monitor, or in the EVF if your eye is at the Viewfinder opening.

The *i* Menu for Photo mode is shown in figure 2.1A, image 2 (with the lens cap on). Following is a list of each default item on the Photo mode's *i* Menu screen and the page number that will give you more detailed information on each setting.

Top Row

A. Set Picture Control (page 200)
B. Image quality (page 175)
C. Flash mode (page 256)
D. Wi-Fi connection (page 537)
E. Release mode (page 177)
F. AF-area mode (page 89, 264)

Bottom Row

G. White balance (page 111)
H. Image size (page 180)
I. Metering (page 235)
J. Active D-Lighting (page 223)
K. Vibration reduction (page 267)
L. Focus Mode (page 261)

Movie Mode *i* Menu

Next, let's examine the *i* Menu that is available when the camera is in Movie mode. The items on this version of the *i* Menu are specific to capturing video only.

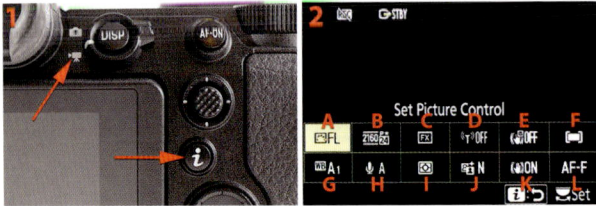

Figure 2.1B: Accessing the Movie mode *i* Menu

To access the Movie mode, switch the Photo/movie selector lever to the bottom position (figure 2.1B, image 1, top red arrow). Then press the *i* button (figure 2.1B, image 1, bottom arrow) to open the *i* Menu on the rear Monitor, or in the EVF if your eye is at the Viewfinder opening.

The *i* Menu for Movie mode is shown in figure 2.1B, image 2 (with the lens cap on). Following is a list of each default item on the Movie mode's *i* Menu screen and the page number that will give you more detailed information on each setting.

Top Row

A. Set Picture Control (page 326)

B. Frame size and rate/Image quality (Movie quality) (pages 316 and 318)

C. Choose image area (page 315)

D. Wi-Fi connection (page 537)

E. Electronic VR (pixel shifting) (page 349)

F. AF-area mode (page 345)

Bottom Row

G. White balance (page 324)

H. Microphone sensitivity (page 350)

I. Metering (page 343)

J. Active D-Lighting (page 337)

K. Vibration reduction (page 347)

L. Focus Mode (page 344)

Using the *i* Menu

There are two ways to use the *i* Menu. One is to highlight an item on it and rotate the camera's command dials to change settings. The second way is to highlight an item and press the OK button or touch the item on the Monitor to open a secondary settings adjustment screen.

We won't discuss how to select and change every item on the *i* Menu. That would be highly repetitive because they all work in basically the same two ways.

Each of the *i* Menu settings is covered in detail later in this book (see page numbers provided). Remember, the *i* Menu is merely a shortcut menu to a selection of the hundreds of settings available in the Z6. Let's examine both setting selection methods.

Changing *i* Menu Settings with the Command Dials

When you have the *i* Menu screen open on your camera's Monitor or in the Viewfinder, you can select a certain setting and simply turn one or more of the camera's command dials to change the setting.

First, let's examine a function that requires the use of only one command dial, and then we will consider one that requires the use of both command dials.

Note: The touch screen becomes disabled when you have turned one of the command dials to change a setting on the *i* Menu. As soon as you finish changing the setting and press OK, the touch screen functionality will be restored.

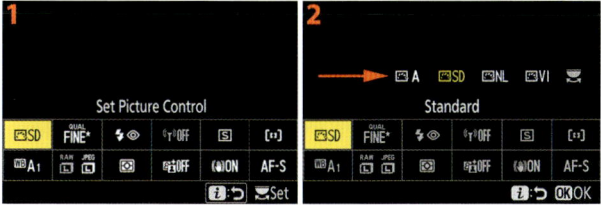

Figure 2.2A: Changing the Picture Control with a single command dial (sample)

Use the following steps to change a setting very quickly by rotating either of the command dials:

1. Press the *i* button to open the *i* Menu and select a setting to change by scrolling to it with the Multi selector pad (figure 2.2A, image 1). For our sample, we will use the Set Picture Control function because it has no subsettings available on the *i* Menu, just the main setting choices (e.g., A, SD, NL).
2. Rotate the rear Main command dial and the choices for that setting (e.g., A, SD, NL) will appear above the *i* Menu (figure 2.2A, image 2, red arrow). If a single line of choices appears, as seen in image 2, then you can turn the rear Main command dial and scroll through each available setting within the selected function (actually, you can turn either dial when there is a single line of settings). When you have highlighted in yellow the selection you want to use (e.g., SD), then press the OK button to lock in the setting.

Now let's consider a sample setting that requires the use of both command dials.

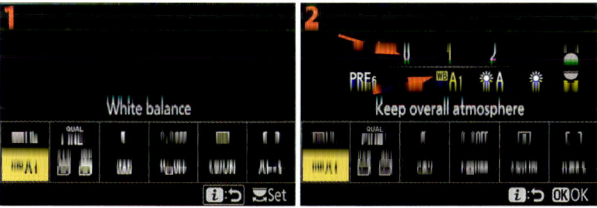

Figure 2.2B: Changing the White balance with both command dials (sample)

Use the following steps to change a setting that requires the use of both command dials to select the setting and a subsetting:

1. Press the *i* button to open the *i* Menu and select a setting to change (e.g., White balance) (figure 2.2B, image 1). We will use the Auto White balance setting as our sample because it not only has several main settings (e.g., A1, Direct sunlight, Cloudy), but it also has subsettings for some of the main settings (i.e., Auto, Fluorescent, K, and PRE).
2. Rotate the rear Main command dial until the WB setting you want to use is highlighted in yellow (e.g., A1; figure 2.2B, image 2, lower red arrow). The sample Auto WB setting has three subsettings: 0, 1, and 2 (upper red arrow), which represent A0 Keep white (reduce warm colors), A1 Keep overall atmosphere, and A2 Keep warm lighting colors. To select a WB subsetting, rotate the front Sub-command dial until the subsetting you want to use is highlighted in yellow. Press the OK button to lock in the setting with its subsetting.

Now let's see how to use the *i* Menu's secondary screen method, which some photographers prefer because it can be easier to see and understand at first.

Changing *i* Menu Settings on a Secondary Screen

Using this method is a bit more like using the camera's normal menu system found under the MENU button. When you press the *i* Button and open the *i* Menu, you will not use the command dials initially to change settings. Instead, you will use a secondary screen, with touch capability, to make changes. Often, this secondary screen will allow you to do more than the previously discussed command dial method. We will again use Set Picture Control and White balance as our samples. Let's see how it works.

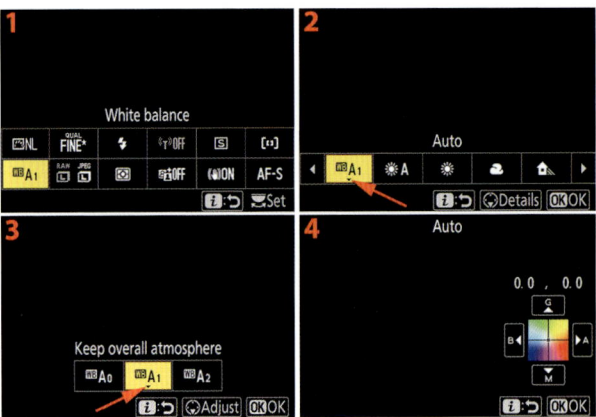

Figure 2.2C: Changing the White balance on the secondary screen (sample)

Use the following steps to change a setting on the *i* Menu by using a secondary screen with touch controls:

1. Press the *i* button to open the *i* Menu, and then select the function you want to change (figure 2.2C, image 1). Press the OK button or tap the option to open the secondary screen. We will use White balance as our sample. Just remember that other functions on the *i* Menu will work in a similar manner to White balance (WB), although most are not as complex. (***Note:*** As we walk through the WB function, keep in mind that our primary concern in this chapter is not how to set White balance, but instead how to use the *i* Menu screens to set any of the functions.)

2. Figure 2.2C, image 2, shows the secondary screen for the White balance setting. You can choose the WB setting you want to use by tapping on the setting, or by scrolling to it and pressing the OK button. In this example, we are adjusting the Auto WB setting because it has subsettings and additional screens. Many other functions on the *i* Menu will not have subsettings and additional screens. In image 2 you will notice that the A1 setting has a tiny down pointer (at the red arrow). This signifies that there is another screen available with subsettings. Scroll down with the Multi selector pad or tap on Details at the bottom of the screen in image 2. This will open the subsettings screen.

3. In figure 2.2C, image 3, you will see the primary subsettings screen, which has three settings: A1, A2, and A3 (A0 Keep white (reduce warm colors), A1 Keep overall atmosphere, and A2 Keep warm lighting colors). You can choose the Auto WB setting you want to use (i.e., A1, A2, or A3) by tapping on the setting, or by scrolling to it and pressing the OK button. However, before you select one of the WB settings, please note that once again, there is a tiny down pointer (at the red arrow) in screen 3. This means there is yet another screen containing subsettings of some type. In this case it is a White balance fine-tuning screen. If you want to fine-tune the White balance you have selected, press down on the Multi selector pad, or tap on Adjust at the bottom of the screen. (***Note:*** Other functions besides WB may have additional screens but may not show the tiny down pointer [e.g., Set Picture Control]. It's a good idea to check each setting for additional screens by scrolling down with the Multi selector pad. If you see a Details or Adjust touch control, even if you don't see a tiny down pointer, there is another screen available—tap the Details or Adjust control to open it. You will better understand why these extra screens are there when you study the camera's menu system in later chapters.)

4. Since we are merely considering how to use the secondary screens and subsettings on the *i* Menu, we will not examine how to fine-tune the White balance here, except to say that you can use the four touch controls on the screen shown in figure 2.2C, image 4. There are four axes that you can use to modify the WB (G green, A amber, M magenta, and B blue). Touch the labeled pointers to move the small black dot in the center of the color box toward or between axes—this will change the WB in a visual way. Press or touch OK to lock in the fine-tuned setting. WB fine-tuning is discussed in much greater detail in this book's chapter on **White balance** (page 107).

Settings Recommendation: Most *i* Menu functions will not be as complex as the White balance function. Usually, a single secondary screen with subsettings will be as deep as the screens go. However, I chose to use the more complex WB function so that you can see the flow of the screens and the controls used to make changes to subsettings. Experiment with each of the settings on the *i* Menu, for both Photo mode and Movie mode. If you need more information on how a certain setting works, use the previously listed page numbers for each of the functions (page 23 for photos and 24 for movies).

Remember that the *i* Menu is merely a selection of the same functions found in the camera's main menu system (accessed by pressing the MENU button). We will discuss each of these functions in detail later in the book.

Playback Quick Menus

The Z6 provides two Quick menus—one for displayed images and one for videos—with several functions when you have a picture or video displayed on the camera's EVF or Monitor screen. These menus allow you to make adjustments to the displayed picture or video in various ways. They are not dependent on whether you have the camera set to Photo or Movie mode. Let's examine the two Quick menus—first the one for displayed images.

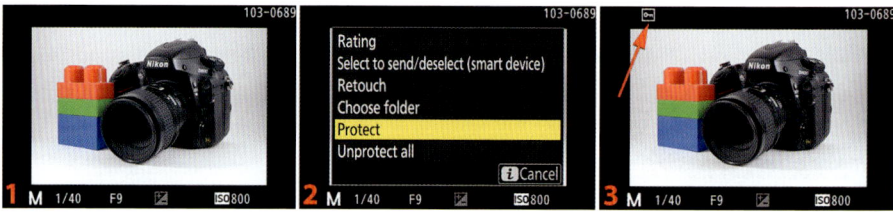

Figure 2.3A: Using the Quick menu for still images

Use the following steps to open the Quick menu for still images:

1. Display an image on the camera's Monitor or in the EVF (figure 2.3A, image 1) and press the *i* button to open the photo Quick menu.
2. The photo Quick menu gives you access to six different functions (figure 2.3A, image 2). Refer to the following page numbers for information about how each function works:
   - Rating (page 159)
   - Select to send/deselect (smart device) (page 535)
   - Retouch (page 567)
   - Choose folder (page 171)
   - Protect (pages 28, 140, 427)
   - Unprotect all (pages 29, 140, 427)

   Let's use the Protect function as our sample. Highlight Protect and press the OK button or tap the option to select it. The camera will now protect the image from accidental deletion and will mark it with a key symbol (figure 2.3A, image 3, red arrow), signifying that the image is protected.

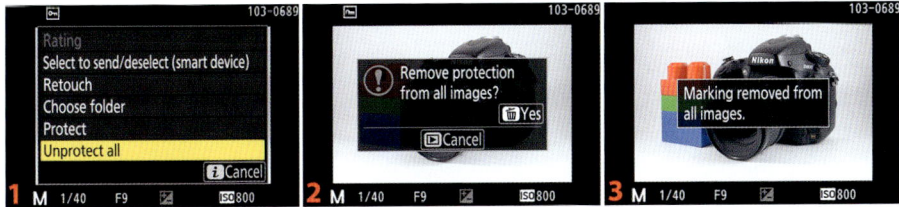

Figure 2.3B: Unprotect all on the photo Quick menu

3 To remove protection from that image, repeat steps 1 and 2. To remove protection from all images, select Unprotect all from the Quick menu (figure 2.3B, image 1). Answer Yes to the *Remove protection from all images?* message (figure 2.3B, image 2). The camera will show an hourglass and then display the message, *Marking removed from all images.*

This example should give you a good base for how to use the Quick menu. Refer to the page numbers beside the other menu items listed above for details on how those functions work. Now let's examine the Quick menu for displayed videos.

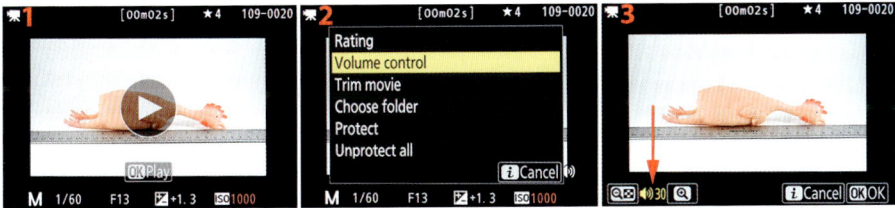

Figure 2.3C: Volume control on the video Quick menu

Use the following steps to open the Quick menu for videos:

1. Display a video on the camera's Monitor or in the EVF (figure 2.3C, image 1) and press the *i* button to open the video Quick menu.
2. The video Quick menu can access six different functions (figure 2.3C, image 2). Refer to the following page numbers for information about how each function works:
   - Rating (page 159)
   - Volume control (see step 3)
   - Trim movie (page 593)
   - Choose folder (page 171)
   - Protect (pages 28, 140, 427)
   - Unprotect all (pages 30, 140, 427)

   To use the Volume control function as our sample, Highlight Volume control and press the OK button or tap the option to select it.
3. The playback volume control for the displayed video is located in the bottom-left corner of the video screen (figure 2.3C, image 3, red arrow). Press the Zoom in button to raise the volume and the Zoom out button to lower the volume. You can also tap the controls to the left and right of the current volume level (30). The range is 0 (off) to 30 (full volume).

Flash Control Screen and Menu

When you have a Speedlight flash unit mounted in the camera's Accessory shoe (hotshoe), the Z6 enables a special Flash control screen. This screen allows you to adjust how the flash works with various modes and compensation types.

To access the Flash control screen, place a flash unit in the camera's Accessory shoe and turn it on. Now press the DISP button until the screen shown in figure 2.4, image 2, appears.

The availability of the Flash control menu items and some of their subsettings is governed by the type of flash unit you have mounted in the hotshoe. I am using a Nikon SB-5000 flash so all features will be available for use.

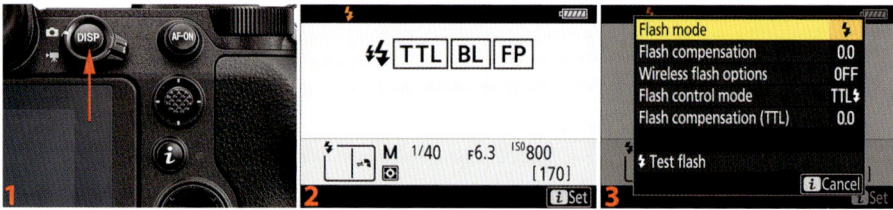

Figure 2.4: Flash control screen

Use the following steps to control a Nikon Speedlight flash unit that is mounted in your camera's hotshoe:

1. Set the Photo/movie selector lever to Photo mode (top position) and then press the DISP button (figure 2.4, image 1) multiple times until the screen shown in figure 2.4, image 2, appears. (**Note:** The Flash control screen and menu are not available in Movie mode.)
2. This is the Flash control screen and it lets you see at a glance which mode, wireless options, and compensation types your camera is using (figure 2.4, image 2). Press the *i* button or tap the Set touch control to open the Flash control menu.
3. The Flash control menu has six functions on it (figure 2.4, image 3). Five of these functions correspond to menu items in the Photo Shooting Menu. Flash control is a deep subject that requires many pages to describe. Therefore, to understand each of these Flash control menu items, please refer to the following page numbers:
   - Flash mode (page 256)
   - Flash compensation (page 260)
   - Wireless flash options (page 244)
   - Flash control mode (pages 238–243)
   - Flash compensation (TTL) (page 240)
   - Test flash is provided to allow you to test fire the flash from the camera without taking a picture. It is available on this Flash control menu only.

Settings Recommendation: This is a useful screen for accessing all the flash control functions in one place. However, understanding each of the Flash control menu items, especially the wireless features (optical and radio), will require a bit of study for a photographer unfamiliar with Nikon's flash unit technology. Remember that this Flash control screen and menu are available. Once you have used the Photo Shooting Menu page references provided to read over a detailed discussion of how each item works, you will be prepared to use the Flash control menu. The Flash control screen and menu provide fast access without digging through multiple Photo Shooting Menus. If you are a regular flash user, learn to use this one well.

Photo Mode

Photo mode gives you six specific screens that you can use to accomplish various things. You can select from the following six screens by setting the Photo/movie selector lever to the top position (Photo mode) and then pressing the DISP button repeatedly (figure 2.5A).

Four of these screens allow you to see your subject and make live adjustments. Two of the screens are opaque and do not show the subject, providing only critical exposure information. Here is a list of the screens in the order the camera displays them when you press the DISP button in Photo mode:

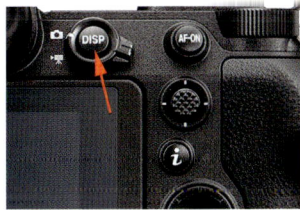

Figure 2.5A: Press the DISP button repeatedly to change Photo mode screens.

- *Indicators on:* A full-featured screen with a large number of symbols reflecting the current state of the camera's settings (figure 2.5B). This screen shows your subject.
- *Simplified display:* A less cluttered screen with the most important symbols (figure 2.5C). This screen also shows your subject.
- *Histogram:* A live histogram screen that allows you to have exceptionally accurate exposures (figure 2.5D). The histogram is superimposed over your subject in the bottom-right area of the screen.
- *Virtual horizon:* A screen to help you keep the camera level in two axes (roll and pitch) when needed (figure 2.5E). This screen shows your subject behind the virtual horizon indicator.
- *Information display:* An opaque screen with the most important shooting information (figure 2.5F).
- *Flash info:* An opaque screen with information on current flash settings (figure 2.5G).

Let's examine each Photo mode screen in detail.

Photo Mode: Indicators On

This is the main screen for using Photo mode and it has many symbols. If you will take a few minutes to explore this screen and learn what each symbol represents, and where to go to adjust its function, you will have better control of your camera later.

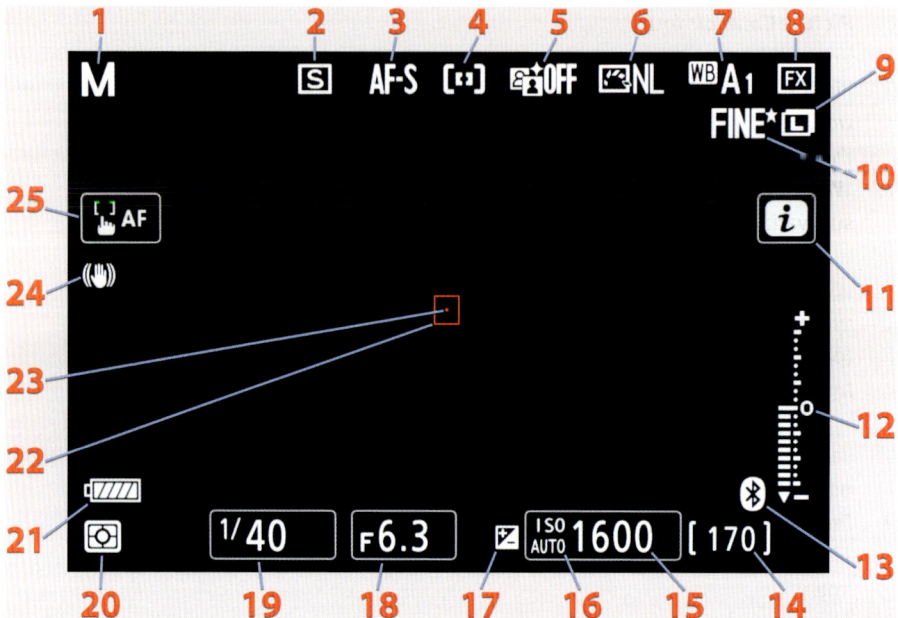

Figure 2.5A: Indicators on – primary Photo mode screen

1. **Shooting mode:** The available selections you will see on the Monitor are Programmed auto (P), Shutter-priority auto (S), Aperture-priority auto (A), and Manual (M). There are also additional modes, including Auto (camera takes full control, becoming a point-and-shoot) and U1, U2, U3 (programmable user modes, see page 474). Turn the Mode dial on top of the camera to select a shooting mode.

2. **Release mode:** Your Release mode choices are Single frame (S), Continuous L (L), Continuous H (H), Continuous H (extended) (H*), and Self-timer (2s to 20s). Access the settings by pressing the Release mode button (looks like a stack of images), just below the MENU button on the camera's back (bottom-right corner), and turning the rear Main command dial for the main settings (and front Sub-command dial for subsettings). For more information, see page 97.

3. **Focus mode:** The available Focus mode settings are Single AF (AF-S), Continuous AF (AF-C), and Manual focus (MF). Access the Focus modes on the *i* Menu (page 82), or by using the *Photo Shooting Menu > Focus mode* function (page 261).

4. **AF-area mode:** Your AF-area mode choices are Pinpoint AF (PIN), Single-point AF, Dynamic-area AF, Wide-area AF (S) (WIDE-S), Wide-area AF (L) (WIDE-L), and Auto-area AF. You will access the AF-area modes on the *i* Menu (page 23), or by using the *Photo Shooting Menu > AF-area mode* function (page 264).

5. **Active D-Lighting:** The available Active D-Lighting settings are Off, Low (L), Normal (N), High (H), Extra High (H*), and Auto (A). You will find the Active D-lighting modes on the *i* Menu (page 23), or by using the *Photo Shooting Menu > Active D-Lighting* function (page 223).

6. ***Picture Control:*** Your Picture Control choices are Auto (A), Standard (SD), Neutral (NL), Vivid (VI), Monochrome (MC), Portrait (PT), Landscape (LS), Flat (FL), and 20 creative Picture Controls (e.g., Dream, Morning, Pop). You may also create custom Picture Controls (page 213). You will find the Picture Controls on the ***i*** Menu (page 23), or by using the *Photo Shooting Menu > Set Picture Control* function (page 200).

7. ***White balance:*** Select from 10 white balance settings, with several settings having sub-variations: Auto (A0, A1, A2), Natural light Auto, Direct sunlight, Cloudy, Shade, Incandescent, Fluorescent (7 sub-variations), Flash, Choose color temperature (K, 2500K to 10000K), and Preset manual (PRE, d–1 to d–6). The camera uses graphical symbols for most of the WB settings. Locate the White balance function on the ***i*** Menu (page 23), or by using the *Photo Shooting Menu > White balance* function (page 197).

8. ***Image area:*** The available in-camera image area crops include FX (36×24), DX (24×16), 1:1 (24×24), and 16:9 (35×20). The EVF or Monitor will display an image cropped to the various selected sizes. You will find the image area crops on the ***i*** Menu (page 23), or by using the *Photo Shooting Menu > Choose image area* function (page 174).

9. ***Image size:*** The Image size settings include Large (L), Medium (M), and Small (S) for JPEG images and Large (RAW L), Medium (RAW M), and Small (RAW S) for NEF (RAW) images. Locate the Image size setting on the ***i*** Menu (page 23), or by using the *Photo Shooting Menu > Image size* function (page 180).

10. ***Image quality:*** The 14 Image quality settings include:
    - NEF (RAW) + JPEG ★
    - NEF (RAW) + JPEG
    - NEF (RAW) + JPEG normal ★
    - NEF (RAW) + JPEG normal
    - NEF (RAW) + JPEG basic ★
    - NEF (RAW) + JPEG basic
    - NEF (RAW)
    - JPEG fine ★
    - JPEG fine
    - JPEG normal ★
    - JPEG normal
    - JPEG basic ★
    - JPEG basic
    - TIFF (RGB)

    Locate the Image quality setting on the ***i*** Menu (page 23), or by using the *Photo Shooting Menu > Image quality* function (page 175).

11. ***i Menu access touch control:*** Touch this symbol to open the i Menu (page 23). Touching the symbol is equivalent to pressing the physical *i* button.

12. ***–/+ Exposure indicator:*** The exposure indicator appears when you are using Manual (M) mode on the Mode dial or whenever the exposure is not good when you are using automatic exposure modes. You can adjust the exposure and watch exposure values change on this –/+ indicator. Your goal is to zero out the indicator for a correct exposure. Use this indicator and the histogram (page 35) when using Manual exposure mode for best results.

13. ***Bluetooth active indicator:*** When you see this symbol on the EVF or Monitor, it means that a Bluetooth connection (page 534) is active between the camera and SnapBridge on your smart device.

14. ***Frame count (images remaining):*** This value shows approximately how many more pictures can be taken and stored on the currently selected memory card. The camera

often underestimates the actual image storage capacity because simple images take less space than more complex images. In other words, the camera will usually hold more images than this number indicates. Also, when you hold the Shutter-release button halfway down, an "r" number will appear in this location (e.g., r16). The "r" number is an estimate of the number of images that can be held by the camera's image buffer during burst shooting before the frame rate will slow down (r16 = 16 images remaining).

15. **ISO sensitivity:** This location displays the current ISO sensitivity value (e.g., ISO 1600). The normal ISO range of the Nikon Z6 is ISO 100 to ISO 51200. The extended range on the low ISO side is Lo 1 to Lo 0.3 (ISO 50 to ISO 80). The extended range on the high ISO side is Hi 0.3 to Hi 2 (ISO 64000 to ISO 204800). Best results are obtained by using the normal ISO range. ISO sensitivity is controlled by holding down the ISO button (just behind the Shutter-release button) and turning the rear Main command dial, or by using the *Photo Shooting Menu > ISO sensitivity settings > ISO sensitivity* function (page 190).

16. **ISO mode:** You have two ISO modes available: ISO (manual ISO sensitivity) and ISO AUTO (automatic, camera-controlled ISO sensitivity). You can change this setting by holding down the ISO button (just behind the Shutter-release button) and turning the front Sub-command dial, or by using the *Photo Shooting Menu > ISO sensitivity settings > Auto ISO sensitivity control* function (page 190).

17. **Exposure compensation:** This symbol will appear only when +/− exposure compensation has been dialed into the camera. You can choose from −5.0 EV to +5.0 EV exposure compensation. Adjust this value by holding down the +/− Exposure compensation button (to the right of the Shutter-release button) and turning the rear Main command dial (the front Sub-command dial will also adjust the value).

18. **Aperture:** Set the aperture by turning the front Sub-command dial. Aperture minimum and maximums vary according to the mounted lens. Manual change is available only in Aperture-priority auto (A) and Manual (M) modes. The camera controls this value in Shutter-priority auto (S) and Programmed auto (P) modes.

19. **Shutter speed:** Set by turning the rear Main command dial. Shutter speeds range from 30 seconds to 1/8000 second (8000), plus X-Sync, Time, and Bulb. Manual change is available only in Shutter-priority auto (S) and Manual (M) modes. The camera controls this value in Aperture-priority auto (A) and Programmed auto (P) modes.

20. **Metering mode:** The metering mode choices are Matrix metering, Center-weighted metering, Spot metering, and Highlight-weighted metering. Adjust this mode by selecting Metering from the *i* Menu (page 23), or by using the *Photo Shooting Menu > Metering* function (page 235).

21. **Battery charge level:** This symbol shows the current battery charge. As the battery is depleted, notches will disappear from the symbol. If this symbol is red, the battery is nearly depleted; please change it before shooting many more shots.

22. **AF point (focus):** Can be moved around the screen with the Multi selector pad or Sub-selector joystick to select the subject for autofocus. This focus point will vary in

size and color according to the AF-area mode selected (#4) and whether the subject is in focus.

23. **Center of frame dot:** This small dot appears when the AF point is directly in the middle of the frame. Unless the OK button has been reassigned to a different function, pressing it will immediately move the focus point to the center position.

24. **In-body VR** (a.k.a. IBIS): This symbol means that In-body VR (Vibration Reduction) is active. Known as "in-body image stabilization" (IBIS) by the rest of the camera industry, this function allows you to handhold your camera at shutter speeds that would normally cause a blurry image from camera shake. You can enable or disable In-body VR, or IBIS, by using the Photo Shooting Menu's Vibration reduction function (page 464)

25. **Touch shooting symbol:** Touch this symbol to enable or disable Touch shutter/AF or Touch AF (page 102). Touch shutter/AF allows you to touch your subject on the camera's Monitor to initiate and lock autofocus and to fire the shutter (take a picture). Touch AF lets you touch the Monitor to autofocus, but not to fire the shutter.

Again, please remember that you will change Photo mode screens by pressing the DISP button. You can scroll through six variations of the Photo mode screens (five if no flash unit is mounted). We've considered the main screen; now let's consider the other five.

Photo Mode: Simplified Display

The second Photo mode screen is called *Simplified display* by Nikon (figure 2.5C). The Simplified display screen is less cluttered, with an almost blank area at the top. It's designed for users who prefer an uncluttered screen while shooting still pictures. It contains a number of symbols shown on the *Indicators on* Photo mode screen, which we examined in the previous subsection. Refer to the symbol descriptions that accompany the Indicators on screen (figure 2.5B) to understand the symbols on the

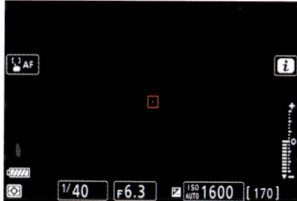

Figure 2.5C: Simplified display for Photo mode

Simplified display screen. If you examine this screen closely, it appears to be the same as the main screen in figure 2.5B, except the top line of symbols are missing.

Photo Mode: Histogram

The *Histogram* screen gives you a small live luminance histogram to help you judge exposure when taking pictures (figure 2.5D, red arrow). In Manual (M) mode, you can adjust the aperture, shutter speed, or ISO sensitivity to correct for under- or overexposure. In other Exposure modes, you can use the +/– Exposure compensation button to push the exposure toward the dark or light sides, making the exposure better.

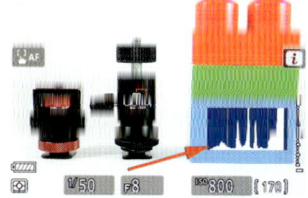

Figure 2.5D: Live histogram for Photo mode

If you want to control all aspects of the exposure, you will certainly enjoy having a live histogram to keep you informed when light levels change in a way that will damage image quality. This is a truly professional tool and one all serious photographers should use regularly, especially in Manual (M) mode!

For more information on using the live histogram for excellent exposure control, see the chapter **Metering, Exposure Modes, and Histogram** (page 67).

Photo Mode: Virtual Horizon

The *Virtual horizon* screen displays roll and pitch from the camera's built-in tilt sensor (figure 2.5E). If the lines are green, it means the camera is level. The tilt sensor senses left and right tilts (roll) and forward and backward tilts (pitch). When the camera is not level in one direction or the other, the line for that direction turns yellow and signifies the approximate degree of tilt. This is very useful when setting up a camera on a tripod. You can take your pictures with the knowledge that the camera is level both left to right and front to back.

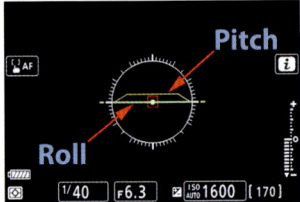

Figure 2.5E: Virtual horizon display for Photo mode

Photo Mode: Information Display

The *Information display* lets you see how the settings are currently configured on the *i* Menu. It also shows you to the current exposure mode (M), shutter speed, aperture, ISO sensitivity, exposure level, and how many more images you can write to the memory card.

If you touch the *i* (Set) control or press the *i* button, the camera will activate the *i* Menu and allow you to make changes to the settings. The Information display is for those who prefer not to use the rear Monitor for composing images. When this screen is active, the camera does not display your subject on the Monitor, but the EVF works normally. This display does not show in the EVF, only on the Monitor.

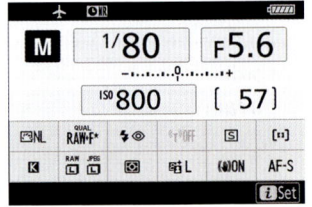

Figure 2.5F: Information display for Photo mode

Photo Mode: Flash Info

We discussed the Flash control screen earlier in this chapter (page 30). This special screen is available only when you have a flash unit mounted and turned on in the camera's Accessory shoe. It shows various information about the flash unit and camera settings.

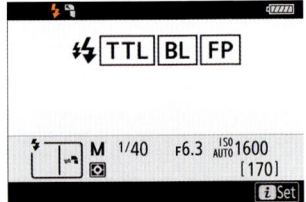

Figure 2.5G: Flash control screen for Photo mode

Additionally, if you touch the *i* (Set) control or press the *i* button, the camera will activate the Flash control menu and allow you to make changes to the flash settings.

You can also control the settings on this menu by using the *Photo Shooting Menu > Flash control* function (page 237), *Photo Shooting Menu > Flash mode* function (page 256), and *Photo Shooting Menu > Flash compensation* function (page 260). This screen is much deeper than it appears at first glance.

Movie Mode

Movie mode gives you four specific screens that you can use to accomplish various things. You can select from the following four screens by setting the Photo/movie selector lever to the bottom position (Movie mode) and then pressing the DISP button repeatedly (figure 2.6A).

Here is a list of the screens in the order the camera displays them when you press the DISP button in Movie mode:

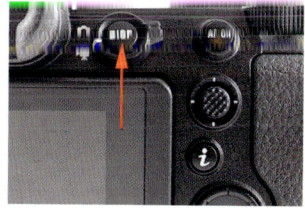

Figure 2.6A: Press the DISP button repeatedly to change Movie mode screens.

- **Indicators on:** A-full featured screen with a large number of symbols reflecting the current state of the camera's video settings (figures 2.6B and 2.6C).
- **Simplified display:** A less cluttered screen with the most important symbols (figure 2.6D).
- **Histogram:** A live histogram screen that allows you to have exceptionally accurate video exposure (figure 2.6E). The histogram is superimposed over your subject in the bottom-right area of the screen, and it stays on the screen during in-camera video recording so that you can quickly make exposure adjustments.
- **Virtual horizon:** A screen to help you keep the camera level in two axes (roll and pitch) when needed (figure 2.6F).

Let's examine each Movie mode screen in detail.

Movie Mode: Indicators On

This is the main screen for using Movie mode and it has many symbols. If you will take a few minutes to explore this screen and learn what each symbol represents, and where to go to adjust its function, you will have better control of your camera later. Let's consider each of the symbols and how to make setting adjustments for each one.

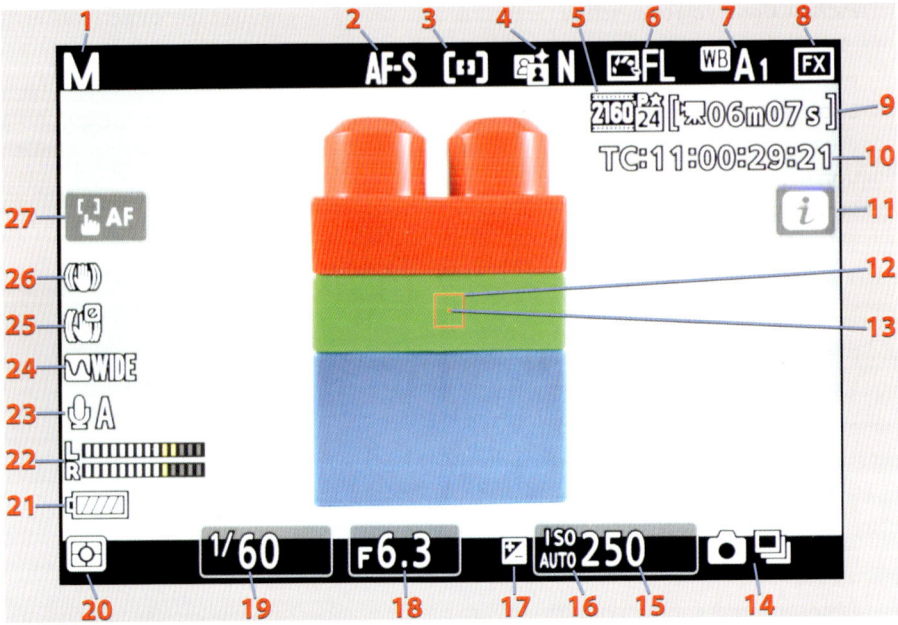

Figure 2.6B: Primary Movie mode screen

1. **Shooting mode:** The available selections you will see on the Monitor are Programmed auto (P), Shutter-priority auto (S), Aperture-priority auto (A), and Manual (M). There are also additional modes including Auto (camera takes full control) and U1, U2, U3 (programmable user modes, see page 475). Turn the Mode dial on top of the camera to select a shooting mode.

2. **Focus mode:** The available Focus mode settings are Single AF (AF-S), Continuous AF (AF-C), Full-time AF (AF-F), and Manual focus (MF). Access the Focus modes on the *i* Menu (page 24), or by using the *Movie Shooting Menu > Focus mode* function (page 344).

3. **AF-area mode:** The AF-area mode choices are Single-point AF, Wide-area AF (S) (WIDE-S), Wide-area AF (L) (WIDE-L), and Auto-area AF. You will access the AF-area modes on the *i* Menu (page 24), or by using the *Movie Shooting Menu > AF-area mode* function (page 345).

4. **Active D-Lighting:** The available Active D-Lighting settings are Off, Low (L), Normal (N), High (H), Extra High (H*), and Same as photo settings. You will find the Active D-lighting modes on the *i* Menu (page 24), or by using the *Movie Shooting Menu > Active D-Lighting* function (page 337).

5. **Frame size/frame rate:** This function is controlled with the Frame size and rate/Image quality setting on the *i* Menu (page 24), or with the Frame size/frame rate function on the Movie Shooting Menu (page 316). Your frame size and rate choices are:

   - 2160p (4K UHD) at 30, 25, or 24 fps
   - 1080p (Full HD) at 120, 100, 60, 50, 30, 25, or 24 fps
   - 1080p at 30 fps x4 (slow-mo)
   - 1080p at 25 fps x4 (slow-mo)
   - 1080p at 24 fps x5 (slow-mo)

6. ***Picture Control:*** Your Picture Control choices are Same as photo settings, Auto (A), Standard (SD), Neutral (NL), Vivid (VI), Monochrome (MC), Portrait (PT), Landscape (LS), Flat (FL), and 20 creative Picture Controls (e.g., Dream, Morning, Pop). You may also create custom Picture Controls (page 330). You will find the Picture Controls on the *i* Menu (page 24), or by using the *Movie Shooting Menu* > *Set Picture Control* function (page 326).

7. ***White balance:*** Select from 10 white balance settings, with several settings having sub-variations: Same as photo settings, Auto (A0, A1, A2), Natural light Auto, Direct sunlight, Cloudy, Shade, Incandescent, Fluorescent (7 sub-variations), Choose color temperature (K, 2500K to 10000K), and Preset manual (PRE, d–1 to d–6). The camera uses graphical symbols for most of the WB settings. Locate the White balance function on the *i* Menu (page 24), or by using the *Movie Shooting Menu* > *White balance* function (page 324).

8. ***Choose image area:*** There are two in-camera image area sizes, FX and DX. The camera will record your video in the size you choose and will adjust the display so that it exactly matches the image area you have chosen. You will find the Choose image area function on the *i* Menu (page 24), or by using the *Movie Shooting Menu* > *Choose image area* function (page 315).

9. ***Time remaining:*** When you are recording a movie, this feature shows you how much time is left before the camera automatically stops recording. In the Nikon Z6, all Frame size/frame rate settings (#5) allow for 29 minutes and 59 seconds of recording time to per video clip, with each clip having a maximum of 4 GB.

10. ***Timecode:*** The Timecode setting is available for capturing in-camera video in MOV format (page 320) only. It displays the hour, minute, second, and frame number for each frame of the video. Use this setting to synchronize the video with other cameras and devices, such as external audio recorders. You can configure the Timecode internal settings (e.g., Count-up method, Timecode origin, Drop frame) by using the *Movie Shooting Menu* > *Timecode* function (page 356).

11. ***i Menu access touch control:*** Touch this symbol to open the *i* Menu (page 24). Touching the symbol is equivalent to pressing the physical *i* button.

12. ***AF point (focus):*** This can be moved around the screen with the Multi selector pad or Sub-selector joystick to select a particular area on the subject for autofocus. This focus point will vary in size and color according to the AF-area mode selected (#3) and whether the subject is in focus.

13. ***Center of frame dot:*** This small dot appears when the AF point is directly in the middle of the frame. Unless it is reassigned to a different function, pressing the Multi selector center button will immediately move the focus point to the center position.

14. ***Release mode (save frame):*** Choose a Release mode (page 97) for taking a single picture while recording a video, or for still photos in 16:9 format when not recording a video. Your choices are Single frame and Continuous. Continuous mode works only when taking still pictures (not while recording a video) and will record an enormous number of images for a maximum of 3 seconds when you press and hold the Shutter-release button. When you're recording a video, the camera will take only one still image per press of the Shutter-release button, regardless of this setting. You can select

a Release mode (save frame) method by pressing the Release mode button (directly below the MENU button) and then turning the rear Main command dial (or the front Sub-command dial).

15. **ISO sensitivity:** This location displays the current ISO sensitivity value (e.g., ISO 1600). The normal ISO range of the Nikon Z6 is from ISO 100 to Hi 2 (ISO 204,800) when using the ISO sensitivity (mode M) setting (page 323). ISO sensitivity is controlled by holding down the ISO button (just behind the Shutter-release button) and turning the rear Main command dial, or by using the Movie Shooting Menu > ISO sensitivity settings > ISO sensitivity (mode M) setting (page 323).

16. **ISO mode:** Choose manual ISO sensitivity (ISO) or ISO Auto. These settings are enabled (On) or disabled (Off) by the Movie Shooting Menu > ISO sensitivity settings > Auto ISO control (mode M) function (page 323). To toggle between manual (ISO) or Auto ISO control, hold down the ISO button and turn the front Sub-command dial.

17. **Exposure compensation:** This symbol will appear only when +/− exposure compensation has been dialed into the camera. Adjust this value by holding down the +/− Exposure compensation button and turning the rear Main command dial. To see the amount of compensation currently dialed in, press and hold the +/− Exposure compensation button.

18. **Aperture:** Set the aperture by turning the front Sub-command dial. Aperture minimum and maximums vary according to the mounted lens. Manual change is available only in Aperture-priority auto (A) and Manual (M) modes. The camera controls this value in Shutter-priority auto (S) and Programmed auto (P) modes.

19. **Shutter speed:** Set the shutter speed with the rear Main command dial. Settings range from 1/30 second to 1/8000 second when using Manual (M) mode only. The camera controls this value in Aperture-priority auto (A), Shutter-priority auto (S), and Programmed auto (P) modes. Even in Shutter-priority auto (S) mode, the camera forces you to use the ISO Auto setting (#16). Only in Manual (M) mode do you have limited control over the shutter speed (1/30 to 1/8000 sec), and the lower number is affected by the Frame rate setting (you will be limited to only as low as 1/60 when using 1080/60p mode, 1/50 in 1080/50p mode, and 1/30 in 1080/30p mode). (**Note:** You can enable or disable ISO Auto in Manual (M) exposure mode by setting Auto ISO control (mode M) to On or Off with Movie Shooting Menu > ISO sensitivity settings > Auto ISO control (mode M). That's right, you can use ISO Auto in Manual (M) mode in case the light changes too quickly for you to manage it with manual controls. This is a powerful feature and safety factor for the Nikon Z6 camera.)

20. **Metering mode:** Movie mode allows you to use three of the four metering modes the camera offers: Matrix metering, Center-weighted metering, and Highlight-weighted metering. To change the metering mode, you must select Metering from the *i* Menu, or use the Movie Shooting Menu > Metering function. You cannot change the metering mode while recording a video.

21. **Battery charge level:** This symbol shows the current battery charge. As the battery is depleted, notches will disappear from the symbol. If this symbol is red, the battery is nearly depleted; please insert a fresh battery before capturing more video.

22. *Microphone sensitivity:* This setting allows you to see the effects of the current Microphone sensitivity setting. The two lines of bars represent the left (L) and right (R) sound channels in action. White means the sound is normal, yellow means the sound is loud, and red means sound is too loud and may be distorted. Microphone sensitivity is controlled by the *Movie Shooting Menu > Microphone sensitivity* function (page 350), or the Microphone sensitivity function on the *i* Menu (page 24).

23. *Microphone mode:* This symbol is part of the Microphone sensitivity setting (#22). You will control which mode the microphone is using: Auto, Manual (in 20 steps), or Microphone off. Choose the mode by using the *Movie Shooting Menu > Microphone sensitivity* setting (page 350), or the *i* Menu's Microphone sensitivity setting (page 24).

24. *Frequency response:* This symbol lets you know whether the microphone's frequency response is set to Wide or Voice. Wide will capture a much broader range of sound and is best for when you want to record all sounds in a scene. The Voice setting limits the sound recording sensitivity to ranges encompassing human voice frequencies, making it best for recording human speech, such as during a public discourse or lecture. This setting is controlled by the *Movie Shooting Menu > Frequency response* function (page 353).

25. *Electronic VR:* This function attempts to reduce handheld camera shake during video recording by shifting the pixels used to record the video in time with slight camera movements. The image or video will be trimmed slightly at its edges as the Electronic VR adjusts the capture. Electronic VR can be used in conjunction with In-body VR (a.k.a. IBIS, or in-body image stabilization, #26) to make rock solid videos while handholding. Be careful not to move the camera abruptly when using Electronic VR because some odd "jumpiness" can occur with rapid movements. This function is best used while not moving or while moving slowly. This setting is controlled by the *Movie Shooting Menu > Electronic VR* function (page 349), or the Electronic VR function on the *i* Menu (page 24).

26. *In-Body VR* (a.k.a. IBIS): This function moves the camera's physical imaging sensor internally to counteract small movements of the camera due to camera shake. It is different than Electronic VR (#25) because it uses mechanical countermotion of the sensor to cancel out handheld shakiness. It is capable of dealing with larger camera movements than the Electronic VR system. When In-body VR (a.k.a. IBIS, or in-body image stabilization) and Electronic VR are used together, it can feel as though you are using a gimble to stabilize the camera. Be careful not to move the camera abruptly because this may result in jumpy movements in your recording. This setting is controlled by the *Movie Shooting Menu > Vibration reduction* function (page 347), or the Vibration reduction function on the *i* Menu (page 24).

27. *Touch shooting control:* Turn Touch AF on or off to control whether or not you can touch your subject on the camera's rear Monitor for autofocus during a video recording. See the **Touch Screen: Shutter Release and Autofocus (Tap Shooting)** subsection of this chapter for detailed information (page 49).

Indicators On (While Recording Video)

The *Indicators on* screen we discussed in the previous subsection changes when you start recording a video. When you press the Movie-record button, several of the controls in the overlay along the top of the screen disappear (figure 2.6C). You can also tell a video is being recorded because there is a REC symbol in the top-left corner, next to the red dot. REC blinks the entire time you are recording.

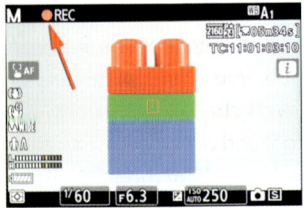

Figure 2.6C: The Indicators on Movie mode screen while recording a video

Movie Mode: Simplified Display

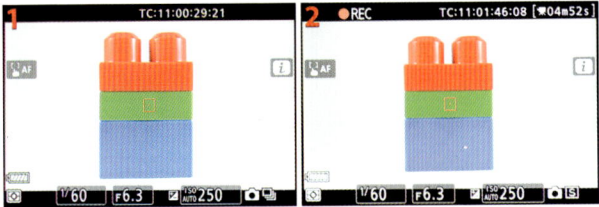

Figure 2.6D: Simplified display Movie mode screens

The *Simplified display* Movie mode screen is a less complex screen for those times when you want little distraction while making a 16:9 format still image or recording a video (figure 2.6D). You can still see the most important controls at the bottom of the screen (e.g., aperture, shutter speed, and ISO sensitivity), but many other symbols are stripped out of the overlay.

Figure 2.6D, image 1, shows the Simplified display screen before a video recording is started, and image 2 shows the same screen while recording a video.

Movie Mode: Histogram

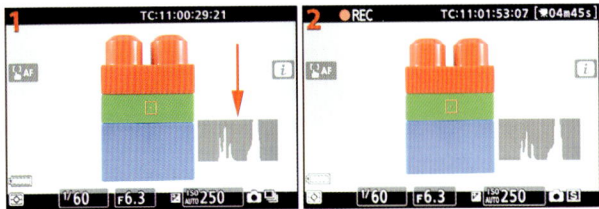

Figure 2.6E: Histogram Movie mode screens

The *Histogram* screen gives you a live histogram to help you judge exposure during video recording (figure 2.6E), or when taking a 16:9 format still image. In Manual (M) mode, you can adjust the aperture, shutter speed, or ISO sensitivity to correct for under- or overexposure. In other Exposure modes, you can use the +/− Exposure compensation button to push the exposure toward the dark or light sides, making the exposure better.

If you are a video perfectionist who wants to control all aspects of the video production, you will certainly enjoy having a live histogram to keep you informed when light levels change in a way that will damage your video's quality. This is a truly professional tool and one all serious videographers should use regularly for in-camera video, especially in Manual (M) mode. While some cameras hide the live histogram screen while recording, the Z6 keeps the histogram available so that you can fine-tune the exposure if needed.

Figure 2.6E, image 1, shows the Histogram screen before a video recording is started, and image 2 shows the same screen while recording a video.

Movie Mode: Virtual Horizon

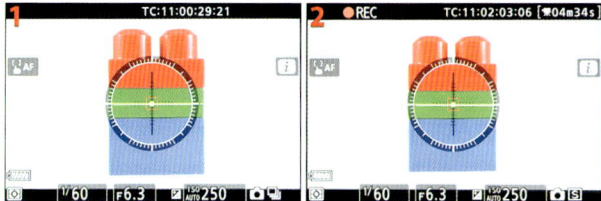

Figure 2.6F: Virtual horizon Movie mode screens

The *Virtual horizon* screen displays roll and pitch from the camera's built-in tilt sensor (figure 2.6F). If the lines are green, it means the camera is level. The tilt sensor senses left and right tilts (roll) and forward and backward tilts (pitch). When the camera is not level in one direction or the other, the line for that direction turns yellow and signifies the approximate degree of tilt.

This is very useful when setting up a camera on a tripod to shoot a video. You can start the video with the knowledge that the camera is level left to right and front to back. While you're shooting a video handheld, this screen may be invaluable in helping you to avoid introducing tilt into an otherwise excellent video.

Figure 2.6F, image 1, shows the Virtual horizon screen before a video recording is started, and image 2 shows the same screen while recording a video.

Control Panel

The Control panel on the Nikon Z6 is much simpler than the Control panel on a Nikon D850. However, it does contain critical exposure information that you can see at a glance, and it allows you to quickly make adjustments without using any item in the rear.

The Control panel has two separate displays—one for Photo mode and the other for Movie mode. Let's consider each of the displays.

Control Panel: Photo Mode

First let's examine the Control panel you will see when the Photo/movie selector lever is set to Photo mode (top position).

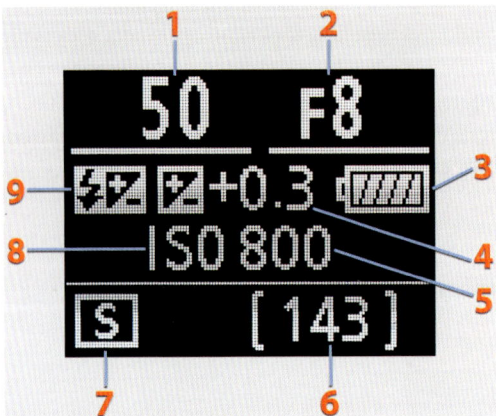

Figure 2.7A: Control panel in Photo mode

1. ***Shutter speed:*** The shutter speed is controlled by turning the rear Main command dial. Your choices are from 30 seconds (30) to 1/8000 second (8000), along with x200 (xSync speed), TIME, and BULB.
2. ***Aperture:*** The aperture is controlled by turning the front Sub-command dial. Your choices are limited to the minimum and maximum aperture openings on the currently mounted lens. For example, the Nikkor Z 24–70mm F/4 S lens has a maximum aperture of f/4 (F4) and a minimum aperture of f/22 (F22).
3. ***Battery charge level:*** The battery charge level shows as a small symbol shaped like an AA battery. As the battery is depleted, notches will disappear from the interior of the symbol. When the battery symbol is down to its last notch, it's time to install a fresh battery and recharge the depleted one.
4. ***Exposure compensation:*** The exposure compensation symbol is composed of a tiny +/– symbol followed by a number. Your compensation choices are –5.0 to +5.0 EV steps. Hold down the +/– Exposure compensation button and turn the rear Main command dial to choose an exposure compensation value. Set it back to +/– 0.0 when you are done.
5. ***ISO sensitivity:*** The ISO sensitivity (page 186) symbol is the acronym ISO or ISO-A followed by a number. Your choices are from ISO Lo 1.0 (ISO 50) to Hi 2.0 (ISO 204800). The normal range is ISO 100 to ISO 51200. Any values above or below the normal range are considered extended ISO values. Best results come from using the normal ISO range. You control the ISO value by holding down the ISO button and turning the rear Main command dial. You can also toggle the camera between manual ISO (ISO) and ISO Auto (ISO-A) by turning the front Sub-command dial (see # 8).

6. ***Number of frames remaining:*** This value is an approximate number of images that can be saved to the XQD or CFexpress memory card. This value is often an underestimate because the camera cannot easily account for the compression level of each image stored. A complex image (e.g., an autumn oak tree with many colorful leaves) will have a larger file size than an image with a simple subject (e.g., a red balloon against a blank white wall). You may often shoot as many as twice the number of images shown when shooting simple subjects. Additionally, if you hold down the Shutter-release button halfway, the camera will display an "r" number (e.g., r16) that represents the approximate number of images the camera's buffer can contain during burst shooting. When that number is exceeded in one burst, the camera's frame rate will slow down.

7. ***Release mode:*** Your Release mode (page 97) choices are Single frame (S), Continuous L (L), Continuous H (H), Continuous H (extended) (H*), and Self-timer (2s). You will change this setting by pressing the Release mode button (below the MENU button) once, and then turning the rear Main command dial until the Release mode you want to use is displayed.

8. ***ISO mode:*** The ISO mode (page 186) has two potential values: ISO (manual ISO sensitivity) and ISO-A (automatic ISO sensitivity). The ISO setting allows you to manually set an ISO sensitivity value by holding down the ISO button and turning the rear Main command dial. Or, you can let the camera set the ISO value automatically by using ISO Auto (ISO-A). You control the ISO mode by holding down the ISO button and turning the front Sub-command dial.

9. ***Flash exposure compensation:*** The Flash exposure compensation symbol is a small lightning bolt followed by +/−. Your compensation choices are −3.0 to +1.0. You will set the flash compensation value in one of three ways:

   - Using the *Photo Shooting Menu > Flash Compensation* setting (page 260). The Flash Compensation setting allows you to set compensation for a flash unit mounted in the camera's Accessory shoe (hotshoe).
   - Using the *Photo Shooting Menu > Flash control > Flash Compensation (TTL)* setting (page 240). The Flash compensation (TTL) setting is tied in with the wireless remote control of multiple flash units while using a WR-R10 Wireless Remote Controller attachment.
   - Using the Flash control menu (page 30) and selecting Flash compensation (page 260) or Flash compensation (TTL) (page 240).

Control Panel: Movie Mode

Next let's examine the Control panel you will see when the Photo/movie selector lever is set to Movie mode (bottom position).

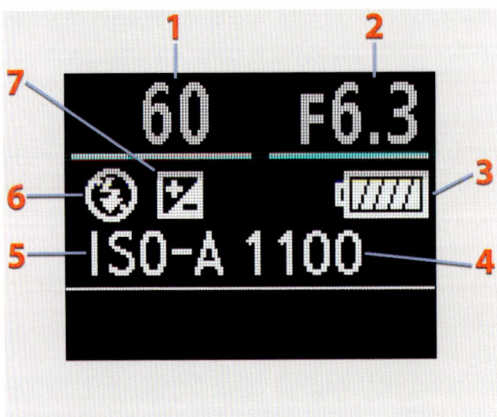

Figure 2.7B: Control panel in Movie mode

1. **Shutter speed:** The shutter speed is controlled by turning the rear Main command dial. Your choices are from 1/30 second (30) to 1/8000 second (8000). The camera's shutter speed should be set to approximately double the frame rate of the video being recorded (e.g., 30 fps should have a shutter speed of 1/60 second).

2. **Aperture:** The aperture is controlled by turning the front Sub-command dial. Your choices are limited to the minimum and maximum aperture openings on the currently mounted lens. For example, the Nikkor Z 24–70mm F/4 S lens has a maximum aperture of f/4 (F4) and a minimum aperture of f/22 (F22).

3. **Battery charge level:** The battery charge level shows as a small symbol shaped like an AA battery. As the battery is depleted, the notches disappear from the interior of the symbol. When the battery symbol is down to its last notch, it's time to install a fresh battery and recharge the depleted one.

4. **ISO sensitivity:** The ISO sensitivity (page 321) symbol is the acronym ISO or ISO-A followed by a number. This location displays the current ISO sensitivity value (e.g., ISO-A 1100). The normal ISO range of the Nikon Z6 is from ISO 100 to Hi 2 (ISO 204,800) when using the ISO sensitivity (mode M) setting (page 323). ISO sensitivity is controlled by holding down the ISO button (just behind the Shutter-release button) and turning the rear Main command dial, or by using the *Movie Shooting Menu > ISO sensitivity settings > ISO sensitivity (mode M)* setting (page 323).

5. **ISO mode:** The ISO mode (page 321) has two potential values: ISO (manual ISO sensitivity) and ISO-A (automatic ISO sensitivity). The ISO setting allows you to manually set an ISO sensitivity value by holding down the ISO button and turning the rear Main command dial. Or, you can let the camera set the ISO value automatically by using ISO Auto (ISO-A). You control the ISO mode by holding down the ISO button and turning the front Sub-command dial. Normally, you will want to use ISO-A when recording video so that the camera can make a quick adjustment if there is a large change in light values, such as when you are recording a video and walk out of a house into the bright sunlight outside.

6. **No flash indicator:** Since you cannot use a flash unit while recording a video, the camera displays a "no flash" symbol as a reminder.

7. **Exposure compensation:** The exposure compensation symbol is composed of a tiny +/– symbol followed by a number. Your compensation choices are –5.0 to +5.0 EV steps. Hold down the +/– Exposure compensation button and turn the rear Main command dial to choose an exposure compensation value. Set it back to +/– 0.0 when you are done.

Next, let's consider the camera's touch screen capability.

Touch Screen

The Z6 has a full-featured touch screen system that can be used to select items on menus, work with pictures displayed on the Monitor, and even focus and take pictures by touching only the Monitor (tap shooting).

As we proceed through the various chapters of this book, you will consistently be reminded of how to choose menu items and change settings by touching the Monitor. Therefore, we will leave those explanations for later chapters. For now, just be aware that virtually any menu item or setting you see on the Monitor can be selected and changed by touching items with your fingertip.

First, let's consider how to use the touch screen to manipulate images and videos you have already taken.

Touch Screen: Playback

The touch screen on your Z6 is somewhat similar to the touch screen on your smartphone. Many of the motions you already use will work in the same way on the camera's Monitor.

Let's examine each of the motions you can make while a picture is on the Monitor.

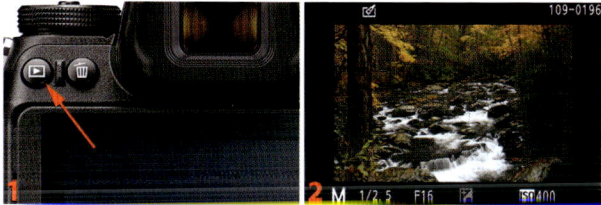

Figure 2.8A: Displaying an image or video

Press the Playback button (figure 2.8A, image 1) to display a sample picture on the screen (image 2). Now let's see what touch motions we can use to work with what's displayed.

Swipe (Flick)

The swipe motion (Nikon calls it a "flick") is very familiar to anyone who has scrolled through a bunch of pictures on a smartphone.

When a picture is displayed on the Monitor (figure 2.8B), you can change to the previous picture by swiping to the right with your fingertip. You can change to the next picture by swiping to the left with your fingertip.

This method works well when you need to examine a few pictures that are near each other on the memory card. But what if you have hundreds of pictures on the card and you want to see different images that are very far apart? Nikon gives you a special Frame advance bar to help you move through a large number of images quickly.

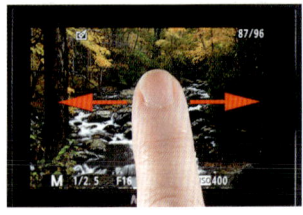

Figure 2.8B: Swipe (flick) to change images

Frame Advance Bar

The Frame advance bar does not show on the screen until you hold your finger on the bottom of the screen. When you touch and hold the bottom, the Frame advance bar will appear under your fingertip (figure 2.8C).

If you slide your finger slowly left or right, the camera will move slowly through the many images stored on the memory card. If you slide your finger more quickly, the camera will jump quickly though the available images.

But what if you want to zoom in to see more image detail, and then zoom back out? The camera gives you two ways to accomplish this: stretch and pinch, and double-tap. Let's examine stretch and pinch first, then double-tap.

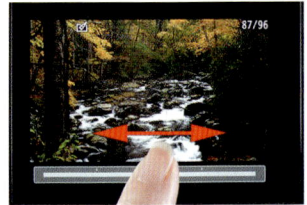

Figure 2.8C: Slide finger on Frame advance bar to change images

Stretch and Pinch

This is a very familiar set of motions for smartphone users and will feel natural for zooming in and out of images on your Nikon Z6 (figure 2.8D).

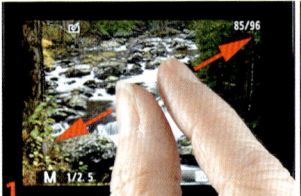
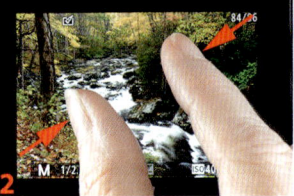

Figure 2.8D: Stretch (spread) to zoom in, pinch to zoom back out

Just like on your smartphone, you can touch two fingertips to the camera Monitor and stretch them apart to zoom in. Pinch the screen, pulling your fingertips back together, to zoom back out.

These stretch-and-pinch gestures allow you to zoom in and out on an image by a variable amount. You can zoom in just a little or all the way to pixel-peeping levels. You can zoom back out by a small amount or all the way back out to normal view. Pull up an image on the Monitor and give it a try.

But what if you want to instantly jump to a 100 percent view to examine the image at the pixel-peeping level? The double-tap method does just that.

Double-Tap

If you regularly examine your images by zooming in to 100 percent on the Monitor, you will find the double-tap method quite convenient (figure 2.8E).

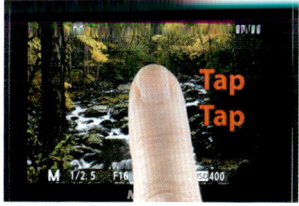

To use this method, display an image on the Monitor and double-tap the picture on the screen at the exact area you want to examine more closely. The camera will immediately jump to a 100 percent, pixel-peeping view of that area to let you validate things like overall sharpness and focus effectiveness. When you are done examining the image at 100 percent, simply double-tap the screen again and the camera will zoom back out to normal view.

Figure 2.8E: Double-tap the screen to zoom in and again to zoom out

The Nikon Z6 also allows you to use the touch-screen to autofocus and take pictures. Let's examine how to choose and use these features.

Touch Screen: Shutter Release and Autofocus (Tap Shooting)

The Nikon Z6 allows you to take pictures and autofocus by merely touching your subject on the Monitor. Let's look at how to use the touch system in both the Photo and Movie modes.

Photo Mode Screen Touch

Nikon calls this Tap shooting and it comes in two parts, Touch shutter/AF and Touch AF.

- **Touch shutter/AF:** When you place your finger on the subject showing on the Monitor, the Z6 will lock autofocus and wait until you lift your finger from the screen before releasing the shutter. As soon as you lift your finger, the camera will fire the shutter and take a picture of the subject.
- **Touch AF:** When you place your finger on the subject showing on the Monitor, the camera will start autofocus on the subject but will not fire the shutter. If you are using AF-F mode, the camera will not refresh the focus until you remove your finger from the screen.

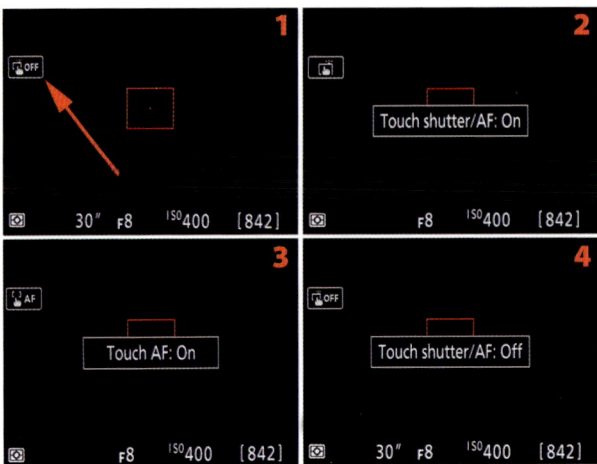

Figure 2.8F: Tap shooting (Touch shutter/AF and Touch AF)

Use the following steps to enable one or both of the Tap shooting methods:

1. Tap on the Touch shutter/AF symbol shown in figure 2.8F, image 1. A popup box will appear with the words *Touch shutter/AF: On* (figure 2.8F, image 2). At this point, both Touch shutter and Touch AF are active (Touch shutter/AF), and the OFF word disappears from the symbol. If you want to use both touch shutter release and touch autofocus, you can skip the following steps (2 and 3) and use Tap shooting.

2. Tap the Touch shutter/AF symbol again and the popup box will reappear with the words *Touch AF: On* (figure 2.8F, image 3). Now only Touch AF is active and the symbol changes to include the initials AF for active autofocus. The touch shutter release is disabled and touching the Monitor will result in autofocus only. If you want to take pictures with the normal Shutter-release button and initiate autofocus by touching the Monitor, the camera is ready. Skip the final step 3.

3. Tap the Touch shutter/AF symbol a final time and a popup box will appear with the words *Touch shutter/AF: Off* (figure 2.8F, image 4). When you see OFF within the touch symbol, you can be sure that the camera will not autofocus or release the shutter in response to screen touches.

Settings Recommendation: Keep this functionality in mind for when you want to fire the shutter with little vibration. Sometimes it will shake the camera less if you lightly touch the Monitor rather than press the Shutter-release or AF-ON button. Could Tap shooting help you when you have accidentally left your electronic shutter release cable at home? This may well be a very convenient function for your photography. I find myself using Tap shooting quite often!

Movie Mode Screen Touch

The Movie mode screen touch is limited to Touch AF. Since the Movie mode is concerned with capturing video, there is no Touch shutter release.

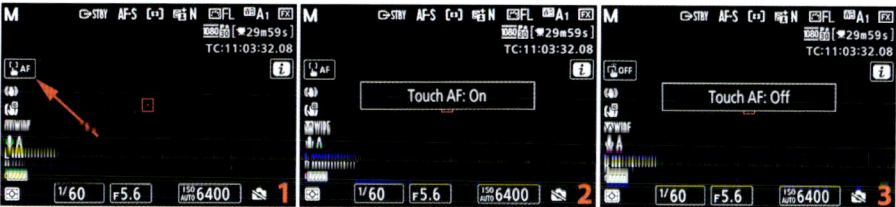

Figure 2.8G: Touch AF for video

Use the following steps to enable or disable Touch AF:

1. Tap on the Touch AF symbol shown in figure 2.8G, image 1 (lens cap on for best control contrast).
2. A popup box will appear with the words *Touch AF: On* (figure 2.8G, image 2), or *Touch AF: Off* (image 3), depending on which mode is currently active. The camera defaults to *Touch AF: On*.
3. Once you have enabled Touch AF, you can then touch your subject on the screen to autofocus. You can touch another area to pull focus to that area at any time.

With a virtually silent Nikkor S lens mounted, you can use Touch AF to autofocus on your subject at will, without making noise or causing vibrations from turning a focus ring.

Author's Conclusion

We've examined the major control screens for the Nikon Z6 camera. While this chapter provides an overview of those screens and how to use them, please remember that the Z6 offers more than one way to do things. These control screens are convenient for quick access to critical functionality, but keep in mind that you can configure the functions found in these control screens in an even more detailed way by using the camera's main menu system. We will discuss the menu system in several upcoming chapters.

Also, it is often possible to assign functions you use frequently to the camera's programmable buttons (page 426) or add them to a special quick-access menu called My Menu (page 602). Later we will discuss how to do both of those things.

In the next chapter, we will discuss several important camera functions, including the light metering system, the camera's exposure modes, and how to use the live EVF histogram and the post-capture histograms for the most accurate exposures you've ever made.

3 Metering, Exposure Modes, and Histogram

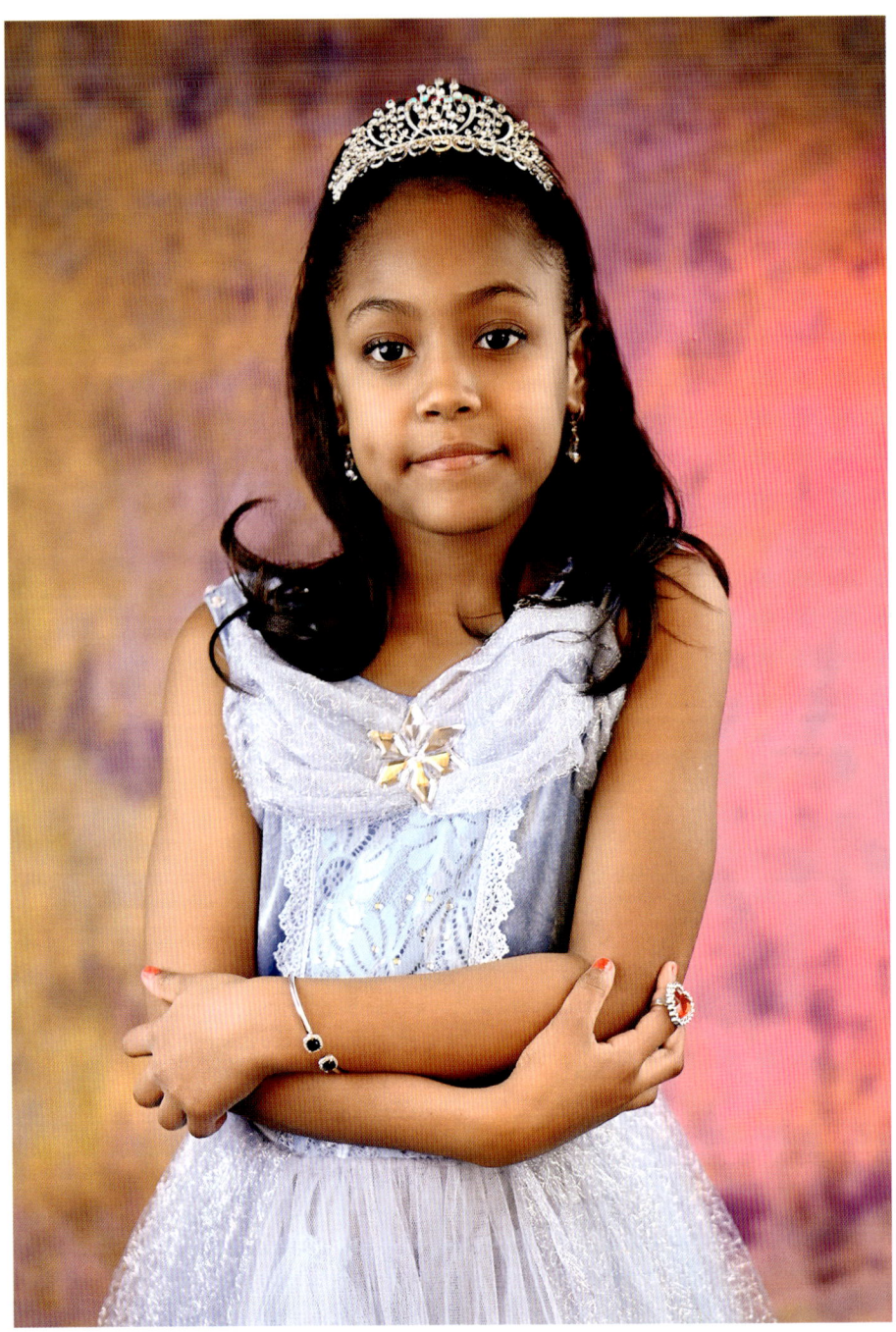

Indecisive Princess Amirah © 2018 Donald E. Jose (*donaldejose*)

I've been using Nikon single-lens reflex (SLR), digital single-lens reflex (DSLR), and now digital single-lens mirrorless (DSLM) cameras since 1980. It seems that with each new camera, there have been improvements in metering and exposure modes. The Nikon Z6 is no exception. Within this camera, Nikon has designed metering and exposure to work not only with still images, but also with up to 4K UHD video.

In this chapter, you'll learn how the exposure metering system and modes work. We'll look at how each of four different light meter types is best used. We'll examine the various modes you can use when taking pictures, and finally, we'll examine how the histogram works on the Nikon Z6.

The histogram readout gives you great control over metering and will help you make the most accurate exposures you've ever made. It is very important that you understand the histogram, so we'll look at it in detail.

This chapter is divided into three parts:

- **Section 1 – Metering:** The Nikon Z6 provides four major light metering systems: Matrix, Center-weighted, Highlight-weighted, and Spot.
- **Section 2 – Exposure Modes:** The camera's Mode dial allows access to various shooting or exposure modes, such as Programmed auto (P), Shutter-priority auto (S), Aperture-priority auto (A), and Manual (M).
- **Section 3 – Histogram:** The histogram is a digital bell-curve readout that shows how well an image is exposed. It's an important tool for advanced photographers. The Z6 gives you not only a regular post-capture histogram, showing how well an image you just took is exposed, but it also offers an in-the-viewfinder live histogram, allowing you to use the histogram as a powerful live exposure indicator. This chapter discusses how to read the histogram and better control your exposures. Let's get started by looking more deeply into the four exposure metering systems.

Section 1: Metering

The basis for the Nikon Z6's exposure meter is the sensor-based, Nikon Advanced Scene Recognition System that meters a wide area of the frame. The camera can set the exposure based on the distribution of brightness, color, distance, and composition when used with a native Nikkor S lens; an FTZ adapter-mounted E, G, P, or D lens that contains a CPU; and many aftermarket lenses. Most people leave their light meter set to Matrix metering and enjoy excellent results.

The Advanced Scene Recognition System measures each scene's light properties, color spectrum, and brightness levels. It then compares your subject against the camera's built-in image database to provide even more accurate autoexposure. With a metering sensor this sensitive, the Z6 can do things with ease that other cameras struggle to accomplish. Let's see how to select one of the Metering modes.

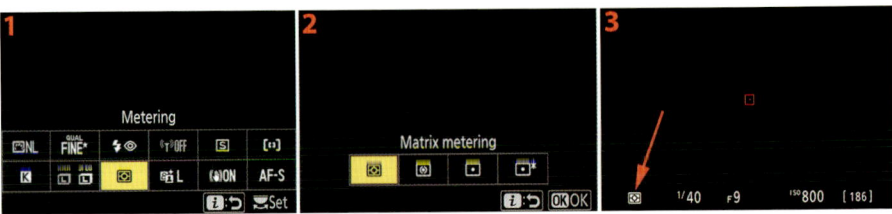

Figure 3.0: Four meter types: Matrix, Center-weighted, Spot, and Highlight-weighted

Use the following steps to select one of the Metering modes:

1. Press the *i* button to open the *i* Menu (figure 3.0, image 1), find the Metering position on the *i* Menu (bottom row, third from the left), and then press the OK button or tap the Metering option to enter the mode selection screen.
2. You will see a series of four metering symbols on the *i* Menu metering mode selection screen, as shown in figure 3.0, image 2. Scroll to the left or right and select the Metering mode you want to use (e.g., Matrix Metering). Your four choices are: Matrix metering, Center-weighted metering, Spot metering, and Highlight-weighted metering. Press the OK button or tap the option on the screen to lock it in.
3. Figure 3.0, image 3, shows where the metering symbol will appear on the camera's rear Monitor or in the electronic viewfinder (EVF) once you have selected a metering mode.

Now, let's examine the four metering types to see which you will use most often.

Matrix Metering

The Nikon Z6 contains the Matrix metering system, one of the most powerful and accurate automatic exposure meters in any camera today.

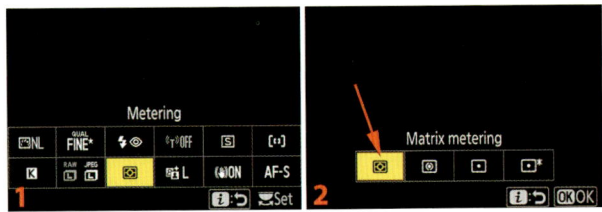

Figure 3.1: The Matrix metering symbol

In the *i* Menu shown in figure 3.1, image 2, you can see the Matrix metering symbol (red arrow). This is the factory default metering style.

How does Matrix metering work? The sensor-based Nikon Advanced Scene Recognition System examines four critical aspects of each picture or video. It compares the levels of *brightness* in various parts of the scene to determine the total range of EV values. It then notices the *color* of the subject and surroundings. If you are using a CPU-equipped S, E, G, P, or D lens, it also determines how far away your lens is focused so it can determine the *distance* to your subject. Finally, it looks at the *compositional* elements of the subject.

When it has all that information, it compares your image to tens of thousands of image characteristics in its image database, uses proprietary Nikon software to make complex evaluative computations, and comes up with an exposure value that is usually right on target, even in complex lighting situations.

Center-Weighted Metering

If you were raised on a classic center-weighted meter and still prefer that type, the Z6's exposure meter can be transformed into a flexible center-weighted meter with variable sized weighting that you can control.

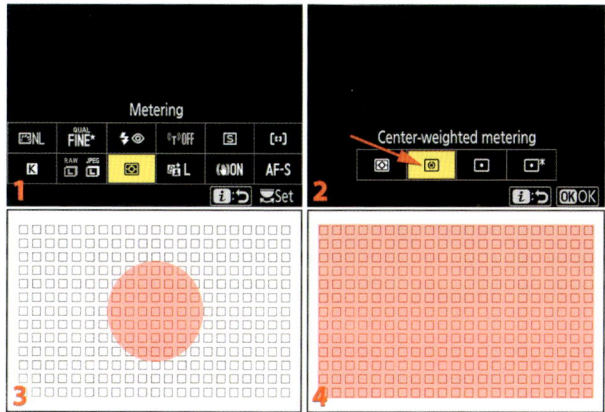

Figure 3.2: Center-weighted metering, 12mm (image 3) and Averaging (image 4)

In figure 3.2, image 2 (red arrow), you can see the Center-weighted metering selection. The Center-weighted meter in the Z6 meters the entire frame, but concentrates 75 percent of the metering into a 12mm circle in the middle of the frame (figure 3.2, image 3). The other 25 percent of metering comes from the rest of the frame outside the circle. You can't actually see a circle in the EVF, so you'll have to imagine it.

If you'd like, you can eliminate the circle and use the entire frame as a basic averaging meter (figure 3.2, image 4). Use *Custom Setting Menu > b Metering/exposure > b3 Center-weighted area* (page 385), to switch between the 12mm metering circle and the entire-frame averaging method. If you set your meter to Average (Avg) in Custom setting b3 Center-weighted area, the light values of the entire frame are averaged to arrive at an exposure value. No particular area of the frame is assigned any greater importance.

This is a little bit like Matrix metering, but without the extra smarts. In fact, on several test subjects, I got similar meter readings from the Average and Matrix meters. However, Matrix metering should do better in difficult lighting situations because it has a database of image characteristics to compare with your current image—including color, distance, and where your subject is located in the frame.

Settings Recommendation: Nikon recommends that you should use Center-weighted metering if you are using a filter with a filter factor over 1x. However, I've been using Matrix metering with polarizer filters with 1.5x and 2x filter factors for many years, and have not had any bad results. Your mileage may vary, so experiment with your filters to see if you detect any Matrix metering exposure problems when using dark filters. If you do, then switch to Center-weighted metering.

Spot Metering

Often only a spot meter will do. In situations where you must get an accurate exposure for a very small section of the frame, or if you must get several meter readings from various small areas—for manual averaging—the Z6 can be adjusted to fit your needs. The camera's Spot meter evaluates only 1.5 percent (4mm) of the frame, so it is indeed a real spot meter.

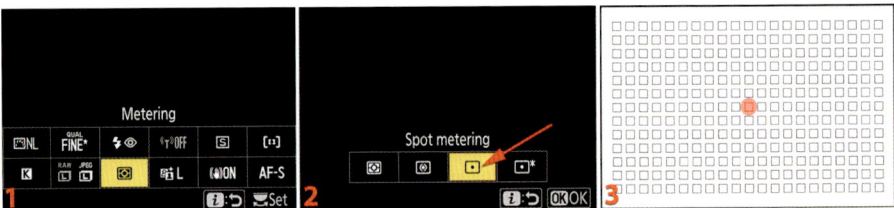

Figure 3.3: Spot metering mode symbol (1) and its size (2)

In figure 3.3, image 1, you can see the Spot metering symbol. The Z6's Spot meter consists of a 4mm circle (0.16 inch) surrounding the currently active single AF point in both Single and Continuous AF modes (AF-S and AF-C). How big is the 4mm spot? The Spot meter barely surrounds an AF point in your viewfinder (figure 3.3, image 3, red circle). In fact, the Spot meter follows the currently active AF point, within the 273 AF points in the Viewfinder, as you move the AF point around the frame with the Sub-selector joystick.

When your Z6 is in Spot meter mode and you move the AF point to some small section of your subject, you can rest assured that you're getting a true spot reading. In fact, you can use your Spot meter to determine an approximate EV range of light values in the entire image by taking multiple manual spot readings from different parts of the subject and comparing the values. If the values exceed 10 EV or 12 EV steps, you have to decide which part of your subject is most important and meter for it.

On an overcast day, you can usually get by with no worries since the range of light is often within the recording capability of the sensor. On a bright, sunny day, the range of light can be more than a single image can record, and you might have to use a graduated neutral-density filter or HDR imaging to rein in the excessive light range.

Just remember that spot metering is often a trade-off. Either you have the ability to ensure that a highly specific portion of an image is exposed with spot-on accuracy (Spot meter) or you can use the camera's multiple averaging skills (Matrix meter) to generally get the correct exposure throughout the frame. The choice is yours, depending on the shooting situation.

If you spot meter the face of someone who is standing in the sun, the shadows around the person will usually be underexposed and have little or no data. If you spot meter the areas in the shadows instead, the person's face is likely to be blown out and lose detail. We'll discuss this more in section 3 of this chapter, which explores the histogram (on page 67).

Settings Recommendation: Use your Spot meter to get specific meter readings of small areas on and around your subject; then make some exposure decisions yourself and your subject should be well exposed. Just remember that the Spot meter evaluates only for the small 4mm area that it sees, so it cannot adjust the camera for anything except that one tiny area. Spot metering requires some practice, but it is a very precise way to obtain exposure readings.

Highlight-Weighted Metering

Highlight-weighted metering is not available for Movie mode (video recording); it works only in Photo mode (still photography).

Some types of photography, such as theater, concert, or other types of event photography, may have a bright subject against a dark background. Since most other meter types tend to average the light in the frame, you may see a burned-out, overly bright subject as the camera tries to compensate for the extreme contrast between the subject and the background.

Highlight-weighted metering causes the camera to pay more attention to the highlights of your subject than to its darker surroundings, often giving you a much better exposure for the subject.

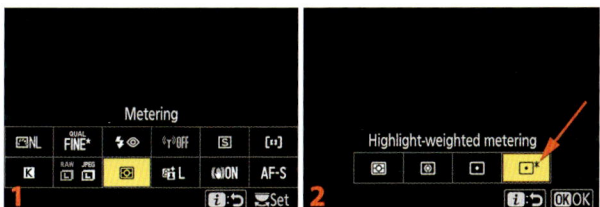

Figure 3.4: Highlight-weighted metering

In figure 3.4, image 2, you can see the Highlight-weighted metering symbol: the small square spot meter symbol with the asterisk on the top-right corner. The Highlight-weighted meter has a special ability to maintain a proper highlight-to-darkness ratio so that the image highlights are exposed correctly.

For instance, if you are photographing a concert singer at a microphone under a spotlight, this type of metering will give you a better exposure of the singer, at the expense of letting the background and surroundings go dark.

I can imagine all types of situations where the subject is bright and the surroundings are dark. The Highlight-weighted meter type should help you create better images under those circumstances.

Settings Recommendation: When you are shooting images where the subject has important bright areas that are surrounded by darker areas, this metering method will help you keep the brighter areas properly exposed. Normally, bright areas on darkness will cause the camera to burn out the highlights while it tries to keep some detail in the dark areas. However, Highlight-weighted metering gives the camera direction to expose for the highlights, letting the dark areas stay dark.

For best results, you may want to consider using NEF (RAW) mode when shooting in this mode. The RAW image will have a lot of hidden detail in the dark areas that can be brought up in image processing software (e.g., Lightroom). Shooting in RAW mode keeps that detail intact so that you can manually bring out dark image detail later. In RAW mode you can make the image more closely match what your eye could see at the event you were photographing. Let Highlight-weighted metering protect the important highlights and then balance the image yourself in your computer.

Section 2: Exposure Modes

My first serious Nikon, back in 1980, was a Nikon FM. I remember it with fondness because that was when I first got serious about making money with photography. It's hard for me to imagine that it has been so long since I bought my FM! Things were simpler back then. When I say simple, I mean that the FM had a basic center-weighted light meter, a manual exposure dial, and manual aperture settings. I had to decide how to create the image in all aspects. It was a camera with only one mode: M, or manual.

Later I bought a Nikon FE and was amazed to use its A mode, or Aperture-priority auto. I could set the aperture manually and the camera would adjust the shutter speed for me. Luxury! The FE had two modes, Manual (M) and Aperture priority (A).

A few more years went by, and I bought a Nikon F4 that was loaded with features and was much more complex. It had four modes, including the two I was used to, M and A, and two new modes, Shutter-priority auto (S) and Programmed auto (P). I had to learn even more stuff! The F4 was my first P, S, A, M camera.

Does this sound anything like your progression? If you're over 50, maybe so; if not, you may just be getting into the digital photography realm with your Z6, and I ought to stop reminiscing and get to the point.

Today's cameras are amazingly complex compared to cameras only a few years ago. Let's examine how we can use that flexibility for our benefit. The Z6 is also a P, S, A, M camera. That's the abbreviated progression of primary shooting modes that allow you to control the shutter speed and aperture. In addition, the Z6 has a fully AUTO mode for when you just want to take good pictures without thinking about exposure. Let's examine each in detail.

There is just one control on the Z6 to set the following modes: AUTO; P, S, A, M; and the user modes (U1, U2, and U3). This special control is called the Mode dial. Let's discuss each exposure mode in detail.

Programmed Auto (P) Mode

Programmed auto (P) mode is designed for those times when you just want to shoot pictures and not think much about camera settings but still want emergency control when needed. The camera takes care of the shutter speed and aperture for you and uses your selected exposure meter to create the best pictures it can without human intervention. You can override the aperture by turning the rear Main command dial.

Figure 3.5A shows the Mode dial set to Programmed auto (P) mode. This mode is called Programmed auto because it uses an internal software program. It tries its best to create optimal images in most situations.

P mode first appeared as a rudimentary AUTO mode on Nikon SLR film cameras and is still on the Mode dial to benefit those who learned to use it in the good old days of film cameras. However, even the User's Manual calls this a "snapshot" mode. P mode can handle a wide variety of situations well, but I wouldn't depend on it for

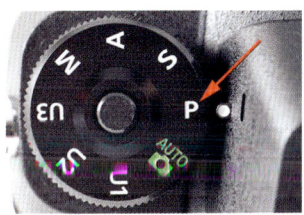

Figure 3.5A: Programmed auto (P) mode

my important shooting. It can be great at a party, for example, where you want some nice snapshots. You don't have to think about camera settings and can just enjoy the party. To many, P mode is *P* for Party.

This is a good mode to use when you want to let the camera control the aperture and shutter while you control the rest of the camera's settings. In a sense, it's like AUTO mode except it doesn't control the ISO sensitivity and it lets you override the aperture in an emergency. You may need more depth of field and decide to use a smaller aperture, and you can override camera control by turning the Main command dial. When you do, the aperture is immediately under your control, while the camera controls the shutter.

P mode comes in two parts: Programmed auto and Flexible program. Flexible program works similarly to Aperture-priority auto (A) mode. Why do I say that? Let me explain by giving an example.

Unexpected Group Shot!

You're shooting at a family party, taking a natural-light snapshot of cousin Jane. The camera, which is in P mode, has selected f/4 for the aperture. Suddenly cousin Bill, aunt Millie, and five more people run to get into the picture. Where you were shooting an individual portrait—using a shallow depth of field to emphasize your subject—now you have a group with more than one row. You (being a well-trained photographer) glance down at your camera and realize that the f/4 aperture won't give you enough depth of field to focus on the front row and still have a sharp image of the back row. You quickly turn the camera's rear Main command dial clockwise to reduce the aperture size for more depth of field.

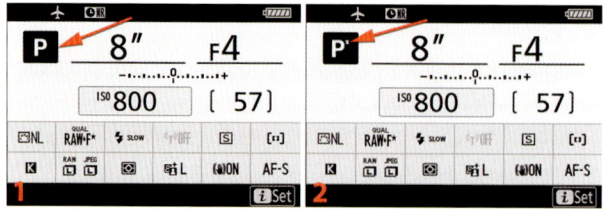

Figure 3.5B: Standard P mode (image 1) and Flexible program P* mode (image 2)

When the camera senses the Main command dial being turned, it realizes that it's being called upon to leave snapshot (standard P) mode and give you aperture control. It displays a small P* on the Information display screen (figure 3.5B, image 2, red arrow) to let you know it realizes you are taking over control of the aperture. Since you are turning the dial clockwise, it obligingly starts cranking down the aperture. After a few rotational clicks to the left, your aperture is now at f/8. You put the camera to your eye, yell "say cheeeeese!" and press the Shutter-release button. You've got the shot! A family memory captured.

What you did in my imaginary scenario was invoke the Flexible program (P*) mode in your Z6. How? As soon as you turned the Main command dial, the Z6 left normal P mode and switched to P* (Flexible program). Before you turned the Main command dial, the Z6 was happily controlling both the shutter speed and the aperture for you. When you turned the dial, the Z6 immediately switched to Flexible program mode and let you have control of the aperture. It then controlled only the shutter speed. In effect, the Z6 allowed you to exercise your knowledge of photography very quickly and assisted you only from that point.

If you turn the Main command dial clockwise, the aperture opening gets smaller (e.g., f/11). If you turn it counterclockwise, the aperture opening gets larger (e.g., f/2.8). Nothing happens if you turn the front Subcommand dial. Can you see why I say Flexible program mode acts like Aperture-priority (A) mode?

Understanding the Extra Clicks

When using P* mode, if you turn the Main command dial counterclockwise until the aperture reaches its maximum size, and then you continue turning the dial, the camera starts counting clicks but does nothing else. To start making the aperture move again, you have to turn back the same number of clicks (up to 15). I have no idea why Nikon does it this way—maybe to allow room for extra aperture click-stops on certain lenses—but it's been like this for many years. It's no big deal, really. Just be aware that this will happen, so you won't think the camera is not working correctly.

Shutter-Priority Auto (S) Mode

Shutter-priority auto (S) is for those who need to control the shutter speed while allowing the camera to maintain the correct aperture for the available light. You'll turn the Main command dial to adjust the shutter speed, while the camera controls the aperture.

Figure 3.6A shows the Mode dial set to S for Shutter-priority auto mode. If you find yourself shooting action, you'll want to keep the shutter speed high enough to capture an image without excessive blurring. Shooting sports, air shows, auto races, or any quickly moving subject requires careful control of the shutter. If you shoot a bird in flight, you'll want to use a fast shutter speed that allows for just a tiny bit of motion blur in its wings while stopping the body of the bird.

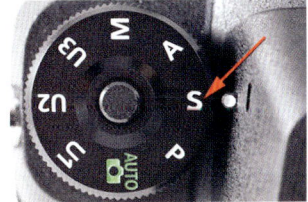

Figure 3.6A: Shutter-priority auto (S) mode

Sometimes you'll want to set your shutter speed to slow settings for special effects or time exposures, such as a small waterfall in a beautiful autumn stream. See figure 3.6B for both effects.

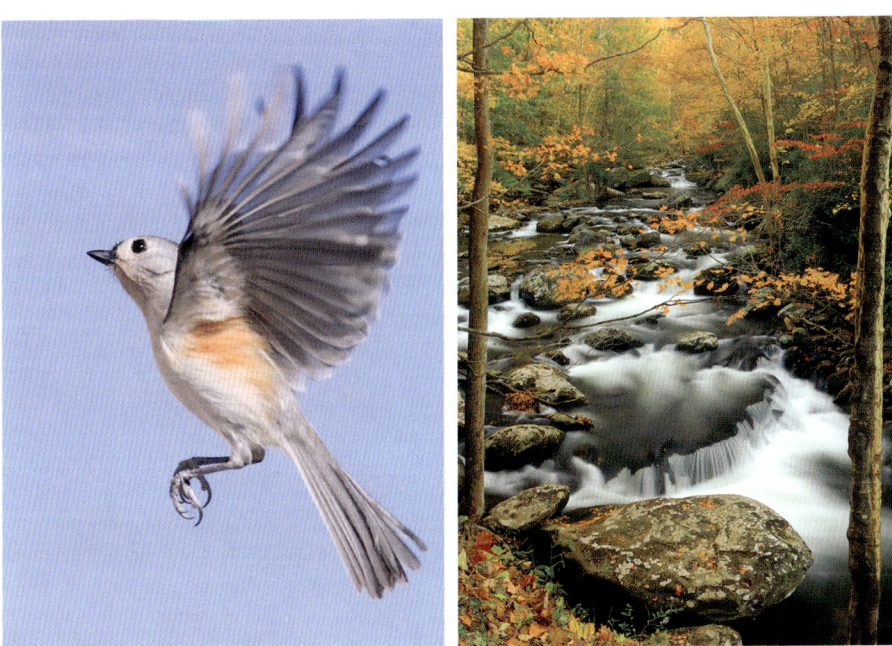

Figure 3.6B: Fast shutter speed to stop bird and slow shutter speed to blur water

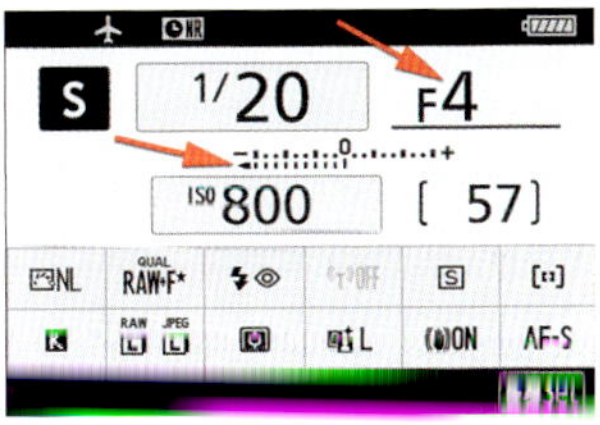

If the light changes dramatically and the camera cannot maintain a correct exposure with your current shutter speed setting, it will inform you by blinking the aperture setting and displaying an exposure indicator showing the amount of under- or overexposure (−/+) in the EVF or on the monitor.

Figure 3.6C: Significant underexposure, items at points of arrows will blink

Figure 3.6C shows the Information display as an example. The aperture indicator (upper red arrow) blinks and the exposure indicator (lower red arrow) appears when the exposure is incorrect.

To change the shutter speed, rotate the rear Main command dial to any value between 30 seconds and 1/8000 second. Turn the wheel counterclockwise for faster shutter speeds or clockwise for slower speeds. The camera will try to adjust the aperture to maintain a correct exposure; if it can't, it will warn you by blinking.

Watch Out for Camera Shake!

Be careful when the shutter speed is set below 1/60 second. Camera shake becomes a problem for many people at 1/30 second and slower. If you are using the camera's in-body image stabilization (IBIS), and you are careful to stand still, brace your arms against your chest, and spread your feet apart with one in front of the other, you'll probably be able to make sharp images at 1/6 to 1/30 second (figure 3.6D, left image). I have regularly been able to shoot handheld in that range with no problem, as long as IBIS is active and I am careful about how I'm holding the camera. Of course, in a slow shutter speed range, your subject must be static.

Surprisingly, your heartbeat and breathing is reflected in your hands during slow shutter speed photography. If you are going to shoot at slow shutter speeds, buy yourself a nice solid tripod (turn IBIS off when on a solid tripod). You'll make much nicer pictures.

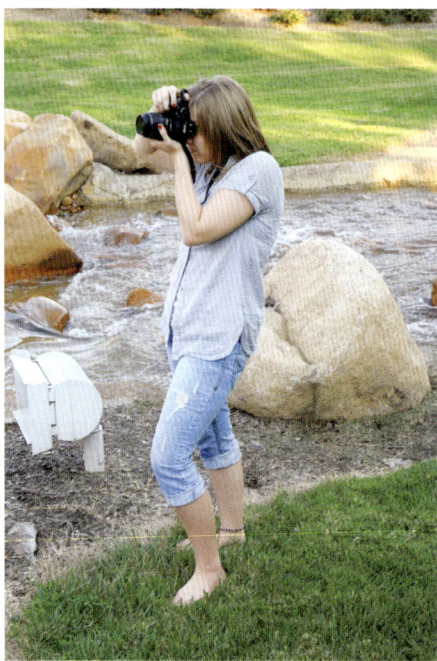
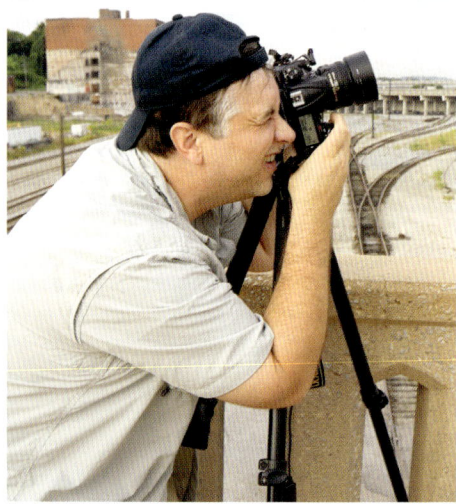

Figure 3.6D: Woman holding camera for steady shooting, and a man using a tripod

Aperture-Priority Auto (A) Mode

Nature and macro shooters, and anyone concerned with carefully controlling depth of field, often leave their cameras set to Aperture-priority auto (A) mode. Figure 3.7A shows the Mode dial set to Aperture-priority auto mode.

Aperture-priority auto mode, or A mode, allows you to control the aperture while the camera takes care of the shutter speed for optimal exposures. To select an aperture, you use the front Sub-command dial. Turn the wheel clockwise for smaller apertures (stopping down) and counterclockwise for larger apertures (opening up).

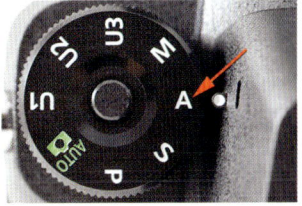

Figure 3.7A: Aperture priority (A) auto

The minimum and maximum aperture settings are limited by the minimum and maximum aperture openings on the lens you're using. Most consumer lenses run from f/3.5 to f/22. More expensive pro-style prime lenses may have apertures as large as f/0.95 (e.g., Nikkor Z 58mm f/0.95 S lens), but pro zoom lenses generally start at f/2.8 and end at f/22–f/32 (e.g., Nikkor Z 24–70mm f/2.8 S lens).

Several of the Nikkor S lenses have a maximum aperture of f/4 to keep the size and weight down, while providing extremely sharp, low-distortion, and virtually aberration-free images and video (e.g., Nikkor Z 24–70mm f/4 S and Nikkor Z 14–30mm f/4 S). These small S lenses are well matched for the light and compact Z-camera bodies.

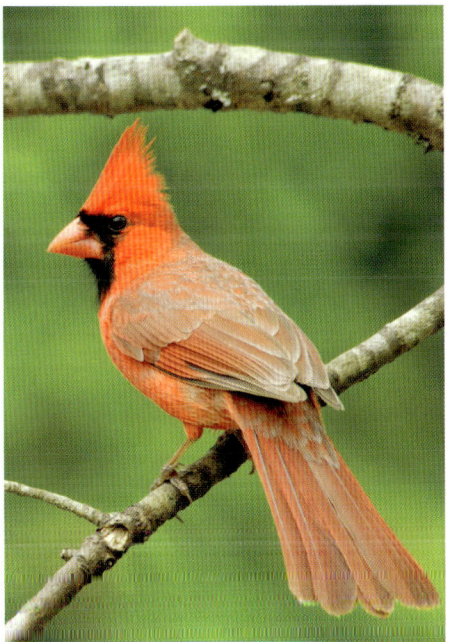
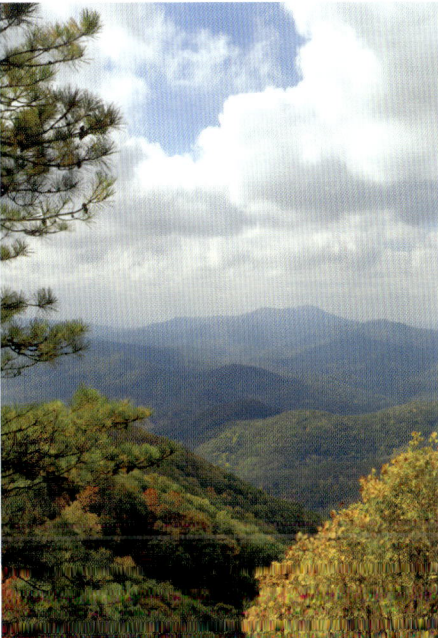

Figure 3.7B: Large aperture to blur background and small aperture for deep focus

The aperture directly controls the amount of depth of field—or zone of sharpness—in an image. Depth of field is an extremely important concept for photographers to understand. Simply put, it allows you to control the range or depth of sharp focus in your images. In the bird image in figure 3.7B, the depth of field is very shallow, and in the scenic shot it is very deep.

Manual (M) Mode

Manual mode gives you complete control of your shutter and aperture so you can make all the exposure decisions, with suggestions from the light meter. Figure 3.8A, image 1, shows the Mode dial set to Manual (M).

You can adjust the aperture with the front Sub-command dial and adjust the shutter speed with the rear Main command dial. In Manual mode you have control over the aperture (for depth of field) and the shutter speed (for motion control). If your subject needs a little more depth of field, just make the aperture smaller, but be sure to slow down the shutter speed as well (or your image may be underexposed). If you suddenly need a faster shutter speed, then set it faster, but be sure to open the aperture to compensate for it. The camera will make suggestions with the meter, but you make the final decision about how the exposure will look.

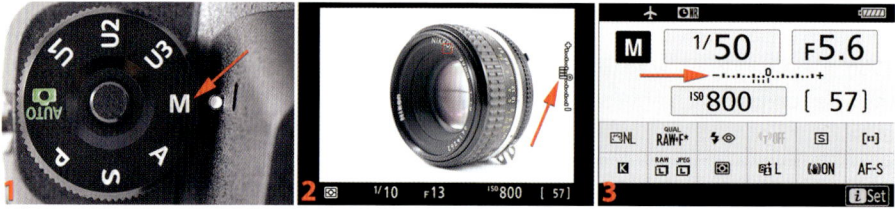

Figure 3.8A: Mode dial set to Manual (M); analog exposure indicator in EVF/Monitor and on the Information display screen

In figure 3.8A, images 2 and 3, notice the electronic analog exposure indicator at the red arrows. This exposure indicator, which is visible in the EVF, on the Monitor, or on the Information display, has a minus sign (−) on one end and a plus sign (+) on the other end. Each dot on the scale represents 1/3 EV step, and each line represents 1 EV step. The exposure indicator in image 2 shows one stop of overexposure (+1 EV), whereas the indicator in image 3 shows one stop of underexposure (−1 EV).

You can control how sensitive this scale is by changing *Custom Setting Menu > b Metering/exposure > b1 EV steps for exposure cntrl*. You can set Custom setting b1 to 1/3 EV step or 1/2 EV step. The camera defaults to 1/3 step.

When you are metering your subject, a dashed bar will appear to the left of the horizontal version of the exposure indicator (figure 3.8A, image 2) on most screens that allow exposure changes, and below the vertical exposure indicator (figure 3.8A, image 3) on the Information display screen. The analog exposure indicator's small dashes extend from the zero in the center toward the plus side to indicate overexposure, or toward the minus side to indicate underexposure. You can gauge the amount of over- or underexposure by the number of dots and lines the bar passes as it heads toward one side or the other.

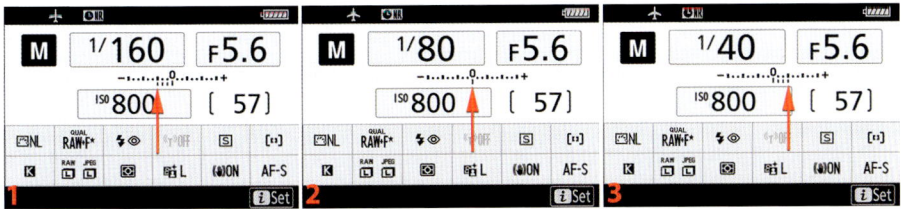

Figure 3.8B: Underexposed, well exposed, and overexposed image

The goal in Manual mode is to make the small bars to the left of or below the exposure indicator disappear. In figure 3.8B, image 1, the image is underexposed by 1 stop (1 EV step). In image 2, the image is well exposed. In image 3, the image is overexposed by 1 stop (1 EV step). To get a good exposure, make sure there are no bars to the left or right of (or above or below, if using the EVF) the 0 position. Manual mode is for taking your time and enjoying your photography. It gives you the most control of how the image looks, but you need more knowledge to get correct exposures.

Settings Recommendation: As a nature photographer, I am mostly concerned with getting a nice sharp image with a deep depth of field. About 90 percent of the time my camera is set to Aperture-priority auto (A) and f/8. I started using this mode back in about 1986 when I bought my Nikon FE, and I have stayed with it since. In A mode, you control the aperture and the camera controls the shutter speed. Sometimes, when I really need extra depth of field, I might stop down to f/11 or f/16. However, in those very small aperture ranges you can lose some image sharpness from diffraction. That lack of sharpness is caused by light rays bouncing off the edges of the aperture blades because the aperture opening is so small.

If I were shooting sports or action, I would have my camera set to Shutter-priority auto (S) most often, which would allow me to control the speed of the shutter and capture those fast-moving subjects without a lot of blur. The camera will control the aperture so I will have to concentrate only on which shutter speed best fits my subject's movement.

I use the other two modes, Programmed auto (P) and Manual (M), only for special occasions. When I want to control the camera absolutely, I use Manual.

I probably use Programmed auto (P) mode least of all. I might use it when I am at a party and just want to take nice pictures for my own use. I let the camera make most of the decisions in P mode, and I still have the ability to quickly jump into Flexible program (P*) mode when events call for a little more aperture control.

Why shouldn't you just use AUTO mode instead? (We'll explore this in the next section.) Well, AUTO mode controls everything, including when to use flash and which ISO sensitivity setting is best; therefore, it may not work well for maximum-quality images in lower light levels. With P mode, the camera controls only the shutter speed and aperture, and you control the rest.

Some new photographers have recently switched from using a point-and-shoot camera or smartphone to the tremendously more powerful Nikon Z6. Most point-and-shoot cameras and smartphones have completely automatic exposure modes. If you have come over from the point-and-shoot or smartphone world, you might enjoy using the AUTO mode at first while learning the more advanced P, S, A, and M modes. Let's look into how AUTO mode works.

Auto Exposure (AUTO) Mode

The AUTO exposure mode (figure 3.9) is for those times when you want to get the picture with no thought as to how the camera works. All you need to be concerned about in AUTO mode is whether the battery is fully charged and how well the image is composed.

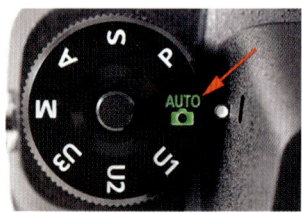

Figure 3.9: AUTO exposure mode

When in AUTO mode, the Z6 becomes a big point-and-shoot camera, like a heavy Nikon Coolpix. Many of its internal modes become automatic, which means you can't change them because the camera decides what is best for each setting. Here is a list of some major functions that become disabled when using AUTO mode:

- White balance
- Picture Control
- Active D-Lighting
- Flash control
- HDR (high dynamic range)
- Auto bracketing
- Multiple exposure

- ISO sensitivity settings
- Time-lapse photography
- Exposure compensation
- Metering mode
- Electronic front-curtain shutter
- Focus shift shooting (stacking)
- Low-light AF

In effect, you relinquish control of the camera's functions for a "guarantee" that some sort of picture will be provided. In most cases, the Z6 will provide its normal excellent images when you select AUTO. However, in difficult circumstances, the camera is free to turn up the ISO sensitivity and extend the Active D-Lighting range to get a picture, even at the expense of image quality.

If you want to loan your camera to a friend who has no interest in how cameras work, the Z6 will happily make nice images for them in AUTO mode. While you are learning to use the more advanced functions of the camera, you too might benefit from using this mode for a while. You'll usually get better pictures when you control the camera, but the Z6 has some very efficient software that will help you if you're not ready to take control.

Settings Recommendation: I don't like to admit it, but I do use AUTO mode sometimes. The Z6 is such a good camera that it will make some nice images without my help. If I have reasonably good light and am not shooting for commercial work, I will switch to AUTO mode just to enjoy taking pictures. Sometimes we need to take ourselves less seriously. AUTO mode lets me do that. Try it!

Bad Exposure Warning

If the light changes drastically and the camera cannot maintain a correct exposure due to your current settings, the offending setting will blink in the Viewfinder and on the Monitor. The camera will also display the −/+ exposure indicator (which you use in Manual mode) with an approximate number of EV steps of over- or underexposure. If you see the aperture or shutter speed setting blinking in any of the displays, along with the −/+ exposure indicator displaying a −/+ EV value, please validate your exposure before taking a picture.

U1, U2, and U3 User Settings

The user modes U1, U2, and U3 on the Mode dial (figure 3.10) allow you to make adjustments to many of the camera's settings and then save them for later use. In a sense, you can use the user settings to make the camera operate in different ways for different styles of photography.

You'll need to configure your camera's settings and then use *Setup Menu > Save user settings > Save to U1 (or U2, U3)* to save the configuration for that specific user setting. Please refer to the chapter titled **Setup Menu** and the heading called **Save User Settings** (page 474) for a thorough discussion of the three user settings, including lists of items that can and cannot be saved to a user setting.

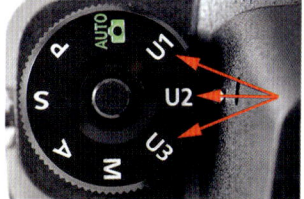

Figure 3.10: User modes U1, U2, and U3

After you have saved your configuration of settings into a user setting (e.g., U1), you can recall them into use by simply selecting that user setting from the Mode dial. This allows you to set your camera up for three very specific purposes and switch to them quickly. Very powerful!

Settings Recommendation: I set U1 for highest-quality NEF (RAW) shooting, U2 for highest-quality JPEG shooting, and U3 for party mode.

Section 3: Histogram

Back in the good old (film) days, we didn't have a histogram, so we had to depend on our experience and light meter to get a good exposure. Because we couldn't see the exposure until after we had left the scene, we measured our success by the number of correctly exposed images we were able to create.

With the exposure meter/histogram combination found in the Z6, and the ability to zoom in to our images with the high-resolution Monitor on the back of the camera, our success rate is much higher than ever before.

The histogram can be as important as the exposure meter, or even more so. The meter sets up the camera for the exposure, and the histogram verifies that the exposure is a good one.

If your exposure meter readout stopped working, you could still get perfect exposures using only the histogram. In fact, I gauge my efforts more by how the histogram looks than anything else. The exposure meter and histogram work together to make sure you get excellent results from your photographic efforts.

- **Live Luminance Histogram:** The Z6 has the ability to display a live luminance histogram right in the EVF and on the Monitor (figure 3.11A). The live histogram reflects the current

exposure of the image displayed. As you change the exposure values, you can instantly see the changes reflected in the histogram, assuring you that your exposure is good or warning you when it is bad. We will review how to read a histogram in the next chapter section. **Technical information:** Figure 3.11A shows a basic luminance histogram, which is a weighted view of the brightness and color in a scene based on how the human eye perceives light. How does the luminance histogram differ from the RGB histograms? The

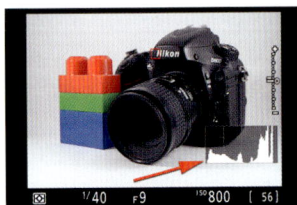

Figure 3.11A: Live luminance histogram

luminance histogram is a representation of the perceived brightness (luminosity) from a combination of the red, green, and blue channels seen in figure 3.11B. In other words, the luminance histogram tries to accurately reflect the light you see by weighting its color values in a particular way. Since the human eye sees green most easily, the luminance histogram is heavily weighted toward green. Notice in figure 3.11B how the luminance histogram at the top (the white one) looks very similar to the green channel histogram below it. Red and blue are also represented in the luminance histogram, but in lesser quantities (59 percent green + 30 percent red + 11 percent blue = luminance). The luminance histogram measures the perceived brightness in 256 levels (0–255). It is an accurate way of looking at the combined color levels in real images. Because it more accurately reflects the way our eyes actually see color brightness, it may be the best histogram for you to use, most of the time.

- **Playback RGB Histogram:** The RGB histogram screen shows an individual histogram for each color channel (figure 3.11B). These are not live histograms. They show up after you take the picture so that you can review how well a picture is exposed. On the top is a luminance histogram, followed by individual red, green, and blue (RGB) channel histo-

grams. If your camera does not display the RGB histogram screen shown in figure 3.11B, you'll need to select the check box found at *Playback Menu > Playback display options > RGB histogram*. This setting enables or disables the RGB histogram screen, which you can then find by displaying an image on the Monitor and scrolling up or down with the Multi selector pad. One important reason to examine the RGB histogram is to see if any single color channel has lost all detail in the

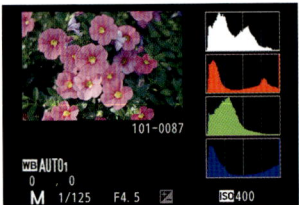

Figure 3.11B: Playback RGB histogram

dark or light areas. Later in this chapter we will examine how you can determine when detail has been lost.

- **Playback Luminance Histogram:** Figure 3.11C shows a slightly larger luminance histogram along with image information. This is not a live histogram. It shows up after you take the picture so that you can review how well a picture is exposed. It works like the previously discussed luminance histogram (figure 3.11A). If your camera does not display the Luminance histogram screen shown in figure 3.11C, you'll need to put a check in the check box found at *Playback Menu > Playback display options > Overview*. This setting enables or disables the Overview screen, which you can then find by displaying an image on the Monitor and scrolling up or down with the Multi selector pad.

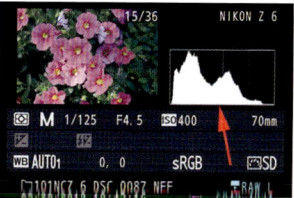

Figure 3.11C: Playback luminance histogram

Understanding the Histogram

The Z6's imaging sensor can record a wide range of light values. Unfortunately, even with the large potential dynamic range the Z6 has, many of the higher-contrast subjects we shoot contain more light range than the camera can capture in one exposure.

Using your Z6's histogram screens will guarantee you a much higher percentage of well-exposed images. It is worth spending time to understand the histogram. It's not as complicated as it looks. Let's look into the histogram so you can determine how well you have captured the light in the scene before your lens. The gray rectangular area in figure 3.11D represents an in-camera histogram. Examine it carefully!

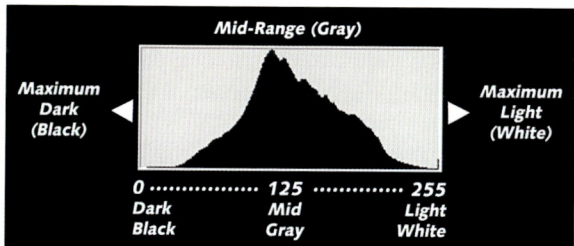

Figure 3.11D: A basic histogram

The histogram is basically a graph of 256 steps that represents the maximum range of light values your camera can capture (0 = pure black and 255 = pure white). In the middle of the histogram are the midrange values that represent middle colors like grays, light browns, and greens. The values from just above zero to just below 255 contain detail.

The actual histogram often looks like a mountain peak, or a series of peaks, and the more there is of a particular color, the taller the peak that represents that color will be.

Sometimes the graph will be rounder on top, and other times it will be flattened or have several peaks.

The left side of the histogram represents the maximum dark values that your camera can record. The right side represents the maximum light values your camera can capture. On either end of the histogram (0 or 255), the light values contain no detail. They are either completely black (0) or completely white (255).

The height of the histogram (top of mountain peaks) represents the amount of individual colors. You cannot easily control this value in-camera, other than changing to a Picture Control with more or less saturated color, so it is for your information only.

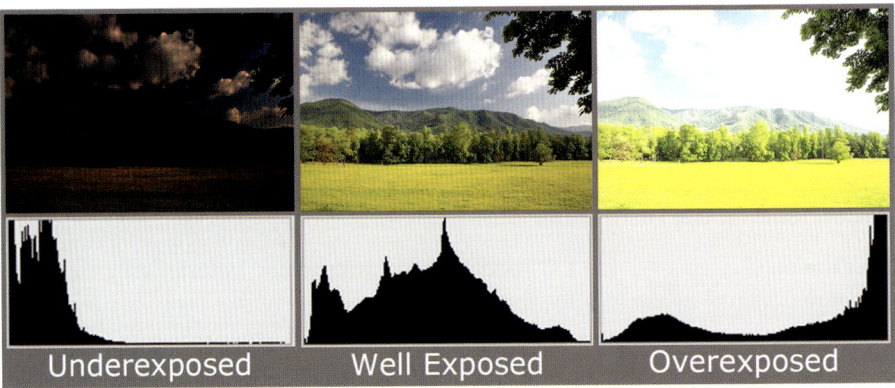

Figure 3.11E: Three histograms: underexposed, well exposed, and overexposed

We are mostly concerned with the left- and right-side values of the histogram because we do have much greater control over those (dark versus light). In figure 3.11E, we see a basic histogram tutorial with three separate histograms that have different exposures of the same subject. Refer to figure 3.11E as we discuss the histogram further.

Simply put, the histogram's horizontal scale is related to the darkness and lightness of the image, and the vertical scale of the histogram (valleys and peaks of the mountains) have to do with the amount of color information.

The left (dark) and right (light) directions of the horizontal scale are very important for your picture taking. If the image is too dark, the light values will be clipped off on the left side; if it's too light, the light values will be clipped off on the right side.

When you see the three histograms next to each other (figure 3.11E), does it make more sense? See how the underexposed histogram is all the way to the left of the histogram window and is clipped mid peak? Note how both edges of the well-exposed histogram just touch the horizontal edges of the histogram window. Finally, notice how the overexposed histogram is crammed toward the right and clipped.

Please note that a histogram does not have to cover the entire window for the exposure to be correct. When there is a very limited range of light, the histogram may be rather narrow. The key thing to remember is that when you see a histogram that is crammed all the way to the left and clipped, some or all of the image is significantly too dark. If the histogram is crammed all the way to the right and clipped, some or all of the image is significantly too light.

It is important that you try to center the histogram without clipping either edge. This is not always possible because the light range is often too great and the sensor or histogram window can't contain it. If you take a picture and the histogram is shifted toward the left or right, you can adjust the exposure and retake the photograph. If there is too much light to allow the histogram to be centered, you must decide which part of the image is more important—the light or dark values—and expose for those values.

If you'd like to learn more about histograms, please download the special resource document titled **A Deeper Understanding of the Histogram** from the resource webpage for this book: **http://reckynook.com/NikonZ6**

Settings Recommendation: The camera's light meter should be used to get the initial exposure only. Then you can look at the histogram to see if the image's light range is contained within the limited range of the sensor. If the histogram is clipped to the right or the left, you may want to add or subtract light with the +/− Exposure compensation button or use Manual mode. Let your light meter get you close, then fine-tune with the histogram. If you master using the histogram, you will have a fine degree of control over where you place the light range of your images.

Highlights (Blink) Mode

There are also other Monitor viewing modes that you can use along with the histogram, such as the Highlights (blink) mode for blown-out highlights (see *Playback Menu > Playback display options* and put a check mark next to Highlights [page 146]).

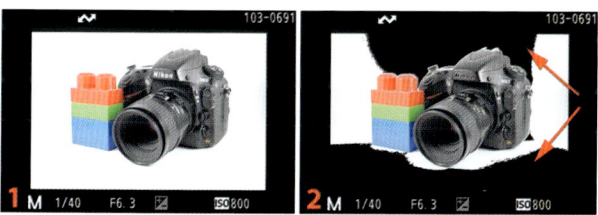

Figure 3.11F: The Highlights (blink) mode

The blink mode will cause your image to flash from light to dark in the blown-out highlight areas, as seen in the white background of my picture in figure 3.11F.

This white-to-black blinking is a rough representation of a histogram in which the highlight value is clipped, and it is quite useful for quick shooting. Using your camera's light meter, histogram, and Highlights (blink) mode together is a powerful way to control your exposures.

Author's Conclusion

This camera certainly gives you a lot of choices for light meters and exposure modes. You can start using this camera at whatever level of photographic knowledge you have. If you are a beginner, use the P mode. If you want to progress into partial automation, use the S or A mode. And if you are a dyed-in-the-wool imaging enthusiast, use the M mode for full manual control of the camera. You have a choice with the Z6!

Understanding and using the histogram will set you apart from many photographers. You will have control over the exposure of your subject in a way that those who do not understand the histogram do not have. Spend time learning to use the histogram for the best image and video exposure.

4 Focus, AF-Area, and Release Modes

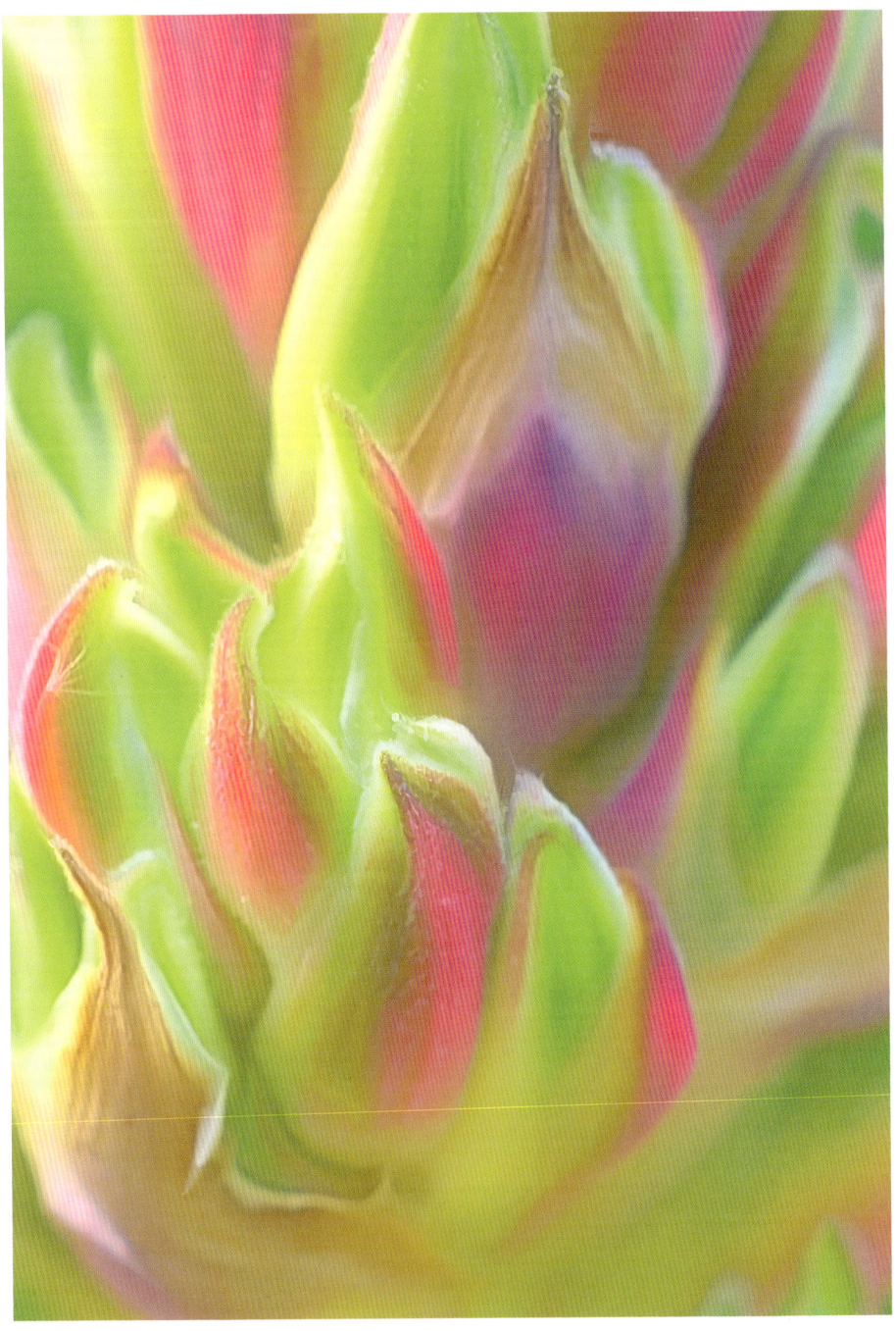

Pastel Blossom © 2019 Don L. Williams (*donlwilliams1966*)

The Focus, AF-area, and Release modes are active settings you'll deal with each time you use your camera. Unlike adjusting settings in the menus, which you'll do from time to time, you'll use these modes every time you create a photo or movie. These critical functions affect how and where the camera focuses on your subject.

To take pictures and make movies, you need to be very familiar with these settings, so this is an important chapter for your mastery of the Nikon Z6. Grab your camera and let's get started!

Autofocus Types

A mirrorless Nikon does not have a separate autofocus (AF) module. Instead, the sensor itself is used for autofocus. Here are the two types of autofocus built into the sensor:

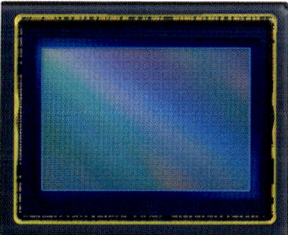

Figure 4.0: The Nikon Z6 sensor directly controls autofocus

- **Phase detection autofocus (PDAF):** The Z6 imaging sensor (figure 4.0) provides focal plane *phase-detection autofocus,* with 273 AF points in a grid-like array covering 90 percent of the electronic viewfinder (EVF) or Monitor. Each of these 273 AF points is composed of a number of photosites (pixels); therefore, thousands of pixels are involved in autofocus. Phase-detection AF is a very fast type of autofocus based on comparing areas of the subject on different parts of the sensor. Specific rows of the sensor are dual-purpose. These special rows can capture normal image data from the subject while also comparing the subject with other rows for autofocus. In other words, all the rows of the sensor can capture image data to make your photograph; however, a limited number of those same rows can also compare areas of the subject to provide autofocus.
- **Contrast detection autofocus (CDAF):** The camera's imaging sensor also provides focal plane *contrast-detection AF,* which uses pixel-level contrast detection. The entire surface of the imaging sensor can be used to detect contrast between light and dark boundaries to provide autofocus. This is a somewhat slower form of autofocus, but it is extremely accurate because it is done at the pixel level. This form of autofocus appears to be used only when you have selected Pinpoint AF (page 264), although, I have read in Nikon literature that the Z6 may also "top off" the phase-detection autofocus with a little contrast-detection, to make the AF very precise.

Shutter-Release Button versus AF-ON Button for Autofocus

In this chapter I will often mention pressing the Shutter-release button halfway down to start autofocus. However, for those who like to use back button focus, the AF-ON button is available. When I mention using the Shutter-release button for autofocus, please keep in mind that you can substitute the AF-ON button. The only difference in how the two work for initiating autofocus is that you press the Shutter-release button halfway down and you press the AF-ON button fully down.

If you prefer to disable the Shutter-release button for autofocus, simply set *Custom Setting Menu > a Autofocus > a7 AF activation* to *AF-ON only* (page 373). Then you can use the AF-ON button for back-button focus and the Shutter-release button will release the shutter but not initiate autofocus. If you leave the camera set to the default of *Shutter/AF-ON* in Custom setting a7, both the Shutter-release button and the AF-ON button will initiate autofocus. Use *AF-ON only* for back-button focus.

Custom Settings for Autofocus

The camera has 13 configurable Custom settings, a1–a13, for autofocus. We will examine each of those Custom settings in the chapter titled **Custom Setting Menu** under the **a Autofocus** subheading (page 364). You may want to read over each of them after reading this chapter.

Three Important Mode Groups

There are three specific mode groups that you should fully understand: Autofocus modes, AF-area modes, and Release modes.

Many people get these modes confused and incorrectly apply functions from one mode to a completely different mode. It *is* a bit confusing at times, but if you read this carefully and try to wrap your brain around the different functionalities provided, you'll have much greater control of your camera later.

First let's examine a list of settings in each of the three mode groups, and then we'll look more closely at each setting.

Focus modes
- Single-servo AF (AF-S)
- Continuous-servo AF (AF-C)
- Full-time AF (AF-F) [Movie mode only]
- Manual focus (MF)

AF-area modes
- Pinpoint AF (PIN) [Photo mode only]
- Single-point AF
- Dynamic-area AF
- Wide-area AF (S)
- Wide-area AF (L)
- Auto-area AF

Release modes
- Single frame (S)
- Continuous [Movie mode only]
- Continuous L (L) [Photo mode only]
- Continuous H (H) [Photo mode only]
- Continuous H (extended) (H*) [Photo mode only]
- Self-timer [Photo mode only]

What's the difference between these mode groups? Think of them like this: The Focus modes control *how* the camera focuses, the AF-area modes control *where* it focuses, and the Release modes control *when* focus happens and how often a picture is taken.

With the controls built into the Z6 body, you'll be able to select whether the camera uses just one or many of its 273 AF points to find your subject. You'll also select whether the camera simply locks focus on a static subject or whether it continuously seeks a new focus when your subject is moving, and how fast (in frames per second) it captures the images.

Settings Recommendation: If you are having trouble remembering what all these modes do—join the club! I've written many books about Nikon cameras and I still sometimes forget what each mode does. I often refer back to my own books to remember all the details. In addition to the printed book, I have an e-book version on my iPad and iPhone.

You'll become familiar with the modes you use most often, and that is usually sufficient. Try to associate the type of mode with its name, and that will make it easier. Learn the difference between a Focus mode (focus *how*), an AF-area mode (focus *where*), and a Release mode (focus *when*).

Accessing the Individual Mode Groups

The Focus modes and AF-area modes are accessible via the *i* Menu; by assigning the *Focus mode/AF-area mode* function to one of the camera's buttons; and by using the Photo and Movie Shooting Menus. The Release modes are available only by pressing the Release mode button. Let's examine each access method, and then we will consider how each works.

Focus and AF-Area Mode Access

To access the Focus and AF-area modes, you can use the *i* Menu, an assigned camera button, or the Photo and Movie Shooting Menus. First, let's see how to access the modes from the *i* Menu.

Access from the *i* Menu

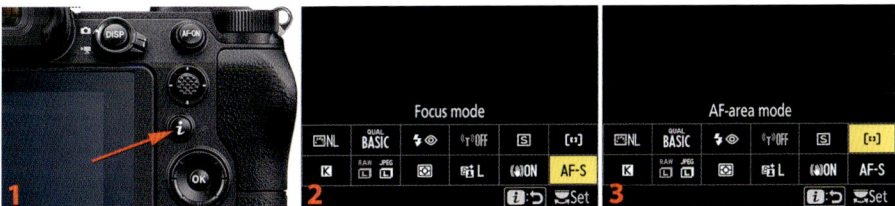

Figure 4.1A: Accessing the Focus and AF-area modes from the *i* Menu

Use the following steps to access the Focus and AF-area modes from the *i* Menu (I left the lens cap on for maximum contrast while examining control locations):

1. Press the *i* button to open the *i* Menu (figure 4.1A, image 1).
2. You will find the Focus mode entry point on the bottom row, last location on the right (figure 4.1A, image 2).
3. You will find the AF-area mode entry point on the top row, last location on the right (figure 4.1A, image 2).

Next, let's consider how to assign a button to Focus and AF-area modes, and then use the button to access the modes.

Access with an Assigned Button

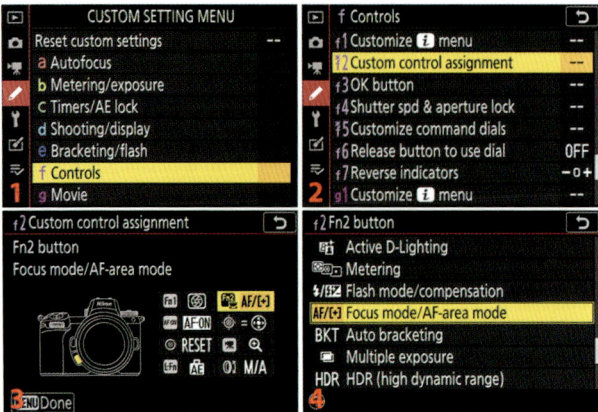

Figure 4.1B: Assigning the Focus and AF-area modes to a camera button

Use the following steps to assign *Focus mode/AF-area mode* to one of the camera's buttons:

1. Choose f Controls from the Custom Setting Menu and scroll to the right (figure 4.1B, image 1).
2. Select f2 Custom control assignment from the f Controls menu and scroll to the right (figure 4.1B, image 2).
3. Choose a camera button to assign (figure 4.1B, image 3). The Fn2 button is the factory default for the Focus/AF-area mode selection, but you may prefer another button. Leave the Fn2 button assigned as it was and skip the next step, or find a different button you want to use, highlight it, and press the OK button to open it.
4. Highlight AF/[+] Focus mode/AF area mode and press the OK button to make the assignment.

Now that you have assigned Focus mode/AF-area mode to one of the buttons, you can use that button at any time to access the Focus and AF-area modes. For more information on making button assignments in general, see **Custom Setting f2: Custom Control Assignment** on page 423.

Now let's see how to use the Fn2 button we just assigned to access the Focus and AF-area modes.

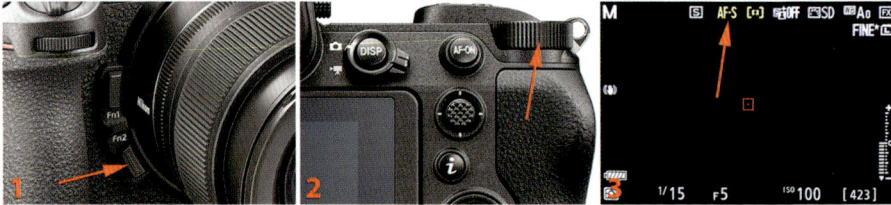

Figure 4.1C: Accessing the Focus modes with an assigned button

Use the following steps to choose a Focus mode with external camera controls:

1. Press and hold the Fn2 button on the front of the camera, or whatever button you assigned in the previous steps (figure 4.1C, image 1).
2. Turn the rear Main command dial on the back of the camera (figure 4.1C, image 2). The Monitor or EVF will display Focus mode symbols at the top (figure 4.1C, image 3, red arrow). The Focus mode will change as you rotate the rear Main command dial. When the Focus mode you want to use is displayed on the screen, stop turning the Main command dial and release the Fn2 button. Next, let's see how to access and change the AF-area modes.

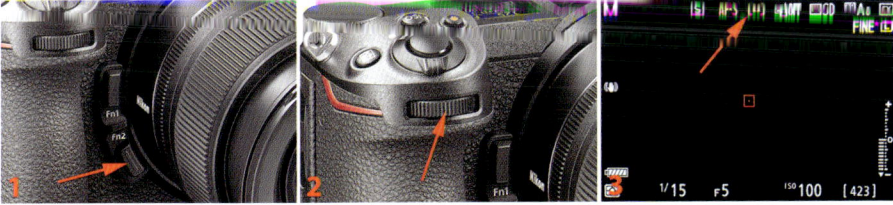

Figure 4.1D: Accessing the AF-area modes with an assigned button

Use the following steps to choose a Focus mode with external camera controls:

1. Press and hold the Fn2 button on the front of the camera (figure 4.1D, image 1).
2. Turn the Sub-command dial on the camera's front handgrip (figure 4.1D, image 2). The Monitor and EVF will display AF-area mode symbols at the top (figure 4.1D, image 3, red arrow). The AF-area mode will change as you rotate the front Sub-command dial. When the AF-area mode you want to use is displayed on the screen, stop turning the Sub-command dial and release the Fn2 button.

Next, let's consider how to access the Focus and AF-area modes from the Photo Shooting Menu and Movie Shooting Menu.

Access from the Photo and Movie Shooting Menus

Use the following steps to choose a Focus mode and an AF-Area mode from the camera's Photo Shooting Menu:

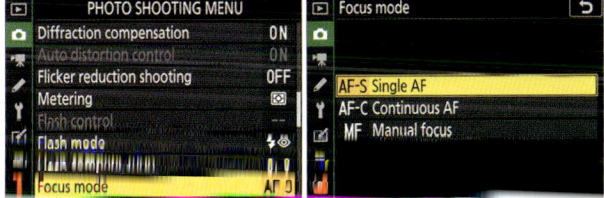

Figure 4.1E: Choosing a Focus mode from the Photo Shooting Menu (still photography)

1. Choose Focus mode from the Photo Shooting Menu (figure 4.1E, image 1) and scroll to the right.
2. Highlight a Focus mode and press the OK button or tap the mode to select it (figure 4.1E, image 2). Next let's see how to select an AF-area mode from the Photo Shooting Menu.

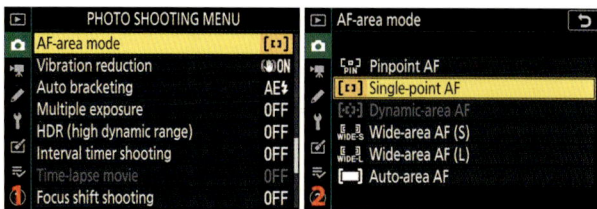

Figure 4.1F: Choosing an AF-area mode from the Photo Shooting Menu (still photography)

3. Choose AF-area mode from the Photo Shooting Menu (figure 4.1F, image 1) and scroll to the right.
4. Highlight an AF-area mode and press the OK button or tap the mode to select it (figure 4.1F, image 2). Pinpoint AF AF-area mode is available only when you are using AF-S (Single AF) Focus mode. Dynamic area AF AF-area mode is available only when you are using AF-C (Continuous AF) Focus mode.

Use the following steps to choose a Focus mode and an AF-Area mode from the camera's Movie Shooting Menu:

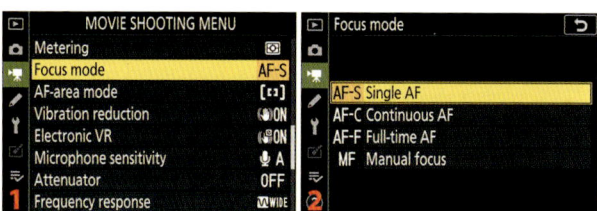

Figure 4.1G: Choosing a Focus mode from the Movie Shooting Menu (video)

1. Choose Focus mode from the Movie Shooting Menu (figure 4.1G, image 1) and scroll to the right.
2. Highlight a Focus mode and press the OK button or tap the mode to select it (figure 4.1G, image 2). Finally, let's consider how to access the AF-area modes from the Movie Shooting Menu.

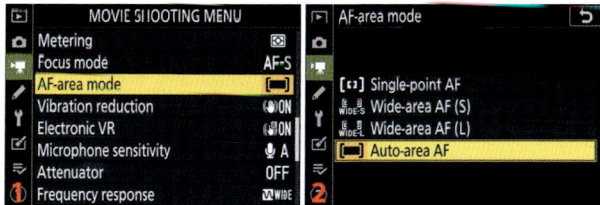

Figure 4.1H: Choosing an AF-area mode from the Movie Shooting Menu (video)

3. Choose AF-area mode from the Movie Shooting Menu (figure 4.1H, image 1) and scroll to the right.
4. Select one of the available AF-area modes and press the OK button or tap the mode to select it (figure 41.H, image 2).

Note: Selecting the Manual focus (MF) Focus mode disables the AF-area modes and they become grayed out and unavailable on the camera's various menus. The camera expects that you will be manually focusing when you are using MF mode, using something like focus Peaking (page 409) to help you get good focus. Keep that in mind as you examine how to use the Focus and AF-area modes in this chapter.

Release Mode Access

Now let's consider how to select a Release mode, first for still photography and then for video.

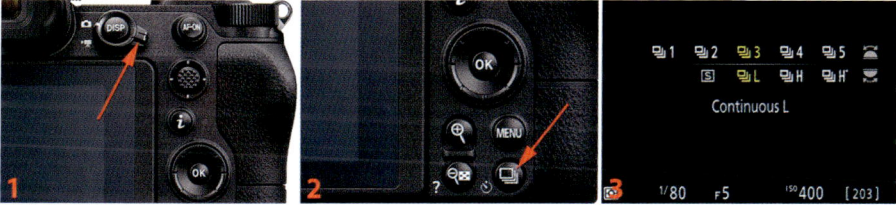

Figure 4.1I: Selecting a Release mode (Photo mode)

Use the following steps to select a Release mode for still photography:

1. Flip the Photo/movie selector lever to its Photo mode position (figure 4.1I, image 1).
2. Press the Release mode button (figure 4.1I, image 2), and the Release mode window will open.
3. The bottom row contains the Release modes (e.g., Continuous L), while the top row contains the subsettings (i.e., 1–5 fps). Turn the rear Main command dial to change the Release mode, and the front Sub-command dial to change the subsetting for that mode (figure 4.1I, image 3). Once you have selected the Release mode you want to use, press the Release mode button again to lock it in.

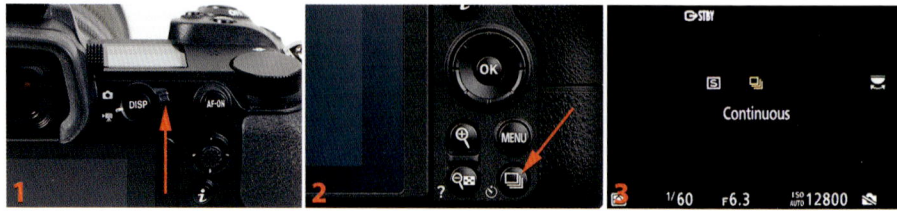

Figure 4.1J: Selecting a Release mode (Movie mode)

Use the following steps to select a Release mode for video capture:

1. Flip the Photo/movie selector lever to its Movie mode position (figure 4.1J, image 1).
2. Press the Release mode button (figure 4.1J, image 2) and the Release mode window will open.
3. Rotate a command dial. Either the rear Main command dial or the front Sub-command dial will change the Release mode. There are no subsettings for the Single frame or Continuous modes (figure 4.1J, image 3). When you have selected the Release mode you want to use, press the Release mode button again to lock it in.

Now let's look more closely at each Focus, AF-area, and Release mode.

Focus Modes

The Focus modes allow you to control how the autofocus works with static and moving subjects in Photo and Movie modes. They allow your camera to lock focus on a subject that is not moving or is moving very slowly (AF-S). They also allow your camera to update focus continuously on a moving subject (AF-C) as long as you hold the Shutter-release button halfway down or the AF-ON button all the way down.

In Movie mode only, you can use full-time autofocus (AF-F), where the camera updates the focus constantly without you holding down any buttons. The Nikon Z6 has Nikon's best-ever AF-F mode, recognized for its continuous-focus capability when making videos.

You can also make use of Manual focus (MF) mode. Plan on using focus Peaking and on-screen symbols, which we will discuss, to assist you in finding the best focus.

Let's consider each of the Focus modes to see when and how you might use them best. I will use the *i* Menu access method for our example screens in the following subsections because I like it best. Just remember that you can also access the Focus modes by using an assigned button (e.g., Fn2) or the Photo and Movie Shooting Menus, as described in the previous **Accessing the Individual Mode Groups** section (page 77).

Single AF (AF-S)

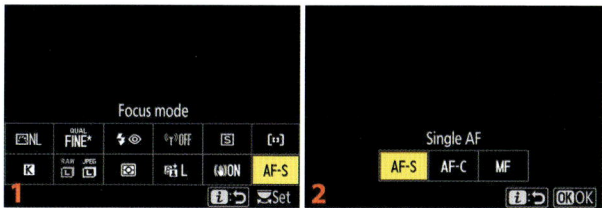

Figure 4.2A: Single AF (AF-S) mode on the *i* Menu (press the *i* button)

Single AF (AF-S) mode (figure 4.2A) works best when your subject is stationary—like a house or landscape. You can use AF-S on slowly moving subjects if you'd like, but you must be careful to keep autofocus adjusted as the subject moves. The two scenarios listed next may help you decide:

- **Subject is not moving:** When you press the Shutter-release button halfway down (or press the AF-ON button fully down), the AF module quickly locks focus on your subject and waits for you to fire the shutter. If your subject starts moving and you don't release and reapply pressure on the Shutter-release button (or AF-ON button) to refocus, the focus will be obsolete and useless. When the camera has the focus locked on your subject, take the picture quickly. This mode is perfect for stationary subjects or, in some cases, very slowly moving subjects.
- **Subject is regularly moving:** This will require a little more work on your part. Since the AF system locks focus on your subject, if the subject moves even slightly, the focus may no longer be good. You'll have to lift your finger off the Shutter-release button and reapply pressure halfway down to refocus (or press the AF-ON button fully down). If the subject continues moving, you'll need to continue releasing and pressing the Shutter-release button (or AF-ON button) halfway down to keep the focus accurate. If your subject never stops moving, is moving erratically, or stops only briefly, AF-S is probably not the best mode to use. In this case, AF-C is better because it never locks focus and the camera is able to better adjust for your subject's movement, keeping it in constant focus.

Continuous AF (AF-C)

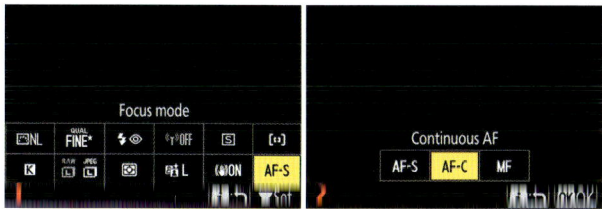

Figure 4.2B: Continuous AF (AF-C) mode on the *i* Menu (press the *i* button)

Continuous AF (AF-C) mode (figure 4.2B) continuously updates the focus while you hold the Shutter-release button halfway down, or the AF-ON button fully down. The slightest camera or subject movement causes the Z6 to refocus. Read these three scenarios carefully:

- **Subject is not moving:** When the subject is standing still, Continuous-servo AF acts a lot like Single-servo AF with the exception that the focus never locks. If your camera or subject moves, the autofocus stepper motor will make small adjustments in the focus position. Because focus never locks in this mode, you'll need to be careful that you don't accidentally move the active AF point(s) off the subject because it may focus on something in the background instead.
- **Subject is moving across the Viewfinder:** If your subject moves from left to right, right to left, or up and down in the Viewfinder, you'll need to keep your AF point on the subject in all AF-area modes. The size of the AF point can be varied from small to large, as we will discuss in the upcoming **AF-Area Modes** section (page 89).
- **Subject is moving toward or away from the camera:** If your subject is coming toward you, or moving away from you, another automatic function of the camera kicks in. It is called *Predictive Focus Tracking,* and it figures out how far the subject will move in the milliseconds before the shutter fires. After you've pressed the Shutter-release button all the way down, predictive focus tracking moves the lens elements slightly to correspond to where the subject should be when the shutter fires a few milliseconds later. In other words, if the subject is moving toward you, the lens focuses slightly in front of your subject so that the camera has time to open the shutter blades, exposing the imaging sensor at the exact moment the subject arrives at the point of best focus.

Full-Time AF (AF-F)

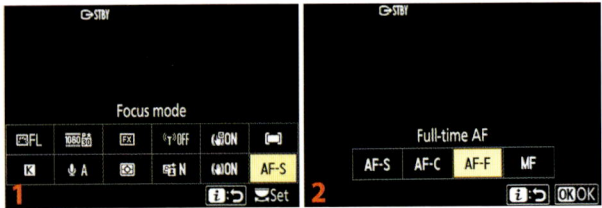

Figure 4.2C: Full-time AF (AF-F) mode on the *i* Menu (press the *i* button)

Full-time AF (AF-F) mode (figure 4.2C) is available in Movie mode only. It is designed to automatically maintain good focus on a detected subject without you pressing any buttons (i.e., Shutter-release or AF-ON). This mode provides constantly updating autofocus that is tempered by the AF-area mode you have selected. The size and shape of the focus square (AF point) changes with the AF-area mode (page 89) you have selected.

In all AF-area modes, except Auto-area AF, you will need to keep the focus square (AF point) on your subject to have accurate focus. Many videographers will use AF-F mode along with Auto-area AF mode, so that the camera will not only constantly update focus, but it will also track the subject, keeping it in good focus.

When using the AF-F Focus mode, the focus doesn't lock on the subject; it updates continuously unless you press the Shutter-release button halfway down or AF-ON button fully down, at which time the camera locks focus only while you hold the button down. If you release pressure from the Shutter-release or AF-ON button, the camera unlocks the focus and instantly resumes continuous autofocus.

In other words, the camera acts as if it is in AF-S mode when you have pressure on the Shutter-release button and AF-C mode when you remove pressure. You really don't need to press the Shutter-release button or AF-ON button, except to force a refocus. The camera will maintain focus on your subject automatically.

Again, your primary job with the AF-F Focus mode is to keep the focus square on your subject (except in Auto-area AF. AF area mode, where the camera automatically tracks your subject).

Manual Focus (MF)

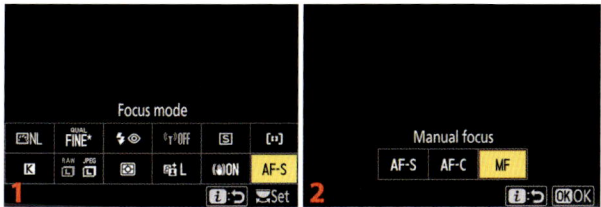

Figure 4.2D: Manual focus (MF) mode on the *i* Menu (press the *i* button)

Manual focus (MF) mode (figure 4.2D) allows you to fully control the focus by turning the focus ring on the lens. You can use your eyes or various focus assistance aids to focus. Let's examine how to enable or disable a couple of important features for using MF.

Visible Focus Point

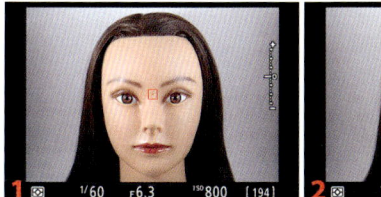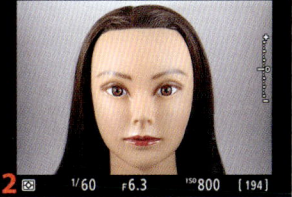

Figure 4.2E: Model Lilly Mae shows us (1) a visible AF point, and (2) a hidden AF point

In Manual Focus mode, you can leave the AF point visible in the Viewfinder (figure 4.2E, image 1), or seen between model Lilly Mae's eyes, or you can turn the AF point off (image 2). The red AF point can be positioned over an area and will turn green when you have turned the focus ring and the area under the focus point has good focus. If you choose not to use the AF point square, the EVF and Monitor will show no AF points at all and you must manually focus by eyesight or use other Manual focus assistance tools, which will we discuss shortly.

Settings Recommendation: Most will leave the AF point enabled.

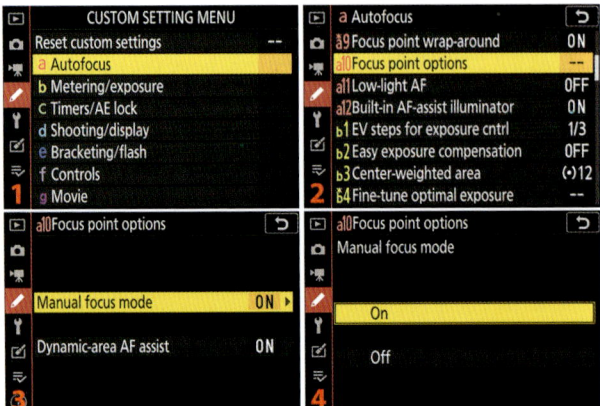

Figure 4.2F: Enabling or disabling the onscreen AF point for Manual focus

Use the following steps to enable or disable the onscreen AF point for Manual focus (MF) mode:

1. Follow the screen flow in figure 4.2F, images 1 to 3 (*Custom Setting Menu > a Autofocus > a10 Focus point options > Manual focus mode*), until you arrive at the final screen shown in image 4.
2. Choose On to enable the onscreen AF point or Off to disable it (figure 4.2F, image 4). Most of us will leave it enabled because it is useful to determine Manual focus in a specific area. Press the OK button or tap the option to lock it in.

Focus Peaking Highlights

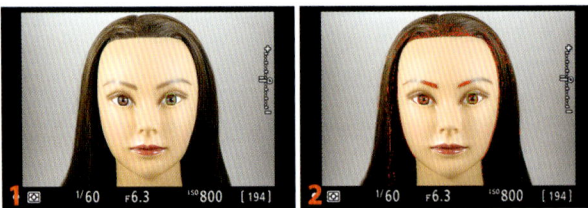

Figure 4.2G: Model Lilly Mae without and with focus Peaking highlights (red)

Peaking highlights (focus peaking) is a function that you can use to help you find the best Manual focus. This feature surrounds the edges of your subject with one of four colors to help you see exactly where the best focus is on your subject. You can see the red Peaking highlights on model Lilly Mae in figure 4.2G, image 2. In image 1, there are no Peaking highlights. In image 2 you can see the highlights in her pupils, eyebrows, and the front of her hairline. Areas highlighted in red are in good focus.

If you use Manual focus, you really should be using Peaking highlights. Let's see how to enable it.

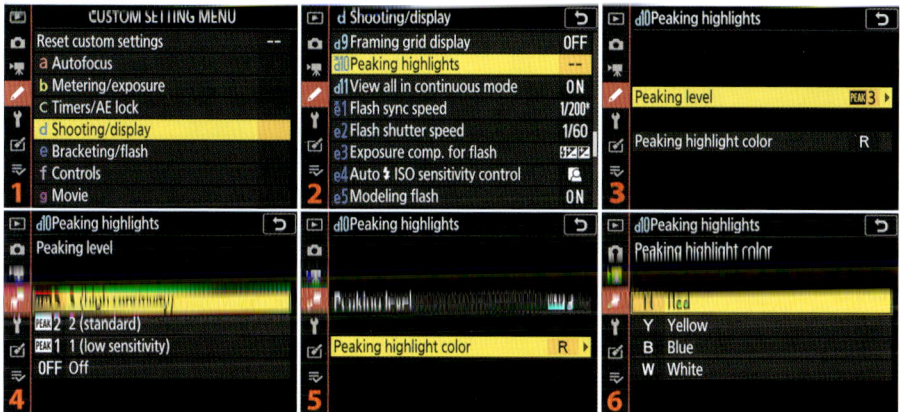

Figure 4.2H: Enabling or disabling focus Peaking highlights

Use the following steps to choose a Peaking level and enable focus peaking:

1. Choose d Shooting/display from the Custom Setting Menu and scroll to the right (figure 4.2H, image 1).
2. Select d10 Peaking highlights from the d Shooting/display menu and scroll to the right (figure 4.2H, image 2).
3. Highlight Peaking level and scroll to the right (figure 4.2H, image 3).
4. Choose a Peaking level from PEAK 3 (high sensitivity) to PEAK 1 (low sensitivity) (figure 4.2H, image 4). Press the OK button or tap the option to lock in the sensitivity and intensity level. The larger the Peaking level number the higher the sensitivity and larger the focus peaking highlight fringe will be. My camera is set to PEAK 3 (high sensitivity). When you choose a Peaking level (anything but Off), you have also enabled focus peaking for manual focusing. There is no other way to enable or disable focus peaking than to select a Peaking level or set it to Off. Now let's choose a peaking color.
5. Select Peaking highlight color and scroll to the right (figure 4.2H, image 5).
6. Choose one of the highlight colors: Red, Yellow, Blue, or White (figure 4.2H, image 6). Press the OK button or tap the option to lock in your choice.

Settings Recommendation: I generally choose the Red setting for the Peaking highlight color because red seems to contrast well with most other colors. Of course, some subjects (especially red subjects) will do better with other colors; therefore, you have a choice of three more when needed.

Now let's examine the use of all of the camera's focusing assistance functions.

Manual Focus Assistance

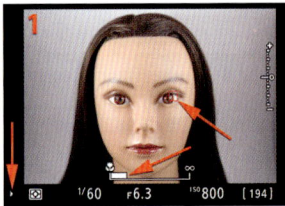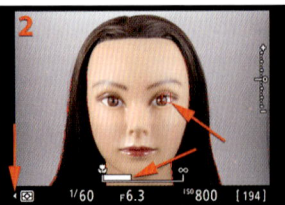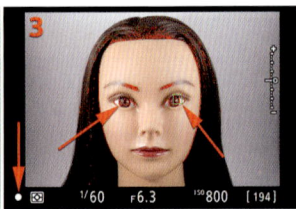

Figure 4.2I: Model Lilly Mae shows off the Z6's Manual focus aids

There are multiple focus aids available to you if you decide to use MF. Figure 4.2I shows model Lilly Mae in various states of focus (or lack thereof). Images 1 and 2 are out of focus, and image 3 is in focus. In image 1, the focus is in front of her face. In image 2, the focus is behind her face. In image 3, good focus is on the pupil of model Lilly Mae's left eye (right side of picture). Let's discuss each image and what the Focus assistance functions are indicating:

- **AF point color:** The AF point stays red when the camera is not focused on anything: red for out of focus, green for in focus. You will notice the AF point is colored red in figure 4.2I, images 1 and 2. The out-of-focus red AF point is on model Lilly Mae's right eye (top arrow in images 1 and 2). Notice, however, that the AF point has turned green in image 3. This green color signifies that the area under the AF point is in good focus.
- **Focus ring direction-turn indicators:** The camera tells you whether the focus is currently in front of or behind your subject, and which direction to turn the focus ring on the lens to obtain better focus. In figure 4.2I, images 1 and 2, the red arrow on the left side of the screen is pointing at the turn direction pointers. Image 1 shows that you need to turn the lens ring to the right (clockwise) to find good focus. That also means the focus is currently in front of Lilly Mae. Image 2 shows that you need to turn the lens ring to the left (counterclockwise) to obtain good focus. That also means the focus is currently behind Lilly Mae's face.
- **In-focus indicator:** This solid white dot appears when good focus has been attained. In figure 4.2I, image 3, the red arrow on the left side of the screen is pointing at a white dot. This dot simply means the focus is good. You can use this dot, which appears between the Focus ring direction indicators, along with those indicators, to see how well the camera is focused on the area under your AF point (which turns red and green according to whether focus is bad or good). For best focus, the dot should show and should not be blinking.
- **Rangefinder scale:** The rangefinder scale at the point of the red arrow at our model's chin in figure 4.2I, images 1 and 2, shows for only a few seconds when you make a focus adjustment. It displays a rough focus range between minimum and infinity focus. It will disappear when you stop turning the Focus ring, as seen in image 3.
- **Focus Peaking:** As previously discussed, Peaking highlights provides a color fringe on the edges of the in-focus areas. In figure 4.2F, image 1, the focus is in front of the model's face, probably near the tip of her nose. Her left eye has just a hint of red Peaking

highlights, signifying that good focus is just beginning to occur in the pupil area but is not quite there yet. In image 2, the focus is well past her face, as can be seen by the Peaking highlights on her hair. In image 3, the picture with good focus, the red Peaking highlights extend from her eyebrows, slightly in front of her eyes, to the hairline at the top of her forehead, showing that the best focus area is no more than an inch from front to back. As you turn the Focus ring on the lens, you will see the red fringe move forward and backward on the subject. You must decide when the red fringe indicates the area that is best in focus.

Using a combination of all these Manual focus assistance functions makes it fairly easy to get good focus when using MF. Learn to use each of them if you plan on using MF often.

Note: For more information on the Focus modes, see the **Photo Shooting Menu** (page 261) and **Movie Shooting Menu** (page 344) chapters.

Settings Recommendation: I leave my camera's Autofocus mode set to AF-S most of the time because I shoot a lot of static nature images and portraits.

If I am shooting sports, though, I switch to AF-C mode so that the camera will keep updating its autofocus as the subject moves very quickly. Wildlife photography is another type of imaging that begs for AF-C, which updates AF continuously when you hold down the Shutter-release button halfway or the AF-ON button all the way.

I am very happy with the AF-F mode when I am capturing video. The camera does a good job keeping the focus continuously on my subject when using AF-F. This is the first Nikon I have ever used that can truly maintain good focus on a subject when using its Live view in video recording, unlike Nikon DSLRs.

AF-Area Modes

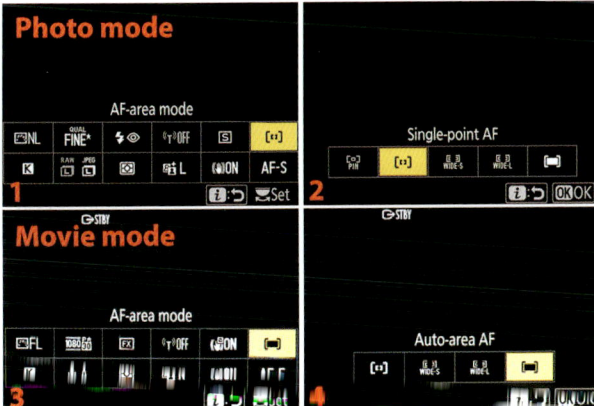

Figure 4.3A: Accessing the AF-area modes on the *i* Menu

The *AF-area* modes are designed to let you control the size of the AF point that shows where the camera is currently focusing. The larger the AF point, the larger the area of the subject that is taken into consideration for what is in good focus.

In this section we will again use the *i* Menu to access the AF-area modes (figure 4.3A). To access the *i* Menu, press the *i* button. Of course, you can also use the Photo and Movie Shooting Menus or an assigned button to access the modes (see pages 78–81 in this chapter).

Be sure that the Photo/movie selector lever is set to the appropriate Photo or Movie mode when you make adjustments. The camera maintains separate settings for the Photo and Movie modes.

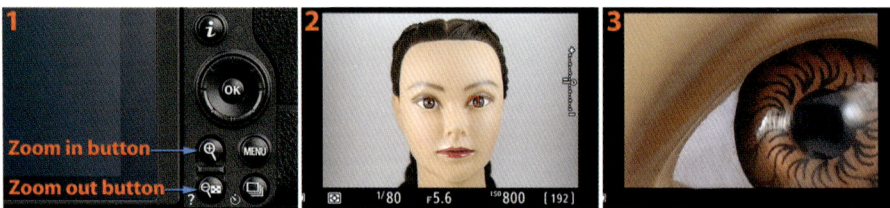

Figure 4.3B: The Zoom in and Zoom out buttons

When you are using the upcoming AF-area modes to focus on your subject, you can zoom in to pixel-peeping level to check how well the focus is working and to fine-tune it if necessary (figure 4.3B). Simply press the Zoom in button to zoom in and the Zoom out button to zoom back out.

Let's examine each of the AF-area modes and discuss what each does.

Pinpoint AF

In figure 4.3C, you can see the red *Pinpoint AF* point square on model Lilly Mae's left eye (right side of picture). This mode allows you to choose a very small area of your subject for autofocus. You can move the AF point to the pupil of an eye or a drop of water on a leaf. It is made to give you precise autofocus so that you can focus on specific areas. This mode does not use phase-detection (PDAF) autofocus; instead, it uses contrast-detection (CDAF) only, which is slower to focus, yet very accurate.

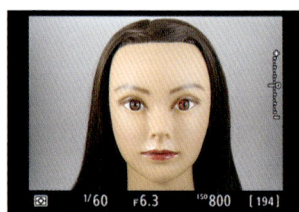

Figure 4.3C: Pinpoint AF AF-area mode

The Pinpoint AF square can be moved around within the 273 AF points in the EVF or on the Monitor by using the Sub-selector joystick or Multi selector pad. When the camera has achieved good focus, the Pinpoint AF square will change from red to green.

Pinpoint AF AF-area mode is available only when you are using the Single AF (AF-S) Focus mode. It is grayed out on the Photo Shooting Menu and not available on the *i* Menu if the camera is using Continuous AF (AF-C). Pinpoint AF is not available in Movie mode.

Single-point AF

In figure 4.3D, you can see the *Single-point AF* point square on model Lilly Mae's left eye (right side of picture). Single-point AF is the preferred mode for many photographers. It has an AF point frame that is larger than the Pinpoint AF frame. Single-point AF is faster than Pinpoint AF and still allows precise location of focus within the 273 AF points in the frame. This mode uses PDAF initially and, according to Nikon, tops off the focus by using CDAF for focus verification.

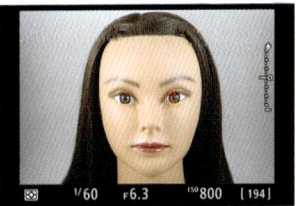

Figure 4.3D: Single-point AF AF-area mode

The Single-point AF square can be moved around within the 273 AF points in the EVF or on the Monitor by using the Sub-selector joystick or Multi selector pad. When the camera has achieved good focus, the square will change from red to green if you are using Single AF (AF-S) Focus mode. If you are using Continuous AF (AF-C) Focus mode, the AF square will stay red because the camera does not stop seeking active focus with AF-C Focus mode.

Single-point AF AF-area mode is available in both AF-S and AF-C Focus modes. It is also available in both Photo and Movie modes.

Dynamic-area AF

In figure 4.3E, you can see the center *Dynamic-area AF* point square—with its surrounding dots representing additional active AF points—on model Lilly Mae's left eye (right side of picture). Dynamic-area AF uses a center active AF point, like Single-point AF, but it surrounds that AF point with eight additional points that are on high alert. If you or the subject moves and the active center AF point loses the subject, one of the surrounding AF points can recapture the subject. All of the AF points within the red AF point frame are actively seeking focus.

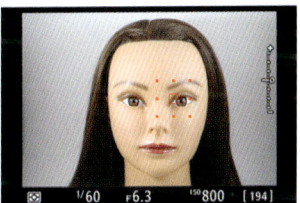

Figure 4.3E: Dynamic-area AF AF-area mode

The Dynamic-area AF frame can be moved around within the 273 AF points in the EVF or on the Monitor by using the Sub-selector joystick or Multi selector pad. The color of the frame does not change from red to green when focus is acquired; rather, it stays red because all the AF points are continuously seeking focus.

Dynamic-area AF is available for Photo mode only, not Movie mode. This AF-area mode is not available when you have the camera set to Single AF (AF-S) Focus mode. You must use Continuous AF (AF-C) Focus mode or Dynamic-area AF will be grayed out on the Photo Shooting Menu and not available on the *i* Menu.

Wide-area AF (S)

In figure 4.3F, you can see the *Wide-area AF (S)* focus frame on model Lilly Mae's left eye (right side of picture). This mode works in a similar manner to Single-point AF, except that it has a wider group of AF points in its frame. The Wide-area AF (S) frame is significantly larger than the Single-point AF frame. All of the invisible focus points within the red focus frame are active.

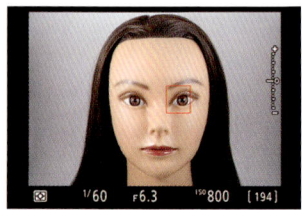

Figure 4.3F: Wide-area AF (S) AF-area mode

The Wide-area AF (S) frame can be moved around within the 273 AF points in the EVF or on the Monitor by using the Sub-selector joystick or Multi selector pad. When the camera has achieved good focus, the frame will change from red to green when you are using Single AF (AF-S) Focus mode. If you are using Continuous AF (AF-C) Focus mode, the frame will stay red because the camera does not stop seeking active focus with AF-C Focus mode.

Wide-area AF (S) AF-area mode is available in both AF-S and AF-C Focus modes. It is also available in Photo and Movie modes.

Wide-area AF (L)

In figure 4.3G, you can see the *Wide-area AF (L)* focus frame surrounding most of the left side of model Lilly Mae's face (right side of picture). This mode works in a similar manner to Wide-area AF (S), except that it has a significantly larger group of AF points within its frame. The Wide-area AF (L) frame is much larger than the Wide-area AF (S) frame, and all of the invisible focus points within the red focus frame are active.

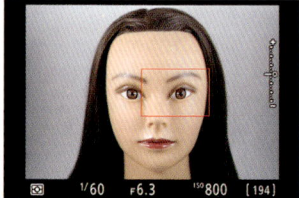

Figure 4.3G: Wide-area AF (L) AF-area mode

This AF point frame can be moved around within the 273 AF points in the EVF or on the Monitor by using the Sub-selector joystick or Multi selector pad. When the camera has achieved good focus, the Wide-area AF (L) frame will change from red to green when you are using Single AF (AF-S) Focus mode. If you are using Continuous AF (AF-C) Focus mode, the frame will stay red because the camera does not stop seeking active focus with AF-C Focus mode.

Wide-area AF (L) AF-area mode is available in both AF-S and AF-C Focus modes. It is also available in Photo and Movie modes.

Auto-area AF

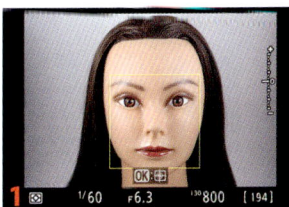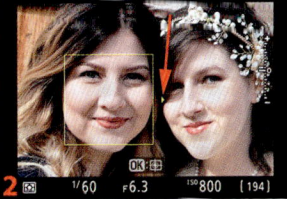

Figure 4.3H: Auto-area AF with one and multiple faces in view

You can see the Auto-area AF yellow focus frame surrounding most of model Lilly Mae's face in figure 4.3H, image 1, and the young woman on the left in image 2. The yellow frame can surround only one face at a time and that face provides the most important autofocus point.

Note: Eye AF was added with the firmware 2.0 update. See document **Eye-AF in Auto-Area AF** at **http://rockynook.com/NikonZ6**.

When there are multiple faces in the frame, the camera allows you to choose which face you want to focus on. Notice in image 2 that the yellow focus frame has a small yellow pointer on the right side (red arrow). This pointer means that you can select the other face(s) in the frame by scrolling in the direction of the pointer with the Multi selector pad, or by touching a different face on the Monitor.

This mode is a clearly a bit more complex than the other AF-area modes. When you are using different Focus modes, the yellow focus frame will do different things:

- **When using AF-S Focus mode:** The yellow focus frame will turn green when the camera achieves good focus, and focus will lock while you hold down the Shutter-release button halfway or the AF-ON button all the way. If you want to update focus, you must use the Shutter-release or AF-ON button again.
- **When using AF-C Focus mode:** The yellow focus frame will turn red while you are holding down the Shutter-release or AF-ON buttons, but it will not turn green nor will the focus lock when good focus is acquired because the focus frame seeks focus continuously. The camera stops updating the focus if you stop pressing the Shutter-release or AF-ON button.
- **When using AF-F Focus mode (Movie):** The yellow focus frame is constantly and automatically seeking focus and may jump around a bit. The camera does its best to maintain good focus as your subject moves in the frame. The yellow focus frame will turn green and the focus will lock while you hold down the Shutter-release button halfway or the AF-ON button all the way. As soon as you release the button, the focus automatically continues updating by itself.

If there are no people in the frame, the camera uses a different focus frame entirely. Let's see how a non-person Auto-area AF focus frame looks and works.

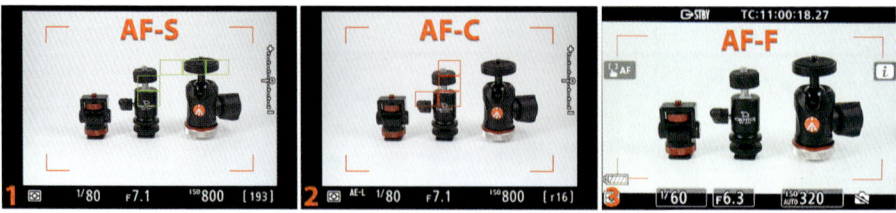

Figure 4.3I: A non-person Auto-area AF autofocus screen

Auto-area AF gives full control of the AF system to the camera. You cannot manually move a focus point around the screen. Focus works only if you keep your subject within the red frame markers near the four corners of the screen (figure 4.3I). The camera will choose a combination of AF points within the frame to achieve the best focus on your subject. You will see a group of green rectangles marking the areas the camera is using for autofocus.

Similar to how the person-based Auto-area AF yellow focus frame works, these non-person AF points have several ways to indicate good AF, according to which Focus mode you have selected:

- **When using AF-S Focus mode** (figure 4.3I, image 1): The small green frames will appear anywhere within the red corner boundaries while you hold down the Shutter-release button halfway or the AF-ON button all the way. The autofocus locks while you hold the button down. If you want to update focus you must release pressure and then press the Shutter-release or AF-ON button again.
- **When using AF-C Focus mode** (figure 4.3I, image 2): A group of small red AF points will appear within the red corner boundaries while you are holding down the Shutter-release or AF-ON button. The group of AF points will not turn green nor will the focus lock when good focus is acquired because the grouped AF points seeks focus continuously. You will see the autofocus update by the movement of the red AF point group as it adjusts focus at the slightest movement of the camera or subject. The Z6 stops updating the focus if you stop holding the Shutter-release or AF-ON button.
- **When using AF-F Focus mode** (figure 4.3I, image 3): No AF points appear within the red corner boundaries. As long as you keep the subject within the corner boundaries the camera will do its best to maintain good focus on your subject. If you hold the Shutter-release button halfway down or the AF-ON button all the way, a group of green AF points will appear and the focus will lock while you hold the button down. As soon as you release the button, the camera continues updating focus automatically, with nothing in the frame to show you what is in focus.

The focus tracking system in the Z6 is a little different than what you are used to with your Nikon DSLRs (firmware C2.00). This will change as Nikon updates the autofocus system with firmware updates. Please check the downloadable resources website (**http://rocky nook.com/NikonZ6**) for updates as Nikon modifies the current system.

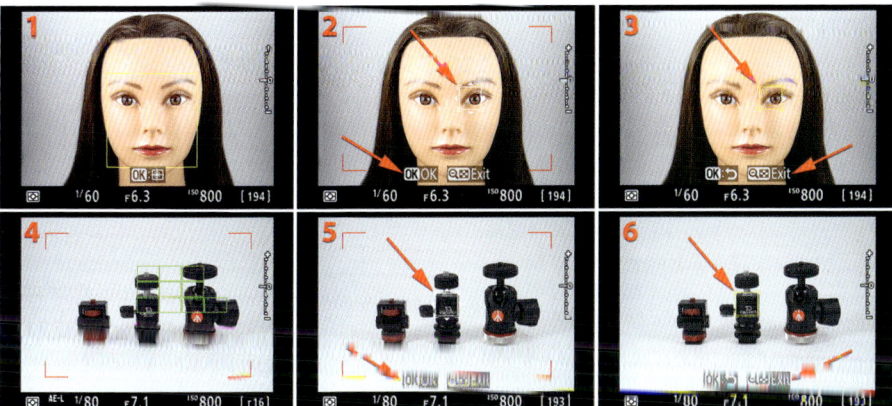

Figure 4.3J: Using focus tracking

Figure 4.3J, images 1–3, show the Auto-area AF screens for a human subject. Images 3–6 show the Auto-area AF screens for a non-human subject.

To track a subject, you can press or touch OK (figure 4.3J, images 2 and 5, bottom red arrows) and a small, white, square targeting reticle will appear on the screen (images 2 and 5, top red arrows). The targeting reticle has small pointers on all four sides, which signify that you can move this tracking frame around the screen with the Sub-selector joystick (or Multi selector pad) until it is over the area you want to track.

Once the white targeting reticle is located exactly on the point of your subject you want to track, you can execute one of four actions to cause the camera to track the subject:

- Press or touch OK again.
- Press the Shutter-release button halfway down.
- Press the AF-ON button all the way down.
- (Movie mode using AF-F Focus mode only): Touch the subject on the screen exactly where you want the camera to track. You can do this even when you are already tracking a subject at another point. You can quickly change to a different subject or different parts of the same subject for tracking by simply touching the screen in the appropriate area. Touch AF (page 102) must be on for this to work.

When you have done one of the four initiating actions from the list, the camera will activate Subject tracking and will attempt to track a moving subject. The white targeting reticle will change to a yellow tracking frame and the pointers around its four edges will disappear (figure 4.3J, images 3 and 6, top red arrow). As you move the camera or the subject moves, the Z6 will try to keep the area under the tracking frame in focus.

To stop tracking your subject, you can execute one of three actions:

- Press or touch OK and the white targeting reticle will reappear.
- Touch the Exit control, if there is one on the screen.
- Press the Zoom out button.

Special considerations: There are several things you need to consider when using Auto-area AF, as follows:

- **Face detection:** If needed, you can enable or disable Auto-area AF face detection by using *Custom Setting Menu > a Autofocus > a4 Auto-area AF face detection*.
- *Tracking sensitivity:* You can set a delay on how long the camera will take to switch to a new subject when it loses your old subject—such as when something temporarily gets between you and your subject, or when the subject accidently moves outside the focus area. Use *Custom Setting Menu > g Movie > g5 AF tracking sensitivity* (page 464). You can select from 1 (High) to 7 (Low). The higher the setting (e.g., 1), the less likely it is that your camera will lose the subject; the lower the setting (e.g., 7), the more likely it is that the subject will be lost due to interference. (**Settings Recommendation:** I set mine to 1, or High.)
- *AF speed:* You can set how fast the camera changes focus when you use Touch AF (page 102) to move the focus between two subjects. Do you want it to snap into focus or gradually change focus (focus pulling)? Use *Custom Setting Menu > g Movie > g4 AF speed* (page 463). You can select from −5 for slower focus changes to +5 for faster focus changes. (**Settings Recommendation:** I set mine to +5 for a fast focus transition. The camera isn't all that snappy when it changes focus areas, even at its fastest setting of +5. Experiment!)

For more information on the AF-area modes, see the **Photo Shooting Menu** (page 264) and **Movie Shooting Menu** (page 345) chapters.

Settings Recommendation: For static or slowly moving subjects, such as landscapes, nature, and outdoors, I use Single AF (AF-S) Focus mode (page 262), Single-point AF AF-area mode (page 264), and Single frame (S) Release mode (page 97) almost exclusively.

If I'm shooting a wedding where the bride and her father are walking slowly down the aisle, Single AF (AF-S) Focus mode (page 262), Wide-area AF (S) AF-area mode (page 265), and Continuous L (L) Release mode (page 97) seem to work well for me, although recently, I have been successfully experimenting with Continuous AF (AF-C) Focus mode (page 262), Auto-area AF mode (page 265), and Continuous H (H) Release mode (page 97).

The Z6 can be accurate at finding and tracking human faces in Auto-area AF mode with reasonable lighting. You must use Auto-area AF mode to let the camera track a face (firmware C2.00). At the time this book was being written, Nikon was about to release a firmware update adding Eye AF to make face tracking even more effective. Please check the downloadable resources website (**http://rockynook.com/NikonZ6**) for updates to this book as Nikon modifies the current system.

I suggest experimentation with all these modes. You will need to use them all for different types of photography, so take the time necessary to learn how each mode functions for your style of shooting.

Release Modes

In the good old film days, the Release modes would have been called motor-drive settings because they are concerned with how often and how fast the camera is capable of taking pictures.

The Release modes are for still photography, not video capture. The five main release modes are available when your camera is in Photo mode:

- Single frame
- Continuous L
- Continuous H
- Continuous H (extended)
- Self-timer

However, since you can take low-res (1920) pictures in Movie mode, either before or during a video capture session, there are also two Release modes for Movie mode:

- Single frame
- Continuous

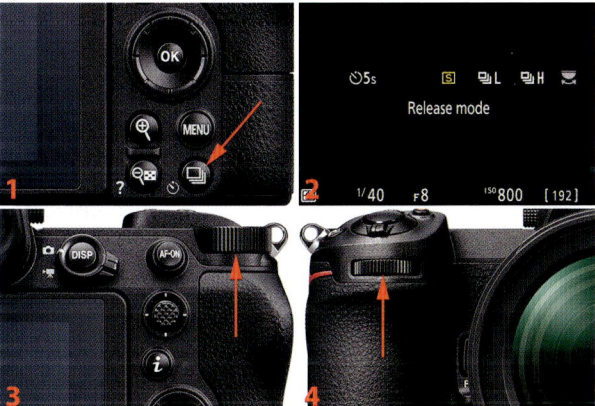

Figure 4.4A: The Release mode/self-timer button (1), Release mode selection screen (2), Main command dial (3), and Sub-command dial (4)

The Z6's Release modes are available for selection by pressing the Release mode button (figure 4.4A, image 1)—which will open the Release mode selection screen (image 2; Photo mode shown)—and turning the rear Main command dial (image 3). Any subsettings are changed by turning the front Sub-command dial (image 4). Remember these controls because we will refer to them as we discuss the individual Release modes.

To access the Release modes, make sure the camera's Photo/movie selector lever (surrounding the DISP button) is set to the correct position (Photo or Movie mode), and then press the Release mode button (figure 4.4A, image 1).

You can see which Release mode (e.g., S, L, H, H*) you currently have selected without opening the camera's menus by glancing at the lower-left corner of the Control panel on top of the camera.

Now let's look more deeply at each of them to see how they can help you capture your subject well. The Release mode screens are presented with the lens cap on for maximum contrast.

Single Frame

Single frame Release mode (figure 4.4B) is the simplest mode. It takes a single picture each time you fully press the Shutter-release button.

There are five modes available in Photo mode, and two modes available in Movie mode, of which Single frame (S) is the first. Open the Release mode screen by pressing the Release mode button (figure 4.4A, image 1). Turn the rear Main command dial until Single frame is highlighted, then press the OK button to lock in the mode.

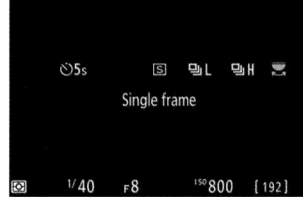

Figure 4.4B: Single frame Release mode

There is no speed in this mode! This is for photographers shooting one picture at a time in Photo mode, or for those capturing one 16x9 picture at a time in Movie mode.

Nature shooters often use this mode because they are more concerned with correct depth of field and excellent composition than blazing speed. This mode also works well for portraits, graduation, weddings, and event shooting. One picture per Shutter-release button press!

When the camera is in Movie mode, Single frame Release mode allows the camera to take one 16x9 picture based on the Frame size/frame rate (page 316) currently configured for Movie mode. You can take one picture at a time when you are not recording a video. When you are recording a video, you can press the Shutter-release button all the way down and the camera will capture one frame from the video as a still picture, without stopping or harming the video recording in progress. You can capture up to 50 still pictures maximum per video recording.

Continuous (Movie mode only)

The *Continuous* Release mode (figure 4.4C) is available in Movie mode only. This mode is not the same as the Continuous L or Continuous H modes in Photo mode. When you are not recording a video, it allows you to take a large number of 16x9 frames in a burst up to three seconds (3 s) long when you hold the Shutter-release button down. When you are recording a video, you can take only one 16x9 frame at a time for each single press of the Shutter-release button.

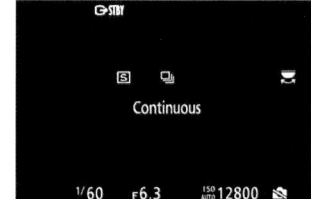

Figure 4.4C: Continuous mode for Movies

To access Continuous mode, make sure the camera is in Movie mode (with the Photo/movie selector lever in the lower position) and open the Release mode screen by pressing the Release mode button (figure 4.4A, image 1). Turn the rear Main command dial until Continuous is highlighted (figure 4.4C), then press the OK button to lock in the mode.

Warning: Be very careful with the Movie mode's Continuous mode (not the Photo mode's Continuous L or H). As previously mentioned, when you are *not* capturing video, you can take pictures with Single frame (one picture at a time) or Continuous (many pictures in a burst). When I say "many pictures," I'm not kidding you. The camera can take literally hundreds of 16x9 images in a few seconds—using the silent electronic shutter—if you hold the Shutter-release button down. Basically, using the Continuous mode while not recording a video is like capturing a manual, three-second-long movie, and having each frame of that movie appear as a single image on your camera's memory card.

Each of these pictures is the equivalent of one 16x9 video frame. Each 1080p picture is about 2 MP in size, while each 4K picture is about 8 MP in size. Even though the camera has a limited buffer, the XQD card's transfer rate is so fast that it almost instantly clears the buffer, meaning you can virtually take as many pictures as you want—or should I say many more than you thought you wanted! The camera attempts to limit your massive individual image intake by stopping the capture at the end of three seconds. However, in those three seconds, you can take *hundreds* of images. I'm not going to tell you how I discovered this, but I bet you can imagine.

On the other hand, when you are recording a video and press the Shutter-release button, regardless of whether you have Single frame or Continuous Release mode selected, the camera will take just one 16x9 photo for each Shutter-release button press, without interrupting the video capture in any way.

Continuous L

Continuous L Release mode (figure 4.4D) allows you to select a frame rate between one and five frames per second (fps). This mode is limited to the Photo mode (see the previous subsection for the Movie mode's form of Continuous release).

To access the mode, open the Release mode screen by pressing the Release mode button (figure 4.4A, image 1), then turn the rear Main command dial until Continuous L is highlighted (figure 4.4D). Now turn the front Sub-command dial and select a frames-per-second rate, from 1 to 5 fps, for shooting with the camera's mechanical shutter. Press the OK button to lock in the mode.

If you are shooting in Silent photography mode (Electronic shutter, page 307), the frame rate will drop to a

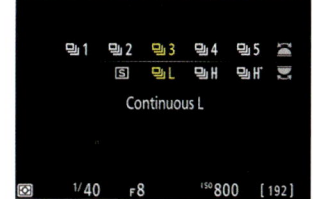

Figure 4.4D: Continuous L (low speed) Release mode

maximum of 4.5 fps for JPEG, TIFF, 12-bit NEF (RAW), or 12-bit NEF (RAW) + JPEG modes; 14-bit NEF (RAW) mode limits the camera to 3.5 fps.

You will see a brief blackout of the EVF or Monitor as each picture is taken when you are using the camera's mechanical shutter.

The camera will provide autofocus (AF) and autoexposure (AE) for every frame when shooting in this mode.

Continuous H

Continuous high speed Release mode (figure 4.4E) is designed for when you want to shoot at the highest frame rate the camera can manage. This mode is not available in Movie mode.

To access the mode, open the Release mode screen by pressing the Release mode button (figure 4.4A, image 1), then turn the rear Main command dial until Continuous H is highlighted (figure 4.4E). Press the OK button to lock in the mode.

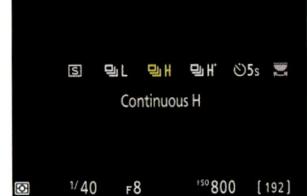

Figure 4.4E: Continuous H (high speed) Release mode

The normal frame rate with the camera's mechanical shutter is 5.5 fps for JPEG, TIFF, 12-bit NEF (RAW), or 12-bit NEF (RAW) + JPEG modes. When shooting in 14-bit NEF (RAW) or 14-bit NEF (RAW) + JPEG modes, the camera is limited to 5 fps when shooting with the mechanical shutter. You will see a brief blackout of the EVF or Monitor as each picture is taken when you are using the camera's mechanical shutter.

If you are shooting in Silent photography mode (Electronic shutter, page 307), the frame rate will drop to a maximum of 4.5 fps for JPEG, TIFF, 12-bit NEF (RAW), or 12-bit NEF (RAW) + JPEG modes. You are limited to 3.5 fps in 14-bit NEF (RAW) or 14-bit NEF (RAW) + JPEG modes.

The camera will provide autofocus (AF) and autoexposure (AE) for every frame when shooting in this mode.

Continuous H (Extended)

Continuous H (extended) Release mode (figure 4.4F) is an especially high-speed mode that has *no EVF or Monitor blackout* when shooting at its maximum rate of 9 frames per second. This mode is not available in Movie mode.

To access the mode, open the Release mode screen by pressing the Release mode button (figure 4.4A, image 1), then turn the rear Main command dial until Continuous H (extended) is highlighted (figure 4.4F). Press the OK button to lock in the mode.

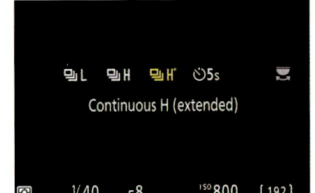

Figure 4.4F: Continuous H (extended) Release mode

As mentioned, the camera is limited to a maximum of 9 frames per second in JPEG, TIFF, 12-bit NEF (RAW), or 12-bit NEF (RAW) + JPEG modes. When shooting in 14-bit NEF (RAW) or 14-bit NEF (RAW) + JPEG modes, the camera is limited to 8 fps when shooting with the mechanical shutter.

If you are shooting in Silent photography mode (Electronic shutter, page 307), the frame rate will remain at 12 fps for JPEG, TIFF, 12-bit NEF (RAW), or 12-bit NEF (RAW) + JPEG modes. However, you are limited to 8 fps in 14-bit NEF (RAW) or 14-bit NEF (RAW) + JPEG modes.

The camera will autofocus for every frame at 12 fps. However, for firmware versions prior to version 2.0, the Z6 cannot meter any frame other than the first one. With firmware 2.0 this limitation was removed and the camera will meter all frames. Be sure to upgrade the firmware!

Note: Flicker reduction (page 234) is disabled when shooting in this mode.

Memory Buffer Information

When you hold down the Shutter-release button in the Continuous Release modes, the camera will fire at the chosen frame rate continuously until you let up on the button or the internal memory buffer gets full.

A chart on page 229 of the older Z6 user's manual, or on pages 234–235 of the new Z7/Z6 user's manual (for firmware C2.00 and greater), displays the number of frames you can expect the buffer to hold before the camera's frame rate slows down. You can also see how many frames (approximately) the buffer will hold in your camera's current configuration by holding down the Shutter-release button halfway. In the bottom-right corner of all the camera's screens you will see an "r" number (e.g., r16) where the frame counter is normally displayed. Whatever number follows the "r" is the number of images your camera's buffer can hold.

Fortunately, the buffer is extended somewhat by having a fast XQD memory card in the camera. The XQD card (and future CFexpress cards, after an upcoming firmware update) allows images to be written so quickly that often the buffer will hold more images than you would expect because one picture is being written to the memory card while one is being taken. The camera may slow down in maximum frame rate, but it will not stop accepting images in Continuous L mode.

If you don't hold the Shutter-release button down continuously and fill up the buffer, you can often shoot a burst of images, hesitate a moment for some images to be written to the card, and then fire off another burst. You may be able to do this until you fill up the memory card!

Self-Timer

Use the *Self-timer* Release mode (figure 4.4G) to cause your camera to take pictures a few seconds after you press the Shutter-release button. The camera will autofocus when you press the Shutter-release button halfway down and start the Self-timer when you press it all the way down. This mode is not available in Movie mode.

To access this mode, open the Release mode screen by pressing the Release mode button (figure 4.4A, image 1),

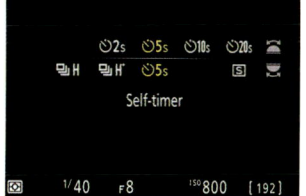

Figure 4.4G: Self-timer Release mode

then turn the rear Main command dial until Self-timer is highlighted (figure 4.4G). Now turn the front Sub-command dial and select a delay timeout (i.e., 2s, 5s, 10s, or 20s). Press the OK button to lock in the mode. The factory default time-out for the Self-timer is 10 seconds.

You can also use *Custom Setting Menu > c Timers/AE lock > c3 Self-timer* to set the time-out to 2, 5, 10, or 20 seconds. And you can use c2 Self-timer to control the number of shots taken for each self-timer cycle (up to 9 shots), and the interval between each shot (from 0.5 to 3 seconds).

If you like to hear that little *beep beep beep* when the Self-timer is counting down the seconds before firing the shutter, you can control that sound with *Setup Menu > Beep options*.

After you press the Shutter-release button in Self-timer mode, the Self-timer lamp will blink about twice per second and the beeping will start (if enabled). When the last two seconds arrive, the Self-timer lamp will shine continuously, and the beeping will double in speed. You are out of time when the beeping speeds up! The image is taken at about the time the beeping stops.

If you want to stop the self-timer, all you have to do is press the MENU or Playback button.

Touch Shutter Release and Autofocus (Tap Shooting)

The Nikon Z6 allows you to take pictures and/or autofocus by merely touching your subject on the camera's Monitor. Nikon calls it Tap shooting and it comes in two parts, Touch shutter/AF and Touch AF.

- **Touch shutter/AF:** When you place your finger on the subject showing on the Monitor, the Z6 will lock autofocus and wait until you lift your finger from the screen before releasing the shutter. As soon as you lift your finger, the camera will fire the shutter and take a picture of the subject.
- **Touch AF:** When you place your finger on the subject showing on the Monitor, the camera will lock autofocus on the subject, but will not fire the shutter. If you are using AF-F mode, the camera will not refresh the focus until you remove your finger from the screen.

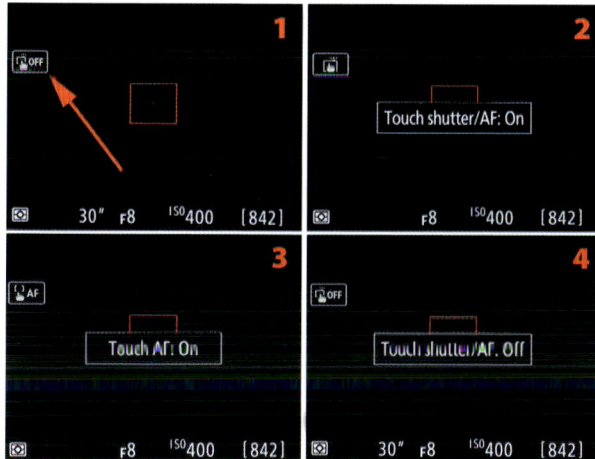

Figure 4.5: Tap shooting (Touch shutter/AF and Touch AF)

Use the following steps to enable one or both of the Tap shooting methods:

1. Touch the Touch shutter/AF symbol shown in figure 4.5, image 1. A popup box will appear with the words *Touch shutter/AF: On* (figure 4.5, image 2). At this point, both Touch shutter and Touch AF are active (Touch shutter/AF), and the OFF word disappears from the symbol. If you want to use both touch shutter release and touch autofocus, you can skip the following steps (2 and 3) and use Tap shooting.

2. Touch the Touch shutter/AF symbol again and the popup box will reappear with the words *Touch AF: On* (figure 4.5, image 3). Now only Touch AF is active and the symbol changes to include the initials AF for active autofocus. The touch shutter release is disabled and touching the Monitor will result in autofocus only. If you want to take pictures with the normal Shutter-release button and initiate autofocus by touching the Monitor, the camera is ready. Skip the final step 3.

3. Touch the Touch shutter/AF symbol a final time and a popup box will appear with the words *Touch shutter/AF: Off* (figure 4.5, image 4). When you see OFF within the touch symbol, you can be sure that the camera will not autofocus or release the shutter in response to screen touches.

Settings Recommendation: Keep this functionality in mind for when you want to fire the shutter with little vibration. Sometimes it will shake the camera less if you lightly touch the Monitor rather than press the Shutter-release or AF-ON button. Could Tap shooting help you when you have accidentally left your electronic shutter release cable at home? This may well be a very convenient function for your photography. I find myself using Tap shooting quite often!

Author's Conclusion

I've followed the development of Nikon autofocus systems since the late 1980s. Autofocus with the Nikon Z6 is a real pleasure. It has a more powerful AF system than many cameras before it, and yet it is somewhat simplified in its operation by comparison. The system can still seem complex, but if you spend some time with this chapter, you should come away with a much greater understanding of the Z6's AF module. You'll better understand how you can adapt your camera to work best for your style of photography. Enjoy your Z6's excellent autofocus system.

Next let's examine the camera's White balance system in detail. White balance is very important for JPEG shooters in particular. It is important to understand how White balance works, even if you shoot only in NEF (RAW) mode. White balance is the base for having good color in your images. Learn to use it well!

5 White Balance

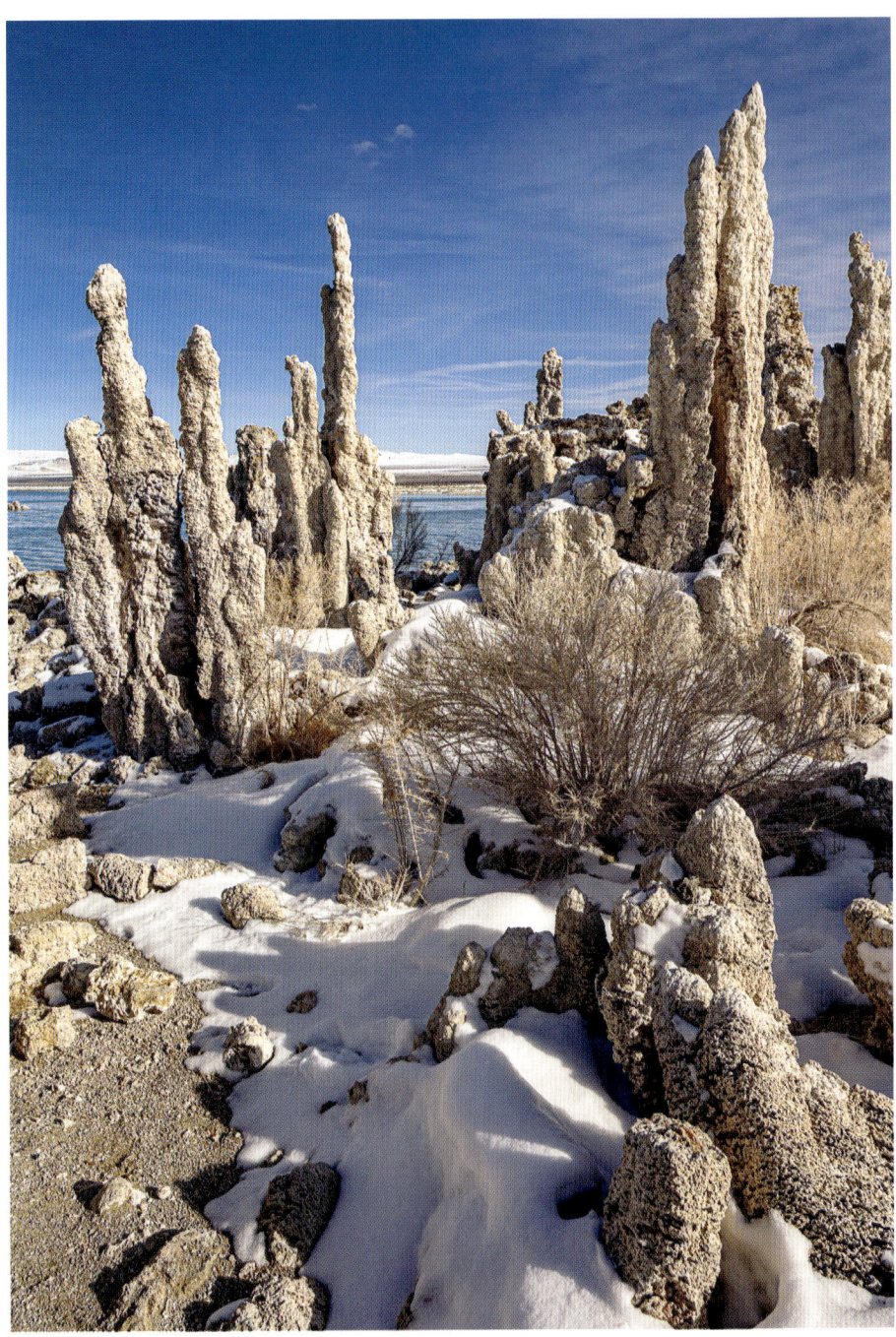

Mono Lake Tufas in Snow © 2019 Eric Bowles (*ericbowles*)

Back in the good old days, photographers bought special rolls of film or filters to meet the challenges of color casts that come from indoor lighting, overcast days, or special situations.

The Z6's two Auto White balance settings do a great job for general shooting. However, discerning photographers learn how to use the White balance controls so they can achieve color consistency in special situations. Fortunately, the Z6's method for balancing the camera to the available light comes with the White balance (WB) controls.

How Does White Balance Work?

Normally, White balance (WB) is used to adjust the camera so that whites are truly white and other colors are accurate under whatever light source you are shooting. You can also use the White balance controls to deliberately introduce color casts into your image for interesting special effects.

The camera's WB color temperature scale is exactly the opposite of the Kelvin scale we learned in school for star temperatures. Remember that a red giant star is cool, whereas a blue/white star is hot. The WB color temperatures are the opposite of that approach because the WB system *adds* color to make up for a deficit of color in the original light of the subject, instead of absorbing and radiating specific color frequencies according to physical temperature the way a "blackbody" does.

Under a fluorescent light, there is a deficit of blue, which makes the subject appear greenish yellow. When the camera adds blue, the image is balanced to a more normal appearance. The White balance for many fluorescent light sources is around 4000K.

Another example might be shooting on a cloudy, overcast day. The cool, ambient light could cause the image to look bluish if left unadjusted. The White balance control in your camera sees the cool color temperature and adds some red to warm the colors a bit. The White balance on a cloudy, overcast day might be about 6000K.

Just remember that we use the real kelvin temperature range in reverse and that red colors are considered warm and blue colors are cool. Even though this is the opposite of what we were taught in school, it fits our situation better. To photographers, blue seems cool and red seems warm! Just don't let your astronomer friends convince you otherwise.

Understanding WB in a fundamental way is simply realizing that light has a range of colors that go from cool to warm. We can adjust our cameras to use the available light in an accurate, neutral, and balanced way that compensates for the actual light source. Or we can allow a color cast to enter the image by unbalancing the settings. In this chapter, we will discuss this from the standpoint of the Z6's camera controls and how they deal with WB.

Color Temperature

The camera's WB range can vary from a very cool 2500K to a very warm 10,000K. Figure 5.0 shows the same picture adjusted in Adobe Photoshop, with the use of photo filters, to three WB settings. Notice how the image in the center is about right; the image on the left is cooler (bluish cast) and the image on the right is warmer (reddish cast). For astronomy mavens, remember that camera White balance color temperature is opposite star color temperature (see previous section).

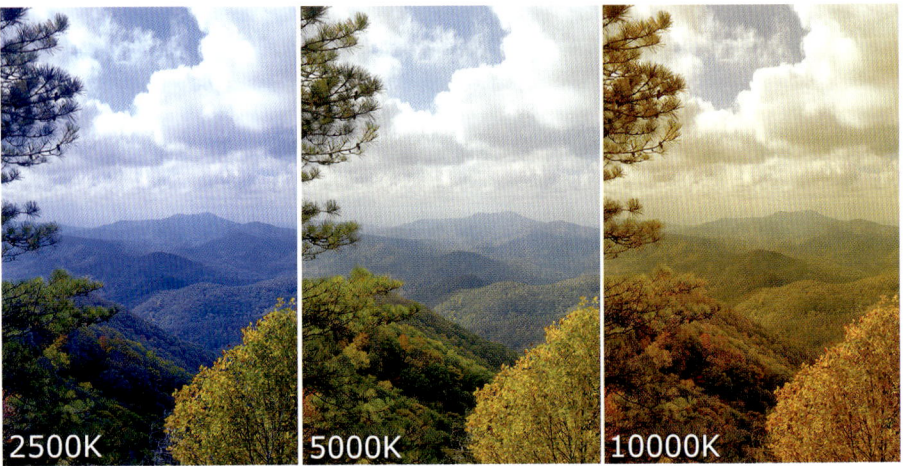

Figure 5.0: Same image with three different WB Color Temperature settings

The same adjustments we used to make with film and filters can now be achieved with the White balance settings built into the Z6. To achieve the same effect as daylight film and a warming filter, simply select the Cloudy White balance setting while shooting in normal daylight. This sets the Z6 to balance at about 6000K, which makes nice, warm-looking images. If you want to really warm up the image, choose the White balance setting called Shade, which sets the camera to 8000K. Or you could set the Z6's White balance to Auto2 (A2), which warms up the colors and automatically adjusts for current light sources.

On the other hand, if you want to make the image appear cool or bluish, try using the Cool-white fluorescent (4200K) or Incandescent (3000K) setting in normal daylight.

Remember, the color temperature shifts from cool values to warm values. The Z6 can record your images with any color temperature from 2500K (very cool or bluish) to 10,000K (very warm or reddish) and any major value in between. There is no need to carry various film emulsions or filters to deal with light color range. The Z6 has very easy-to-use color temperature controls and a full range of color temperatures available. The WB symbols, official names, kelvin values, and specifications—in camera order—are as follows:

A   Auto (3500K to 8000K): This mode uses the following symbols: *AUTO0 Keep white (reduce warm colors)* automatically adjusts the WB with a bias toward cooler coloration. *AUTO1 Keep overall atmosphere* automatically adjusts the WB with coloration that most people would consider normal colors for the subject. *AUTO2 Keep warm lighting colors* tends to make the image a little warmer than normal, which is quite appealing to most people. When you are using a G, E, D, or S Nikkor lens, the WB is adjusted automatically with any of the three Auto types.

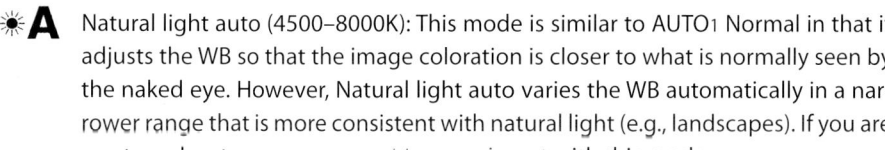 Natural light auto (4500–8000K): This mode is similar to AUTO1 Normal in that it adjusts the WB so that the image coloration is closer to what is normally seen by the naked eye. However, Natural light auto varies the WB automatically in a narrower range that is more consistent with natural light (e.g., landscapes). If you are a nature shooter, you may want to experiment with this mode.

Direct sunlight (5200K). This mode is best used when you are photographing subjects in direct sunlight.

Cloudy (6000K): This mode allows you to warm up the image on an overcast day.

Shade (8000K): This mode helps overcome the strong blue tint caused by a blue sky when you are photographing a subject in the shade.

Incandescent (3000K): This mode allows the camera to produce correct and consistent coloration when the main light source is an older style incandescent light (older type light bulb).

Fluorescent (2700K to 7200K): This mode has seven subtypes, including Sodium-vapor lamps (2700K), Warm-white fluorescent (3000K), White fluorescent (3700K), Cool-white fluorescent (4200K), Day white fluorescent (5000K), Daylight fluorescent (6500K), and High temp. mercury-vapor (7200K). Refer to the listing on the bulb or bulb packaging in order to determine the correct type.

Flash (5400K): This mode is best used when you want to match the color of your Nikon Speedlight output and maintain consistent color between frames.

K (2500K–10,000K): Choose a color temperature manually from a range of color temperatures. This mode allows you to very carefully match the exact color of the lighting on a subject for more critical work.

PRE (Preset manual): White balance is measured from actual ambient light by using a white or gray card under that light source. This value can then be stored in the camera's memory (d–1 to d–6) for future reuse under the same lighting.

When Does White Balance Matter?

Most of us will use Auto White Balance because the camera does a great job at detecting the color temperature of ambient light and adjusting the camera so that colors appear accurate.

When you are shooting JPEG or TIFF images, you should make sure the White balance is correct for the current ambient light by using Auto or by manually choosing an appropriate

WB setting. If you use the wrong WB value for JPEG or TIFF images, it is hard to correct the color balance later during post-processing. It can be done, but it is not easy. Therefore, it is important to get the WB set correctly for JPEGs and TIFFs. But what about RAW images?

Many ask the question: Should I worry about WB if I shoot in NEF (RAW) mode? The quick answer is no, but that may not be the best answer. When you take a picture using NEF (RAW) mode, the sensor image data has no White balance, sharpening, or color saturation information applied. Instead, the information about your camera settings is stored as markers along with the RAW black-and-white sensor data. Color information, including White balance, is applied permanently to the image only when you post-process and save the image in another format, such as JPEG or TIFF.

When you open the image in Nikon Capture NX-D, Photoshop, Lightroom, or another RAW conversion program, the camera settings are applied to the sensor data in a *temporary* way so that you can view the image on your computer screen. If you don't like the White balance or almost any other setting you used in-camera, you can simply change it in the conversion software, and the image will look as if you used the new setting when you first took the picture.

Does that mean you should not be concerned about WB settings if you shoot RAW most of the time? No! The human brain can quickly adjust to image colors and perceive them as normal, even when they are not. The brain does its own automatic white balancing. When you are looking at a white object under direct sunlight does it not appear white to you? How about a white object under fluorescent light? It still appears white to you. Your brain adjusts the white point for you so that colors look normal to you under almost any light source, even though there may actually be a wide variance in color temperature.

This is one of the dangers of not using correct WB. Because an unbalanced image on your computer screen is not being compared to another correctly balanced image side by side, there is some danger that your brain may accept the slightly incorrect camera settings as normal, and your image will be saved with a color cast.

As a rule of thumb, if you use your WB correctly at all times, you'll consistently produce better images. You'll do less post-processing if the WB is correct in the first place. As RAW shooters, we already have a lot of post-processing work to do. Why add WB corrections to the workflow, unless necessary?

Additionally, you might decide to switch to JPEG mode in the middle of a shoot, and if you are not accustomed to using your WB controls, you'll be in trouble. When you shoot JPEGs, your camera will apply the WB information directly to the image and save it on your memory card—permanently. Be safe; always use good WB technique!

Now let's consider how to adjust the White balance.

Methods for Adjusting White Balance

There are three methods for setting the White balance in the Nikon Z6. Let's discuss each of them.

- **WB on the i Menu:** You can quickly access the White Balance settings by selecting White balance from the *i* Menu (press the *i* button). You will need to make sure the Photo/movie selector switch is set to the correct position for still photography or video recording. Different WB settings can be used for photos and video.
- **WB on the Photo and Movie Shooting Menus:** The White balance settings on the Photo Shooting Menu affect still images only, while the WB settings on the Movie Shooting Menu affect videos only. With one minor difference, which we will discuss, both of the menus work exactly the same. Different WB settings can be used for photos and video.
- **Assigning White Balance to a camera button:** If you change White balance very frequently, you can assign the White balance function to a camera button, such as Fn1 or Fn2. You can adjust the White balance for taking pictures by having the Photo/movie selector switch set to still image mode, or for recording video by having the Photo/movie selector switch set to Movie mode.

Now let's consider each of these White balance adjustment methods.

White Balance on the *i* Menu

The majority of photographers and videographers will use the Z6's *i* Menu to choose an appropriate WB value, simply because the White balance setting is easily available there. Let's examine how to use the *i* Menu for choosing a White balance.

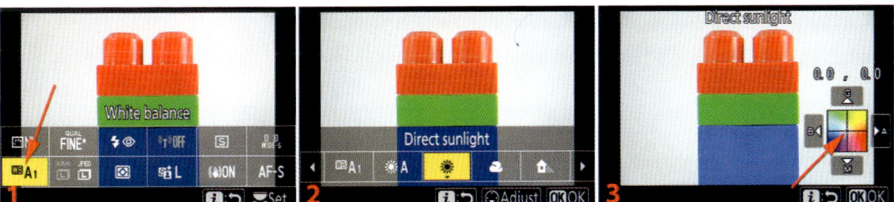

Figure 5.1A: Choosing a WB value from the *i* Menu

Use the following steps to choose a White balance value:

1. With your subject showing on the screen, press the *i* button to open the *i* Menu. Choose the White balance position on the bottom row, first position on the left (figure 5.1A, image 1), and then press the OK button or tap the WB position with your fingertip.
2. Select one of the White balance values (e.g., Direct sunlight) and press or touch OK (button or screen control) to lock it in. If you want to fine-tune the White balance color setting, you may do so by highlighting a WB value and pressing down on the Multi selector pad or by tapping Adjust (figure 5.1A, image 2).

3. To fine-tune the current Auto WB, you have four color axes available: green (G), amber (A), magenta (M), and blue (B). Move the little black square (figure 5.1A, image 3, red arrow) toward any of the axes or between two of them. You will see the color change on your subject as you move the square. When you are satisfied with the fine-tuning, press or touch OK to lock it in.

Four of the WB choices have an intermediate screen (Auto, Fluorescent, K, and PRE). Let's see how to use the additional screens.

Auto White Balance on the *i* Menu

The Auto WB setting has an additional screen that allows you to choose and fine-tune one of the three Auto WB settings (A0, A1, or A2). Let's see how (using the *i* Menu with a lens cap on for maximum screen contrast).

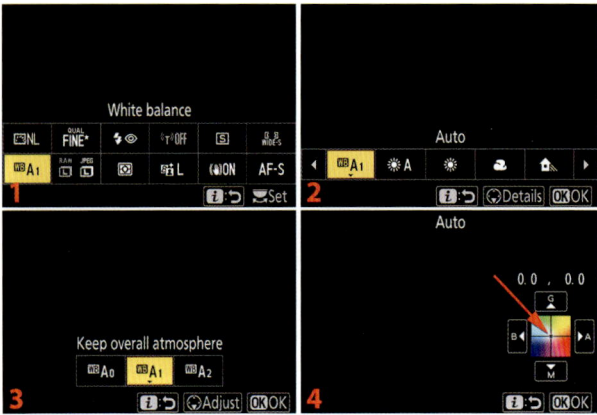

Figure 5.1B: Choosing and fine-tuning an Auto WB from the *i* Menu

Use the following steps to choose and/or fine-tune one of the three Auto WB types:

1. With your subject showing on the screen, press the *i* button to open the *i* Menu. Choose the White balance position on the bottom row, first position on the left (figure 5.1B, image 1), and press the OK button or tap the WB position.
2. Scroll to the Auto WB item on the left and press or touch OK (e.g., A1) to lock in the current Auto WB setting (figure 5.1B, image 2). If you want to change to a different Auto WB setting, scroll down with the Multi selector pad or tap the Details control. The next screen allows you to choose one of the three WB values (i.e., A0, A1, or A2).
3. Select one of the three Auto WB values: A0 Keep white (reduce warm colors), A1 Keep overall atmosphere, or A2 Keep warm lighting colors (figure 5.1B, image 3). If you want to fine-tune the White balance color setting, you may do so by highlighting one of the Auto WB values and pressing down on the Multi selector pad or by tapping on Adjust (figure 5.1B, image 3).

4. To fine-tune the current Auto WB, you have four color axes available: green (G), amber (A), magenta (M), and blue (B). Move the little black square (figure 5.1B, image 4, red arrow) toward any of the axes or between two of them. You will see the color change on your subject as you move the square. When you are satisfied with the fine-tuning, press or touch OK to lock it in.

Fluorescent White Balance on the *i* Menu

The Fluorescent WB setting has an additional screen that allows you to choose and fine-tune one of the seven available fluorescent types.

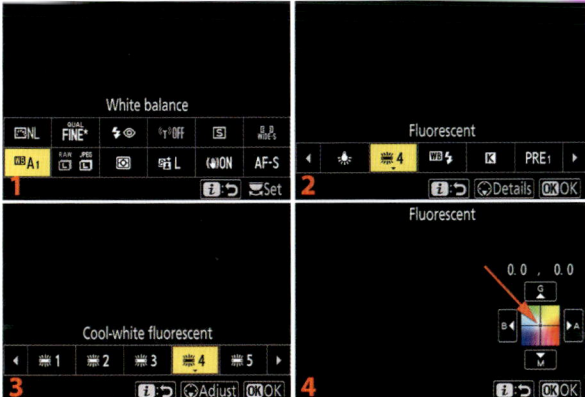

Figure 5.1C: Choosing and fine-tuning a Fluorescent WB setting from the *i* Menu

Use the following steps to choose and/or fine-tune a Fluorescent WB type:

1. With your subject showing on the screen, press the *i* button to open the *i* Menu. Choose the White balance position on the bottom row, first position on the left (figure 5.1C, image 1), and then press the OK button or tap the WB position.
2. Scroll to the Fluorescent WB item and press or touch OK (e.g., 4) to lock in the current Fluorescent WB setting (figure 5.1C, image 2). If you want to change to a different Fluorescent WB setting, scroll down with the Multi selector pad or tap the Details control. The next screen allows you to choose one of the seven WB values.
3. Select one of the seven Fluorescent WB values (figure 5.1C, image 3): Sodium-vapor lamps (1), Warm-white fluorescent (2), White fluorescent (3), Cool-white fluorescent (4), Day white fluorescent (5), Daylight fluorescent (6), or High temp. mercury-vapor (7). If you want to fine-tune the White balance color setting, you may do so by highlighting one of the Fluorescent WB values and pressing down on the Multi selector pad or by tapping on Adjust (figure 5.1C, image 3).
4. To fine-tune the current Fluorescent WB, you have four color axes available: green (G), amber (A), magenta (M), and blue (B). Move the little black square (figure 5.1C, image 4, red arrow) toward any of the axes or between two of them. You will see the color change on your subject as you move the square. When you are satisfied with the fine-tuning, press or touch OK to lock it in.

K White Balance on the *i* Menu

The K WB setting has an additional screen that allows you to choose and fine-tune a specific color temperature in the range of 2500K to 10000K.

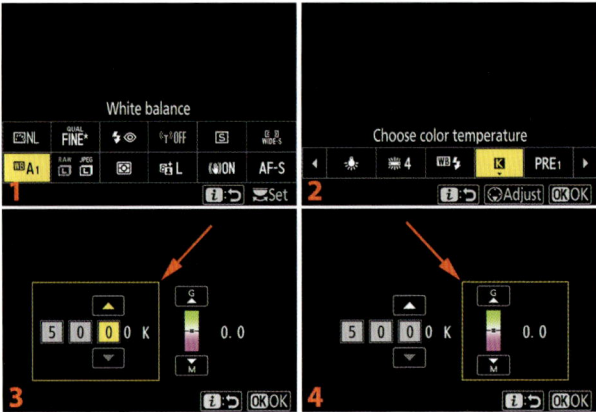

Figure 5.1D: Choosing and fine-tuning a K WB setting on the *i* Menu

Use the following steps to choose and/or fine-tune a K White balance type:

1. With your subject showing on the screen, press the *i* button to open the *i* Menu. Choose the White balance position on the bottom row, first position on the left (figure 5.1D, image 1), and press the OK button or tap on the WB position.
2. Scroll to the K WB item and press or touch OK (e.g., 4) to lock in the current K WB setting (figure 5.1D, image 2). The default is 5000K. If you want to change to a different K WB setting, scroll down with the Multi selector pad or tap the Adjust control. The next screen allows you to choose from a range of WB values.
3. Make sure the yellow box is surrounding the left (5000K) area of the screen (figure 5.D, image 3, red arrow). There are three adjustable up/down settings. Tap on the up/down pointers or press up or down on the Multi selector pad to choose a value for each of the three adjustment fields. The available range is 2500K to 10000K. Press or touch OK to lock in the specific K WB value.
4. If you want to fine-tune the White balance color setting, you may do so by moving the yellow box to the right. This is the fine-tuning section for the K WB screen. Pressing down on the Multi selector pad or tapping on the lower (M) pointer with your fingertip adds magenta to the current White balance (figure 5.1D, image 4). Pressing up on the Multi selector pad or tapping on the upper (G) pointer with your fingertip adds green to the current K White balance. You will immediately see the fine-tuning color changes in your subject. When fine tuning a specific K value, you cannot add blue (B) or amber (A), as with previous WB settings. When you are satisfied with the fine-tuning, press or touch OK to lock it in.

PRE White Balance on the *i* Menu

The PRE WB setting has an additional screen that allows you to choose from or create saved WB settings.

This setting is one of the camera's prime ways to let you create WB settings and save them for immediate and later use. These saved preset values are created by reading a white or gray card under the current ambient light.

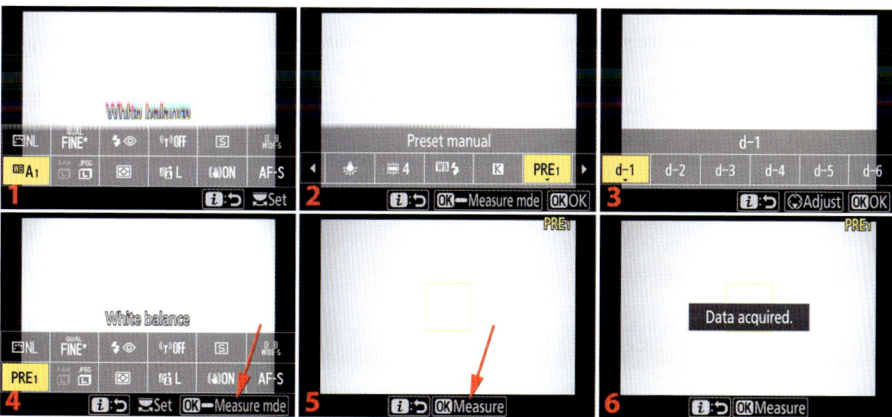

Figure 5.1E: Choosing and/or creating a measured WB reading from the *i* Menu

Use the following steps to choose or create a measured PRE WB:

1. Point the camera's lens at a well-lit white or gray card—don't worry about focus—and press the *i* button to open the *i* Menu. Choose the White balance position on the bottom row, first position on the left (figure 5.1E, image 1), and press the OK button or tap on the WB position.
2. Scroll to the PRE WB item (e.g., PRE1) and press or touch OK to lock in the current PRE WB setting (figure 5.1E, image 2). If, instead, you want to measure the light and create a new PRE WB setting, scroll down with the Multi selector to open the next screen.
3. Choose one of the available PRE memory locations (d-1 to d-6). You will place the upcoming white or gray card reading into one of these six memory locations for immediate and future use (figure 5.1E, image 3). When you have selected the memory location (e.g., d-1) where you want to receive the white or gray card reading, press or touch OK to return to the main *i* Menu screen.
4. You will note that the *i* Menu screen now has a new touch control named OK–Measure mde (figure 5.1E, image 4, red arrow). Tap on OK–Measure mde and the camera will switch the measurement screen.
5. PRE1 (or whichever PRE-number you chose) will be flashing in the top right corner of the measurement screen (figure 5.1E, image 5). This screen allows you read the ambient light reflected from your white or gray card and then store that in one of six PRE WB memory locations (d-1 to d-6) for immediate or later use. Make sure the white or

gray card is close to the front of the lens—without casting a shadow on the card that might influence the reading—and press or touch OK Measure. The camera will not try to focus on the card so you can place it close to the lens to prevent reading anything from the background. You will hear the shutter open and close as the camera makes a White balance reading of the card.

6. If the WB reading was successful, you will see a screen like the one shown in figure 5.1E, image 6. The camera will inform you: *Data acquired*. The WB reading has been stored in the memory location (d–1 to d–6) you chose. You can now take pictures with accurate white balance while remaining under the current light source. You can also return later to the same light source, if it has not changed, and reuse the WB reading you just stored, by selecting the memory location again (see steps 1 and 2). If the WB reading was unsuccessful, the camera will inform you: *Unable to measure white balance. Please try again*. If you see this message, the light may be too dim, the card may have a very bright reflection or an intruding shadow, or the color or pattern of the card may be unacceptable to the camera. If the reading was unsuccessful, reposition the camera or change cards and try again.

Note: You can fine-tune this PRE WB setting by tapping on the Adjust control seen in figure 5.1E, image 3. Use the instructions seen under figure 5.1C, image 4 (step 4) to fine-tune the WB setting.

WB on the Photo and Movie Shooting Menus

This method involves using either the Photo Shooting Menu or Movie Shooting Menu screens to select the appropriate White balance. As an example, we will use the Photo Shooting Menu; however, the Movie Shooting Menu works in the same manner with a couple of minor differences, which we will discuss.

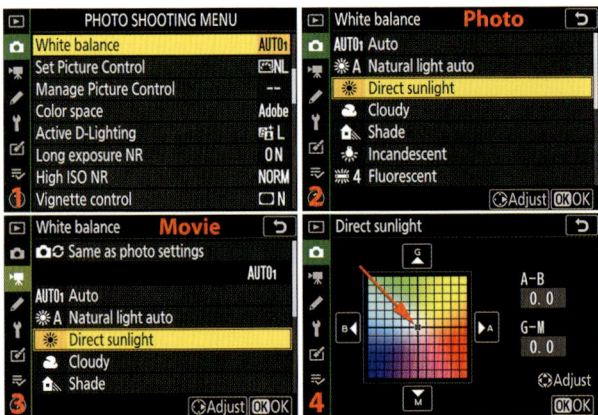

Figure 5.2A: Choosing a WB value from the Photo or Movie Shooting Menu

Use the following steps to choose a White balance value:

1. Choose White balance from the Photo or Movie Shooting Menu and scroll to the right (figure 5.2A, image 1).
2. Select one of the White balance values (e.g., Direct sunlight) and press or touch OK to lock it in. Figure 5.2A, image 2, shows the screen from the Photo Shooting Menu, and figure 5.2A, image 3, shows the screen from the Movie Shooting Menu. There are two minor differences in the Movie Shooting Menu:
   a. The Photo Shooting Menu (image 2) has a Flash WB setting (not shown) that does not exist on the Movie Shooting Menu. One does not use a Nikon Speedlight flash while capturing video, so the setting is not available on the Movie Shooting Menu.
   b. The Movie Shooting Menu (image 3) has a setting called Same as photo settings. This setting tells the camera to use the same WB settings for both still images and video, using the Photo Shooting Menu settings for both.
   If you want to fine-tune the White balance color setting, you may do so by highlighting a WB value and scrolling to the right with the Multi selector pad or by tapping on Adjust (figure 5.2A, image 2).
3. To fine-tune the current Auto WB, you have four color axes available: green (G), amber (A), magenta (M), and blue (B). Move the little black square (figure 5.2A, image 4, red arrow) toward any of the axes or between two of them. You will see the color change on your subject as you move the square. When you are satisfied with the fine-tuning, press or touch OK to lock it in.

Four of the WB choices have an intermediate screen (Auto, Fluorescent, K, and PRE). Let's see how to use the additional screens.

Auto White Balance on the Photo/Movie Shooting Menus

The Auto WB setting has an additional screen that allows you to choose and fine-tune one of the three Auto WB settings (AUTO0, AUTO1, or AUTO2). Let's see how.

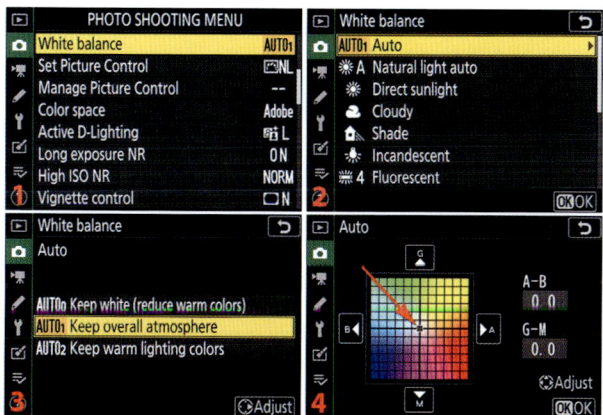

Figure 5.2B: Choosing and fine-tuning Auto WB from the Photo/Movie Shooting Menu

Use the following steps to choose and/or fine-tune one of the three Auto WB types:

1. Choose White balance from the Photo or Movie Shooting Menu and scroll to the right (figure 5.2B, image 1).
2. Scroll to the Auto WB item (e.g., AUTO1) and press or touch OK to lock in the current Auto WB setting (figure 5.2B, image 2). If you want to change to a different Auto WB setting, scroll to the right with the Multi selector pad. The next screen allows you to choose one of the three WB values (i.e., AUTO0, AUTO1, or AUTO2).
3. Select one of the three Auto WB values: AUTO0 Keep white (reduce warm colors), AUTO1 Keep overall atmosphere, or AUTO2 Keep warm lighting colors (figure 5.2B, image 3). If you want to fine-tune the White balance color setting, you may do so by highlighting one of the Auto WB values and scrolling to the right with the Multi selector pad or by tapping on Adjust (figure 5.2B, image 3).
4. To fine-tune the current Auto WB, you have four color axes available: green (G), amber (A), magenta (M), and blue (B). Move the little black square (figure 5.2B, image 4, red arrow) toward any of the axes or between two of them. When you are satisfied with your fine-tuning, press or touch OK to lock it in.

Settings Recommendation: I often use AUTO1 White balance on my Z6 for general-purpose photography. The only time I use anything but AUTO1 is when I am shooting special types of images. For instance, if I am shooting an event with flash and I want consistent image color, I often choose the Flash White balance setting. Or, if I am shooting landscapes under direct sunlight, I often shoot with the Natural light auto White balance setting. Other than special occasions, Auto White balance works very well for me. Give it a try, along with each of the others in their respective environments. Experimenting is part of improving our digital photography. A few years back, we carried different film emulsions and colored filters to get these same effects. Now it's all built in!

Fluorescent White Balance on the Photo/Movie Shooting Menus

The Fluorescent WB setting has an additional screen that allows you to choose and fine-tune one of the seven available fluorescent types.

Use the following steps to choose and/or fine-tune a Fluorescent WB type:

1. Choose White balance from the Photo or Movie Shooting Menu and scroll to the right (figure 5.2C, image 1).
2. Scroll to the Fluorescent WB item (e.g., 4) and press or touch OK to lock in the current Fluorescent WB setting (figure 5.2C, image 2). If you want to change to a different Fluorescent WB setting, scroll to the right with the Multi selector pad. The next screen allows you to choose one of the seven WB values.

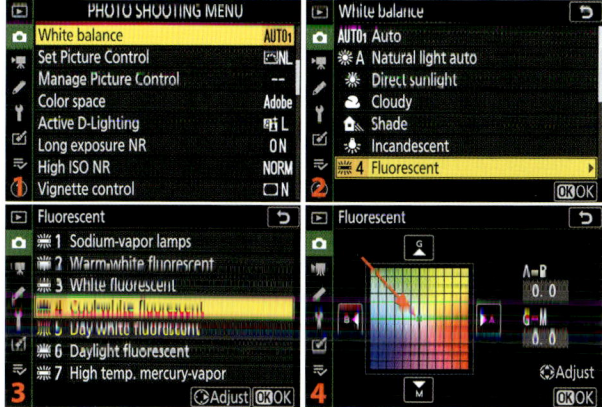

Figure 5.2C: Choosing and fine-tuning Fluorescent WB on the Photo/Movie Shooting Menu

3. Select one of the seven Fluorescent WB types (figure 5.2C, image 3) and press or touch OK to lock it in. If you want to fine-tune the White balance color setting, you may do so by highlighting one of the Fluorescent WB values and scrolling to the right with the Multi selector pad or by tapping on Adjust (figure 5.2C, image 3).

4. To fine-tune the current Fluorescent WB, you have four color axes available: green (G), amber (A), magenta (M), and blue (B). Move the little black square (figure 5.2C, image 4, red arrow) toward any of the axes or between two of them. When you are satisfied with your fine-tuning, press or touch OK to lock it in.

K White Balance on the Photo/Movie Shooting Menus

The K WB setting has an additional screen that allows you to choose and fine-tune a specific color temperature in the range of 2500K to 10000K.

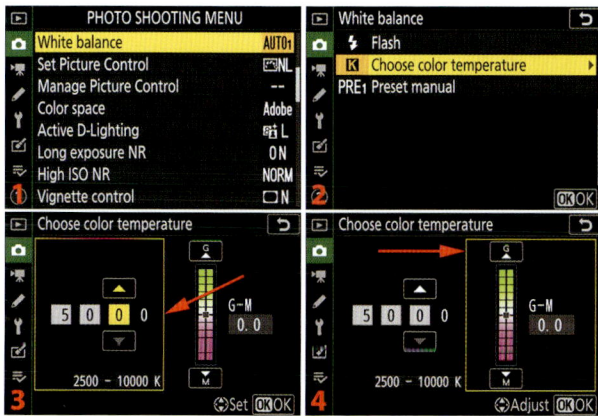

Figure 5.2D: Choosing and fine-tuning a K WB on the Photo/Movie Shooting Menu

Use the following steps to choose and/or fine-tune a K White balance type:

1. Choose White balance from the Photo or Movie Shooting Menu and scroll to the right (figure 5.2D, image 1).
2. Scroll to the K Choose color temperature item and press or touch OK to lock in the current K WB setting (figure 5.2D, image 2). The default is 5000K. If you want to change to a different K WB setting, scroll to the right with the Multi selector pad. The next screen allows you to choose from a range of WB values.
3. The yellow box should be surrounding the left (2500–10000K) area of the screen (figure 5.2D, image 3, red arrow). There are three adjustable up/down settings. Tap on the up/down pointers or press up or down on the Multi selector pad to choose a value for each of the three adjustment fields. The available range is 2500K to 10000K. Press or touch OK to lock in the specific K WB value.
4. If you want to fine-tune the White balance color setting, you may do so by moving the yellow box to the right. This is the fine-tuning section for the K WB screen. Pressing down on the Multi selector pad or tapping on the lower (M) pointer adds magenta to the current White balance (figure 5.2D, image 4). Pressing up on the Multi selector pad or tapping on the upper (G) pointer adds green to the current K White balance. You will immediately see the fine-tuning color changes in your subject. You cannot add blue (B) or amber (A), as with previous WB settings, when fine-tuning a specific K value. When you are satisfied with your fine-tuning, press or touch OK to lock it in.

PRE White Balance on the Photo/Movie Shooting Menu

The PRE (Preset manual) WB setting has additional screens that allow you to choose, name, and protect saved WB readings. These saved preset values are ones you've created previously by reading a white or gray card under the current ambient light (page 115).

Additionally, you can select another image to use as a WB source, copying the WB from an older image to a saved PRE memory location for use when making new images and videos.

Let's examine each of the subsettings within the PRE WB setting.

Choosing an Existing PRE White Balance

The PRE WB method for the Photo/Movie Shooting Menus is a little complicated because there are several subsettings to consider.

First, let's examine how to choose an existing PRE WB measurement you have previously stored (page 115) in the camera's six PRE memory locations (d-1 to d-6).

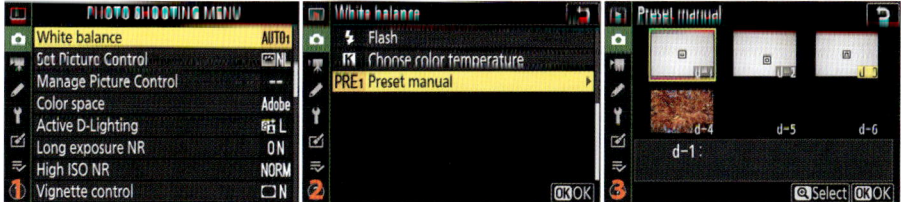

Figure 5.2E: Choosing an existing (pre-measured) PRE WB setting

Use the following steps to choose or create a measured PRE WB:

1. Choose White balance from the Photo or Movie Shooting Menu and scroll to the right (figure 5.1E, image 1).
2. Scroll to the Preset manual item (e.g., PRE1) and scroll to the right (figure 5.1E, image 2).
3. Highlight one of the existing stored PRE WB measurements (d–1 to d–6) and press or touch OK to lock in that setting (figure 5.1E, image 2).

Next let's examine how to fine-tune a Preset manual WB setting.

Fine-Tuning an Existing PRE White Balance

Previously we examined how to take a PRE measurement from a white or gray card to balance the camera to the available light (page 115), and we also looked at how to select an existing PRE WB (previous subsection). What if you want to fine-tune one of the d–1 to d–6 Preset manual in mired values before you use it? Let's see how.

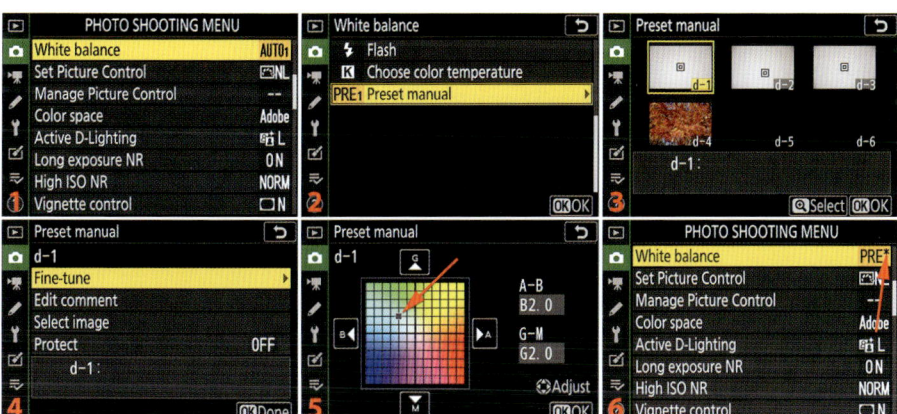

Figure 5.2F: Fine-tuning a Preset manual WB value

Use these steps to fine-tune a Preset White balance value:

1. Follow the screen flow shown in figure 5.2F, images 1 and 2 (*White balance > Preset manual*), until you arrive at the third screen in the series.

2. Tap with your fingertip to select one of the memory locations (d–1 to d–6) or use the Multi selector pad to scroll to the memory location you want to fine-tune (figure 5.2F, image 3). Press the Zoom in button or tap on Select to open the Preset manual menu. **Note:** Don't use the OK button in this case because that will merely select the d–1 Preset for use and not allow you to fine-tune the value. You must use the Zoom in button or tap on Select.

3. Choose Fine-tune from the Preset manual menu and scroll to the right (figure 5.2F, image 4).

4. Use the Multi selector pad to adjust the color balance in 0.25- or 0.5-mired increments (figure 5.2F, image 5), according to the direction you press on the Multi selector pad (i.e., up/down = 0.25 mired; left/right = 0.5 mired; and one full step = 5 mired). You can also tap on the arrows on the four sides of the color box with your fingertip to modify the color values. Scroll around in the color box toward whatever color you want to add to the currently stored White balance (B2.0 and G2.0 are selected in figure 5.2F, image 5). You'll see the color-mired values change on the right side of the screen in the fields next to A–B and G–M. Each full step (e.g., G1.0 to G2.0) is equal to about 5 mired.

5. Press or touch OK to save your adjustments to the stored White balance. When you return to the main Photo or Movie Shooting Menu screen you will see that PRE* appears next to White balance (figure 5.2F, image 6). The asterisk shows that this particular Preset manual WB has been fine-tuned.

What Is Mired?

In this chapter I mention adjusting the White balance in mired increments. **Mired** stands for **micro reciprocal degree**. It is a unit of measurement used to express color temperature value differences. It is based on a just-noticeable difference between two light sources and founded on the difference of the reciprocal of their kelvin color temperatures (not the temperatures themselves). The use of mired values dates back to 1932 when Irwin G. Priest invented the method. It is based on a mathematical formula, as follows: $M = 1{,}000{,}000/T$, where M is the desired mired value and T is the color temperature in units of kelvin. Most of us don't need to be concerned about understanding the term "mired." Just realize that it means a visual difference between color values.

Editing a Preset Manual (PRE) WB Comment Field

You can edit (add text to) the comment field of an existing PRE WB memory location (d–1 to d–6) to help you remember what type of light was measured and stored in that Preset manual setting.

Let's see how to change the comment to something that will remind you of this measured WB setting's purpose.

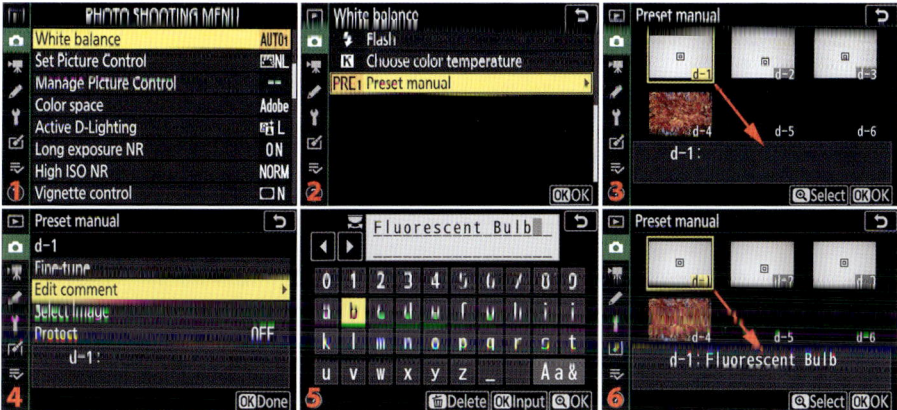

Figure 5.2G: Editing the comment field

Here are the steps to edit a WB setting's comment field:

1. Follow the screen flow shown in figure 5.2G, images 1 and 2 (*White balance* > *Preset manual*), until you arrive at the third screen in the series.
2. Select the memory location for which you want to edit the comment (d–1 to d–6) and press the Zoom in button or tap on Select with your fingertip (figure 5.2G, image 3). This will open the Preset manual menu. Don't use the OK button in this case because that will merely select the d–1 Preset for use and won't allow you to edit the comment field. You must use the Zoom in button or the Select touch control. Also, notice at the tip of the red arrow in image 3 there is no text after d–1 in the comment field. Let's use this field to identify under what type of light source the PRE reading was taken.
3. Choose Edit comment from the menu and scroll to the right (figure 5.2G, image 4).
4. The character-selection panel will now appear (figure 5.2G, image 5). Use the touch screen arrows to move the cursor in the data entry field and then tap on the characters you want to use in each space. Tap on the Aa& button to change case and to select symbols. Select Delete to delete the current character. Press or touch OK to save the PRE memory location comment.
5. The White balance memory location screen will now appear with the new memory location comment displayed (figure 5.2G, image 6, red arrow). Here, the PRE comment field for memory location d–1 was changed to Fluorescent Bulb.

Settings Recommendation: Unfortunately, you cannot create a PRE comment at the time you make a Preset manual reading from a white or gray card (page 115); you will have to use this Edit comment item in the Photo or Movie Shooting Menu. At the very least, I think you should be able to make a PRE WB reading here in this function and then name it. However, you must make the reading under the *i* Menu or from a button with White balance assigned to it (page 126) to create a new PRE WB measurement, and then you must come here and set up the comment field. This separation is not well thought out, in my opinion.

Using the White Balance from a Previous Image (Select Image)

This setting allows you to select an image you have already successfully taken and then store the WB information from that image in a PRE memory area (d–1 to d–6) to use it for new images. The thumbnail of the image will appear in the PRE location you select. Let's see how.

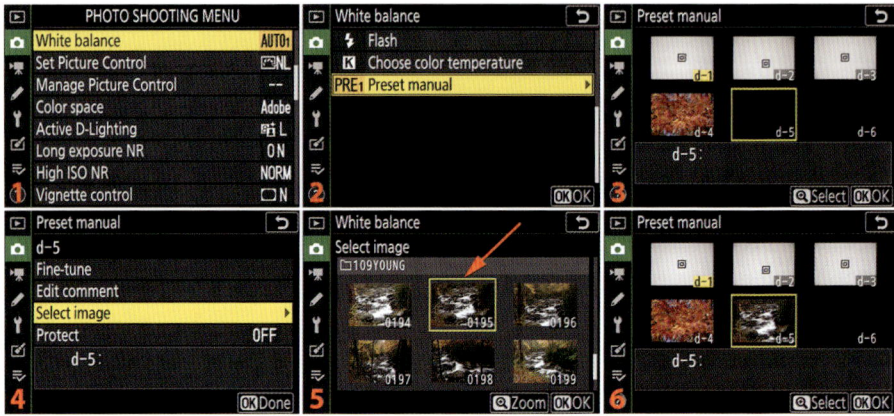

Figure 5.2H: Using White balance from a previously taken image

Here are the steps to recover the White balance setting from an image stored on your camera's memory card:

1. Follow the screen flow shown in figure 5.2H, images 1 and 2 (*White balance > Preset manual*), until you arrive at the third screen in the series.
2. Choose a memory location to which you want to save the White balance setting from an existing picture. I chose d–5 (figure 5.2H, image 3). Press the Zoom in button or tap on Select to choose the memory location. This opens the Preset manual menu. ***Note:*** Don't use the OK button at this time because that will merely select the d–5 Preset for use and will not allow you to select a previously taken image. You must use the Zoom in button or the Select touch control.
3. Choose Select image from the Preset manual menu and scroll to the right (figure 5.2H, image 4). Select image will be grayed out if there are no images on your current memory card.
4. You will now see the Select image screen (figure 5.2H, image 5). Navigate through the available image thumbnails until you find the one you want to use for White balance information. You can zoom in to look at a larger version of the image by pressing the Zoom in button or by tapping on the Zoom control. Press or touch OK to choose the image.
5. A thumbnail of the image will appear in your selected Preset White balance memory location and is saved there for future use (figure 5.2H, image 6). The White balance setting from that picture is now the White balance setting for the camera, until you change it.

Protecting a White Balance Preset

You may have gone to great efforts to create a particular PRE WB value that you will use frequently. Maybe you have a studio with a certain type of lighting that does not vary, and you want to have a dependable Preset manual value available for it. Let's see how to protect a saved Preset (d–1 to d–6) value.

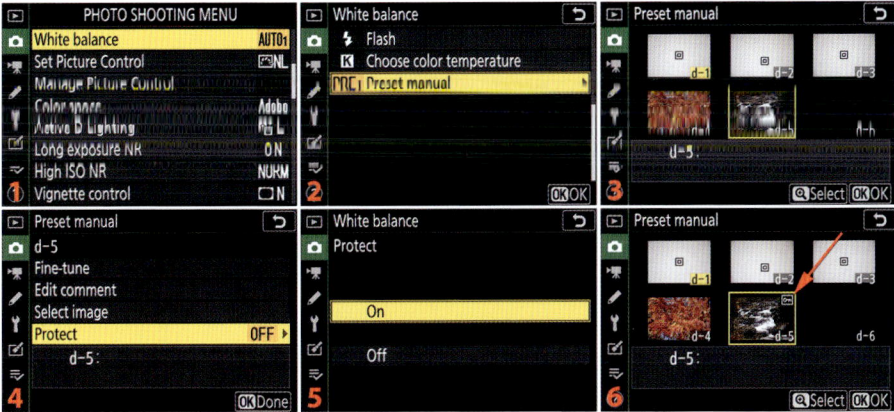

Figure 5.2I: Protecting a Preset manual White balance from deletion or change

Here are the steps to protect a White balance Preset manual value:

1. Follow the screen flow shown in figure 5.2I, images 1 and 2 (*White balance > Preset manual*), until you arrive at the third screen in the series.
2. Choose the memory location you want to protect (d–1 to d–6). We will use Preset manual d–5 (figure 5.2I, image 3) as our example. Press the Zoom in button or tap on Select to select the Preset memory location. This opens the Preset manual menu. **Note:** Don't use the OK button at this time because that will merely select the d–1 Preset for use and will not allow you to protect the Preset manual value. You must use the Zoom in button or the Select touch control.
3. Choose Protect from the Preset manual menu and scroll to the right (figure 5.2I, image 4).
4. Choose On to protect or Off to remove protection from the selected White balance memory location. I am protecting d–5, so I chose On (figure 5.2I, image 5).
5. The camera will display the White balance screen with a protection symbol (a tiny key) showing on the memory location you protected. The key symbol at the point of the red arrow in figure 5.2I, image 6, shows that memory location d–5 is locked from deletion and change. You cannot modify the protected value in any way, including fine-tuning or editing the comment field, until you remove the protection.

Now let's examine how to use an assigned camera button for White balance operations.

Using an Assigned Camera Button for White Balance

The camera's Fn1 button defaults from the factory to White balance. Therefore, unless it has been changed, you will be able to use the Fn1 button immediately to execute various WB operations.

Just in case you want to assign White balance to a different button or change Fn1 back to White balance (if it was changed), let's review how to assign White balance to a camera control.

Assigning White Balance to a Camera Control

Let's briefly examine how to assign White balance to the Fn1 button, in case your camera has been changed. You can assign White balance to another control if you would prefer.

If you press the Fn1 button and the White balance screen appears, you can skip figure 5.3A and its four steps.

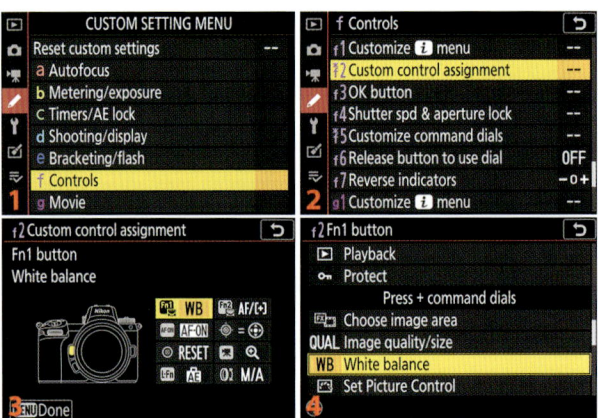

Figure 5.3A: Assigning White balance to the Fn1 button

Use the following steps to assign White balance to the Fn1 button, or another camera control (we will use the Fn1 button as our example):

1. Choose f Controls from the Custom Setting Menu and scroll to the right (figure 5.3A, image 1).
2. Select f2 Custom control assignment from the f Controls menu and scroll to the right (figure 5.3A, image 2).
3. Highlight the Fn1 button (or some other control, if you prefer) and then press the OK button to enter the assignment screen (figure 5.3A, image 3).
4. Scroll up or down with the Multi selector pad until you locate White balance (WB) on the menu (figure 5.3A, image 4). Highlight White balance and then press the OK button to assign White balance to the Fn1 button.

Now that we have assigned White balance to the Fn1 button, let's see how to use the Fn1 button to execute White balance operations.

Using an Assigned Button for White Balance Operations

In the previous subsection we assigned White balance to the Fn1 button (which is also the factory default). Let's now examine how to use the Fn1 button to control White balance.

Choosing a White Balance with the Fn1 Button

To use a button to call up the White balance (WB) system, you will need to choose a capture mode (photo or video), press and hold the assigned button down, and rotate the rear Main command dial to select a White balance type and the front Sub-command dial to select a subtype—if there is one.

First let's examine how to select a White balance with no subtype (Direct sunlight).

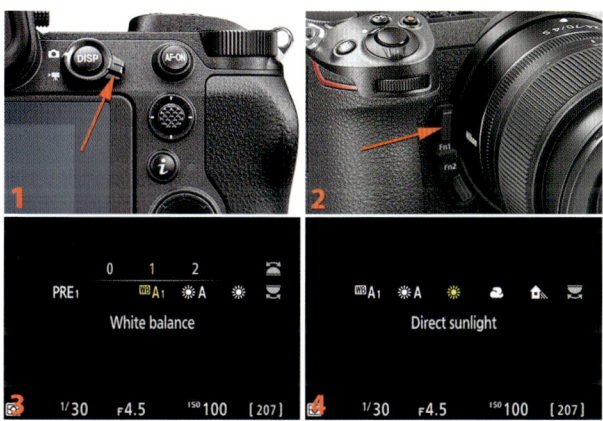

Figure 5.3B: Choosing a WB type with the Fn1 button

Use the following steps to choose a White balance type with the Fn1 button (or a different assigned button):

1. Set the Photo/Movie selector (figure 5.3B, image 1, red arrow) to Photography mode (top position) or Movie mode (bottom position).
2. Press and hold the Fn1 button, or other assigned button (figure 5.3B, image 2), and the White balance screen will appear (figure 5.3B, image 3). While still pressing the Fn1 button, rotate the rear Main command dial and you will see 10 White balance types scroll across the screen.
3. Stop turning the rear dial when the White balance you want to use is highlighted in yellow (figure 5.3B, image 4). The name of the White balance type will show just below the highlighted symbol for that WB, such as the one currently selected (Direct sunlight). Simply release the Fn1 button when you have selected a particular White balance and you are ready to take pictures or capture video with the selected White balance.

Now that we have seen how to select a White balance that has no subtypes (Natural light auto, Direct sunlight, Cloudy, Shade, and Incandescent), let's examine White balance settings that do have subtypes (Auto, Fluorescent, K, and PRE).

Auto White Balance Selection by Assigned Button
The Auto WB setting has three available subtypes. Since each is an Auto WB setting, they each have a range of color temperatures they can automatically select from, varying from as cool as 3500K to as warm as 8000K.

Remember, Nikon Z6 Kelvin White balance is backwards from the blackbody radiation Kelvin color temperatures we learned about in school because the camera *adds* colors to balance for a deficit of certain colors radiating from your subject.

Here is a description of the three Auto subtypes:

- **AUTO0 – *Keep white (reduce warm colors):*** This Auto setting tends to cool down the image by selecting from a cooler white balance (e.g., in the direction of 3500K).
- **AUTO1 – *Keep overall atmosphere:*** This Auto setting is more neutral and is probably perferred for most general photography and video, where the photographer/videographer is not overly concerned about maintaining a singular white balance, yet wants nicely balanced colors. This setting tends to keep the white balance around the 5000K range, but can move up or down the Kelvin scale as needed, within the 3500K to 8000K range.
- **AUTO2 – *Keep warm lighting colors:*** This Auto setting is for those of us who love the feel of warmer pictures. If you used a warming filter on your film camera, this setting is for you. This setting will tend to automatically select white balance in the warmer range toward 8000K, without warming up the image too much.

Let's examine how to select an Auto setting and one of its subtypes.

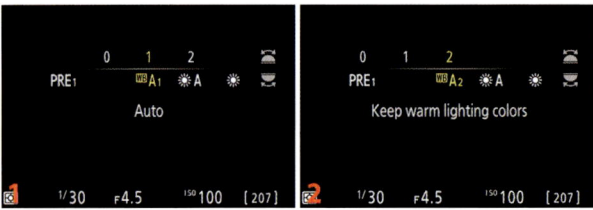

Figure 5.3C: Choosing Auto WB and a subtype

Use the following steps to choose Auto WB and one of its three subtypes:

1. Press and hold the Fn1 button while rotating the rear Main command dial until Auto is selected (figure 5.3C, image 1).
2. While still holding the Fn1 button, rotate the front Sub-command dial. You may select from A0, A1, or A2, also known as: 0 Keep white (reduce warm colors), 1 Keep overall atmosphere, and 2 Keep warm lighting colors (figure 5.3C, image 2).
3. When you have selected Auto WB and one of its three subtypes, release the Fn1 button and go make pictures or movies with your selected White balance.

Fluorescent White Balance Selection by Assigned Button

The Z6 offers seven different Fluorescent White balance settings so that you can carefully match your White balance to the ambient fluorescent light type.

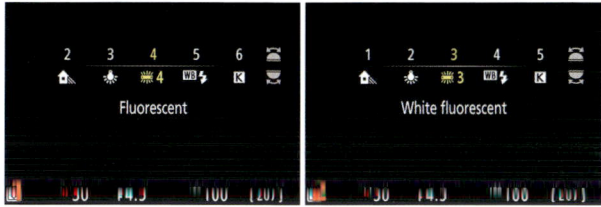

Figure 5.3D: Selecting the Fluorescent White balance and one of its subtypes

Use the following steps to choose Fluorescent WB and one of its seven subtypes:

1. Press and hold the Fn1 button while rotating the rear Main command dial until Fluorescent is selected (figure 5.3D, image 1).
2. While still holding the Fn1 button, rotate the front Sub-command dial. You may select from: 1 Sodium-vapor lamps, 2 Warm-white fluorescent, 3 White fluorescent, 4 Cool-white fluorescent (default), 5 Day white fluorescent, 6 Daylight fluorescent, and 7 High temp. mercury-vapor (figure 5.3D, image 2).
3. When you have selected Fluorescent WB and one of its seven subtypes, release the Fn1 button and the new White balance is locked in.

K White Balance Selection by Assigned Button

The K WB setting allows you to select a specific Kelvin color temperature from a range of 2500K to 10000K. Let's see how.

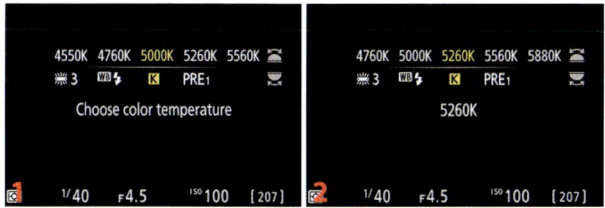

Figure 5.3E: Choosing a specific Kelvin WB color temperature

Use the following steps to choose a specific Kelvin (K) WB color temperature:

1. Press and hold the Fn1 button while rotating the rear Main command dial until Choose color temperature is selected (figure 5.3E, image 1).
2. While still holding the Fn1 button, rotate the front Sub-command dial. You may select from a large Kelvin color temperature range of 2500K to 10000K (figure 5.3E, image 2).
3. When you have selected Choose color temperature and a specific Kelvin WB value (e.g., 5260K), release the Fn1 button to lock in the new White balance.

PRE White Balance Selection by Assigned Button

This setting allows you to choose a Preset manual (PRE) White balance that has been previously created. You can also use a white or gray card and do a WB reading for immediate use or to store for future use. The camera provides six Preset manual WB memory locations (d–1 to d–6) for your use.

Let's examine how to choose and existing PRE WB and also how to make a new one.

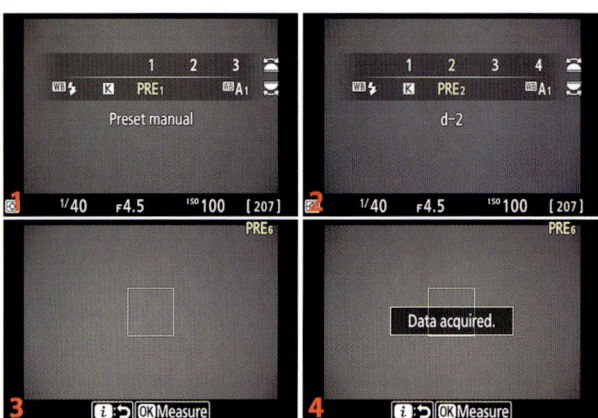

Figure 5.3F: Selecting a Preset manual (PRE) WB setting and/or making a new one

Use the following steps to choose an existing Preset manual (PRE) WB setting and/or obtain a measurement from a gray or white card to make and store a new PRE WB setting:

1. Press and hold the Fn1 button while rotating the rear Main command dial until Preset manual is selected (figure 5.3F, image 1).
2. While still holding the Fn1 button, rotate the front Sub-command dial. You may select from six Preset manual memory locations: PRE1 (d–1) to PRE6 (d–6), as seen in figure 5.3F, image 2. Once you have selected an existing PRE WB setting, you can simply release the Fn1 button and use the previously saved Preset manual WB value. Or you can make a new PRE WB reading by following the next two steps.
3. With a Preset manual memory location selected (e.g., PRE6), release and repress the Fn1 button. You will need to hold the Fn1 button down for a couple of seconds and then the screen shown in figure 5.3F, image 3, will display with a PRE symbol and number blinking in the top right corner (e.g., PRE6). Point the lens at a white or gray card, while under the ambient light you want to measure. At the bottom of the screen (image 3) is a touch control called Measure. Tap on the Measure control or press the OK button to do a reading of the light reflected from your white or gray card.
4. If the WB measurement was successful, you will see the screen shown in figure 5.3F, image 4, with the message: *Data acquired*. If the white balance measurement was unsuccessful, you will instead see the message: *Unable to measure white balance. Please try again*. If the reading fails, please refer to the side bar below titled: **White Balance Tips and Tricks**.

This WB function and the WB function found under the *i* Menu (page 199) are the two ways the camera has provided to let you make accurate, measured white balance readings when you must maintain consistent colors, such as when doing product shots in a studio. Learn to use both of them so that you can make a WB reading when you need it.

White Balance Tips and Tricks

When measuring WB with a gray or white card, keep in mind that your camera does not need to focus on the card. In PRE mode, it will not focus anyway because it is only trying to read light values, not take a picture. The important thing is to put your lens close enough to the card to prevent it from seeing anything other than the card. Three or four inches (about 75mm to 100mm) away from the card is about right for most lenses.

Be careful that your lens does not cast a shadow onto the card in a way that lets your camera see some of the shadow. This will make the measurement less accurate. Also, be sure that your source light does not produce glare on the card. This problem is not common because most cards have a matte surface, but it can happen. You may want to hold the card at a slight angle to the source light if the light is particularly bright and might cause glare.

Finally, when the light is dim, use the white side of the card because it is more reflective. This may prevent a *no Gd* reading in low light. The gray card may be more accurate for color balancing, but it might be a little dark for a good measurement in dim light. If you are shooting in normal light, the gray card is best for balancing. You might want to experiment in normal light to see which you prefer.

Auto White Balance Considerations

Auto White balance works very well in the Z6. As the camera's RGB meter senses colors, it does its best to balance to any white or midrange grays it can find in the image. However, the color will vary a little on each shot. If you shoot only in Auto WB mode, your camera considers each image a new WB problem and solves it without reference to the last image taken.

That's not a problem unless you must maintain a very tightly controlled color balance, in which case you should not use Auto WB. Instead, you should do a white or gray card reading (page 115) and arrive at a very specific White balance for your needs.

For the majority of us, using one of the three Auto White balance settings (AUTO1 to AUTO3) is fine. Nikon's color science is excellent and is recognized as one of the best available. Therefore, you can feel confident in using Auto WB for most of your photography and videography.

Remember that it is very important to get the white balance right when you are shooting in JPEG or TIFF modes. It is hard to change color balance when the color settings have been baked into the image file. On the other hand, shooting in NEF (RAW) mode frees you from some of the worry of White balance accuracy. You can change the WB on a RAW file after the fact and it will be as if you had used the new WB when you first took the picture.

Learn to use RAW mode, if you haven't already, and post-process your own images! This is the closest thing we have to the chemical darkrooms of old (we miss you, Ansel Adams).

You have a robust digital darkroom. Learn to use WB effectively and shoot in RAW mode for best results.

Author's Conclusion

With these simple tips and some practice, you can become a Z6 White balance expert. On pages 62–65 of the new Z7/Z6 User's Manual, you'll find WB information, if you want another perspective on Nikon WB.

Learn to use the color temperature features of your camera to make superior images. You'll be able to capture very accurate colors or make pictures with intentional color casts to reflect how you feel about your images. Practice a bit and you'll find it easy to remember how to set WB in the field.

Now, let's move on to the reference section of this book (chapters 6–12), with a detailed consideration of all the menu items and the hundreds of individual settings inside your powerful Nikon Z6 camera.

6 Playback Menu

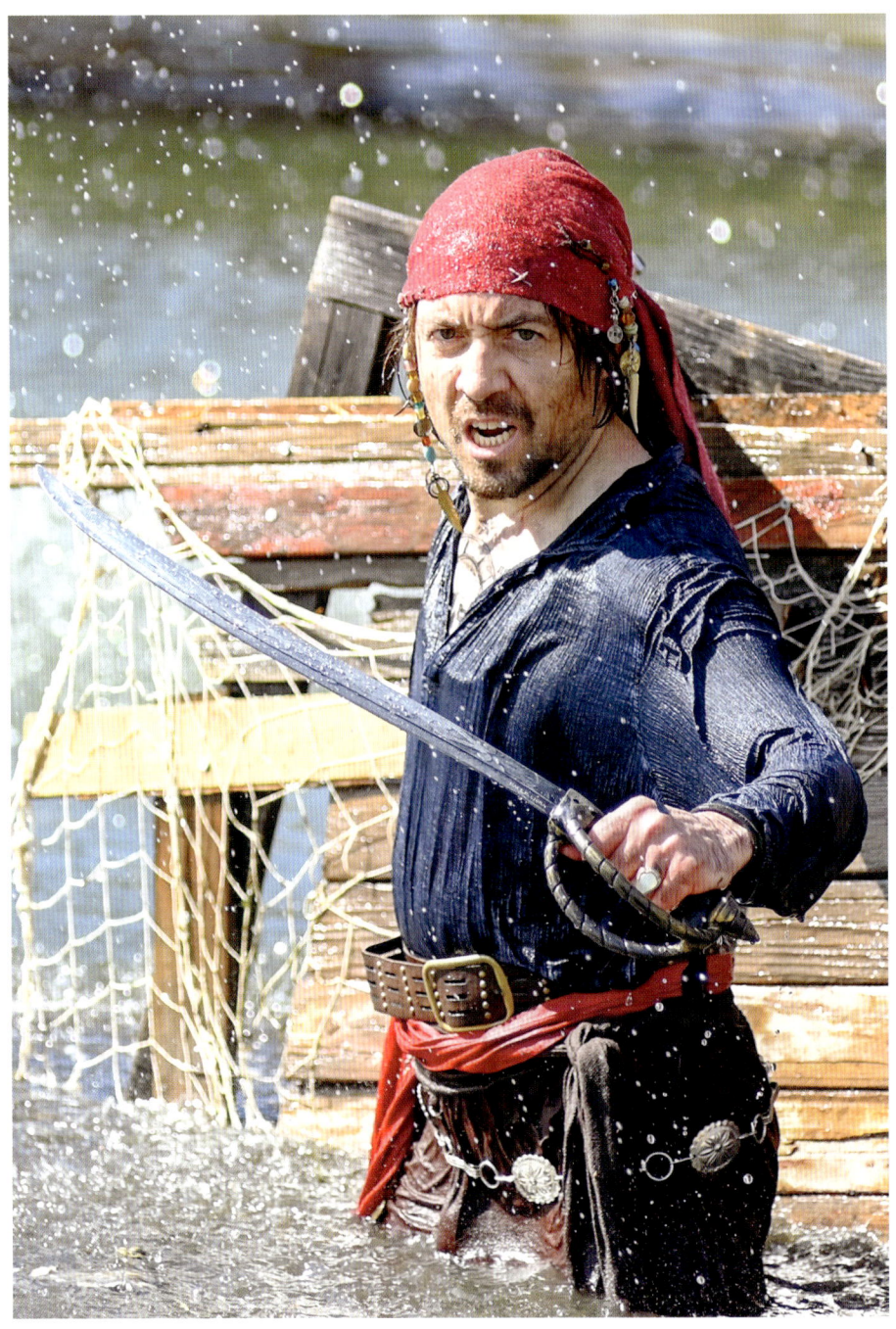

JS, the Cosplay Pirate © 2019 Wen Wu (*wwp512*)

The Nikon Z6 has a big 3.2-inch, 2.1-million pixel, tilting, touch sensitive, TFT LCD, rear Monitor, which you can use to examine the images you have taken in great detail. You can zoom in past the 100 percent pixel-peeping level to make sure an image is sharp enough. You can review, delete, rotate, rate, and examine detailed shooting information on each picture. You can even use the Monitor or EVF (electronic viewfinder) to view a slide show, or use the HDMI port to output the slide show to a larger device, such as a television (HDTV).

The Playback Menu has everything you need to control your camera's image playback and copying functions. You'll be taking thousands of pictures and will view many of them on the Monitor or in the EVF; therefore, it's a good idea to learn how to use the Playback Menu well.

This chapter, and the next several chapters, will consider the camera's menu systems. The Z6 has seven primary menu systems—along with several supplementary menus—with hundreds of configuration options. We'll examine each setting in each menu, starting with the Playback Menu.

To open the camera's menu system, press the Menu button on the lower–right back of the camera.

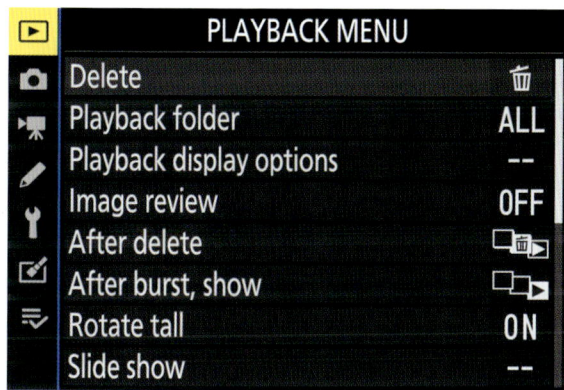

Figure 6.0: Playback Menu

The Playback Menu is first in the list of menus (figure 6.0) and it contains the following functions:

- **Delete:** Allows you to delete all or selected images from your camera's memory card(s).
- **Playback folder:** Allows you to set which image folders your camera will display, if you have multiple folders on the camera's memory card(s).
- **Playback display options:** Controls how many informational screens the camera will display for each image.
- **Image review:** Turns the camera's post–shot automatic image review on or off.
- **After delete:** Determines which image is displayed next when you delete an image from a memory card.

- *After burst, show:* Allows you to choose whether the camera Monitor displays the first or last picture from a burst series of images taken in Continuous release mode.
- *Rotate tall:* Allows you to choose whether portrait-orientation (vertical) images display in an upright position or lying on their side on the horizontal Monitor.
- *Slide show:* Allows you to display all the images on your camera's memory card(s) in a sequential display, like the slide shows of olden days. No projector is required.
- *Rating:* Rate a picture on a sliding scale of 1 to 5 stars, or mark an image for deletion.

Let's examine each of these settings in detail, with full explanations on how, why, and when to configure each item.

Delete

The *Delete* function allows you to selectively delete individual images from a group of images in a single folder or multiple folders on your camera's memory card. It also allows you to clear all images in the folders without deleting the folders. This is similar to a card formatting operation that affects only images, and not folders. However, if you have protected images, this function will not delete them.

There are three parts to the Delete menus:

- *Selected:* Deletes only selected images.
- *Select date:* Deletes all images taken on a certain date.
- *All:* Deletes all images in the folder you currently have selected with the Playback folder function (see the next main section).

Selected

Figure 6.1A shows the menu screens you'll use to control the Delete function for selected images.

Notice in image 3 of figure 6.1A that there is a list of images, each with a number in its lower-right corner. These numbers run in sequence from 1 to however many images you have in your current image folder or on the entire memory card. The number of images shown will vary according to how you have the Playback folder settings configured. (See the next section of this chapter, **Playback Folder**.)

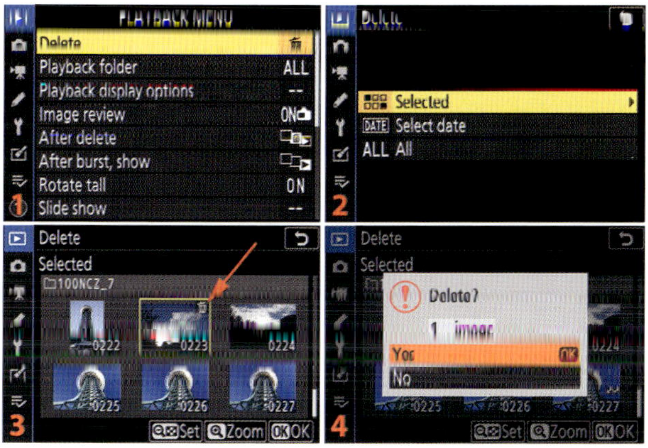

Figure 6.1A: Delete menu screens for the Selected option

If you have Playback folder set to Current (factory default), the camera will show you only the images found in your current Playback folder. If you have Playback folder set to All, the Z6 will display all the images it can find in all the folders on your camera's memory card.

Here are the steps to delete one or more images:

1. Select Delete from the Playback Menu and scroll to the right (figure 6.1A, image 1).
2. Choose Selected and scroll to the right (figure 6.1A, image 2).
3. Locate the images for deletion with the Multi selector and then press the checkered Zoom out button—or touch the image thumbnail(s) with your fingertip—to select and mark the image(s) for deletion. You will mark or unmark images for deletion by toggling a small trash can symbol on and off on the top right of the selected image(s) (red arrow in figure 6.1A, image 3).
4. Select the images you want to permanently delete, then press or touch the OK control. A screen will appear and ask you to confirm the deletion of the image(s) you have selected (figure 6.1A, image 4).
5. To finish deleting the image(s), select Yes and then press or touch the OK control. To cancel, select No and press or touch the OK control (figure 6.1A, image 4).

Settings Recommendation: This function is useful when you are reviewing your images and want to delete multiple images. Simply mark and delete the image(s) you no longer want by using the steps listed above.

There is a simpler and faster way to delete a single image. Simply display the image you no longer want on the camera's monitor and press the Delete (garbage can) button twice. The image shown in figure 6.1B has been displayed on the monitor and the Delete button has been pressed once, which opens a *Delete?* screen. Press the Delete button once more, or touch Yes with your fingertip, to finish deleting the unwanted image.

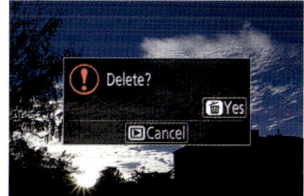

Figure 6.1B: Press the Delete button twice to delete a single displayed image.

Select Date

Using the Select date method to delete images is simple. When you preview your images for deletion, you won't be shown a list of all the images, as with the Delete option. Instead, the Select date screen (figure 6.1C, image 3) will give you a list of dates with a single representative image following each date.

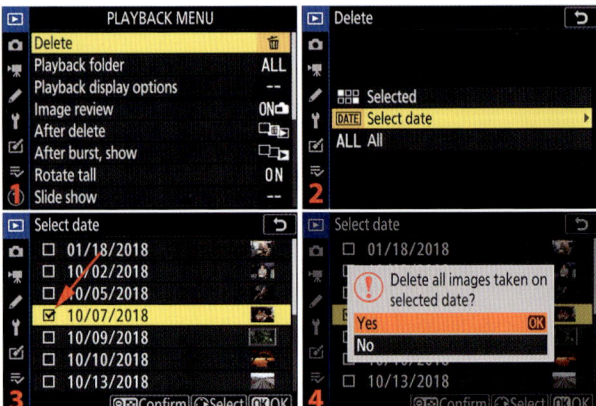

Figure 6.1C: Delete menu screens for the Select date option

Here are the steps to delete images by Select date:

1. Select Delete from the Playback Menu and scroll to the right (figure 6.1C, image 1).
2. Choose Select date and scroll to the right (figure 6.1C, image 2).
3. Notice that there's a check box to the left of each date (figure 6.1C, image 3). Check a box by scrolling up or down to the date of your choice with the Multi selector pad and then scroll to the right to place a check mark in the box(es), or you can touch the box(es) you want to select with your fingertip. Placing a check mark in the box(es) tells the camera to later delete all images that were taken on a checked date. If the single tiny representative image next to the date is not sufficient to help you remember which images you took on that date, you can view the whole bunch. Press the checkered Zoom out button, or touch Confirm, and the Z6 will display the images for that date. If you want to examine an image more closely, you can press and hold the Zoom in button, or touch Zoom with your fingertip, to temporarily zoom in on individual images. When you're satisfied that none of the images for that date are worth keeping, and while you are still examining images for a single date, press or touch OK to select the date, then press the Zoom out button—or touch Back (not shown)—to return to the list of all available dates.
4. Make sure the date(s) you want to delete are checked as described in step 3, and then press or touch the OK control to start the image deletion process (figure 6.1C, image 3).
5. A final screen will ask you to confirm your deletion (figure 6.1C, image 4). This screen has a big red exclamation point and asks, *Delete all images taken on selected date?* Select Yes and press or touch the OK control, and the images will be deleted. Be careful! Select No and press or touch the OK control to cancel the operation.

Settings Recommendation: Be *very* careful with this function! It could permanently delete hundreds of images all at once. Use the listed steps to carefully review the dated images to make sure you don't accidentally delete important pictures.

All

This option is like formatting the memory card, except that it will not delete folders. It will delete only images—except for protected images (figure 6.1D). Using this option is a quick way to format your card while maintaining your favorite folder structure and keeping protected images in them.

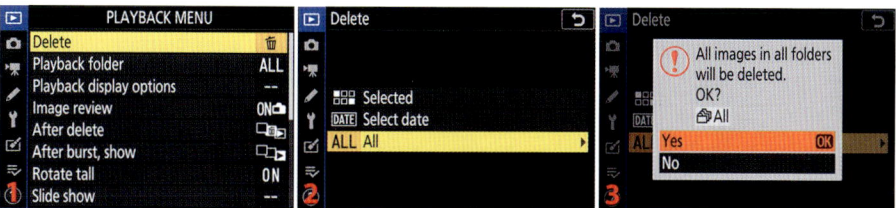

Figure 6.1D: Delete menu screens for the All option

Here are the steps to delete all images on the card (or in the current folder):

1. Select Delete from the Playback Menu and scroll to the right (figure 6.1D, image 1).
2. Select All and scroll to the right (figure 6.1D, image 2).
3. Select Yes from the next screen with the big red exclamation point and dire warning of imminent deletion (figure 6.1D, image 4). **Be very careful from this point forward!** If you have Playback folder (next chapter section) set to NCZ_6, the camera will delete all images in **every** folder that was created by the Z6, and the warning will say, *All images will be deleted. OK?,* followed by *NCZ_6.* If you have Playback folder set to Current, the camera will delete only the images in the folder that is currently in use, and the warning will say, *All images will be deleted. OK?,* followed by *Current.* If you have Playback folder set to All, the camera will delete all images in all folders, and the warning will say, *All images in all folders will be deleted. OK?,* followed by *All.* The camera is prepared to delete every image in every folder (created by any camera) if *Playback Menu > Playback folder > All* is selected. (See the next main section for information on the Playback folder option.) When you select Yes and tap the OK control, the images will be deleted.

Being the paranoid type, I tested this thoroughly and found that the Z6 really will not delete protected and hidden images, and it will keep any folders you have created. However, if you are a worrier, maybe you should transfer the images off the card before deleting any images.

Settings Recommendation: I don't use the *Delete > All* function often since I usually don't create special folders for each type of image. If you maintain a series of folders on your memory card(s), you may enjoy using the *Delete > All* function. Most of the time, I just use *Delete > Selected* to remove particular images. Any other time I want to clear the card, I use the Format memory card function on the Setup Menu. We'll discuss formatting the memory card in the chapter titled **Setup Menu,** under the heading **Format Memory Card** on page 472.

Protecting Images from Deletion

The Nikon Z6 will allow you to protect images from accidental deletion when you use the Delete function. Using this method will *not* protect images from deletion when you format the memory card.

To mark an image as protected from deletion, you will use the Help/protect button, as shown in figure 6.1E and the upcoming steps.

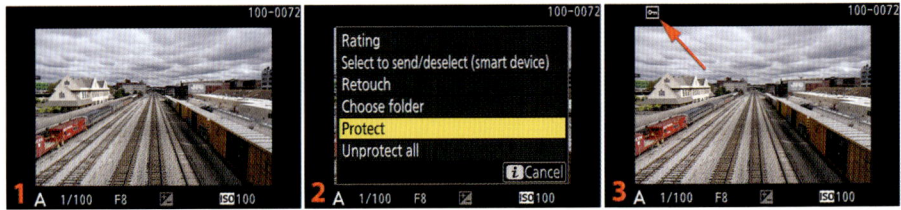

Figure 6.1E: Protecting images from deletion

Use the following steps to protect individual images from accidental deletion (figure 6.1E):

1. Display an image on the Monitor (figure 6.1E, image 1).
2. Press the *i* button just below the Sub-selector joystick and the photo Quick Menu will open (figure 6.1E, image 2). Choose Protect from the menu and a small key symbol will appear in the upper left of the Monitor, signifying that this image is protected from the Delete function (figure 6.1E, image 3—red arrow).

Settings Recommendation: You can either use this photo Quick Menu choice, or you can assign the Protect function to one of the camera's buttons for faster image protection by configuring the *Custom Menu > f controls > f2 Custom control assignment* function. Follow the instructions starting on page 423 to choose an appropriate physical button and make the Protect assignment.

You can remove image protection on individual images by following the previous steps again, which will remove the key symbol and protected status.

Recovering Deleted Images

If you accidentally delete an image or a group of images, or even if you format the entire memory card and then realize that you didn't really mean to, all is not lost. Immediately remove the card from your camera and do not use it until you can run image recovery software on the card. Deleting or formatting doesn't permanently remove the images from the card. It merely marks the images as deleted and removes the references to them from the memory card's file allocation table (FAT). The images are still there and can usually be recovered as long as you don't write any new data to the card before you try to recover them.

It's wise to have a good image recovery program on your computer at all times. Sooner or later you'll have a problem with a card and will need to recover images. Many of the better brands of memory cards include recovery software, either on the card itself, or as a downloadable app.

To find recovery software, do a Google search for your card's brand name followed by "image recovery software." Sometimes it's free, other times it costs a few dollars. However, it is best to have the software on hand for emergencies.

Playback Folder

The *Playback folder* setting allows your camera to display images during preview and slide shows. You can have the Z6 show you images created by the Z6 *only*, in all folders; images that were created by the Z6 and any other Nikon cameras, in all folders; or only the images in the current folder.

If you regularly use your memory card in multiple cameras, as I do, and sometimes forget to transfer images, adjusting the Playback folder setting is a good idea. I use a D500, D850, Z7, and Z6 on a regular basis. Often, I'll grab a 64 GB XQD card out of one of the cameras and stick it in another one for a few shots. If I'm not careful, I'll later transfer the images from one camera and forget that I have folders created by the other camera on the memory card. It's usually only after I have formatted the card that I remember the other camera's images on my memory card. The Z6 comes to my rescue with its *Playback folder > All* function.

With All set, I can see all the images in all folders created by all Nikon cameras on both memory cards.

Let's look at how the Playback folder function works by first looking at what each selection does, and then examining the steps needed to select the best function for you (figure 6.2).

The three selections are as follows:

- *NCZ_6:* The camera will display images created by the Z6 from all folders on both memory cards. This is good to use if you are interested in seeing only Z6-created images, wherever they may reside.
- *All:* The Z6 will obligingly show you every image—created by any Nikon camera it can find—in all of the folders on both memory cards. During playback, or before deletion, the Z6 will display images from other Nikon cameras you've used with the current memory card. Each camera usually creates its own unique folders, and normally the other folders are not visible. When you select All, the Z6 intelligently displays its own images and any other Nikon-created images in any folder on the two cards.

- **Current:** This is the most limited playback mode. Images in the image folder the camera is currently using will be displayed during playback, whether the images were created by the Z6 or another Nikon camera. No other images or folders will be displayed.

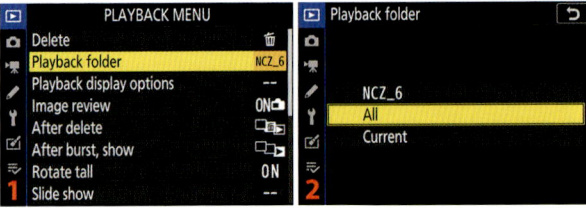

Figure 6.2: Selecting a Playback folder source

Use the following steps to select the folder(s) from which your camera will display images:

1. Select Playback folder from the Playback Menu and scroll to the right (figure 6.2, image 1).
2. Select NCZ_6, All, or Current and press the OK button or tap your selection (figure 6.2, image 2).

Settings Recommendation: Using anything except All makes it possible for you to accidentally lose images. If you don't have any other Nikon cameras, this may not be a critical issue. However, if you have other Nikon cameras around that use XQD cards, you will likely switch memory cards between them. If there are images on any of your memory cards, don't you want to see them and know they are there? Until I started using the All setting, I was sometimes formatting cards with forgotten images on them. Use All!

Playback Display Options

The *Playback display options* selection allows you to customize how the Z6 displays several histogram and data screens for each image. You get to those screens by displaying an image on the camera's Monitor and scrolling up or down with the Multi selector.

When you want to see a lot of detailed information about each image, you can program your camera to display your preferred data screens. Or, if you would rather take a minimalist approach to viewing image information, simply turn off some of the screens.

If you turn off certain screens, the camera still records the information—such as lens used, shutter speed, and aperture—and adds it to the metadata embedded within each image. However, with no Playback display options selected, you'll see only one basic file information screen when you view images.

With some or all of the Playback display option screens enabled, you can use the Multi selector to scroll up or down and examine detailed data on any image. In other words, you can scroll through your images by pressing left or right on the Multi selector (or swiping with your finger), and you can also scroll through the data screens for that image by pressing up or down on the Multi selector. You cannot swipe up and down to see any selected Playback display options screens. You must use the Multi selector.

Here are the selections in this menu:

Add info
- Focus point

Additional photo info
- Exposure info
- Highlights
- RGB histogram
  Shooting data
- Overview
- None (image only)

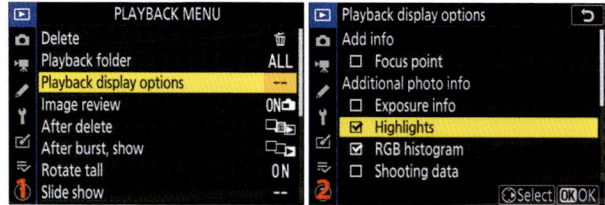

Figure 6.3A: Playback display options menu screens

Use the following steps to enable or disable any of the seven playback display screens:

1. Select Playback display options from the Playback Menu and scroll to the right (figure 6.3A, image 1).
2. Choose any of the seven available Playback display options by highlighting a line in yellow with the Multi selector pad and then scrolling to the right to put a check mark in the box for that item, or you may tap a box to add or remove a check mark (figure 6.3A, image 2). You must scroll down to see the final two menu selections, Overview and None (image only). In figure 6.3A, image 2, only Highlights and RGB histogram are selected. After you have put check marks in the boxes for all the screens you want to use, press or touch the OK control.

Now, let's look at what each of these selections accomplish (figures 2.3B to 2.4L).

Focus Point

If you are curious about *how* the autofocus (AF) points are focused on your subject (the focus mode), and *where* the points are focused (the AF-area mode) during an exposure, use this mode to easily find out.

These are the six AF-area modes that you can use to decide where on your subject is the most important area for autofocus:

- Pinpoint AF
- Single-point
- Dynamic-area AF (shows only center AF point of nine-point pattern)
- Wide-area AF (S)
- Wide-area AF (L)
- Auto-area AF

When you are using the first five AF-area modes, you'll see a single red AF indicator that varies in size with each mode, showing where the camera was focused when you took the picture (figure 6.3B, images 2–5).

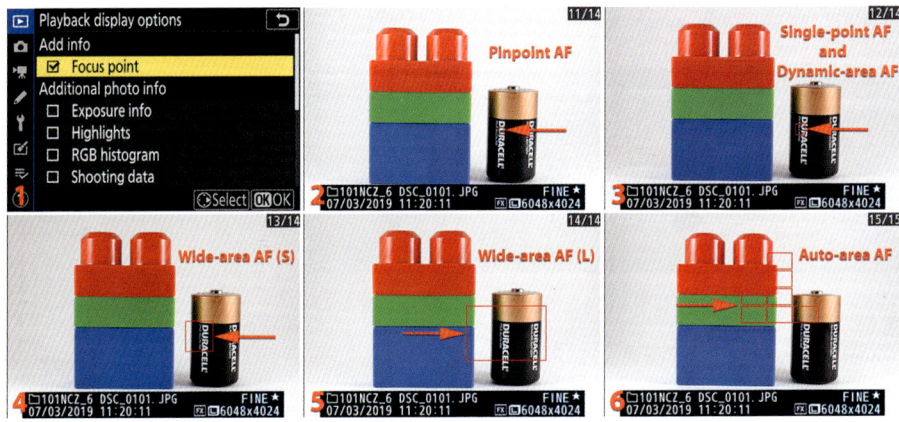

Figure 6.3B: Focus point display

The pattern of focus points for Auto-area AF, shown in red in figure 6.3B, image 6, will vary in number and location, as the camera examines the entire frame to seek likely focus points.

We will discuss the use of the AF-area modes (where the image focuses), in the chapter titled **Photo Shooting Menu,** under the heading **AF-Area Mode,** on page 264. We also touched on using the AF-area modes in the chapter titled **Camera Control Screens,** on page 23.

Exposure Info

Exposure info provides a simple screen that, in addition to displaying your subject, shows the image number, exposure mode, shutter speed, aperture, exposure compensation, and ISO sensitivity (figure 6.3C, image 2).

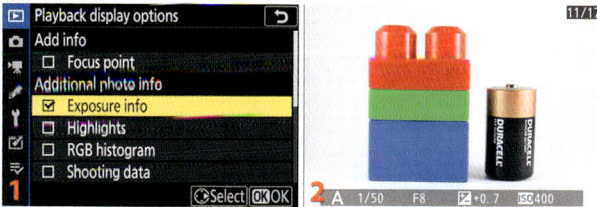

Figure 6.3C: The Exposure info screen

The gray bar along the bottom of the screen in figure 6.3C, Image 2 shows the Exposure Info (e.g., 1/50, F8, ISO 400). Here is a list of the items seen in the gray bar and what they mean:

- **A:** Exposure mode. The letter represents one of the selections on the Mode dial on top left of the camera:
  - P = Programmed auto
  - S = Shutter priority auto
  - A = Aperture priority auto
  - M = Manual exposure
  - Auto = Automatic exposure (point-and-shoot mode)
  - U1 to U3 = User programmable modes, uses one of the first five modes in this list (a–e), per selection by the photographer (page 475).
- **1/50:** Shutter speed. This value can vary between 30 seconds and 1/8000 second, or X-sync (1/200), Time, and Bulb.
- **F8:** Aperture. The maximum and minimum values of the aperture setting will vary with the mounted lens (e.g., f/1.8 to f/32).
- **+/− +0.7:** Exposure value (EV) compensation. Can be set between five EV steps overexposure (+5.0) and five EV steps underexposure (−5.0), in one third EV step increments (1 EV step = 1 stop).
- **ISO 400:** ISO sensitivity. Normal ISO sensitivity range is from ISO 100 to ISO 51200. The ISO can be extended outside the normal range in both directions, from Lo 1.0 (ISO 32) to Hi 2.0 (204800). ISO sensitivity roughly equals the older ASA film sensitivity standard.
- **11/17:** Image number/total images in current folder. The number shown in the top right of figure 6.3C, image 2, is a simple numeric count of the images in the current folder (11/17). The first number (11) is the number of the currently displayed image. The second number (17) is the total number of images in the current folder. In other words, this image is number 11 of 17 images in this particular folder. This image number has no relationship with the actual file name of the image; it is merely an image-count-per-folder number. **Note:** We will discuss how to create and change folders in the **Setup Menu** chapter under the **Storage Folder** heading on page 168.

Settings Recommendation: I like this simple screen, which shows only the important exposure information, and its uncluttered look does not distract from viewing my latest image.

Highlights

If you decide to use the Highlights selection, as shown in figure 6.3D, you will use what I call the "blink mode" screen. When any area of the image is overexposed, that area will blink white and black repeatedly.

This is to warn you that the areas of the image that blink white and black are overexposed and have lost detail. You will need to use exposure compensation or manually control the camera to contain the exposure within the dynamic range of the camera's sensor.

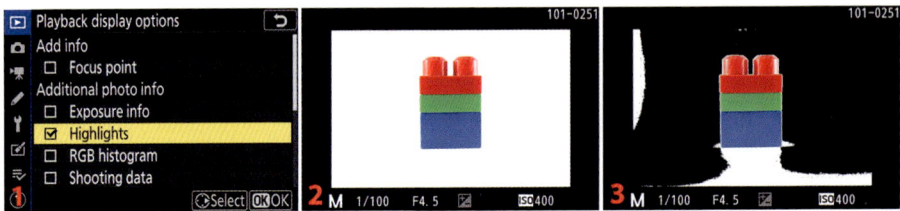

Figure 6.3D: Highlights display

Look at the white area behind the blocks in figure 6.3D, screens 2 and 3. Notice how it is white (blown out) in image 2 and mostly black in image 3. The blinking area of the image is completely blank from overexposure and has lost all detail.

If you examine the RGB histogram (see next subheading, figure 6.3E) for an overexposed (blown-out) image, you'll see that it's cut off, or clipped, on the right side. Current software can't recover much, if any, image data from the blown-out areas. The exposure has exceeded the recording capacity of the sensor. We discussed how to deal with images that have light ranges that exceed the sensor's recording capacity in the chapter **Metering, Exposure Modes, and Histogram** on page 67.

Highlights mode conveniently warns you when the exposure has surpassed what the sensor can capture *in a JPEG image* (a RAW image may have a little more detail), and lets you know that portions of the image may be overexposed. Generally, for best results, adjust the exposure until the blinking goes away (or almost goes away).

RGB Histogram

A histogram is a digital readout that shows the range of light and color in an image. If there is too much contrast, the histogram display will be cut off. We'll examine the histogram in more detail later. For now, let's see how to turn the display on and off.

I like this feature because it allows me to view not just a basic luminance (brightness) histogram as some cameras do, but also all three color (chrominance) histograms—red, green, and blue—on one screen (figure 6.3E, image 2). The Z6 stacks the four histograms on the right side of the screen, with luminance on top (white histogram) and the RGB color histograms below.

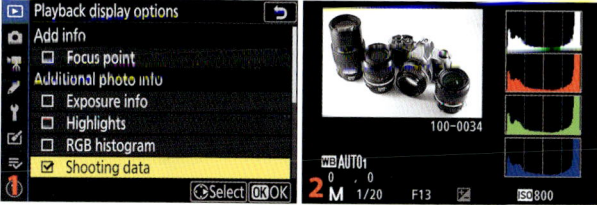

Figure 6.3E: RGB histogram display

It is quite useful to see each color channel in its own histogram because it is possible to overexpose or underexpose one color channel only. The white luminance histogram usually looks similar to the green channel histogram because green is the most common color and the luminance histogram is weighted toward green. We discussed the luminance histogram, and the three RGB channel histograms, in the chapter titled **Metering, Exposure Modes, and Histogram** on page 67.

Shooting Data

This setting gives you four additional image shooting data screens to scroll through (figure 6.3F).

The Shooting data screens insert a transparent, black rectangle over the image they represent; therefore, you will see the same picture beneath the five overlays. The data on these screens includes the following information.

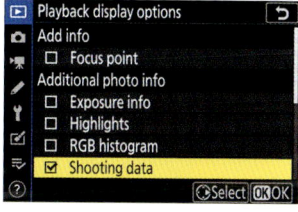

Figure 6.3F: Shooting data screens

Shooting data, screen 1 (figure 6.3G)
- Meter type (e.g., Matrix), Shutter speed (e.g., 1/30), and Aperture (e.g., F11)
- Exposure mode (e.g., P, S, A, M) and ISO sensitivity (e.g., 800)
- Exposure compensation value (e.g., 0.0)
- Lens focal length (e.g., 49mm)
- Lens overview data (e.g., 24–70mm/2.8)
- AF mode (e.g., AF-S) and AF-area mode (e.g., Single-point AF)
- VR mode (i.e., Off, Normal, Sport)
- White balance type (e.g., Auto, Direct sunlight)
- Color Space (e.g., sRGB, Adobe RGB)

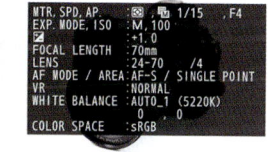

Figure 6.3G: Shooting data, screen 1

Shooting data, screen 2 (figure 6.3H)
- Flash type
- Commander mode (CMD, requires a separate Speedlight or SU-800 unit)
- Flash sync mode
- Flash control and compensation
- Commander mode info (if used)

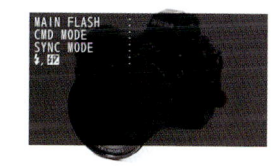

Figure 6.3H: Shooting data, screen 2

Shooting data, screen 3 (figure 6.3I)
- Picture control type: Auto, Standard, Neutral, Vivid, Monochrome, Portrait, Landscape, and Flat (or one of the creative Picture Controls—e.g., Dream, Pop)
- Picture Control adjustments: Quick sharpening, Sharpening, Mid-range sharpening, Clarity, Contrast, Brightness, Saturation, and Hue

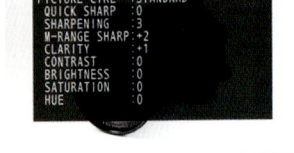

Figure 6.3I: Shooting data, screen 3

Shooting data, screen 4 (figure 6.3J)
- High ISO noise reduction, Long exposure noise reduction
- Active D-Lighting (i.e., Off, Low, Normal, High, Extra high, Auto)
- HDR exposure differential (e.g., Auto, 1 EV) and smoothing (e.g. Low, High)
- Vignette control (i.e., Off, Low, Normal, High)
- Retouch history
- Image comment

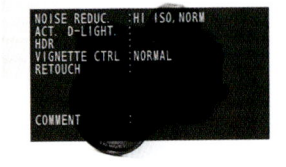

Figure 6.3J: Shooting data, screen 4

Overview

This screen provides an overview of the image detail for each picture (figure 6.3K). It is packed with information on each image, all in one convenient place.

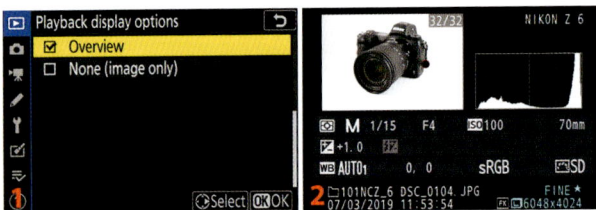

Figure 6.3K: Overview screen

With this screen and the always-available File information screen (figure 6.3M), you will have enough information to determine the most important details about a particular image. Whether you select any other screens is entirely up to you and is determined by how much information you want for each image you have taken.

None (Image Only)

This setting is designed to give you a somewhat larger view of the current image, using all of the available screen space to show the image (figure 6.3L, image 2). There are no text overlays—the image is shown by itself.

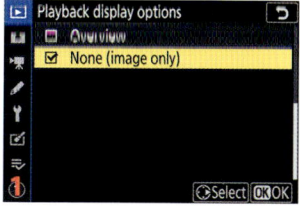 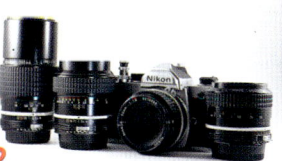

Figure 6.3L: None (image only) display

This is a good selection for when you want to zoom in on the image to look at details. Since only the image is displayed, it is easier to scroll around within it for deep looks when using the camera's two zoom buttons (zoom in and out), or stretch and pinch gestures on the monitor. You can zoom all the way in to 24× the normal image view. There is a tremendous level of detail buried inside each 24.5-megapixel image. You have an easy way to view it with None (image only).

File Information

This File information screen is not selectable under the Playback display options for the simple reason that it is always turned on and available for each image (figure 6.3M).

You cannot turn it off, although if you have *Playback display options > Focus point* enabled, the Focus point and File information screens will be combined into just one screen. File information includes a large, clear view of the picture with only basic image information.

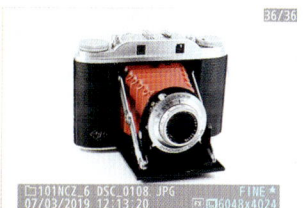

Figure 6.3M: File information screen

This screen provides the following information: image number in folder (22), total images in current folder (217), folder name (100NCZ_6), image file name (DSC_0027.jpg), JPEG compression level and/or RAW size (e.g., FINE, RAW L, RAW L+FINE), date (10/09/2018), time (12:40:42), Image area (FX, DX, 1:1, 16:9), Image size (L, M, S), and image pixel count (6048 × 4024).

GPS Screen

If you take a picture with a GPS unit attached and active on your Z6, you'll have an additional screen available (figure 6.3N)—even if you don't have Shooting data selected.

The GPS screen will not show up unless a GPS unit was attached to the camera when you took the picture, or you inserted GPS data into the image from your smartphone.

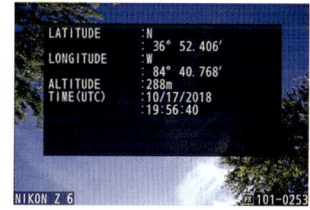

Figure 6.3N: GPS screen

There are a lot of screens to scroll through, but they provide a great deal of information about the image. Look how far we've come since the days when cameras wrote date information on the lower-right portion of an image (permanently marking it) or between the frames on pro-level cameras.

Settings Recommendation: The screens I use frequently on my Z6 are as follows: Exposure info (figure 6.3C), Highlights (figure 6.4D), RGB histogram (figure 6.3E), Overview (figure 6.3K), and None (image only) as seen in figure 6.3L.

The Exposure info screen gives me just the basics when I need to see what exposure settings I've used on an image.

The Highlights screen is useful because I can see at a glance where I have overexposed an image and can take corrective action. The black-and-white blinking areas grab my attention, and I can change my settings and then retake the shot for an immediate improvement.

The RGB histogram is also important to me because it allows me to see all the color channels, just in case one of them is being clipped off on the light or dark sides (no detail). It also allows me to see if I am keeping my exposure balanced for light and dark.

The Overview screen gives me, at a glance, most of the important information I need to know about the image, along with a larger luminance histogram. If I had only one screen, I'd want it to be the Overview screen.

I like None (image only) because I love to drill down into my images to see what detail I've been able to capture. I enjoy this setting because it lets me examine the image without text overlays. And it's also nice to view the composition of the image with no distractions.

The Shooting data and Focus point screens are not very important to me, unless I need that metadata for a special purpose. Also, if I have the Shooting data screens enabled, I'll have to scroll through four more screens to get to the screens I like to use. However, those are my personal preferences. If you want to examine a large amount of extra image data, then you should enable the other screens, too. Nikon gives us very thorough picture detail screens. Use what you like best.

Image Review

Image review displays an image you've just taken on your camera's Monitor or in the EVF (electronic viewfinder). With this function set to On, you will see each picture just after you take it. You can review the image for quality and usefulness.

With Image review set to Off, you won't see each picture unless you press the Playback button afterward. This saves battery life, which can be important for a camera using Live view all the time. If you prefer to review every image after you take it, then you'll need to set this feature to On.

You can control how long each image is displayed on the Monitor before it shuts off by adjusting *Custom Setting Menu > c Timers/AE lock > c3 Power off delay > Image review*. This custom image review time can be adjusted to display pictures from 2 seconds to

10 minutes. We'll discuss the image review timeout setting In more detail under **Image Revlew** on page 395. There are three Image review settings. Let's examine each of them.

- **On:** Shows the picture on the Monitor or EVF after each shutter release. After the review timeout, the screen will return to its normal state. If your eye is looking through the EVF, the camera will display the image there. If you are holding the camera away from your eye, the Z6 will display the image on the rear monitor instead. Keep in mind that reviewing images on the EVF will prevent you from using the EVF to take pictures until you have reviewed the image for the specified timeout period (default 4 seconds), or you have half pressed the Shutter-release button to force the review off and normal viewing back on. Therefore, if you are shooting bursts of images, or need to be able to take another picture with no delay, you may not want Image review enabled for the both the Monitor and the EVF. The next setting may be better for you.
- **On (monitor only):** Shows the picture on the rear Monitor only. This works more like a DSLR, giving you the ability to review images immediately after taking them. You may find this setting the most useful one since you can ignore the monitor if you are in a situation where you must take more images quickly while using the EVF.
- **Off:** The Monitor or EVF does not display the image you just took. You must press the Playback button to see it on the current display (Monitor or EVF).

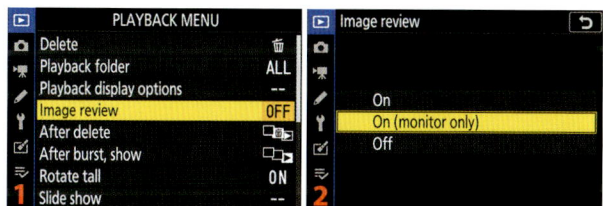

Figure 6.4: Enabling Image review

Here are the steps to choose an Image review setting:

1. Choose Image review from the Playback Menu and scroll to the right (figure 6.4, image 1).
2. Select On, On (monitor only), or Off from the Image review screen (figure 6.4, image 2) and press the OK button or tap the option to lock in the setting.

Note: The current setting you have selected with the Monitor mode button (page xi), on the left side of the Viewfinder bump, will affect how Image review works, as follows:

- **Proritize viewfinder** or **Automatic display switch:** The camera will automatically switch the image review between the EVF and Monitor according to whether or not your eye is at the Viewfinder.
- **Viewfinder only:** The rear Monitor will not display images for review. Only the EVF will be able to display images for review.

- *Monitor only:* The EVF will not display images for review. Only the rear Monitor will display images for review.

   Settings Recommendation: Mirrorless cameras use more battery power than DSLRs, especially when using the rear Monitor. Therefore, you should consider carefully if you really need to review every image after you take it. With Image review set to Off, the only way to view an image after taking it is to press the Playback button.

   I am an unashamed image chimper (see sidebar **Are You a Chimper, Too?**) and if there's time and I have extra batteries, I examine every image. My main style of shooting (landscapes) often allows me time to examine each image. However, shooting weddings, graduations, and other events often does not allow one time to admire each image between shots. If you are shooting a sports event and blasting through hundreds of shots per hour, there certainly isn't time to view each image.

   It all boils down to how you shoot. If you aren't inclined to view your images as you take them, then it may be a good idea to set Image review to Off—merely to save battery life.

> **Are You a Chimper, Too?**
>
> "Chimping" means reviewing images on the Monitor or EVF after each shot. I guess people think you look like a monkey if you review each image. Well, I do it anyway! Sometimes I even make monkey noises when I'm chimping my images. Try saying, "Ooh, Ooh, Ooh, Ah, Ah, Ah" when you're looking at an image and are happy with it. That's chimping with style, and it's the reason the word was coined.

After Delete

If you delete an image during playback (Image review), another of your other images will be displayed on the camera's Monitor. The *After delete* function lets you select which image is displayed after you delete an image. The camera can display the next image or the previous image, or it can detect which direction you were scrolling—forward or backward—and let that determine which image appears after you have deleted one. The three selections on the After delete menu are:

- *Show next:* If you delete an image and it wasn't the last image on the memory card, the camera will display the next image on the card. If you delete the last image on the card, the previous image will be displayed because there is no next image. Show next is the factory default behavior of the Z6.
- *Show previous:* If you delete an image that is not the first image on the memory card, the previous image will then be displayed. If you delete the first image on the memory card, the camera will display the next image because there is no previous image.
- *Continue as before:* This weird little setting shows the flexibility of computerized camera technology in all its glory. If you are scrolling to the right (the order in which the images were taken) and decide to delete an image, the camera uses the Show next method to display the next image. If you happen to be scrolling to the left (opposite

from the order in which the images were taken) when you delete a picture, the camera will use the Show previous method instead.

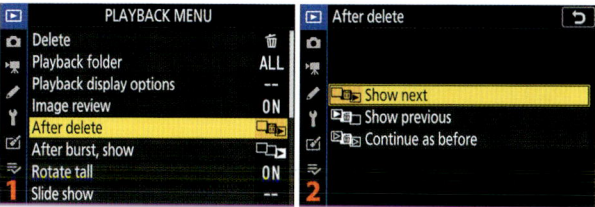

Figure 6.5: After delete

Use the following steps to choose an After delete setting:

1. Choose After delete from the Playback Menu and scroll to the right (figure 6.5, image 1).
2. Highlight one of the three settings from the After delete screen (figure 6.5, image 2) and press the OK button or tap the option to lock in the setting.

Settings Recommendation: When I delete an image, I'm not overly concerned about which image shows next—most of the time. However, this functionality is handy for certain styles of shooting and when I am deleting rejects.

For instance, some sports or wildlife shooters might like to move backward through a long sequence of images, starting with the last image taken. They can then delete the images that are not usable in the sequence, and the camera will immediately show the previous image for review. When they reach the first image in the sequence, the entire series is clean and ready to use.

I set my camera to Continue as before because, after I delete an image, it will resume the direction in which I had been scrolling.

After Burst, Show

The *After burst, show* function will work only if you have *Image review* (page 150) turned off. When you are taking pictures in one of the burst modes using Continuous L (low), Continuous H (high), or Continuous H* (high extended) Release mode (page 97), you can use this function to choose whether the camera displays the first or last photo in the series of images on the camera's Monitor or EVF for review.

Since Image review must be turned off, the camera will not display an image at all until you press the Playback button. When you press Playback, the camera will display the first or last image in the burst series, according to how you have this function configured.

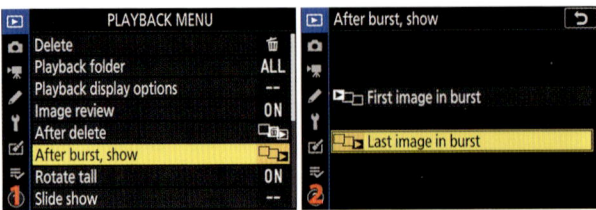

Figure 6.6: After burst, show

Use the following steps to choose an After burst, show setting:

1. Choose After burst, show from the Playback Menu and scroll to the right (figure 6.6, image 1).
2. Select either First image in burst or Last image in burst (figure 6.6, image 2) and press the OK button to lock in your choice. You can also tap on one of the settings for immediate selection.

Settings Recommendation: After testing this function, I chose the *First image in burst* setting so that I could easily scroll forward through all the images in the series. If you prefer to see the last image for validation, choose the other option.

I don't generally use this function because I prefer the Image review function's way of doing things. If Image review and the camera's Monitor are both enabled, and you quickly look at the Monitor after a long burst series, you will see individual images in the series scroll by on the Monitor as the camera writes the images to the memory card. The number of images you actually see is affected by the speed of the memory card.

Rotate Tall

When you shoot a portrait-oriented (vertical) image with the camera rotated sideways, the image can later be viewed as a horizontal image lying on its side or as a smaller, upright (tall) image on the camera's horizontal (wide) Monitor.

If you view the image immediately after taking it, the camera's software assumes you are still holding the camera in the rotated position and the image will be displayed correctly for that angle. Later, if you are reviewing the image with the camera's playback functionality and have *Rotate tall* set to On, the image will be displayed as an upright, vertical image that is smaller so it will fit on the horizontal Monitor. You can zoom in to see sharpness detail if needed.

If you would rather have the camera leave the image lying on its side while in a horizontal view, you'll need to choose Off. The following two settings are available.

- ***On:*** When you take a vertical image, the camera will rotate it so you don't have to turn your camera to view it naturally during playback. This resizes the view of the image so that a vertical image fits in the horizontal frame of the Monitor. The image will be a bit smaller than normal. When you first view the image after taking it, the camera does not rotate it because it assumes you are still holding the camera in a vertical orientation. It also senses which end of the camera is up—if the Shutter-release button is up or down—and displays the image accordingly.

- **Off:** Vertical images are left in a horizontal direction, lying on their side; you'll need to turn the camera to view the images in the same orientation as when they were taken. This provides a slightly larger view of a portrait-oriented image.

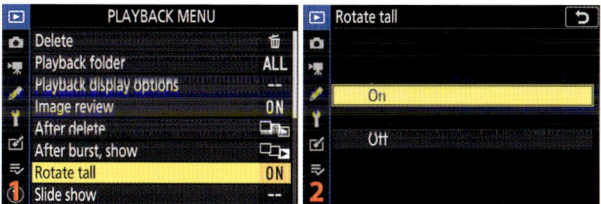

Figure 6.7: Rotate tall

Use these steps to choose a Rotate tall setting:

1. Choose Rotate tall from the Playback Menu and scroll to the right (figure 6.7, image 1).
2. Select On or Off from the Rotate tall screen (figure 6.7, image 2) and press the OK button to lock in your choice. You can also tap on one of the settings for immediate selection.

Besides this Rotate tall function, the camera evidently has built-in auto image rotation, which causes the Z6 to record the angle at which you are holding the camera body as part of the image's metadata. This is important so that an image will report how it should be displayed on the camera's Monitor and later on your computer and smart devices. Who wants to manually rotate images later to look at them on your computer monitor or smart device screen? The built-in auto image rotation prevents that.

In Nikon DSLRs released before the Z6, Auto image rotation was a Playback menu function that could be enabled or disabled. However, in the Z6 (firmware C2.00) the function appears to be an automatic function that cannot be disabled. There are no function listings for Auto image rotation in the User's Manual. However, auto image rotation is mentioned as being a Playback operation in the new Z7/Z6 User's Manual on page 210.

Basically, Rotate tall and the camera's built-in auto image rotation work together to display your image in the correct orientation. Rotate tall gives you the choice of how the image is viewed based on the orientation information it finds in the image's metadata. Auto image rotation causes the camera to store how the image was taken so it will know whether the image has a vertical or horizontal composition. It can then report this information to the Rotate tall function.

Settings Recommendation: I leave Rotate tall set to On. That way, I can view a portrait-oriented image in its natural, vertical orientation without turning my camera. Be sure you understand the relationship between this function and auto image rotation, which stores orientation data with the picture.

Slide Show

Slide show allows you to display an automatic, sequenced show of images and movies on your camera's Monitor. With the Z6's big 3.2-inch, high-resolution Monitor, it should be a satisfying viewing experience for one or two people.

If the camera Monitor is not large enough, you can connect the camera to a high-definition television (HDTV) and do a slide show for an even larger group. Connecting to an HDTV requires the separate purchase of an HDMI (type A) to mini-HDMI (type C) cable.

When you are ready for your show, you can control how long each image is displayed with the Frame interval setting. First, let's see how to start a Slide show (following the Z6's menu order), and then we'll see how to change the Image type for display and the Frame interval timing.

Starting a Slide Show

You can start the Slide show immediately, and it will commence with a default display time (Frame interval) of two seconds (2s) per image, displaying the images and movies it finds on your camera's memory card(s).

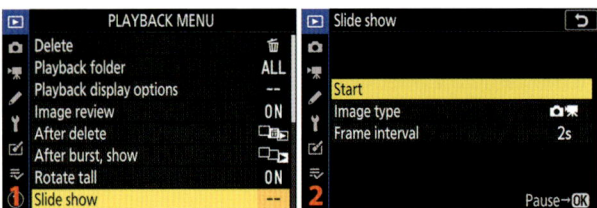

Figure 6.8A: Starting a Slide show

Use the following steps to start a Slide show immediately:

1. Select Slide show from the Playback Menu and scroll to the right (figure 6.8A, image 1).
2. Select Start and the Slide show will begin immediately (figure 6.8A, image 2), using the default Image type (Still images and Movies) and Frame interval timing (2 s).

You can easily change the way the camera chooses which Image type to display during the Slide show. The next subsection shows how.

Selecting an Image Type for a Slide Show

As you will notice in figure 6.8B, image 2, you can set the camera to display Still images and movies, Still images only, Movies only, or By rating (page 159).

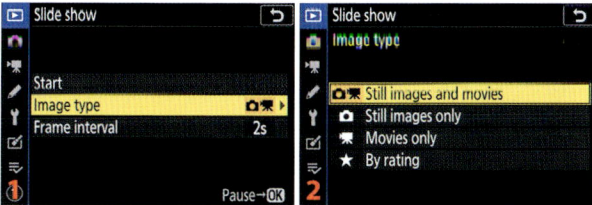

Figure 6.8B: Selecting the Slide show Image type

Use the following steps to change the Image type for display:

1. Select Image type from the Slide show screen (figure 6.8B, image 1).
2. Choose one of the three listed image types (figure 6.8B, image 2) and press the OK button to lock in your choice. You can also tap on one of the settings for immediate selection.

Note: If Movies only is grayed out and unavailable, it simply means you have no movies on the memory cards inserted in the camera.

Now let's consider how to change the amount of time before the camera changes to the next image or movie in the slide show.

Changing a Slide Show's Frame Interval

If you want to allow a little more time for each Still image to display, or between each Movie, you'll need to change the Frame interval (display time). Your Frame interval choices are as follows.

- **2 s:** 2 seconds
- **3 s:** 3 seconds
- **5 s:** 5 seconds
- **10 s:** 10 seconds

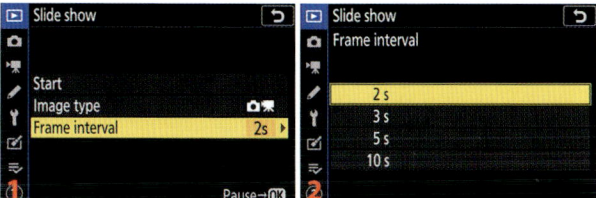

Figure 6.8C: Selecting the Slide show Frame interval

Use these steps to change the Slide show's Frame interval:

1. Choose Frame interval from the Slide show menu and scroll to the right (figure 6.8C, image 1).

2. Select one of the four choices from 2 s to 10 s (figure 6.8C, image 2) and press the OK button to lock in your choice. You can also tap on one of the settings for immediate selection.

To start the Slide show after you change the Frame interval, repeat the steps shown in the previous subsection, **Starting a Slide Show** (page 156). The Slide show will now run at the speed you chose.

    Settings Recommendation: I usually set the Frame interval to 3 s. If the images are especially beautiful, I might set it to 5 s. I've found that 2 s is not quite enough, and 5 s or 10 s may be too long. I wish there were a four-second setting, but 3 s seems to work well most of the time.

Slide Show Camera Control Options

Several options affect how the images are displayed during a slide show. None of these options are in the camera menus; they are available through the camera's physical controls. Your options are as follows:

- *Skip back/Skip ahead:* During the slide show you can go back to the previous image for another viewing by simply pressing left on the Multi selector pad. You can also see the next image with no delay by pressing right on the Multi selector pad. This is a quick way to skip images or review previous images without stopping the slide show.
- *View additional photo information:* While the slide show is running, you can press up or down on the Multi selector pad to view the additional data screens. The screens you will see depends on how you have your camera's Playback display options configured for Highlights, Focus point, RGB histogram, and Shooting data (see the section called **Playback Display Options** earlier in this chapter). If any of these screens are available, they can be used during the slide show.
- *Pause slide show:* During the slide show you may want to Pause, change the Frame interval, or even Exit the show. If you press the OK button, the slide show will be suspended and you will see the Pause screen (figure 6.8D). To select one of the choices on the screen, do one of the following: Tap on your choice to immediately execute it, highlight the item and press the OK button, or scroll to the right with the Multi selector pad. Here are the choices:

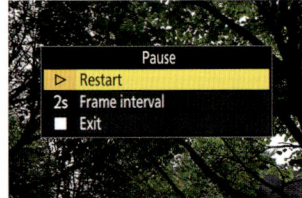

Figure 6.8D: Slide show Pause and Restart

  - *Restart:* This option immediately continues the slide show, starting with the image following the last one that was viewed.
  - *Frame interval:* This option takes you to a screen that allows you to change the display time to one of four values: 2 s, 3 s, 5 s, or 10 s. After you choose the new Frame interval, select Restart to continue the slide show where you left off.

- **Exit:** This option exits the slide show immediately. It is unrelated to the next three items in the main list, which provide alternate ways to exit a slide show without accessing up the Pause screen.
- **Exit to the Playback Menu:** If you want to quickly exit the slide show, simply press the MENU button and you'll jump directly back to the Playback Menu.
- **Exit to playback mode:** You can press the Playback button to stop the slide show and switch to a normal full-frame or thumbnail view of the last image seen in the slide show. This exits the show on the last image viewed.
- **Exit to shooting mode:** If you press the Shutter-release button halfway down, the slide show will stop. The camera is now in shooting mode, meaning it is ready to take some pictures.

Note: When a video is playing on the monitor, you can press the Zoom in button—to the left of the Menu button—to raise the movie's volume, or press the Zoom out button to lower the volume.

Rating

The *Rating* system in the Z6 allows you to add your own personal one- to five-star rating to a displayed image (figure 6.9).

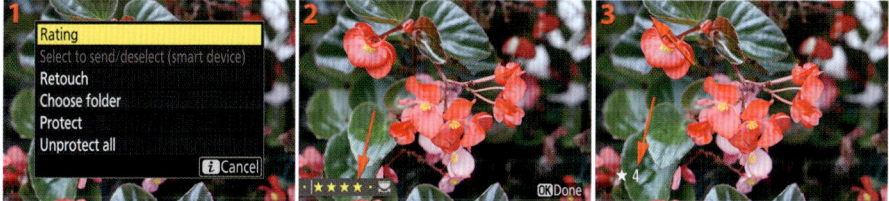

Figure 6.9: Adding a star (★) rating to your pictures

Use the following steps to add a star (★) rating to an image:

1. Press the Playback button and then find an image you want to rate. With the picture displayed on the screen, press the *i* button and choose Rating from the menu (figure 6.9, image 1).
2. Use the Multi selector pad to scroll to the right (or left) until you have displayed the number of stars you want to use as the rating for this image (figure 6.9, image 2, red arrow). You can also slide your fingertip back and forth on the bar in the bottom-left area of the screen, or tap the dots individually until they turn into a star. Choose from one (★) to five stars (★ ★ ★ ★ ★). Here, I selected four stars.
3. Press or touch the OK control to lock in the rating. The Monitor will now display a rating (e.g., ★ 4) in the bottom-left area of the image (figure 6.9, image 3, red arrow).

Note: You can also assign the Rating system option to one of the camera's program-mable buttons, using *Custom Setting Menu > f Controls > f2 Custom control assignment* (see page 423).

Author's Conclusion

We have configured all aspects of the camera's image Playback system. By now you should be pretty well informed on how to use the Playback functions to view your images on the camera Monitor or a smart device (smartphone or tablet).

Let's move on to the next menu system in the camera, the Photo Shooting Menu. This is one of the most important menus for photographers because it affects how the camera is configured to shoot still pictures.

7 Photo Shooting Menu

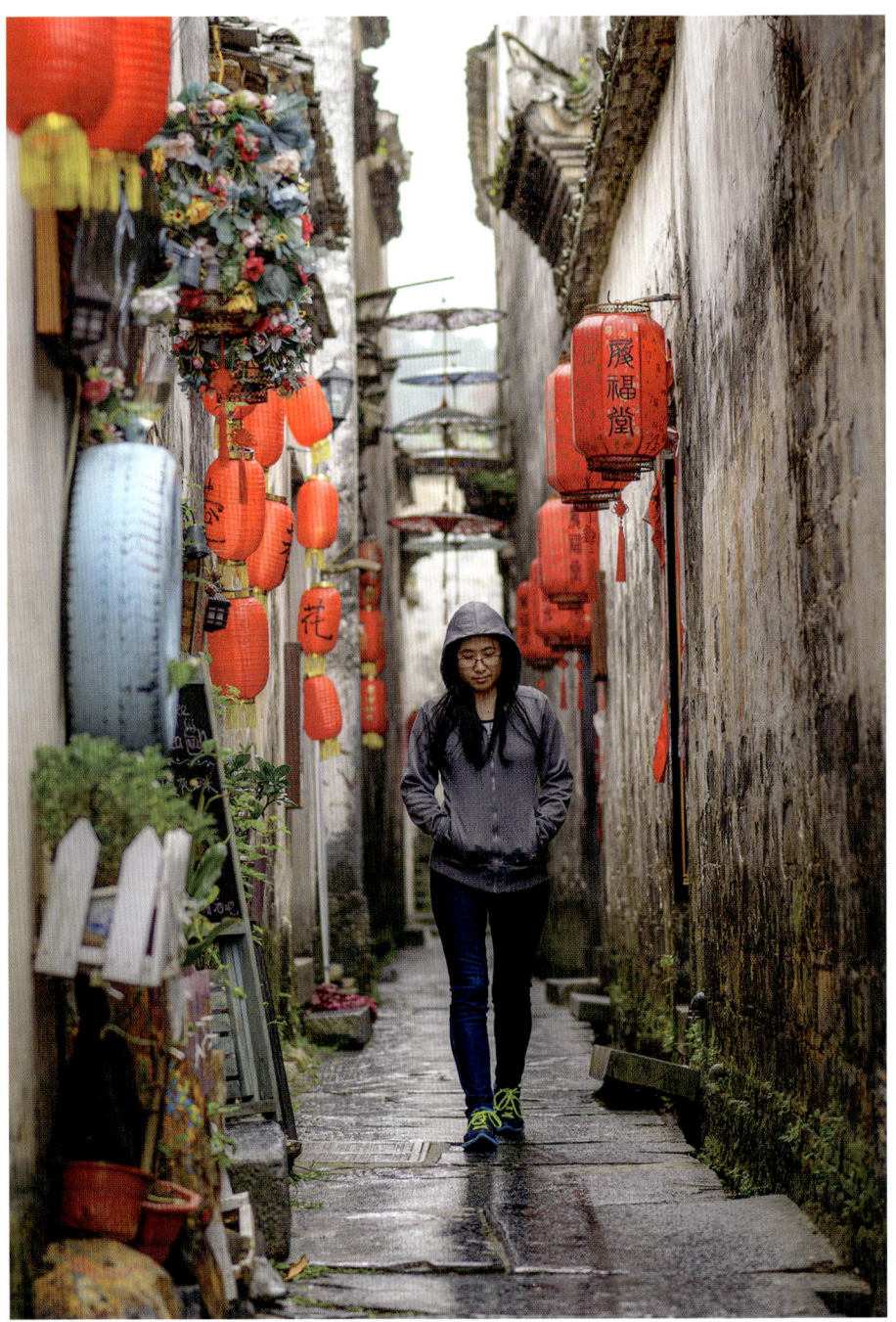

Tenmuki in Xidi Village © 2019 Wen Wu (*wwp512*)

The Photo Shooting Menu settings are some of the most-used functions in the camera. Spend time thoroughly learning about each of these selections because you will use them often. They affect how your camera takes pictures in all sorts of ways. Let's see how to get your new camera ready for thousands of pictures to come.

Configuring the Photo Shooting Menu

Press the MENU button on the back of your Z6 to locate the Photo Shooting Menu, which corresponds to the camera icon in the toolbar on the left side of the Monitor (figure 7.0).

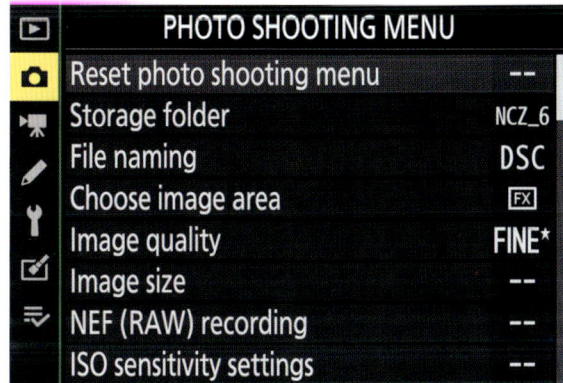

Figure 7.0: Photo Shooting Menu

We will examine each of the settings on the Photo Shooting Menu in great detail. Have your camera in hand, and maybe even the camera manuals if you are interested in what they say about certain settings (page numbers provided). Remember that it's *entirely optional* to use the camera manuals. This book is a comprehensive reference, but sometimes it is good to get an alternate view for deeper understanding. The Nikon Z7/Z6 User's Manual, and also the Reference Manual, although somewhat dense, are still good references.

If you take time to think about and configure each of these settings at least once, you'll learn a lot more about your new camera. There are a lot of settings to learn about, but don't feel overwhelmed. Some of these settings can be configured and then forgotten, and you'll use other settings more often. We'll look at each setting to see which ones are most important to your style of shooting.

Here is a list and overview of the 33 items found on the Z6 Photo Shooting Menu:

- **Reset photo shooting menu:** Restores the factory default settings in the Photo Shooting Menu.
- **Storage folder:** Selects the folder (e.g., 100NCZ_6) into which subsequent images will be stored on the camera's memory card(s).

- **File naming:** Lets you change three characters of the image's file name so that it is personalized.
- **Choose Image area:** Allows you to choose one of the FX (36 × 24), DX (24 × 16), 1:1x (24 × 24), and 16:9 (36 × 20) Image area modes.
- **Image quality:** You can select from 14 image quality types, such as JPEG fine, NEF (RAW), or TIFF. The camera adds a star symbol (★) next to certain JPEG quality types (e.g., JPEG fine ★) to signify that it will use high-image-quality priority, which will vary JPEG image size according to complexity (higher complexity = larger file size). If there is no star (e.g., JPEG fine), the camera will use file-size priority, which will compress complex images more than simple images, to provide a similar file size.
- **Image size:** Allows you to choose whether to shoot Large, Medium, or Small images in NEF (RAW), JPEG, or TIFF formats. The Nikon Z6 has three NEF (RAW) image sizes (RAW L, RAW M, and RAW S) along with three JPEG and TIFF sizes (L, M, and S).
- **NEF (RAW) recording:** Allows you to choose the image compression type and bit depth for NEF (RAW) files, including RAW L (Large), RAW M (Medium), and RAW S (Small). You can select Lossless compressed, Compressed, or Uncompressed for the RAW compression type, and 12-bit or 14-bit for the bit depth (page 185) of each image.
- **ISO sensitivity settings:** Allows you to manually set the camera's ISO sensitivity within a normal range from ISO 100 to ISO 51200, or you can extend the ISO downward and upward outside the normal ISO range, setting the ISO as low as ISO 50 (Lo 1.0) and as high as ISO 204800 (Hi 2.0). You can also choose to let the camera automatically decide the ISO sensitivity for you with the Auto ISO sensitivity control.
- **White balance:** You can choose from 10 preset White balance (WB) types (e.g., Direct sunlight, Shade, Flash), or you can directly choose a WB value from 2500K to 10,000K (Choose color temperature). You can also directly measure the ambient light's color balance (PRE) by using a white or gray card.
- **Set Picture Control:** You can choose from eight normal Picture Controls (e.g., Standard, Neutral, Vivid) that modify how JPEG pictures look. Additionally, the Nikon Z6 has 20 creative Picture Controls for JPEG special effects (e.g., Dream, Somber, Dramatic).
- **Manage Picture Control:** Lets you save, load, rename, or delete custom Picture Controls from your camera's internal memory or memory card. You can modify and save any of the camera's normal or creative Picture Controls to suit your needs, giving them a name of your choosing.
- **Color space:** Your camera can use either the commercial-printing standard Adobe RGB or the Internet-use and home-printing standard sRGB color space.
- **Active D-Lighting:** Allows you to select from five levels of automatic contrast correction (artificial dynamic range increase) for your images, along with disabling the contrast correction (Off). As Active D-Lighting (ADL) increases in power (Low to Extra High), the camera will pull more and more details out of the shadows. ADL also tends to protect the highlights. There can be additional noise in the darker areas when extra shadow detail is revealed.
- **Long exposure NR:** Uses the "dark-frame subtraction" method to significantly reduce noise (bright spots and fog) in long exposures. This is a powerful and useful function if

you make long exposures, because it is not as damaging to the image as blurring noise reduction.

• **High ISO NR:** Gives you three levels (Low, Normal, High) of a blurring and resharpening method to remove random grainy noise from images shot with high ISO sensitivity values. It tends to reduce the sharpness and clarity of the image, especially at higher levels.

• **Vignette control:** This function allows you to automatically remove various amounts of the corner darkness (vignetting) resulting from using certain lenses at maximum aperture. Provides for three levels (Low, Normal, High) of vignette control when using a lens of the S, G, E, or D types. Excludes PC lenses.

• **Diffraction compensation:** Allows the camera to reduce the lack of sharpness caused by diffraction of light rays through a small lens aperture (e.g., f/11, f/16, f/22).

• **Auto distortion control:** With an S, G, E, or D type Nikkor lens, the camera can automatically reduce barrel distortion when using a wide-angle lens, and pincushion distortion when using a telephoto lens.

• **Flicker reduction shooting:** Allows the camera to reduce the effects of flicker under lighting such as fluorescent and mercury vapor. While in use, the EVF and Monitor may display the word FLICKER.

• **Metering:** Gives options for the camera's light meter types. Choose from Matrix, Center-weighted, Spot, and Highlight-weighted metering.

• **Flash control:** Provides a means for your Z6 to control wireless flash units (e.g., SB-5000, SB-500), either by optical or radio control.

• **Flash mode:** Allows options to select from various flash modes, such as Fill flash, Red-eye reduction, or Slow sync.

• **Flash compensation:** Gives options to set Flash compensation in a range of from –3.0 EV to +1.0 EV, in 1/3 EV steps.

• **Focus mode:** Provides choices for a Focus (autofocus) mode, which are Single AF (AF-S), Continuous AF (AF-C), and Manual focus (MF).

• **AF-area mode:** Allows choices for the camera's six AF-area modes (e.g., Pinpoint AF, Single-point AF, Dynamic-area AF).

• **Vibration reduction:** Offers options to set the camera's vibration reduction (VR) methods: Normal, Sport, and Off.

• **Auto bracketing:** Allows you to choose one of five types of bracketing (e.g., AE & Flash, WB, ADL) when you are using Auto bracketing (page 269).

• **Multiple exposure:** Allows you to make from 2 to 10 exposures in a single frame and then combine the exposures in interesting ways.

• **HDR (high dynamic range):** You can create a two-exposure HDR image. The camera will automatically combine them. Use for JPEG or TIFF images only.

• **Interval timer shooting:** You can put your camera on a tripod and set it to make one to several exposures at customizable intervals.

• **Time-lapse movie:** Allows you to create Full HD or 4K UHD time-lapse movies in-camera. 8K movie production requires third-party software.

- **Focus shift shooting:** The camera varies its focus over a series of images (up to 300), with customizable intervals and focus depths. The images can later be combined—in your computer, not in the camera—into one image with very deep depth of field.
- **Silent photography:** Allows you to do silent photography, where the camera uses its electronic shutter to make exposures with no noise.

Before we get into the configuration of the camera, you need to know a little about saving your configuration to one of the cameras User settings (U1, U2, or U3). Afterward, we will consider each of these 33 Photo Shooting Menu functions in more detail.

Each saved User setting allows you to save a particular camera configuration. You can then recall one of your three custom configurations when you need to use the camera for a different style of photography, by selecting a User setting on the Mode dial.

User Settings U1, U2, and U3

User settings U1, U2, and U3 are memory locations to which you can assign specific camera configurations for the Photo Shooting Menu, Movie Shooting Menu, Custom Setting Menu, and various other camera settings. Later, you can recall each of the three carefully crafted camera configurations for specific styles of photography. Let's briefly discuss how the User settings work.

If you configure your camera's internal settings in a particular way and want to save that setup for future use, simply go to *Setup Menu > Save user settings > Save to U1 [or U2, U3] > Save settings*. This is optional, in case you don't want to use the User settings on the Mode dial (figure 7.1). However, it is a convenient way to configure your camera for specific shooting situations so you can change comprehensive setups quickly. Here is how I have my Z6's User settings configured:

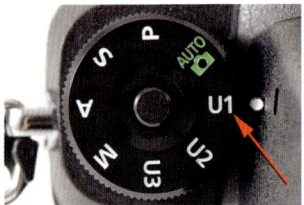

Figure 7.1: U1, U2, and U3 user settings

- **User Setting U1:** My highest-quality RAW setting for images that will be post-processed and commercially printed using the CMYK process (e.g., in a book or magazine). I shoot in NEF (RAW) Image quality with Lossless compressed and 14-bit depth in NEF (RAW) recording, Adobe RGB Color space, ISO 100, and Neutral Picture Control.
- **User Setting U2:** My highest-quality JPEG setting for images that will be used with little post-processing, printed on inkjet-type printers (giclée), or any circumstance where the highest-quality, immediate-use JPEG is required. I take the pictures using JPEG fine ★ Image quality (high-quality priority compression), Adobe RGB Color space, ISO 100, and Standard Picture Control.
- **User Setting U3:** My party and Internet-use setting. I use JPEG fine Image quality (size priority compression), sRGB Color space, ISO 400 with Auto ISO sensitivity control set to On and Maximum sensitivity set to 1600, and Standard Picture Control.

The three user settings on the Mode dial allow you to store more than just Photo Shoot-ing Menu, Movie Shooting Menu, and Custom Setting Menu items. They can also store a specific configuration for many other settings, such as flash modes, Exposure compensa-tion, Metering, Focus modes, AF-area modes, Bracketing, and more. Nikon has given you a powerful and flexible way to configure our cameras for specific shooting needs.

We'll discuss the detailed configuration of these three settings in the chapter titled **Setup Menu** under the subheading **Save User Settings** (page 474). For now, just keep in mind that you can save the settings you make to the 33 upcoming Photo Shooting Menu items in a cumulative way within one of the three User settings. After you configure many functions of your camera, you can save the changes, for instance, to the U1 User setting with *Setup Menu > Save user settings > Save to U1 > Save settings*. If you want to review how to save your Photo Shooting Menu configuration, please review the **Save User Settings** information on page 474.

There are several Photo Shooting Menu options that cannot be saved and stored in the User settings, as follows:

- Storage folder
- Choose image area
- Manage Picture Control
- Multiple exposure

- Interval timer shooting
- Time-lapse movie
- Focus shift shooting

The above-listed Photo Shooting Menu functions are independent of the user settings that can be saved. If you modify one of these five functions, it will function the same way no matter what user setting you have selected.

Now, let's examine how to configure each of the camera's Photo Shooting Menu settings.

Reset Photo Shooting Menu

Reset Photo Shooting Menu does what it says—it resets the Photo Shooting Menu's 33 func-tions back to their factory default configuration. Be careful with this selection because you might have put a lot of work into configuring the menu. Make sure you really want to reset the entire Photo Shooting Menu before proceeding. If so, here's how to use it.

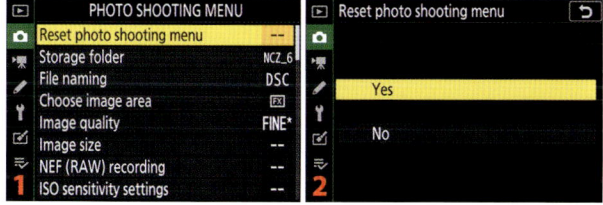

Figure 7.2: Resetting the Photo Shooting Menu

Following are the steps to reset the Photo Shooting Menu:

1. In the Photo Shooting Menu select Reset Photo Shooting Menu, and then scroll to the right (figure 7.2, screen, image 1).
2. Choose Yes or No (figure 7.2, screen, image 2) and press the OK button or tap your selection.

Settings Recommendation: This is an easy way to start fresh with the Photo Shooting Menu. I use this when I purchase a preowned camera and want to clear someone else's settings or if I simply want to start over.

Storage Folder

(User's Manual: Page 125, Reference Manual: Page 159)

The Z6 automatically creates a folder named 100NCZ_6 on its primary memory card. The first three digits in **100**NCZ_6 are the folder number, and the last five characters in 100**NCZ_6** are the folder name. You can change both of these.

If you want to store images in separate folders on the memory card, you might want to create a new number/folder, such as 101PORTR for portraits or 200LANDS for landscapes. Each folder you create can hold 999 images, and using *Storage folder,* you can select any folder as the default folder.

This is a good way to isolate certain types of images while on a photographic outing. Maybe you'll put nature pictures in a folder named 100NATUR and people shots in 101PEOPL. You can name the number and folder according to your needs.

Whenever the camera senses that the current folder contains 999 images or when an image reaches a file number of 9999, a new folder is created, with the value of the first three digits of the folder name increased by one. If you are using a folder named 100NCZ_6, the camera will automatically create a new folder called 101NCZ_6 when you exceed 999 images or reach image number 9999.

If you try to create a folder name that already exists, the camera doesn't give you a warning; it simply switches to the already existing folder. Let's look at how to rename an existing folder, create a new folder with a number and name of your choice, and choose an existing folder from a list of all folders on the memory card.

Rename

The *Rename* function allows you to change the folder name of an existing folder from the default of NCZ_6 to any five-character name you desire. For instance, I am fortunate that my last name is only five characters, so I renamed my folder to YOUNG. Once renamed, my folder number and name will look like this: 101YOUNG. Let's see how to rename the folder.

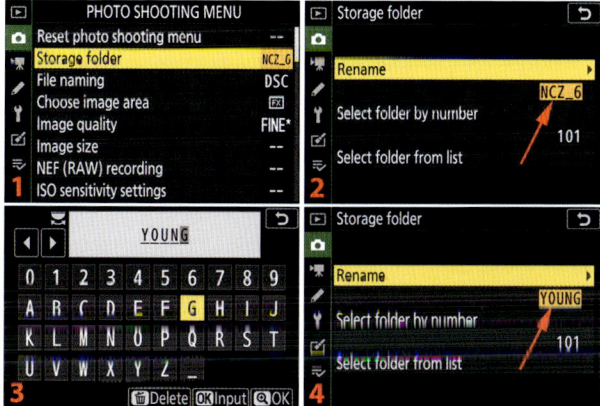

Figure 7.3A: Renaming the camera's default folder name

Use the following steps to rename the default folder:

1. Follow the screen flow shown in figure 7.3A, images 1 and 2 (*Storage folder* > *Rename*) until you arrive at the third screen in the series.
2. Use the touch screen shown in figure 7.3A, image 3, to create a new five-character folder name in the text field at the top of the screen. If you do not use all five characters, the camera will insert an underscore for any character you leave blank. To create the new name, use the left- and right-arrow touch buttons in the top-left corner of image 3 to select a character position from the five characters. Tap Delete at the bottom of image 3 to delete the current character. Tap the characters from the source list to insert them in the text field. There are uppercase characters only, along with numbers. Press or touch OK to save your work, or press the MENU button to cancel. Notice in figure 7.3A, image 4, that the name was changed to YOUNG as soon as I selected OK.

Select Folder by Number

The *Select folder by number* function allows you to select an existing folder by number or create a new one with a new number. Let's examine how to do it.

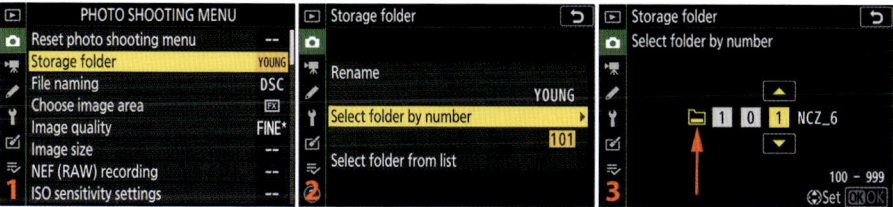

Figure 7.3B: Creating and numbering a new folder

Use these steps to create or select a folder with a number of your choice:

1. Follow the screen flow shown in figure 7.3B, images 1 and 2 (*Storage folder* > *Select folder by number*) until you arrive at the third screen in the series.
2. You will now see a screen that allows you to enter a folder number between 100 and 999 (figure 7.3B, image 3). Create your new number by scrolling up or down in any of the three available number positions. This number will have NCZ_6 appended to it when you are done—unless you have changed the default folder name—and a new folder by that name (or your new name) will appear on the camera's current primary memory card. Notice the little folder symbol at the red arrow in image 3. This little folder appears only when you have an existing folder with the number shown on the screen. If I were to change the number to 201 or 102, the little folder would disappear because my camera does not have a folder named 201NCZ_6 or 102NCZ_6. When I save the settings from image 3, the camera will not create a new folder named 101NCZ_6 because it clearly already exists (small folder showing at red arrow). Instead, the camera will simply switch to that folder. If there is no folder showing where the red arrow is pointing, the camera will create a new folder instead of switching to an existing one.
3. Press or touch OK to create the new folder or switch to an existing folder.

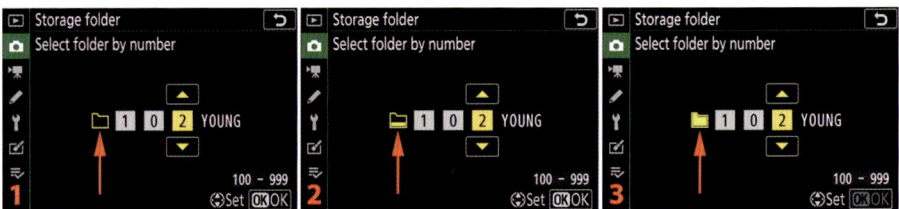

Figure 7.3C: Folder states

When you see a tiny folder symbol to the left of a folder number, as shown in figure 7.3B, images 1–3 (red arrows), you should take note of how full the folder is. If there is not a folder showing there, the folder number and name does not yet exist, and selecting OK will create it. If there is an empty folder, as seen in image 1, the folder exists but has no images in it and selecting OK will create it. If there is a folder that shows partially full, as seen in image 2, there are between 1 and 998 images in the folder and selecting OK will select it. If the folder is full, as seen in image 3, the folder contains 999 images and will not be available for selection; the OK touch control will be grayed out and the OK button will not work.

What if you want to simply start using an existing folder, choosing it from a list of folders instead of making a new one? Let's find out.

Select Folder from List

The *Select folder from list* function allows you to choose an existing folder from a list of folders on your camera's memory card(s).

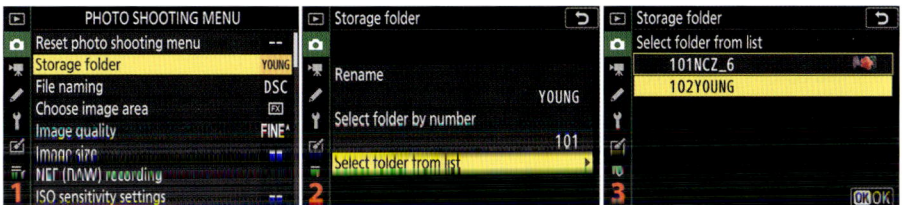

Figure 7.3D: Selecting an existing folder from the list of available folders

Use the following steps to choose an existing folder from a list of folders:

1. Follow the screen flow shown in figure 7.3D, images 1 and 2 (*Storage folder > Select folder from list*) until you arrive at the third screen in the series.
2. Choose a folder from the list of current folders (figure 7.3D, image 3). If your Z6 has only one folder, that is all you will see in image 3 (most likely 100NCZ_6). Press or touch OK and all images will now be saved to the chosen folder until you exceed 999 images in the folder or manually change to another. Please note that the folders 100NCZ_6 and 101NCZ_6 clearly have images in them because you can see an image thumbnail to the right of the folder name. However, folder 102YOUNG is empty and no thumbnail appears.

Note of caution: If you are using a folder numbered 999 (e.g., 999NCZ_6) and the camera records the 999th image in that folder, or if it records an image with the number 9999, the Shutter-release button will be disabled until you change to a different folder. Normally, when those conditions occur, the camera increases the folder number by one and creates a new folder with the new number, and the next image simply goes into the new folder. However, if you are using folder number 999 (999NCZ_6), the camera cannot create a new folder because it cannot go any larger than 999 on a folder number. Therefore, it locks the Shutter-release button until you remove the memory card containing folder 999NCZ_6 or create a new folder manually. In my opinion, it is not wise to create a folder numbered 999, especially if you shoot a lot of images and may exceed 999 pictures in the folder.

Additionally, if the current folder is numbered 999 (e.g., 999NCZ_6) and it contains 992 images or a file numbered 9992 or higher, video recording may be disabled.

Settings Recommendation: As memory cards increasingly hold more data, I can see a time when this functionality will become very important. Last year, I shot around 250 GB of image files. With the larger memory cards now moving into the terabyte range, I can foresee a time when the card(s) in my camera will become a yearlong backup source. At the present time, I do not use the Storage folder functionality all that much, but I guarantee you I will in the near future. This is a good function to learn how to use!

File Naming

File naming allows you to control the first three letters of the file name for each of your images. The default is DSC, but you can change it to any three alphanumeric characters provided by the camera. The Z6 defaults to using the following file naming convention for your images:

- sRGB color space: **DSC_1234.JPG**
- Adobe RGB color space: **_DSC1234.JPG**

According to the color space you are using, the camera adds an underscore character to the end of the three DSC characters in sRGB or to the beginning in Adobe RGB.

I use this feature on my camera in a special way. Because the camera can count images in a sequence (see Custom setting d7 on page 405) from 0001 to 9999, I use File naming to help me personalize my images. The camera cannot count images higher than 9999. Instead, it rolls back over to 0001 for the 10,000th image.

When I first got my Z6, I changed the three default characters from DSC to 1DY. The 1 tells me how many times my camera has passed 9999 images, and DY are my initials, thereby helping me protect the copyright of my images in case they are ever stolen and misused.

Because the camera's image File number sequence counter rolls back over to 0001 when you exceed 9999 images, you need a way to keep from accidentally overwriting images from the first set of 9999 images you took. I use this method:

- First 9999 images: 1DY_0001 through 1DY_9999
- Second 9999 images: 2DY_0001 through 2DY_9999
- Third 9999 images: 3DY_0001 through 3DY_9999
- Fourth 9999 images: 4DY_0001 through 4DY_9999
- Fifth 9999 images: 5DY_0001 through 5DY_9999

See how simple that is? The listed numbers show a range of just under 50,000 images. Since the Z6's shutter is tested to the pro level of 200,000 images, you will surely need to use a counting system like this one.

My system works up to only 89,991 images (9999 × 9). If you wanted to start your camera at 0 instead (0DY9999), you could count up to 99,990 images.

If Nikon would ever give us just one extra digit in our image counter, we could count in sequences of just under 100,000 images instead of 10,000 images. I suppose that many of us will have traded on up to the next Nikon DSLR before we reach enough images that this really becomes a constraint.

This is merely the way I'm using this useful feature in my Z6. If my method doesn't work for you, you could use the three characters to classify your image names in all sorts of creative ways.

Let's examine how to rename the first three characters of a file name.

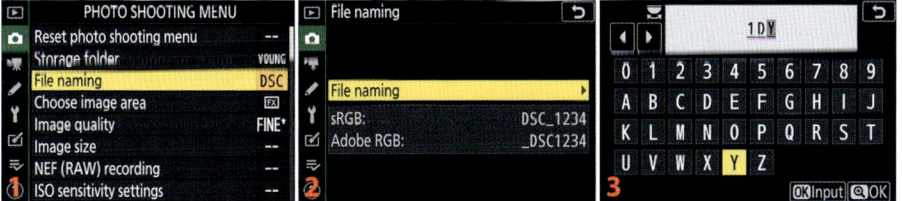

Figure 7.4: Creating a new three-letter file name

Here are the steps to set up your custom file naming characters:

1. Follow the screen flow shown in figure 7.4, images 1 and 2 (*File naming > File naming*) until you arrive at the third screen in the series.
2. Use the touch screen shown in figure 7.4, image 3, to create a new three-character file name in the text field at the top of the screen. You must use all three characters. You cannot delete characters; you can only replace them. To create the new name, tap on the arrows in the top-left corner of image 3 to select a character position from the three characters. Tap the characters from the source list to insert them in the text field. There are uppercase characters only, along with numbers. Press or touch OK to save your work, or press the MENU button to cancel.

Settings Recommendation: We discussed how I use these three custom characters in the beginning of this section. You may want to use all three of your initials or some other numbers or letters. Some will even leave these three letters at their default of DSC. I recommend at least using your initials so that you can easily identify the images as yours. If you use my method, just be sure to watch for the images to roll over to 9999 so that you can rename the first character for the next sequence of 9999 images. With the longevity of a Nikon and your prolific shooting habits, I am sure the numbers will be rolling over often!

File Number Sequence

Custom Setting Menu > d Shooting/display > d7 File number sequence controls the File number sequence. That function works along with File naming to let you control how your image files are named. If File number sequence is set to Off, the Z6 will reset the four-digit number—after the first three custom characters in File naming—to 0001 each time you format your camera's memory card. As soon as I got my camera, I made sure File number sequence was set to On so it would remember the sequence all the way up to 9999 images. The factory default is On for File number sequence, but I would check it just in case. I want to know exactly how many pictures I've taken over time. We'll talk more about File number sequence in the chapter titled **Custom Setting Menu** (page 405).

Choose Image Area

The Z6 camera offers four *Image area* formats: FX, DX, 1:1, and 16:9. Each format or ratio is a crop of the 36×24 mm FX sensor. When you select one of the four Image area formats, the Viewfinder (EVF) and Monitor adjust to that format instantly, making it easy to see what the camera will capture with the selected Image area.

Let's examine each of the four Image area formats. Each is displayed in figure 7.5A so that you can compare how the various ratios crop the sensor's full view. The five pictures in figure 7.5A are of my 2002 Nikon D100 6-megapixel DSLR—the first DSLR I felt comfortable enough to use at a wedding. It's hard to imagine it has been 17 years since those film-versus-digital days. Anyway, I digress…

To display the Image area formats properly, I did not vary the camera position at any point when taking these images so that you can see how the change in Image area crop affects the size of the subject.

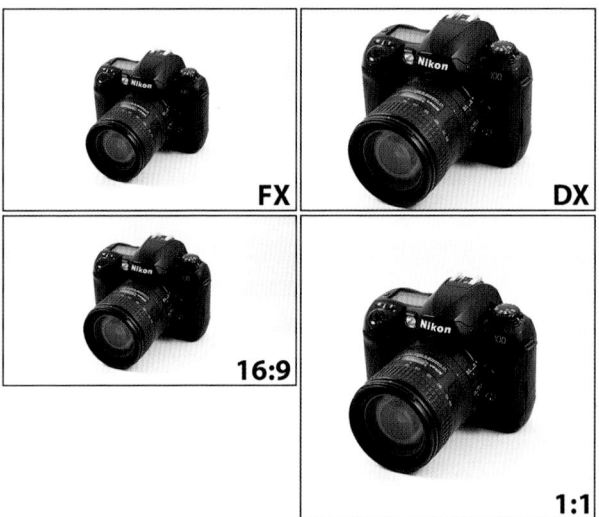

Figure 7.5A: The five Image area formats

Following is a detailed list of specifications for the four available image areas, including sensor format (mm), Image size, pixel count, and megapixel (MP) rating.

Image Area	Large	Medium	Small
FX Image area (36 × 24 mm)	6048 × 4024 – 24.3 MP	4528 × 3016 – 13.7 MP	3024 × 2016 – 6.1 MP
DX Image area (24 × 16 mm)	3936 × 2624 – 10.3 MP	2944 × 1968 – 5.8 MP	1968 × 1312 – 2.6 MP
1:1 Image area (24 × 24 mm)	4016 × 4016 – 16.1 MP	3008 × 3008 – 9.0 MP	2000 × 2000 – 4.0 MP
16:9 Image area (36 × 20 mm)	6048 × 3400 – 20.6 MP	4528 × 2544 – 11.5 MP	3024 × 1696 – 5.1 MP

Now let's see how to select one of the Image area formats for those times you need to vary the image area in-camera.

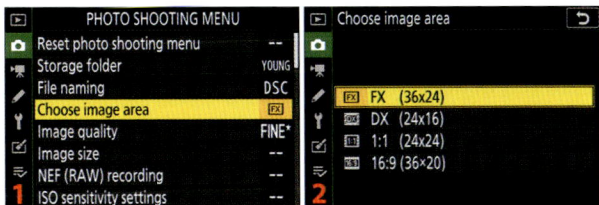

Figure 7.5B: Choosing an Image area format

Use the following steps to select one of the Image area formats:

1. Select Choose image area from the Photo Shooting Menu and scroll to the right (figure 7.5B, images 1).
2. Select one of the four Image area crops (e.g., FX (36×24)) and then press the OK button (figure 7.5B, image 2) or simply tap on the item you want to choose.

Settings Recommendation: If you are primarily a JPEG shooter who does not post-process RAW images, you may find these on-the-fly formats (crops) useful. Most RAW shooters will prefer to crop the image manually in the computer after carefully developing it to its best potential. Based on the pixel ratio (6048 × 4024 = 24,337,152), the Nikon Z6 provides 24.5 MP images with great depth and cropping potential. However, if you just want some quick DX or square (1:1) JPEG images, why not experiment with these settings?

Image Quality

Image quality is simply the type of image your camera creates. You can shoot with several distinct image formats: NEF (RAW), JPEG, JPEG★, and TIFF.

We'll examine each format in detail and discuss the pros and cons of each. When we are done, you will have a better understanding of the formats and will be able to choose an appropriate one for each of your styles of shooting. Following are the screens and steps to select an Image quality setting.

Setting Image Quality with the Menu System

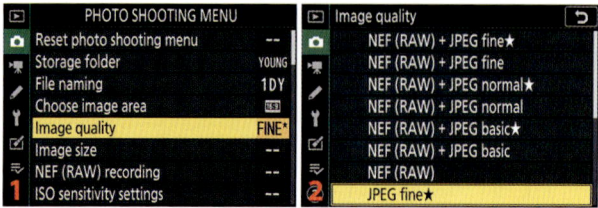

Figure 7.6A: Choosing an Image quality setting

Use these steps to select an image quality via the Photo Shooting Menu:

1. Select Image quality from the Photo Shooting Menu and scroll to the right (figure 7.6A, image 1).
2. Choose one of the 14 Image quality types listed (figure 7.6A, image 2) and press the OK button or simply tap on the item you want to choose. You may have to scroll down on the Image quality screen to find your choice.

Setting Image Quality with the *i* Menu

You can also display the *i* Menu on the Monitor or in the EVF and choose the Image quality setting from there. This method can be much faster than using the menus. If you learn the location of the *i* button by feel, you won't even have to take your eye away from the Viewfinder to change settings. Here's how.

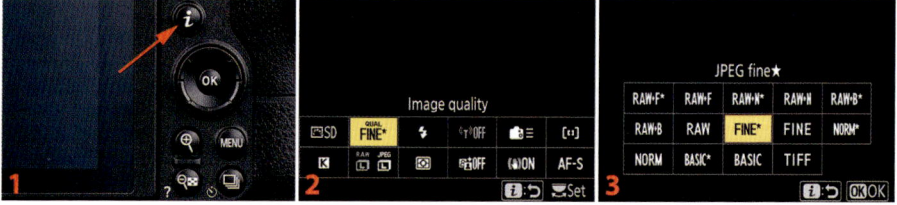

Figure 7.6B: Setting the Image quality with the *i* Menu

Use these steps to select an image quality from the *i* Menu:

1. Press the *i* button to open the *i* Menu (figure 7.6B, image 1).
2. Select the Image quality function shown in figure 7.6B, image 2, by scrolling to it with the Multi selector pad and pressing the OK button, or by tapping on it.
3. The main Image quality screen will show, with its 14 selections in little rectangles (figure 7.6B, image 3). Choose an Image quality by scrolling to it with the Multi selector pad, or just tap on your choice (e.g., Fine ★), and then press or touch OK.

The camera supports the following 14 Image quality types (figure 7.6A, image 2):

- NEF (RAW) + JPEG fine ★
- NEF (RAW) + JPEG fine
- NEF (RAW) + JPEG normal ★
- NEF (RAW) + JPEG normal
- NEF (RAW) + JPEG basic ★
- NEF (RAW) + JPEG basic
- NEF (RAW)

- JPEG fine ★
- JPEG fine
- JPEG normal ★
- JPEG normal
- JPEG basic ★
- JPEG basic
- TIFF (RGB)

Which Image Quality Format Should I Use?

New photographers may feel unsure about which format is best to use. In fact, it is a good idea to use all three formats at different times. The 14 choices you have are composed of just three actual Image quality types: NEF, JPEG, and TIFF. Here, we will briefly discuss the basics of the formats:

- **NEF (RAW):** The 12- or 14-bit NEF (RAW) format is designed for those photographers who have the time and inclination to post-process each image after-the-fact. The camera merely captures light information when shooting in RAW but does not process the data into a usable image. It is up to you to develop a workflow that allows finalizing the image within your computer. The reward for this extra work is the highest possible image quality that can be achieved with the camera. **Note:** The Z6 also has an NEF (RAW) processing function on the **Retouch Menu** (page 567) that allows you to convert to JPEG from a RAW file on the memory card.
- **JPEG:** The 8-bit JPEG format is for when you must have a finished image right now! The image comes out of the camera ready to use. JPEG is a lossy format, however, as it discards a considerable amount of image data when the camera converts the 12- or 14-bit RAW file to 8 bits. The image data that is left is of high quality and is ready to use. However, a JPEG cannot be modified and resaved more than a time or two without JPEG compression losses damaging the image. Use JPEG when you have to use the image right away or when you do not have the time or inclination to work with RAW images. JPEG files are significantly smaller than NEF (RAW), according to the complexity of the scene and compression ratio used. The camera uses the following compression ratios for a JPEG file: JPEG fine = 1:4, JPEG normal = 1:8, and JPEG basic = 1:16. The star symbol (★) that follows some of the JPEG choices (e.g., JPEG fine★) represents what Nikon called "Optimal quality" in previous cameras. If a JPEG mode does not have the star, it means the camera is using what Nikon calls "Size priority." Size priority uses a higher compression ratio for images that are more complex leading to lower image quality. On the other hand, the JPEG images with a ★ use a variable compression ratio so that as image complexity rises so does picture quality. File sizes on a ★-level image will be larger for more complex images.
- **TIFF (RGB):** The 8-bit TIFF file type, as created by the camera, is basically like a JPEG with no compression routines applied. The image file can be used immediately without

conversion. To create a TIFF file, 12- or 14-bit sensor data is converted by the camera into an 8-bit file, discarding considerable data, so TIFF is initially a lossy format—losing from 4 to 6 bits of image data. However, once the file is created, you can modify and resave it without compressing the data or losing any more image detail. If you are in a situation that requires an immediate-use file and a JPEG won't do because image modification is required, and you have no interest in or experience with NEF (RAW) files, the TIFF format is a good candidate. The biggest drawback to a TIFF file is its very large file size. Unless you are using a high-capacity memory card, you shouldn't plan on shooting a large number of TIFF files.

Combined NEF and JPEG Shooting (Two Images at Once)

Some shooters use the six storage modes at the top of the list in figure 7.6A, image 2, whereby the Z6 takes two images at the same time—NEF (RAW) + JPEG fine, normal, or basic (and JPEG★ versions). This gives you the best of both worlds in that the camera captures a NEF (RAW) file and at the same time creates a JPEG file each time you press the Shutter-release button. Here are the first six modes found at the top of the *Photo Shooting Menu > Image quality* setting list:

- NEF (RAW) + JPEG fine★
- NEF (RAW) + JPEG fine
- NEF (RAW) + JPEG normal★
- NEF (RAW) + JPEG normal
- NEF (RAW) + JPEG basic★
- NEF (RAW) + JPEG basic

With these combined modes, you can use the NEF (RAW) file to store all the image data and later process it into a masterpiece, and you can use the JPEG file immediately with no adjustment.

There is no need to go into any amount of detail about these modes since the NEF (RAW) + JPEG modes have the same features as each individual mode. In other words, the RAW file in NEF (RAW) + JPEG mode is just like a normal RAW file if you were using the standalone NEF (RAW) mode. The JPEG in the NEF (RAW) + JPEG mode is just like a standalone JPEG fine, normal, or basic image without the NEF (RAW) file.

Which format do I prefer? Why, NEF (RAW), of course! However, it does require a bit of a commitment to shoot in this format. The camera is simply an image-capturing device, and you are the image manipulator. You decide the final format, compression ratios, sizes, color balances, and so on, instead of letting Nikon's software engineers decide. You create the final image when *you* post-process it with your computer and save it in a final format, such as JPEG. Your RAW file stays untouched and ready for reuse.

By shooting in NEF (RAW) mode, you have the absolute best image your camera can produce. It is not modified by the camera's software and is ready for your personal touch.

If you get nothing else from this section of the chapter, remember this: When your camera is processing the images in *any* way, it is modifying or discarding image data. There is only a finite amount of data for each image that can be stored on your camera, and later on the computer. With JPEG or TIFF mode, your camera optimizes the image according to the assumptions recorded in its memory. Image data is permanently discarded, in varying amounts.

If you want to keep *all* of the image data that was recorded with your images, you must store your originals in RAW format. Otherwise, you'll never again be able to access that original data to change how the image looks. A RAW file is the closest thing to a film negative or a transparency that your digital camera can make (if you are old enough to remember when we all shot film). That's important if you want to modify the image later. If you are concerned with maximum quality, you should shoot and store your images in RAW format.

Later, when you have the urge to make another masterpiece out of the original RAW image file, you'll have all of the original picture data intact for the highest-quality image.

I shoot in NEF (RAW) format for my most important work and JPEG fine for the rest. Some people find that JPEG fine is sufficient for everything they shoot. These individuals generally do not like working with files in computer or do not have time to do so. NEF (RAW) files are not yet usable images and must be converted to another format. You'll use both RAW and JPEG, I'm sure. The format you use most often will be controlled by your time constraints and digital workflow. Most of us use TIFF only when we convert a RAW file in-computer into that format. I rarely, if ever, shoot images in TIFF. There are just not enough benefits in TIFF files to deal with the larger files and slower transfer speeds, in my opinion. Shoot RAW for the best and JPEG for the rest!

RAW Conversion and Image Editing Software

There are many different software apps you can use to post-process RAW files into JPEGS. Some are free and others you have to pay for. Here is a list of software to consider.

Free Software:

Nikon Capture NX-i: Basic RAW conversion, JPEG image editing, and image management software

Nikon Capture NX-D: Advanced RAW conversion software with powerful Color Point technology, JPEG image editing, and basic image management

Here is a download link to obtain both of Nikon's free software packages (Nikon Capture NX-i and NX-D):

https://downloadcenter.nikonimglib.com/en/products/261/VCNXSP.html

For-Pay Software:

Adobe Lightroom: RAW conversion, JPEG image editing, and comprehensive image management software designed specifically for photographers

Adobe Photoshop: RAW conversion, JPEG image editing, and graphical design software for photographers and graphic designers

Many other free and for-pay apps are available for Mac, Windows PC, and Linux (and even smart devices). Do a Google search for "RAW conversion software" and "Image-editing software."

Image Size

Image size lets you shoot with your camera set to various megapixel (M) ratings. The default Image size setting for the Z6 is Large (L), or 24.3 M (megapixels) for JPEG, NEF (RAW), and TIFF files. You can change this megapixel rating by selecting one of four Image area sizes (FX, DX, 1:1, or 16:9), as discussed earlier in the chapter (page 174).

This setting is relatively simple because it just affects the megapixel size of the image. Let's see how to set the Image size for all five Image area formats.

Image Size for JPEG/TIFF Files

Following are the screens and steps to select the Image size for JPEG and TIFF images (figure 7.7A). Both have the same megapixel size but, of course, the image file size (megabytes) will vary. As discussed earlier in the chapter, JPEG files are compressed while TIFF files are uncompressed. Both have 8 bits of color depth. The actual megapixel (M) size of each Image size selection is listed in figure 7.7A, image 3.

The *Image size* pixel ratio (e.g., 6048 × 4024) and megapixel size (e.g., 24.3 M) will vary for each of the *Image area* settings (i.e., FX, DX, 1:1, 16:9), as discussed a few pages back (page 174). The values displayed in this subsection are based on the FX Image area setting (figure 7.7A, image 3). If you change to a different Image area format, these Image size values will vary accordingly.

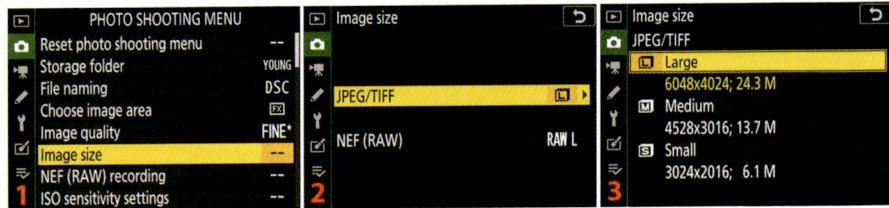

Figure 7.7A: Choosing an Image size setting for JPEG and TIFF images

Use these steps to choose a JPEG/TIFF Image size for FX shooting:

1. Follow the screen flow shown in figure 7.7A, images 1 and 2 (*Image size > JPEG/TIFF*), until you arrive at the third screen in the series.
2. Choose one of the three Image size settings listed for JPEG and TIFF files (Large, Medium, or Small). Figure 7.7A, image 3, represents the FX setting from the previously considered Choose image area function (page 174). Press the OK button or tap your selection to choose the size.

Image Size for NEF (RAW) Files

The Z6 has three NEF (RAW) Image sizes for more flexibility than previous Nikon HD SLR cameras. You can select from RAW L (Large), RAW M (Medium), and RAW S (Small). Figure 7.7B, image 3, shows the various megapixel (M) sizes for each Image size setting.

As mentioned previously, the *Image size* values will vary according to which *Image area* (FX, DX, 1:1, 16:9) you selected previously (page 174). We are using the FX Image area values in this subsection.

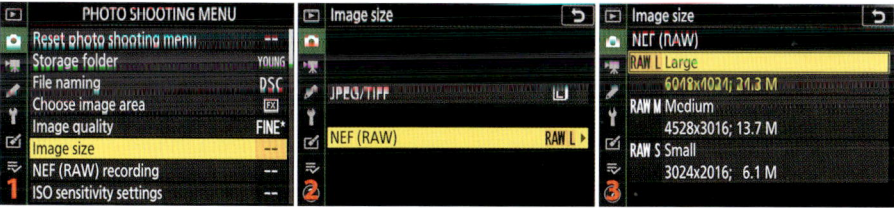

Figure 7.7B: Choosing an Image size setting for NEF (RAW) images

Use these steps to choose a NEF (RAW) Image size for FX shooting:

1. Follow the screen flow shown in figure 7.7B, images 1 and 2 (*Image size > NEF (RAW)*), until you arrive at the third screen in the series.
2. Choose one of the three Image size settings listed for NEF (RAW) files. Figure 7.7B, image 3, represents the FX setting from the previously considered Choose image area function (page 174). Press the OK button or tap your selection to choose the size.

Setting the Image Size Using the *i* Menu

You can also display the *i* Menu on the Monitor or in the EVF and choose the Image size setting from there. This method can be faster than using the menus. As mentioned in previous sections, if you learn the location of the *i* button by feel, you won't even have to take your eye away from the Viewfinder to change settings. Here's how it works.

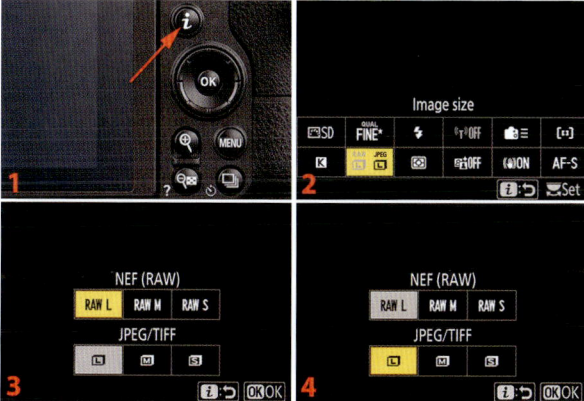

Figure 7.7C: Setting the Image quality with the *i* Menu

Use these steps to select an image size from the *i* Menu:

1. Press the *i* button to open the *i* Menu (figure 7.7C, image 1).
2. Select the Image size function shown in figure 7.7C, image 2, by scrolling to it with the Multi selector pad and pressing the OK button, or by tapping the icon.
3. The main Image size screen will show, with its two subsections, one for NEF (RAW) (figure 7.7C, image 3) and one for JPEG/TIFF (figure 7.7C, image 4). Choose an Image size by scrolling with the Multi selector pad or by tapping your choice (e.g., RAW L for RAW files, or L for JPEG/TIFF), and then press or touch OK.

Settings Recommendation: You'll get the best images at the Large (L) setting, of course. Using the smaller sizes won't affect the quality of a small print, but it will limit your ability to enlarge your images. I recommend leaving your camera set to Large (L or RAW L) unless you have a specific reason to shoot smaller images (e.g., social media usage) or you have low-capacity memory cards, which is anything under 32 GB with the Z6.

NEF (RAW) Recording

NEF (RAW) recording is composed of two menu choices—NEF (RAW) compression, which affects image file size, and NEF (RAW) bit depth, which affects color quality. Let's examine each choice.

NEF (RAW) Compression

In previous sections, we discussed how JPEG files have levels of compression that vary the size of a finished image file. NEF (RAW) also has compression choices, though not as many. The nice thing about the RAW compression methods is that they don't throw away massive amounts of image data like JPEG compression does. NEF (RAW) is not considered a lossy format because the file stays complete, with virtually all the image data your camera captured.

One of the compression methods, called Compressed, is very slightly lossy. The other, Lossless compressed, keeps all the image data intact. Let's discuss how each of the available compression methods works. There are three NEF (RAW) formats available: NEF (RAW) Lossless compressed, NEF (RAW) Compressed, and NEF (RAW) Uncompressed. Here are details on each of the choices:

- **NEF (RAW) Lossless compressed:** This is the best choice for most photographers. According to Nikon, this compression will not affect image quality because it is a "reversible" compression algorithm. Because Lossless compressed shrinks the stored file size by 20 to 40 percent—with no image data loss—it's my favorite compression method to use. It works somewhat like a ZIP file on your computer—it compresses the file but allows you to use it later with all the data still available.

- **NEF (RAW) Compressed:** Before the newest generation of cameras, this mode was known as "visually lossless." The image is compressed and the size is reduced by 35 to 55 percent, depending on the amount of detail in the image. A small amount of data is lost in this compression method. Most people won't be able to see the loss because it doesn't affect the image visually. While I've never seen any loss in my images using this method, I've read that some notice slightly less highlight detail. Nikon says that this is a nonreversible compression, so once you've taken an image using this mode, any small amount of data loss is permanent. If this concerns you, then use the Lossless compressed method discussed above. It won't compress the image quite as much but is guaranteed by Nikon to be a reversible compression that in no way affects the image.

- **NEF (RAW) Uncompressed:** No compression is applied to the image. The main drawback to this mode is that your image files will be larger, so it will take larger storage media to store your image files. With Lossless compressed available, I feel that this method is semi-obsolete.

Selecting a NEF (RAW) Compression Level

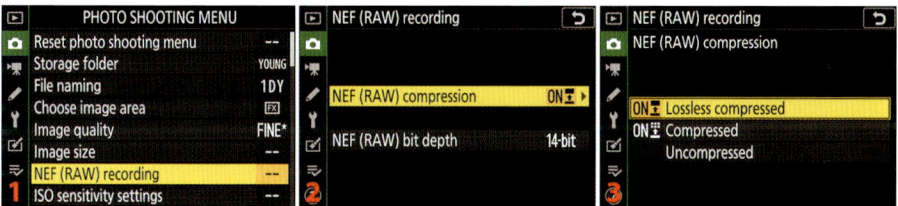

Figure 7.8A: RAW (NEF) compression

Here are the steps to select one of the NEF (RAW) compression types:

1. Follow the screen flow shown in figure 7.8A, images 1 and 2 (*NEF (RAW) recording > NEF (RAW) compression*), until you arrive at the third screen in the series.
2. Select one of the three compression methods (figure 7.8A, image 3) and then press the OK button or tap your selection to save it.

Settings Recommendation: I shoot in Lossless compressed RAW most of the time because I'm concerned with maximum quality along with good storage capacity. The Lossless compressed method makes the most sense to me. It gives me a file size significantly smaller than the Uncompressed setting's results. With Lossless compressed is available I do not use Compressed. Even though I might not be able to see any image quality loss, it bothers me that it is there, if only slightly. A few extra percentage points of compression is not worth the potential small data loss to me. If I were running out of card space but wanted to keep shooting RAW, I might consider changing to Compressed temporarily. Otherwise, it's Lossless compressed for me!

Card Capacity Reporting

Why does your memory card's remaining image capacity seem to stay the same in NEF Lossless compressed and Compressed modes as in Uncompressed mode? Shouldn't it show lots more capacity in the compressed modes since they make the image smaller by 20 to 55 percent? The reason your camera does not show any increased image capacity on the Control panel in the compressed modes is because the Z6 has no idea how well it will be able to compress a particular image.

An image with a large amount of blank space, such as an expanse of sky, will compress a lot more efficiently than an image of a forest with lots of detail. The camera shows a certain amount of image storage capacity in NEF (RAW) modes—about 1100 Lossless compressed, 14-bit, RAW L images with a 64-gigabyte card (your results may vary). However, you'll find that in the compressed modes, the Z6 often does not decrease the image capacity by one for each picture taken, as it does in Uncompressed mode.

This means that the camera will decrease the number of available images only every couple of shots, according to how well it was able to compress each image. When the card is full, it might contain as much as twice as many images as it initially reported it could hold. Basically, your Z6 deliberately underreports storage capacity when you are shooting in either of the NEF (RAW) compressed modes.

NEF (RAW) Bit Depth

NEF (RAW) bit depth is a special feature for those of us concerned with capturing the best color in our images. The Z6 has three color channels: one each for red, green, and blue. It combines those color channels to form all the colors you see in your images. You may have seen the acronym RGB in your camera study. RGB stands for red, green, blue—the three color channels. Let's talk about how bit depth, or the number of colors per channel, can make your pictures even better.

With the Z6, you can select the bit depth stored in an image. More bit depth equals potentially better color gradations. The default for the Z6 is 14-bit (16,384 colors for each RGB channel), or you can switch it to 12-bit (4,096 colors per RGB channel). The more color bit depth in your images, the better they can look—if there is a lot of color in your subject in the first place.

Why would anyone set their camera to a lower bit depth and reduce its color capacity and smoothness? Older Nikons used to suffer from a slower frame rate when shooting bursts of images in continuous high-speed shooting mode. The Z6 does not have slower frame rates from 14-bit shooting.

However, a 14-bit image file is bigger and will make the internal buffer space in the camera hold less. Also, the additional file size from the greater color capacity in a 14-bit image can lead to a little slower image writing to the memory cards and also slower transfer to the computer later.

Therefore, people who are concerned about maximum camera speed will sometimes shoot in 12 bit mode. A photographer shooting a football game will not have as great a concern for maximum color depth but is more concerned with shooting speed to capture the shot. On the other hand, a landscape artist wants as much color depth as the pictures can contain. Beautiful color gradations and maximum color fidelity is the priority.

The good thing for Z6 users is that shooting speed is barely affected by using the best bit depth (14-bit).

Selecting a Bit-Depth

As mentioned earlier, the Z6 has the following two bit depths available for RAW L images:

- **12-bit:** 4,096 colors per channel
- **14-bit:** 16,384 colors per channel

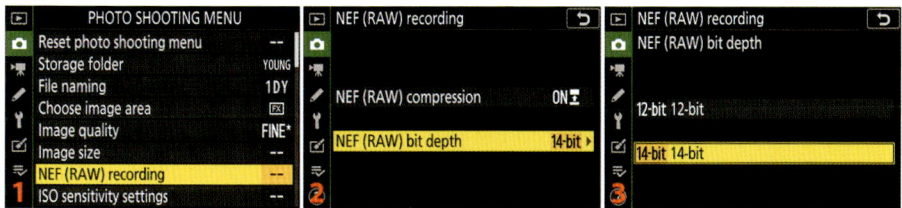

Figure 7.8B: Choosing an NEF (RAW) bit depth

Here are the steps to choose a bit depth:

1. Follow the screen flow shown in figure 7.8B, images 1 and 2 (*NEF (RAW) recording > NEF (RAW) bit depth*) until you arrive at the third screen in the series.
2. Select 12-bit or 14-bit from the menu (figure 7.8B, image 3) and press the OK button or tap your choice to save the selection.

Settings Recommendation: Which bit depth setting is best? Well, I always use 14-bit because I want all the color my camera can capture for the best pictures later. If you read my tutorial on bit depth in the next section, you'll understand why I feel this way. However, my style of shooting is nature oriented, so I am concerned with capturing every last drop of color I can.

There is one small disadvantage to using the 14-bit mode. If you choose 14-bit, be aware that your file sizes could be 10 to 20 percent larger than they would be in 12-bit. There is a lot more color information being stored, after all; therefore, 14-bit is best overall for image color quality, even if the file size is a little larger. Memory card sizes and computer hard drives are less expensive these days.

Channel and Bit Depth Discussion

Many experienced Z6 users may already understand this bit-depth information. However, I decided to include this short tutorial in the book because it is important information for a digital photographer. This information is a good review for most of us.

- **12-bit image:** An image from your camera is an RGB image. As mentioned previously, RGB stands for red, green, blue. Each of the colors has its own "channel." If you are shooting in 12-bit mode, your camera will record up to 4,096 colors for each channel—which means there will be up to 4,096 different reds, 4,096 different greens, and 4,096 different blues. Lots of color! In fact, almost 69,000,000,000 (69 billion) colors (4,096 × 4,096 × 4,096).
- **14-bit image:** However, if you set your camera to 14-bit mode, instead of just 4,096 different colors per channel (as in 12-bit mode), the camera can now store 16,384 different colors in each channel. Wow! That's quite a lot more color, almost 4,400,000,000,000 (4.4 trillion) shades (16,384 × 16,384 × 16,384). Is that important? Well, it can be, because the more color information you have available, the better the image. I always use the 14-bit mode because it allows for smoother color changes when a large range of color is actually in the image. I like that!
- **8-bit image:** Of course, once you shoot and save your image as an 8-bit JPEG or 8-bit TIFF, most of those colors are compressed or thrown away. Shooting a TIFF or JPEG image in-camera [as opposed to a RAW L (Large) image] means that the Z6 converts from a 12- or 14-bit RGB file down to an 8-bit file. An 8-bit file can hold only 256 different colors per RGB channel, or a little over 16,700,000 (16.7 million) colors (256 × 256 × 256). That sounds like quite a lot of color, and it is. However, when you compare the 16.7 million colors in a camera-created 8-bit JPEG or TIFF image to the potential 4.4 trillion colors in a 14-bit NEF (RAW) file, the 8-bit color potential is relatively small in comparison.

Settings Recommendation: I always shoot in the 24.3 MP, RAW L (Large), 14-bit format so that I can later make full use of all those potential extra colors to create different looks for a single image, if I'd like. The RAW file remains untouched and ready for reuse.

In my opinion, a 14-bit Lossless compressed NEF (RAW L) is the best way to store your Z6 images long-term, with all potential color information included in the file. Only when I am shooting extremely time-sensitive pictures, or just-for-fun party pictures, will I consider using JPEG.

ISO Sensitivity Settings

ISO sensitivity settings give you control over the light sensitivity of the imaging sensor, including whether you manually control the ISO or the camera sets it automatically.

An ISO sensitivity number, such as 200 or 3200, is an agreed-upon sensitivity level for the image-capturing sensor. Virtually everywhere one goes in the world, all camera ISO numbers will mean the same thing. With that fact established, camera bodies and lenses can be designed to take advantage of the ISO sensitivity ranges they will have to deal with.

In figure 7.9A we see the external camera controls used to change the ISO sensitivity on the Z6. This is the easiest method to change the camera's ISO sensitivity setting, although it doesn't involve the Photo Shooting Menu, which we are now examining.

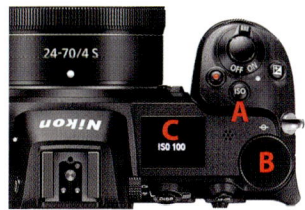

Here are the steps you'll use to manually adjust the camera's ISO:

Figure 7.9A: External controls to set ISO manually

1. Using the controls seen in figure 7.9A, hold down the ISO button (red letter A).
2. Rotate the rear Main command dial (red letter B) counterclockwise to increase the ISO sensitivity (red letter C) or clockwise to decrease sensitivity.
3. Release the ISO button to set the value.

Settings Recommendation: You can also view the ISO sensitivity value in the lower-right area of the EVF and on the Monitor. If you use the EVF and memorize the location of the ISO button and rear Main command dial, you can set the ISO without removing the camera from your eye.

ISO Sensitivity

You can also use ISO sensitivity settings directly from the Photo Shooting Menu to change the camera's ISO sensitivity. Figure 7.9B shows the three screens used. Select your favorite ISO sensitivity for the circumstances in which you find yourself.

Notice in image 3 of figure 7.9B that you have a scrollable list of ISO sensitivity settings, from Lo 1 (~ISO 50) to Hi 2 (ISO 204800). The "normal" ISO range for the Z6 is ISO 100 to 51200. Following is a list of what the Lo and Hi numbers mean and the normal ISO range. Nikon does not publish what the actual Lo and Hi numbers represent, so these figures are approximations (~).

1. *Lo 1:* ~ISO 50
2. *Lo 0.7:* ~ISO 64
3. *Lo 0.3:* ~ISO 80
4. *Normal ISO range:* ISO 100 to ISO 51200
5. *Hi 0.3:* ~ISO 64000
6. *Hi 0.7:* ~ISO 80000
7. *Hi 1:* ~ISO 102400
8. *Hi 2:* ~ISO 204800

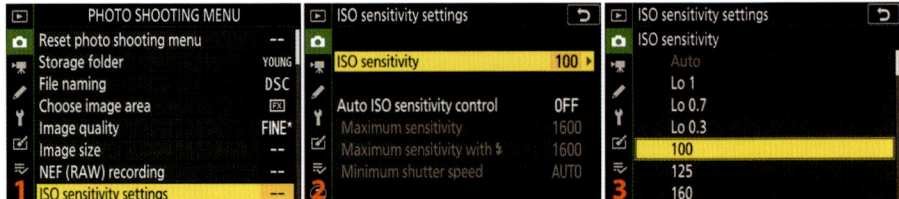

Figure 7.9B: Setting ISO sensitivity from the Photo Shooting Menu

Here are the steps to select an ISO sensitivity setting:

1. Follow the screen flow shown in figure 7.9B, images 1 and 2 (*ISO sensitivity settings > ISO sensitivity*) until you arrive at the third screen in the series.
2. Scroll up or down in the ISO sensitivity menu until you highlight the ISO value you want to use (figure 7.9B, image 3) and press the OK button or tap the ISO value to save the ISO sensitivity setting.

The minimum ISO sensitivity for the Z6 is ~ISO 50 (Lo 1). As shown in the previous ISO sensitivity list, the camera's ISO sensitivity can be adjusted in a range from ISO 50 (Lo 1) to ISO 204800 (Hi 2), in 1/3 or 1/2 EV steps. The ISO step increment is controlled by *Custom Setting Menu > b Metering/exposure > b1 EV steps for exposure control,* and, again, can be set to 1/3 or 1/2 EV step. We'll look at this more carefully in the chapter titled **Custom Setting Menu** (page 382).

Select your favorite ISO sensitivity setting, using either the external camera controls or the Photo Shooting Menu's ISO sensitivity settings function.

If you want, you can simply let your camera decide which ISO it would like to use. Let's consider this often-misunderstood feature in detail.

Two Automatic ISO Sensitivity Modes

There are two ways to let the camera automatically adjust the ISO sensitivity so that you can focus on composition and capturing images while the camera automatically controls the exposure. The two methods are: *ISO sensitivity Auto mode,* and *Auto ISO sensitivity control*. Here is a short description of each of these:

- **ISO sensitivity Auto mode** (figure 7.9C): This mode is available when the camera is put into point-and-shoot mode, or AUTO on the Mode dial. It makes the camera fully automatic so you do not have to be concerned with anything other than composing and taking pictures. ISO sensitivity may get high quickly when light levels drop. From personal testing, my Nikon Z6 uses a range from ISO 100 to ISO 12800 when this mode is in use. Unlike with the Auto ISO sensitivity control (next bullet), there is no way to control which ISO sensitivity the camera will select. I have not seen the camera go outside the ISO 100–12800 range under the brightest or darkest light levels. Of course, this could change with a firmware update, so test this for yourself if you are inclined to use point-and-shoot mode often.

- *Auto ISO sensitivity control* (figure 7.9D): This mode allows for finer control of the automatic ISO mode. You can select a minimum and maximum ISO sensitivity value, for the camera by itself or when a Speedlight flash unit is attached, and a minimum shutter speed. Controlling the minimum shutter speed allows you to protect image sharpness.

Now, let's consider each of these methods in more detail.

ISO Sensitivity Auto Mode

By using AUTO mode on the Mode dial and the Auto setting under ISO sensitivity settings, you allow the camera to take full control of adjusting the ISO sensitivity—and most other camera settings (e.g., shutter speed, aperture, metering, autofocus)—to help you get a good picture under difficult conditions.

You may have noticed that there is a grayed-out Auto setting at the top of the ISO sensitivity settings menu in figure 7.9B, image 3. The same setting is not grayed out in figure 7.9C because I set the camera to AUTO on the Mode dial.

The ISO sensitivity can be controlled by the Auto mode selected in figure 7.9C, image 2, while many other camera settings are automatically controlled by the AUTO mode on the Mode dial, as seen in figure 7.9C, image 1. Let's see how.

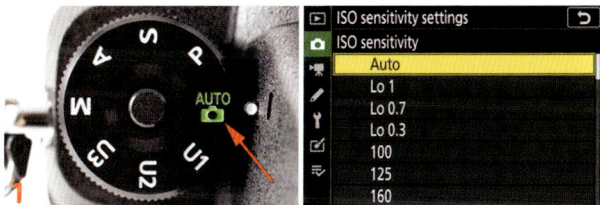

Figure 7.9C: AUTO on the Mode dial and the ISO sensitivity Auto setting

Here are the steps to use ISO sensitivity Auto mode:

1. Set the camera to AUTO mode on the Mode dial (figure 7.9C, image 1).
2. Figure 7.9C, image 2, continues where figure 7.9B, image 3 ends. Select Auto from the top of the list of available ISO sensitivity values (image 2). If the camera is not set to AUTO mode on the Mode dial, the Auto ISO sensitivity selection will be grayed out and unavailable (as seen in figure 7.9B, image 3).

Settings Recommendation: Normally, the AUTO mode on the Mode dial will obey the regular ISO sensitivity setting you choose—such as ISO 100—and will not vary from that ISO value, using the other camera settings, such as aperture and shutter speed, to control the exposure. However, what is the point of using AUTO mode on the Mode dial if you then have to worry about the ISO sensitivity? If you are handing off exposure decisions to the camera so that you can simply take pictures without worrying about anything except composing the image, why not have the camera also control the ISO sensitivity?

This setting is best used for situations where the images are for fun (e.g., at a party), not for commercial use, because the ISO can go as high as 12800, which may introduce noise into your pictures. Maybe you could assign this setting to your "party" User setting (U1, U2, U3). The finer control you have with the Auto ISO sensitivity control (next subsection) is better for commercial photography.

Auto ISO Sensitivity Control (ISO-Auto)

You may have noticed in figure 7.9B, image 2, that another setting is available, *Auto ISO sensitivity control,* which defaults to Off. This setting allows the camera to control the ISO sensitivity and shutter speed according to the light levels sensed by the Z6's metering system. Figure 7.9D shows the Photo Shooting Menu screens used to enable Auto ISO sensitivity control.

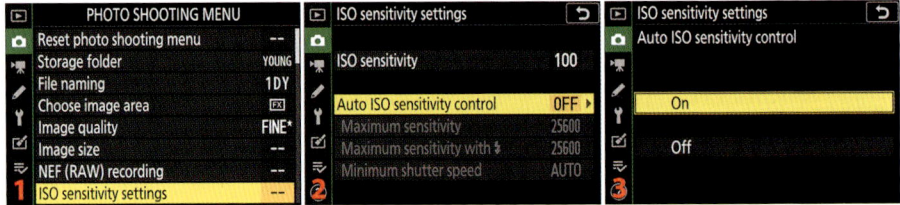

Figure 7.9D: Enabling Auto ISO sensitivity control

Here are the steps to enable the Auto ISO sensitivity control:

1. Follow the screen flow shown in figure 7.9D, images 1 and 2 (*ISO sensitivity settings > Auto ISO sensitivity control*) until you arrive at the third screen in the series.
2. Choose either On or Off (figure 7.9D, image 3) and press the OK button or tap your selection to save it.

Once you've set Auto ISO sensitivity control to On, you should immediately set two values, according to how you shoot: Maximum sensitivity (for both camera and flash) and Minimum shutter speed, as seen in figure 7.9D, image 2, below the Auto ISO sensitivity control setting. These settings will become available once you have enabled the Auto ISO sensitivity control. Let's discuss each of them.

Maximum Sensitivity

The *Maximum sensitivity* and *Maximum sensitivity with flash* settings are safeguards for you (figure 7.9E). They allow the camera to adjust its own ISO sensitivity from the minimum value you have set in *ISO sensitivity* (figure 7.9B) to the value set in *Maximum sensitivity* (figure 7.9E), according to light conditions.

In other words, the value you set in ISO sensitivity becomes a floor value (lowest ISO) the camera will not go below (e.g., 100), and the *Maximum sensitivity* setting becomes a ceiling value (highest ISO) the Z6 will not go above (e.g., 1600). With these settings, you can control the exact range of ISO sensitivity values you want the camera to use.

The Z6 will maintain the lowest ISO sensitivity it can to take the picture. However, if needed, it can rapidly rise to the Maximum sensitivity level to "get the picture" no matter what.

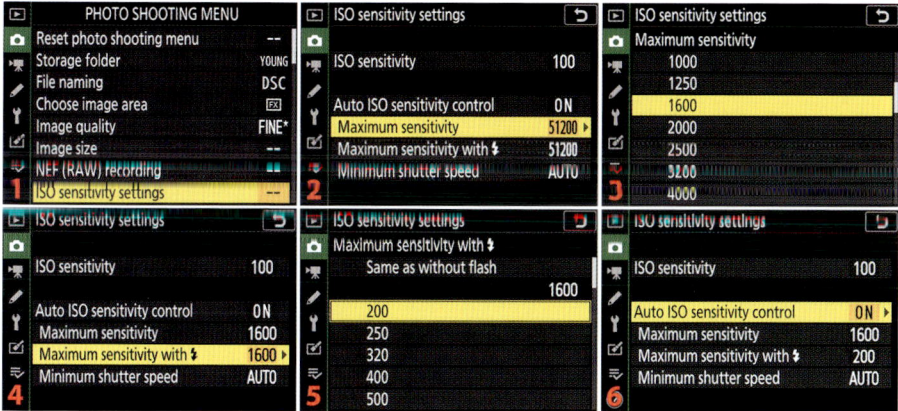

Figure 7.9E: Auto ISO sensitivity control—Maximum sensitivity

Use the following steps to select a maximum ISO sensitivity for nonflash and flash use (two menu items):

1. Choose ISO sensitivity settings from the Photo Shooting Menu and scroll to the right (figure 7.9E, image 1).
2. Make sure you have enabled the Auto ISO sensitivity control, as shown in figure 7.9D, images 2 and 3, and then select Maximum sensitivity (figure 7.9E, image 2).
3. In figure 7.9E, image 3, you have a selection of ISO values from ISO 200 to Hi 2 (ISO 204800), and you can choose the one you want to use for Maximum sensitivity. Highlight a Maximum sensitivity value (e.g., 1600) and press the OK button or tap the option to select it.
4. The camera will return to the ISO sensitivity screen shown in figure 7.9E, image 4. The Z6 automatically sets the Maximum sensitivity with [flash] value, according to what you set under Maximum sensitivity. If you are using a flash unit and want a different Maximum sensitivity for the flash unit, scroll to the right. Otherwise, if no special flash unit settings are needed, you are ready to take pictures and can skip the following screens and steps.
5. In figure 7.9E, image 5, you will notice there is a setting called Same as without flash, which, when selected, allows you to tie all Maximum sensitivity values to the value for nonflash (image 3). The current nonflash value is shown directly below the words Same as without flash (I selected ISO 400). If you want, you can have separate values for nonflash and flash use, by selecting a different value for each of the screens in images 3 and 5. Press the OK button or tap your selections to save your values.
6. The final screen (figure 7.9E, image 6) shows that the lowest ISO the camera will use (the floor value) is ISO 100. The Maximum sensitivity for non-flash photography (the ceiling value) is ISO 1600, and the Maximum sensitivity for [flash] is ISO 200.

These settings allow the camera take the ISO sensitivity all the way up to ISO 1600 for non-flash pictures in a low-light situation. It is the maximum ISO value the camera will use to get a good exposure when the light drops. Most photographers will keep this value somewhat low to prevent noisy images.

However, what happens when the camera reaches the Maximum sensitivity setting and there still isn't enough light for a good exposure? Let's find out by examining the next part of the Auto ISO sensitivity control: Minimum shutter speed.

Settings Recommendation: My personal maximum is ISO 1600, unless I am shooting very critical images in low light. You should experiment to see what your own tolerance for high ISO noise may be and set your camera accordingly.

Minimum Shutter Speed

Because shutter speed helps control how sharp an image can be—depending on camera shake and subject movement—you will need some control over the minimum shutter speed while the Auto ISO sensitivity control is enabled (figure 7.9F).

The Minimum shutter speed setting lets you to select the minimum shutter speed the camera will allow when the light diminishes. In exposure modes Programmed auto (P mode—camera controls shutter and aperture) and Aperture-priority (A mode—camera controls shutter and you control aperture), the camera will not go below the Minimum shutter speed unless the Maximum sensitivity setting still won't give you a good exposure. We will discuss this more in a moment, but first let's see how to choose a Minimum shutter speed.

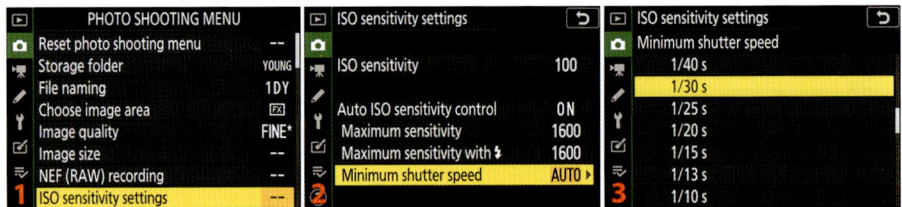

Figure 7.9F: Auto ISO sensitivity control—Minimum shutter speed

Here are the steps to select a Minimum shutter speed value:

1. Follow the screen flow shown in figure 7.9F, images 1 and 2 (*ISO sensitivity settings > Minimum shutter speed*) until you arrive at the third screen in the series.
2. Either leave the camera set to the default Auto, which lets the camera decide which shutter speed to use (we will discuss Auto in the next subsection), or select a different speed, such as the 1/30 s chosen in figure 7.9F, image 3, and press the OK button or tap your selection to save the setting. The shutter speed range you can select manually is from 30 seconds (30 s) to 1/4000 s.

This is the answer to our question in the last section about what happens when there is not enough light and the camera has reached the Maximum sensitivity level. Take careful note of this: even though you've selected a Minimum shutter speed, the camera *will go below the Minimum shutter speed* when the Maximum sensitivity ISO number has been reached and the light is still too low for a good exposure.

In other words, in Programmed auto (P) or Aperture-priority (A) exposure modes, if you get into low light and try to take pictures, the camera will attempt to keep the ISO sensitivity as low as possible until the shutter speed drops to your selected Minimum shutter speed. Once the camera hits the selected Minimum shutter speed value—like the 1/30s shown in figure 7.9F, image 3—the ISO sensitivity will begin to rise up to your selected Maximum sensitivity value, like the ISO 1600 shown in figure 7.9F, image 3.

Once the camera hits the Maximum sensitivity value, if there still isn't enough light for a good exposure, it won't keep raising the ISO sensitivity. Instead, the camera will now go below your selected Minimum shutter speed, dropping below the 1/30s shown in figure 7.9F, image 3. Be careful, because if the light gets that low, your camera can go all the way down to a shutter speed of 30 seconds to get a good exposure. You had better have your camera on a tripod and have a static subject with shutter speeds that low.

Look at the Minimum shutter speed value as the lowest "safe" speed, after which you'll put your camera on a tripod. Most people can handhold a camera down to about 1/60s if they are careful, and maybe to 1/30s if they're extra careful and brace themselves. The Z6 has the excellent in-body image stabilization (IBIS), which helps a great deal, but still, when you get to very slow shutter speeds, it can be blur city for your images. It's even worse with telephoto lenses. Camera movement is greatly magnified with a long lens, and a Minimum shutter speed of 1/250s to 1/500s or more may be required.

The next section discusses an excellent solution the Nikon Z6 gives us for those times when we are using a longer lens requiring a faster shutter speed to maintain sharp images—the Auto Minimum shutter speed setting.

Auto Minimum Shutter Speed

There is an important principle in photography called the "reciprocal of focal length shutter speed rule." You may know the rule, but a short review won't hurt. This impressive-sounding rule simply means that you should use a tripod (no handholding) whenever the shutter speed in use is below the reciprocal of the lens's focal length.

For example, if you are using a 50mm zoom position on your lens, you should not use a shutter speed below 1/50s without having the camera on a tripod. With a 105mm focal length, the minimum handheld shutter speed is 1/100s or 1/125s. There is no 1/105s available, so you can use the closest one. If you are using a 300mm lens, you should not use a shutter speed below 1/300s.

The reason this rule exists is because a longer focal length tends to magnify the subject and any vibrations you introduce when you press the shutter-release button. With a shutter speed below the reciprocal of the lens focal length, you can introduce movement just from your heartbeat or natural hand shakiness.

If you are going to handhold the camera at slower shutter speeds, you need to learn how to brace yourself properly. It's best to use a tripod any time you have to shoot below the reciprocal of the lens's length. Otherwise, you will be known for your well-exposed, yet blurry images (from camera shake). Although lenses with vibration reduction (VR) and in-body image stabilization (IBIS) can help, they are not a cure-all for camera shake at slow shutter speeds.

When using the Auto ISO sensitivity control, you have an opportunity to implement the reciprocal of focal length shutter speed rule in an automatic fashion. It is even more important when using one of the Image area formats, such as DX, because these crop modes have a narrower field of view that tends to magnify camera shake. For instance, the DX field of view is 1.5× the FX field of view, which has the effect of magnifying camera shake (e.g., by 1.5× for DX).

The Nikon Z6 has an Auto setting for Minimum shutter speed, which allows the camera to sense what focal length is currently in use and prohibits the camera from using a minimum shutter speed that would cause camera shake, except when the light gets too low.

If the camera can't get enough light to correctly expose the image in any other way— such as by raising the ISO sensitivity to the Maximum sensitivity level, or by using flash—it will discard the reciprocal of focal length rule by slowing the shutter speed to a value below the reciprocal of the focal length (as slow as 30 seconds, if necessary), potentially leading to camera shake.

Let's see how to select the Auto Minimum shutter speed mode.

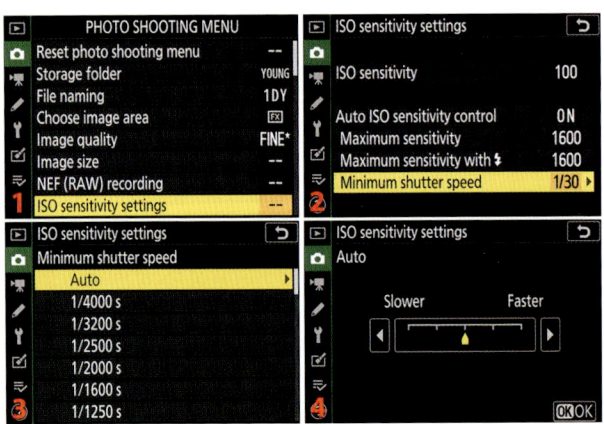

Figure 7.9G: Auto ISO sensitivity control—Auto Minimum shutter speed

Use these steps to enable Auto Minimum shutter speed:

1. Follow the screen flow shown in figure 7.9G, images 1 and 2 (*ISO sensitivity settings > Minimum shutter speed*) until you arrive at the third screen in the series.
2. Select Auto from the top of the Minimum shutter speed list and scroll to the right (figure 7.9G, image 3).
3. Adjust the Auto Minimum shutter speed fine-tuning scale (figure 7.9G, image 4). Each position on the scale is the equivalent of one stop (1 EV). The camera will use the reciprocal of the focal length of the mounted lens if the yellow pointer is set in the center as

seen in figure 7.9G, image 4. If you move it one notch to the right of center, the camera will switch to the reciprocal of the focal length plus one stop. If you are using a 50mm lens, the reciprocal of 50mm plus one stop is 1/100s (1/50s plus 1 EV) for the camera's minimum shutter speed. If you move the scale one notch to the left of center, the camera will use 1/25s instead (1/50s less 1 EV). Here is a list matching what each position on the scale represents if you are using a 50mm lens: 1/13s, 1/25s, 1/50s, 1/100s, 1/200s. Of course, these numbers will vary with the focal length of the lens mounted on the camera.

4. Press or touch OK to lock in the fine-tuned Auto Minimum shutter speed.

Settings Recommendation: When I use the Auto ISO sensitivity control with my Z6, I set my camera to Auto Minimum shutter speed. Why worry about having to adjust a setting just because I changed lenses? The camera is smart enough to know what to do and tries to protect me from losing sharpness from camera shake.

However, I am also cognizant that slow shutter speeds will cause camera shake; therefore, I use a tripod when the shutter speed may drop to a value that I cannot successfully handhold while still having a sharp image.

Note: Shutter-priority (S) and Manual (M) modes allow you to control the camera in a way that overrides certain parts of the Auto ISO sensitivity control.

In Manual mode (M), the camera relinquishes all control of the shutter and aperture. It can adjust only the ISO sensitivity by itself, so it can obey the Maximum sensitivity but the Minimum shutter speed is overridden and does not apply.

In Shutter-priority mode (S), the camera can control the aperture, but the shutter speed is controlled only by the camera user. So, the Auto ISO sensitivity control can still control the Maximum sensitivity but has lost control over the Minimum shutter speed.

Also, it may be a good idea to enable High ISO NR (page 227) when you use the Auto ISO sensitivity control. This is especially true if you leave the camera set to the default Maximum sensitivity value of 51200. Otherwise, your images may have excessive noise when the light drops.

In summation: If Auto is selected for Minimum shutter speed, the camera will decide which shutter speed to use as a minimum based on the focal length of the lens in use, for both CPU and registered non-CPU lenses.

Enabling ISO-AUTO with External Controls

If you like to use external controls to make adjustments when possible (don't we all?), be aware that you can conveniently turn the Auto ISO sensitivity control on and off with the ISO button, the front Sub-command dial, and the Control panel (or Information display). Figure 7.9H shows the controls.

You will need to configure Auto ISO sensitivity control before you use the external controls or the camera will use factory defaults.

Here are the steps you'll use to manually enable or disable ISO-AUTO (ISO-A):

1. Using the controls seen in figure 7.9H, hold down the ISO button (red letter A).
2. Rotate the front Sub-command dial (red letter B) to enable or disable ISO-A, the Auto ISO sensitivity control. The ISO-A symbol will appear on the Control panel (C), along with the current ISO sensitivity value (ISO-A 100). You will see the camera toggle between ISO and ISO-A as you turn the front Sub-command dial. Release the ISO button to set the value. You can also see the ISO Auto notification on the bottom right areas of the Viewfinder and the Monitor.

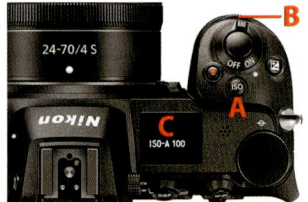

Figure 7.9H: Enabling Auto ISO sensitivity control with external camera controls

When, Why, and How Should I Use ISO-AUTO?

How much automation do you need to produce consistently excellent images? Let's explore how and when automatic, self-adjusting ISO might improve or degrade your images. What is this feature all about? When and why should I use it? Are there any compromises in image quality when using this mode?

Normally, you set your camera to a particular ISO number, such as 100 or 400, and shoot your images. As the light gets darker, or in the deep shade, you might increase the ISO sensitivity to continue taking handheld images.

However, if lighting conditions are rapidly changing or otherwise becoming difficult to maintain, why not let the camera help you adjust instantly? If you absolutely must get the shot, the Auto ISO sensitivity control will work nicely. Here are a few scenarios:

- **Scenario #1:** Let's say you are a photojournalist and you're taking flash pictures of a celebrity as she disembarks from her airplane, walks into the terminal, and drives away in her limousine. Under these circumstances, you are shooting in widely varying light conditions but you have little time to check your ISO settings or shutter speeds.
- **Scenario #2:** You are a wedding photographer shooting in a church that doesn't allow the use of flash. As you follow the bride and groom from the dark inner rooms of the church out into the lobby and finally up to the altar, your light conditions vary constantly. You have no time to deal with the fluctuations in light by changing your ISO because things are moving too quickly.
- **Scenario #3:** You are at a party and you want some great pictures. You really don't want to be bothered with camera configuration at this time but still want some well-exposed images. Light will vary as you move around the room, talking, laughing, and snapping pictures.

These scenarios present excellent examples for using the Auto ISO sensitivity control. The camera will use your normal settings, such as your normal ISO sensitivity, shutter speed, and aperture, until the light will not allow those settings to provide an accurate exposure.

Only then will the camera raise the ISO sensitivity or lower the shutter speed to keep functioning within the shutter/aperture parameters you have set.

Look at ISO-AUTO as a failsafe for times when you must get the shot but have little time to deal with camera settings, or when you don't want to vary the shutter/aperture settings but still want to be assured of a well-exposed image.

Unless you are a private detective shooting handheld telephoto images from your car, or you are a photojournalist or sports photographer who must get the shot every time regardless of maximum quality, I personally would not recommend leaving Auto ISO sensitivity control set to On all the time. Use it only when you really need to get the shot under any circumstances!

Of course, If you are unsure of how to use the correct ISO for the light level due to lack of experience, don't be afraid to experiment with this mode. At the very worst, you might get noisier-than-normal images. Keep in mind that it may not be a good idea to depend on this mode over the long-term because noisy images are not very nice.

Are There Any Drawbacks to Using ISO-AUTO?

Maybe! It really depends on how widely the light conditions vary when you are shooting. Most of the time, your camera will maintain the normal range of ISO settings in Auto ISO sensitivity control, so your images will be their normal low-noise, sharp masterpieces. However, at times, the light may be so low that the ISO may exceed low-noise range and will start getting into the noisier ranges above ISO 1600.

Just be aware that the Auto ISO sensitivity control can and will push your camera's ISO sensitivity into a range that causes noisier images when light levels drop, if you have allowed it. Use it with this understanding and you'll be fine.

The Auto ISO sensitivity control is yet another feature of our powerful Nikon cameras. Maybe not everyone needs this failsafe feature, but for those who do, it must be there. I will use it myself in circumstances where getting the shot is the most important thing and where light levels may get too low for normal ISO image-making.

Even if you think you might only use it from time to time, do learn how to use it for those times. Experiment with the Auto ISO sensitivity control. It's fun and can be useful!

White Balance

White balance (WB) is designed to let you capture accurate colors in each of your camera's RGB color channels. Your images can reflect realistic colors if you understand how to use the WB settings.

This is one of the more important things to learn about digital photography. If you don't understand how white balance works, you'll have a hard time when you want consistent color across a number of images.

In this chapter we will look at WB briefly and learn only how to select the various White balance settings. This is such an important concept to understand that an entire chapter—titled **White Balance**—is devoted to this subject (page 107). Please read that chapter carefully. It is critical that you thoroughly learn to control the WB settings. A lot of what you'll do in computer post-processing of images requires a good understanding of white balance control.

White Balance from the Photo Shooting Menu

First let's examine how to set a White balance from the Photo Shooting Menu and then from the *i* Menu.

Most photographers leave their cameras set to Auto White balance (Figure 7.10A). This works fine most of the time because the camera is quite capable of rendering accurate color. However, it's hard to get exactly the same white balance in each consecutive picture when you are using Auto mode. The camera has to make a new WB decision for each picture in Auto. This can cause the WB to vary a little from picture to picture.

For many types of photography this isn't a problem (e.g., Landscapes), but if you are doing product photography in a studio, surely your client will want the pictures to be the same color as the product. White balance lets you control that carefully when needed.

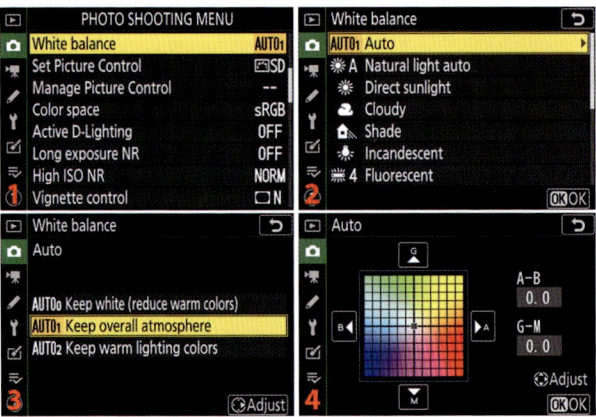

Figure 7.10A: Choosing a White balance setting

The steps to select a White balance setting are as follows:

1. Follow the screen flow shown in figure 7.10A, images 1 and 2 (*White balance > Auto*, or another selection such as *White balance > Direct sunlight*) until you arrive at the third screen in the series.
2. If you choose Auto, Fluorescent, Choose color temperature, or Preset manual you will need to select from an intermediate screen, similar to the one shown in figure 7.10A, image 3, for Auto WB. The other settings will skip image 3 and go directly to image 4. Auto presents three settings: Auto0 Keep white (reduce warm colors), Auto1 Keep

overall atmosphere, and Auto2 Keep warm lighting colors. Fluorescent presents seven different types of fluorescent lighting. Choose color temperature allows you to select a color temperature manually from a range of 2500 K (cool looking) to 10000 K (warm looking). Preset manual (PRE) shows six WB memory locations d-0 through d–6 and allows you to select one of them. If you are unsure which is best, choose Auto1 Normal for now. The chapter titled **White Balance** (page 112) will explain how to use all these settings; therefore, consider this section an introduction to how to choose a white balance. Press the OK button or tap your selection to choose a value. If you would like to fine-tune the highlighted value, scroll to the right, or tap the Adjust control (see step 3).

3. If you select the Adjust control, you'll arrive at the Auto WB fine-tuning screen. With this screen you can adjust how this particular WB setting records color by introducing a color bias toward green (G), amber (A), magenta (M), or blue (B). You do this by moving the little black square in the middle of the color box toward the edges of the box in any direction, by selecting the little (G, A, M, B) squares. If you make a mistake, simply move the black square back to the middle of the color box. After you have finished adjusting (or not) the colors, press or touch OK to save your setting. Most people select OK as soon as they see the fine-tuning screen so they do not change the default settings for this particular White balance setting.

White Balance from the *i* Menu

You can also access the White balance selection and fine-tuning screens for the currently selected WB by following this procedure:

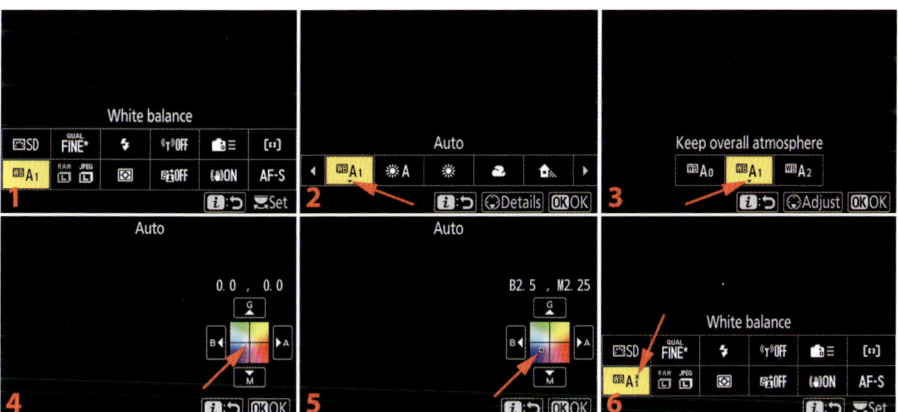

Figure 7.10B: Setting White balance with the *i* Menu

Use the following to set the White balance or fine-tune it:

1. Press the *i* button on the camera's rear panel to open the *i* Menu (figure 7.10B, image 1). Select the White balance setting from the menu and then press the OK button.

2. The White balance secondary screen will now display (figure 7.10B, image 2). You can choose a WB setting from this screen by swiping the bar containing WB settings right or left and then tapping on your choice, or by scrolling to it with the Multi selector pad and pressing the OK button. Note that below the WB A1 choice there is a tiny down indicator (at the red arrow). Press down on the Multi selector pad, or tap the Details control and the camera will either move to an intermediate screen (for Auto, Fluorescent, Choose color temperature, or Preset manual only) or will move to the WB fine-tuning screen.

3. As noted in figure 7.10B, image 3, since we are examining the Auto WB, we see an intermediate screen offering three types of Auto WB (A0, A1, A2). The Z6 has A1 selected, which is equivalent to Keep overall atmosphere (don't warm up or cool down the image). You can select the WB A1 setting by selecting OK and skipping the following WB fine-tuning steps. You can also choose A0 (cool image down) or A2 (warm image up), instead of A1 at this point. If you want to fine-tune your WB selection, note again in image 3 that below the WB A1 choice there is a tiny down indicator (at the red arrow). To open the fine-tuning screen, press down on the Multi selector pad, or touch the Adjust control.

4. With the fine-tuning screen shown in figure 7.10B, images 4 and 5, you can adjust how this particular WB setting records color by introducing a color bias toward green (G), amber (A), magenta (M), or blue (B). You do this by moving the little black square in the middle of the color box toward the edges of the box in any direction (see red arrows in images 4 and 5), by touching the little (G, A, M, B) squares, or using the directional Multi selector pad. If you make a mistake, simply move the black square back to the middle of the color box. After you have finished adjusting (or not) the colors, press or touch OK to save your setting. Most people press or touch OK as soon as they see the fine-tuning screen, so they do not change the default color settings for the selected WB.

5. Notice at the red arrow in figure 7.10B, image 6, that is pointing to a small asterisk displayed above the WB A1 setting. This asterisk shows that the WB value has been fine-tuned and has colors different from the factory default. To return the WB value back to its default values and get rid of the asterisk, move the little black square to the center of the color box, as seen in figure 7.10, image 4.

Settings Recommendation: Until you've read the chapter on white balance, I suggest that you leave the camera set to one of the Auto WB selections. However, please do take the time to understand this setting by reading the dedicated chapter carefully. Understanding White balance is especially important if you plan on shooting JPEGs regularly.

Set Picture Control

Set Picture Control allows you to choose a Picture Control for a shooting session. Nikon's Picture Control system lets you control how your JPEG image appears in several ways. Each control has a specific effect on the image's appearance. If you shot film a few years ago, you will remember that each film type has a distinct look. No two films produce color that looks the same.

In today's digital photography world, Picture Controls give you the ability to impart a specific look to your images. You can use Picture Controls as they are provided from the factory, or you can fine-tune Sharpening, Contrast, Brightness, Saturation, and Hue.

We'll discuss how to fine-tune a Nikon Picture Control later in this section. In the next section, Manage Picture Control, we'll discuss how to save a modified Picture Control under your own Custom Picture Control name. You can create up to nine Custom Picture Controls.

I'll refer to Picture Controls included in the camera as Nikon Picture Controls because that's how Nikon refers to them. In some Nikon literature, you may also hear them called Original Picture Controls. If you modify and save a Nikon Picture Control under a new name, it becomes a Custom Picture Control. I'll also use the generic name of Picture Control when referring to any of them.

The cool thing about Picture Controls is that they are shareable. If you tweak a Nikon Picture Control and save it under a name of your choice, you can then share your control with others. Compatible cameras, software, and other devices can use these controls to maintain the look you want from the time you press the Shutter release button until you print the picture.

Nikon Picture Controls

Nikon provides eight normal Picture Controls, all of which allow you to change the general look of your JPEG images. They also include 20 special creative Picture Controls, which we will examine in the next subsection.

Keep in mind that Picture Controls are primarily designed to be used with JPEG images. JPEGs have baked-in permanent colors that are difficult to change after the fact without damaging the quality of the image from re-compression losses. Therefore, once you have created the JPEG image, it is best used as is.

While you can use a normal or creative Picture Control on a NEF (RAW) image, the color information is not baked into a RAW file, but is, instead, stored with the image in a non-permanent way—as markers in the image metadata. Later you can change to a different Picture Control (general look) in your computer, using free software, such as Nikon Capture NX-D. Then you can resave the RAW file as a JPEG with the new look.

In figure 7.11A, I took a gray-card-balanced picture of my *X-rite Colorchecker Classic* color chart for each of the eight normal Nikon Picture Controls.

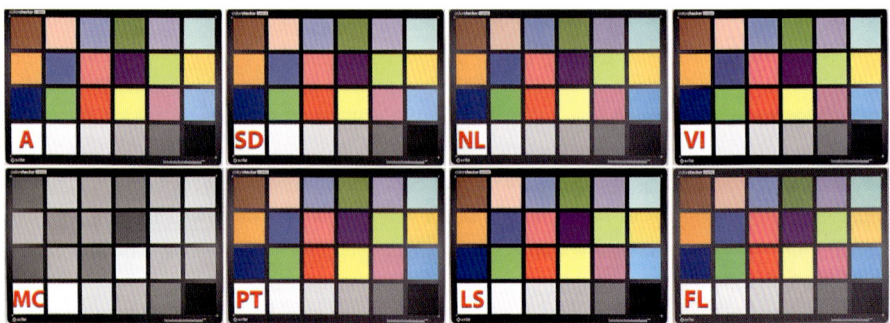

Figure 7.11A: Nikon Picture Controls

Each color chart picture is labeled in the lower-left corner, matching this list:

- Auto (A)
- Standard (SD)
- Neutral (NL)
- Vivid (VI)

- Monochrome (MC)
- Portrait (PT)
- Landscape (LS)
- Flat (FL)

Figure 7.11A provides a look at the differences in color saturation and shadow with the various normal Picture Controls. Due to limitations in printing, it may be hard to see the variations, but they would be clearly visible in a picture.

Saturation and Contrast depth increase within these Picture Control choices, in this order: FL (very low) > NL (low) > SD (medium) > VI (high). PT appears to be a modified form of the NL control, and LS seems to be a modified form of the VI control. The Auto Picture Control is constantly variable, according to subject.

The following is an overview of what Nikon says about Picture Controls and what I see in my sample color chart images taken with the various controls (figure 7.11A).

- **A,** or **Auto,** is a variable Picture Control using the Standard Picture Control as its base. It automatically decides—based on subject contrast, color, and exposure—how to make the image look. Use Auto if you have little interest in controlling the overall look of the image, or if you do not have enough photographic experience and want your camera to do it for you. The Auto control is constantly variable according to subject. For instance, if you are shooting portraits, the camera may make the subject appear a little softer than the Standard Picture Control, or it may make the sky and foliage more saturated than the Standard Picture Control it is based on.
- **SD,** or **Standard,** is Nikon's recommendation for getting "balanced" results. Nikon recommends SD for most general situations. Use this if you want a balanced image and do not want to post-process it. It has what Nikon calls "standard image processing." The SD control provides what I would call medium saturation, with darker shadows to add contrast. If I were shooting JPEG images in a studio or during an event, I would seriously consider using the SD control. I would compare this setting to Fuji Provia or Kodak Kodachrome 64 slide films.

- **NL,** or **Neutral,** is excellent for an image that will be extensively post-processed in a computer. It has a wide dynamic range, surpassed only by the Flat (FL) Picture Control. It too is a balanced image setting, but it applies minimal camera processing, so you'll have room to do more with the image during post-processing. NL has less saturation and weaker shadows, so the image will be less contrasty (wider dynamic range). Basically, the NL control will give you extra dynamic range in each image due to more open shadows and slightly less saturated colors. If you've ever shot with Fuji NPS film or Kodak Portra negative films and liked them, you'll like this control.

- **VI,** or **Vivid,** is for those of us who loved Fuji Velvia slide film. This setting places emphasis on saturating primary colors for intense imagery. The contrast is higher for striking shadow contrast, and the sharpness is higher, too. If you are shooting JPEGs and want to imitate a saturated transparency film like Velvia, this mode is for you! If you look at the red block in the VI example in figure 7.11A, you'll see that it's pushed into deep saturation, almost to the point of oversaturation. Plus, the greens and blues are extra strong. That means your nature shots will look saturated and contrasty. Be careful when you are shooting on a high-contrast day, such as in direct sunshine in the summer. If you use the VI control under these conditions, you may find that your images are too high in contrast. It may be better to back off to the SD or NL control when shooting in bright sunshine. You will need to experiment with this to see what I mean. On a cloudy or foggy low-contrast day, when the shadows are weak, you may find that the VI control adds pleasing saturation and contrast to the image.

- **MC,** or **Monochrome,** allows the black-and-white lovers among us to shoot in toned black-and-white. The MC control basically removes the color by desaturation. It's still an RGB color image, but the colors have become levels of gray. It does not look the same as black-and-white film, in my opinion. The blacks are not as deep, and the whites are not as bright. To me, it seems that the MC control is fairly low contrast, and that's where the problem lies. Good black-and-white images should have bright whites and deep blacks. To get images like that from a digital camera, you'll have to manually work with the image in a graphics program like Photoshop, using the Channel Mixer (see the upcoming **Note on Photoshop for Z6 Black-and-White Images**). However, if you want to experiment with black-and-white photography, this gives you a good starting point. Additionally, two extra settings in the MC control allow you to experiment with Filter effects and Toning. We'll look at these settings in the upcoming section called **MC Picture Control Filter Effects and Toning**. The MC control creates a look that is somewhat like Kodak Plus-X Pan negative film, with blacks that are not as deep.

- **PT,** or **Portrait,** is a control that "lends a natural texture and rounded feel to the skin of portrait subjects" (Nikon's description). I've taken numerous images with the PT control and shot the same images with the NL control. The results are very similar. I'm sure that Nikon has included some software enhancements specifically for skin tones in this control, so I would definitely use this control for portraits. The results from the PT control look a bit like smooth Kodak Portra or Fuji NPS negative film.

- **LS,** or **Landscape,** is a control that "produces vibrant landscapes and cityscapes," according to Nikon. That sounds like the VI control to me. I shot a series of images using both the LS and VI controls and got similar results. Compared to the VI control, the LS control seemed to have slightly less saturation in the reds and a tiny bit more saturation in the greens. The blues stayed about the same. It seems that Nikon has created the LS control to be similar to, but not quite as drastic as, the VI control. In my test images, the LS control created smoother transitions in color. However, there was so little difference between the two controls that you'd have to compare the images side by side to notice. Maybe this control is meant to be more natural than the super-saturated VI control. It will certainly improve the look of your landscape JPEG images. The look of this control is somewhere between Fuji Provia and Velvia. You get great saturation and contrast, with emphasis on the greens and blues in natural settings.

- *FL,* or **Flat,** is a control that allows you to preserve details "over a wide tone range, from highlights to shadows." If you are a JPEG or TIFF shooter and need maximum dynamic range in your image but do not want to use HDR (high dynamic range) imaging (where you shoot several images at different exposures and then combine them), you may be able to use this Picture Control as a substitute. The Z6 has a wide dynamic range already, with excellent detail in the shadow areas; therefore, a very low contrast Picture Control setting can help maintain maximum dynamic range in a single image. You may also use this Picture Control when you are shooting video and later want to professionally color grade the results. It is hard to compare this Picture Control to a certain film stock; I have never shot any film with contrast and saturation this low.

Creative Picture Controls

Nikon also included 20 creative Picture Controls for JPEG photographers who want to have some fun with their images. Each creative Picture Control is designed to resemble a filter you might see on a social media site or smartphone.

I photographed my X-rite color chart with each of the 20 creative Nikon Picture Controls included with the Nikon Z6.

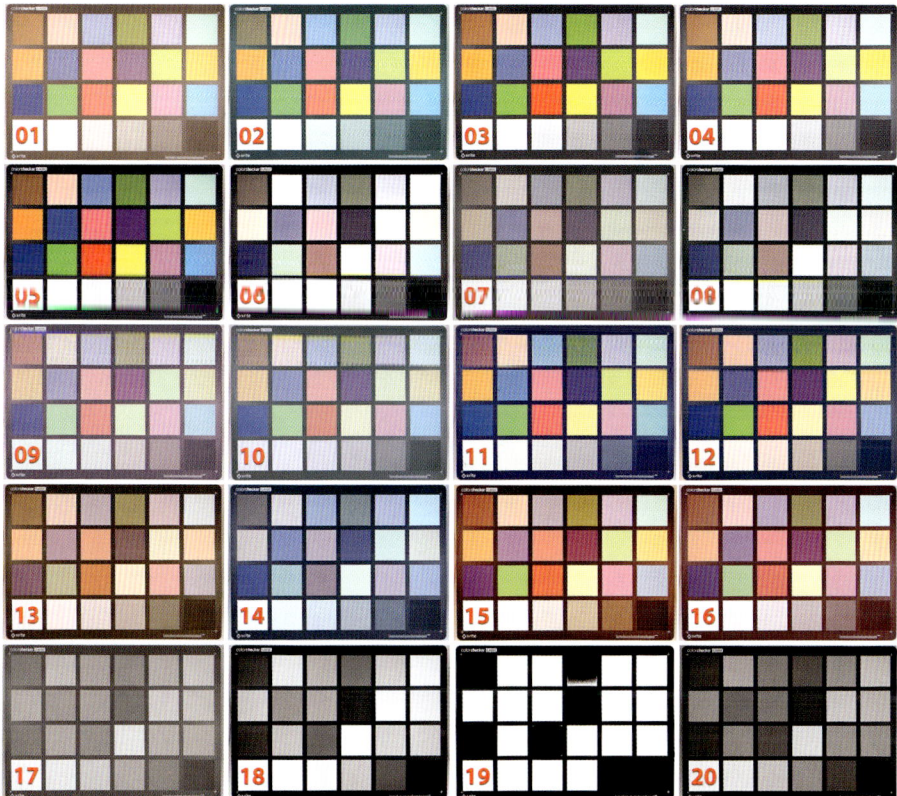

Figure 7.11B: Creative Nikon Picture Controls

Each creative Picture Control shown in figure 7.11B is labeled with its number in the lower-left corner, matching the Picture Control names this list:

- 01 Dream
- 02 Morning
- 03 Pop
- 04 Sunday
- 05 Somber
- 06 Dramatic
- 07 Silence
- 08 Bleached
- 09 Melancholic
- 10 Pure
- 11 Denim
- 12 Toy
- 13 Sepia
- 14 Blue
- 15 Red
- 16 Pink
- 17 Charcoal
- 18 Graphite
- 19 Binary
- 20 Carbon

Describing these creative Picture Controls is difficult because there are so many variations. You may want to experiment with each of these special Picture Controls to see if you like any of them. It can be fun to use them for some unique looks.

Selecting, Fine-Tuning, and Resetting a Picture Control

Now that we have examined the various types of Picture Controls and how they might provide a certain stylistic look to your pictures, let's explore how to select your favorite Picture Controls and discover how to fine-tune them to better meet your needs.

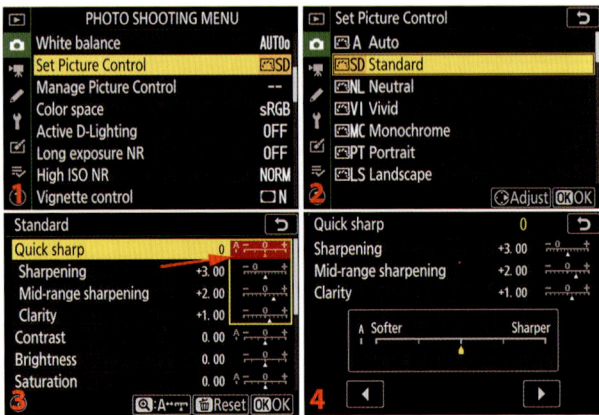

Figure 7.11C: Choosing a Nikon Picture Control from the menus

Here are the steps to choose a Picture Control from the Photo Shooting Menu:

1. Select Set Picture Control from the Photo Shooting Menu and scroll to the right (figure 7.11C, image 1).
2. Choose one of the Nikon Picture Controls from the Set Picture Control screen (figure 7.11C, image 2), such as the SD control we have selected. At this point, you can simply press or touch OK, or just tap the control you want, and the control you've chosen will be available for immediate use. It will show up as a two-letter name in the Photo Shooting Menu next to Set Picture Control. You can see this in figure 7.11C, image 1, where SD is shown next to Set Picture Control. If you want to fine-tune the Picture Control, you can highlight the control and scroll to the right or tap the Adjust control (image 2).
3. The Picture Control fine-tuning screen is shown in figure 7.11C, image 3. You can adjust Sharpening, Clarity, Contrast, Brightness, Saturation, and Hue by scrolling up or down to select an item, or by tapping the adjustment name (e.g., Contrast, Brightness). Once a line is highlighted, you can scroll right or left (+/−) to fine-tune the value of that line item. If you would like to use a larger screen to make fine-tuning adjustments, tap on the area I highlighted in red on any setting and a secondary fine-tuning screen will open.
4. The Quick sharp secondary screen looks different from the other options' secondary screens (figure 7.11C, image 4). Quick sharp causes you to adjust three settings at once: Sharpening, Mid-range sharpening, and Clarity, where the other secondary screens (e.g., figure 7.11D, image 2) adjust only one item at a time. To use Quick sharp, tap the

left and right arrows at the bottom of the screen (image 4). You can adjust all three settings by 2.00 steps toward Softer or 2.00 steps toward Sharper. All three settings will be adjusted at once. (**Note:** You can adjust these three items individually by not using Quick sharp, but by selecting each setting individually.)

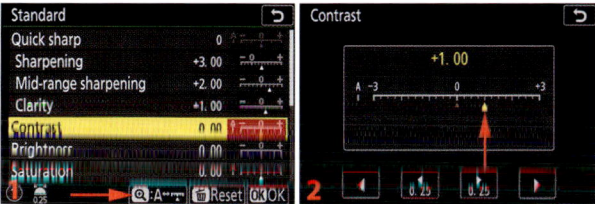

Figure 7.11D: Fine-tuning a single item

5. Contrast, Brightness, Saturation, and Hue (not shown) remain individual adjustments only (Hue is on the next adjustment screen page, available by scrolling down in figure 7.11D, image 1). You can also individually adjust Sharpening, Mid-range sharpening, and Clarity by selecting each of them in the same manner as we are doing now with Contrast. From the screen shown in figure 7.11D, image 1, you can make Contrast adjustments directly without using the secondary screen shown in figure 7.11D, image 2. To adjust Contrast by –/+ 1.00 step, scroll left or right with the Multi selector pad, one press for each 1.00 step increment, left for – and right for +. To adjust in much finer 0.25 step increments, turn the front Sub-command dial left or right, one click for each 0.25 step increment. If you prefer, you can set the Contrast setting to Auto mode, asking the camera to decide how much contrast to use, by examining the subject. To select Auto mode, scroll all the way to the left until AUTO shows where 0.00 is currently displayed, or you can press the Zoom in button to the left of the Menu button, or you can tap on the A control (red arrow). Auto mode is available for the Quick sharp, Contrast and Saturation settings only. Now let's see how to use the secondary fine-tuning screen. To open the secondary screen, tap the area I highlighted in red for the Contrast control. I have not found a way to open the secondary screen without tapping the adjustment area of a setting on the primary screen.

6. Figure 7.11D, image 2, displays the secondary fine-tuning screen. You have a range of –3.00 (–3) to +3.00 (+3) steps of contrast adjustment. Use the outside left and right pointers on the bottom of the screen to adjust in –/+ 1.00 increments, or use the inside pointers to adjust in –/+ 0.25 increments. Press the Back control in the top-right corner of the screen when you are done, which will save the settings and return you to the main adjustment screen (image 1).

Now that you have adjusted a Nikon Picture Control away from its factory default settings, it would be good to know how to return the control to its default settings. Let's consider how to reset a Picture Control (figure 7.11E).

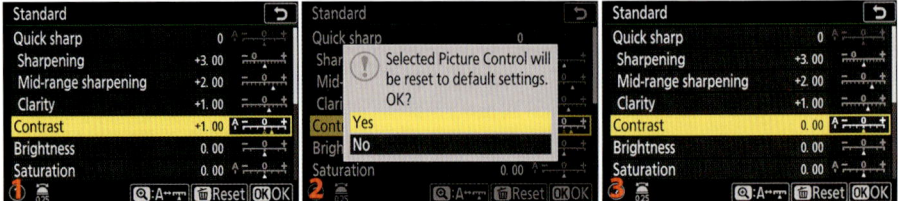

Figure 7.11E: Resetting a Nikon Picture Control

Use the following steps to reset a Picture Control:

1. Open the adjustment screen for the Picture Control you want to reset. We are resetting the Standard (SD) Picture Control in which we previously adjusted the Contrast by +1.00 steps Sharper (figure 7.11E, image 1). To reset the SD Picture Control only, press the Delete button (garbage can), or tap the Reset control at the bottom of the screen.
2. A box will appear that says, *Selected Picture Control will be reset to default settings. OK?* (figure 7.11E, image 2). Select Yes and press the OK button or tap Yes to reset the Picture Control. In figure 7.11E, image 3, you will notice that Contrast has been reset to 0.00. If we had adjusted any or all of the other settings in addition Contrast, resetting the control would have returned everything to factory default settings.

Note: If you choose to modify a Picture Control using Quick Sharp or with the individual line item settings (e.g., Contrast, Brightness), it is not yet a Custom Picture Control because you have not saved it under a new name. Instead, it is merely a modified Nikon Picture Control. We'll discuss how to name and save your own Custom Picture Controls in the upcoming section, **Manage Picture Control** (page 330).

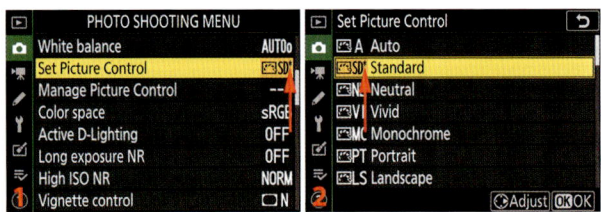

Figure 7.11F: An adjusted Nikon Picture Control (see asterisks)

Figure 7.11F, images 1 and 2 (red arrows) show an asterisk after the Standard control (SD*). This asterisk appears after you have made a modification to any of the Picture Control's inner settings (e.g., Contrast). The asterisk will go away if you reset the Picture Control to its factory settings.

Selecting or Fine-Tuning a Picture Control from the *i* Menu

Because many of us change Picture Controls often, Nikon has given us a fast way to access the Picture Control menu (figure 7.11G)—the *i* Menu. Let's see how to use it.

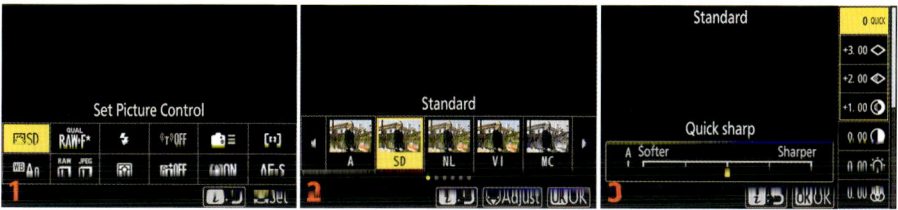

Figure 7.11G: Using the *i* Menu to open Set Picture Control

Use the following steps to set a Picture Control, or fine-tune it by using the *i* Menu:

1. Press the *i* button on the camera's back, just below the Sub-selector joystick. The *i* Menu will open (figure 7.11G, image 1). Enter the Picture Control selection screen by scrolling to the Set Picture Control location and pressing the OK button, or by tapping the location.

2. The Picture Control selection screen allows you to select one of the camera's eight regular Picture Controls, or one of the 20 Creative Picture Controls, by scrolling left or right with the Multi selector pad and highlighting the control, or by swiping with your fingertip and tapping the Picture Control you want to select (figure 7.11G, image 2). When you have the control selected, press or touch OK to choose the control. If you want to fine-tune the control, press down on the Multi selector pad with the Picture Control you want to adjust highlighted, or tap the Adjust control.

3. The Picture Control fine-tuning screen will appear, allowing you to choose each of its internal settings for adjustment by scrolling or swiping up or down on the settings list on the right and then selecting the setting you want to adjust (figure 7.11G, image 3). Once you have the setting highlighted (e.g., Quick sharp), tap the Softer or Sharper side, or scroll left or right. You can adjust this particular setting by –/+ 2.00 steps and many of the other settings by –/+ 3.00 steps.

The *i* Menu works in a similar manner to the discussion we had in the previous subsection for selecting and fine-tuning a Nikon Picture Control from the Photo Shooting Menu. It may be faster to use the *i* Menu to access the Picture Controls, or you might want to assign Set Picture Control to one of the camera's programmable buttons, such as Fn1 or Fn2 (page 423). (**Hint:** Use *Custom Setting Menu > f Controls > f2 Custom control assignment.*)

MC Picture Control Filter Effects and Toning

The Monochrome, or MC, Picture Control has some added features that are enjoyable for those who love black-and-white photography. We will examine the MC control in more detail so you can make use of its special features.

As shown in figure 7.11H, there are Filter effects that simulate the effect of yellow (Y), orange (O), red (R), and green (G) filters on a monochrome image. Yellow, orange, and red (Y, O, R) change the contrast of the sky in black-and-white images. Green (G) is often used in black-and-white portrait work to change the appearance of skin tones. You do not have to buy filters for your lenses; they are included in your Z6!

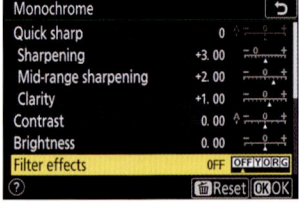

Figure 7.11H: Filter Effects

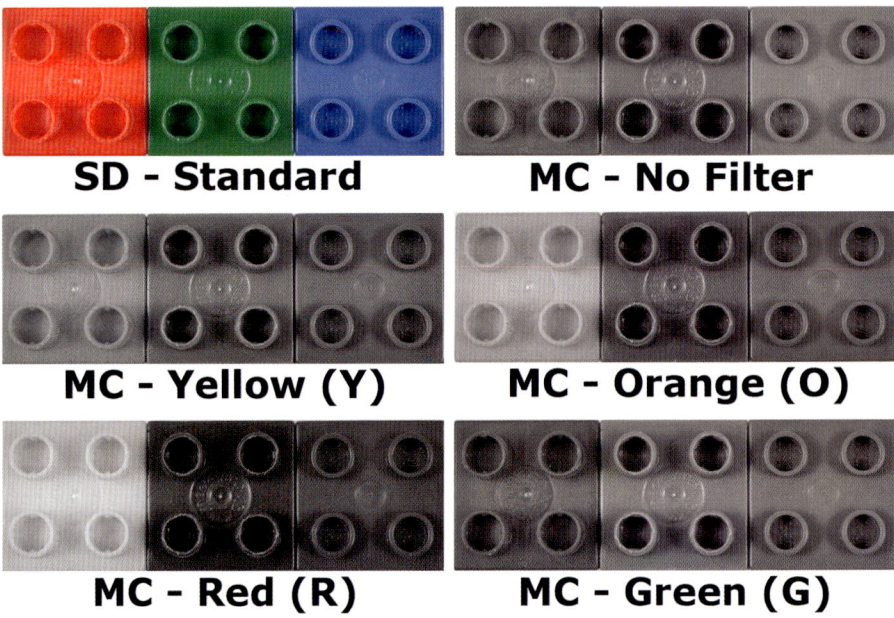

Figure 7.11I: Monochrome Filter effects compared

In figure 7.11I, you'll see an unretouched sample of a color SD Picture Control (for comparison) alongside the five flavors of Monochrome (MC) Filter effects. It is rather interesting how the yellow, orange, red, and green filters affect the RGB Lego blocks. The Filter effects settings are more pronounced than those you would achieve using a glass filter attached to your lens. Now, let's examine the MC Toning effects.

As shown in figure 7.11J, 10 variable Toning effects are available—B&W (standard black-and-white), Sepia, Cyanotype, Red, Yellow, Green, Blue Green, Blue, Purple Blue, and Red Purple. Each of the Toning effects is variable within itself, and you can adjust the saturation of the individual tones. In figure 7.11J, I cranked them all the way up to the maximum setting, which tends to oversaturate the toning color. I wanted you to clearly see the maximum potential of the Toning settings.

Compare how the RGB-colored blocks look under the various toning settings. In each example, three blocks are stacked with red on top, green in the middle, and blue on the bottom. Clearly, the toned blocks all look similar in brightness (with only minor variation) to the B&W blocks, showing that the underlying image for each of the color tones is simply black-and-white.

Note on Photoshop for Z6 Black-and-White Images

Since the RGB color channels are still intact in the camera's black-and-white image, you can use Photoshop's Channel Mixer *(Image Menu > Adjustments > Channel Mixer…)* to manipulate the color channels and improve the blacks and whites. If you use Photoshop to play with the channels, be sure to check the Monochrome box on the Channel Mixer window. If you don't, you'll simply add color back into your black-and-white image. The fact that you must check the Monochrome box proves that a Z6 black-and-white image is really just a color image with the colors desaturated to levels of gray. The good thing about this is that you now have room to play with the three color channels, similar to how you use filters when shooting black-and-white film. You can increase or decrease contrast by moving the channel sliders until you are happy with the results. There is a lot of discussion of these techniques on the Internet. Why not join the Nikonians.org forum to discuss how to best achieve beautiful black-and-white images? Look for the Nikonians Gold Membership discount coupon in the front of this book.

You can shoot a basic black-and-white image, use filters to change how colors appear, or tone the image in experimental ways. Can you see the potential for a lot of fun with these tones?

In the Monochrome menu screen at the top left of figure 7.11J, notice that to the right of the word Toning is a row of tiny colored rectangles. The first rectangle is half black and half white; that is the normal black-and-white (B&W) selection, and it has no extra toning. Next to that you'll see a golden-brown rectangle; that is the Sepia toning effect (selected). To the right of that is the bluish Cyanotype effect. The smaller rectangles that follow the first three selections are the other available colors for toning.

Figure 7.11J (physical controls) and figure 7.11K (touch controls) show how to adjust the depth of color saturation for the 10 available toning colors. Each color has seven major saturation gradations available, as shown in the little bar tinted the same color as the one you have selected for toning—in this case, Sepia. This saturation adjustment bar allows you to select the depth of saturation for each of the colors. In figure 7.11J, the setting has been moved from Sepia, 4.00 (default) to Sepia, 5.00. The higher the number, the deeper the saturation, and vice versa.

Use these steps to adjust the depth of color saturation for toning an image (figure 7.11J):

1. Scroll to Toning on the Monochrome screen, and then press left or right on the Multi selector pad to select a color (e.g., B&W, Sepia, Cyanotype). Alternatively, you can touch the small toning box (figure 7.11J, red arrow) and a larger version will open (figure 7.11K), allowing you to use touch controls to make adjustments.
2. As shown in figure 7.11J, to make adjustments to the saturation level of the Toning color, first press down on the Multi selector pad to select the saturation adjustment

bar below the color selections, and then press right or left to make one-step saturation adjustments. The available saturation adjustment range is from 0.00 to 7.00, with the default being level 4.00 saturation. For adjustments finer than one step, turn the front Sub-command dial in 0.25 increments to select more or less color saturation. Alternatively, if you use the touch controls seen in figure 7.11K, you can touch a tone (color) to select it, and then use the slider touch controls to adjust the color saturation.

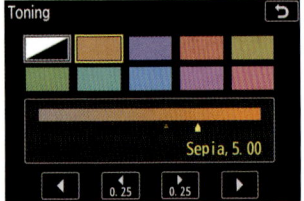

Figure 7.11K: Toning saturation touch controls (see figure 7.11J)

3. Make your Toning saturation-level selection and then press the OK button to lock in the new saturation level.

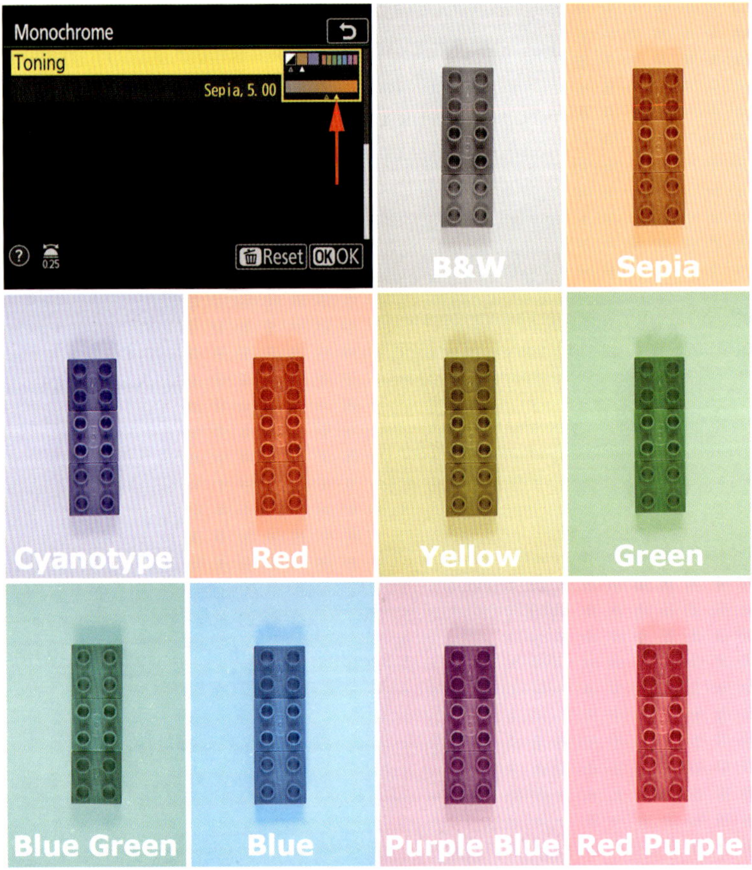

Figure 7.11J: Monochrome Toning screen and samples

I'm sure you will agree that Nikon's Picture Control system is very powerful and flexible, especially for those who like to shoot mostly JPEG images. Now, let's see how to go about managing your own Custom Picture Controls in our next section, **Manage Picture Control**.

Manage Picture Control

The *Manage Picture Control* function is designed to allow you to create and store Custom Picture Control settings for future use. You can take an existing Nikon Picture Control—A, SD, NL, VI, MC, PT, LS, FL, or one of the 20 Creative Picture Controls—and make modifications to it, and then rename it.

If you modify a Picture Control using the Set Picture Control function discussed in the previous section, you simply create a one-off setting. If you'd like to go further and create your own named Custom Picture Controls, the Z6 is happy to oblige. There are four choices on the Manage Picture Control screen:

- Save/edit
- Rename
- Delete
- Load/save

Let's look at each of these settings and see how to manage Picture Controls effectively.

Save/Edit a Custom Picture Control

There are six screens used to Save/edit a Nikon Picture Control (figure 7.12A), storing the results for later use as a Custom Picture Control.

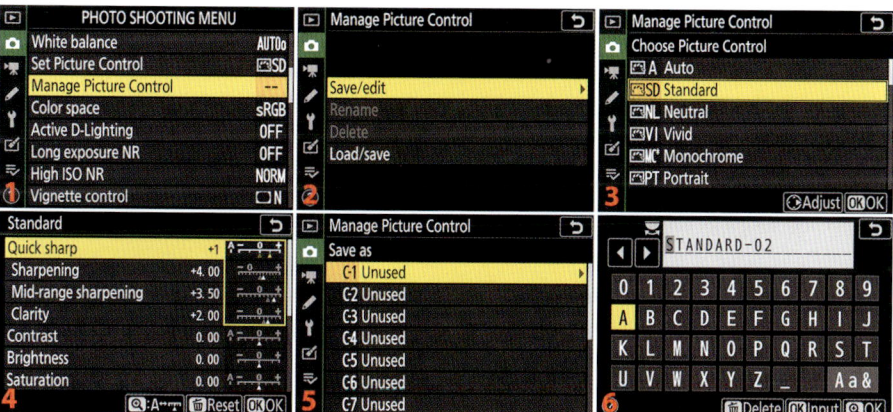

Figure 7.12A: Save/edit a Custom Picture Control

Here are the steps to edit and save a Picture Control with modified settings and a new name:

1. Select Manage Picture Control from the Photo Shooting Menu and scroll to the right (figure 7.12A, image 1).
2. Highlight Save/edit and scroll to the right (figure 7.12A, image 2).

3. Choose a Picture Control that you want to use as a base for your new settings and then scroll to the right (figure 7.12A, image 3). We will modify the SD Standard Picture Control and save it under a different name.

4. Make your adjustments to Sharpening, Contrast, and so forth. I simply used the Quick sharp setting and added +1 to it, increasing the overall effect of Standard by +1 (out of 2). When you have modified the control in a way that makes it yours, press or touch OK (figure 7.12A, image 4). If you want to abandon your changes and start over, you can simply press the Delete button or tap Reset, and it will reset the control to factory specs.

5. Select one of nine storage areas named C-1 to C-9 and scroll to the right (figure 7.12A, image 5). In figure 7.12A, image 5, they are all currently marked as Unused. I can save as many as nine different Custom Picture Controls here for later selection with Set Picture Control.

6. You will now see the Rename screen (figure 7.12A, image 6), which works just like the other touch screens you have used to rename things. Insert a new name for the control by selecting characters from the list at the bottom of the screen and tapping the Input control at the bottom of the screen for each character. You can tap the characters you want to use and they will appear in the position marked with the dark-gray cursor in the name field (STANDARD-02). You can tap on the left/right arrows in the top-left corner to move left and right in the name field. To change case from upper to lower, tap the Aa& button in the lower-right corner of the screen (just above OK). If you make a mistake, position the dark-gray cursor over the error and tap Delete at the bottom of the screen. When you have the name completed, press or touch OK to save it. The word *Saved* will appear briefly on the Monitor. The camera will create a default name for you by appending a dash and two numbers at the end of the current control name in case you do not want to change the name yourself. I left it at the default of STANDARD-02.

Once you have created and saved a Custom Picture Control, you can still tell which control was used as its base, just in case you name it in a way that does not suggest its origins. Notice the red arrow in figure 7.12B pointing to the Picture Control type that is the base for our new control. STANDARD-02 is the control we just created in the previous steps, and it was derived from an SD Nikon Picture Control, as shown by the SD label at the top right of the screen.

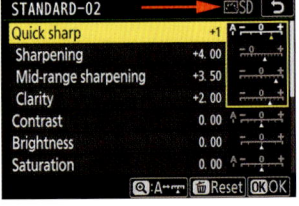

Figure 7.12B: Identifying the base of a Custom Picture Control

You can switch between your Custom Picture Controls and the basic Nikon Picture Controls by using Set Picture Control (see previous section titled **Set Picture Control** on page 200). In other words, each of your newly named Custom Picture Controls will appear in the Set Picture Control menu (below the Nikon Picture Controls and Creative Picture Controls) for later selection.

Now, let's look at how to rename an existing Custom Picture Control.

Rename a Custom Picture Control

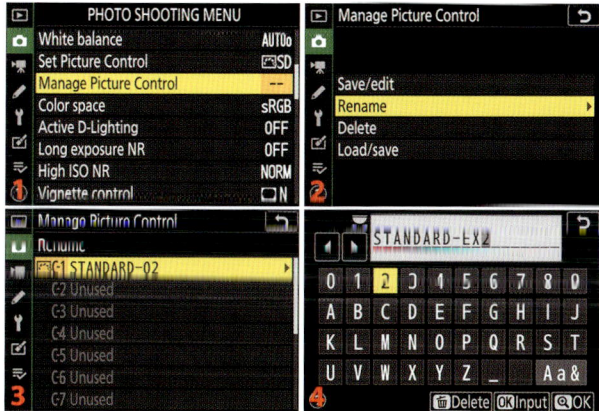

Figure 7.12C: Rename a Custom Picture Control

If you decide to rename an existing Custom Picture Control, you can do so with the following steps:

1. Select Manage Picture Control from the Photo Shooting Menu and scroll to the right (figure 7.12C, image 1).
2. Select Rename and scroll to the right (figure 7.12C, image 2).
3. Select one of your Custom Picture Controls from the list (C-1 to C-9) and scroll to the right (figure 7.12C, image 3). I selected to rename STANDARD-02. This is the Custom Picture Control we created in the preceding subsection. You will now be presented with the Rename screen (figure 7.12C, image 4). Insert characters in the new name by positioning the gray cursor where you want a character to appear and selecting a character from the list at the bottom of the screen. You can tap the characters you want and they will appear in the position marked with the dark-gray cursor in the name field (STANDARD-02). You can use the left/right arrows in the top-left corner to move the gray cursor left and right in the name field. To change case from upper to lower, touch the Aa& control in the lower-right corner of the screen (just above OK). If you make a mistake, position the dark-gray cursor over the error and tap Delete at the bottom of the screen. When you have the name completed, press or touch OK to save it. You will see the word *Saved* appear briefly on the Monitor. I renamed the STANDARD-02 Custom Picture Control STANDARD-EX2.

Interestingly, you can have more than one control with exactly the same name in your list of Custom Picture Controls. The camera does not get confused because each control has a different location (C-1 to C-9) to keep it separate from the rest. However, I don't suggest that you give several custom controls the same name. How would you tell them apart?

When a Custom Picture Control is no longer needed, you can easily delete it; let's see how.

Delete a Custom Picture Control

You cannot delete a Nikon Picture Control or a Creative Picture Control. In fact, they don't even appear in any of the Manage Picture Control menu screens.

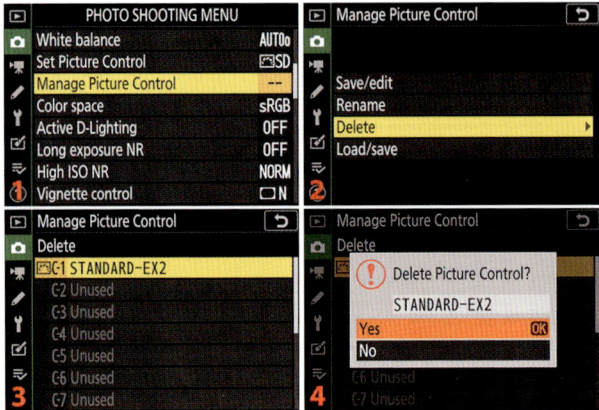

Figure 7.12D: Deleting a Custom Picture Control

However, you can delete one or more of your Custom Picture Controls with the following screens and steps:

1. Follow the screen flow shown in figure 7.12D, images 1 and 2 (*Manage picture control > Delete*) until you arrive at the third screen in the series.
2. Select one of the nine available Custom Picture Controls and scroll to the right, or tap the control (figure 7.12D, image 3).
3. Choose Yes at the *Delete Picture Control?* prompt (figure 7.12D, image 4) and press or touch OK to delete the unneeded control.

Now, let's move to our final menu selection from the Manage Picture Control screen, Load/save.

Load/Save a Custom Picture Control

There are three parts to the Load/save function. They allow you to copy Custom Picture Controls to and from the memory card, or delete them from the card.

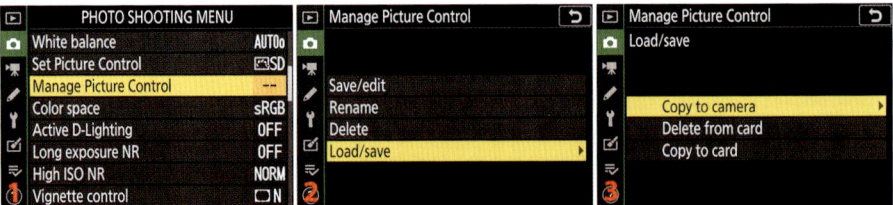

Figure 7.12E: Load/save a Custom Picture Control

Here are the three selections on the Load/save menu, as shown in figure 7.12E, image 3:

- **Copy to camera:** Loads Custom Picture Controls from the memory card into your camera. You can store up to nine controls in your camera's nine available memory locations (C1–C9).
- **Delete from card:** Displays a list of any Custom Picture Controls found on the memory card. You can selectively delete them.
- **Copy to card:** Allows you to copy your carefully crafted Custom Picture Controls (C1–C9) from your camera to a memory card. You can then share them with others. The camera will display up to 99 control locations (01–99) on any single memory card.

Let's examine each of these selections and see how best to use them.

Copy to Camera

You can use the Copy to camera function to copy Custom Picture Controls from your camera's memory card to the camera's Set Picture Control menu. Once you have transferred a Custom Picture Control from your memory card to your camera, it will show up in the *Photo Shooting Menu > Set Picture Control* menu.

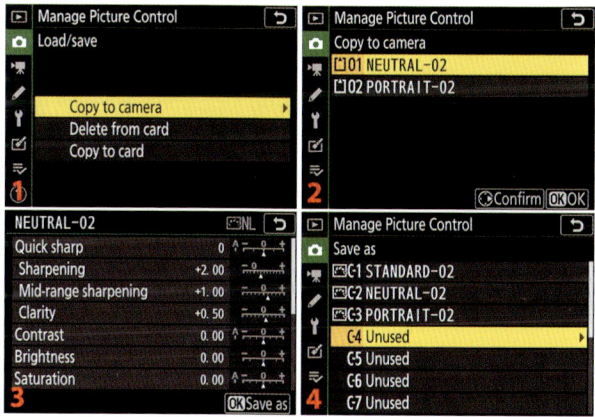

Figure 7.12F: Manage Picture Control – Copy to camera

Here are the steps to copy a Custom Picture Control from the memory card to the camera itself:

1. Figure 7.12F continues from the previous screen shown in figure 7.12E (*Manage Picture Control > Load/save > Copy to camera*). Choose Copy to camera and scroll to the right (figure 7.12F, image 1).
2. You will be presented with the list of Custom Picture Controls that are currently on the memory card (figure 7.12F, image 2). If there are no controls on the memory card, the camera will display a screen that says, *No Picture Control file found on memory card.* Figure 7.12F, image 2, shows two controls—NEUTRAL-02 and PORTRAIT-02. Select a

control from the list and press or touch OK. (If you scroll to the right instead, you will be able to examine and adjust the control's settings before saving it to your camera, as seen in figure 7.12F, image 3. If you don't want to modify it, simply press or touch OK.)

3. You will now see the Manage Picture Control Save as menu, which lists any Custom Picture Controls already in your camera (figure 7.12F, image 4). Select one of the Unused memory locations and scroll to the right.

4. You'll now be presented with the Rename screen, just in case you want to change the name of the Custom Picture Control (figure 7.12G). If you don't want to change the name, simply press or touch OK and the custom control will be added to your camera's Set Picture Control menu. It is okay to have multiple controls with exactly the same name. The camera keeps each control separate in its list of controls (C–1 to C–9). However, I always rename them to prevent future confusion. Insert a new name for the control

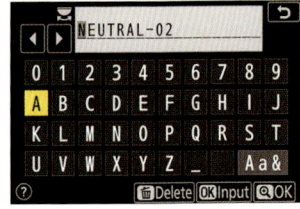

Figure 7.12G: Manage Picture Control – Choose a new name (or Rename)

by selecting characters from the list at the bottom of the screen, and tap Input at the bottom of the screen for each character. You can tap on the characters you want to use and they will appear in the position marked with the dark-gray cursor in the name field (NEUTRAL-02). You can use the left/right arrows in the top-left corner to move left and right in the name field. To change case from upper to lower, tap on Aa& in the lower-right corner of the screen (just above OK). If you make a mistake, position the dark-gray cursor over the error and tap Delete at the bottom of the screen. When you have the name completed, press or touch OK to save it. The word *Saved* will appear briefly on the Monitor. The name is limited to 19 characters.

Now let's examine how to delete a Custom Picture Control that you no longer need from where it is stored on the memory card.

Delete from Card

Once you've finished loading Custom Picture Controls or optional Nikon Picture Controls to your camera, you may be ready to delete a control or two from the memory card. You could format the memory card, but that will blow away all images and Picture Controls on the card. The Delete from card function is a less drastic method that allows you to be more selective in removing Picture Controls.

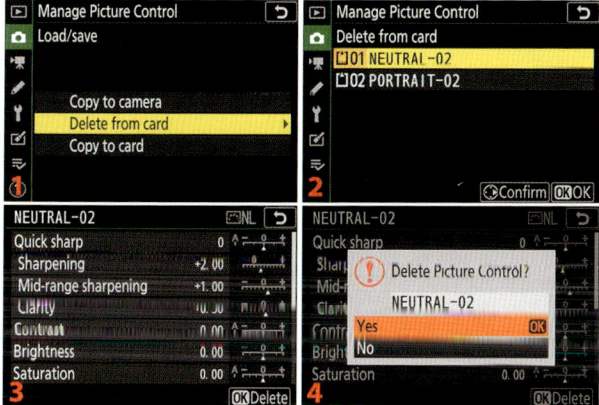

Figure 7.12H: Manage Picture Control – Delete from card

Here are the steps used to remove Custom Picture Controls from your camera's memory card:

1. Figure 7.12H continues where figure 7.12E ended. Choose Delete from card from the Load/save menu and scroll to the right (figure 7.12H, image 1).
2. Choose one of the Custom Picture Controls that you want to delete (figure 7.12H, image 2). I chose NEUTRAL-02. You can confirm that you are deleting the correct control by scrolling to the right, which gives you the fine-tuning screen with current adjustments for that control (figure 7.12H, image 3). If you are sure this is the control you want to delete, move on to the next step by pressing or touching OK.
3. You will be shown a screen that asks, *Delete Picture Control?* Choose Yes or No (figure 7.12H, image 4). If you choose Yes, the Picture Control will be deleted from the memory card. If you choose No, the camera will return to the previous screen. Press or touch OK to execute your choice.

Next, let's examine the method for copying a carefully crafted Custom Picture Control to a memory card so that you can share it with others or store it off-camera.

Copy to Card

After you create up to nine Custom Picture Controls using the instructions in the previous few sections, you can use the Copy to card function to save them to a memory card. Once they are on a memory card, you can use your custom controls on your other Nikons or share them with your friends who have compatible Nikon cameras.

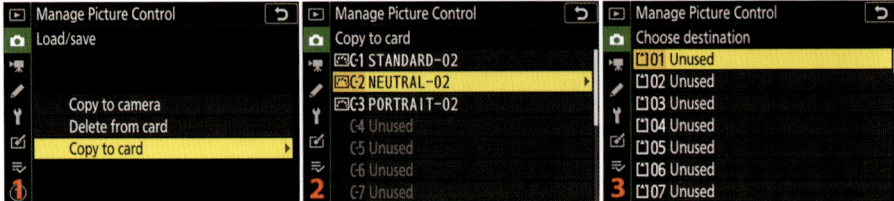

Figure 7.12I: Manage Picture Control – Copy to card

When your Custom Picture Controls are ready to go, use the following steps to copy them to a memory card:

1. Figure 7.12I continues where figure 7.12E ends. Choose Copy to card from the Load/save menu and scroll to the right (figure 7.12I, image 1).
2. Select one of your current Custom Picture Controls from the Copy to card menu and scroll to the right (figure 7.12I, image 2). I chose NEUTRAL-02 to copy to the memory card.
3. Now you'll use the Choose destination menu to select the location in which you want to save the custom control (figure 7.12I, image 3). You have 99 choices; select any Unused location. You do not have to save to the next available Unused location since any of the 99 numbers are available. Be careful, though! If you select a location with an existing Custom Picture Control already there and save it, the camera will immediately overwrite the existing control with no warning. When you are ready, press the OK button or tap the Unused location and you'll briefly see a screen that says *Data saved to memory card*. Your Custom Picture Control is now ready to distribute to the world or load onto another of your compatible Nikon cameras.

Where Is the Custom Control Stored on the Memory Card?

If you take the time to look at the contents of your camera's memory card on your computer once you've saved a Custom Picture Control, you'll find a new folder called NIKON with a subfolder called CUSTOMPC. This folder contains any Custom Picture Controls you might have saved, each with a file name ending in ".NP3." For instance, the NEUTRAL-02 Custom Picture Control we saved to the memory card in destination 02 is saved to the memory card as PICCON02.NP3 in the CUSTOMPC subfolder. If I had used the first destination location (01), the file name would have been PICCON01.NP3. Therefore, you should realize that the memory card destination locations 01–99 are actually individual files in the CUSTOMPC folder, with a range of file names from PICCON01.NP3 to PICCON99.NP3P. Now you can access the saved custom controls for sharing or for backup to your computer.

Color Space

Using a *Color space* is an interesting and important part of digital photography. They help your image files fit into a much broader range of imaging devices. Software, printers, monitors, and other devices recognize which Color space is attached to your image and use it, along with other color profiles, to help balance the image to the correct output colors for the device in use.

The color spaces available on the Nikon Z6—sRGB and Adobe RGB—each have a different gamut, or range of color. We'll discuss which might be better after we look into how to select one of the Color spaces.

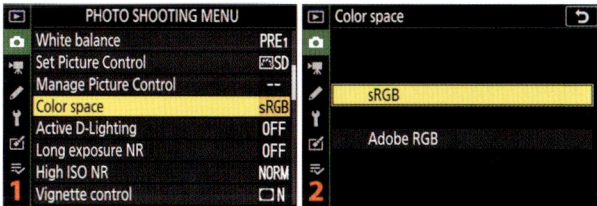

Figure 7.13A: Choosing a Color space

Here's how to select your favorite Color space:

1. Choose Color space from the Photo Shooting Menu and scroll to the right (figure 7.13A, image 1).
2. Select the Color space setting that you want to use, keeping in mind that Adobe RGB has a larger color gamut (figure 7.13A, image 2). Adobe RGB is better for commercial printing and publication, whereas sRGB may be better for social media use, snapshots, home printing, and movies. Press the OK button or tap your selection to lock it in.

Now, let's look a little more deeply into how Color space works.

Which Color Space Is Best Technically?

There is a large color space used by the graphics industry called CIELAB, which approximates human vision (figure 7.13B). Adobe RGB covers about 50 percent of the CIELAB color space, whereas sRGB uses only 35 percent. In other words, Adobe RGB has a wider gamut. That means Adobe RGB gives your images access to significantly higher levels of color, especially cyans and greens.

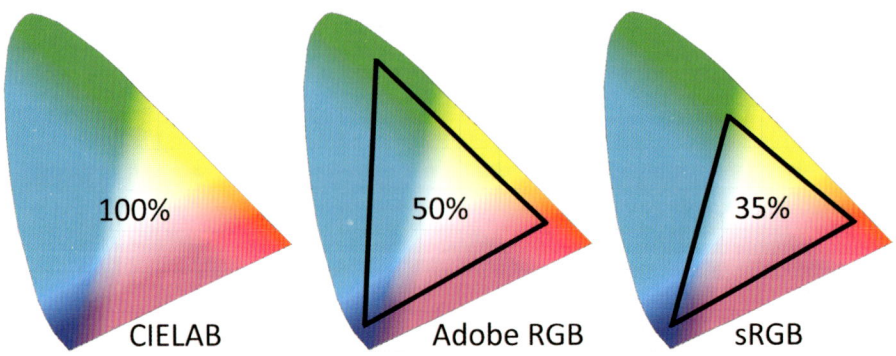

Figure 7.13B: Color space graphs

Another important consideration for those who will be sending their work to companies that use commercial digital printing—such as book and magazine publishers—is that Adobe RGB maps very well to the CMYK offset printing process. If you are shooting commercial work, you may want to seriously consider Adobe RGB if you want your images to look their best in print. Stock photography shooters are nearly always required to shoot in Adobe RGB.

For home use, such as printing on personal inkjet printers, posting images on the web, and printing images at the local superstore, the sRGB color space is fine.

Once a JPEG file is created—in-camera or in-computer—the color gamuts for both Adobe RGB and sRGB are compressed into the same number of color levels. A JPEG has only 256 levels for each of its red, green, and blue (RGB) channels. However, since Adobe RGB takes its colors from a wider spectrum, you will have a better representation of reality when there are lots of colors in your image.

Of course, when shooting in NEF (RAW), the Color space setting is just a convenience for initial display in your computer before the RAW file is converted to another format, such as JPEG. A RAW file's Color space can be changed after the fact to Adobe RGB, sRGB, or to another Color space if one is available in your RAW conversion software.

To simplify your RAW workflow, you still may want to consider using Adobe RGB so that you don't have to add Color space conversion to the tasks you must perform for RAW conversion. If you are a commercial shooter, just leave your camera set to Adobe RGB for convenience. Again, *it really doesn't matter* when you are shooting in NEF (RAW) format because the Color space can easily be changed after the fact in post-processing, with no damage to the image. If you are a RAW shooter and regularly post-process your images, you should consider using Adobe RGB, just for convenience.

There are some drawbacks to using Adobe RGB, though, for non-commercial photographers. The sRGB color space is widely used in home printing and display devices. Even many local labs print using sRGB because so many point-and-shoot digital camera users bring their pictures to them in that format. If you try to print directly to some inkjet printers using the Adobe RGB color space, the colors may not be as brilliant as with sRGB because many inkjets are designed for home printing and sRGB. For internet usage, such as for posting images on social media, sRGB is the expected norm and may make more saturated-looking JPEG images on most computer monitors and smart devices.

For JPEG or TIFF shooters, it is much more critical that the best Color space setting is used because once the image is made, the Color space cannot be changed. Yes, you can modify and resave a JPEG file, changing its color balance somewhat, but that lowers the quality of a JPEG image due to re-compression losses, and it is hard to get a good color balance when major changes of that type are made. If you are shooting JPEG, get it exactly right when you take the picture and your images will be much better. JPEGs are not really designed for heavy post-processing—they should be considered a final product. If you really want to modify your images after the fact, learn how to process RAW files instead.

If you are shooting JPEG images professionally, such as for stock images, or magazine and book printing, most places expect you'll be using Adobe RGB. It has a wider gamut of colors, so it's the quality standard for commercial printing.

Technical Note: If you print to devices that do not support color management, use ExifPrint, or print directly on some household printers or at superstore kiosk printers, the print's colors may not be as vivid when using Adobe RGB. JPEG pictures taken in Adobe RGB color space are DCF compliant. Applications and devices that support the DCF protocol will automatically select the correct color space. If you shoot in TIFF, the camera will imbed an ICC color profile when you shoot in Adobe RGB. Applications and devices that support color management will automatically select the correct color space setting when using the TIFF file. It is a good idea to familiarize yourself with the capabilities of the device you are about to use so you can determine its color space capabilities. Nikon Capture NX-D software automatically selects the correct color space when opening your pictures.

Settings Recommendation: I use Adobe RGB most of the time because I shoot a lot of nature with a wide range of color and I don't want to change Color spaces later during final RAW to JPEG conversion. I want color that's as accurate as my camera will give me. Adobe RGB has a wider range of colors, so it can be more accurate when a wide range of colors is present in your subject. If you are shooting Optimal quality JPEGs (e.g., JPEG fine ★) for commercial purposes, I would still carefully consider using Adobe RGB. Even with a JPEG's more limited color capacity, the colors in the JPEG represent a broader range of color when you use Adobe RGB. However, if you are just shooting JPEG snapshots or movies, there is no need to worry about this. Leave the camera set to sRGB and have fun.

Active D-Lighting

Active D-Lighting is used to help control contrast in your images. Often, the range of light within a scene is broader than your camera's sensor can fully capture.

Although the Z6 has excellent dynamic range, it is still possible for the range of light in some situations to exceed the range of the sensor's light-capturing capability. Or, you may just want to have less image contrast.

The Z6 allows you to "D-Light" the image, bringing out additional shadow detail, or in other words, lower the image contrast. This extends the dynamic range by opening up the shadows and protecting the highlights. One of the downsides of using Active D-Lighting could be additional noise in shadow details. The Z6 has excellent noise control, though, so this is less of a problem than with older cameras. Active D-Lighting has these six levels:

- Auto (A)
- Extra high (H*)
- High (H)

- Normal (N)
- Low (L)
- Off (no Active D-Lighting)

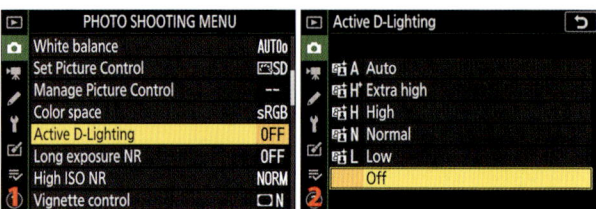

Figure 7.14A: Choosing an Active D-Lighting level

Here are the steps to select an Active D-Lighting level:

1. Choose Active D-Lighting from the Photo Shooting Menu and scroll to the right (figure 7.14A, image 1).
2. Select one of the Active D-Lighting levels (figure 7.14A, image 2), or select Off, and press the OK button or tap the option to save your setting. Refer to figure 7.14C to see how each level affects the image.

Additionally, you can open the Active D-Lighting menu without using the Photo Shooting Menu directly. Instead, you can press the *i* button and select it from the Quick Menu screen (figure 7.14B).

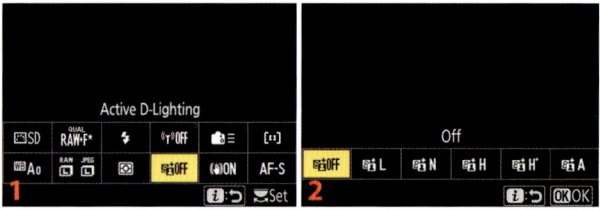

Figure 7.14B: Opening Active D-Lighting from the *i* Menu screen

Use these steps to change Active D-Lighting quickly:

1. Press the *i* button once (figure 7.14B, image 1), which will cause the *i* Menu screen to appear. Scroll to the Active D-Lighting position and press the OK button or tap on the Active D-Lighting symbol. This will open the secondary screen (figure 7.14B, image 2).
2. Choose the setting you want to use and press or touch OK to save the setting (figure 7.14B, image 2).

Now let's take a look at how Active D-Lighting affects a series of images (figure 7.14C).

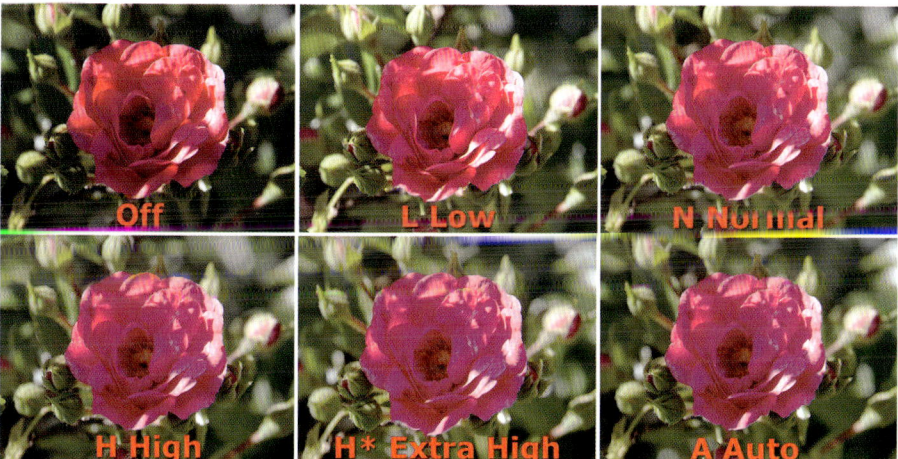

Figure 7.14C: Active D-Lighting samples

Basically, Active D-Lighting will help bring out detail in areas of your image that are hidden in shadow due to excessive image contrast. It also tends to protect the highlights from blowing out (becoming pure white with no detail). Figure 7.14C shows a series of six images with Active D-Lighting set to its various levels. I chose a rosebush scene with heavy shadow and bright highlights (heavy contrast) to see how these six settings performed.

Notice how the Active D-lighting system tends to progressively open the shadows and rein in the highlights. It lowers the overall contrast of the image. At the H* Extra high level, the colors may change a little and you may have a slight HDR (high dynamic range) look, with lower shadow-to-highlight contrast.

Settings Recommendation: You should experiment with the Active D-Lighting settings to see which you like best. Active D-Lighting has the effect of lowering contrast, and some people do not like low-contrast images. Also, whenever you recover lost detail from shadows, there may be extra noise in the recovered areas.

This function can be useful for JPEG shooters in particular. Since you shouldn't modify a JPEG file after shooting it, it's important that the image is created exactly right in the first place. When you are shooting in a high-contrast setting, such as in direct sunlight, some degree of Active D-Lighting may help rein in the contrast.

I am quite impressed with the intelligence of the camera, and when I must get a good shot, such as at a wedding ceremony, I may use Active D-Lighting to keep shadow detail open. It has the added benefit of reining in the highlights, too, so I keep more detail in a bride's dress, which can be hard to do when shooting with flash in a lowlight room.

Experiment with this by shooting images in a high-contrast and a low-contrast setting at all the various levels of Active D-Lighting. You'll see how the camera reacts and you can better decide how you'll use this functionality.

Long Exposure NR

Long exposure NR (noise reduction) is designed to combat visual noise in long exposures. Long-exposure noise is a little different from grainy-looking high-ISO sensitivity noise due to its cause. Nikon says long-exposure noise appears as "bright spots, randomly spaced bright pixels, or fog." Why does this happen? During longer exposures, the imaging sensor can start to warm up a little, especially in warm ambient temperatures. This causes a condition called amp noise, in which warmer sections of the imaging sensor start to display more foggy noise than other sections.

Additionally, when pixels are left turned on for a length of time, a few of them may become brighter than normal and record an improper color, often bright red. Those off-color hot pixels should be removed by the camera. Long exposure NR does just that. (For an explanation of the differences between stuck pixels, hot pixels, and dead pixels, download the **Pixel Problems** document from the downloadable resources website: **http://rocky nook.com/NikonZ6**.)

Long-exposure noise is best handled by this Long exposure NR function, whereas high-ISO noise is well handled by High ISO NR (see the next section). Sometimes, when you are shooting long exposures at higher ISO settings, both may be needed!

Nikon warns that images taken at shutter speeds over 1 second without Long exposure NR may exhibit more long-exposure noise than is acceptable for normal images. There are two settings for Long exposure NR, as shown in figure 7.15.

- *On:* When you select On and the exposure lasts over 1 second (e.g., 2 sec, 10 sec, 30 sec), the camera will take two exposures with the exact same time for each. The first exposure is the normal picture-taking exposure. The second exposure is a dark-frame subtraction exposure, made for the same length of time as the first one but with the shutter closed. The noise (hot pixels and fog) in the dark frame image is examined and then subtracted from the original image. It is really quite effective and beats having to blur the image to get rid of noise. I've taken exposures of around 30 seconds and had perfectly usable results. The only drawback is that the exposure time is doubled because two exposures are made. The dark frame exposure is not written to the memory card, so you'll have only one image, with much less noise, in the end. While the dark frame image is being processed, the words *Job nr* will blink on camera displays. During this second exposure, while *Job nr* is flashing, you cannot use the camera. If you turn it off while *Job nr* is flashing, the camera still keeps the first image; it just doesn't do any noise reduction on it. If Long exposure NR is set to On, the frame advance rate may slow down a little in Continuous release mode, and the capacity of the in-camera memory buffer will drop while the image is being processed.
- *Off:* If you select Off, you will have no long-exposure noise reduction with exposures over 1 second.

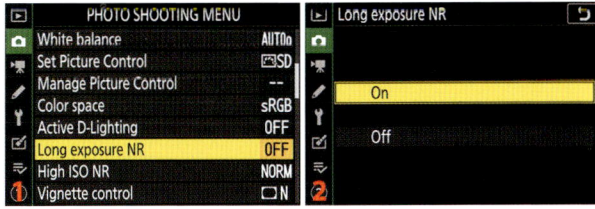

Figure 7.15: Choosing a Long exposure NR setting

Here are the steps to choose a Long exposure NR setting:

1. Choose Long exposure NR from the Photo Shooting Menu and scroll to the right (figure 7.15, image 1).
2. Highlight either On or Off (figure 7.15, image 2) and press the OK button or tap the option to save your setting.

Settings Recommendation: I like the benefits of Long exposure NR. I shoot a lot of waterfall and stream shots where I often need exposures of several seconds to really blur the water. Also, I like to take midnight shots of the sky and shots of city scenes at night. Even though it may slow down the frame rate slightly and allow me fewer images in the in-camera memory buffer for burst shooting, I still use it most of the time.

If I were a sports or action shooter using Continuous release mode, I might leave Long exposure NR turned Off. It's unlikely I would be using exposures over 1 second, and I would want maximum frames per second as well as the ability to cram as many images into the camera buffer as possible. I wouldn't want my camera to slow down while writing images to the memory card.

Your style of shooting will govern whether this function is useful to you. Ask yourself one simple question: "Do I often shoot exposures more than 1 second in length?" If so, you may want Long exposure NR set to On. Compare how the images look with and without it, especially nighttime shots. I think you'll like Long exposure NR.

High ISO NR

High ISO NR (High ISO Noise Reduction) lessens the effects of digital noise in your images when you use high ISO sensitivity (exposure gain) settings by using a blurring and resharpening method. Nikon doesn't specify the exact ISO level at which High ISO NR kicks in. I suspect that a small amount of noise reduction occurs at around ISO 400–800 and gradually increases as the ISO gets higher.

The Z6 has better noise control than most cameras, so it can shoot up to ISO 1600 with little noise. However, no digital camera (that I know of) is completely without noise, so it's a good idea to use some noise reduction above a certain ISO sensitivity.

If High ISO NR is turned Off, the camera still does a small amount of noise reduction—less than the Low setting. Therefore, at higher ISO settings there will always be some noise reduction.

You can control the amount of noise reduction by choosing one of the four High ISO NR settings: High, Normal, Low, or Off. Shoot some high-ISO exposures and decide for yourself which settings you are comfortable with.

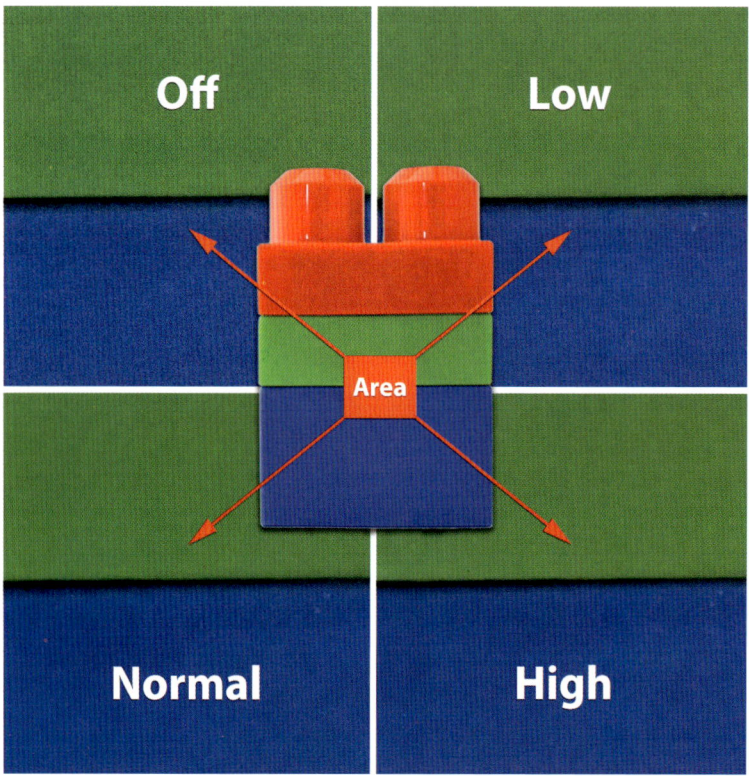

Figure 7.16A: High ISO NR – Off to High correction samples

Figure 7.16A is a sample image of my RGB blocks at ISO 25600 with High ISO NR set to Off, Low, Normal, and High settings. The red rectangle in the little picture of the blocks indicates the area that is shown in the four larger images. These images of the dark subject were shot with no flash, at the camera's highest normal ISO sensitivity setting. It is a worst-case noise scenario (other than the "Hi" ISOs above the normal range).

High ISO NR works by first blurring and then resharpening the image more and more as you increase the setting from Low to High. By blurring the image, the camera blends the grainy noise into the surroundings to make it less visible. Some mild resharpening is applied to restore image sharpness. This whole process tends to make the image lose a little detail at the highest noise reduction settings.

However, the noise (grain) pattern is better than many cameras I've used. This is one excellent FX camera! Let's see how to enable the various High ISO NR levels.

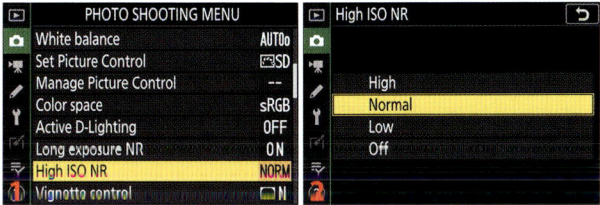

Figure 7.16B: Setting High ISO NR

Use the following steps to choose a High ISO NR setting:

1. Choose High ISO NR from the Photo Shooting Menu and scroll to the right (figure 7.16B, image 1).
2. Highlight one of the noise reduction levels: High, Normal, Low, or Off (figure 7.16B, image 2) and then press the OK button or tap the option to save your setting.

Settings Recommendation: I leave High ISO NR set to Low or Normal. I do want some noise reduction above ISO 1600. However, since any form of noise reduction blurs the image, I don't go too far with it. I shoot RAW, so it really makes no difference because I can change everything later in the computer. If I were shooting JPEGs, it would make a serious difference. Why not test a few images at high ISO sensitivity settings with High ISO NR turned On to see which setting you like? Remember that you can use a different choice for each Photo shooting menu bank setting (A–D) to configure your camera for different shooting styles.

Note: If you choose Off, the camera still does a tiny bit of noise reduction, if needed. Nikon says that it does less noise reduction than the Low setting when set to Off.

What Is Noise?

Have you ever tried to listen to a high-fidelity sound system while children are playing in the same room? It seems like the louder you turn up the music, the louder the kids get. However loud the volume of the music player, the children laughing and running around degrades the pure sound you desire. There is a high child-to-music noise ratio that interferes with your enjoyment of your songs. After a while, you simply have to ask the kids to leave the room.

Noise in a digital image is somewhat similar. You want pure, clean images when you take pictures, but digital noise interferes with the clarity. The higher you turn the camera's ISO sensitivity, the more digital noise degrades your image. The noise-to-signal ratio can damage the picture. How can you make the visual noise go away? Use High ISO NR, that's how!

Vignette Control

Vignette control allows you to reduce the amount of vignetting (slight darkening) that many lenses produce in the corners at wide-open apertures. The angle at which light strikes a sensor on its edges is greater than the angle at which rays go straight through the lens to the center areas of the sensor. Due to the increased angle, some light falloff occurs at the extreme edges of the frame, especially at wide apertures. In recognition of this fact, Nikon has provided the Vignette control setting. It can reduce the vignetting effect to a large degree for Nikkor type G, E, D, and S lenses (excluding PC lenses). If more vignette control is required, you can use Photoshop or Nikon Capture NX-D (or other software) to remove it.

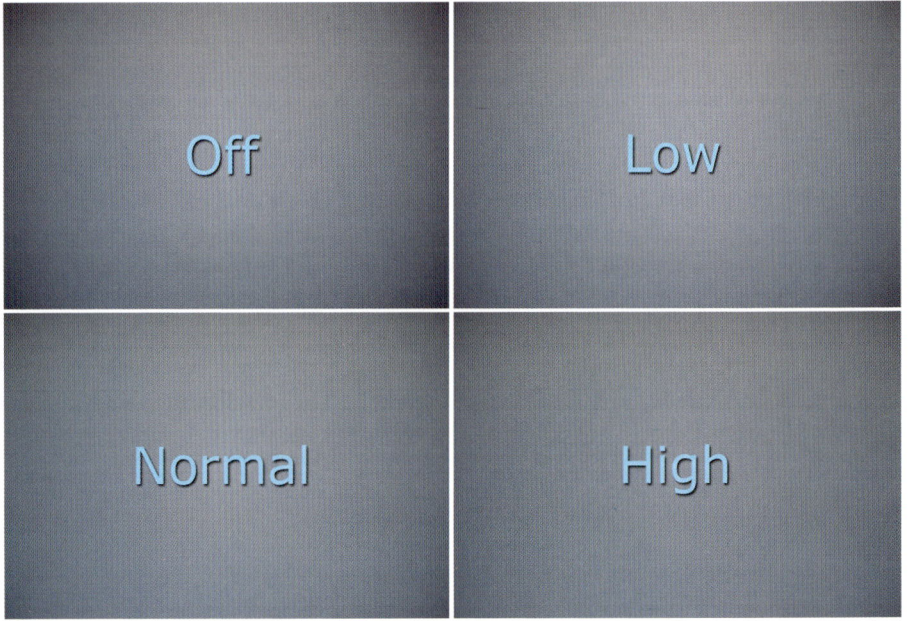

Figure 7.17A: Vignette control choices

Figure 7.17A shows a sample of what the Vignette control can accomplish on its own. I shot four pictures of the sky with an AF-S Nikkor 50mm f/1.4G lens at f/1.4 (wide-open aperture). Each picture has more Vignette control applied, from Off to High. Let's see how to configure the Vignette control for edge light falloff reduction with your lenses.

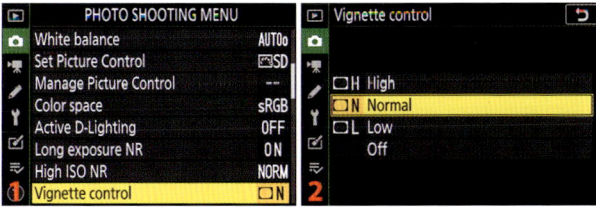

Figure 7.17B: Vignette control range

Here are the steps to choose a Vignette control level for your Z6ı

1. Choose Vignette control from the Photo Shooting Menu and scroll to the right (figure 7.17B, image 1).
2. Highlight a level you want from the list: High, Normal, Low, Off (figure 7.17B, image 2). Then press the OK button or tap the option to lock in the level.

Settings Recommendation: The camera defaulted to Normal from the factory, so I have been shooting most of my images with it set to Normal. I like this control. It does help remove vignetting in the corners when I shoot with the aperture wide open. I have not noticed any additional noise or image degradation in the corrected areas. I suggest leaving your camera set to Normal at all times unless you are shooting with a lens that has a greater tendency to produce vignetting, in which case you can increase it to High. Even High does not seem to fully remove the vignetting when a lens is wide open, so this is not an aggressive algorithm that will leave white spots in the corners of your images. Why not shoot a few shots with your lenses at wide aperture and see how Vignette control works with your lens and camera combinations?

Remember, you can remove vignetting in the computer with post-processing software if the camera's Vignette control setting does not entirely remove the problem.

Diffraction Compensation

Diffraction compensation is designed to help reduce diffraction unsharpness in your images caused by using small apertures (e.g., f/11, f/16, f/22). When light hits the edge of an aperture blade it deflects slightly, arriving at the sensor at a slightly different angle than the light going through the middle of the aperture. This tends to cause the image to be less sharp than an image taken at a larger aperture (e.g., f/4, f/5.6, f/8).

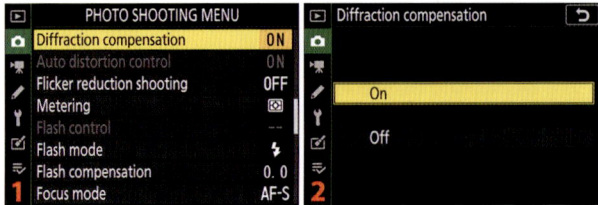

Figure 7.18: Enabling Diffraction compensation

Use the following steps to enable or disable Diffraction compensation:

1. Choose Diffraction compensation from the Photo Shooting Menu and scroll to the right (figure 7.18, image 1).
2. Highlight your choice: On or Off, and press the OK button or tap the option to lock in the setting (figure 7.18, image 2).

Settings Recommendation: Diffraction has been a problem for as long as lenses and apertures have existed. For many years, photographers have tried use mid-sized apertures instead of small apertures to prevent diffraction. I set this function to On and I am happy to have it. I tested it on some landscapes and it does make a difference in sharpness. The Z6 is capable of extra sharpness and this is one of the reasons. Why not test this for yourself and see if you have sharper images with Diffraction compensation enabled? It defaults to enabled and I left it that way permanently on my Z6.

Auto Distortion Control

Auto distortion control is designed to automatically reduce barrel and pincushion distortion in your images. It will try to keep lines straight but may crop the edges of your image in the process. This function may be best used by architectural photographers who are concerned about keeping lines and edges straight, for obvious reasons.

The Auto distortion control is designed to be used with Nikkor G, E, and D lenses; not PC, fisheye and aftermarket lenses, nor movies. Using the control may slow down the image processing functions of the camera as distortion is calculated and removed.

What is barrel and pincushion distortion?

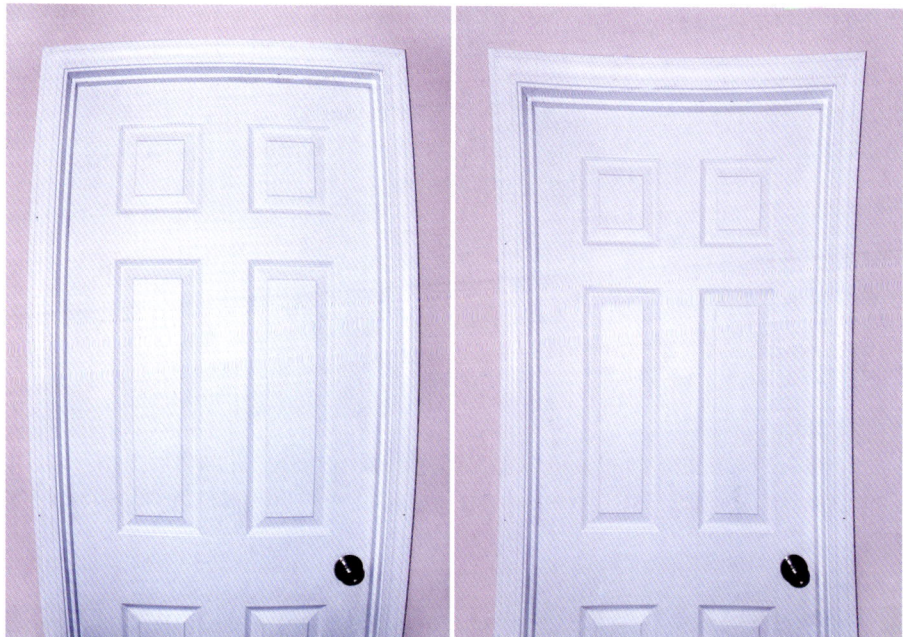

Figure 7.19A: Extreme examples of barrel (left) and pincushion (right) distortion

Figure 7.19A shows a greatly exaggerated example of the two distortion types. If you have a lens that does this, you might want to dispose of it, unless it is a fisheye or extreme wide angle, of course.

To prevent even mild cases of these two distortion types from ruining images that contain straight lines, you can use this control. Of course, if you are out shooting nature shots or portraits, it is unlikely that you will gain much benefit from this function. If you need automatic barrel and pincushion distortion control, you will already know it from previous work.

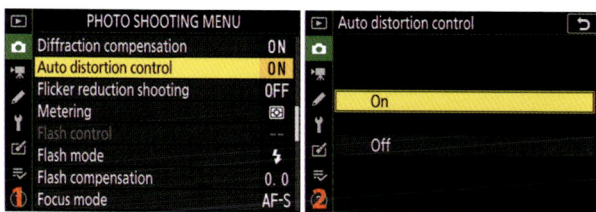

Figure 7.19B: Auto distortion control

Use these steps to enable or disable Auto distortion control:

1. Choose Auto distortion control from the Photo Shooting Menu and scroll to the right (figure 7.19B, image 1).
2. Highlight On or Off (figure 7.19B, image 2) and press the OK button or tap the option to save the setting.

Settings Recommendation: If you are a photographer who really needs this function, you will already know it. If you question whether it will benefit you, it probably won't. I prefer to remove distortion using software on my computer because I am working with a much larger image and can more easily see what needs to be done. This is an automatic function in the Z6 and, like most automatic functions, does great sometimes but has little benefit most of the time. However, this may be a handy function for times when you are out in the field shooting and you need some distortion correction immediately. Just watch out and allow for edge cropping.

Flicker Reduction Shooting

Flicker reduction helps control the banding or flicker you may see when photographing under certain lighting types, such as fluorescent and mercury-vapor lighting. These types of lights do not output a constant stream of light. Instead, they rapidly pulse the light at a rate that is much faster than a human can normally detect. However, this flickering light can affect photographs and cause exposure problems.

The Nikon Z6 has the ability to time the taking of a photograph to reduce the effects of this flickering. When you press the Shutter-release button under those types of lights, the camera will attempt to fire the shutter during a full brightness pulse of the light, leading to better exposures. If you rarely shoot important pictures under fluorescent or mercury-vapor lighting, you may want to ignore the function.

Let's see how to enable and disable Flicker reduction.

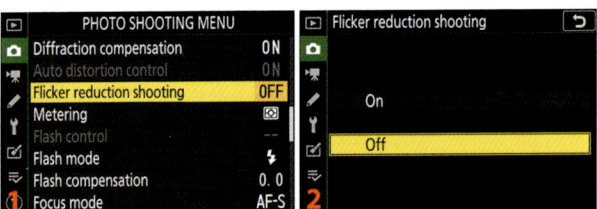

Figure 7.20: Enabling or disabling Flicker reduction

Use these steps to enable or disable the Flicker reduction function:

1. Choose Flicker reduction shooting from the Photo Shooting Menu and scroll to the right (figure 7.20, image 1).
2. Highlight On or Off on the menu (figure 7.20, image 2) and press the OK button or tap your selection to save the setting.

Note: The frame rate can be affected when Flicker reduction is enabled. If you are shooting in Continuous H (Extended) mode (page 100), with Custom Setting d4 Exposure delay mode enabled (page 402), in HDR mode (page 283), or at a shutter speed slower than 1/100s, Flicker reduction shooting is automatically disabled.

Settings Recommendation: I enable Flicker reduction shooting only when I shoot events where there is fluorescent light (graduations and weddings).

If you are primarily an outdoor sports shooter and photograph under natural light only, you can safely disable the function. Doing so will ensure that you have the maximum shooting frame rate. Be careful, though, if you are shooting night sports under artificial lighting.

Metering

The Metering function allows you to control the type of light meter your camera uses to choose a good exposure. There are four types of meters available in the Nikon Z6. Here is a description of each type:

- *Matrix metering:* The camera meters a wide area of the frame using a matrix of zones and an internal database of patterns from thousands of images. It uses these patterns along with tone distribution, color, composition, and subject distance to capture the best exposure for the subject. Matrix metering is accurate in most cases and is generally used as a default setting by most photographers.
- *Center-weighted metering:* The camera measures light from the entire frame but con- centrates 75 percent of its metering attention on a 12mm circle in the middle of the frame with only 25 percent for the areas outside the circle (firmware version C2.00). Also, the camera can be set to use the entire frame and average the light reading from across 100 percent of the frame instead of concentrating 75 percent on the 12mm circle in the middle of the frame and 25 percent outside that circle. For more information see the *b3 Center-weighted area* function in the **Custom Setting Menu** chapter (page 385).
- *Spot Metering:* The camera allows you to use a tiny 4mm spot for metering. The 4mm spot is about 1.5 percent of the frame so it can provide accurate metering of a specific area on your subject, allowing you to manually figure an average, or concentrate on the most important area of your subject for best exposure. This spot meter is movable and surrounds the currently active autofocus point; therefore, when you move the AF point in this mode, you are also moving the spot meter. Just move the AF point with the Sub- selector joystick to the area of the subject you want to meter and the camera will make the exposure based on a small 4mm area surrounding the currently active AF point.
- *Highlight-weighted metering:* The camera meters for highlights in this mode, mostly ignoring surrounding darkness. If you are shooting a concert with a performer in a spot- light, this mode is excellent. It also works well for direct flash of human subjects against a somewhat distant dark background.

All metering modes have a metering range of from −3 to +17 EV. Let's examine how to choose the best meter style for your subjects, from both the Photo Shooting Menu and the *i* Menu.

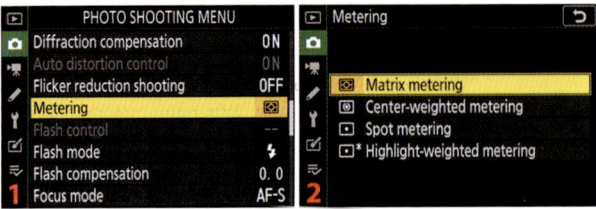

Figure 7.21A: Metering modes on the Photo Shooting Menu

Use these steps to choose a Metering mode from the Photo Shooting Menu:

1. Choose Metering from the Photo Shooting Menu and scroll to the right (figure 7.21A, image 1).
2. Referring to the previous list of metering modes, highlight your Metering mode choice (figure 7.21A, image 2) and press the OK button or tap your choice to use that Metering type.

An even faster way to access the Metering mode types is to use the *i* Menu. Let's see how.

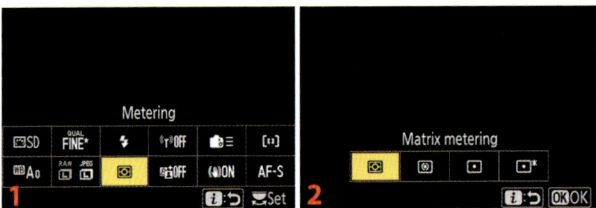

Figure 7.21B: Metering modes on the *i* Menu

Use these steps to choose a Metering mode from the *i* Menu:

1. Press the *i* button on the back of the camera and the *i* Menu will open (figure 7.21B, image 1). Scroll to the Metering position on the menu and press the OK button or tap the Metering icon. The Metering secondary screen will open.
2. Referring to the previous list of metering modes, highlight your Metering mode choice (figure 7.21B, image 2) and press the OK button or tap your selection to use that Metering type.

Settings Recommendation: The majority of photographers will leave their Metering mode set to Matrix metering. This is a well-established and often uncannily accurate form of exposure metering. Nikon has been working on their Matrix metering algorithms for many years, and the Nikon Z6 has benefitted from that work. If you have special needs, such as for spot metering or for shooting highlighted subjects, you also have those choices. Center-weighted metering is an old style of metering that comes from the days of film glory. It works pretty well and some people prefer it, especially those who cut their teeth on old film cameras with center-weighted metering only. Use whichever one you like best or need at that time. I've found that Matrix metering works best for me most of the time.

Flash Control

The Nikon Z6 has one of the most advanced flash control systems of any mirrorless camera, with the ability to control multiple banks of external flash units by radio and/or optical control. In figure 7.22A, you will find a dressed-up Nikon Z6 with a Nikon SB-5000 Speedlight flash unit and a WR-R10 Wireless Remote Controller (radio transmitter) kit mounted.

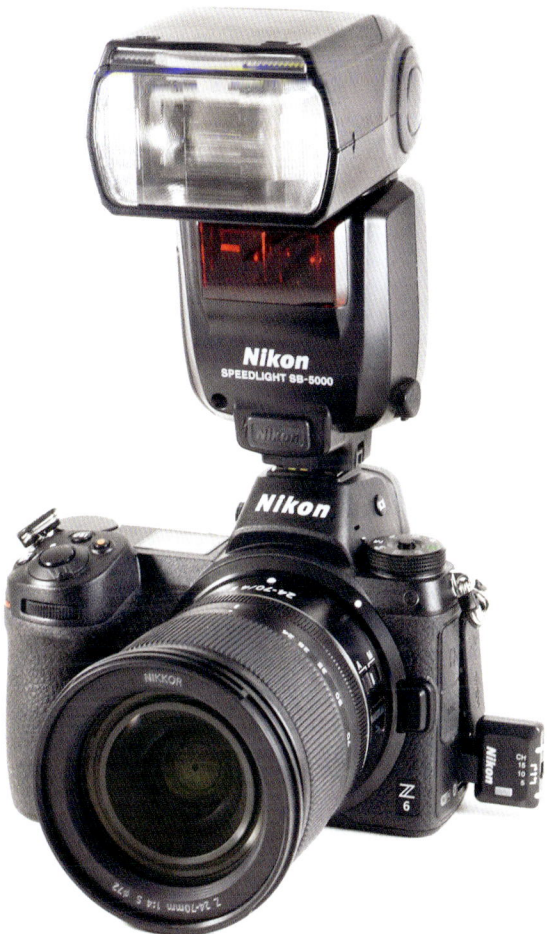

Figure 7.22A: Nikon Z6 with WR-R10 receiver and SB-5000 flash

Using Older Nikon Speedlights with the Nikon Z6

Some older Nikon Speedlights will not open the Flash control menu on the Z6. It will stay grayed out and unavailable. In this book, I will discuss using the SB-500 and SB-5000 flash units with the Z6 camera because those two flash units are specifically mentioned in the User's Manual as being fully compatible. There is no harm in testing your recent older Nikon flash unit with the Z6 to see if it will open the Flash control menu. One qualifier, though: I would not even mount a Speedlight flash older than the SB-800 on a current Nikon camera, as it could damage the camera. The Nikon Z6 is fully compatible with i-TTL mode on all Speedlight flash units produced after the SB-800 and will take correctly exposed pictures with them.

I tested an SB-900 and SB-910 flash unit with my Nikon Z6 and the resulting pictures were exposed correctly. Therefore, if you do not have an SB-500 or SB-5000 Speedlight, you can continue using your older Nikon flash units for normal i-TTL flash photography.

You cannot use the Commander mode of master-flash compatible units (e.g., SB-700, SB-900, SB-910, SU-800) from within the Z6's Flash control menu because it remains grayed out when an older Speedlight is mounted. However, you can use the Commander settings in the LCD screen on the back of the Speedlight flash itself to control Nikon's optical Creative Lighting System (CLS). In other words, the camera allows the built-in Commander (master flash) modes of the SB-700, SB-900, SB-910, and the SU-800 wireless commander to work as expected.

Note: Several older Nikon Speedlights will work fine in the i-TTL modes with the Z6, including the SB-910, SB-900, SB-800, SB-700, SB-600, SB-400, and SB-300; however, there are limitations on other modes. Please refer to the chart in the new Z7/Z6 Nikon User's Manual on pages 179–181 that shows which modes are compatible for each Speedlight.

Using the SB-500 and SB-5000 Speedlights for Flash Photography

The SB-500 and SB-5000 Speedlights are mentioned in the Nikon manuals as the most efficient flash units for use on the Z6. You can use either of these two Speedlights to control multiple banks of remote Nikon Speedlights, either by using the optical Creative Lighting System (CLS) or by radio control with a WR-R10 Wireless Remote Commander kit (figure 7.22A).

Let's examine how to use either of the Nikon-suggested flash units for Flash control. First, let's examine the five available Flash control modes (figure 7.22B, image 3).

- *(TTL) TTL:* The camera will take pictures using the excellent i-TTL (TTL-BL or balanced fill-flash) mode built into the Speedlight. The flash fires in two stages. Nikon calls stage one "monitor preflash." The flash emits a series of almost invisible flashes before the main flash burst fires (stage two). The preflashes allow the camera's RGB flash sensor to examine all areas of the frame for reflectivity. The Z6 then uses the Matrix meter and distance information from a Nikkor D, G, E, or S lens to calculate a flash output that is balanced between the main subject and the ambient lighting. You must use Matrix or Center-weighted metering for this mode to work. When the Spot meter is used, the camera automatically switches out of balanced fill-flash mode and enters Standard i-TTL (TTL). This mode ignores the background's ambient light and concentrates on whatever the camera's selected AF point is focused on. For the most accurate flash output for a specific subject, just set your camera to use its Spot meter (page 56), and the flash will meter for the subject only. TTL and TTL-BL mode are available for both the SB-500 and SB-5000. You can manually select TTL or TTL-BL with the *i* button on the back of the SB-5000 flash (using the Mode menu item); however, with the SB-500, the selection is done automatically.

- *(A) Auto external flash:* This mode uses an older style of reflective light sensing to arrive at a fairly accurate flash. It is the equivalent of using A mode (non-TTL auto) on older Speedlight flash units. This mode also supports auto-aperture flash. If you use a non-CPU lens and do not specify a focal length and maximum aperture (page 429), this mode will be selected automatically. Auto external flash mode is limited to the SB-5000 Speedlight and will not appear on the Flash control mode menu for lesser flash units.

- *(GN) Distance-priority manual:* Allows you to input the distance to your subject and the flash unit will adjust itself automatically for a proper exposure. This mode is limited to the SB-5000 Speedlight and will not appear on the Flash control mode menu for lesser flash units.

- *(M) Manual:* With this mode you can choose the flash output manually, based on a percentage of full power. The flash starts out in 1/1 mode, which means it will provide the maximum flash output it can generate. It can be adjusted in 1/3 EV steps down to 1/256, which is 1/256th of a full power flash. This mode is available for both the SB-5000 and SB-500 Speedlights (plus some other smaller units, such as the SB-400 and SB-300).

- *(RPT) Repeating flash:* The flash will fire repeatedly with a strobe-like effect while the shutter is open. You can set the Output, Times, and Frequency. *Output* means the flash power level (from 1/8 to 1/256), *Times* means the number of times the flash fires (from 2 to 20 times), and the *Frequency* means the Hz rate (times per second) the flash fires (from 1 to 100 Hz). This mode is limited to the SB-5000 Speedlight and will not appear on the Flash control mode menu for lesser flash units.

Note: As we go through the following items, please keep in mind that the new Nikon Speedlight units (SB-5000 and SB-500) work more closely with your camera than previous Nikon cameras and Speedlights. This means any changes you make on the Flash unit's LCD menu will be reflected in the camera's menu settings immediately, and any changes you make in the camera's menu settings will show up in the Speedlight's LCD menus and screens. The Speedlight and camera update each other's settings through the Accessory shoe contact points. In my opinion, this makes things much nicer for flash photography!

Now let's examine the screens and steps needed to choose one of these five modes and adjust it to fit your needs.

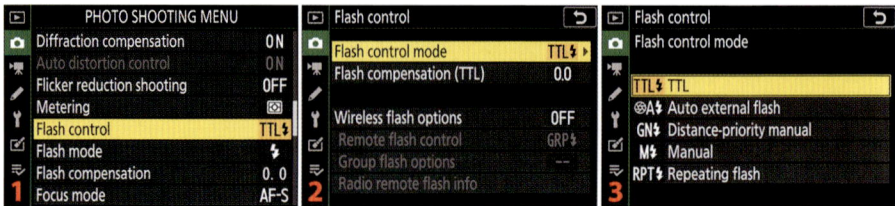

Figure 7.22B: Using Flash control mode

Use the following steps to choose a Flash control mode:

1. Follow the screen flow shown in figure 7.22B, images 1 and 2 (*Flash control > Flash control mode*) until you arrive at the third screen in the series.
2. Choose one of the five Flash control modes and press the OK button or tap the item to lock in the setting (figure 7.22B, image 3).

Now let's look closely at how to configure each of the five Flash control mode settings.

TTL Mode Configuration

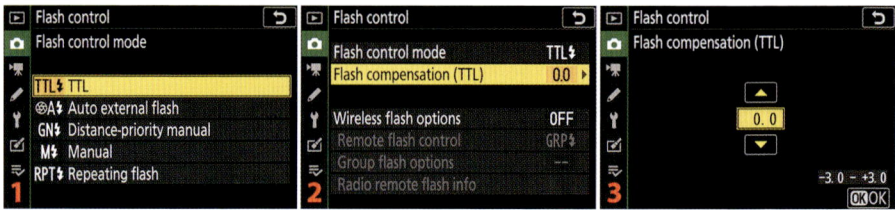

Figure 7.22C: Configuring TTL mode

Use these steps to configure the TTL mode (continuing from where figure 7.22B, image 3, ends):

1. Choose TTL from the Flash control mode menu and press the OK button or tap on TTL (figure 7.22C, image 1).
2. If you want to use flash compensation for the SB-5000 flash, scroll down to the Flash compensation (TTL) menu item and scroll to the right (figure 7.22C, image 2). Otherwise, skip steps 2 and 3. (See the upcoming special note for compensation for flash units other than the SB-5000.)
3. Choose a flash compensation amount using the up/down arrows, from −3.0 to +3.0 EV steps, and press or touch OK to lock in the value (figure 7.22C, image 3). (**Note:** If you are using an SB-5000, you will see that the LCD on the back of the flash unit now reflects the value you just selected in the camera menu. If you change it on the flash unit directly, you will see the camera menus update to the new value.)

Note: The compensation steps above apply to the SB-5000 flash only and most likely to future Nikon flagship Speedlights.

Settings Recommendation: I sometimes shoot with the flash underexposed by 1/3 EV step when I am very close to my subject and the background is a little dark. I find my flash units shoot a little too brightly for up-close use in those circumstances, so I might dial mine back a little. What is so convenient with the Z6 and SB-5000 flash cooperation is that I can select a compensation value on either the flash unit or within the camera, whichever is easier, and the other device will automatically update its value to match.

(A) Auto External Flash Configuration

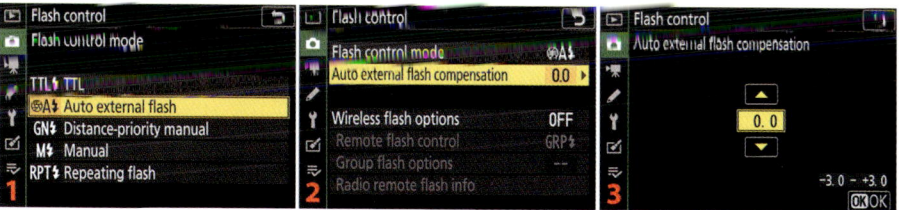

Figure 7.22D: (A) Auto External Flash mode configuration

Use these steps to configure the (A) Auto external flash mode (continuing from where figure 7.22B, image 3, ends):

1. Choose Auto external flash from the Flash control mode menu and press the OK button or tap on Auto external flash (figure 7.22D, image 1).
2. If you want to use flash compensation for the SB-5000 flash, scroll down to the Auto external flash compensation menu item and scroll to the right (figure 7.22D, image 2). Otherwise, skip steps 2 and 3.
3. Choose a compensation amount with the up/down arrows, from −3.0 to +3.0 EV steps, and press or touch OK to lock in the value (figure 7.22D, image 3). The camera and an SB-5000 flash will share and display the compensation values you just entered, on their LCD screens.

(GN) Distance-Priority Configuration

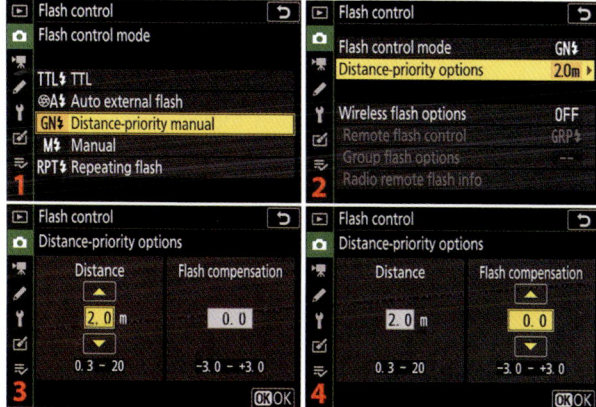

Figure 7.22E: Distance-priority mode configuration

Use these steps to configure the (GN) Distance-priority manual mode (continuing from where figure 7.22B, image 3, ends):

1. Choose Distance-priority manual from the Flash control mode menu and press the OK button or tap on Distance-priority manual (figure 7.22E, image 1).
2. Scroll down to the Distance-priority options menu item and then scroll to the right (figure 7.22F, image 2).
3. You now have two options to configure: Distance and Flash compensation (figure 7.22E, images 3 and 4). Carefully measure the distance between your subject and the camera with a tape measure, or by using lens-marking information, and select that value from the Distance up/down menu (figure 7.22E, image 3), then press or touch OK. The Distance scale is marked in meters (m); therefore, if you are unfamiliar with the metric system, have a meter/foot conversion calculator available or use a metric tape measure. Alternatively, you can just estimate and use a smaller aperture for more depth of field to accommodate for minor distance errors. You can choose from 0.3m to 20m Distance.
4. If you would like to use Flash compensation, scroll to the right and enter a value from −3.0 to +3.0 EV steps in the up/down menu, and then press or touch OK to lock in the value (figure 7.22E, image 4). The camera and an SB-5000 flash will share and display the compensation values you just entered, on their LCD screens.

(M) Manual Configuration

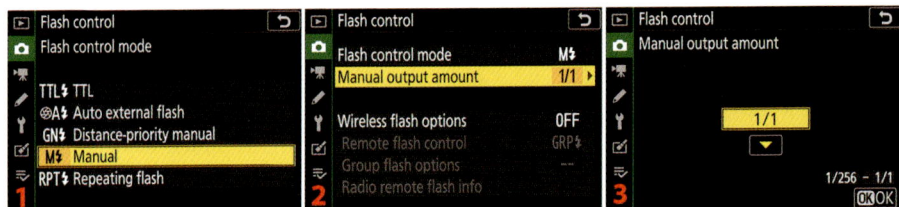

Figure 7.22F: (M) Manual mode configuration

Use these steps to configure the (M) Manual mode (continuing from where figure 7.22B, image 3, leaves off):

1. Choose Manual from the Flash control mode menu and press the OK button or tap on Manual (figure 7.22F, image 1).
2. Scroll down to the Manual output amount menu item and then scroll to the right (figure 7.22F image 2).
3. Now you must select a power output setting (Manual output amount) for the Speedlight to use (figure 7.22F, image 3). By using the up/down menu, you can choose from 1/1 (full power) all the way down to 1/256 (1/256th of a full power flash) in 1/3 EV step increments. Press or touch OK to lock in the value.

(RPT) Repeating Flash Configuration

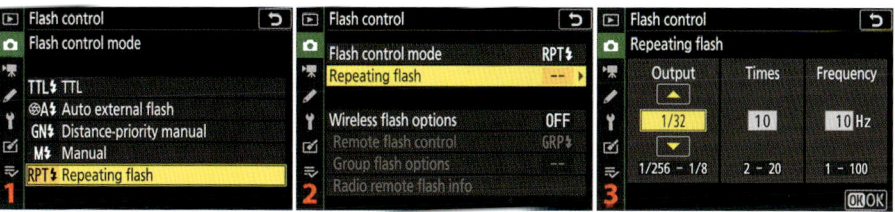

Figure 7.22G: (RPT) Repeating flash mode configuration

Use these steps to configure the (**RPT**) Repeating flash mode (continuing from where figure 7.22B, image 3, leaves off):

1. Choose Repeating flash from the Flash control mode menu and press the OK button or tap on Repeating flash (figure 7.22G, image 1).
2. Scroll down to the Repeating flash menu item and then scroll to the right (figure 7.22G, image 2).
3. Now you must select from three values to set up the strobing effect (figure 7.22G, image 3): Output—or how powerful the flash is—from 1/8 to 1/256 power; Times—or how many times the flash pulse fires—from 2 to 20 times; and Frequency—or how fast the flash pulse fires—from 1 to 100 pulses per second (Hz). When you have all three subsettings configured, press or touch OK to lock in the values.

Wireless Speedlight Control

The Nikon Z6 has the capability of using Commander mode master-flash units to provide optical Nikon CLS (creative lighting system) services. This will let you use older master-flash, Commander-capable units like the SB-700, SB-800, SB-900, SB-910, and SU-800 to control multiple banks of remote Speedlights. Unfortunately, you must use Master mode and the LCD screen on the accessory-shoe mounted commander unit to control Nikon CLS Commander mode settings because the camera provides no menus screens to direct the older Speedlights. The *Photo Shooting Menu > Flash control* menu is grayed out and unavailable when an older flash unit is mounted.

However, when a Nikon SB-500, SB-5000, or later compatible Speedlight is mounted, the Flash control menu becomes available, and you have full ability to control the attached Speedlight and remote units with the camera's Flash control screens. You can use optical control, radio control (via the WR-R10 receiver), or a combination of both optical and radio. When you use the combined optical and radio systems, you can have older and newer Speedlights working together in a unified system.

A few pages back, figure 7.22A shows a fully loaded Nikon Z6 with the SB-5000 and the WR-R10 receiver mounted on the camera. The SB-5000, of course, mounts on the camera's Accessory shoe, whereas the WR-R10 receiver mounts in the Accessory terminal socket, just below the HDMI port, under the largest rubber cover. Figure 7.22H shows a closeup of the WR-R10 receiver plugged directly into the Z6. Let's see how it mounts.

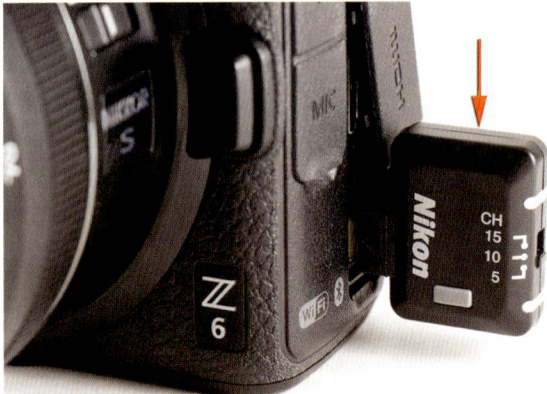

Figure 7.22H: Mounting the WR-R10 Wireless Remote Controller in the Accessory terminal

Use these steps to mount the WR-R10 wireless remote controller in the camera's Accessory terminal:

1. Open the large rubber cover nearest the back of the camera (figure 7.22H).
2. Be sure the WR-R10 wireless remote controller is facing toward the front of the camera and carefully push the WR-R10's male connector into the female Accessory terminal— into the lower connector, just below the HDMI connector.

Note: Be careful with the camera once the WR-R10 is mounted because it protrudes awkwardly and it may be possible to break the WR-R10 or camera by hitting the WR-R10 against something. I have been unable to find an extension cable that would mount the WR-R10 in a less exposed manner. You cannot use the HDMI port while the WR-R10 is inserted because it covers part of the HDMI connector.

Additionally, since we are using a WR-R10 controller and pairing it with an SB-5000 Speedlight, you will need to configure the type of pairing (Pair or Pin) used in the *Setup Menu > Wireless remote (WR) options* function (page 525) before using the upcoming Wireless flash options.

Next, let's see how to use the camera's Wireless flash options and its subfeatures: Remote flash control, Group flash options, and Radio remote flash info.

Wireless Flash Options

When you turn the camera on with a WR-R10 receiver mounted, or a compatible Speedlight (SB-500 or SB-5000), or a combination of the WR-R10 receiver and a compatible Speedlight, the Flash control menu will allow you to enable the Wireless flash options.

These three options allow you to use Nikon's Advanced Wireless Lighting (AWL)—a subset of Nikon CLS   to control remote flash units as a "Commander" master flash. Let's examine the three available options. The options are available according to what type of Commander unit is mounted in the Accessory shoe; therefore, the camera menu offers only one or two of these options at a time. Following are all three options:

- **Optical AWL:** When you are using a Nikon SB-500 or SB-5000 Speedlight—or any compatible future Speedlights—you can use the mounted flash unit as a master-flash unit (Commander) to control multiple banks of remote Speedlight flash units. The mounted Commander Speedlight will emit low-intensity optical preflashes that send controlling information to the remote units, telling them how to expose the subject.
- **Optical/radio AWL:** This combination mode is available only when the SB-500 is mounted *along with* the WR-R10 Wireless Remote Controller kit. This allows you to use the relatively inexpensive SB-500 as a Commander Speedlight (master) in combination with the WR-R10 radio receiver, to use optical and radio control at the same time. This mode does allow you to easily control up to six banks (A–F) of remote (slave) Speedlights. Up to three banks (A–C) are devoted to Optical AWL and up to three banks (D–F) are relegated to Radio AWL. The actual number of banks you can control is set by the capabilities of the mounted units. For instance, the SB-500 can normally control only two banks (A–B) for optical, while the WR-R10 controls banks D–F. When using SB-500 as a optical wireless commander, you will be able to control banks A–C for Optical AWL (via the Commander menu on the external master unit) and D–F for Radio AWL (via the camera's menu).
- **Radio AWL:** In this mode all six available banks for the remote (slave) units (A–F) are controlled by the WR-R10 receiver. You must use remote flash units that support Radio AWL, such as the Nikon SB-5000 (or compatible future flash units).

Now, let's consider how to select one of these options. Use the following screens and steps to configure the Wireless flash options, according to which units are mounted on the camera:

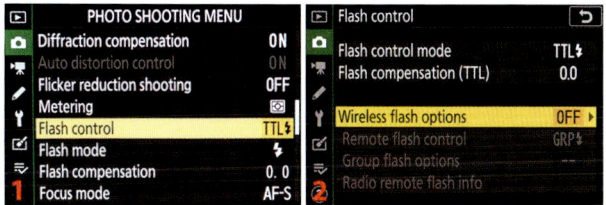

Figure 7.22I: The Flash control's Wireless flash options

1. Select Wireless flash options from the Flash control menu and then scroll to the right (figure 7.22I).

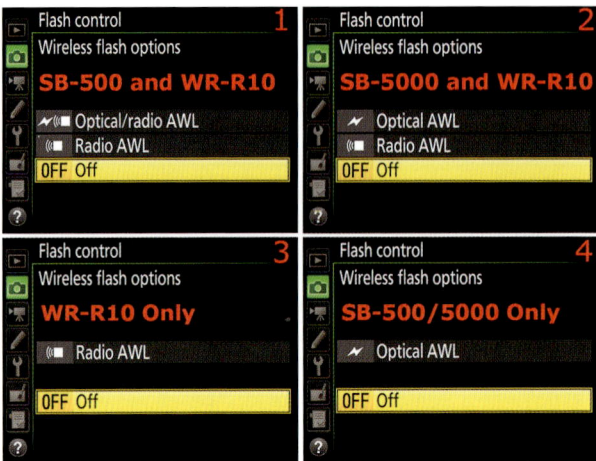

Figure 7.22J: AWL combinations per flash and radio unit mounted

2. You will see a single Wireless flash options screen, with one of the menu selections shown in figure 7.22J, images 1–4. Each of the screens shown represent a different combination of Speedlight and WR-R10 radio unit, per the following descriptions (see bold red text in figure 7.22J, images 1–4):

   a. Figure 7.22J, image 1, displays the available options for using an SB-500 and the WR-R10 receiver (Optical/radio AWL or Radio AWL).

   b. Figure 7.22J, image 2, shows the available options when you have an SB-5000 and a WR-R10 receiver mounted (Optical AWL or Radio AWL).

   c. Figure 7.22J, image 3, displays the single Radio AWL option you have available when you have just the WR-R10 radio receiver unit mounted.

   d. Figure 7.22J, image 4, shows the single Optical AWL option you have when either the SB-500 or SB-5000 (or compatible future Speedlight) is mounted, but no WR-R10 transmitter is in the Ten-pin remote terminal. (**Note:** While the SB-5000 Speedlight is capable of receiving radio signals through the WR-R10 receiver, it is not capable of replacing the WR-R10 as a radio Commander unit for radio control of remote Speedlights.)

   e. Select one of the Wireless flash options from the menu and press the OK button or tap the option to lock in your choice.

Settings Recommendation: After experimenting quite a bit to fully understand these settings, I am now using an SB-500 in the camera's Accessory shoe and the WR-R10 kit in the Accessory terminal to control remote flash units by radio and optical *at the same time* (see figure 7.22J, image 1), to control up to five banks of flash units. With this arrangement, you may control up to two banks of remote Speedlights *optically* (A and B; C is not available in this mode). Then, you can adjust the camera's radio settings for the WR-R10 radio transmitter and control up to an additional three banks (D–F) by *radio signal*. This arrangement allows you to use your older Speedlight flash unit(s) along with new SB-500 or SB-5000 flash unit(s) for simultaneous optical and radio control.

If you prefer to use an older Speedlight flash unit that has a Commander mode as the *optical* master flash, you can configure the flash using the LCD menu on the master flash itself. It will then directly control up to three banks (A–C) without changing any settings in the camera. If you like, you can then add a WR-R10 unit in the accessory shoe to control banks D–F by *radio*. In other words, when you have an older flash unit or the SU-800 wireless commander unit in the camera's hotshoe, acting as a master flash for *optical* control, you will be able to control banks D–F for *radio* control only within the camera using the *Flash control > Group flash options* function when a WR-R10 unit is mounted.

However, if you are missing some of the equipment necessary to power both radio *and* optical Speedlight control, you can do one or the other (optical or radio), with one of the combinations shown in figure 7.22J. The only difficulty you will encounter is that you must control your Commander master flash outside of the camera's menu system when you have no WR-R10 receiver unit to use along with the older Commander master-flash unit. The camera's Flash control menu will be grayed out and unavailable when any older flash technology is mounted in the camera's hotshoe. Therefore, be prepared to use normal Optical AWL from the older Speedlight (or SU-800) LCD menu directly, like you have in the past.

On the other hand, if you have a new SB-5000 Speedlight, you can control Optical AWL from the camera's Flash control menu or the LCD menu on the flash itself. The Z6 or SB-5000 will accept settings changes on their respective menus and then transmit the changes immediately to the other device.

Special note: Please do not be put off by the complexity of this flash configuration system. The Nikon Z6 gives you some truly flexible ways to control multiple banks of flash units optically and by radio. It took me a while to really get comfortable with it, but now that I understand it, it is certainly worthwhile for when I need to use multiple Speedlight flash units to light a scene.

Now, let's go a little deeper into the usage of Nikon SB-5000 Speedlights and the WR-R10 receiver for wireless radio remote control.

When you are using an SB-5000 Speedlight and WR-R10 controller, you will have all Remote flash control menu choices available to you. Using a different Speedlight, including the SB-500, will limit your menu choices.

We will consider the following settings primarily based on a Z6 with an SB-5000 Speedlight flash unit on the Accessory shoe individually and also with a WR-R10 controller in the Accessory terminal.

Remote Flash Control and (GRP) Group Flash Options

The Group flash options allow you to control your remote flash groups in the way most familiar to users of older, optical-only Nikon CLS standards.

This subsection continues where the choices found in figure 7.22J leave off. After you have chosen which AWL method you will use (Optical/radio AWL, Radio AWL, or Optical AWL), you will need to choose a Remote flash control type, and then set the Group flash options that appear on the camera's menu (figure 7.22K, image 3).

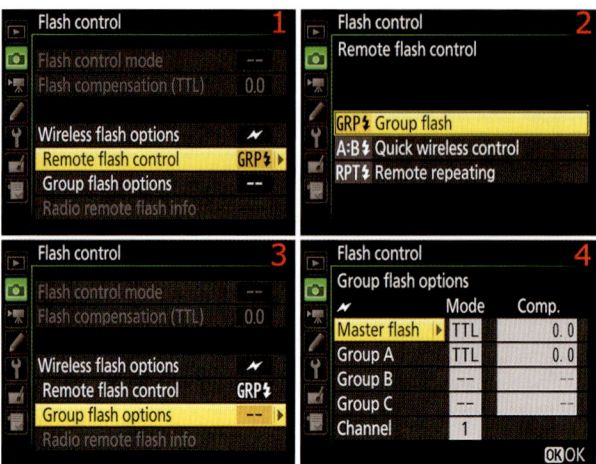

Figure 7.22K: Using Remote flash control and Group flash options

Use the following steps to set the Remote flash control and resulting Group flash options settings:

1. After setting the Wireless flash options, as shown in figure 7.22J, choose Remote flash control and scroll to the right (figure 7.22K, image 1).

2. Highlight the GRP Group flash setting and then press the OK button or tap the option to select it (figure 7.22K, image 2). Please note that using a flash unit other than the SB-5000 will disable any changes to the Remote flash control function, leaving it set to GRP Group flash. No other Remote flash control setting is available unless you use the SB-5000 flash unit (or a compatible future flash unit).

3. Your camera's menu will now show the words Group flash options just below Remote flash control (figure 7.22K, image 3). Select Group flash options and scroll to the right.

4. The final screen in the series (figure 7.22K, image 4) allows you to adjust the Group flash options for the Master flash and the Groups (A–C). It also allows you to set a channel for communicating with the remote flash unit optically. I chose Optical AWL (see figure 7.22L, image 1) for the first look at these settings because this is the most familiar Commander mode setting for previous Master flash configuration. If you have used Nikon CLS is the past, you have seen this final screen (image 4) many times. In a moment we will consider what the final screens looks like for Radio AWL and Optical/radio AWL. But first, let's examine what each of the settings do.

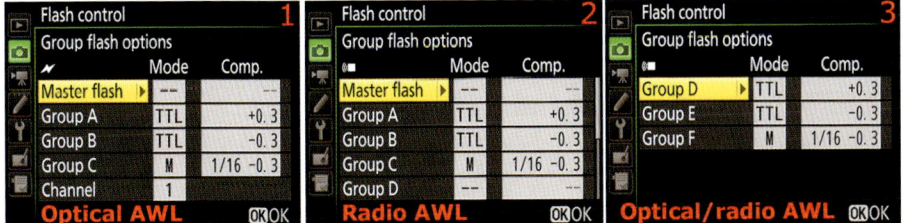

Figure 7.22L: Group flash options settings (per-type screen choices in figure 7.22K, image 4)

5. There are three columns in the Group flash options screen (figure 7.22L, images 1–3). The first column represents the Master flash and remote flash group headings (Group A to Group F). In the first column of the Group flash options screens, you will notice some differences, according to which AWL type you have selected. The following list describes the differences in the first column of figure 7.22L, images 1–3:

- **Optical AWL:** In figure 7.22L, image 1 (Optical AWL), the camera will offer the Master flash setting, up to three groups (A–C), and the Channel (1–4) selection.

- **Radio AWL:** In figure 7.22L, image 2 (Radio AWL), you will note there are extra Groups (A–F) available. You cannot see past Group D (Groups E and F) on the Radio AWL screen unless you scroll down. You can control up to six groups of Speedlight units with the Radio AWL selection—if you have a WR-R10 receiver mounted. You do not have a Channel selection in the camera itself when using Radio AWL because the WR-R10 receiver has a physical switch on it offering three channels (CH) 5, 10, and 15. You must set the radio-controlled Speedlight (e.g., SB-5000) to the same Channel setting as the WR-R10 receiver with the flash unit's controls (for instance, the SB-5000 has an *i* button menu with a Channel setting).

- **Optical/radio AWL:** In figure 7.22L, image 3 (Optical/radio AWL), you will notice that you see only Groups D, E, and F. Where are Groups A, B, and C? Well, this mode is available only when you have an older Commander master flash unit on the Accessory shoe (e.g., SB-700, SB-800, SB-900, SB-910, and SU-800). Groups A–C are controlled by the mounted Commander master flash itself and you do not make any adjustments in the Z6's Group flash options screen. All adjustments for Groups A–C are instead made on the Commander master flash unit's LCD menu on back of the master flash unit. Only Groups D–F can be adjusted from the camera's Group flash options menu. To make this clearer: With this hybrid Optical/radio AWL setting, the master flash unit itself controls Groups A, B, and C, while the Z6 controls Groups D, E, and F. (**Note on pairing the WR-R10 and the SB-5000:** If you cannot get your remote SB-5000 to pair with the WR-R10 receiver after setting the Channel [CH] for each unit, make sure you have selected a Mode [e.g., TTL] for the Group [D, E, or F] that is controlling the remote flash SB-5000 unit. **Note on using an SB-500:** The Group flash options screen combines the screens in images 1 and 3 when you have an SB-500 mounted on the Accessory shoe. You must scroll up and down in the screen to see all the available Groups. The SB-500 provides only Groups A and B, but not C, for the optical side of the equation. The WR-R10 receiver will control Groups D, E, and F for the radio side.) *Note:* I have included a quick step-by-step configuration for optical and radio combination control of multiple remote flash units using a low-cost SB-500 Speedlight as the master flash. See the subsection titled **Step-by-Step Simultaneous Optical AWL and Radio AWL Configuration** on page 251.

6. The second column in the Group flash options screens shown in figure 7.22L, images 1–3, represents the Mode setting, which includes the four selections in the following list of Mode types:

- **TTL mode:** The TTL setting allows you to use the full power of i-TTL technology. By leaving Mode set to TTL (figure 7.22L) for the Groups (A–F), you derive maximum flexibility and accuracy from all your flash units. In TTL mode, the Comp. setting will display exposure values from +3.0 EV to −3.0 EV, a full six-stop range of exposure compensation for each group of Speedlights. You can set the Comp. in 1/3 EV steps for very fine control. In all three screens in figure 7.22L, Group A and Group B is set to TTL mode with +0.3 EV Comp. for Group A and −0.3 EV Comp. for Group B.

- **A mode:** The A mode for non-CPU lenses, and the Auto Aperture mode for lenses with a CPU, are older, non–i-TTL technologies included for people who are accustomed to using older flash systems. In these two modes, flash output is automatically adjusted according to the amount of light reflected back from your subject. The two A modes work basically the same as TTL mode, without the extra smarts provided by the amazing i-TTL mode. The SB-5000's light sensor for non-TTL-auto flash measures the reflected light from the subject. The SB-5000 then controls the output level of the main flash burst, with input from the camera and lens, which includes the ISO sensitivity, exposure compensation, and the size of the aperture. A mode use is most accurate when you are using lenses having a CPU that transmits data to the camera and flash (G, D, and E lenses). If you are using a non-CPU lens with no maximum aperture information entered into the camera, the flash is forced into using only reflected light from the subject to judge proper exposure.

- **M mode:** This allows you to set different levels of flash output in 1/3 EV steps for the Speedlights in Group A, B, and C. The settings you can put in the Comp. field are between 1/1 (full power) and 1/256 in 1/3 EV steps. The intermediate 1/3-step settings are presented as decimals following the power fraction (e.g., 1/16 −0.3). In all three screens in figure 7.22L, Group C is set to M mode at 1/16 power, less −0.3 EV step (1/3 EV step below 1/16 power). This mode requires you to experiment while getting the settings just right, but then provides very stable exposures.

- **−− mode (do not fire mode):** The Speedlight in the Accessory shoe will not fire the main flash burst in this mode. It will fire the monitor preflashes because it uses them to determine exposure and communicate with the external flash groups for Optical AWL. It is often best to set Master flash to −− Mode so that the master flash does not influence the lighting in your carefully arranged Groups of Speedlights (as seen in figure 7.22L, images 1 and 2). When you set −− Mode for any of the Groups (A–F), that entire group of flashes will not fire any flash output. You can use this mode to temporarily turn off one of the flash groups for testing purposes.

7. The third column represents flash Comp. (compensation) for the Master flash and remote Group flashes. When using TTL, A mode, or Auto Aperture mode, you can set exposure compensation from ⁺3.0 to −3.0 EV. When using Manual (M) mode, you can select the flash output power from 1/1 (full flash output) to 1/256 (1/256th of full flash output).

8. Once you have configured the options, press or touch OK to lock in the settings.

Step-by-Step Simultaneous Optical AWL and Radio AWL Configuration

Let's examine how to configure a complex master flash setup for both optical and radio control of multiple remote flash units. This configuration requires the use of an inexpensive SB-500 Speedlight as a master flash unit for *optical* control (or alternatively an older commander flash unit—discussed at the end of this subsection), a WR-R10 wireless remote controller for *radio* control, and two or more remote (slave) flash units.

Some slave units will need to have Optical AWL remote capability (e.g., SB-600, SB-700, SB-800, SB-900, SB-910) and some will need to have Radio AWL remote capability (e.g., SB-5000). Also, the WR-R10 and SB-5000(s) will need to have been previously paired (Refer to *Setup menu > Wireless remote (WR) options > Link mode,* on page 525, for Paring instructions.)

Configure SB-500 Master flash without WR-R10 inserted:

1. Put the SB-500 flash unit in camera's Accessory shoe and turn it on. Do not insert the WR-R10 unit into the camera's Accessory terminal until instructed!
2. Set *Photo Shooting Menu > Flash Control > Wireless flash options* to Optical AWL.
3. Set *Photo Shooting Menu > Flash Control > Group flash options > Group A* and/or *B* to TTL and then set a communication Channel (1 to 4).
4. Configure the remote flash units to use Groups A and/or B and the communications channel you are using (1–4) and set the remote flash units to Remote (slave) mode.
5. Turn SB-500 flash off (you must turn it off before configuring the WR-R10).

Configure WR-R10 wireless remote controller:

1. Flip WR-R10 switch to channel 5, 10, or 15.
2. Insert WR-R10 into Accessory terminal.
3. Configure remote SB-5000(s) to channel 5, 10, or 15 to match WR-R10.
4. Set *Photo Shooting Menu > Flash Control > Wireless flash options* to Radio AWL.
5. Set Photo *Shooting Menu > Flash Control > Group Flash options Groups D, E,* or *F* to TTL.
6. Configure remote (slave) flash units to match the communications channel set on the WR-R10 (5, 10, or 15) and the Group(s) set (D–F) in *Group flash options* (must be SB-5000s or newer radio flashes, older non-radio flash units won't work)
7. Set slave flash units to Remote (slave) mode.

Prepare to take pictures:

1. Check that the Link light on the WR-R10 and SB-5000 (slaves) are both green.
2. Turn SB-500 flash on.

3. Set *Photo Shooting Menu* > *Flash Control* > *Wireless flash options* to Optical/radio AWL. The CMD light on the SB-500 should shine.
4. Take pictures.

Using older Speedlight commander flash units as master flash: As previously mentioned, an alternate form of this method is to use an older Speedlight flash unit with master flash capability (e.g., SB-700, SB-800, SB-900, SB-910, SU-800) and configure it directly on the flash unit's LCD screen, for *optical* control of remote (slave) flash units (beyond the scope of this book, see your Speedlight flash user's manual).

Put the older Commander flash unit in the camera's Accessory shoe instead of the SB-500 mentioned previously. The Flash mode screens in the camera will be grayed out and unavailable in the Photo Shooting Menu, so you can ignore the camera for the optical configuration. Use the older flash unit to control your optical remote Speedlights.

Follow the steps under the previous **Configure WR-R10 wireless remote controller** to configure the WR-R10 for radio control of the SB-5000 flash unit(s). In this manner, you can simultaneously use older flash units to control the optical remote flash units and a WR-R10 to control the radio remote flash units.

Remote Flash Control and (A:B) Quick Wireless Control Options

The Quick wireless control options allow you to blend the power output of your remote flash groups in a very creative way.

This subsection continues where the choices found in figure 7.22J leave off. After you have chosen which AWL method you will use (Optical/radio AWL, Radio AWL, or Optical AWL), you will need to choose the Remote flash control type named A:B Quick wireless control and then modify the Quick wireless control options from the camera's menu that shows below Remote flash control (figure 7.22M, image 3).

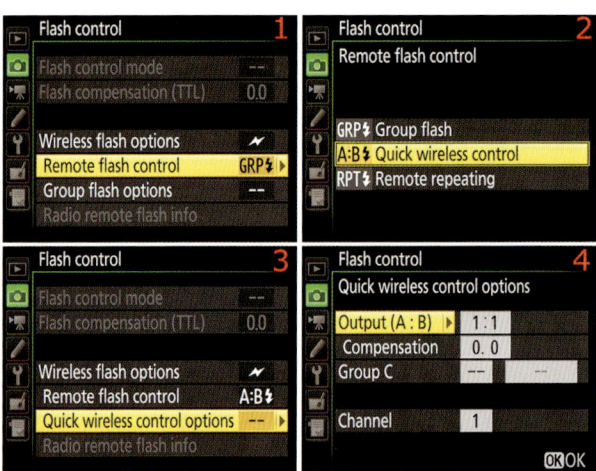

Figure 7.22M: Using Remote flash control and Quick wireless control options

Use the following steps to set the A:B Quick wireless control options:

1. After having previously set the Wireless flash options in figure 7.22J, choose Remote flash control and scroll to the right (figure 7.22M, image 1).
2. Choose the A:B Quick wireless control setting and press the OK button or tap on the item to select it (figure 7.22M, image 2). Please note that using a flash unit besides the SB-5000 will disable any changes to the Remote flash control function, leaving it set to GRP Group flash. No other Remote flash control setting is available unless you use the SB-5000 flash unit (or a compatible future flash unit).
3. Your camera's menu will now show the words Quick wireless control options just below Remote flash control (figure 7.22M, image 3). Select Quick wireless control options and scroll to the right.
4. The final screen in the series (figure 7.22N), which is the same screen as figure 7.22M, image 4 (except with adjustments added), allows you to adjust the Quick wireless control options. You can control three Groups of remote Speedlights: Groups A, B, and C. The SB-5000 master flash will not fire anything except the optical communication preflashes so it cannot be used for primary lighting and has no Master flash selection on this screen. Groups A and B will use TTL only and you can adjust a blend of power between the two groups by adjusting the Output (A:B) setting. You can select from –:1 to 1:–, and a range

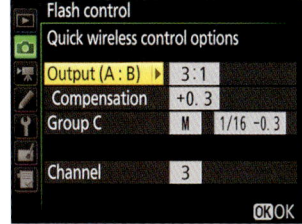

Figure 7.22N: Quick wireless control options with adjustments

of settings in between. The –:1 setting means that Group A will not fire, while Group B does fire. The 1:– setting means that Group A will fire, while Group B does not fire. The in-between settings range from 1:8, which means that Group A is 8 times *less* powerful than Group B, to 8:1, which means that Group A is 8 times *more* powerful than Group B. You can select 1:1 to make both flashes use equal TTL-based output power. Following is a list of all the settings in the Output (A:B) up/down menu:

Output (A:B) Settings
–:1, 1:8, 1:6, 1:4, 1:3, 1:2, 1:1.5, 1:1, 1.5:1, 2:1, 3:1, 4:1, 6:1, 8:1, 1:–

5. Once you have arrived at the proper blend of flash output between Groups A and B, you can also add from +0.3 to –0.3 compensation, which affects both A and B equally. Additionally, you can use Group C in Manual (M) mode only. You can adjust the flash output in Group C from 1:1 (full power) to 1/256 (1/256th of full power) in 1/3 EV step increments. Group C in figure 7.22N is set to 1/16 –0.3, which is 1/3 EV step below 1/16 of full power. This allows you to use Group C as a fill flash group or as the primary group with Groups A and B providing blended and compensated fill flash. (**Note:** If you are using Radio AWL instead of Optical AWL, the screen shown in figure 7.22N will not have the Channel selection since that is controlled by a physical switch on the WR-R10 receiver.)
6. Once you have configured the options, press or touch OK to lock in the settings.

Remote Flash Control and (RPT) Remote Repeating Options

The Remote repeating options allow you to set up a creative strobing (multiple-exposure) effect with remote groups of Speedlight flash units.

This subsection continues where the choices found in figure 7.22J leave off. After you have chosen which AWL method you will use (Optical AWL or Radio AWL), you will need to choose the Remote flash control type named RPT Remote repeating. Then you must configure the Remote repeating options setting that shows below Remote flash control (figure 7.22O, image 3).

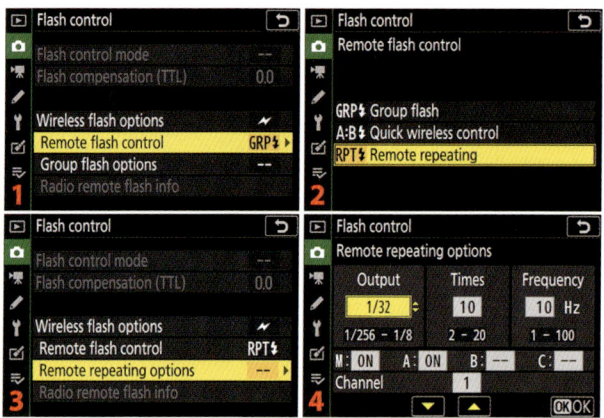

Figure 7.22O: Using Remote flash control and Remote repeating options

Use the following steps to set the RPT Remote repeating options:

1. After having previously set the Wireless flash options in figure 7.22J, choose Remote flash control and scroll to the right (figure 7.22O, image 1).
2. Choose the RPT Remote repeating setting and press the OK button or tap the option to select it (figure 7.22O, image 2). Please note that using a flash unit other than the SB-5000 will disable any changes to the Remote flash control function, leaving it set to GRP Group flash. No other Remote flash control setting is available unless you use the SB-5000 flash unit (or a compatible future flash unit).
3. Your camera's menu will now show the words Remote repeating options just below Remote flash control (figure 7.22O, image 3). Select Remote repeating options and scroll to the right.

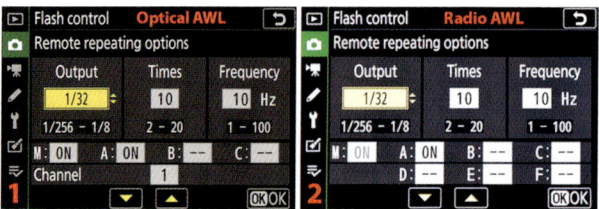

Figure 7.22P: Remote repeating options for Optical and Radio AWL

4. The final screen in the series (figure 7.22P)—which is the same screen as figure 7.22O, image 4—allows you to adjust the Remote repeating options. Scroll left or right to an item or touch it with your fingertip to select it for adjustment. Use the small yellow up/down arrows at the bottom of the screen to make adjustments to the currently selected item. You must enter three values to set up the strobing effect: Output—or how powerful the flash is—from 1/8 to 1/256 power; Times—or how many times the flash pulse fires—from 2 to 20 times; and Frequency—or how fast the flash pulse fires   from 1 to 100 pulses per second (Hz). On the lower part of the screen, you can control up to three Groups of remote Speedlights in manual mode, including Groups A–C in Optical AWL mode and Groups A–F in Radio AWL mode. You can use the Master flash (M) as an additional flash by setting it to On. Any Group set to On will participate in the repeating flash output. In both of the screens shown in figure 7.22P, only Groups A and B are active (set to ON). If you are using Optical AWL, you will need to choose a Channel (1–4) for the Master flash to transmit to the remote flashes. If you are using Radio AWL, the channel is set with a physical switch on the WR-R10 receiver unit.

5. Once you have configured the options, press or touch OK to lock in the settings.

Radio Remote Flash Info

The Radio remote flash info function simply allows you to see the Speedlight unit being controlled by the WR-R10 receiver and which Group that flash is working under.

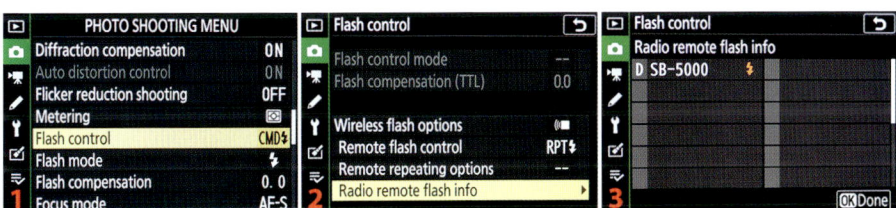

Figure 7.22Q: Radio remote flash info

Use the following steps to examine the Speedlights being controlled by radio transmitter unit:

1. Follow the screen flow shown in figure 7.22Q, images 1 and 2 (*Flash control > Radio remote flash info*) until you arrive at the third screen in the series.

2. The final screen (figure 7.22Q, image 3) shows that my Z6 is controlling a single SB-5000 Speedlight and it is using Group D to do so (D SB-5000). When you have examined your Speedlight configuration, press or touch OK to finish.

Note: Silent photography mode (page 307) disables the use of a flash unit powered by the camera.

Flash Mode

The Z6 has four basic flash modes that will present themselves according to which ex-posure mode on the Mode dial (P,S,A,M) you have selected. Let's examine each of them, with their combinations, on the Flash mode screen (see figures 7.23A–7.23D). Press the *i* button (or touch *i* Set) with the Flash mode screen open to access the Flash mode menu to change flash modes.

Fill Flash (Front-Curtain Sync)

In Front-curtain sync mode (figure 7.23A, red arrow), the camera tries to balance the light if you're using a lens that has a CPU in it. A CPU lens, such as a Nikkor G, D, E, or S lens, can balance ambient light and light from the flash equally and makes the lighting look very natural.

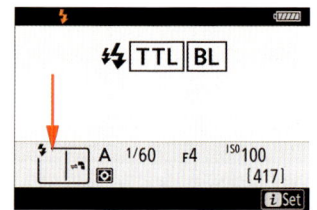

Figure 7.23A: Fill flash (front-curtain sync)

If you use this correctly outdoors, it will be hard to tell that you were using flash, except for the catch light in your subject's eyes and the lack of damaging shadows. The flash simply fills in some extra light without over-powering the ambient light.

In a situation where there is very little ambient light, the camera will use only the flash to get a correct exposure. It balances with ambient light only if there is enough.

There is a side effect to using this mode with slow shutter speeds. Front-curtain sync causes the flash to fire as soon as the front shutter curtain is out of the way and before the rear shutter curtain starts closing. If there is some ambient light, the shutter speed is long (like 1/2 second), and the subject is moving, you'll see a well-exposed subject with a blurry trail in front of it. The flash correctly exposes the subject as soon as the front curtain gets out of the way, but the ambient light continues exposing the subject before the rear curtain closes. This effect can be seen at shutter speeds as fast as 1/60s if the ambient light is strong enough and the subject is moving.

Use this Flash mode for general flash photography. Just keep the camera's shutter speed at reasonable levels (1/60 to 1/250).

Red-Eye Reduction

Red-eye reduction mode (figure 7.23B, red arrow) causes the mounted Speedlight to flash a moderately bright strobe three times in the face of your subject before the Front-curtain sync flash fires. The intention is that the three extra flashes before the main flash burst will cause your subject's pupils to close somewhat and reduce the red-eye effect. Otherwise, this mode performs the same as Front-curtain sync.

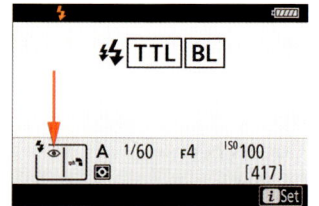

Figure 7.23B: Red-eye reduction

Slow Sync + Red Eye

Slow sync + red-eye combines two modes, Slow sync and Red-eye reduction, so you can take portraits indoors using ambient light while still using fill-flash to get rid of unwanted shadows (figure 7.23C, red arrow).

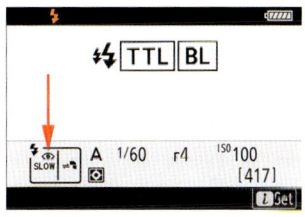

Figure 7.23C: Slow sync + red eye

Slow sync flash causes the camera to fire three moderate bursts of light into your subject's face to reduce red-eye, while allowing the camera to leave its shutter open for a normal nonflash exposure time to record ambient light. The main flash burst then fires to provide some fill flash for shadow reduction and to balance with the ambient light.

The exposure will be heavily influenced by ambient light with flash providing only balanced fill light. When you are shooting in a darker environment, you should have your camera on a tripod to prevent blurry pictures. Shutter speeds can get quite low while using this mode in low light because the camera considers ambient light more important than the flash fill light.

In low light, you should ask your subject to remain perfectly still, or there is a chance of subject ghosting.

Slow Sync

Slow sync mode lets the camera use ambient light to make a good exposure and then fires the flash to add some extra light, rounding out the shadows or better exposing a foreground subject (figure 7.23D, red arrow). Ambient light rules in this mode!

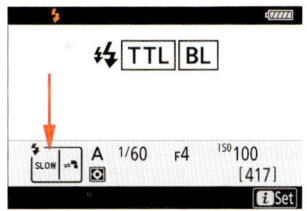

Figure 7.23D: Slow-sync

Use this mode in people shots outdoors or where you want ambient light to provide the primary exposure and you want the flash to add a sparkle to your subjects' eyes and remove dark shadows from their faces. You can get some beautifully balanced outdoor portraits with Slow sync.

You normally don't have to worry about red eye outdoors because ambient light is bright enough to constrict your subject's pupils; therefore, this mode works well for natural-scene portraits. If red eye becomes a concern due to light levels dropping and subject pupils enlarging, switch to Red-eye reduction with slow sync mode instead (previous subsection).

Slow sync is closely related to Front-curtain flash, except that with Slow sync the ambient light is more important than the light from the flash. Be careful when using this mode indoors because it will expose for ambient light first and will only assist with some flash fill light.

You can get some terrible ghosting and blurry handheld shots when using Slow sync indoors in lower light levels. Use a tripod in low light.

Rear-Curtain Sync

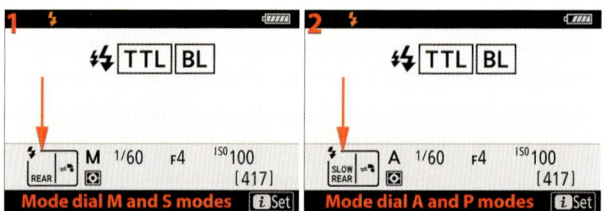

Figure 7.23E: Rear-curtain sync

Rear-curtain sync (figure 7.23E, red arrows) is the opposite of Front-curtain sync. The flash waits to fire until just before the rear curtain starts to close. The entire shutter speed time just ends when the flash fires. This causes a ghosting effect to the rear of moving subjects when slower shutter speeds are used.

When you press the Shutter-release button, the front curtain opens, ambient light starts hitting the sensor, and the sensor starts recording the subject. Just as the shutter's rear curtain is about to close, the flash fires, exposing the subject at its current position.

The subject was fully exposed by the flash at the end of the shutter speed time, so the ambient light had time to register the subject before the flash fired. If the subject is moving, this can produce a blurred ghost behind the well-exposed subject, if a slow shutter speed is used.

Note: In certain modes on the Mode dial (i.e., M and S), the word REAR will appear in the Flash mode box (figure 7.23E, image 1, red arrow). In other modes (i.e., A and P), the words SLOW and REAR will appear in the Flash mode box (red arrow). This is because the shutter speed is controlled by the camera in those A and P modes and the shutter speeds can get rather slow if needed, without your control. In M and S modes on the Mode dial, you control the shutter speed, so only the word REAR appears in the Flash mode box.

Flash Off

The No-flash mode disables the flash altogether so you can take pictures without the flash influencing the exposure (figure 7.23F, red arrow). This is the equivalent of removing the flash unit from the Accessory shoe or turning it off. It's a nice way to temporarily disable the flash unit without removing it, while you take some ambient light pictures.

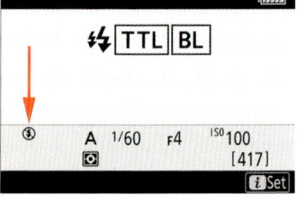

Figure 7.23F: Flash off

Next let's see how to select a Flash mode and then discuss what each does. Nikon gives Z6 users three different ways to access the Flash mode settings. We'll examine each.

Flash Modes from the Photo Shooting Menu

First, we'll examine how to access and set a Flash mode using the Photo Shooting Menu.

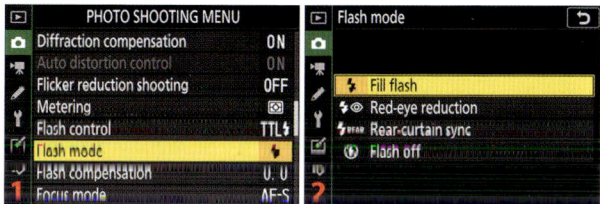

Figure 7.23G: Selecting a Flash mode

Use the following steps to select a Flash mode:

1. Choose Flash mode from the Photo Shooting Menu and scroll to the right (figure 7.23G, image 1).
2. Highlight one of the four Flash modes from the list and press the OK button or tap on the option to select it (figure 7.23G, image 2).

Flash Modes from the *i* Menu

Next, let's examine the second way the Z6 allows you to set one of the flash modes: choosing one from the *i* Menu.

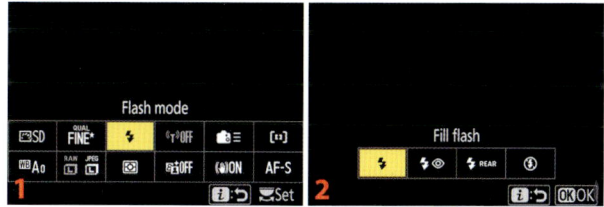

Figure 7.23H: Selecting a Flash mode from the *i* Menu

Use the following steps to choose a Flash mode from the *i* Menu:

1. Press the *i* button and the *i* Menu will open (figure 7.23H, image 1). Scroll to the Flash mode icon and press the OK button or tap the icon to open the Flash mode secondary screen.
2. Highlight or touch one of the Flash mode symbols and press or touch OK to choose it (figure 7.23H, image 2).

Flash Modes from the Flash Information Screen

The *i* Menu also offers a third way to access the Flash modes: the Flash information screen.

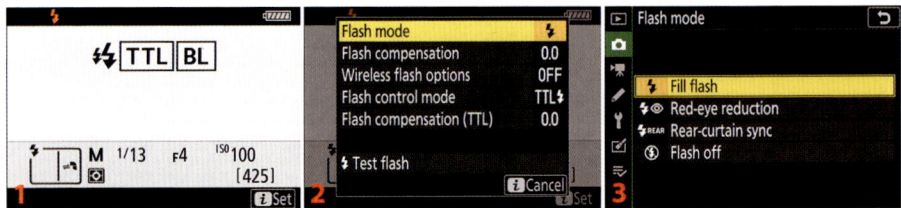

Figure 7.23I: Flash modes from the Flash information screen

Use the following steps to choose a Flash mode from the *i* Menu's Flash information screen:

1. Press the *i* button and the *i* Menu will open (seen in figure 7.23I, image 1), then press the DISP button multiple times until the Flash information screen appears (figure 7.23I, image 1).
2. Press the *i* button again and the Flash information menu will open (figure 7.23I, image 2). Choose Flash mode from the menu and press the OK button or tap the option to open the Flash mode secondary screen.
3. Choose one of the Flash modes from the list of modes by highlighting it and pressing the OK button or by tapping on the option (figure 7.23I, image 3).

More information on using the special Flash information screen and menu is found in the chapter **Camera Control Screens** (page 30).

Settings Recommendation: I generally use the *i* Menu to directly choose the Flash mode I need at the moment. You may find the *i* Menu to be the fastest way to access the modes; however, there are two additional ways, as described above.

Most of the time I use Fill flash because it tends to balance so well with ambient light or provide artificial light when there is insufficient ambient light for a good exposure. However, I sometimes use Red-eye reduction when I am shooting individual or group pictures with direct flash. Rear curtain sync is fun to use when you want to have a ghosted trail following your subject when shooting with a slow shutter speed. No flash mode is there for when I need to temporarily disable the flash unit without turning the flash off or removing it from the camera.

Flash Compensation

Flash compensation allows you to control the brightness of your subject in relation to the background. By increasing the exposure on your subject, it becomes brighter while the background stays relatively the same. You can also choose to give less exposure to your subject relative to the background.

Basically, Flash compensation helps you balance the exposure of your subject and the background behind your subject, helping get rid of unwanted highlights or reflections. It is different from general camera +/– exposure compensation, which just averages the exposure for the entire frame. Flash compensation has more smarts when it comes to exposing your subject in relation to the background. Let's see how to use it.

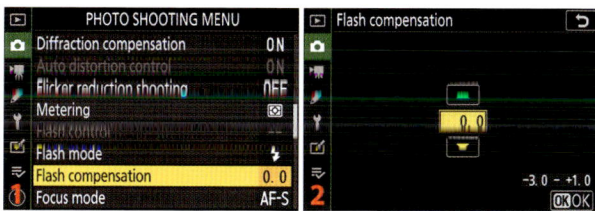

Figure 7.24: Flash +/– compensation

Use the following steps to add or subtract flash exposure on your subject:

1. Choose Flash compensation from the Photo Shooting Menu and scroll to the right (figure 7.24, image 1).
2. Use the up/down arrows to add up to +1.0 EV step or subtract down to –3.0 EV steps exposure for your subject, in 1/3-step increments. Press or touch OK to set the value.

Settings Recommendation: I find this to be a useful function when I am shooting some weddings and graduation ceremonies. If shooting a wedding in a darker environment, it is sometimes difficult to maintain detail in the bride's white dress because the flash adjusts for a dark background and then slightly blows out detail in the dress. By taking a few test shots, you can determine if removing 1/3 to 1/2 steps of exposure will help maintain the detail. You get the idea. You have the power to control the flash exposure on your subject in relation to the background. Experiment with this setting so you can locate it and use it when needed.

Flash compensation can be assigned to a camera button, with *Custom Setting f2 Custom control assignment* (page 423) or to the *i* Menu with *Custom Setting g1 Customize i menu* (page 452).

Focus Mode

Focus mode allows you to control *how* the camera focuses on your subject. It can use three methods:

- **Single AF (AF-S):** This focus setting is best used for stationary or slowly moving subjects. The camera will obtain an initial focus and lock focus on the subject. If the subject moves, the focus may become invalid and will need to be updated.

- *Continuous AF (AF-C):* This focus method is best for rapidly moving subjects or subjects that rarely stop moving. The camera acquires focus but never locks the focus. Instead, it keeps trying to maintain good focus on your subject as long as your subject is under the current AF point area (see AF-area modes on page 264).
- *Manual focus (MF):* You must manually turn the focus ring on the lens to focus on the subject. Many people will use focus Peaking to assist with manual focusing. We will discuss focus Peaking when we talk about *Custom Setting d10 Peaking highlights* (page 409).

The camera gives us two menu systems to change focus modes, and the programmable Fn2 button is assigned to Focus modes as a factory default. Since we are working with the Photo Shooting Menu, let's first examine how to select a focus mode with the Photo Shooting Menu and the *i* Menu, and then we will look into using the Fn2 button.

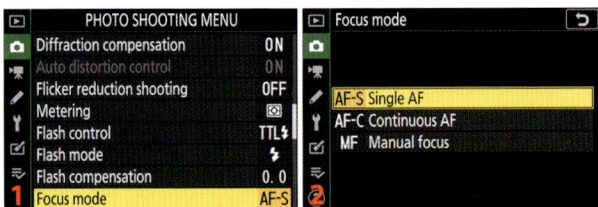

Figure 7.25A: Selecting a Focus mode from the Photo Shooting Menu

Use the following steps to choose a Focus mode from the camera's Photo Shooting Menu:

1. Choose Focus Mode from the Photo Shooting Menu and scroll to the right (figure 7.25A, image 1).
2. Referring to the previous list, highlight a Focus mode and press the OK button or tap the mode to set it (figure 7.25A, image 2).

Next, let's examine how to select the same Focus modes from the *i* Menu.

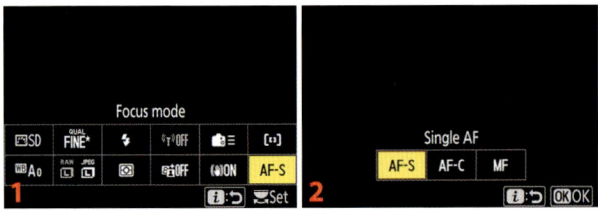

Figure 7.25B: Selecting a Focus mode from the *i* Menu

Use the following steps to select a Focus mode from the *i* Menu:

1. Press the *i* button on the camera's back to open the *i* Menu. Choose Focus mode by highlighting its symbol and pressing the OK button or by tapping the symbol (figure 7.25B, image 1). The secondary screen will open.

2. Referring to the previous list, choose one of the Focus modes (AF-S, AF-C, or MF) by highlighting its symbol and pressing the OK button or by tapping the symbol (figure 7.25B, image 2).

Next let's see how to use the assigned Fn2 button to access the Focus mode system.

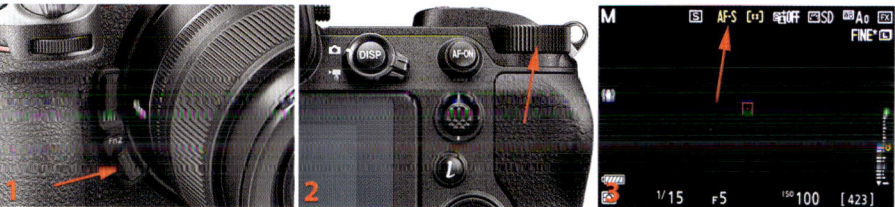

Figure 7.25C: Using the Fn2 button to choose a Focus mode

Use the following steps to choose a Focus mode with external camera controls:

1. Press and hold the Fn2 button on the front of the camera (figure 7.25C, image 1).
2. Turn the rear Main command dial on back of the camera (figure 7.25C, image 2).
3. The Monitor and EVF will display Focus mode symbols at the top (figure 7.25C, image 3, red arrow). The Focus mode will change as you rotate the rear Main command dial. When the Focus mode you want to use is displayed on the screen, stop turning the Main command dial and release the Fn2 button.

Note: See the chapter titled: **Autofocus, AF Area, and Release Modes** (page 82) for deeper information on using Focus modes and their relationship with the AF-area and Release modes.

Settings Recommendation: Most of the time, I find myself using Single AF (AF-S) focus mode. I do a lot of nature photography and landscapes. I find that a single, well-placed focus point allows me to control the focus for the most important area of my subject, allowing me to use the camera's aperture to control depth of field to cover the zone of sharp focus I need for my subjects.

However, those who are shooting moving subjects may need a little more help with keeping a subject in good focus. AF-C allows you to make the autofocus system maintain focus on a moving subject. You may need to also experiment with various AF-area modes since they control what area of your subject is covered by focus points. There is a very strong relationship between the Focus modes and the AF-area modes. Study the chapter that discusses those subjects and then experiment, for better understanding.

Sometimes, especially when I am shooting macro shots, I like to manually focus the camera so I will use the MF mode. Or, I will touch up the focus by turning the focus ring on the lens after autofocus has been established. I always use focus Peaking in those cases so I can easily see exactly where the focus is sharpest on my subject. You will need all these focus modes at one time or another. Learn them well!

AF-Area Mode

The AF-area mode system allows you to choose a single focus point (AF point), or a group of AF points selected from the camera's 273 AF points, to cover your subject and help capture it in sharp focus. The available AF point(s) are surrounded by a red frame, dots, or a partial frame, to give you some idea of the area covered by the AF point(s).

In figure 7.26A you will see six camera screens. Each screen shows the symbol of one of the available AF-area modes (upper red arrow) and the area of the subject the AF point(s) cover (lower red arrow). Let's examine each of the AF-area modes.

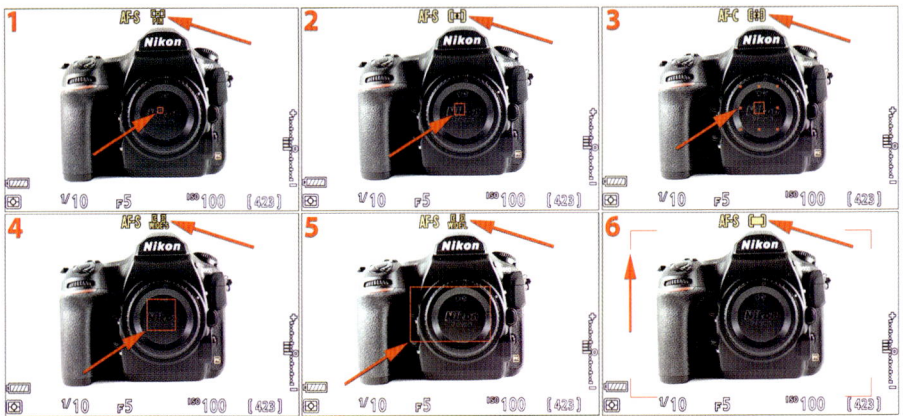

Figure 7.26A: AF-area modes

Here is a description of each of the AF-area modes. The numbers in the list match the numbers in figure 7.26A, images 1–6:

1. *Pinpoint AF:* This mode allows you to choose a very small area of your subject for auto-focus. You can move the AF point to the pupil of an eye or a drop of water on a leaf. It is made to give you precise autofocus so that you can focus on very specific areas. This mode does not use phase detection (PDAF): instead it uses contrast detection (CDAF) only, which is slower to focus yet very accurate. Pinpoint AF AF-area mode is available only when you are using the Single AF (AF-S) Focus mode. It is grayed out on the Photo Shooting Menu and not available on the *i* Menu if the camera is using Continuous AF (AF-C).
2. *Single-point AF:* This is the preferred mode for many photographers. It has an AF point frame that is larger than the Pinpoint AF frame. This mode uses PDAF initially and tops off the focus by using CDAF for focus verification. It is much faster and still allows precise location of focus within the 273 AF points in the frame. Single-point AF AF-area mode is available in both AF-S and AF-C Focus modes.
3. *Dynamic-area AF:* This mode provides a nine-AF-point frame that can be moved within the 273 AF points in the frame. It uses a center active AF point, like Single-point AF, but it surrounds that AF point with eight additional points that are on high alert. If you or the

subject move and the active center AF point loses the subject, one of the surrounding AF points can recapture the subject. Dynamic-area AF AF-area mode is available for still photography only, not video. Also, this AF-area mode is not available when you have the camera set to AF-S Focus mode. You must use AF-C Focus mode or Dynamic-area AF will be grayed out on the Photo Shooting Menu and not available on the *i* Menu.

4. ***Wide-area AF (S):*** This mode works in a similar manner to Single-point AF except that it has a wider group of AF points in its frame. As you can see, the focus frame is larger in figure 7.26A, image 4, compared to Single-point AF in image 2. Wide-area AF (S) AF-area mode is available in both AF-S and AF-C Focus modes.

5. ***Wide-area AF (L):*** This mode also works in a similar manner to Single-point AF except that it has a much wider group of AF points in its frame. You can see that the focus frame is significantly larger in figure 7.26A, image 5, compared to Wide-area AF (S) in image 4. Wide-area AF (L) AF-area mode is available in both AF-S and AF-C Focus modes.

6. ***Auto-area AF:*** This mode gives full control of the AF system to the camera. The entire 273-point frame is involved in autofocus. The camera will choose a combination of AF points within the frame to get best focus on your subject. You will see groups of rectangles marking the areas the camera is using for autofocus. If a human face is detected in the frame, a yellow square will surround the face and attempt to focus on that face. If multiple people are in the frame, the yellow square for the active face will add a directional arrow beside the yellow frame. This indicates that you can choose another face for best focus by scrolling with the Multi selector. If you want to choose just one person or some other subject to track, you can press the OK button and choose some part of your subject with the small white frame (targeting reticule) that appears and then press the OK button again—or the AF-ON button. The camera will activate Subject tracking and will attempt to track a moving subject with the white frame. Press OK again to stop Subject tracking. Auto-area AF AF-area mode is available in both AF-S and AF-C Focus modes.

Now let's consider how to choose an AF-area mode. Similar to choosing a Focus mode in the last section, there are three ways to choose your favorite AF-area mode: on the Photo Shooting Menu, on the *i* Menu, and with the Fn2 button.

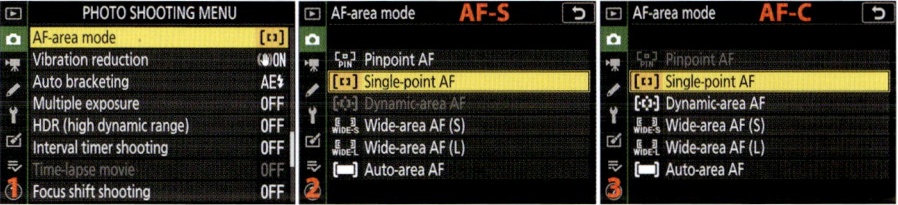

Figure 7.26B: AF-area modes on the Photo Shooting Menu

Use the following steps to choose an AF-area mode from the camera's Photo Shooting Menu:

1. Choose AF-area Mode from the Photo Shooting Menu and scroll to the right (figure 7.26B, image 1).
2. Referring to the previous list, highlight an AF-area mode and press the OK button or tap the mode to choose it (figure 7.25B, images 2 and 3). The AF-area mode secondary screen offers choices according to whether you are using AF-S Focus mode or AF-C Focus mode. Images 2 and 3 are the same screen, showing your choices when the camera is using different Focus modes. Grayed-out AF-area mode items are not available in that particular Focus mode.

Next, let's examine how to select the same AF-area modes from the *i* Menu.

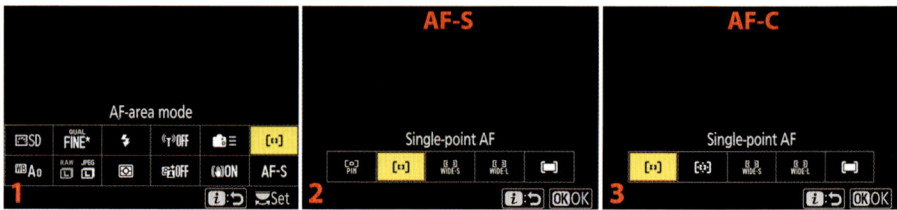

Figure 7.26C: AF-area modes on the *i* Menu

Use the following steps to select an AF-area mode from the *i* Menu:

1. Press the *i* button on the camera's back to open the *i* Menu. Choose AF-area mode by highlighting its symbol and pressing the OK button or by tapping the symbol (figure 7.26, image 1). The secondary screen will open.
2. Referring to the previous list, choose one of the AF-area modes by highlighting its symbol and pressing the OK button or by tapping the symbol (figure 7.26C, images 2 and 3).
3. As with the Photo Shooting Menu, the camera will present choices according to which Focus mode (AF-S or AF-C) you selected in the previous chapter section.

Next let's see how to use the assigned Fn2 button to access the Focus mode system.

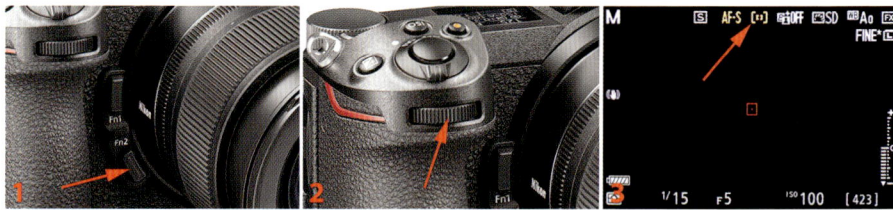

Figure 7.26D: Using the Fn2 button to choose an AF-area mode

Use the following steps to choose an AF-area mode with external camera controls:

1. Press and hold the Fn2 button on the front of the camera (figure 7.26D, image 1).
2. Turn the Sub-command dial on the camera's front handgrip (figure 7.26D, image 2).
3. The Monitor and EVF will display AF-area mode symbols at the top (figure 7.26D, image 3, red arrow). The AF-area mode will change as you rotate the front Sub-command dial. When the AF-area mode you want to use is displayed on the screen, stop turning the Sub-command dial and release the Fn2 button.

Note: See the chapter titled **Focus, AF Area, and Release Modes** (page 89) for deeper information on using AF-area modes and their relationship with the Focus and Release modes.

Vibration Reduction

Vibration reduction (VR) attempts to counteract small movements of the camera due to shaky hands or slow shutter speeds. It is designed to keep the image sharp while using up to five stops slower shutter speeds than normal. For instance, if you can handhold a camera and get sharp images at 1/60 second, then, if you are careful, you may be able to handhold the camera and get comparatively sharp images at 1/2 second.

Therefore, if you normally use the reciprocal of focal length rule and shoot handheld at a minimum of 1/500 second with a 500mm lens, you may be able to get sharp images of static subjects at 1/15 second. I am sure that is pushing things a bit, but the point is that IBIS VR allows you to get sharp images where you normally would have to use a tripod.

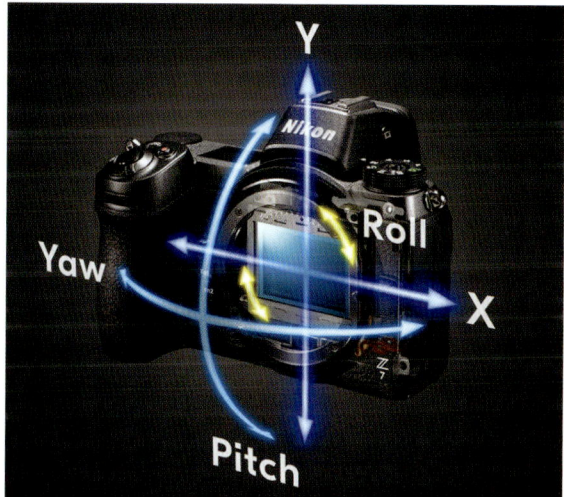

Figure 7.27A: In-body image stabilization (IBIS), aka Vibration reduction (VR) [image © Nikon]

The Vibration reduction function is different in Nikon Z cameras compared to Nikon DSLRs. Current Nikon DSLRs do not have in-body image stabilization (IBIS), where the Z cameras do. IBIS is a vibration reduction (VR) system where the sensor assembly can move in up to 5-axes to counter camera vibration (figure 7.27A): left and right (X), up and down (Y), pitch, yaw, and roll. Best results are achieved when using Nikkor Z-mount lenses. If you are using an F-mount, AF-S Nikkor lens on an FTZ adapter, the camera provides up to 3-axis IBIS (pitch, yaw, and roll).

Vibration reduction for Nikon DSLRs is handled within Nikkor lenses marked with the VR symbol only. At the time of this book's publication, there are no Nikon DSLR bodies using IBIS. Even if IBIS VR were developed for Nikon DSLRs, it would not be possible to see its effects in an optical viewfinder the same way you can see the effects of VR in a Nikkor lens, although IBIS would still work great for image stabilization.

With a Z camera, when you are using a Nikkor lens with VR built in, the camera and lens communicate and work together to get the best vibration reduction. Let's see how to choose the best IBIS VR for your needs.

Vibration Reduction Modes

There are two VR modes available, along with Off (no VR). Let's examine what each mode is designed to accomplish:

- **On Normal:** This mode is designed for shooting static subjects. If you are handholding the camera, or it is on a wobbly tripod or on a monopod, this is the best mode to use. Do not use IBIS VR when on a solid tripod or unexpected results might occur (e.g., odd-looking background effects).
- **SPT Sport:** This mode is designed for shooting sports where subjects are moving rapidly and unpredictably. Use this mode for panning. The Z6 will detect when you are panning with your subject and turn off IBIS for horizontal movement. It will correct for vertical movement only when panning. When the subject stops moving and panning ceases, IBIS will again work for both horizontal and vertical vibration reduction.
- **Off:** The camera disables the IBIS system for the Z6 and Z-mount lenses.

The Vibration reduction menu item on the Photo Shooting Menu and in the *i* Menu will become grayed out and unavailable when an AF-S Nikkor lens with VR is mounted on the camera with the FTZ adapter. To control VR in that case, simply use the VR On/Off switch found on the side of Nikkor VR lenses. The VR On/Off switch will enable in-lens and in-body image stabilization at the same time. When a Nikkor lens having no VR (e.g., AF-S Nikkor 50mm f/1.4G) is mounted, the Vibration reduction menus become available again.

Now, let's see how to choose an IBIS VR mode from the Shooting Menu and the *i* Menu.

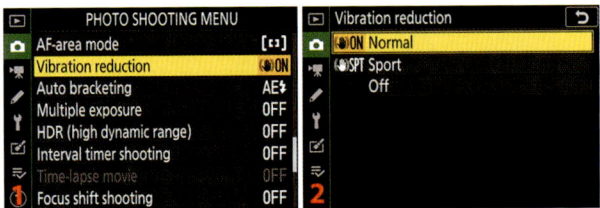

Figure 7.27B: Selecting an IBIS VR mode from the Photo Shooting Menu

Use the following steps to choose a Vibration reduction mode from the camera's Photo Shooting Menu:

1. Choose Vibration reduction from the Photo Shooting Menu and scroll to the right (figure 7.27B, image 1).
2. Referring to the previous list, highlight a Vibration reduction mode and press the OK button or tap the mode to select it (figure 7.27B, image 2).

Next, let's examine how to select the same Vibration reduction modes from the *i* Menu.

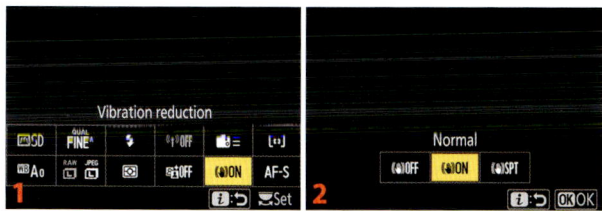

Figure 7.27C: Selecting an IBIS VR mode from the *i* Menu

Use the following steps to select a Vibration reduction mode from the *i* Menu:

1. Press the *i* button on the camera's back to open the *i* Menu. Choose a Vibration reduction mode by highlighting its symbol and pressing the OK button or by tapping the symbol (figure 7.27C, image 1). The secondary screen will open.
2. Referring to the previous list, choose one of the Vibration reduction modes (i.e., OFF, ON, SPT) by highlighting its symbol and pressing or touching OK (figure 7.7C, image 2).

Settings Recommendation: In my experience with my Nikon Z6, I can regularly get sharp images of static subjects at 1/6 second. With a little bracing against something, I have created sharp images in the 1 to 2 second range.

Another of the marvelous things about IBIS in the Z6 is that it will work for virtually any lens mounted on the camera or on an adapter. Even older F-mount, manual focus AI and AI-S lens favorites, along with non-VR autofocus lenses, will have IBIS.

Auto Bracketing

Auto bracketing set lets you choose how bracketing works for each of the camera's bracketing methods. You can set up bracketing for the exposure system (AE), flash, White balance (WB), and Active D-Lighting (ADL).

Let's start by reviewing the five types of bracketing on the Z6. I'll explain how to use bracketing in an upcoming subsection:

- **AE & flash bracketing:** When you set up a session for bracketing, the camera will cause any type of normal pictures you take to be bracketed, whether they are standard exposures or you are using flash. See how to bracket in the next subsection.
- **AE bracketing:** Your bracketing settings will affect only the camera exposure system and not the flash.

- **Flash bracketing:** Your bracketing settings will affect only the flash system and not the camera exposure.
- **WB bracketing:** White balance bracketing works the same as exposure and flash bracketing, except it is designed for bracketing color in mired values, instead of bracketing light in EV step values. WB bracketing is not available with image quality settings of NEF (RAW) or NEF (RAW) + JPEG.
- **ADL bracketing:** In this case, you are bracketing Active D-Lighting (ADL) in up to five separate exposures. The next higher level of ADL is used on each selected exposure.

AE & Flash Bracketing (Includes AE Only and Flash Only)

AE & flash bracketing (exposure bracketing) allows you to bracket a series of images using ambient light and/or a Speedlight flash unit. You can later combine these images into a high dynamic range (HDR) image with greater than normal dynamic range, as seen in figure 7.28A.

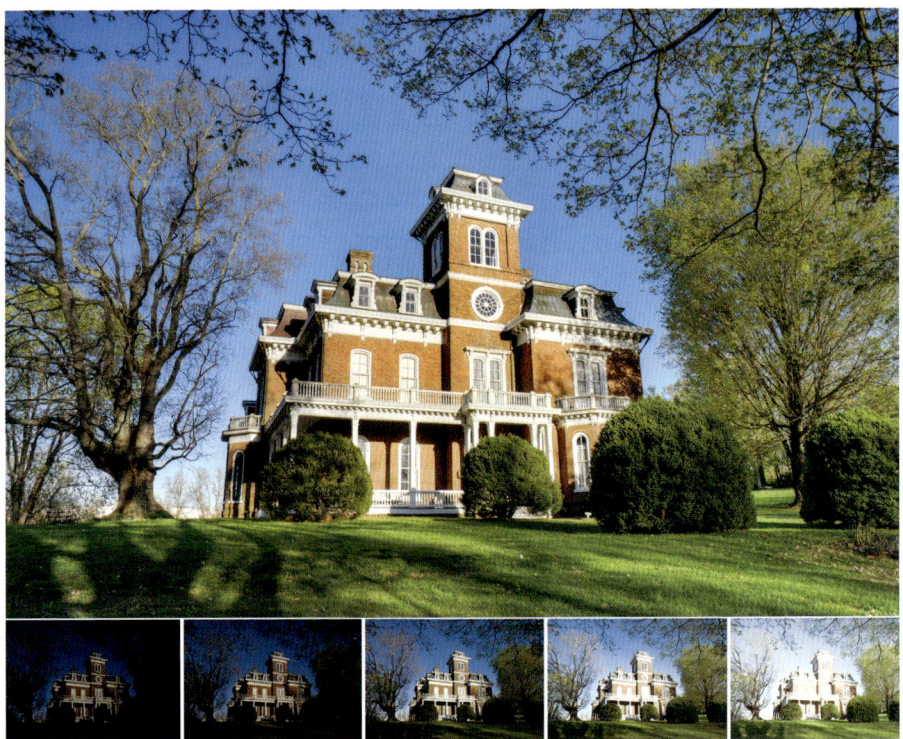

Figure 7.28A: Five-image bracket combined in Photomatix Pro to a single HDR image

In figure 7.28A you will find a sample five-image bracket with 1.0 EV step between each exposure. I combined the five images using Photomatix Pro software (**www.hdrsoft.com**) and was pleased with the final result. The main image was created with a bracketed series of five shots (the pictures underneath the main image) using the same settings shown on the Information display screen in figure 7.28C, image 1, as discussed in step 4 of the bracketing step-by-step method.

AE & flash bracketing, AE bracketing, and Flash bracketing all use bracketing in exactly the same manner and are all considered in this one section.

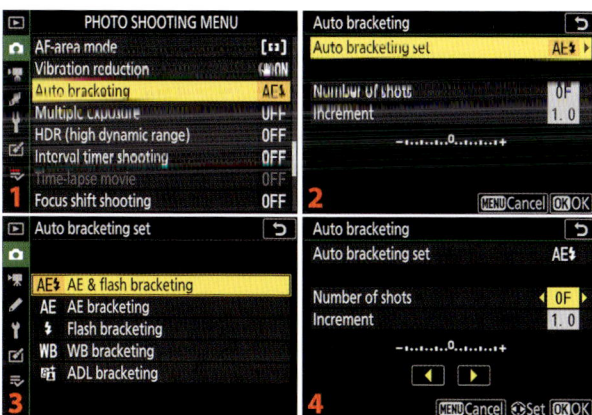

Figure 7.28B: AE and flash bracketing (top three types in screen 2)

Here are the steps to configure AE and flash bracketing for results similar to what is seen in figure 7.28A:

1. Select Auto bracketing from the Photo Shooting Menu and scroll to the right (figure 7.28B, image 1).
2. Highlight Auto bracketing set and scroll to the right (figure 7.28B, image 2). We will return to this screen for further adjustments after we have selected the type of bracketing we want to do.
3. Choose AE & flash bracketing, AE bracketing, or Flash bracketing and press the OK button or tap the item to lock in the setting (figure 7.28B, image 3).
4. The camera will return to the screen shown in figure 7.28B, image 2. We will now make adjustments to the Number of shots and Increment (or Amount for ADL) subsettings (figure 7.28B, image 4).

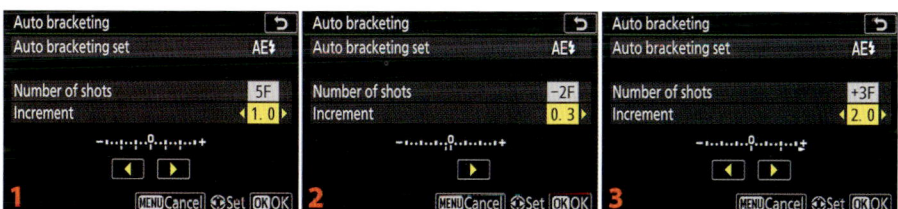

Figure 7.28C: Auto bracketing (AE & flash)

5. Figure 7.28C continues where figure 7.28B ends. We will now adjust the Number of shots and Increment subsettings. Highlight the item you want to change and scroll left or right with the Multi selector or tap on the left/right arrows to change the value. The symbols will initially be Number of shots: 0F and Increment: 1.0 (if not previously changed), and there may be no lines hanging below the −/+ scale. You will set both of those values as you create the bracket. The number of shots in the bracket appears at the end of the Number of shots line (e.g., 5F, −2F, and +3F) as shown in each screen in figure 7.28C. The amount of exposure difference appears at the end of the Increment line (e.g., 1.0, 0.3, and 2.0). Number of shots can be set to as many as 9 frames (9F) in an AE & flash bracketing, AE bracketing, or Flash bracketing bracket, and the Increment of exposure difference can range from 0.3 EV to 3.0 EV steps between frames. The number of small vertical lines hanging below the −...... 0 ......+ scale equals the number of shots in the bracket. The position of those lines represents the EV spread of the shots in the bracket. In figure 7.28C, image 1, for instance, you can count five lines hanging below the −/+ scale, and there is one stop of exposure between each line. Those five shots are represented by the 5F in image 1, and the 1.0 after Increment represents the 1 EV step (1 stop) exposure differential between each frame.

6. The Number of shots value can have a plus sign (+3F), minus sign (−2F), or no sign (5F) next to it (figure 7.28C). Select a number with a plus sign if you want the bracket to take only normal and overexposed shots. Select a number with a minus sign if you want the bracket to take only normal and underexposed shots. If you want the bracket to take exposures that are evenly distributed on both sides of the scale, select a number that has no plus or minus sign in front of it.

7. As previously mentioned, the Increment value controls the EV steps between each exposure in the bracket. This value appears at the right of Increment on each screen in figure 7.28C as 1.0, 0.3, and 2.0. You can select an EV step value between each image in the bracket, in steps of 1/3, and 1/2 EV. (The EV step value is set in *Custom Setting Menu > b Metering/exposure > b2 EV steps for exposure cntrl*. You can use *Custom Setting Menu > e Bracketing/flash > e7 Bracketing* order to set the order of the exposures. Once you have entered all the values you want to change, press or touch OK to lock in the values. We'll discuss this in chapter 9 in the section titled **Custom Setting e7: Bracketing Order** (page 421). The default order is *normal > underexposed > overexposed*. You can change it to *underexposed > normal > overexposed* if you'd like.) Following are detailed explanations of the values on images 1, 2, and 3 of figure 7.28C:

- *Figure 7.28C, image 1* shows a five-shot bracket with 1.0 EV step between each image. You can tell there are five shots by the 5F at the top center along with the number of lines hanging below the scale. The 1.0 means that there is 1.0 EV step (1 stop) between each exposure in the bracket. The fact that the 5F has no plus or minus sign in front of it tells us that the bracket uses exposures that are normal, overexposed, and underexposed.

- *Figure 7.28C, image 2* shows a two-image bracket with 0.3 EV steps (1/3 stop) between each exposure. Notice the minus sign before the 2F symbol (−2F). This means that the bracket is configured to take only normal and underexposed shots—no overexposed ones. The bracketed images are on the minus side of the −/+ scale.

- *Figure 7.28C, image 3* represents a three-image bracket with 2.0 EV steps between each exposure. The bracket is configured to take only normal and overexposed shots as indicated by the plus sign (+3F).

8. Figure 7.28D shows the camera's screen with the symbols for AE & Flash bracketing [AE BKT] (upper red arrow) and the +/− scale (lower red arrow). The +/− scale looks like a normal exposure scale; however, it is actually a bracketing scale in this instance. Once you have configured your bracket, press the Shutter-release button to take each bracketed picture in the series. Figure 7.28D's symbols (5 lines sticking out from the left of the +/− scale) show that this bracket

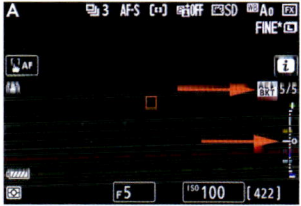

Figure 7.28D: Capturing the bracketed images

is for 5 frames (5F), with both two overexposed (+) images, one normal exposure (0), and two underexposed (−) images in the bracket. As you take each image, one of the lines that stick out to the left of the −/+ scale will disappear and the first number in the 5/5 next to AE BKT will reduce by one until all the frames are captured. When they are all gone (0/5), your bracket is complete. If you have your camera set to Continuous L or Continuous H release mode, you can shoot the all of frames in your bracket by holding down the Shutter-release button. Once the bracket is complete (all the lines are gone), the camera will stop firing.

Note about flash bracketing: If you are using a Speedlight flash unit to light the bracketed series, it may or may not be able to keep up with bracketed shots taken in Continuous-release mode. If you fully dump the flash power between shots, you'll have to wait for the next shot.

Settings Recommendation: I normally bracket with a 1 EV step value (1 stop) so I can get a good spread of light values in high dynamic range (HDR) images. In most cases, I will do a three- to five-image bracket, with one or two images overexposed and one or two images underexposed by 1 stop. This type of bracketing allows me to combine detail from the highlight and dark areas in-computer for the HDR exposures everyone is experimenting with these days.

WB Bracketing

The process for *WB bracketing* (white balance bracketing) is similar to the process for flash or exposure bracketing; you even use the same controls. No form of AE or flash bracketing will work during the time that Auto bracketing set is set to WB bracketing.

WB bracketing does not work when your camera is in NEF (RAW) and NEF (RAW) + JPEG modes. In fact, the bracketing controls will not even respond unless you are using a JPEG only mode because White balance information is stored with the RAW image but is not directly applied to the image. You can change the White balance after the fact when you are shooting RAW, so bracketing a RAW image does not make sense.

Now let's examine how to select WB bracketing, and then bracket the white balance.

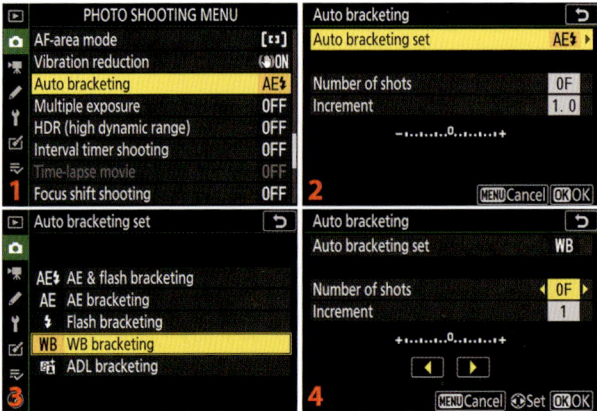

Figure 7.28E: Auto bracketing set – WB bracketing

Here are the steps to configure WB bracketing:

1. Select Auto bracketing from the Photo Shooting Menu and scroll to the right (figure 7.28E, image 1).
2. Highlight Auto bracketing set and scroll to the right (figure 7.28E, image 2). We will return to this screen for further adjustments after we have selected the type of bracketing we want to do.
3. Choose WB bracketing and press the OK button or tap the option to lock in the setting (figure 7.28E, image 3).
4. The camera will return to the screen shown in figure 7.28E, image 2. We will now make adjustments to the Number of shots and Increment (or Amount for ADL) subsettings (figure 7.28E, image 4).

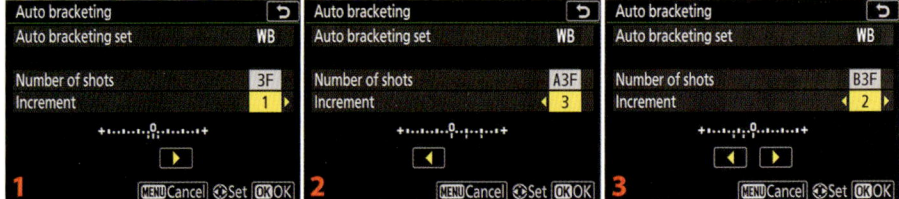

Figure 7.28F: WB bracketing (White balance)

5. Choose the number of shots in the bracket, examples of which are 3F, A3F, or B3F, as seen in figure 7.28F at the end of the Number of shots line. Press left or right on the yellow arrows, or scroll with the Multi selector pad, to select the number of shots, up to nine shots total (9F). In figure 7.28F, the 3F, A3F, and B3F symbols show the number of images (3), as do the lines hanging below the +/+ scale. Table 7.1 and step 4 describe what these mean.

Camera Displays	No. of Shots	WB Increment	Bracketing Order
0F	0	1	0
A2F	2	1A	0 > 1A
B2F	2	1B	0 > 1B
A3F	3	1A	0 > 2A > 1A
B3F	3	1B	0 > 1B > 2B
3F	3	1A, 1B	0 > 1A > 1B
5F	5	1A, 1B	0 > 2A > 1A > 1B > 2B
7F	7	1A, 1B	0 > 3A > 2A > 1A > 1B > 2B > 3B
9F	0	1A, 1B	0 > 4A > 3A > 2A > 1A > 1D > 2B > 3B > 4B

Table 7.1. Camera display symbols, number of shots, amber/blue changes, and bracketing order

6. You control the white balance color differences by bracketing toward amber or blue (A or B), using the symbols on the screen, as described in table 7.1. Each increment of color difference is called a *mired* and is controlled by the number displayed at the end of the Increment line, in figure 7.28F (i.e., 1, 3, 2). Change the mired Increment number by tapping the left or right yellow arrows or by scrolling with the Multi selector pad. Each number represents multiple mired. Choose 1, 2, or 3, where 1=5 mired, 2=10 mired, and 3=15 mired. Figure 7.28F, image 1, shows a 5 mired difference (1), image 2 shows a 15 mired difference (3), and image 3 shows a 10 mired difference (2). Once you have entered all the values you want to change, press or touch OK to lock in the values. Following are detailed explanations of the values on images 1, 2, and 3 of figure 7.28F:

   - **Figure 7.28F, image 1** shows a three-image bracket, with a 5 mired difference (1) in color between each image. One has more amber, one is normal, and one has more blue (3F).
   - **Figure 7.28F, image 2** shows a three-image bracket with a 15 mired difference (3) between each image, in the amber direction only (A3F).
   - **Figure 7.28F, image 3** shows a three-image bracket with a 10 mired color difference (2) in the blue direction only (B3F). If you do not see an A (A3F) or B (B3F) in the Number of shots position (e.g., 3F), it simply means that the bracket goes in both directions, such as *amber > normal > blue* or *normal > amber > blue*, according to how you have *Custom Setting Menu > e Bracketing/flash > e7 Bracketing order* set.

7. Press the Shutter-release button to take the bracketed picture series. Interestingly, you do this by taking just *one* picture. The camera takes that picture, reapplies the color filtration for each image in the bracket, and then saves each image as a separate image file with a new consecutive file number and bracketed color value. This works very differently from AE or flash bracketing, where you have to fire off each individual frame of the bracket. WB bracketing is very easy because you only have to set up the bracket and take one picture. The series of images in the bracket (up to nine) simply appears on your memory card. Nikons are fun!

How Does Mired Work?

Changes to mired simply modify the color of your image, in this case toward amber (reddish) or blue. In effect, changing mired toward amber or blue warms or cools the image. The color changes are applied directly to the image by the camera when shooting JPEGs or are saved as markers when shooting RAW images. You don't have to worry about mired values unless you are a color scientist.

You can just determine whether you like the image the way it is or would prefer that it be warmer or cooler and bracket accordingly. WB bracketing toward the A direction warms the image, whereas the B direction cools it. Technically, a mired is calculated by multiplying the inverse of the color temperature by 106.

I'd rather let my camera figure mired values and then judge them with my eye, wouldn't you? Remember, if you shoot in RAW, you can modify color values later in your computer. Otherwise, they are applied permanently to JPEG files.

ADL Bracketing

ADL bracketing (ADL stands for Active D-Lighting) is designed to let you shoot a normal image and then a series of up to four additional images with Active D-Lighting applied to each at progressively higher levels.

As you set ADL bracketing from two to five shots, you are setting the camera to switch to a higher ADL level for each consecutive shot. The progressive levels are Off, L Low, N Normal, H High, and H* Extra High.

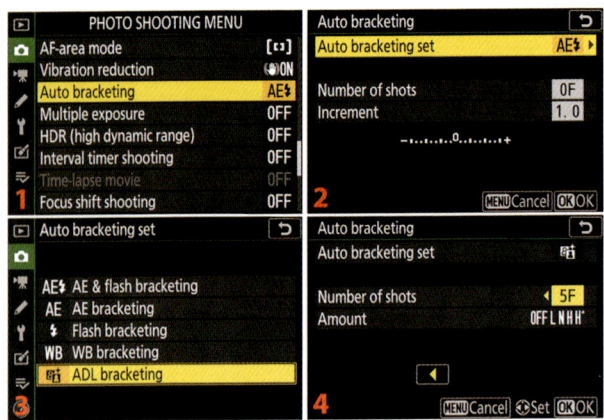

Figure 7.28G: Auto bracketing set – ADL bracketing

Here are the steps to use ADL bracketing:

1. Select Auto bracketing from the Photo Shooting Menu and scroll to the right (figure 7.28G, image 1).

2. Highlight Auto bracketing set and scroll to the right (figure 7.28G, image 2). We will return to this screen for further adjustments after we have selected the type of bracketing we want to do.

3. Choose ADL bracketing and press the OK button or tap the option to lock in the setting (figure 7.28G, image 3).

4. The camera will return to the screen shown in figure 7.28G, image 2. We will now make adjustments to the Number of shots and Amount subsettings.

5. Figure 7.28G, image 4, shows a bracket of five frames (5F), which means the camera will use all five available levels of Active D-Lighting (Off, L Low, N Normal, H High, and H* Extra high) as the five images are taken (Auto Active D-Lighting is ignored). You will also see the Amount field, which shows the full progression of the ADL bracket (OFF L N H H*), which stands for Off (OFF), Low (L), Normal (N), High (H), and Extra high (H*). Once you have entered all the values you want to change, press or touch OK to lock in the values.

6. Press the Shutter-release button to take each shot in the bracketed series. If you have your camera set to one of the Continuous-release modes (CL or CH), and are using AE & Flash bracketing, AE bracketing, Flash bracketing, or ADL bracketing—but not WB bracketing—you can shoot all frames in your bracket by holding down the Shutter-release button. Once the bracket is complete, the camera will stop firing.

Settings Recommendation: This is a great way to capture important shots and try to get extra shadow detail and highlight protection in some of them. You may not need ADL bracketing on all shots, but on important images where you are slightly off on your exposure selection, ADL will help to open shadows and mildly protect the highlights. Of course, if you shoot in RAW mode, you can apply ADL in-computer. I don't bracket ADL very often, but I'm glad to know it's there when I need it.

Note concerning all bracketing types: One final note about bracketing of any type: Turn it off when you're done by setting Number of shots to 0F! I often forget and then wonder why my camera keeps under- and overexposing a series of images. Only after wasting several images do I realize I left bracketing turned on. You'll see what I mean if you use AE & flash bracketing often, as I do.

Multiple Exposure

Multiple exposure is the process whereby you take more than one exposure on a single frame, or picture. Multiple exposure normally requires you to figure out the exposure values carefully for each exposure segment so that in the final picture, all the combined exposures equal one normal exposure. In other words, if you are going to create a nonmasked double exposure, your background will need two exposures at half the normal exposure value to equal one normal exposure.

The Z6 allows you to figure out your own exposure settings and input them manually, or you can use the Overlay mode to help with exposure calculations.

There are five steps to setting up a Multiple-exposure session, which we will examine in detail. The basic steps are as follows:

- Choose whether you are shooting one multiple-exposure image or a series of images.
- Select the number of individual shots you want to take, which will be combined into a multiple-exposure image.
- Select an Overlay mode to determine how you want to control exposure.
- Decide whether to keep the intermediate images that are combined to create the single multiple-exposure image, or delete the intermediate images and keep only the single multiple-exposure image.
- Optional step: You can choose a previously taken image as the first image in the multipleexposure series.
- Shoot the pictures that the camera will combine into one multiple-exposure image.

Let's discuss how to implement these steps. First, we will examine a simple double—exposure combination (figure 7.29A).

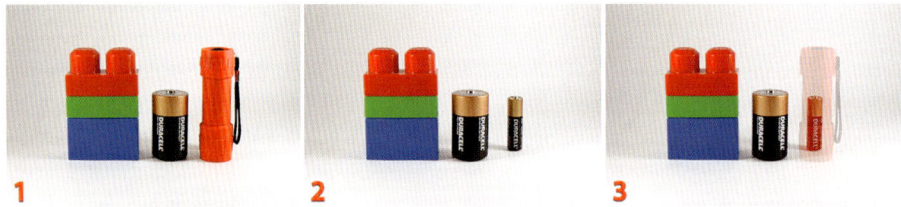

Figure 7.29A: Double-exposure image

In figure 7.29A, image 1, you see the first of two pictures that will be combined to create the third picture. The first picture received 1/2 of a normal exposure. The tall red flashlight was placed in front of the small battery and the picture was taken. The second image also received 1/2 of a normal exposure with the red flashlight removed. Image 3 is images 1 and 2 combined. Since the blocks and large battery received 1/2 exposure twice (1/2 exposure in two images), they are recorded with one full exposure in the combined picture. However, the red flashlight was in the first image only and received only 1/2 exposure, so it is somewhat transparent in the third image, allowing you to see the small battery through the flashlight.

Note: For my Multiple exposure sequence, I used Multiple exposure mode: On (single photo), Number of shots: 2, Overlay mode: Average (AVG), Keep all exposures: On, and Overlay shooting: On. If you choose to enable Keep all exposures, the individual intermediate exposures will be fully exposed, but will be combined at some fraction of their normal exposure value to create the single multiple exposure image. That's why the individual images in figure 7.29A, images 1 and 2, do not look underexposed, even though the camera is truly using only 1/2 exposure for each image. For more information about Keep

all exposures, see the downloadable document titled **How Does "Keep All Exposures" Work?** on the downloadable resources website: **http://rockynook.com/NikonZ6.**
Now let's discuss the multiple-exposure settings.

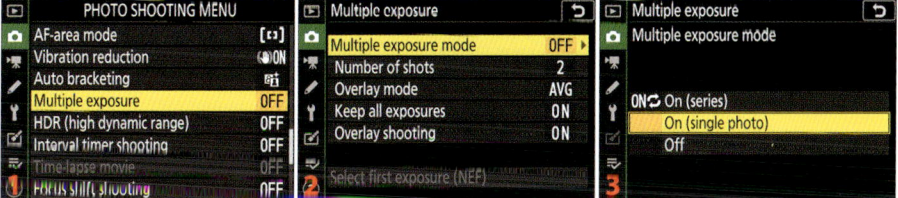

Figure 7.29B: Setting up Multiple exposure basics

Use the following steps to configure one or a series of multiple exposures:

1. Select Multiple exposure from the Photo Shooting Menu and scroll to the right (figure 7.29B, image 1).
2. Choose Multiple exposure mode from the Multiple exposure menu and scroll to the right (figure 7.29B, image 2).
3. Now choose whether you want one multiple exposure sequence or a series of multiple exposure sequences (figure 7.29B, image 3). If you choose On (single photo) the camera will automatically set Multiple exposure mode to Off after you have created one multiple-exposure picture. If, instead, you choose On (series) the camera will stay in Multiple exposure mode, allowing you to create many multiple exposures, until you manually set it to Off with this setting (image 3). Press the OK button or tap the option to lock in your choice.

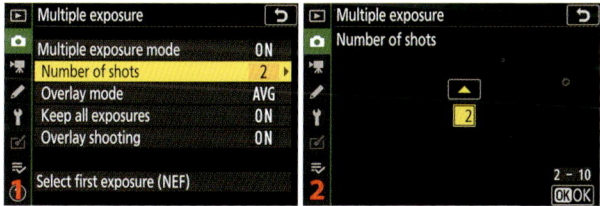

Figure 7.29C: Choosing the Number of shots in the multiple exposure

4. Select Number of shots and scroll to the right (figure 7.29C, image 1).
5. Use the up/down menu to choose the number of individual shots that will be combined into a final multiple-exposure picture (figure 7.29C, image 2). Select a number from 2 to 10 and then press or touch OK to save the setting.

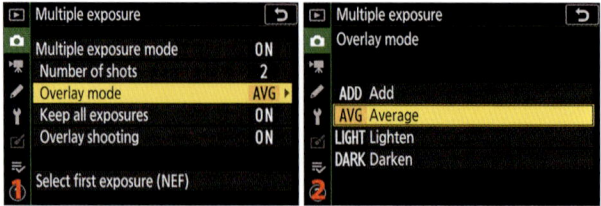

Figure 7.29D: Choosing an Overlay mode for proper exposure

6. Select Overlay mode and scroll to the right (figure 7.29D, image 1).
7. Select one of the Overlay modes, as discussed in table 7.2, and press the OK button or tap your selection (figure 7.29D, image 2).

Overlay Mode	Description
Add	All exposures are overlaid (combined) as they were taken, no exposure adjustments are made for individual image density.
Average	The camera will meter for a normal exposure and then divide the exposure in half for two shots. For three shots, it will divide the exposure by 1/3, four shots by 1/4, eight shots by 1/8, and so forth. In other words, it will divide the normal exposure for a single shot by the number you entered on the Number of shots screen so that when you are done, you have the equivalent of a single good exposure. This was called Auto gain in previous Nikon cameras.
Lighten	The Z6 will compare all the pixel values in each exposure and use only the brightest pixels to create the final combined image.
Darken	The Z6 will compare all the pixel values in each exposure and use only the darkest pixels to create the final combined image.

Table 7.2: Overlay mode choices and descriptions

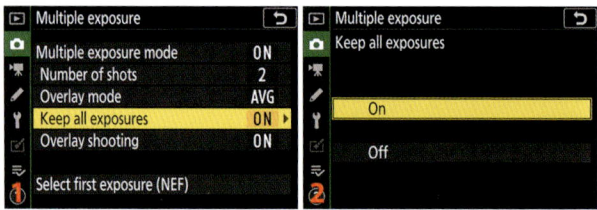

Figure 7.29E: Keep (or not) the individual images that make up the multiple exposure

8. Choose Keep all exposures from the menu and scroll to the right (figure 7.29E, image 1).
9. Select On if you want to keep each of the intermediate images that are combined into the final multiple-exposure picture. An example of these intermediate images is seen in figure 7.29A, images 1 and 2. If you do not have a use for the intermediate images, select Off and the camera will keep only the final combined multiple-exposure image. Press the OK button or tap the option to lock in your choice.

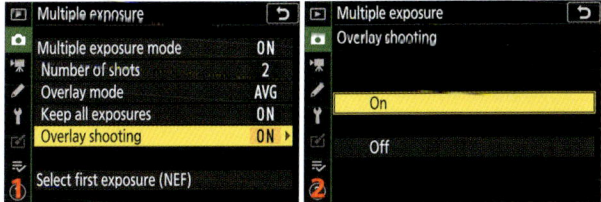

Figure 7.29F: Overlay shooting – see superimposed earlier images

10. Choose Overlay shooting from the Multiple exposure menu and scroll to the right (figure 7.29F, image 1).

11. If you want to see earlier images in the sequence superimposed over the view through the lens, select On. Otherwise, select Off. Press the OK button or tap the option to save the setting (figure 7.29F, image 2).

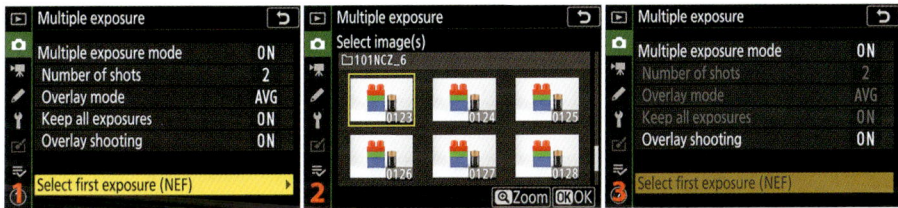

Figure 7.29G: Select the first image included in a multiple-exposure picture (optional)

12. *Please note:* This is an *optional* step and is not required for normal multiple-exposure images. You may use this special setting to start with a previously taken primary image to which other intermediate images will be added. Highlight Select first exposure (NEF) and scroll to the right (figure 7.29G, image 1).

13. Choose a NEF (RAW) image to use as the first image in the group of intermediate images (figure 7.29G, image 2). Although other intermediate images can be JPEG images, this first one must be a NEF (RAW) image. Once you have selected a RAW image to use as a base, press or touch OK and the camera will return to the main Multiple exposure screen, ready to start the Multiple exposure sequence. If you are creating a fresh multiple exposure picture, you can safely skip steps 12 and 13.

Once you've selected the basic values for Multiple exposure mode, the camera will remember your multiple exposure settings, and you may reuse them for the next session.

Note: If you do a lot of multiple exposures, you can assign one of the camera's programmable buttons to allow you to select Multiple exposure settings with external camera controls. We will consider how in the chapter **Custom Setting Menu,** under the subheading **f2 Custom control assignment** (page 423).

Changes During a Multiple-Exposure Session

Nikon has provided an *i* Menu with action choices that allow you to modify a multiple exposure session—one with at least three images in the sequence—that is in progress (figure 7.29H). Here is a description of each:

- **View progress:** Allows you to see a preview of the multiple exposure at the current point.
- **Retake last exposure:** If you are unhappy with the latest intermediate exposure, you can ask the camera to discard and retake the exposure.
- **Save and exit:** Stops the multiple-exposure session at the current point and assembles the final picture from images taken so far.
- **Discard and exit:** Exits the multiple-exposure session and throws away the current multiple-exposure picture. If you previously set *Keep all exposures* to On, the camera will not throw away the intermediate images.

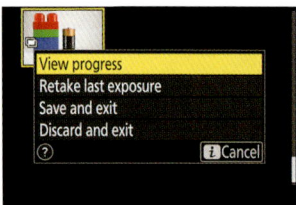

Figure 7.29H: Multiple exposure *i* menu.

Use the following steps to access and use the multiple-exposure *i* Menu:

1. While a multiple exposure is in session and you have taken at least two intermediate images, press the Playback button (▶). This will open the last of the intermediate images so you can see it on the Monitor.
2. Press the *i* button and the menu in figure 7.29H will display.
3. Make your selection and press the OK button to proceed with one of the self-explanatory actions, or press the *i* button again to cancel and return to the current multiple-exposure session.

Settings Recommendation: Multiple exposure images can be a lot of fun to create. I often shoot Multiple exposure images with two people in the frame. One person leaves after the first half of the exposure is taken, while the other carefully stays still. When finished, you will have a normal picture of one person and the background, but the person who left halfway through the Multiple exposure will be ghosted (figure 7.29I). That means you'll be able to see the background right through them. It's even more fun if you have the person who leaves touch the other person during the first half of the Multiple exposure. Maybe have them put a hand on the other person's shoulder or wrap their arms around him.

If the person who stays for the entire exposure is very careful not to move at all, they will remain sharp and the image will certainly raise eyebrows later.

You can also do this with just one person, as the second picture in figure 7.29I shows. Just make sure they leave halfway through the Multiple exposure.

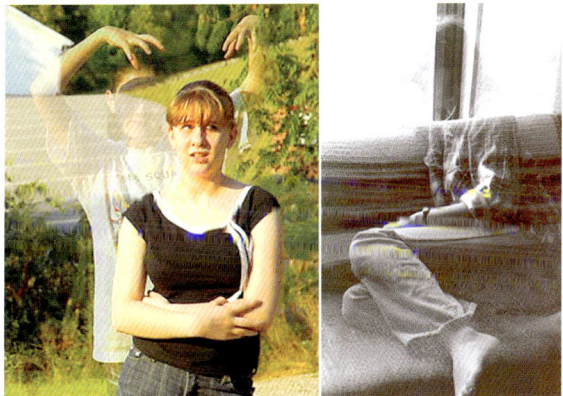

Figure 7.29I: Sample double-exposure images

HDR (High Dynamic Range)

HDR (high dynamic range) directs the camera to combine two JPEG or TIFF exposures into a single image. It is not available in NEF (RAW) modes.

HDR combines details from an underexposed shot and an overexposed shot into one well-exposed picture with much greater dynamic range than normal. In figure 7.30A, you can see a sample. The two images on the left were combined, in-camera, to create the third image.

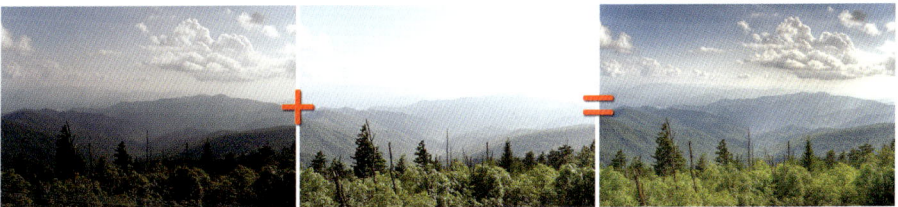

Figure 7.30A: HDR combination sample

HDR (high dynamic range) in the Z6 is a form of bracketing that allows you to create an HDR image without setting up a bracketing series. There are three settings to choose from under HDR (high dynamic range):

- **HDR mode:** This setting has three options: On (series), On (single photo), and Off. When On (series) is selected, the camera will keep shooting its two-image HDR brackets until you set HDR mode to Off. When On (single photo) is chosen, the camera will make a single HDR bracket for one image (figure 7.30A). Off means the camera does not create an HDR image.

- **Exposure differential:** You can choose how many stops (EV) there will be between the two images that are later combined. The choices are 1 EV, 2 EV, 3 EV, and Auto. Use 1, 2, or 3 EV when you want to make the decision; choose Auto when you want to let the camera decide. If you control the amount of Exposure differential, be careful to choose only what is needed or you may experience under- or overexposure in the final combined image. If a two-image exposure bracket is insufficient, you may want to investigate the exposure bracketing system connected to the BKT button. (**Note:** We previously discussed how to use the camera's bracketing system in this chapter under the heading **Auto Bracketing** [page 269]. With it you can do up to a nine-shot bracket.)

- **Smoothing:** This allows you to choose smoothing for the boundaries between the two images. Three choices are available: Low, Normal, and High. Each subject's boundaries are different, so you may have to experiment with these settings. Higher values make a smoother combined image. Watch out for uneven shading with some subjects.

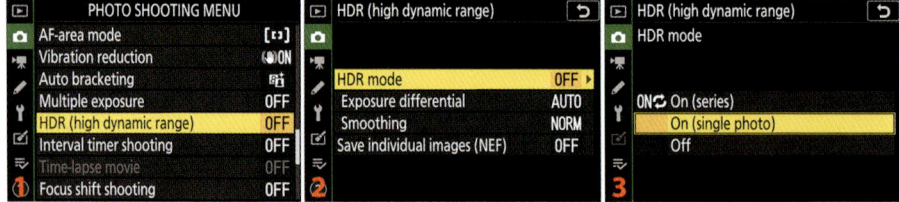

Figure 7.30B: Choosing an HDR mode

First, let's examine how to configure the three settings and prepare for HDR imaging. Use these steps to enable HDR mode for a single picture or a series:

1. Follow the screen flow shown in figure 7.30B, images 1 and 2 (*HDR (high dynamic range) > HDR mode*) until you arrive at the third screen in the series.
2. Decide whether you want to make one or a series of HDR images and choose accordingly: On (series) for a series of images or On (single photo) for a single image (figure 7.30B, image 3).
3. Press the OK button or tap your selection to prepare the camera for shooting in HDR mode.

When the Z6 is set to HDR mode, you will see the acronym HDR displayed on the camera's EVF and Monitor. It will go away when HDR mode is set to Off. Now let's look into configuring the Exposure differential setting.

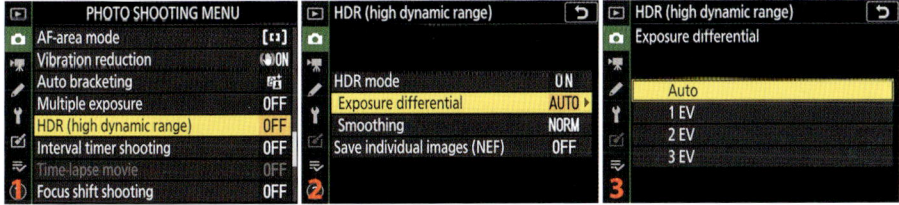

Figure 7.30C: Choosing an Exposure differential setting

Use the following steps to choose an Exposure differential setting:

1. Follow the screen flow shown in figure 7.30C, images 1 and 2 (*HDR (high dynamic range)* > *Exposure differential*) until you arrive at the third screen in the series.
2. Choose one of the four settings, according to how much exposure variance you want between the two images that will be combined into one (figure 7.30C, image 3). Use Auto to let the camera decide, or choose from 1 EV to 3 EV. If you have a high-contrast subject, you may want to try the 3 EV level first to see if it works best. For low- to medium-contrast subjects, choose 1 EV or 2 EV. Press the OK button or tap the option to lock in your choice.

Next, let's see how to configure the Smoothing selection for the best image edge boundary control.

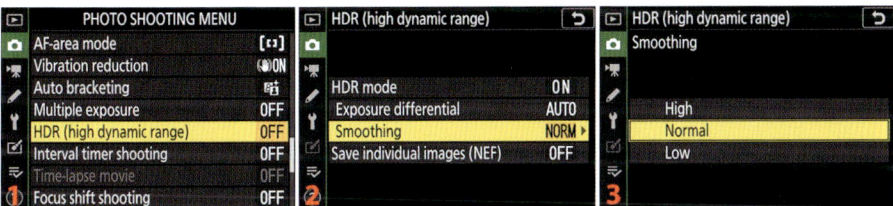

Figure 7.30D: Choosing a Smoothing setting

Use these steps to configure Smoothing for the HDR image combination:

1. Follow the screen flow shown in figure 7.30D, images 1 and 2 (*HDR (high dynamic range)* > *Smoothing*) until you arrive at the third screen in the series.
2. Select High, Normal, or Low (figure 7.30D, image 3). You will need to experiment and observe the differences in image boundaries when you vary this setting. Press the OK button or tap the option to choose your Smoothing level.

Finally, let's see how to save intermediate images as NEF (RAW) files.

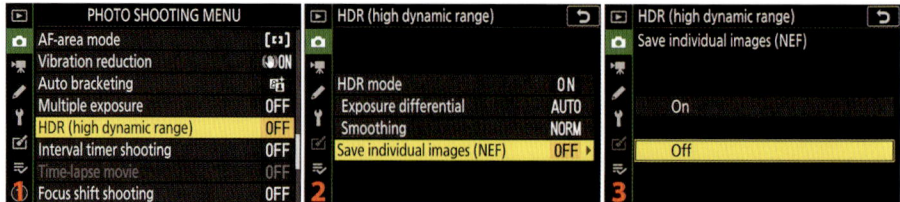

Figure 7.30E: Saving intermediate images as NEF files

Use the following steps to save the two intermediate files as Large NEF files, regardless of the camera's current Image quality and Image size settings:

1. Follow the screen flow shown in figure 7.30E, images 1 and 2 (*HDR (high dynamic range)* > *Save individual images (NEF)*) until you arrive at the third screen in the series.
2. Select On or Off and press the OK button or tap the option to save the setting (figure 7.30E, image 3).

If you do not use this setting, the camera will not keep the intermediate files at all. Instead, you will just have the one HDR image.

Now it's time to take some HDR pictures. Here are some things you will need to know during and after the HDR process:

- The camera will take two exposures when you press the Shutter-release button all the way down once. It is a good idea to have the camera on a tripod during low-light HDR operations or you may have some nasty, blurry images as a result. If you do choose to handhold in low light, please brace yourself and do not allow camera movement. When light is very bright, the HDR process can be quite fast. It is much slower when light is low, taking several seconds to deliver a combined image.
- **HDR** will be displayed in the EVF and on the Monitor as soon as you enable HDR (high dynamic range).
- **Job** and **HDR** will flash on the small top Control panel during image combination.
- The edges of the image may be cropped, so do not allow important parts of the subject to touch the edges if possible.
- If you detect shadows around bright objects or halos around dark objects, you can reduce this effect by setting Smoothing to a lower level.
- You cannot select any form of NEF (RAW) shooting when HDR (high dynamic range) mode is enabled, only JPEG or TIFF. Also, HDR (high dynamic range) mode is grayed out on the Photo Shooting Menu when you set Image quality using NEF (RAW).

Note: You can assign one of the camera's programmable buttons to allow you to select HDR settings with external camera controls. See the section **f2 Custom Control Assignment** (page 423) in chapter 9.

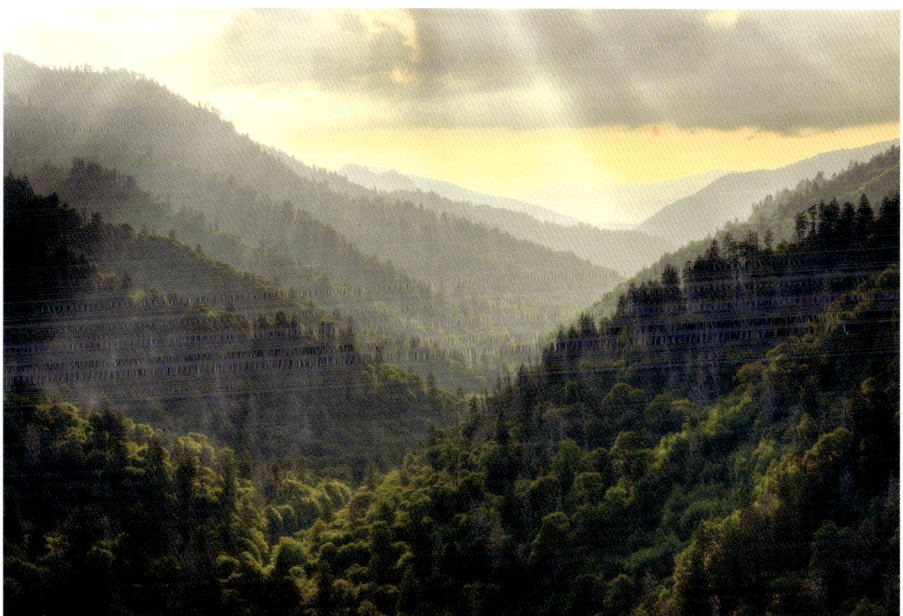

Figure 7.30F: Morton's Overlook with sunbeams in the Great Smoky Mountains, Tennessee, near sunset. Five-image HDR with 1 stop EV difference between each image. Combined in Photomatix Pro 5. AF-S Nikkor 24–70mm f/2.8G ED lens at 70mm, f/22, ISO 100, on tripod.

Settings Recommendation: I am a big fan of bracketing and HDR. You'll often find me on top of some Appalachian mountain shooting a five-bracket HDR shot of the valley below. Beautiful things can be done with HDR. I do not like the shadowless HDR images that some photographers shoot. To me they look fake and seem faddish. However, HDR, when used correctly, can help create images the camera could not normally take due to excessive light range.

Photoshop has built-in software for HDR, or you can buy a less costly dedicated package, such as Photomatix Pro by HDRsoft. I've been using Photomatix Pro for several years to combine my bracketed images into carefully tone-mapped HDR images.

There are some limitations to in-camera HDR, which is why people who are serious about it use the main bracketing system and combine their images using dedicated HDR software (figure 7.30E). However, HDR (high dynamic range) in the Z6 is an easy way to knock off a few quick HDR images for those times when only an HDR will do. Give it a try!

Interval Timer Shooting

Interval timer shooting allows you set up your camera to shoot a series of images over a long period of time so you can capture events such as flower petals opening. Interval timer shooting is somewhat different than Time-lapse movie (page 295) because an Interval timer shooting session is usually measured in hours or days, instead of minutes, and no automatic movie creation is done at the end. At the end of an Interval timer shooting session, you will have a large number of images that you can assemble into a movie in your computer or use individually. There are five steps to configuring an Interval timer shooting session:

- Choose a start date and time
- Choose an interval between pictures
- Choose the number of intervals and the number of pictures per interval
- Enable or disable Exposure smoothing
- Enable or disable Silent photography

Let's carefully consider how to configure your Interval timer choices.

Configuring an Interval Timer Shooting Session

The series of screens we will now consider may look a little daunting at first; however, if you take the setup one step at a time, you will quickly learn to do Interval timer shooting. First, let's see how to choose when the picture taking begins and ends.

Note: You can start the timer immediately by choosing the Start selection from the menu. However, we will save that step for last because we have configured nothing for the Interval timer. Therefore, we will skip Start at the top of the Interval timer shooting menu (figure 7.31A, image 2) and begin by setting up Choose start day/time.

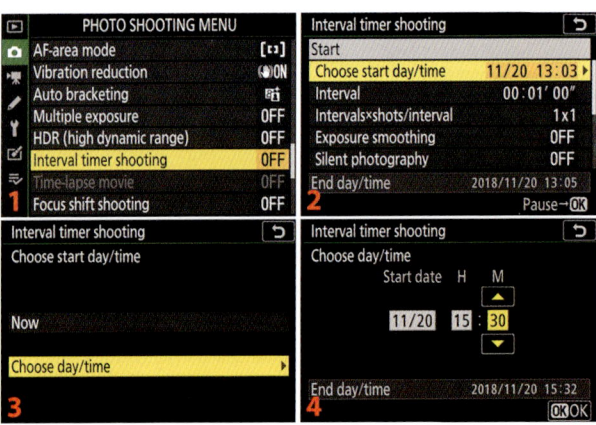

Figure 7.31A: Interval timer shooting configuration

Use the following steps to configure an Interval timer shooting session:

1. Select Interval timer shooting from the Photo Shooting Menu and scroll to the right (figure 7.31A, image 1).
2. Skip over the Start selection for now because we have not configured any of the Interval timer settings yet (figure 7.31A, image 2). Later, after you have configured the Interval

timer, you can simply come back and select Start to begin the timer. The camera will remember the settings from your last configuration of the Interval timer and you can use them again by selecting Start and pressing the OK button or by tapping Start with your fingertip.

3. Highlight Choose start day/time and scroll to the right (figure 7.31A, image 2).

4. The Choose start day/time menu will display two choices, Now and Choose day/time (figure 7.31A, image 3). Choose Now if you want to start the timer three seconds after you select Start and then press the OK button. If you would rather select a specific date and time to start the timer, select Choose day/time from the menu and scroll to the right.

5. The Choose day/time screen will now appear (figure 7.31A, image 4). The Start date is always presented in the Month/Day (MM/DD) format, while the time is presented in a 24-hour (international time) format. If you are not using the Now selection from the previous step, move to the Start date field and use the up/down menu to enter a month and day, such as 11/20.

6. Next, scroll over to the H and M fields and enter an hour in international time format (e.g., 15 = 3 p.m.). Enter the time at which you want the intervals to begin. The selectable hour (H) range is from 00 (midnight) to 23 (11 p.m.). After you have entered an hour setting, enter a minute setting. The selectable minute (M) range is from 00 to 59. Once you've entered the time, press or touch OK to lock it in. In figure 7.31A, image 4, my camera reflects a start time of 11/20 15:30 (November 20 at 3:30 p.m.) in the adjustable settings, and an ending time of 11/20 15:32 (November 20 at 3:32 p.m.) in the informational display at the bottom of the screen. Now let's choose an Interval that will elapse before more pictures are taken.

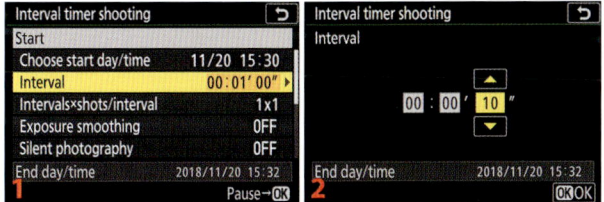

Figure 7.31B: Choosing an Interval

7. The camera will now return to the Interval timer shooting menu. Choose the Interval setting on the Interval timer shooting screen and scroll to the right (figure 7.31B, image 1).

8. You will now see the interval selection fields with selections representing Hours: Minutes' Seconds" in the following format (figure 7.31B, image 2): 00:00' 00". The first two zeros represent the hours, the second set represents minutes, and the third set represents seconds. We will start out with an Interval of 10 seconds, so let's set the screen to look like this: 00: 00' 10". Once you've entered the Interval, press or touch OK to lock it in. Now the camera will wait the length of time you set in the Interval field between each series of pictures.

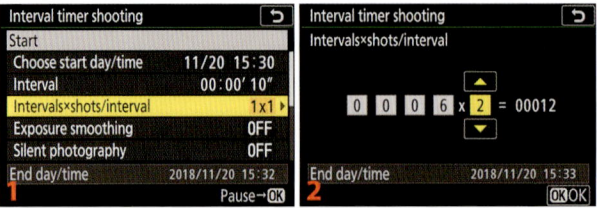

Figure 7.31C: Choosing the number of intervals and number of shots per interval

9. Now we'll choose the number of intervals and shots per interval by selecting Intervals×shots/interval and scrolling to the right (figure 7.31C, image 1).

10. You will be presented with a screen where you can select the number of intervals (Intervals) and the number of shots per interval (shots/interval), as seen in figure 7.31C, image 2. Number of intervals × number of shots = total shots. These values are gathered in this format: 0000 × 0 = 0000. You can set the number of intervals (0000) anywhere from 0001 to 9999. You can set the number of shots taken per interval anywhere from 1 to 9. If, for example, you want to shoot six Intervals, and take two pictures during each Interval, set your camera so that it looks like this: 0006 × 2 = 00012 (figure 7.31C, image 2). This means there will be six Intervals (0006) of 10 seconds each (set in step 7) and the camera will take two pictures for each interval (x 2), for a total of 12 pictures (00012). In other words, 2 pictures will be taken every 10 seconds over a period of 60 seconds, for a total of 12 images at the end of the series (0006 intervals × 10 seconds each = 60 seconds). Press or touch OK to lock in the Intervals×shots/interval value. **Note:** The maximum number of images that can be taken in one Interval timer session is 89991. Additionally, if you have the camera set to single frame release mode, the camera will instead use Continuous Low release mode. You can choose a frames-per-second (fps) rate for Continuous Low in *Custom Setting d1 CL mode shooting speed,* which defaults to 3 fps (page 398).

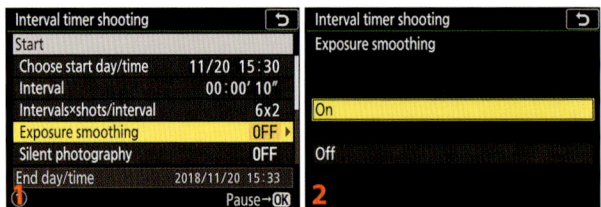

Figure 7.31D: Choosing an Exposure smoothing setting

11. Next, you may select Exposure smoothing (figure 7.31D, image 1), which allows the camera to adjust the exposure of an image so it matches the exposure of the previous image, when using P, S, and A modes on the Mode dial. If you use M mode, you must have *Photo Shooting Menu > ISO sensitivity settings > Auto ISO sensitivity control* set to On (page 190), or Exposure smoothing will not work. Choose Exposure smoothing from the Interval timer shooting screen and scroll to the right (figure 7.31D, image 1).

Note: If you have very long Intervals, and you are shooting outdoors, there may be such large changes in brightness that the camera cannot overcome it and smoothing will not work. In that case, you will need to shorten the Intervals or accept the brightness changes.

12. Select On or Off for Exposure smoothing and press the OK button or tap the option to lock in the setting (figure 7.31D, image 2).

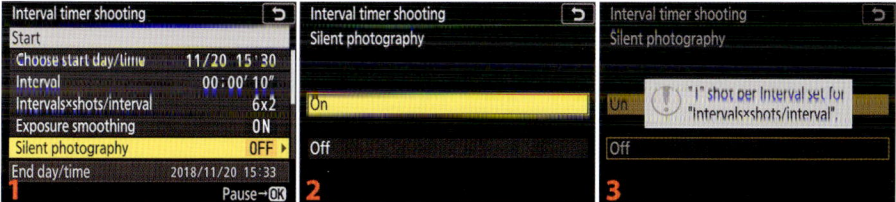

Figure 7.31E: Enabling or disabling Silent photography

13. Next, you may highlight Silent photography on the Interval timer shooting menu and scroll to the right (figure 7.31E, image 1).
14. Select On to use the camera's electronic shutter instead of the mechanical shutter or select Off to cancel (figure 7.31E, image 2). If you select On, no sound will be heard during the Interval timer shooting session. Though the camera will be silent, it will display each image on the Monitor as it is captured. Unfortunately, if you enable Silent photography and have previously selected more than one shot per interval (steps 9 and 10), the camera will reset the shots per interval setting back to 1 (figure 7.31E, image 3). A message will pop up on the screen that says, *"1" shot per interval set for "Intervals×shots/interval"* as soon as you select On. To take more than one shot per interval, you must not use Silent photography! *Note:* Using Silent photography mode disables the following camera features:

- ISO sensitivity of Hi 0.3 to Hi 2
- Flash photography
- Exposure delay mode
- Flicker reduction
- Bracketing

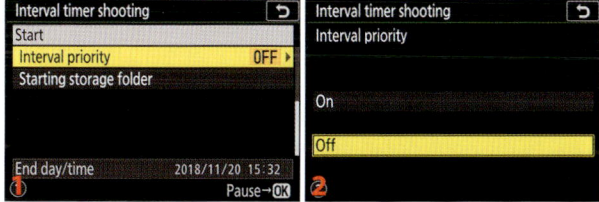

Figure 7.31F: Enabling or disabling Interval priority

15. In some Interval timer shooting situations you might find yourself in the unenviable position of needing an exposure time that is longer than the Interval time, leading to underexposed images if the Interval timing is obeyed. To remedy that problem, Nikon has provided the Interval priority setting, allowing you to set priority for the Interval timing or the exposure timing. Choose Interval priority from the Interval timer shooting menu and scroll to the right (figure 7.31F, image 1).

16. Select On and press the OK button or touch On with your fingertip to set the priority on the Interval timing for exposure modes P and A. This setting does *not* apply to the M or S exposure modes. Be aware that if you have selected On, the camera *will not* complete a good exposure when the exposure time is longer than the Interval time. The Interval timing will have priority. If you feel the exposure time is more critical than the Interval time, then set Interval priority to Off and press the OK button or touch Off with your fingertip. ***Note:*** If On is selected, be sure that the Minimum shutter speed under the Auto ISO sensitivity control settings is faster than the Interval setting (see: *Photo Shooting Menu > ISO sensitivity settings > Auto ISO sensitivity control > Minimum shutter speed,* on page 192). Also, you should use manual focus. However, if you do use autofocus, use *Release* priority under *Custom Setting Menu > a Autofocus > a1 AF-C priority selection* (page 365) or *Custom Setting Menu > a Autofocus > a2 AF-S priority selection* (page 366), according to whether you are using AF-C or AF-S Focus modes. The camera will not take a picture when it is not in focus unless Release priority is selected, which, of course, may be a good thing for most of us. *Note:* If Interval priority is enabled, Bracketing is disabled.

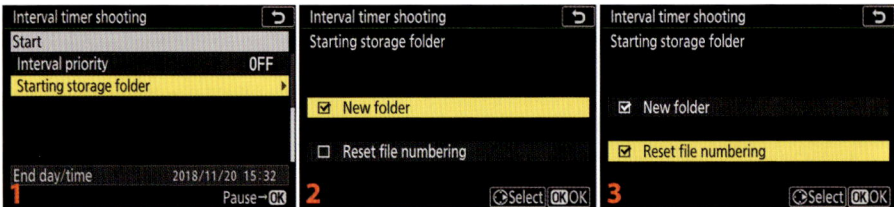

Figure 7.31G: Selecting a Starting folder and file numbering

17. You can choose to have the camera create a new folder for each Interval timer shooting session so each session is stored separately. You can also choose to set image numbering back to 0001 at the beginning of each session (e.g., DSC-0001.jpg). Choose Starting storage folder from the Interval timer shooting menu and scroll to the right (figure 7.31G, image 1).

18. If you want to use a separate new folder for each Interval timer shooting session, highlight New folder and scroll to the right, or tap on the small box to the left of New folder to add a check mark (figure 7.31G, image 2). Now, when the camera starts a new Interval timer shooting session, it will first create a new folder. For instance, I was taking normal pictures using a folder named 200YOUNG. When I put a check mark next to New folder (enabled it) and started an Interval timer shooting session, the camera created a new folder named 201YOUNG and saved all the images from that session in

the new folder. You can also choose to use continuous image numbering or start over with 0001 with each new session. If you prefer to use new image numbers for each session, go to the next step instead of selecting OK. Otherwise, to keep using current sequential image numbers, press or touch OK and skip step 19.

19. If you would like each Interval timer shooting session to have new file numbers starting at 0001, highlight Reset file numbering and scroll to the right or tap on the small box to place a check mark in the box (figure 7.31G, image 3). Press or touch OK to lock in your choices.

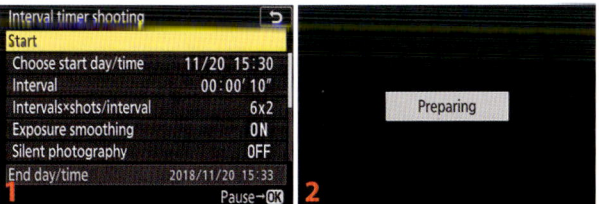

Figure 7.31H: Starting the Interval timer shooting session

20. Now that you have all the previous options set, you are ready to Start the Interval timer using the settings displayed on the Interval timer shooting screen (figure 7.31H, image 1). When you select Start, as shown in image 1, and press the OK button, a *Preparing* message will appear briefly on your camera's Monitor (figure 7.31H, image 2), and then the Interval timer shooting session will begin. Normally, the rear Monitor will be turned off during a session. However, if you press the Shutter-release button halfway, the Monitor will turn on and you will see *Interval timer shooting* appear briefly on the screen, then you will see the abbreviated word INTVL flashing. INTVL will continue to flash as long as the Interval timer is in operation. Additionally, the Memory card access lamp on back of the camera will flash approximately every three seconds while the Interval timer shooting session is active.

Pause, Cancel, or Restart an Interval Timer Shooting Session

You may need to pause or cancel the Interval timer while it is counting down to the start time you set in Shooting options, or when the timer is already active and taking pictures. The Interval timer will continue to function and count down even if you have switched the camera off. Therefore, once you have activated the timer you will need to use the screens shown in figure 7.31I to pause or cancel it. Let's see how to do it.

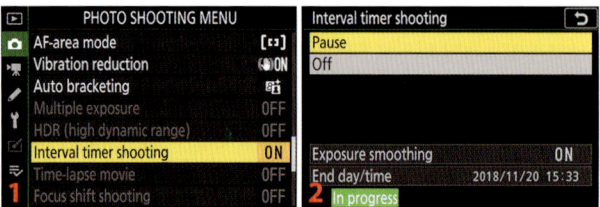

Figure 7.31I: Pausing or canceling an Interval timer shooting session

Use these steps to pause or cancel an Interval timer shooting session:

1. Select Interval timer shooting from the Photo Shooting Menu and scroll to the right (figure 7.31I, image 1).
2. Choose Pause to temporarily stop the timer, or Off to cancel the session (figure 7.31I, image 2).
3. Press the OK button or tap the option to lock in your choice.

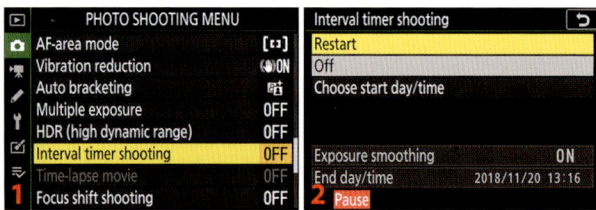

Figure 7.31J: Restarting or canceling an Interval timer shooting session

If you have previously paused the Interval timer and would like to restart or cancel it, use the following steps:

1. Select Interval timer shooting from the Photo Shooting Menu and scroll to the right (figure 7.31J, image 1).
2. Select Restart, which allows you to continue your Interval timer session, or Off, which lets you cancel the session (figure 7.31J, image 2).
3. Press the OK button or tap the option to lock in your choice.

Note: If the memory card fills up during a shooting session and has no more room for images, the timer will remain active, but the camera will stop taking pictures. You can resume shooting after you have either deleted some pictures or inserted another memory card.

Interval timer shooting will pause if you select the Self-timer. You must disable the Self-timer before you can restart the Interval timer.

During pauses, you can replace batteries and memory cards without ending the Interval timer session. To restart the session and continue where it left off, you must use the Photo Shooting Menu screens shown in figure 7.31J.

Please remember that pausing the session does not affect Interval timer settings. If, for any reason, the camera cannot continue Interval timer photography, it will display a warning on the Monitor.

Skipping Intervals: The camera will skip an interval if any of the following occurs for longer than eight seconds:

- Any photographs from the previous session are not yet taken
- The memory card is full
- Single-servo AF is active and the camera is unable to focus (the camera refocuses before each shot)

The camera will then try again at the next interval. Following are some things you need to be aware of when using the Interval timer shooting system:

- *User Settings and Auto Mode:* Changing to a different User setting position, or selecting Auto mode, on the Mode dial (U1, U2, U3, AUTO) will interrupt the Interval timer and *Shooting paused* will display on the Monitor. You can restart the session when you have changed the settings (see figure 7.31J).
- *Bracketing Info:* Be sure to adjust any bracketing for the exposure, flash, or Active D-Lighting (ADL) before you start Interval timer shooting. Bracketing overrides the number of shots, so you may not get what you expected if any kind of bracketing is active. Also, according to Nikon, "If White balance bracketing is active during an Interval timer session, the camera will take one shot at each interval and process it to create the number of copies specified in the bracketing program."
- *Power adapter for long shooting sessions:* The optional EH-7P USB Charging AC Adapter cannot be used to power the camera when it is turned on. It is designed to charge the camera's EN-EL15b battery while the camera is off. When you are shooting images over long periods of time, make sure you have a full battery or are connected to a full-time power source, such as the Nikon EH-5c AC adapter (with EP-5b power connector).

Settings Recommendation: Please learn to use this function! It is complicated, but if you read this section carefully and practice using Interval timer shooting as you read, you'll learn it quickly. This type of photography allows you to shoot things like flowers gradually opening or the sun moving across the sky. Have some fun with it!

Time-Lapse Movie

Time-lapse movie is a cousin of Interval timer shooting (see the previous section). The primary difference is that Time-lapse movie is designed to create a silent time-lapse movie when you are done shooting. During time-lapse creation, the camera automatically takes pictures at intervals you select during setup and later assembles them into a time-lapse movie.

Let's examine how to set up a short time-lapse sequence using Time-lapse movie.

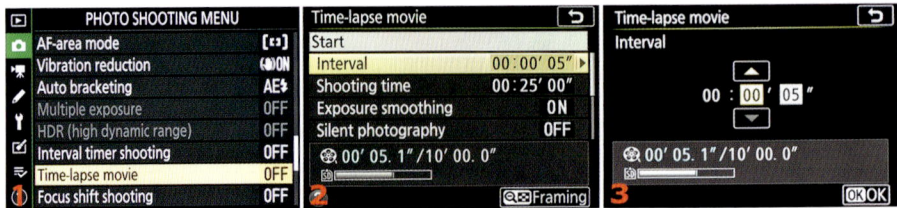

Figure 7.32A: Configuring a Time-lapse Interval

Here are the steps to set up a Time-lapse movie:

1. Choose Time-lapse movie from the Photo Shooting Menu and scroll to the right (figure 7.32A, image 1).
2. We are skipping the Start selection at this time, until we have fully configured the Time-lapse movie settings. Select Interval from the Time-lapse movie screen and scroll to the right (figure 7.32A, image 2). You can check the Framing the camera will use with the current settings by pressing the Zoom out button or by tapping the Framing symbol on the bottom right of the screen.
3. Set the picture Interval in minutes and seconds. You can choose from 1 second to 10 minutes (figure 7.32A, image 3). The hours column is not available to adjust from the Interval screen. I entered 00' 05" in image 3, which means I have selected a 5-second interval. The camera will take a picture every 5 seconds during the Shooting time period set in step 4. Press or touch OK to lock in your setting and return to the Time-lapse movie screen.

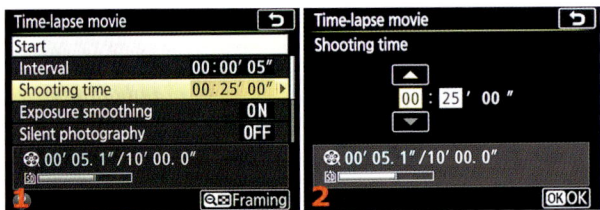

Figure 7.32B: Choosing a Shooting time

4. Select Shooting time from the Time-lapse movie screen and scroll to the right (figure 7.32B, image 1).
5. Choose a Shooting time over which the picture Interval will be executed (figure 7.32B, image 2). You can choose from 1 minute (00:01) to 7 hours 59 minutes (07:59). The seconds column is not available to adjust from the Shooting time screen. I entered 25 minutes (00:25' 00") in image 2, which means the camera will take a picture every 5 seconds (the Interval set in step 3) over a 25-minute period (the Shooting time). Press or touch OK to lock in your setting and return to the Time-lapse movie screen.

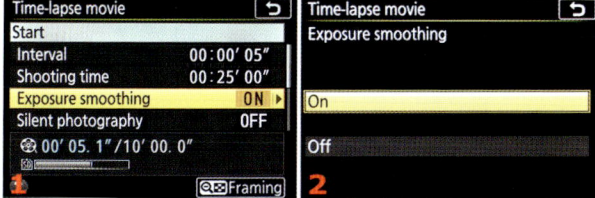

Figure 7.32C: Selecting Exposure smoothing

6. Next, you may select Exposure smoothing, which prevents abrupt exposure changes between images when you are using P, S, and A exposure modes. If you use M mode, you must have *Photo Shooting Menu > ISO sensitivity settings > Auto ISO sensitivity control* set to On, or Exposure smoothing will not work. Choose Exposure smoothing from the Time-lapse movie screen and scroll to the right (figure 7.32C, image 1).

7. Select On or Off for Exposure smoothing (figure 7.32C, image 2) and press the OK button or tap your selection to lock in the value and return to the Time-lapse movie screen.

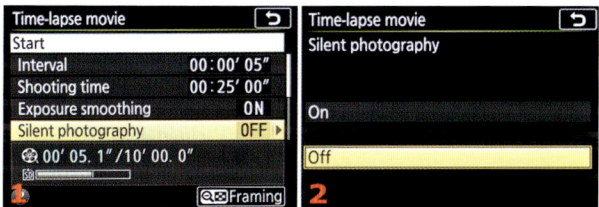

Figure 7.32D: Silencing the shutter

8. If you are capturing the Time-lapse movie in an area where it is important to be quiet, you may want to silence the camera's shutter. Select Silent photography from the Time-lapse movie menu and scroll to the right (figure 7.32D, image 1).

9. Choose On to use the silent electronic shutter or Off to use the normal mechanical shutter. Press the OK button or tap your selection to lock in the value and return to the Time-lapse movie screen (figure 7.32D, image 2). Now, scroll down to find the final three Time-lapse movie settings.

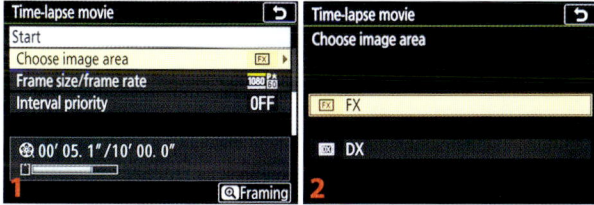

Figure 7.32E: Setting the Image area

10. Select Choose image area from the Time-lapse movie screen and scroll to the right (figure 7.32E, image 1).

11. Choose FX or DX as the Image area for this Time-lapse movie (figure 7.32E, image 2) and press the OK button or tap your selection to lock in the value.

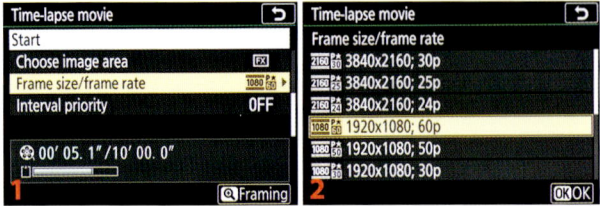

Figure 7.32F: Setting the Frame size/frame rate

12. Choose Frame size/frame rate from the Time-lapse movie screen and scroll to the right (figure 7.32F, image 1).
13. Choose one of the eight Frame size/frame rate settings (figure 7.32F, image 2; there are no slow-mo settings) and press or touch OK to return to the main screen.

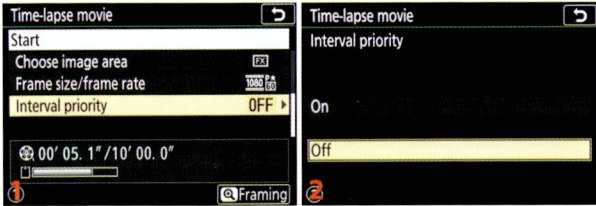

Figure 7.32G: Setting the Interval priority

14. When you are shooting time-lapse sequences with a short Interval time, you might run into a situation where the image exposure time on a dark night is longer than the Interval time, causing the camera to underexpose your images when the Interval expires and cuts the exposure short. Interval priority helps solve that problem. You can tell the camera whether the exposure of images is more important than the Interval (Off), or whether the Interval is more important than the exposure (On). If you choose On, make sure you are not consistently underexposing your images. This setting applies only to P and A exposure modes: S and M modes ignore this setting. Select Interval priority and scroll to the right (figure 7.32G, image 1).
15. Choose On to give priority to the Interval or select Off to give priority to the image exposure time. Press the OK button or tap on the option to lock in your setting and return to the main screen (figure 7.32G, image 2).

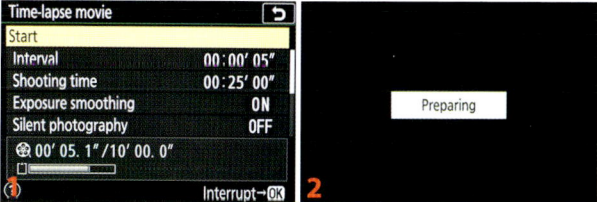

Figure 7.32H: Starting the Time-lapse movie sequence

16. Make sure your camera is on a tripod and ready for shooting the time-lapse sequence, and then select Start from the Time-lapse movie menu (figure 7.32H, image 1).

17. The camera will display a screen that says, *Preparing* (figure 7.32H, image 2), for about three seconds and will begin shooting your sequence. During the time-lapse sequence you will see moving chevron (pointer) symbols where the image count normally appears on the upper Control panel, and the images will briefly appear on the Monitor as they are captured. If you choose to end the sequence early, simply press the OK button and the camera will stop taking pictures. Other than the fact that the camera stops taking pictures and the chevron symbol stops moving on the Control panel, there is nothing externally visible that lets you know the Time-lapse movie sequence stopped when you pressed the OK button.

Note: Before you start a time-lapse sequence, check the framing and exposure by taking a picture from the position you will use to capture the time-lapse movie. It is often best to shoot in Manual (M) exposure mode with everything preset to a particular aperture, shutter speed, and ISO sensitivity. When shooting in M mode, if you are worried about ambient light changes affecting the exposure during the time-lapse session, simply enable *Photo Shooting Menu > ISO sensitivity settings > Auto ISO sensitivity control.* Use the ISO-Auto setting from the Photo Shooting Menu because the Time-lapse movie function is just a series of still images joined together and is not a true video. Auto ISO allows the camera to vary the ISO sensitivity within a range you can set and will prevent inconsistencies in exposure during the sequence. Additionally, it is a good idea to choose a White balance setting other than Auto to keep the colors the same across all the images in the time-lapse movie.

If you have selected a long shooting time, you may want to consider connecting the camera to the optional Nikon EH-5c AC adapter for continuous power (you'll also need the Nikon EP-5B power supply connector if you do).

Why is Time-lapse movie grayed out?: Time-lapse movie is not available (it's grayed out) if Shutter speed is set to Bulb; when you are in the middle of a bracket sequence; if the camera is connected via an HDMI cable to an external device for movie recording; or when HDR, Multiple exposure, or Interval timer shooting is enabled.

Time-sequence length calculation: The total number of frames in the movie can be calculated by dividing the shooting time by the interval. Then you calculate the movie length by dividing the number of frames by the frame rate (e.g., 30p, 24p) you've selected in *Time-lapse movie > Frame size/frame rate.* Remember, the Time-lapse movie system makes short movies based on the Frame size/frame rate and Image area configured under the Time-lapse movie menu and not the same ones found on the Movie Shooting Menu.

What you will see while shooting: As previously mentioned, while you're recording the time-lapse sequence, chevron symbols will move on the Control panel where the image count normally displays. The normal shutter speed and aperture settings will be displayed on the Control panel between frames (unless the frames are too loosely spaced in time), allowing you to make adjustments if needed (according to the exposure mode you are using). The exposure meter will not turn off during shooting. To stop the sequence outright, press the OK button or turn the camera off.

A movie is made: When the sequence is complete, the camera will automatically assemble a short, silent movie based on the frame rates you selected in the Movie Shooting Menu. You can identify the time-lapse movie by the fact that it shows a Play touch button on the screen with the first frame of the movie sequence.

Settings Recommendation: This function is convenient for those of us who would like to experiment with or shoot interesting time-lapse sequences. Try shooting some short sequences of an event and see how easy it is!

Focus Shift Shooting

Focus shift shooting allows the camera to vary its focus over a series of up to 300 images, with customizable intervals and focus steps. The resulting image series can later be combined in your computer into one image with very deep depth of field.

How Does Focus Shift Shooting Work?

To test the Focus shift shooting (known as *focus stacking*) function, I chose a red block as my closeup subject (figure 7.33A). I decided I wanted about 4 inches of sharp focus to fully cover my subject. I focused my camera on the 5-inch mark on the ruler and since I was using f/9, I knew there would be a little sharpness in front of the focus position due to depth of field.

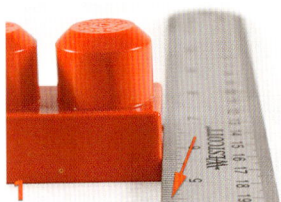 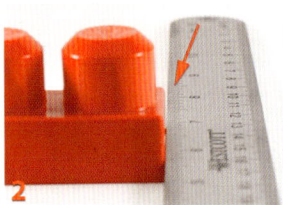 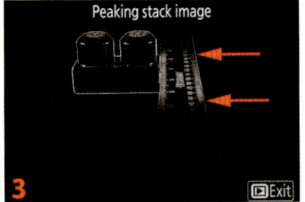

Figure 7.33A: Beginning focus position at 4.5 inches, ending position at 8.5 inches

The two ruler pictures shown in figure 7.33A, images 1 and 2, are the first and last images of a nine-shot Focus shift shooting session. In the ruler picture shown in figure 7.33A, images 1, you can see that mostly sharp focus starts at about 4.5 inches and full sharpness begins at about 5 inches. The ruler picture shown in figure 7.33A, image 2, shows that the final zone of sharpness extends to about 8.5 inches; and is still mostly sharp out to about 9 inches.

After combining the nine images, the 3.5-inch zone of full sharpness covered my subject with room to spare. Using focus stacking was an elegant solution for what I needed to do.

In figure 7.33A, image 3, you see a Peaking stack image, which, if enabled, allows you to see a black-and-white focus Peaking representation of the zone of sharp focus for your subject.

Let's examine how the focus stacking system handled my needs (figure 7.33B).

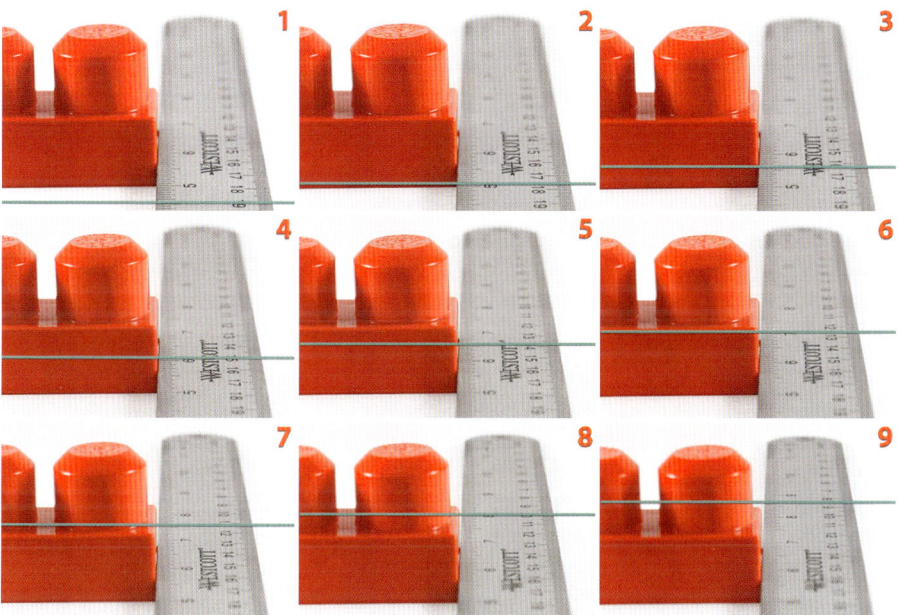

Figure 7.33B: Actual focus movement with *No. of shots* at 9 and *Focus step width* at 5

In the nine frames shown in figure 7.33B, the camera kept moving the focus from its starting position of 5 inches to its ending position of about 8.5 inches on the ruler. The most important settings were *No. of shots* set to 9 and *Focus step width* set to 5.

In figure 7.33B, image 1, I have the lens focused on the number 5 on the ruler, and at f/9 the depth of field extends some sharpness toward the camera as shown by the thin green line at 4.5 inches. I started the automatic Focus shift shooting function and the camera took 9 pictures (No. of shots) while automatically moving the focus forward by 5 steps (Focus steps width) for each frame. You do not need to take each picture individually; the camera will do it for you. As you examine figure 7.33B, images 1 to 9, note that the horizontal green line shows approximately where the primary focus position is on each frame.

The camera moved the point of focus forward automatically for each new frame (starting at 5 inches and ending at 8.5 inches).

When the Focus shift shooting process was complete, I had the full subject covered with good focus, within a series of nine pictures that needed to be combined in the computer. The camera only takes the pictures; it will not assemble the final image. Let's see how to configure the camera to do a Focus shift shooting session.

Configuring Focus Shift Shooting

There are seven configurable settings in the Focus shift shooting function, plus a Start setting to begin the automatic focus shifting process. First, let's discuss what each setting does, and then we will configure each setting individually.

- *Start:* This setting starts the automatic shooting process. The camera will take the pictures without you having to press the Shutter release button. As soon as you select Start and press the OK button, the camera will start taking all the pictures in the series.
- *No. of shots:* This setting allows you to tell the camera how many shots you want it to take. You can choose a number from 1 to 300, for up to 300 images in the Focus shift shooting series. For figure 7.33B, I selected nine shots.
- *Focus step width:* This setting controls how far forward the focus is shifted before the next shot is taken. You can see the action of this setting by examining the position of the green lines in figure 7.33B, images 1 to 9.
- *Interval until next shot:* This setting allows you to introduce a time delay, in seconds, between each picture in the Focus shift shooting series. If you select 00, the camera will not use a delay between frames and will attempt to shoot at about 5.5 frames-per-second. If you do not use the default of 00, you will need to select the number of seconds between each frame, from 01 to 30 seconds.
- *First-frame exposure lock:* If you set this to On, the camera will use the same exposure for each picture in the stack series. If set to Off, the camera will adjust exposure for each picture.
- *Peaking stack image:* The directs the camera to create an image showing the approximate range of sharp focus in high-contrast black-and-white (figure 7.33A, image 3). This is like black-and-white focus Peaking for the entire range of focus for all the combined images.
- *Silent photography:* This setting allows you to silence the camera's shutter by switching from the mechanical shutter to the electronic shutter. You will hear the mirror raise on the first frame of the Focus shift shooting series, and then each subsequent frame will be silent, except for the last frame when the mirror is lowered.
- *Starting storage folder:* This setting causes the camera to create a new folder for each Focus shift shooting series so that each series is separated from any previous series. You can also use this setting to start image numbering over at 0001 (e.g., DSC-0001.jpg) for each Focus shift shooting series.

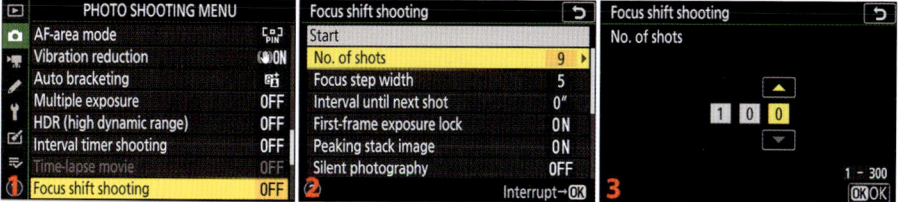

Figure 7.33C: Configuring a Focus shift shooting series

Use the following steps to configure a Focus shift shooting series:

1. Select Focus shift shooting from the Photo Shooting Menu and scroll to the right (figure 7.33C, image 1).
2. We will skip the Start setting initially, beginning instead with No. of shots, so that we can configure the camera for our current needs (figure 7.33C, image 2). Choose No. of shots and scroll to the right.
3. The camera presents a series of three up/down menus, which can be used to create a No. of shots value from 001 to 300 (figure 7.33C, image 3). Choose the number of frames you want in your Focus shift shooting series and then press or touch OK.

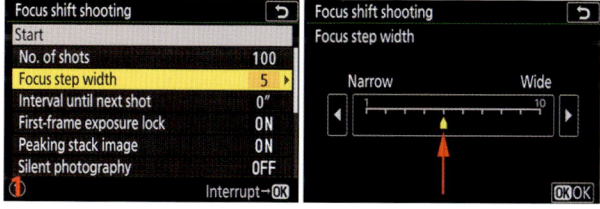

Figure 7.33D: Configuring the Focus step width setting

4. Choose Focus step width from the menu and scroll to the right (figure 7.33D, image 1).
5. The camera presents you with a Focus step width selector bar (figure 7.33D, image 2). Tap the arrows on the left or right of the selector bar (or use the Multi selector pad) to move the yellow pointer toward 1 or 10. The default value is 5, as indicated by the yellow pointer at the red arrow in image 2. The Focus step width has no easily measurable value since the actual focus movements will be affected by how close you are to your subject and the zoom setting of your lens (field of view). You will need to experiment with this value by measuring the depth of focus you need for a macro subject, or by guesstimating with a larger subject like a landscape. If you need smaller focus steps, move the yellow pointer toward 1. If you need larger steps, move it toward 10. Press or touch OK after you have chosen a value.

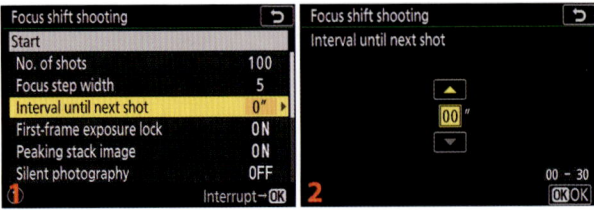

Figure 7.33E: Configuring Interval until next shot

6. Highlight Interval until next shot and scroll to the right (figure 7.33E, image 1).
7. Use the up/down menu to select a value from 00" to 30" (figure 7.33E, image 2). If you select 00", the camera will not use a delay between frames and will attempt to shoot a rapid succession of frames at ~5.5 frames per second. If you want more time between frames, choose from as low as 1 second (01") to as long as 30 seconds (30") between each frame of the Focus shift shooting series. Press or touch OK after you have chosen a value. **Note:** If you are using flash to light your subject, you may need to allow a second or two between frames for the flash to recycle. Experiment with this!

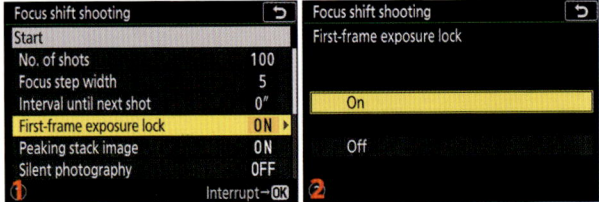

Figure 7.33F: Configuring First-frame exposure lock

8. Choose First-frame exposure lock and scroll to the right (figure 7.33F, image 1).
9. Highlight On or Off and press the OK button or tap your selection to lock it in (figure 7.33F, image 2).

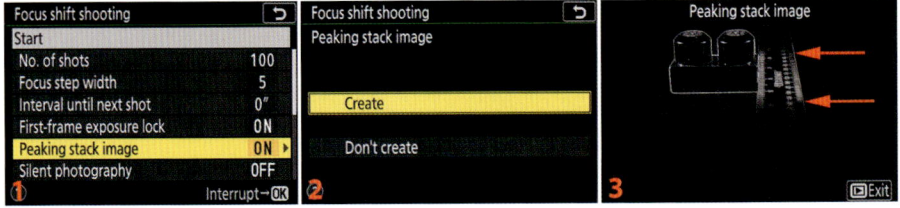

Figure 7.33G: Configuring Peaking stack image

10. Choose Peaking stack image and scroll to the right (figure 7.33G, image 1).
11. If you choose Create from the menu (figure 7.33G, image 2), the camera will display a Peaking stack image like you see in figure 7.33G, image 3. This high-contrast image displays only the edges of your subject in white lines on black. This image stays on the screen for about four seconds and then it disappears; however, you can recall it

later (see figure 7.33H). When the focus session is over, the final image of the session will display for about four seconds and then the Peaking stack image will appear for an additional four seconds. During the time it is displayed you can quickly see the range of focus captured. I marked the approximate range of the zone of sharpness in my sample focus stack (red arrows in figure 7.33G, image 3). If you don't want a Peaking stack image to be created, choose Don't create from the menu instead (image 2). Highlight your choice and press the OK button or tap on the item to lock in the setting. Now let's see how to review the Peaking stack image.

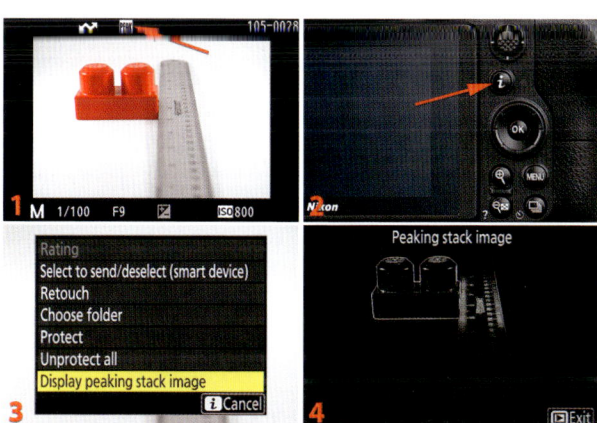

Figure 7.33H: Reviewing the Peaking stack image

12. If you previously enabled Create in step 11, all images in the Focus stack shooting session will be marked with a PEAK word at the top of the screen (figure 7.33H, image 1). If you want to review the Peaking stack image, display one of the pictures from the stack and press the *i* button (figure 7.33H, image 2). The *i* Menu will display, with Display peaking stack image as the last choice on the menu (figure 7.33H, image 3). Select that item and press the OK button or touch it with your fingertip and the Peaking stack image will appear on the Monitor (figure 7.33H, image 4). When you are finished examining the Peaking stack image, press the Playback button or tap Exit.

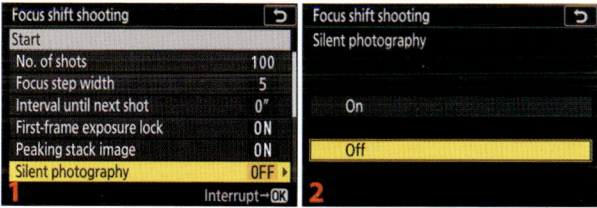

Figure 7.33I: Configuring Silent photography

13. To silence the camera, highlight Silent photography and scroll to the right (figure 7.33I, image 1).

14. Select On to silence the shutter by using the camera's electronic shutter instead of its mechanical shutter (figure 7.33I, image 2). If On is selected, the entire Focus shift shooting series will silent. Choose Off to continue using the normal mechanical shutter with its resulting sounds. Press the OK button or tap your selection to lock it in.

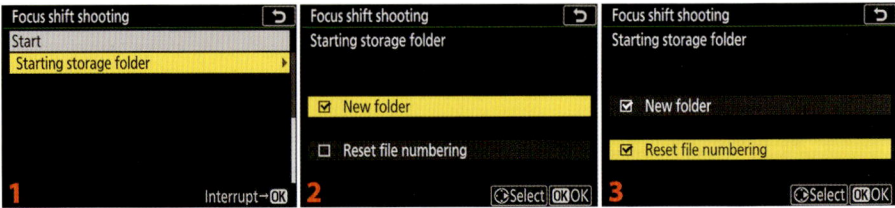

Figure 7.33J: Configuring Starting storage folder

15. You can choose to have the camera create a new folder for each Focus shift shooting series so that each series is stored separately. You can also choose to set image numbering back to 0001 at the beginning of each session (e.g., DSC-0001.jpg). Choose Starting storage folder from the Focus shift shooting menu and scroll to the right (figure 7.33J, image 1).

16. If you want to use a separate new folder for each Focus shift shooting session, highlight New folder and scroll to the right (figure 7.33J, image 2) or tap the little box to the left of New folder to add a check mark. Now when the camera starts a new Focus shift shooting series, it will first create a new folder. For instance, I was taking normal pictures using a folder named 300YOUNG. When I put a check mark next to New folder (enabled it) and started a Focus shift shooting series, the camera created a new folder named 301YOUNG and saved all the session images in the new folder. You can also choose to keep using current sequential image numbering or start over with 0001 with each new series. If you would prefer to use new image numbers for each series, go to the next step instead of selecting OK. Otherwise, to keep using current sequential image numbers, press or touch OK and skip step 14.

17. If you would like each Focus shift shooting series to have brand-new file numbers starting at 0001, highlight Reset file numbering and scroll to the right or tap the box to place a check mark in it (figure 7.33J, image 3). Press or touch OK to lock in your choice.

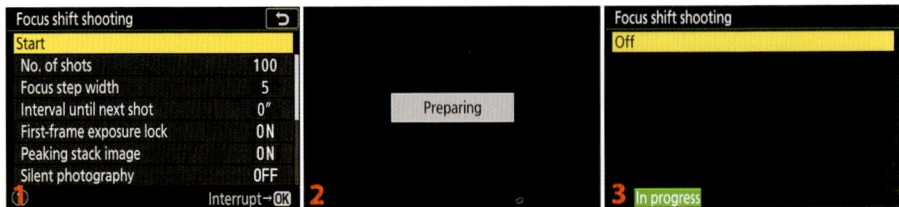

Figure 7.33K: Starting a Focus shift shooting series

18. After you have completed choosing the settings above, it's time to actually capture the Focus shift shooting series of images that will later be combined into a final image with deep depth of field. Before you execute the next step, be sure your camera is on a tripod, focused, in the exposure mode you want to use, and fully ready to take the focus-shifted (stacked) images. Scroll up to Start at the top of the menu and press the OK button (figure 7.33K, image 1).

19. A popup box with the word *Preparing* will show on the screen (figure 7.33K, image 2) and the camera will begin taking pictures without you having to press the Shutter-release button. The focus point will move forward for each image. When the process is complete you will have a series of images on your memory card that are ready to be combined in your computer. You can interrupt an active Focus shift shooting session by pressing the OK button or by tapping on Interrupt/OK in between pictures.

20. If you press the Menu button during the session, the In progress screen shown in figure 7.33K, image 3, will appear. You can press the OK button or touch Off with your fingertip to stop the Focus shift shooting session part of the way through its sequence without losing any of the images already captured.

Note: Assembling the stacked images into a final combined image with deep depth of field in your computer is beyond the scope of this book. However, there are good resources for learning about combining images.

Photoshop has a built-in utility to combine focus-stacked images through a process called focus blending. Do a YouTube search for "Photoshop focus blending," and you will find some good video resources.

Many experienced focus stack shooters often recommend Helicon Focus software. You can review the software here:

http://www.heliconsoft.com

Enjoy the new focus stacking capability found in your Nikon Z6. Hopefully, in the future, Nikon will provide image combination within the camera so you don't have to use a computer.

Silent Photography

Silent photography allows you to make the camera shoot silently. The Z6 will use its electronic shutter to make exposures with no noise. This mode is best used in environments where camera noise is not allowed or could draw unwanted attention to the photographer.

There are a couple of things to be aware of when using this mode:

- **Rolling shutter effect:** If the subject or photographer is moving quickly (e.g., Panning), the subject might appear to lean in the direction of the motion in an odd fashion. This is caused by the fact that Silent shooting uses the camera's electronic shutter only, and each row of the sensor is read in quick succession from top to bottom. As the camera or subject moves, the subject is shifted slightly for each row of the imaging sensor, as that row is read by the camera. This introduces a weird distortion that makes the subject appear to lean in the direction of the motion. Silent shooting might not be a good idea when the subject or the camera is moving at a higher than normal speed. For more information do a Google search on "rolling shutter versus global shutter."

• **Banding under certain types of lighting:** Certain types of pulsed lighting (e.g., fluorescent, mercury-vapor, and sodium) can cause a banding or flickering effect as the light varies during the time of the exposure. It's best to use the normal shutter when shooting under pulsed (non-continuous) lighting.

• **Slower burst shooting:** Using this mode when burst shooting can drop the frame rate (fps) by about 1 to 1.5 frames per second. There is a chart on page 82 of the downloadable Reference Manual that lists the frame rates in and out of Silent mode.

• **No flash photography allowed:** Short-duration flash photography will cause banding or bright spots in your subject. You must use continuous lighting of some form, or good ambient light, to take pictures in Silent photography mode.

Now let's see how to select Silent photography.

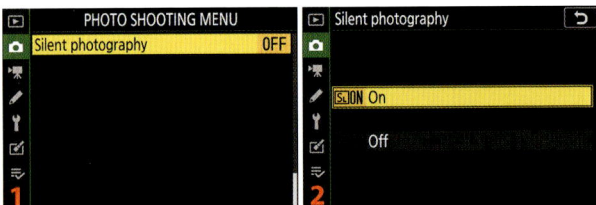

Figure 7.34: Selecting Silent photography

Use the following steps to select Silent photography:

1. Choose Silent photography from the Photo Shooting Menu and scroll to the right (figure 7.34, image 1).
2. Highlight SL On or Off on the Silent photography menu to enable or disable silent shooting. Press the OK button or tap on your choice to lock in the feature.

Note: Enabling Silent photography mode will automatically disable the following: the Speedlight flash unit (no flash is allowed), Beep sound, Long exposure NR, and the Electronic front-curtain shutter. If you are photographing flashing lights, such as an ambulance, there might be banding or bright spots in your images.

Settings Recommendation: Silent photography is great for environments such as outdoor weddings (no flash is available), photographing grizzly bears in Alaska, or sneaky pictures of family and friends—anywhere photographers do not want to call attention to themselves. Any time you want your camera to stop making noise while taking pictures, the camera or subject is not moving rapidly, and the lighting is continuous, true Silent shooting is a great feature to have.

Author's Conclusion

Congratulations on configuring the camera for still image capture! If you save the current Photo Shooting Menu settings to one of the camera's three User settings (U1, U2, or U3) with *Setup Menu > Save user settings,* you will have configured only one of the camera's User settings. Now, configure the camera a different way and save it to one of the other User settings (U2 or U3).

Taking advantage of the camera's three User settings gives you a great deal of flexibility in how your camera operates. You can switch between three different camera configurations very quickly

Next, let's examine the Movie Shooting Menu to learn how to set up the camera for capturing excellent video.

8 Movie Shooting Menu

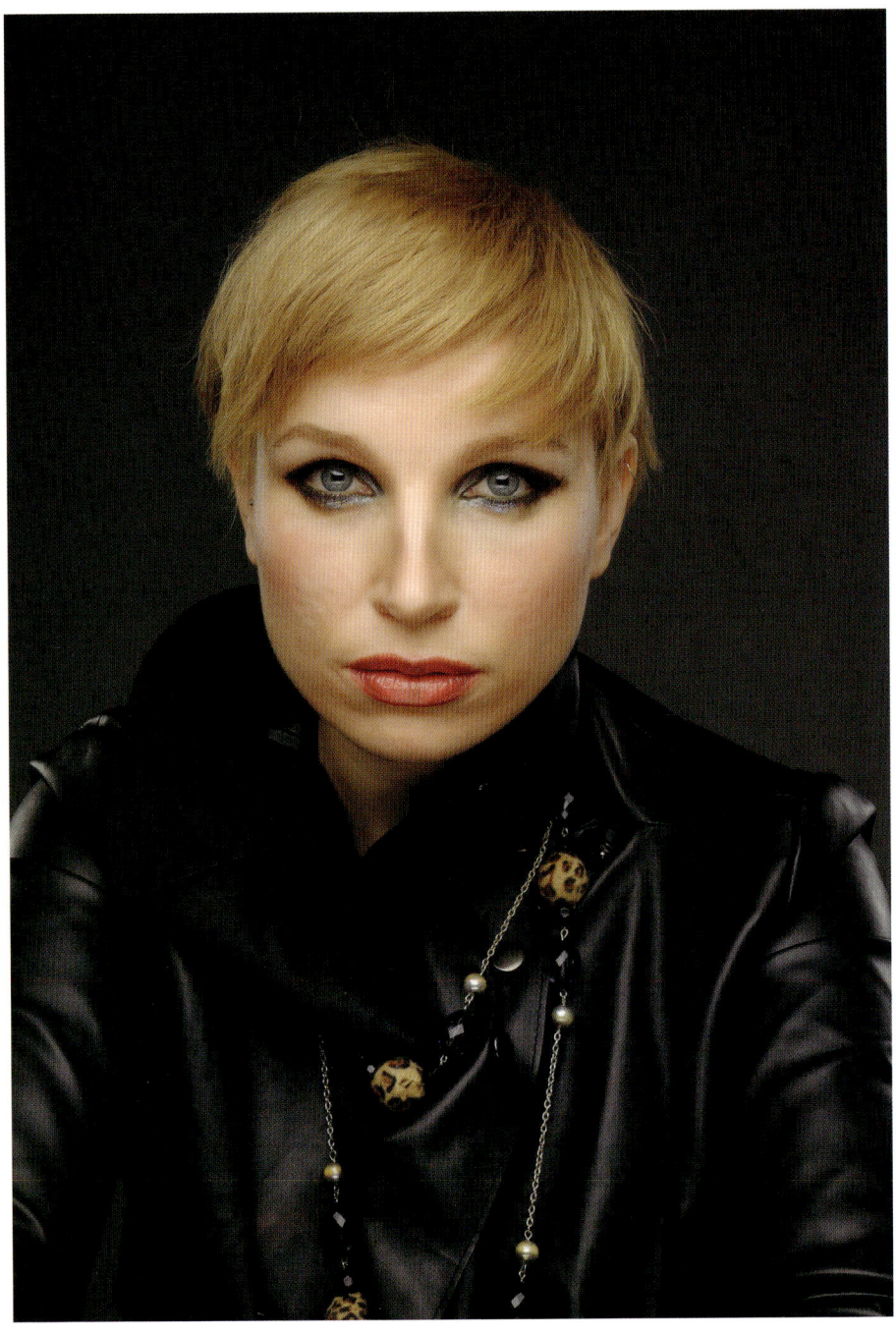

Societies Masterclass Model Shoot © 2019 Garrett Hayes (*Garrett Hayes*)

The Movie Shooting Menu is a menu subsystem similar to the Photo Shooting Menu discussed in the previous chapter. The Movie Shooting Menu applies its settings to the creation of videos instead of still pictures.

In older Nikon cameras the video functions could be a little harder to locate because they were appended to some of the still picture menus. However, Nikon now wisely uses a completely separate menu for movie functions. These easy-to-locate functions will make it much easier to configure your camera for high-quality video capture.

Following is a list and overview of the 27 Items found on the Z6 Movie Shooting Menu:

- **Reset movie shooting menu:** Restores the factory default settings in the Movie Shooting Menu for the currently selected User setting (i.e., U1, U2, U3).
- **File naming:** Lets you change three characters of the image file name so it is personalized.
- **Choose image area:** Allows you to choose whether the camera uses FX or DX mode when shooting videos.
- **Frame size/frame rate:** Use this function to choose the frame size (i.e., 2160p, 1080p) and the frame rate (i.e., 120p, 100p, 60p, 50p, 30p, 25p, 24p, and slow-mo).
- **Movie quality:** Lets you select the bit rate (Mbps) of the movie for controlling overall quality.
- **Movie file type:** Allows you to select the file type (container) of the movie. Your two choices are MOV and MP4.
- **ISO sensitivity settings:** Allows you to select an upper limit for Auto ISO, from ISO 200 to Hi 2 (ISO 204800). You can also choose your own manual ISO sensitivity.
- **White balance:** Chooses from nine White balance types, including several subtypes, and it includes the ability to measure the color temperature of the ambient light (Preset manual).
- **Set Picture Control:** Chooses from eight regular Picture Controls, or 20 creative Picture Controls, each of which modify how the video looks.
- **Manage Picture Control:** Saves, edits, loads, renames, or deletes custom video Picture Controls in your camera's internal memory or on its memory card.
- **Active D-Lighting:** Helps preserve details in both highlights and shadows so your video recordings will have a more "natural" level of contrast.
- **High ISO NR:** Uses a blurring and resharpening method, with selectable levels, to help remove noise from videos shot with high ISO sensitivity values.
- **Vignette control:** For certain lenses with corner vignetting, the camera will lessen the darkened-corner effect.
- **Diffraction compensation:** Reduces the aperture-blade diffraction effect caused by capturing video with a small aperture.
- **Auto distortion control:** Attempts to reduce or remove barrel and pincushion distortion in your video frames.
- **Flicker reduction:** Reduces banding and flickering that occurs when you record video under fluorescent, mercury-vapor, and sodium lighting by attempting to match the frequency of the local power supply (e.g., 50Hz, 60Hz).

- **_Metering:_** Allows you to choose the type of light meter your camera will use while capturing video. Choose from Matrix, Center-weighted, and Highlight-weighted exposure metering.
- **_Focus Mode:_** Allows you to choose a Focus mode for video capture (_how_ the camera focuses). Your choices are: Single AF (AF-S), Continuous AF (AF-C), Full-time AF (AF-F), and Manual focus (MF).
- **_AF-area mode:_** Allows you to choose an AF-area mode for video capture (_where_ the camera focuses). Your choices are: Single-point AF, Wide-area AF (S) [WIDE-S], Wide-area AF (L) [WIDE-L], and Auto-area AF.
- **_Vibration reduction:_** Choose a vibration reduction (VR/IBIS) method, including ON Normal, SPT Sport, and Off.
- **_Electronic VR:_** Allows the camera to use sensor pixel-shifting in an attempt to stabilize vibration during a handheld video recording. This is not the same as physical VR or IBIS. This method actually shifts the video frame on the sensor slightly, to mitigate shakiness.
- **_Microphone sensitivity:_** Gives you control over the sensitivity of the built-in stereo mic and any external mic plugged into the audio-in (MIC) port.
- **_Attenuator:_** If enabled, this allows the camera to automatically control the microphone gain so that loud sounds will not cause audio distortion.
- **_Frequency response:_** Allows you to set one of two audio recording modes: Wide, which records a full range of sounds, or Voice, which asks the camera to narrow its audio frequency response to the human voice range.
- **_Wind noise reduction:_** Gives you a low-cut filter to remove a portion of the rumbling noise made when wind blows on the built-in microphone. This setting does _not_ work with external stereo microphones plugged into the MIC port.
- **_Headphone volume:_** Provides a way to control the headphone volume level. You can adjust the volume from 0 to 30.
- **_Timecode:_** Allows you to store the hour, minute, second, and frame number for each frame in your video recording. This function is available only when using the MOV movie format (container).

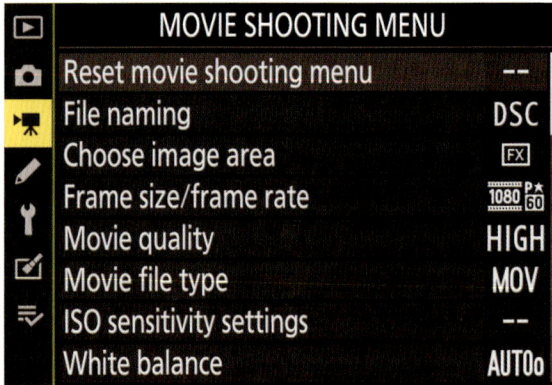

Figure 8.1: The Movie Shooting Menu

Figure 8.1 shows the location of the Movie Shooting Menu, which is the third menu down on the left. Its symbol is a movie camera on a tripod (in yellow).

Let's examine each of these Movie Shooting Menu functions in much greater detail.

Reset Movie Shooting Menu

Reset movie shooting menu does what it says—it resets the Movie Shooting Menu back to factory defaults. If you want start fresh with all the settings in the Movie Shooting Menu, use this function.

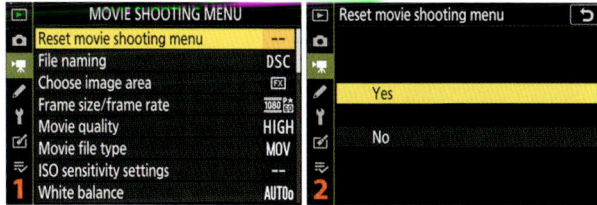

Figure 8.2: Resetting the Movie shooting menu back to factory defaults

Here are the steps to reset the Movie Shooting Menu:

1. Select Reset movie shooting menu and scroll to the right (figure 8.2, image 1).
2. Choose Yes or No and press the OK button or tap the option to lock it in (figure 8.2, image 2).

Settings Recommendation: This is an easy way to start fresh because it's a full reset of all the Movie Setting Menu values. I use this when I purchase a preowned camera and want to clear someone else's settings or if I simply want to start fresh.

File Naming

File naming allows you to change the first three characters (prefix) in the video's file name to three characters of your choice. The default is DSC. You could use your initials, a combination of letters and numbers, all letters, or all numbers.

Following is how to modify the first three characters (prefix) of the video file name.

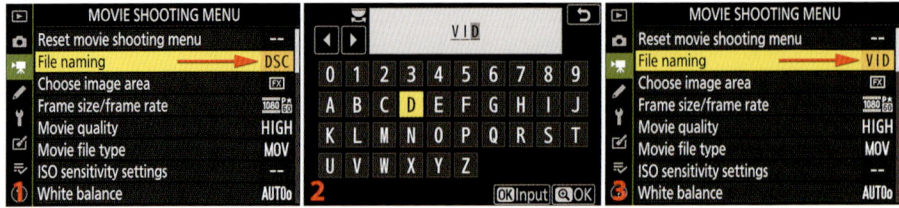

Figure 8.3: Renaming the file name prefix

Here are the steps to set up your custom File naming characters:

1. Select File naming from the Movie Shooting Menu and scroll to the right (figure 8.3, image 1).
2. From the screen shown in figure 8.3, image 2, insert a new prefix by selecting characters, with your fingertip, from the alpha-numeric list at the center of the screen and they will appear in the position marked with the dark-gray cursor in the prefix name field (VID). You can tap on the left/right arrows in the top-left corner to move left and right in the name field, or you can tap on the individual character locations in the new prefix name. When you have the name completed, tap OK or press the Zoom in button to save it.
3. My camera is now using the prefix VID for all video files. Notice how the red arrows in images 1 and 3 point to the previous (DSC) and new (VID) prefixes. The new prefix will now be the first three characters of each image file name (figure 8.3, image 3).

Settings Recommendation: Because I shoot only a moderate number of videos in comparison to the large number of still images I create, I am not concerned with tracking when a video file name exceeds 9999 and rolls back over to 0001. Therefore, I simply add the prefix VID to my video files.

This works identically to the File naming function in the Photo Shooting Menu. If you will recall, there is a suggestion in chapter 7, **Photo Shooting Menu,** for tracking the number of still image files your camera has created (see page 172) so that you can keep up with it when your camera rolls the file name over to 0001 after exceeding 9999 files (i.e., when you exceed DSC-9999, the camera rolls the filename over to DSC-0001).

However, unless you bought your Z6 to use primarily to shoot video, you will probably shoot less video compared to still images. In that case, you may not be concerned with exceeding 9999 videos. If you are concerned with tracking when your camera's videos roll over from 9999 to 0001, review both this section and the similar section in chapter 7, under **File Naming** (page 172).

Choose Image Area

(User's Manual: Pages 133, Reference Manual: Page 235)

Choose Image area is designed to allow you to use the normal FX view for most videos and to take advantage of the extra apparent reach of the DX crop mode when you need it for something like videoing distant and/or small subjects.

In figure 8.4A, please compare the field of view for the left (FX) and right (DX) Image areas

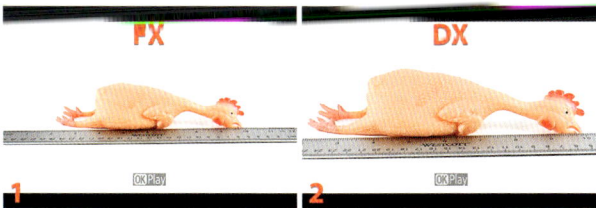

Figure 8.4A: FX and DX video modes

You can see two sample videos I created from exactly the same camera position. The FX mode obviously has a wider field of view for the video frame, whereas the DX mode has a stronger apparent telephoto effect.

The camera will automatically adjust the frame size to fit the screen when using either of the two modes. In other words, you will see no box with a grayed-out area like you see in Nikon DSLRs when you select the DX mode for still images. Instead, the camera simply presents the exact field of view you will see in your video.

This is much simpler to use when shooting a video because you don't have to worry about trying to keep the video within certain lines on the Monitor. The video simply fits the screen and shows only what the camera is actually recording.

Selecting an Image Area Mode

As previously mentioned, you can choose one of two Image area modes (FX or DX) for video recording in all video modes. Let's examine how to do so.

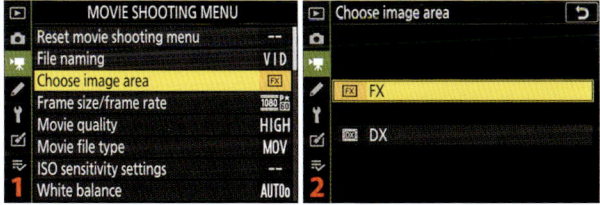

Figure 8.4B: Choose an Image area mode

Use the following steps to choose one of the two Image area modes:

1. Select Choose image area from the Movie Shooting Menu and scroll to the right (figure 8.4B, image 1).
2. Choose either the FX or DX mode (figure 8.4B, image 2), according to whether you need a normal view or a 1.5x cropped telephoto view (figure 8.4A), and press the OK button or tap the option to lock in your choice.

Note: This function is also available on the *i* Menu. Press the *i* button to open the menu and you will find this function on the top row, third from left.

Settings Recommendation: For general video recording, I leave the camera set to FX mode. However, when I want to video something smaller or farther away, such as birds in a tree or a bear across a meadow, I will switch to DX mode to maximize the apparent telephoto view of my subject. The DX mode is convenient for those who need to video things at a distance and would like the subject to appear larger on the screen.

Frame Size/Frame Rate

The Nikon Z6 provides 10 normal-speed *Frame size/frame rate* settings and three slow-motion (slow-mo) settings. Table 8.1 shows the Frame size (pixels) and frame rate (e.g., 60p, 30p) for each option, along with recording speed and whether FX and DX mode is available for that option.

Option	Frame Size (pixels)	Frame Rate	Recording Speed, FX versus DX
3840 × 2160; 30p	3840 × 2160	30p	Normal speed, FX or DX
3840 × 2160; 25p	3840 × 2160	25p	Normal speed, FX or DX
3840 × 2160; 24p	3840 × 2160	24p	Normal speed, FX or DX
1920 × 1080; 120p	1920 × 1080	120p	DX only
1920 × 1080; 100p	1920 × 1080	100p	DX only
1920 × 1080; 60p	1920 × 1080	60p	Normal speed, FX or DX
1920 × 1080; 50p	1920 × 1080	50p	Normal speed, FX or DX
1920 × 1080; 30p	1920 × 1080	30p	Normal speed, FX or DX
1920 × 1080; 25p	1920 × 1080	25p	Normal speed, FX or DX
1920 × 1080; 24p	1920 × 1080	24p	Normal speed, FX or DX
1920 × 1080; 30p	1920 × 1080	30p ×4	Slow-mo: e.g., record 1 minute, playback 4 minutes, DX only
1920 × 1080; 25p	1920 × 1080	25p ×4	Slow-mo: e.g., record 1 minute, playback 4 minutes, DX only
1920 × 1080; 24p	1920 × 1080	24p ×5	Slow-mo: e.g., record 1 minute, playback 5 minutes, DX only

Table 8.1: Frame size/frame rate options and speeds (figure 8.5, image 2)

Normal-speed videos play back the same number of minutes you recorded. If you record for 10 minutes, the video will be 10 minutes long. Slow-mo videos are recorded at four or five times the rated speed. For instance, a 1920 × 1080; 30p ×4 video is recorded at 120 frames per second (30 × 4 = 120), but it is played back at 30 fps. If you capture slow-mo video for 3 minutes, the playback will be 12 minutes (3 × 4 = 12). Let's see how to choose a frame size and frame rate.

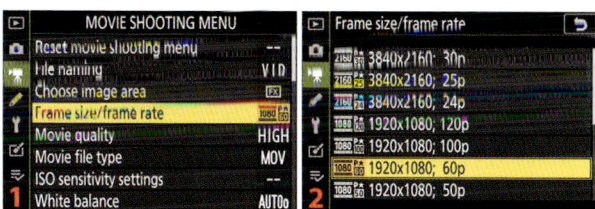

Figure 8.5: Choosing a Frame size/frame rate setting for the video

The following steps allow you to select a Frame size/frame rate for your next movie:

1. Choose Frame size/frame rate from the Movie Shooting Menu and scroll to the right (figure 8.5, image 1).
2. Choose a size (i.e., 1280×720, 1920×1080, 3840×2160) and rate (i.e., 60p, 50p, 30p, 25p, 24p) for your movie from the list of 13 Frame size/frame rate choices (figure 8.5, image 2), and then press the OK button to lock in the setting.

Basically, the Z6 can record video in Full HD (1080p) and 4K UHD (2160p), along with 1080p slow-mo. The 4K UHD (ultrahigh definition) video modes—at full FX resolution—are a welcome addition for many advanced videographers. If you have the equipment necessary to display 4K video, why not enjoy the higher resolution and sharper display?

Just keep in mind that a 4K video is quite large, requiring a larger memory card and greater hard drive storage on your computer. Plus, it is harder to work with the video files later because the file size is significantly larger. The mode in which you shoot most often will most likely be governed by available computer hardware capacity and processing power.

Note: The actual frame rates (e.g., 24p, 30p) for recording video do not exactly match the numbers provided. The majority of companies that publish frame rates are, in a sense, rounding up from the actual values. Here is a list of the actual fps values:

- 120p = 119.88 fps progressive
- 100p = 99.90 fps progressive
- 60p = 59.94 fps progressive
- 30p = 29.97 fps progressive
- 24p = 23.976 fps progressive

Note: This function is also available on the *i* Menu. Press the *i* button to open the menu and you will find this function on the top row, second from left.

Settings Recommendation: I tend to prefer the cinematic look provided by one of the 24p modes. That's what we see when we go to the movies. However, if you want to use a somewhat faster frames-per-second rate for action, select 30p, which gives you 30 frames per second in progressive (p) mode for less motion blurring.

I am experimenting with the new 4K video modes and I am finding them delightful to use. I still tend to shoot at 24p in 4K mode because of the cinematic look. You will need to experiment and determine your favorite video modes. Being able to shoot up to ~30 minutes of 4K video for each clip is quite powerful, as long as you have enough memory card space!

If you want to shoot some slow-motion video, you will need to set the camera to one of the three DX-only, 1920 × 1080 (Full HD), slow-mo modes. Just remember that a few minutes of slow-mo shooting will create a much longer video (4 or 5 times longer) than normal recording speed will create (up to 12 or 15 minutes for the up to 3 minutes recorded). For more information on shooting slow motion, I suggest discussing this subject in the **Nikon Video** forum at **www.Nikonians.org**.

Also, please investigate using an external recorder, such as the Atomos Ninja V, to record 4K 10-bit 4:2:2 N-Log video through the HDMI port. There are no time limits for this type of recording and the quality is on the professional level. Here's a link: **https://www.atomos. com/ninjav**

Movie Quality

Movie quality affects the "bit rate" (Mbps) at which the movie is shot. The bit rate decides the quality level of the movie, much like how the JPEG type (Fine, Normal, Basic) sets the quality of a JPEG still image. The higher the bit rate, the better the video quality. For video written to the memory card, two bit rates are available: High quality and Normal. The Frame size/frame rate of the video controls how these are applied.

If your camera's Movie quality menu selection is grayed out and unavailable, it is because you have one of the three 4K UHD (2160p) video modes selected. In the three 4K modes, the camera defaults to High quality mode at all times.

Table 8.2 shows a list of Frame size/frame rates, Movie quality bit rates, and maximum video lengths controlled by the bit rate.

Frame Size/ Frame Rate	Bit Rate: High Quality	Bit Rate: Normal Quality	Maximum Length High Quality and Normal
3840 × 2160; 30p	144 Mbps	N/A	29 min 59 sec
3840 × 2160; 25p	144 Mbps	N/A	29 min 59 sec
3840 × 2160; 24p	144 Mbps	N/A	29 min 59 sec
3840 × 2160; 120p	144 Mbps	N/A	29 min 59 sec
3840 × 2160; 100p	144 Mbps	N/A	29 min 59 sec
1920 × 1080; 60p	56 Mbps	28 Mbps	29 min 59 sec
1920 × 1080; 50p	56 Mbps	28 Mbps	29 min 59 sec
1920 × 1080; 30p	28 Mbps	14 Mbps	29 min 59 sec
1920 × 1080; 25p	28 Mbps	14 Mbps	29 min 59 sec
1920 × 1080; 24p	28 Mbps	14 Mbps	29 min 59 sec
1280 × 720; 60p	28 Mbps	14 Mbps	29 min 59 sec
1280 × 720; 50p	28 Mbps	14 Mbps	29 min 59 sec
1920 × 1080; 30p x4	N/A	36 Mbps	Record: 3 min, Playback: 12 min
1920 × 1080; 25p x4	N/A	36 Mbps	Record: 3 min, Playback: 12 min
1920 × 1080; 24p x5	N/A	29 Mbps	Record: 3 min, Playback: 15 min

Table 8.2: Movie quality affects video recording length and quality

Now let's examine how to select one of the two Movie quality choices.

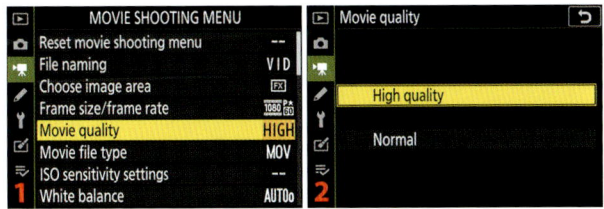

Figure 8.6: Choosing a Movie quality (bit rate)

Use these steps to choose a Movie quality:

1. Select Movie quality from the Movie Shooting Menu and scroll to the right (figure 8.6, image 1).
2. Choose High quality or Normal (figure 8.6, image 2) and then press the OK button or tap on your choice to lock in the setting.

The Movie quality setting is applied to compressed (H.264 MPEG-4 AVC) video written to the camera's memory cards only. Streaming uncompressed video through the HDMI port to an external video recorder is not affected by this setting.

Note: This function is also available on the *i* Menu. Press the *i* button to open the menu and you will find this function on the top row, second from left, under the *Frame size and rate/Image quality* setting.

Settings Recommendation: Because I am interested in maximum video quality, I leave my camera set to High quality. Any important video that will be displayed on a local computer or HDTV for friends and family to view deserves the High quality setting. (All video shot in 4K mode is fixed at High quality.)

However, if you are shooting some fun video for uploading to certain social media sites, which may compress the video to the max—destroying its high quality in the process—you could select Normal. Or, if your camera is low on card space and you need to cram as much video onto the card as possible, use the Normal setting.

Movie File Type

The default video file format (container) used by the Z6 is the popular MOV format (Apple QuickTime). However, you may also choose the even more popular MP4 format (MPEG-4 Part 14), which is closely related to the QuickTime format but may be better for streaming over the internet. Both of these file types should be compatible with virtually all computer and smart device movie player apps. See the sidebar titled **What Is a Container?**

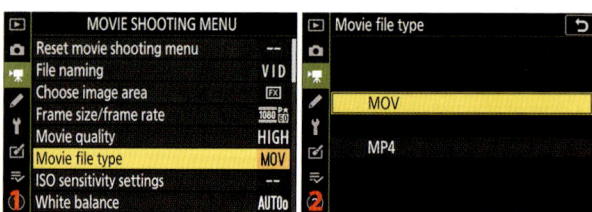

Figure 8.7: Choosing a Movie file type

Use the following steps to select your favorite Movie file type (container):

1. Select Movie file type from the Movie Shooting Menu and scroll to the right (figure 8.7, image 1).
2. Choose either the MOV or MP4 file type and press the OK button or tap on your choice to lock in the setting (figure 8.7, image 2).

Settings Recommendation: I generally choose the MOV format for my best videos because I am a Mac user and prefer the MOV file type. These days, almost any computer will play a MOV file, so it doesn't matter as much as when a MOV file was exclusive to the Apple world.

When I am shooting fun videos that I plan to upload to Facebook or YouTube, I often switch to the MP4 format because it is so highly accepted by social media in general.

Honestly, I can't tell much difference in the video quality between the two formats and the file size doesn't really seem much different—although the MOV file can be slightly larger sometimes.

Use whichever format you find most convenient for your purposes. If you need more information on video file types (containers), stop into the Nikonians.org **Nikon Video** forum and ask a few questions of the helpful experts there. Here's a convenient link: **www.nikonians.org/forum/402/nikon-video**

What Is a Container?

You may use container formats very often, although you may have not realized it. Every time you play a video on your smart device or computer, you are using an app that reads and plays certain containers. The last three letters of a video file name (e.g., myvideo.*mp4*) tells you which container is used for that video. For instance, I am sure you've heard of WAV, AVI, MOV, FLV, and the various MPEG formats (e.g., MP4). These are all container formats that are commonly played on your computer, smartphone, or tablet. The Z6 allows you to use a MOV or MP4 container (Movie file type). Basically, once you have recorded H.264 MPEG-4 AVC compressed video to your camera's memory card, the video signal must be placed into a specific container file type (MOV or MP4), which will contain not only the video, but also the audio (sound) signal.

ISO Sensitivity Settings

Movie *ISO sensitivity settings* give you control over the light sensitivity of the imaging sensor while capturing a video, whether you manually control it or the camera sets it automatically.

Because light levels in a scene will often vary as you move the camera, it is more critical that you allow the Z6 to adjust its ISO sensitivity automatically; otherwise, you could easily end up with under- or overexposed video. At times, you may want to leave the camera on one ISO setting—and you can—such as when you are shooting under controlled lighting. However, in general, it is better to allow the camera to adjust the ISO sensitivity on the fly so you can concentrate on capturing the best video compositions.

Let's examine the various settings within the ISO sensitivity settings function. Specifically, we will examine how to use automatic ISO sensitivity and manual ISO sensitivity while shooting video.

Maximum Sensitivity

The *Maximum sensitivity* setting is a safeguard for you (figure 8.8A, image 2). It allows the camera to automatically adjust its ISO sensitivity within a specific range, from a minimum value of ISO 100 (controlled by the camera) to whatever value you have set in Maximum sensitivity (up to Hi 2 or ISO 204800), according to light conditions.

This setting gives the camera freedom to immediately change the ISO sensitivity value to one that will give you an acceptable exposure, allowing you to concentrate on capturing the best movie instead of constantly trying to maintain the best exposure. The camera will try to maintain the lowest ISO sensitivity it can to make a good video. However, if needed, it can rapidly raise the ISO to the Maximum sensitivity level.

When you are using P, S, or A auto exposure modes, the camera will *always* use automatic ISO sensitivity for video, using whatever you set as the Maximum sensitivity value as its highest potential setting and ISO 100 as its lowest potential setting. Only when using manual exposure mode (M) can you turn off automatic ISO sensitivity and use manual ISO sensitivity. We will discuss how to do that in the next subsection, **Auto ISO Control (Mode M)**. First, though, let's see how to set the camera's Maximum sensitivity for video.

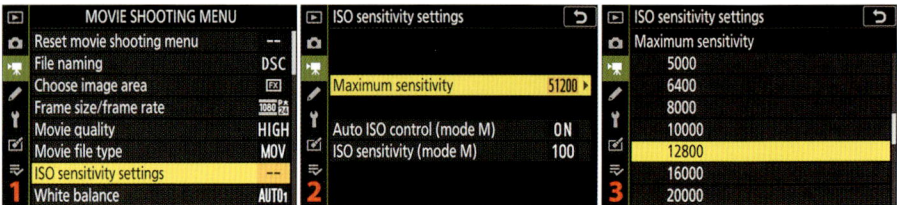

Figure 8.8A: Auto ISO sensitivity control – Maximum sensitivity

Use the following steps to choose a Maximum sensitivity (ISO) for your video:

1. Follow the screen flow shown in figure 8.8A, images 1 and 2 (*ISO sensitivity settings > Maximum sensitivity*) until you arrive at the third screen in the series.
2. Select an ISO sensitivity value to be used as the automatic maximum ISO if the light drops below normal (figure 8.8A, image 3). My camera has ISO 12800 selected. Press the OK button or tap the option to lock in the ISO value.

When you are using P, S, or A exposure modes, the camera ignores the values set in *Auto ISO control (mode M) and ISO sensitivity (mode M)* settings (discussed in the next two chapter subsections).

The Z6 will attempt to use a lower ISO sensitivity until it can no longer make good video without raising the ISO value. My camera's factory default Maximum sensitivity value was set to ISO 51200. This default setting will let the camera take the ISO sensitivity all the way up to a maximum ISO 51200 in a low-light situation (or up to ISO 204800 if adjusted). However, if you think a certain high ISO value may cause too much noise to appear in your video, you may want to reduce the ISO value. I keep my camera's Maximum sensitivity set to ISO 12800.

Auto ISO Control (Mode M)

Auto ISO control (mode M) is designed to let the camera automatically adjust the ISO sensitivity even when you are using manual (M) exposure mode, applying the Maximum sensitivity (ISO) set in the previous subsection. This mode has no effect when you are using auto exposure modes P, S, or A.

However, when you are using exposure mode M, you can disable Auto ISO control (mode M), and the camera will use only the manual ISO value you set in the ISO sensitivity (mode M) setting (next subsection).

In other words, Auto ISO control (mode M) allows you to choose whether to use automatic ISO control or manual ISO control. Often, you may want to manually control the camera in *most* aspects (e.g., aperture, shutter speed), while still taking advantage of automatic ISO sensitivity. Or, you can set Auto ISO control (mode M) to Off and manually control *all* aspects of the video capture, including ISO sensitivity. Let's examine how to adjust Auto ISO control (mode M).

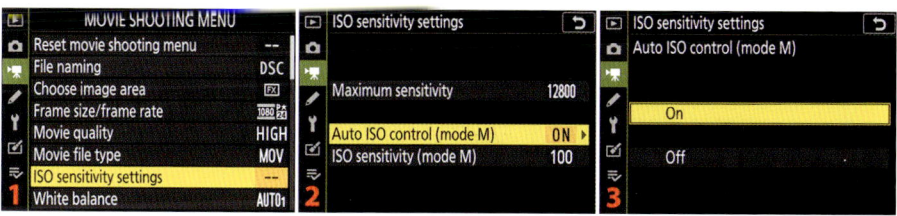

Figure 8.8B: Enabling Auto ISO control (mode M)

Use the following steps to enable or disable the Auto ISO control (mode M):

1. Follow the screen flow shown in figure 8.8B, images 1 and 2 (*ISO sensitivity settings > Auto ISO control (mode M)*), until you arrive at the third screen in the series.
2. Select On or Off from the Auto ISO control (mode M) menu (figure 8.8B, image 3) and then press the OK button or tap the option to save the setting.

Once you've set Auto ISO control (mode M) to On, you should immediately set the Maximum sensitivity (ISO) that you want to use while shooting a video.

Now let's discuss how to set the single ISO sensitivity you will use when capturing video in manual exposure mode, with the Auto ISO control (mode M) set to Off.

ISO Sensitivity (Mode M)

ISO sensitivity (mode M) allows you to choose a certain ISO sensitivity value to use in manual (M) exposure mode only. This value is applied only when you have Auto ISO control (mode M) set to Off (previous subsection), and it has no effect when you are using P, S, or A auto exposure modes.

Notice in figure 8.8C, image 3, that you have a scrollable list of ISO sensitivity settings. It extends from ISO 100 to ISO 204800 (Hi 2). Let's see how to adjust for pure manual exposure (no ISO automation at all).

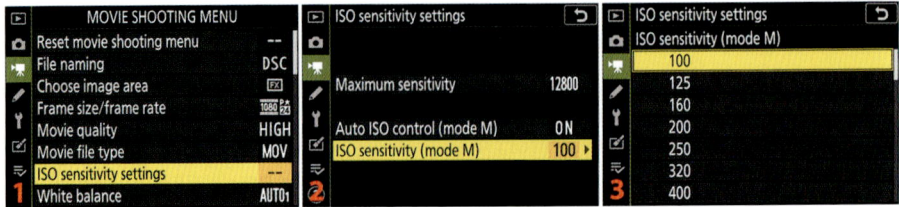

Figure 8.8C: Setting ISO sensitivity

Here are the steps to select an ISO sensitivity setting:

1. Follow the screen flow shown in figure 8.8C, images 1 and 2 (*ISO sensitivity settings > ISO sensitivity (mode M)*), until you arrive at the third screen in the series.
2. Scroll up or down in the ISO sensitivity (mode M) menu until you highlight the ISO value you want to use while capturing video (figure 8.8C, image 3). You can choose an ISO value from ISO 100 to Hi 2 (ISO 204800). Press the OK button or tap on your choice to save the setting.

Settings Recommendation: Most of the time I leave my Z6 set to a Maximum sensitivity of ISO 12800 for video capture. I appreciate the fact that Nikon has given us the ability to use automatic or manual ISO values even when capturing video in manual (M) exposure mode. When I am shooting serious video outside, I will often use Auto ISO control (mode M). I especially like that setting to prevent large changes in ambient light from ruining the video. However, sometimes, such as when I am videoing something under studio lighting, I will use a single manual ISO sensitivity value by setting Auto ISO control (mode M) to Off, and then setting an ISO value for the session with the ISO sensitivity (mode M) setting (e.g., ISO 100).

White Balance

The *White balance (WB)* settings for video recording work basically the same way they do for making still images. You can select a specific WB type, such as Direct sunlight, Fluorescent, or Cloudy, or you can let the camera decide which WB to use with the Auto WB modes.

If you prefer to be extremely accurate, you can choose a specific Kelvin color temperature from 2500K to 10000K, or you can do an ambient light reading from a white or gray card for the best color temperature matching.

Virtually everything you know about WB for still images works the same way for video recording. To prevent this section from repeating material covered in other chapters, we will consider only how to make a WB selection in this section. For deeper information on how to use White balance, see the more detailed white balance information found in the chapter titled **White Balance** on page 107.

Now, let's examine how to select a particular WB value for your video.

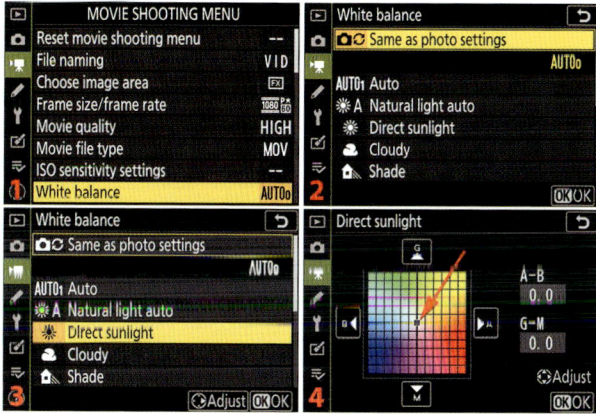

Figure 8.9A: Choosing a WB value for video recording

The steps to select a White balance setting for video recording are as follows:

1. Select White balance from the Movie Shooting Menu and scroll to the right (figure 8.9A, image 1).
2. If you prefer to use a carefully prepared WB value currently in use in the Photo Shooting Menu for still images, you can highlight the Same as photo settings selection and press or touch OK to use the same settings you were using previously for your still images (figure 8.9A, image 2). If this setting is satisfactory, you can skip the following steps. To use a different WB for video recordings than you use for still images, proceed with step 3.
3. Choose a White balance type, such as Auto or Direct sunlight, from the menu and scroll to the right (figure 8.9A, image 3).
4. If you choose Auto, Fluorescent, Choose color temp., or Preset manual you will need to select from an intermediate screen with additional choices, similar to the one shown for the Fluorescent WB in figure 8.9B. The Auto WB screen presents three settings: Auto0 Keep white (reduce warm colors), Auto1 Keep overall atmosphere, and Auto2 Keep warm lighting colors. Fluorescent presents seven different types of fluorescent lighting (as seen in figure 8.9B). Choose color temp. allows you to select a color temperature manually from a range of 2500 K (cool or bluish looking) to 10000 K (warm or reddish looking). Preset manual (PRE) provides stored White balance memory locations d–1 through d–6 and allows you to choose one of them to store or reuse a certain WB setting. (**Note:** These Preset manual values are stored separately from any Preset manual values you've created in the Photo Shooting Menu for still photography.) If this seems a bit overwhelming, just choose Auto1 Normal for now. The chapter titled **White Balance** will explain how to use all these settings for both video and still images (see page 107). Once you have selected the WB value you

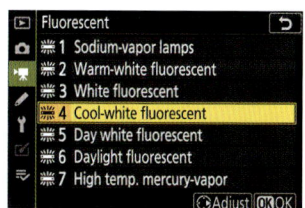

Figure 8.9B: Sample Fluorescent intermediate screen

want to use, either press or touch OK to lock in the WB value and skip step 5, or scroll to the right to fine-tune the value.

5. If you want to fine-tune the WB value, you will use the screen shown in figure 8.9A, image 4. You can make an adjustment to how you want this White balance to record color by introducing a color bias toward green (G), amber (A), magenta (M), or blue (B). You do this by using the Multi selector pad to move the little black square in the middle of the color box (image 4, red arrow) toward the edges of the box in any direction. If you make a mistake, simply move the black square to the middle of the color box. You can also introduce the bias by touching the four little arrow pointers (G, A, M, B) on the four sides of the color box. Most people do not change this setting. After you have finished adjusting (or not adjusting) the colors, press or touch OK to save your setting. Most people select OK as soon as they see the fine-tuning screen so they don't change the default settings for that particular White balance.

Note: This function is also available on the **i** Menu. Press the **i** button to open the menu and you will find this function on the bottom row, first on the left.

 Settings Recommendation: I generally leave my camera set to the *Same as photo settings* selection when I am shooting video (figure 8.9A, image 2). A nature photographer can generally shoot both still images and video with similar WB values. However, your style of video may require a WB setting completely different from the setting you use to shoot still images. The camera offers you the ability to have separate WB values for both photos and video.

Set Picture Control

Set Picture Control allows you to use the same Picture Control you have set in the Photo Shooting Menu (for taking pictures), one of eight regular Nikon Picture Controls, or one of 20 Creative Picture controls, to impart a certain look to your video. Set Picture Control works in a similar way for both video and still images. In fact, the factory default for this function is the same as the settings you last used when taking pictures (figure 8.10A).

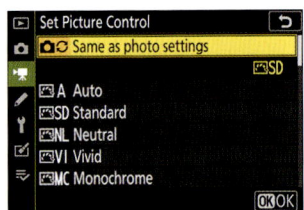

Figure 8.10A: Picture Control settings for video

Each Picture Control has individual settings for Sharpening, Mid-range sharpening, Clarity, Contrast, Brightness, Saturation, and Hue; plus it has a Quick sharp setting that quickly modifies Sharpening, Mid-range sharpening, and Clarity as a group.

 Here is a list of each choice on the Set Picture Control menu and what each one does for your videos:

- **Same as photo settings:** Uses the same Picture Control settings as when you were last taking still pictures (factory default).

- **A Auto:** Uses the Standard Picture Control as a base, but changes how the camera approaches portraiture and landscapes. When a human face is detected, the camera will adjust the hues and tones of the skin for a softer, more pleasing look. When using this mode for landscapes, the foliage and sky will be a bit more saturated (tending more toward the Vivid Picture Control without being so strong). Other subjects will be rendered like the Standard Picture Control.
- **SD Standard:** A Picture Control setting that gives a medium level of Sharpening, Mid-range sharpening, Clarity, Contrast, Brightness, Saturation, and Hue. This is a good general-purpose Picture Control for video; it's not too saturated and not too weak colored.
- **NL Neutral:** A Picture Control setting that gives a low level of Sharpening, Mid-range sharpening, Clarity, Contrast, Brightness, Saturation, and Hue. Good for videos with subjects that require low saturation and contrast.
- **VI Vivid:** A Picture Control setting that gives a high level of Sharpening, Mid-range sharpening, Clarity, Contrast, Brightness, Saturation, and Hue. Use this Picture Control for nature videos where you want very saturated reds, blues, and greens. This is not a good Picture Control to use for videos where skin tones are important because the VI control uses very strong colors and high contrast.
- **MC Monochrome:** A Picture Control for those who like to shoot old-style, black-and-white videos. The standard settings within the control are medium in level, which means you may want to experiment with the contrast settings. This control also provides filter effects that allow you to use the equivalent of a yellow, orange, red, or green filter for special effects. Additionally, you can use toning to tint the video in interesting ways. Toning filter options include B&W, sepia, cyanotype, red, yellow, green, blue green, blue, purple blue, and red purple.
- **PT Portrait:** This Picture Control uses settings that make it good for videos featuring people, in which skin tones are important. It is a bit more saturated and contrasty than the NL Neutral control, but not quite as strong as the SD Standard control, and no where near as strong as the VI Vivid control.
- **LS Landscape:** This Picture Control is designed for those who want natural landscape videos without the extra saturation of the VI Vivid control. While this control does add some additional saturation to natural colors, they are not garish or oversaturated.
- **FL Flat:** This Picture Control is designed for professional videographers. It has very low sharpening, contrast, and saturation. A video shot with this control will have maximum dynamic range (low contrast) and weaker colors. It allows the videographer to grade the video in professional video editing software (e.g., Final Cut Pro X, Adobe Premier Pro CC), selectively adding the needed amounts of saturation, sharpening, and contrast in a computer software program.

In addition, Nikon has provided 20 special Creative Picture Controls. Each of these has filtered color or black-and-white tones that impart a different look than normal to your videos. We have discussed these controls in our previous chapter on still photography. Please refer to **Set Picture Control** (page 200) for a look at color styles based on an X-rite color chart. These creative controls give you room to have some fun with your family video, or even impart a certain look that is rare in commercial videos. These will require experimentation on your part to fully understand what each control does.

If you leave this function set to *Same as photo settings,* the camera will use the same Picture Control settings for both still images and video. By selecting any of the listed Picture Controls instead of *Same as photo settings,* you are separating Picture Control Use for still image and video shooting. Each will use their own settings, instead of sharing Picture Control settings.

Now let's consider how to select one of the Picture Controls for shooting a video with a specific look.

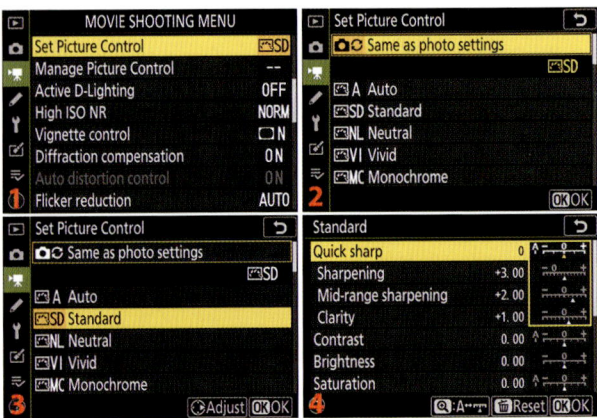

Figure 8.10B: Choosing a Picture Control

Use the following steps to choose a Picture Control:

1. Select Set Picture Control from the Movie Shooting Menu and scroll to the right (figure 8.10B, image 1).
2. If you prefer to use the same Picture Control settings for still images and videos, simply leave the selection set to Same as photo settings (figure 8.10B, image 2). The camera will then use the settings you have configured for still images when you are shooting videos. Press or touch OK to lock in the Same as photo settings selection (default) and skip the following steps.
3. If you prefer to use different settings for still images and videos, scroll down and select one of the eight Picture Controls (figure 8.10B, image 3), or scroll even farther down and find the 20 Creative Picture Controls (figure 8.10C). Press or touch OK to choose that Picture Control, unless you would like to fine-tune its internal settings. If so, scroll to the right to open the adjustment screen.

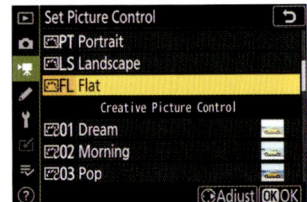

Figure 8.10C: Creative Picture Controls

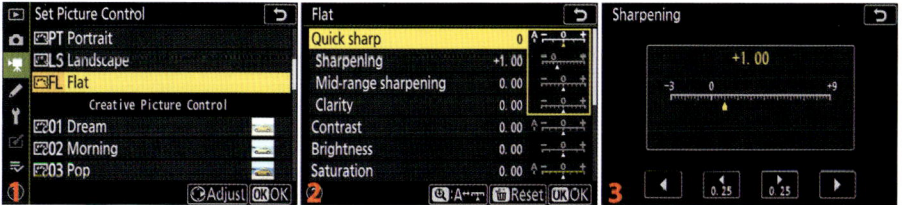

Figure 8.10D: Using touch controls to access and adjust internal settings

4. You now have access to the Quick sharp, Sharpening, Mid-range sharpening, Clarity, Contrast, Brightness, Saturation, and Hue settings for any of the Picture Controls (figure 8.10D, image 2). Use the Multi-selector pad to make your adjustments by scrolling up or down to select a setting and then scrolling left (–) or right (+) to adjust the setting. Or, you can tap the –/+ adjustment slider for one of the settings and open a touch screen to make the adjustment (figure 8.10D, image 3). Tap the pointer buttons to change the setting and then tap the back arrow in the top-right corner to lock in the setting. The name of each setting is self-explanatory. If you adjust a Picture Control, a small asterisk will appear to the right of the control name in camera menus, letting you know that this is a modified Picture Control. When you are done, press or touch OK to lock in your settings. To reset a Picture Control's internal settings, press the Delete button (garbage can) or tap Reset, and then choose Yes when prompted with the screen that says *Selected Picture Control will be reset to default settings. OK?*

As previously mentioned, this Set Picture Control function for videos is very similar to the Set Picture Control function for still images. To prevent duplication of material, we have only considered how to select the controls in this chapter. For a much more detailed discussion of how the Picture Controls work, including the internal adjustments within each control, please reread the section **Set Picture Control** in chapter 7, **Photo Shooting Menu,** on page 200.

Note: This function is also available on the *i* Menu. Press the *i* button to open the menu and you will find this function on the top row, first on the left.

Settings Recommendation: I normally leave my camera set to the SD Standard Picture Control, unless I am shooting nature videos. I like the idea of separating my use of Picture Controls for still images and video. When I am shooting nature videos on an overcast, low-contrast day, I will often use the VI Vivid Picture Control to add a little snap to the video. If I am shooting nature in direct sunshine, I do not like the extra high contrast of the VI Vivid Picture Control and therefore use the LS Landscape Picture Control.

If I am shooting a high school graduation or wedding, I will usually use the PT Portrait Picture Control to prevent odd skin coloration in my human subjects. If I plan to grade the video myself in my computer, I will use the FL Flat Picture Control to record as much dynamic range as I can in the video for later manipulation in software.

This is a very subjective setting. You will need to experiment with the various Picture Controls to see what they can add to your videos. Each of them has a certain look that can be useful at different times.

Manage Picture Control

Manage Picture Control is designed to allow you to create and store Custom Picture Control settings for future video use. You can take an existing Nikon Picture Control (A, SD, NL, VI, MC, PT, LS, or FL) or an existing Creative Picture Control (e.g., Dream, Sepia, Charcoal), make modifications to it, and then rename it.

If you modify a Picture Control using the Set Picture Control function discussed in the previous section, you simply create a one-off setting. If you'd like to go further and create your own named Custom Picture Controls, the Z6 is happy to oblige.

Any changes you make to a Nikon Picture Control within this function affect that particular control for video use only. The camera saves Custom Picture Controls separately for still images and video. You will not see custom controls for still images on the video menu, and vice versa.

Let's look at each of these settings and examine how to manage Picture Controls effectively.

Save/Edit a Custom Picture Control

There are six screens used to save and edit a Nikon Picture Control (figure 8.11A)—storing the results for later use as a Custom Picture Control.

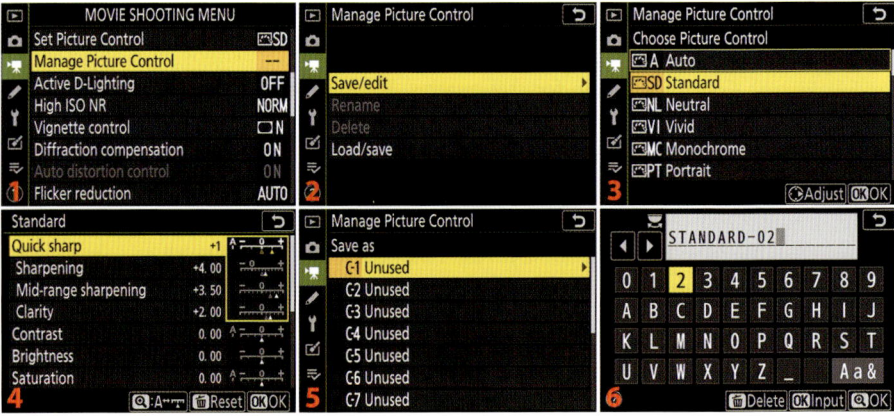

Figure 8.11A: Save/edit a Custom Picture Control

Here are the steps to edit and save a Picture Control with modified settings for use in your video productions:

1. Select Manage Picture Control from the Movie Shooting Menu and scroll to the right (figure 8.11A, image 1).
2. Highlight Save/edit and scroll to the right (figure 8.11A, image 2).

3. Choose a Picture Control that you want to use as a base for your new settings and then scroll to the right (figure 8.11A, image 3). I am modifying the SD Standard Picture Control and will save the new control under a different name.

4. Make your adjustments to Sharpening, Contrast, and so forth. I simply used the Quick sharp setting and added +1 to it, increasing the overall effect of Sharpening by 1 (out of 2). When you have modified the control in a way that makes it yours, press or touch OK (figure 8.11A, image 4). If you want to abandon your changes and start over, you can simply press the Delete button (garbage can) or tap Reset and reset the control to factory specs.

5. Select one of nine storage areas named C-1 to C-9 and scroll to the right (figure 8.11A, image 5). Only seven of the nine storage areas are viewable without scrolling down. In figure 8.11A, image 5, they are all currently marked as Unused. I can save as many as nine different Custom Picture Controls here for later selection with Set Picture Control.

6. You will now see the Rename screen (figure 8.11A, image 6), which works just like the other screens you have used to rename things. Insert a new name for the control by tapping on characters at the center of the screen and they will appear in the position marked with the dark-gray cursor in the name field (Standard-02). You can tap on the left/right arrows in the top-left corner to move left and right in the name field. To change case from upper to lower, tap the Aa& button in the lower-right corner of the screen (just above OK). If you make a mistake, position the dark-gray cursor over the error and select Delete. When you have the name completed, press or touch OK to save it. The word *Saved* will briefly appear on the Monitor. The camera will create a default name for you by appending a dash and two numbers at the end of the current control name. I left it at the default of STANDARD-02.

7. Press or touch OK when you have entered the name of your Custom Picture Control.

Once you have created and saved a Custom Picture Control, you can still tell which control was used as its base, just in case you name it in a way that does not suggest its origins.

Notice the red arrow in the upper-right area of the screen in figure 8.11B. This is the control we just created in the previous steps (STANDARD-02) and it is derived from an SD Nikon Picture Control, as shown by the SD label at the red arrow.

Your camera is now set to your Custom Picture Control. You switch between your Custom Picture Controls and the basic Nikon Picture Controls by using Set Picture Control (see the previous section titled **Set Picture Control** on page 326). In other words, each of your newly named Custom Picture Controls will appear at the end of the Set Picture Control menu for later selection.

Now, let's examine how to rename an existing Custom Picture Control.

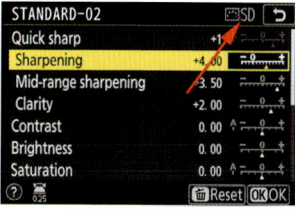

Figure 8.11B: Identifying the base of a Custom Picture Control

Rename a Custom Picture Control

Now that you have created and saved a new Custom Picture Control or two, you may want to rename one of them. Here's how.

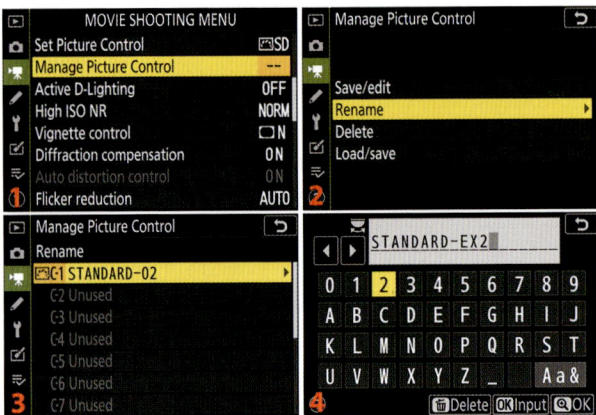

Figure 8.11C: Rename a Custom Picture Control

Use the following steps to rename an existing Custom Picture Control for video use:

1. Select Manage Picture Control from the Movie Shooting Menu and scroll to the right (figure 8.11C, image 1).
2. Select Rename and scroll to the right (figure 8.11C, image 2).
3. Select one of your Custom Picture Controls from the list (C–1 to C–9) and scroll to the right (figure 8.11C, image 3). I selected to rename STANDARD-02. This is the Custom Picture Control we created in the preceding subsection.
4. You will now be presented with the Rename screen (figure 8.11C, image 4). Insert a new name for the control by tapping on the characters at the center of the screen and they will appear in the position marked with the dark-gray cursor in the name field (STANDARD-EX2). You can tap on the left/right arrows in the top-left corner to move left and right in the name field. To change case from upper to lower, tap the Aa& button in the lower-right corner of the screen (just above OK). If you make a mistake, position the dark-gray cursor over the error and select Delete. When you have the name completed, press or touch OK to save it. The word *Saved* will briefly appear on the Monitor. The name is limited to a maximum of 19 characters. I renamed the STANDARD-02 Custom Picture Control STANDARD-EX2.
5. Press or touch OK when you have completed the new name.

Note: You are able to have more than one control with exactly the same name in your list of Custom Picture Controls. The camera does not get confused because each control has a different location (C-1 to C-9) to keep it separate from the rest. However, I don't suggest that you give several custom controls the same name. How would you tell them apart?

When a Custom Picture Control is no longer needed, you can easily delete it. Here's how.

Delete a Custom Picture Control

You cannot delete a Nikon Picture Control or a Creative Picture Control. In fact, they don't even appear in any of the Manage Picture Control menu screens.

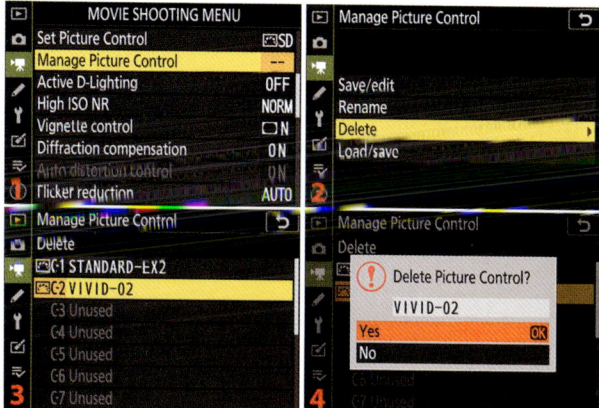

Figure 8.11D: Delete a Custom Picture Control

However, you can delete one or more of your video Custom Picture Controls with the following steps:

1. Follow the screen flow shown in figure 8.11D, images 1 and 2 (*Manage Picture Control > Delete*) until you arrive at the third screen in the series.
2. Select one of your nine available Custom Picture Controls and select the item you want to delete (figure 8.11D, image 3). I selected VIVID-02 for deletion.
3. Choose Yes at the *Delete Picture Control?* prompt (figure 8.11D, image 4) and then press or touch OK to delete the custom Picture Control.

Now, let's move to our last menu selection from the Manage Picture Control screen: Load/save.

Load/Save a Custom Picture Control

There are three parts to the Load/save function. They allow you to copy Custom Picture Controls to and from the memory card, or delete them from the card.

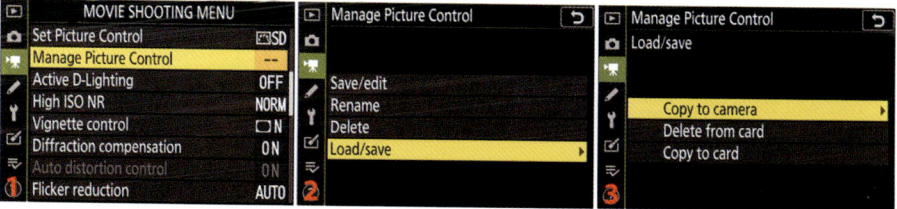

Figure 8.11E: Load/save a Custom Picture Control

Here are the three selections on the Load/save menu, as shown in figure 8.11E, image 3:

- **Copy to camera:** Loads Custom Picture Controls from the memory card into your camera. You can store up to nine controls in your camera's nine available memory locations (C1–C9).
- **Delete from card:** Displays a list of any Custom Picture Controls found on the memory card. You can selectively delete them.
- **Copy to card:** Allows you to copy your carefully crafted Custom Picture Controls (C1–C9) from your camera to a memory card. You can then share them with others. The camera will display up to 99 control locations (01–99) on any single memory card.

Let's examine each of these selections and see how best to use them.

Copy to Camera

You can use the *Copy to camera* function to copy Custom Picture Controls from your camera's memory card to the camera's Set Picture Control menu for video use. Once you have transferred a Custom Picture Control from your memory card to your camera, it will show up in the *Movie Shooting Menu > Set Picture Control* menu.

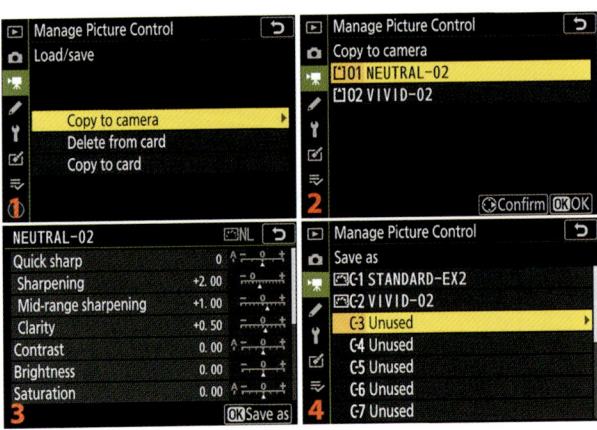

Figure 8.11F: Manage Picture Control – Copy to camera

Here are the steps to copy a Custom Picture Control from the memory card to the Set Picture Control menu:

1. Figure 8.11F continues from the last screen shown in figure 8.11E (Load/save on the Manage Picture Control menu). Choose Copy to camera and scroll to the right (figure 8.11F, image 1).
2. You will be presented with the list of Custom Picture Controls that are currently on the memory card (figure 8.11F, image 2). If there are no controls on the memory card, the camera will display a screen that says, *No Picture Control file found on memory card.* My camera in figure 8.11F, image 2, shows two controls—NEUTRAL-02 and VIVID-02. Choose a control from the list and press or touch OK. (If you scroll to the right instead,

you will be able to examine and adjust the control's settings before saving it to your camera [figure 8.11F, image 3]. If you don't want to modify it, simply select OK.)

3. You will now see the Manage Picture Control Save as menu, which lists any Custom Picture Controls already in your camera (figure 8.11F, image 4). Select one of the Unused memory locations and scroll to the right.

4. You'll be presented with the Rename screen (figure 8.11G), just in case you want to change the name of the Custom Picture Control. If you don't want to change the name, simply press or touch OK and the custom control will be added to your camera's Set Picture Control menu. It is possible to have multiple controls with exactly the same name. The camera keeps each control separate in its list of controls (C-1 to C-9). However, I always rename them to prevent

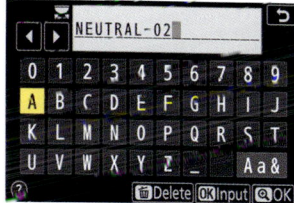

Figure 8.11G: Choose a new name (or rename)

future confusion. To create a different name, tap on the characters at the center of the screen and they will appear in the position marked with the dark-gray cursor in the name field (NEUTRAL-02). You can tap on the left/right arrows in the top-left corner to move left and right in the name field. To change case from upper to lower, tap the Aa& button in the lower-right corner of the screen (just above OK). If you make a mistake, position the dark-gray cursor over the error and select Delete. The name is limited to a maximum of 19 characters. When you have the name completed, press or touch OK to save it. The word *Saved* will briefly appear on the Monitor.

Delete from Card

Once you've finished loading Custom Picture Controls for video to your camera, you may be ready to delete a control or two from the memory card. You could format the memory card, but that will blow away all images and Picture Controls on the card. A less drastic method that allows you to be more selective in removing Picture Controls is the Delete from card function.

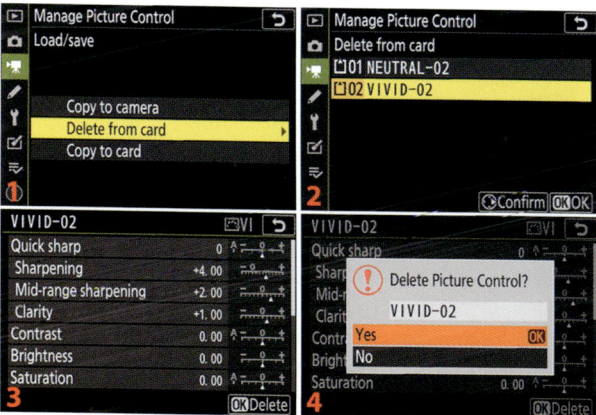

Figure 8.11H: Manage Picture Control – Delete from card

Here are the steps used to remove Custom Picture Controls for video from your camera's memory card:

1. Figure 8.11H continues from the last screen shown in figure 8.11E. Choose Delete from card from the Load/save menu and scroll to the right (figure 8.11H, image 1).
2. Choose one of the Custom Picture Controls that you want to delete (figure 8.11H, image 2). I chose VIVID-02. You can confirm that you are deleting the correct control by scrolling to the right, which gives you the fine-tuning screen with current adjustments for that control (figure 8.11H, image 3). If you are sure that this is the control you want to delete, move on to the next step by pressing or touching OK.
3. You will be shown a screen that asks, *Delete Picture Control?*, with the control's name shown below (VIVID-02). Choose either Yes or No (figure 8.11H, image 4). If you choose Yes, the Picture Control will be deleted from the memory card. If you choose No, the camera will return to the previous screen. Press or touch OK to execute your choice.

Copy to Card

After you create up to nine Custom Picture Controls for video using the instructions in the last few sections, you can use the Copy to card function to save them to a memory card. Once they are on a memory card, you can share your custom video controls with friends who have compatible Nikon cameras.

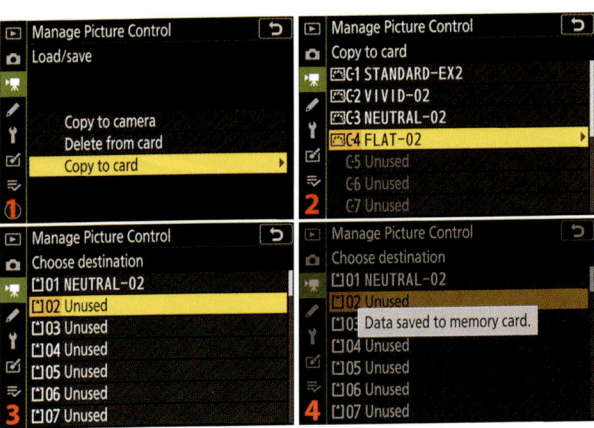

Figure 8.11I: Manage Picture Control – Copy to card

When your Custom Picture Controls for video are ready to go, use the following steps to copy them to a memory card:

1. Figure 8.11I continues from the last screen shown in figure 8.11E. Choose Copy to card from the Load/save menu and scroll to the right (figure 8.11I, image 1).
2. Select one of your current Custom Picture Controls from the Copy to card menu and scroll to the right (figure 8.11I, image 2). I chose FLAT-02 to copy to the memory card.

3. Now you'll use the Choose destination menu to select the location in which you want to save the custom control (figure 8.11I, image 3). You have 99 choices; select any Unused location by scrolling down.
4. Press the OK button or tap on an Unused location and you'll briefly see a message that says, *Data saved to memory card.* Your Custom Picture Control is now ready to distribute to the world or load onto another of your compatible Nikon cameras.

Active D-Lighting

The *Active D-Lighting* function allows you some contrast control while capturing video. If shadows are deeper than you'd like, you can open them up somewhat and maintain more dark detail. If the highlights are in danger of burning out to pure white, you can rein them in a little and preserve more highlight detail.

We discussed Active D-Lighting in detail in the **Photo Shooting Menu** chapter on page 223. Refer to that section for deeper information. Active D-Lighting works the same for both still images and video. Here is a review of how it works.

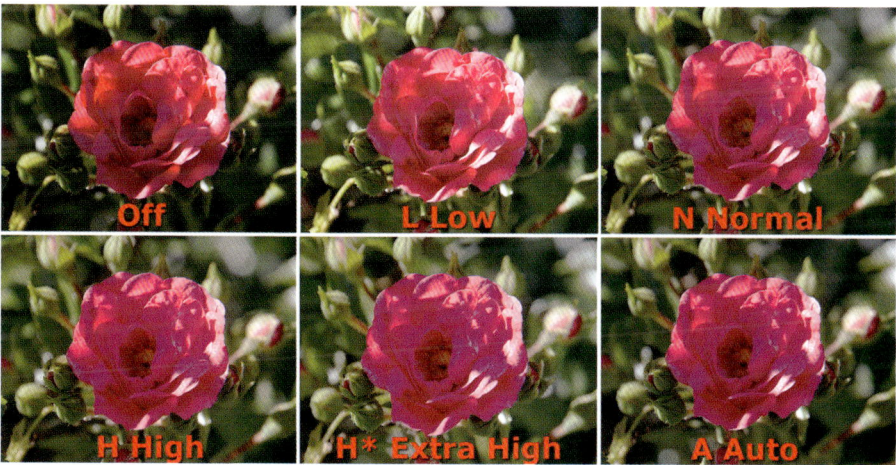

Figure 8.12A: Active D-Lighting controls contrast

Notice in the images of a rose (figure 8.12A) how the various levels of Active D-Lighting affect the image or video [including the A (Auto) selected under *Same as photo* settings]. The shadows are progressively opened up while the highlights are protected from becoming blown out.

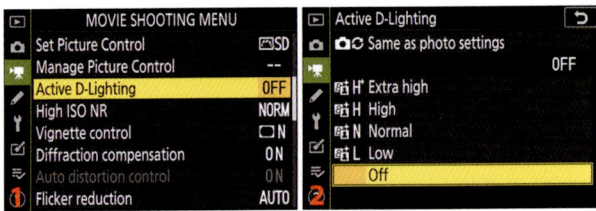

Figure 8.12B: Choosing an Active D-Lighting level

Use the following steps to select an Active D-Lighting level:

1. Choose Active D-Lighting from the Movie Shooting Menu and scroll to the right (figure 8.12B, image 1).
2. Select one of the four levels of Active D-Lighting: H* Extra high, H High, N Normal, or L Low (figure 8.12B, image 2). You can also choose Off (no Active D-Lighting) or Same as photo settings, which carries over your favorite Active D-Lighting setting from the Photo Shooting Menu (page 223). Highlight your choice and press the OK button or tap the option to lock in your setting.

Note: This function is also available on the *i* Menu. Press the *i* button to open the menu and you will find this function on the bottom row, fourth from the left.

Settings Recommendation: When I am shooting video on a sunny day, I will usually add some Active D-Lighting, either L Low or N Normal. When there is a lot of contrast, such as with direct sun, shadow detail can be hard to see and brighter subjects tend to become overexposed due to bright reflections. Some level of Active D-Lighting can be useful to contain excessive contrast. Why not experiment by shooting video with various levels until you determine what works best for you?

High ISO NR

High ISO NR (High ISO Noise Reduction) lessens the effects of digital noise in your videos when you use high ISO sensitivity settings.

The Z6 has better noise control than most cameras, so it can record video with an ISO setting of up to 3200 with little visible noise. However, no digital camera is completely without noise, so it's a good idea to use some noise reduction above a certain ISO sensitivity.

If High ISO NR is turned Off, the camera still does a small amount of noise reduction—less than the Low setting. Therefore, at higher ISO settings there will always be some noise reduction.

You can control the amount of noise reduction by choosing one of the four High ISO NR settings: High, Normal, Low, or Off.

We covered how High ISO NR works in greater detail in the **Photo Shooting Menu** chapter on page 227. The function works the same for both images and video. Review that section if you need deeper information on how High ISO NR works.

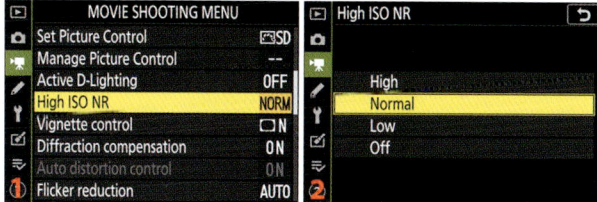

Figure 8.13: Setting High ISO NR

Use the following steps to choose a High ISO NR setting for video:

1. Choose High ISO NR from the Movie Shooting Menu and scroll to the right (figure 8.13, image 1)
2. Select one of the noise reduction levels: High, Normal, Low, or Off (figure 8.13, image 2) and then press the OK button or tap on the level to save your setting.

Settings Recommendation: I leave High ISO NR set to Low or Normal. I do want some noise reduction above ISO 1600 for videos. However, since any form of noise reduction blurs the video slightly, I don't go too far with it. Shoot some high-ISO videos and decide for yourself which settings you are comfortable with.

Vignette Control

Vignette control allows you to reduce the amount of vignetting (slight darkening) that many lenses have in the corners of the frame at various apertures. The angle at which light strikes a sensor on its edges is greater than the angle at which rays go straight through the lens to the center areas of the sensor. Because of the increased angle, some light falloff occurs at the extreme edges of the frame, especially at wide apertures. In recognition of this fact, Nikon has provided the Vignette control setting. It can reduce the vignetting effect to a large degree for Nikkor type G, E, D, and S lenses (excluding PC lenses).

Let's see how to configure the Vignette control for edge light falloff reduction with your lenses.

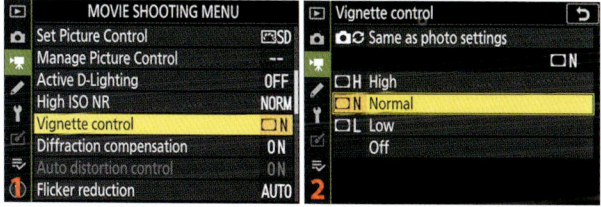

Figure 8.14: Vignette control range

Here are the steps to choose a Vignette control level for your Z6:

1. Choose Vignette control from the Movie Shooting Menu and scroll to the right (figure 8.14, image 1).
2. Highlight a level from the list: High, Normal, Low, Off (figure 8.14, image 2). Then press the OK button or tap on the item to lock in the level.

Settings Recommendation: A new Z6 defaults to Normal, so I have been capturing most of my video with it set to Normal and I like this setting. It does help remove vignetting in the corners. I have not noticed any additional noise or image degradation in the corrected areas. I suggest leaving your camera set to Normal at all times unless you are shooting with a lens that has a greater tendency to vignette, in which case you can increase the setting to High. Even High does not seem to fully remove vignetting when a lens is wide open, so this is not an aggressive algorithm that will leave white spots in the corners of your images. I suggest making a few videos with your lenses at wide aperture and see how Vignette control works with your lens and camera combinations.

Diffraction Compensation

The Diffraction compensation function is designed to help reduce diffraction unsharpness in your videos caused by using small apertures (e.g., f/11, f/16, f/22). When light hits the edge of an aperture blade it deflects slightly, arriving at the sensor at a slightly different angle than the light going through the middle of the aperture opening. This tends to cause a video to be less sharp than a one shot at a larger aperture (e.g., f/4, f/5.6, f/8).

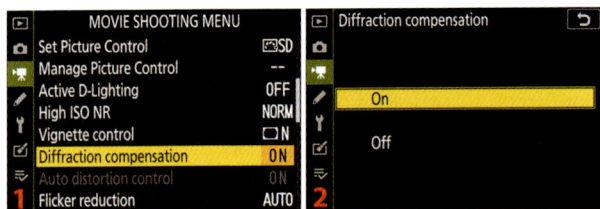

Figure 8.15: Enabling Diffraction compensation

Use the following steps to enable or disable Diffraction compensation:

1. Choose Diffraction compensation from the Movie Shooting Menu and scroll to the right (figure 8.15, image 1).
2. Highlight your choice: On or Off, and then press the OK button or tap on the item to lock in the setting (figure 8.15, image 2).

Settings Recommendation: Diffraction has been a problem for as long as lenses and apertures have existed. Photographers have tried to take pictures and videos at mid-sized apertures instead of small apertures to prevent diffraction. I set this function to On and I am happy to have it. I tested it on some videos and it does make a difference in sharpness.

The Z6 is capable of extra sharpness and this function is one of the reasons. Why not test this for yourself and see if you have sharper video with Diffraction compensation enabled? It defaults to On and I left it that way permanently on my Z6.

Auto Distortion Control

Auto distortion control is designed to automatically reduce barrel and pincushion distortion in your videos. This function may be best used by architectural photographers who are concerned about keeping lines and edges straight, for obvious reasons.

The Auto distortion control is designed to be used with Nikkor G, E, and D lenses, and not with PC, fisheye, or aftermarket lenses. When my Nikkor Z 24–70mm F/4 S lens was mounted, this function was grayed out and unavailable. Therefore, certain S lenses may not allow you to use this feature (it may not be necessary).

To prevent even mild cases of these two distortion types from affecting straight lines in your videos, you can use this function. Of course, if you are out shooting nature videos, it is unlikely you will gain much benefit from this function. If a lens you are using needs automatic barrel and pincushion distortion control, you will probably know it from previous work.

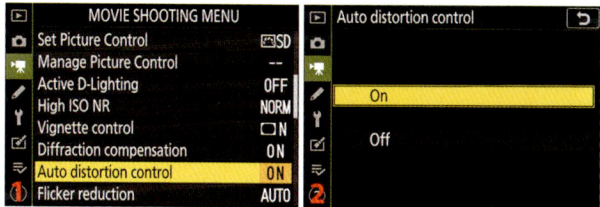

Figure 8.16: Auto distortion control

Use these steps to enable or disable Auto distortion control:

1. Choose Auto distortion control from the Movie Shooting Menu and scroll to the right (figure 8.16, image 1).
2. Highlight On or Off (figure 8.16, image 2) and then press the OK button or tap on your choice to save the setting.

Settings Recommendation: If you are a videographer who needs this function, you will already know it. If you question whether it will benefit you, it probably won't. This is an automatic function in the Z6 and, like many automatic functions, it does great sometimes and has little benefit most of the time. However, this may be a handy function when you are out in the field making videos and you immediately need some distortion correction.

Flicker Reduction

Flicker reduction helps reduce the banding effect we've all seen in videos, where darker-than-normal bands travel down the screen during playback. When you record video under certain types of lighting, especially fluorescent, mercury-vapor, and sodium lights, your video may be more susceptible to banding (flicker).

To help prevent this banding effect, it's a good idea to enable Flicker reduction. You may want to start by selecting Auto Flicker reduction (figure 8.17, image 2), which directs the camera to detect the frequency of the flickering and to time the video frame capture in a way that reduces banding.

If you do not have good results with Auto, you can try the 50Hz or 60Hz setting (figure 8.17, image 2); choose whichever one gives you the best results.

When subjects are especially bright, flicker may be worse. In this case, it is a good idea to use a smaller aperture (e.g., f/8 or smaller).

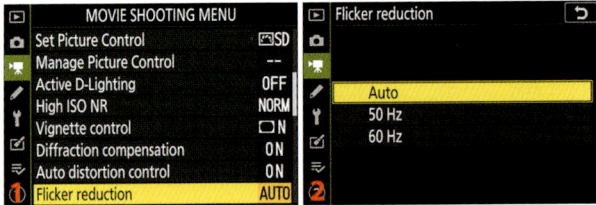

Figure 8.17: Choosing a Flicker reduction setting

Use these steps to select a Flicker reduction setting:

1. Choose Flicker reduction from the Movie Shooting Menu and scroll to the right (figure 8.17, image 1).
2. Select one of the Flicker reduction settings: Auto, 50 Hz, or 60 Hz (figure 8.17, image 2) and then press the OK button to save your setting.

Settings Recommendation: I usually start with Auto mode, and if that doesn't work, I try the 50Hz and 60Hz settings to see what happens. Another way to control banding, besides using the Flicker reduction, is to shoot the video in Manual (M) exposure mode and experiment with a shutter speed setting that more closely matches the frequency of the local electricity supply. If the frequency of electricity in your area is 50Hz, use a shutter speed of 1/100 sec, 1/50 sec, or 1/24 sec. For 60Hz (United States), try 1/125 sec, 1/60 sec, or 1/30 sec.

Metering

The *Metering* function allows you to control the type of light meter your camera uses to make a good exposure. There are three types of meters available in the Nikon Z6 for video. Here is a description of each type:

- **Matrix metering:** The camera meters a wide area of the frame using a matrix of zones. It uses these patterns along with tone distribution, color, composition, and subject distance to capture the best exposure for the subject. Matrix metering is accurate in most cases and is generally used as a default setting by most videographers.
- **Center-weighted metering:** The camera measures light from the entire frame but concentrates 75 percent of its metering attention on a 12mm circle in the middle of the frame, with only 25 percent for the areas outside the circle (firmware version C 2.00). However, the camera can be set to use the entire frame and average the light reading across 100 percent of the frame. For more information see the *b3 Center-weighted area* function in the **Custom Setting Menu** chapter (page 385).
- **Highlight-weighted metering:** The camera meters for highlights in this mode, mostly ignoring surrounding darkness. For example, if you are videoing a concert with a performer in a spotlight, this mode is excellent.

Let's examine how to choose one of the meter styles for your videos.

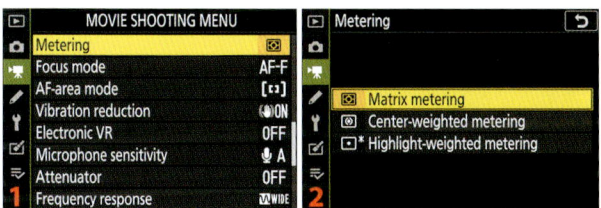

Figure 8.18: Metering modes on the Photo Shooting Menu

Use these steps to choose a Metering mode from the Movie Shooting Menu:

1. Choose Metering from the Movie Shooting Menu and scroll to the right (figure 8.18, image 1).
2. Highlight your Metering mode choice and press the OK button or tap your choice to use that Metering type (figure 8.18, image 2).

Note: This function is also available on the *i* Menu. Press the *i* button to open the menu and you will find this function on the bottom row, third from left.

   Settings Recommendation: The majority of photographers will leave their Metering mode set to Matrix metering. This is a well-established and often uncannily accurate form of exposure metering. Nikon has been working on their Matrix metering algorithms for many years and the Nikon Z6 has benefitted from that work. If you have special needs, such as for shooting highlighted subjects, you also have that choice. Center-weighted metering is an old style of metering that comes from the days of film glory. It works pretty well and some people prefer it, especially those who cut their teeth on old film cameras with center-weighted metering only. Use whichever one you like best or need at the time. I've found that Matrix metering works best for me most of the time.

Focus Mode

Focus mode allows you to control *how* the camera focuses on your subject. You will need various autofocus capabilities for static and moving subjects. It can use four methods:

- **Single AF (AF-S):** This focus setting is best for static or slowly moving subjects. The camera will obtain an initial focus and lock focus on the subject. If the subject moves, the focus may become invalid and will need to be updated.
- **Continuous AF (AF-C):** This focus method is best for rapidly moving subjects or subjects that rarely stop moving. The camera acquires focus but never locks the focus. Instead, it keeps trying to maintain good focus on your subject as long as your subject is under the current AF point area (see AF-area modes on page 345).
- **Full-time AF (AF-F):** This mode works like a combination of AF-S and AF-C. When you initially focus on a non-moving subject, the camera may lock focus on the subject. However, if the subject moves, or if you move the camera, the Z6 will update and maintain focus on your subject until it, or you, stops moving, at which point the focus will lock again.
- **Manual focus (MF):** You must manually turn the focus ring on the lens to focus on the subject. Many people will use focus Peaking to assist with manual focusing. We will discuss focus Peaking when we talk about **Custom Setting d10 Peaking Highlights** (page 409).

Let's see how to select a Focus mode.

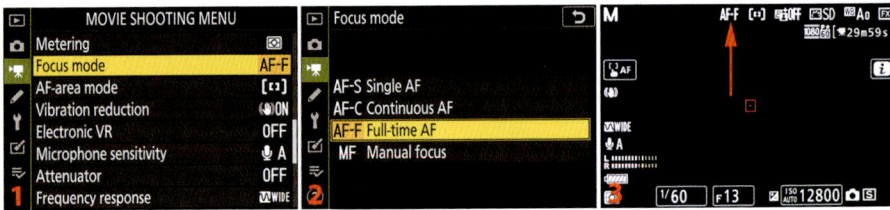

Figure 8.19: Choosing a Focus mode

Use the following steps to choose a Focus mode for video capture:

1. Choose Focus mode from the Movie Shooting Menu and scroll to the right (figure 8.19, image 1).
2. While referring to the previous list, select a Focus mode and press the OK button or tap your choice to lock it in (figure 8.19, image 2).

3. In figure 8.19, image 3, the location of the Focus mode (red arrow) is shown on the video screen (Monitor or EVF). You can immediately change to a different Focus mode by pressing and holding the Fn2 button on the camera's front while turning the rear Main command dial (unless Fn2 has been assigned to a different function).

Note: This function is also available on the *i* Menu. Press the *i* button to open the menu and you will find this function on the bottom row, last item on the right.

Settings Recommendation: Experiment to find the Focus mode that is best for you. For most of us the Full-time AF (AF-F) mode is preferred because it lets the camera control autofocus. The Z6 usually does a good job with automatic focus, so I use AF-F often for family videos.

Hardcore enthusiasts and commercial videographers will use manual focus lenses, often with special rings added to a lens's focus ring to assist with focus control. In that circumstance Manual focus (MF) with focus Peaking (page 409) may be best.

If you prefer to use back button focusing or to simply focus on a certain spot, such as when creating a video in your studio, you can use Single AF (AF-S) or Continuous AF (AF-C).

AF-Area Mode

The *AF-area mode* system allows you to choose a single focus point (AF point), or a group of AF points selected from the camera's 273 AF points, to cover your subject and help capture it in sharp focus.

The available AF point(s) are surrounded by a red frame (Single-point AF and Wide-area AF), or a partial frame (Auto-area AF), to give you some idea of the area covered by the AF point(s)—except for Auto-area AF, which lets the camera control the autofocus by selecting your subject automatically in the frame. For Single-point AF and Wide-area AF modes, you can move the red focus frame anywhere you choose in the EVF or Monitor (90% of the screen is available for choosing the AF-area).

Figure 8.20A shows the location of the AF-area mode symbol (upper arrows), along with the autofocus frame size for each mode (lower arrows).

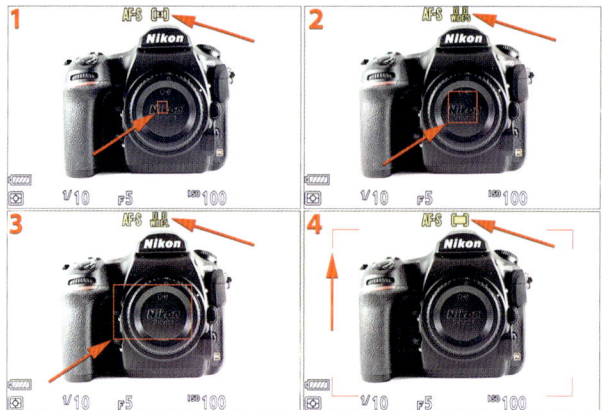

Figure 8.20A: Each of the four AF-area modes available for video

Let's examine each of the AF-area modes shown in figure 8.20A. The numbers in figure 8.20A match the numbers in this list:

1. **Single-point AF:** This is the preferred mode for many videographers. Its small AF point frame can be moved to specific areas of the subject. Single-point AF AF-area mode is available in both AF-S and AF-C Focus modes.
- **Wide-area AF (S):** This mode works in a similar manner to Single-point AF but it has a wider group of AF points in its frame. The Wide-area AF (S) focus frame is larger as seen in figure 8.20A, image 2, compared to Single-point AF in image 2. Wide-area AF (S) AF-area mode is available in both AF-S and AF-C Focus modes.
- **Wide-area AF (L):** This mode also works in a similar manner to Single-point AF but it has a much wider group of AF points in its frame. The focus frame is significantly larger as seen in figure 8.20A, image 3, compared to Wide-area AF (S) in image 2. Wide-area AF (L) AF-area mode is available in both AF-S and AF-C Focus modes.
- **Auto-area AF:** This mode gives full control of the AF system to the camera. The entire 273-point frame is involved in autofocus. The camera will choose a combination of AF points within the frame to obtain the best focus on your subject. You will see one rectangle, or groups of small rectangles, marking the areas the camera is using for autofocus. If a human face is detected in the frame, a yellow square will surround the face and will attempt to maintain focus on that face. If multiple faces are in the frame, the yellow square for the active face will add a directional arrow beside the yellow frame. This indicates that you can choose another face for best focus by scrolling with the Multi selector or Sub-selector joystick. If you want to choose just one person or some other subject to track, you can press the OK button, choose some part of your subject with the small white frame (targeting reticule) that appears, and press the OK button again—or the AF-ON button. The camera will activate Subject tracking and will attempt to track a moving subject with the white frame. Press OK again to stop Subject tracking. Auto-area AF AF-area mode is available in both AF-S and AF-C Focus modes.

Now let's consider how to choose an AF-area mode.

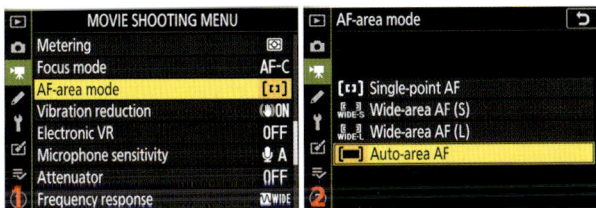

Figure 8.20B: Choosing an AF-area mode

Use the following steps to choose an AF-area mode for video:

1. Choose AF-area mode from the Movie Shooting Menu and scroll to the right (figure 8.20B, image 1).
2. Referring to the previous list, highlight one of the AF-area modes and press the OK button or tap the mode to lock it in (figure 8.20B, image 2). You can immediately change to a different AF-area mode by pressing and holding the Fn2 button on the camera's front while turning the front Sub-command dial (unless Fn2 has been assigned to a different function).

Note: This function is also available on the *i* Menu. Press the *i* button to open the menu and you will find this function on the top row, last item on the right.

 Settings Recommendation: Unless I am using manual focus (MF Focus mode), I will usually use the Continuous AF (AF-C) Focus mode (page 344) and Auto-area AF AF-area mode. I like the way the Z6 handles autofocus when using that combination. I have also found subject tracking to be pretty reliable when shooting videos, as long as the subject is not moving too quickly.

 Of course, you may prefer to use the other AF-area modes, according to your subject. Try shooting a video with each of these AF-area modes, in both AF-S and AF-C Focus mode (page 344), just to learn how well the camera focuses for you.

Vibration Reduction

Vibration reduction (VR) attempts to counteract small movements of the camera due to shaky hands. It is designed to keep the image sharp, even when you are handholding the camera and following your subject.

 The Vibration reduction function is different in the Nikon Z cameras compared to Nikon DSLRs. Current Nikon DSLRs do not have in-body image stabilization (IBIS), whereas the Z cameras do. IBIS is a vibration reduction (VR) system where the sensor assembly can move in up to 5-axes to counter camera vibration: left and right (X), up and down (Y), pitch, yaw, and roll. Best results are achieved when using Nikkor Z-mount lenses. If you are using an F-mount, AF-S Nikkor lens on an FTZ adapter, the camera provides up to 3-axis IBIS (pitch, yaw, and roll).

When you are using a Nikkor lens having VR built in, the camera and lens communicate and work together to get the best vibration reduction. With the Z6's IBIS you may well be able to get steady video, even without your camera mounted in a balanced video frame device.

There are two VR modes available, along with Off (no VR). Let's examine what each mode is designed to accomplish:

- **On Normal:** This mode is designed for shooting static subjects. If you are handholding the camera, walking around, or videoing a slowly moving subject, this is the best mode to use.
- **SPT Sport:** This mode is designed for shooting sports where athletes, or other subjects, are moving around rapidly and unpredictably. Use this mode for panning. The Z6 will detect when you are panning with your subject and turn off IBIS for horizontal movement. It will correct for vertical movement only when panning. When the subject stops, IBIS will again work for both horizontal and vertical vibration reduction.
- **Off:** The camera disables the IBIS system for the Z6 and Z-mount lenses.

The Vibration reduction menu item on the Photo Shooting Menu and in the *i* Menu will become grayed out and unavailable when an AF-S Nikkor lens with VR is mounted on the camera with the FTZ adapter. To control VR in that case, simply use the VR On/Off switch found on the side of Nikkor VR lenses. The VR On/Off switch will enable or disable in-lens and in-body image stabilization at the same time. When a Nikkor lens having no VR (e.g., AF-S Nikkor 50mm f/1.4G) is mounted, the Vibration reduction menus become available again.

Now, let's see how to choose an IBIS VR mode.

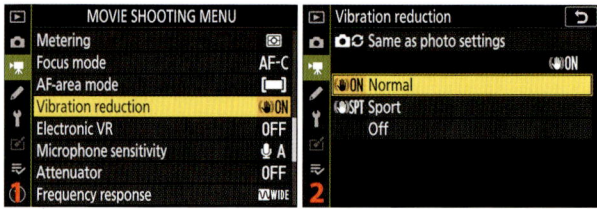

Figure 8.21: Selecting an IBIS/VR mode from the Movie Shooting Menu

Use the following steps to choose a Vibration reduction mode from the camera's Movie Shooting Menu:

1. Choose Vibration reduction from the Movie Shooting Menu and scroll to the right (figure 8.21, image 1).
2. Referring to the previous list, highlight a Vibration reduction mode and press the OK button or tap the mode to lock it in (figure 8.21, image 2).

Note: This function is also available on the *i* Menu. Press the *i* button to open the menu and you will find this function on the bottom row, next to the last item on the right.

Settings Recommendation: I normally use *On Normal* IBIS mode. I video mostly static or slowly moving subjects, such as cascading rivers, waterfalls, mountains, meadows, and sunsets. If I were videoing an action event, such as a football game, I would definitely consider using the *SPT sport* mode.

Another marvelous thing about IBIS in the Z6 is that it will work for virtually any lens mounted on the camera or on an adapter. Even older F-mount, manual focus AI and AI-S lens favorites, along with non-VR autofocus lenses, will have IBIS. Many videographers appreciate that the camera offers IBIS, even with their old, favorite, manual-focus, cine lenses.

Electronic VR

Electronic VR gives you a way to stabilize your videos when you shoot handheld. This is not the same thing as the physical sensor-shifting IBIS technology discussed in the previous subsection. Instead, Electronic VR works by pixel-shifting the video frame to add stability.

In other words, as slight vibrations occur during handheld video capture, the image recorded by the sensor will change position slightly. The camera attempts to shift the pixels that are capturing video, in time with the vibration from minor camera shake.

Electronic VR works alongside the normal in-body image stabilization (IBIS) and lens vibration reduction (VR) found in most newer Nikkor lenses, to keep the frame more stable.

Let's see how to configure Electronic VR.

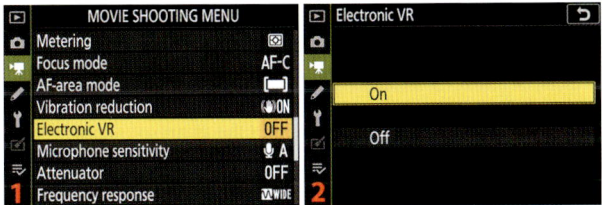

Figure 8.22: Selecting Electronic VR

Use the following steps to enable or disable Electronic VR:

1. Choose Electronic VR from the Movie Shooting Menu and scroll to the right (figure 8.22, image 1).
2. Select On or Off to enable or disable Electronic VR and then press the OK button or tap the option to save your choice (figure 8.22, image 2).

Settings Recommendation: This function may be useful if you are not moving around much while shooting a video handheld. However, if you are shooting a video while walking around, Electronic VR may tend to make the video look jumpy. For serious videos, I would stick with normal IBIS or lens VR, but for fun videos, you might want to give it a try. Experiment with this function before putting it to serious use, especially for a commercial video!

Microphone Sensitivity

Microphone sensitivity allows you to choose how sensitive the camera's audio recording circuit is to sound. You can use your Z6's internal stereo microphone or an Accessory-shoe mounted microphone such as the Nikon ME-1 stereo mic.

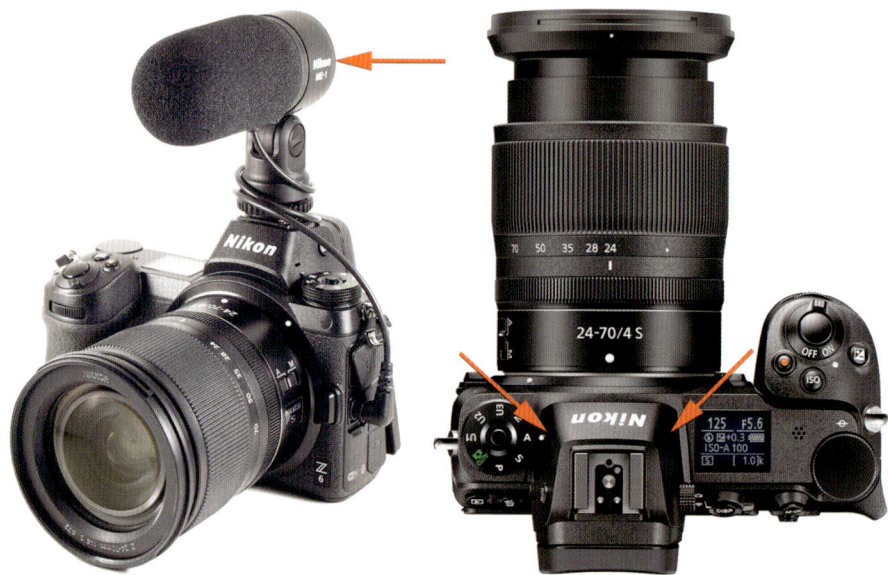

Figure 8.23A: External Nikon ME-1 mic and the built-in left and right stereo mic ports

In figure 8.23A you can see the two main types of microphones. One is an external, accessory shoe–mounted microphone that plugs into the audio-in port found on the side of the camera under the rubber flap labeled MIC (image on left). The other is the built-in stereo microphone on the top front of the camera (image on right; the stereo left and right ports are at the two red arrows). When you plug in an external mic, the camera automatically disables the built-in stereo mic.

There are three available Microphone sensitivity settings. Let's learn how to use them.

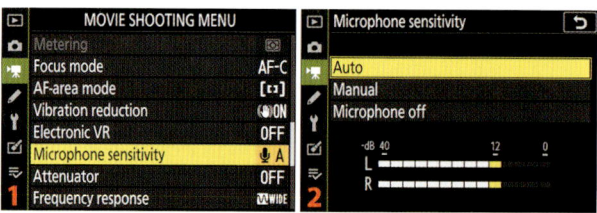

Figure 8.23B: Choosing a Microphone sensitivity setting

The following steps allow you to select a Microphone sensitivity setting for your next movie:

1. Select Microphone sensitivity from the Movie Shooting Menu and scroll to the right (figure 8.23B, image 1).
2. Choose Auto, Manual, or Microphone off (figure 8.23B, image 2). These settings are live, so you can test them immediately. Press the OK button or tap the option to lock in the Microphone sensitivity setting.

If you decide to adjust the microphone sensitivity manually, instead of using Auto mode (as selected in figure 8.23B, image 2), you will need to use the Manual sensitivity setting (as selected in figure 8.23C).

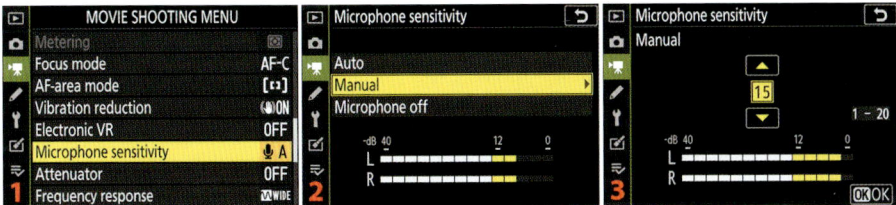

Figure 8.23C: Choosing a Microphone sensitivity setting manually

Use these steps to choose a sound level manually:

1. Follow the screen flow shown in figure 8.23C, images 1 and 2 (*Microphone sensitivity > Manual*), until you arrive at the third screen in the series.
2. Select a level for the microphone from the up/down menu by scrolling up or down with the Multi selector pad or by tapping the up/down arrows. You can choose from level 1 to level 20. The higher the number, the greater the mic sensitivity, and vice versa. The microphone's factory default setting is level 15 (figure 8.23C, image 3). These settings are live, so you will be able to test them immediately. Press or touch OK to lock in your choice.

As displayed in figure 8.23D, image 2, you can also choose to disable the microphone completely and record a silent movie by selecting the Microphone off setting. Use this setting if you are using a clapperboard for synchronization and an external sound-recording device.

The Microphone off setting will separate sound recording from the camera body or attached mic, removing the little squeaks, clicks, and whines that all cameras make while autofocusing, zooming, and changing apertures, or from the sound of a cooling fan in an external recorder mounted in the camera's accessory shoe.

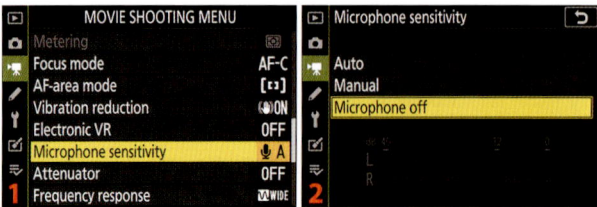

Figure 8.23D: Disabling the internal microphone and audio-in MIC port

Use these steps to turn the internal stereo microphone off and disable the MIC audio-in port on the camera:

1. Choose Microphone sensitivity from the Movie Shooting Menu and scroll to the right (figure 8.23D, image 1).
2. Select Microphone off from the menu to disable the internal stereo mic and the audio-in MIC port (figure 8.23D, image 2). Press the OK button or tap on Microphone off to lock in your choice.

Settings Recommendation: For basic video using the built-in stereo mic, or even with an external Accessory-mounted mic, such as the Nikon ME-1, the Auto setting seems to perform well.

Experiment with this setting at Auto and Manual to see which works best for you. Auto sensitivity works for most of us, and Manual sensitivity is better for those with more critical needs.

If you are using an external video recorder and streaming uncompressed video from the HDMI port, you will generally set the camera's Microphone sensitivity setting to Microphone off and use an external audio recorder and a sound synchronization device.

Attenuator

The microphone *Attenuator* is a function that will automatically adjust the sensitivity of the microphone when there are large changes in the sound level. For instance, you might be recording a local sports event and suddenly someone scores, causing the crowd to go wild. The Attenuator will automatically reduce the mic sensitivity to help prevent overwhelming the camera's audio circuit. Let's see how to enable it.

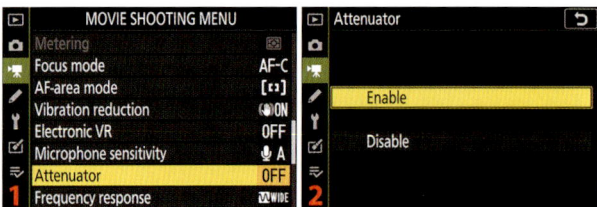

Figure 8.24: Enabling or disabling the microphone Attenuator

Use the following steps to enable or disable the mic Attenuator:

1. Select Attenuator from the Movie Shooting Menu and scroll to the right (figure 8.24, image 1).
2. Choose Enable to use the Attenuator or select Disable to turn it off. Press the OK button or tap an option to lock it in (figure 8.24, image 2).

Settings Recommendation: Whenever I am capturing video at any type of event where loud sounds suddenly occur—or there is constant loud ambient sound—I use the Attenuator to prevent audio distortion. However, I do not use the Attenuator for normal video. Why not experiment with this setting to see if you find it useful?

Frequency Response

The *Frequency response* function allows you to choose two different ranges of audio-frequency response to use while recording sound for a video. Sound is a very important part of quality video recording!

Maybe you want to record a video in the wilds of the jungle and would like to pick up the sound of every birdsong, leaf rustle, and buzzing insect. On the other hand, you could be recording a video of a famous lecturer and would rather not pick up the sounds of people walking by, a bird singing outside the window, and road traffic outside.

The Nikon Z6 gives you better control of sound quality than many Nikons before it. With a combination of the Microphone sensitivity, Attenuator, and Frequency response functions, you can capture some very high-quality sound. Microphone sensitivity affects how sensitive the microphone is, the Attenuator prevents distortion from loud sounds, and Frequency response determines which sound frequencies the mic is most sensitive to. We've already considered Microphone sensitivity and the Attenuator, so now let's see how Frequency response works.

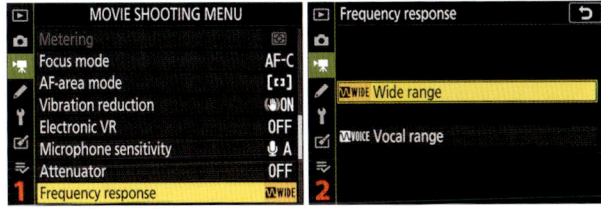

Figure 8.25: Choosing a microphone frequency response setting

Use the following steps to choose a Frequency response setting for your camera's microphone:

1. Select Frequency response from the Movie Shooting Menu and scroll to the right (figure 8.25, image 1).

2. Choose one of the two Frequency response settings (figure 8.25, image 2). Select Wide range for those times when you want to record every sound near your camera. This setting is best for nature, travel, and general family videos. Choose Vocal range when you are recording a person or group of people talking. This setting helps eliminate spurious background noises. Press the OK button or tap your selection to lock it in.

Settings Recommendation: Because I am a nature photographer, I often use the Wide range setting when shooting video in the Great Smoky Mountains. However, when recording a wedding ceremony, I use the Vocal range setting so that I won't get so much spurious noise from the audience.

Test these two settings carefully for your style of photography to see which works best for you. Most people use Wide range for general video recording.

Wind Noise Reduction

The *Wind noise reduction* function helps remove that aggravating sound you hear when wind blows on the camera's stereo microphone ports. This function will not work with external, accessory shoe–mounted, stereo microphones; it works only with the internal stereo mic.

Have you ever recorded a video on a beautiful, breezy spring day, only to later find that you have recorded that distinctive rumbling sound of wind blowing across the mic ports instead of the clear sound you desired?

While that sound may not be completely eliminated without using special external microphones designed to deal with it, it can be significantly reduced with a selective low-cut filter, which removes or cuts low-frequency noises like wind rumbles.

Fortunately for Z6 users, Nikon has included a low-cut filter setting for when you are recording video. If you turn this filter on, you can remove a portion of wind noise when recording outside.

However, if you are recording an orchestra, with deep cello and bass parts, a low-cut filter may take away some of the depth in the recording, so maybe it shouldn't be left on all the time. Let's see how to enable and disable the Wind noise reduction low-cut filter.

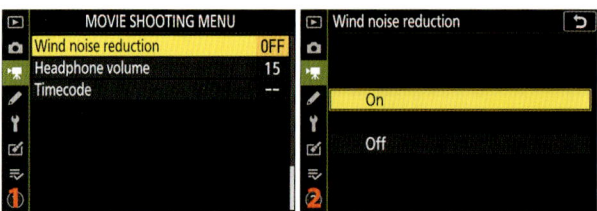

Figure 8.26: Using the Wind noise reduction low-cut filter

Use the following steps to choose a Wind noise reduction setting for your camera's microphone:

1. Select Wind noise reduction from the Movie Shooting Menu and scroll to the right (figure 8.26, image 1).
2. Choose On to enable the filter or Off to disable it, and then press the OK button or tap your selection to lock it in (figure 8.26, image 2).

Settings Recommendation: I use this wind noise filter selectively. Most of the time I am using an external Nikon ME-1 Accessory-shoe mounted microphone, which has a foam screen around the mic to reduce or eliminate most wind noise. I do use Wind noise reduction when I am outside using the built-in stereo mic to record family events, such as a cookout in Great Smoky Mountains National Park.

Headphone Volume

The Headphone port under the rubber Connector cover is an excellent addition to the Nikon Z6 (figure 8.27A). It allows you to plug in a headphone set to isolate yourself from surrounding sounds and focus on hearing what the camera is actually recording. This is important for those who are concerned about maximum sound quality.

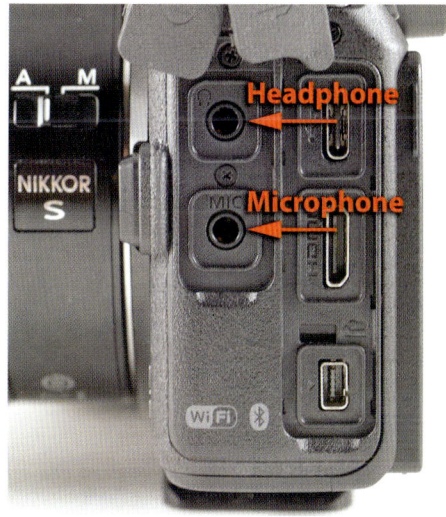

Figure 8.27A: Headphone and Microphone ports

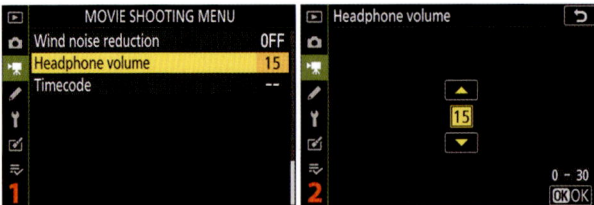

Figure 8.27B: Choosing a Headphone volume output level

Use these steps to select a Headphone volume to use while recording your video:

1. Choose Headphone volume from the Movie Shooting Menu (figure 8.27B, image 1).
2. Tap the up/down arrow pointers or press up or down on the Multi selector pad to adjust the headphone volume (figure 8.27, image 2). You can select from a range of 0 to 30. Press or touch OK to lock in your setting.

Settings Recommendation: The headphone you use doesn't have to be an expensive outfit to be effective. I often use a set of normal isolation earbuds, like the ones you would plug into your smartphone or iPod. Earbud headsets can be stored in a small pocket in your camera bag, so they will always be with you.

I have found that output level 15 is about right for me. However, my hearing isn't as good as it was when I was young due to listening to my Walkman (remember those?) at high volume as a kid. Be careful not to go too loud because sudden sound increases might damage your hearing. You may be more comfortable with the volume around 10 or 12.

Timecode

The *Timecode* function allows you to do commercial-level synchronization of your camera with other devices, such as additional video recorders and sound recorders. Since sound, for instance, is often recorded separately from the video stream in commercial recording, there needs to be an accurate way to synchronize an external sound recorder with your camera's video stream. Nothing is more distracting in a video than sound being out of sync with the video frames (remember the old Kung Fu movies?).

Basically, Timecode is a clock that counts in video frames. Timecode clocks can be synchronized so that the timecodes are identical on each device. Synchronizing two timecode clocks to run independently yet remain in time with each other is called "jam-synching" or "jamming." Do some Internet research on those words to learn more about jamming.

Timecode relies on high-precision timecode clocks. When synchronized (jam-synched), two timecode clocks should run for a period of time without "drifting" or losing their synchronization. The more accurate the clocks, the longer the two devices will remain synched. Over time you may have to resynch the two clocks to make sure they are keeping the same time. Here is a sample Timecode readout, with the numbers on the top row and an explanation on the bottom row:

```
00:00:00.00
HH:MM:SS.FF
```

In the explanation line HH stands for hours, MM for minutes, SS for seconds, and FF for frames. When you enable the Timecode feature, your camera's video recording screens will display the Timecode in this format:

```
TC: 00:00:00.00
```

A full discussion of using Timecode to synchronize your camera with another device is beyond the scope of this book. However there are quite a few good videos on YouTube about this subject. Let's discuss how to select the Timecode settings and what each does.

Note: The Timecode is not displayed on the video itself; it is recorded as part of the video's metadata for synchronizing purposes.

Recording Timecodes

Recording timecodes has three settings. Let's examine each one:

- **On:** Timecodes will appear on the camera's display screens using the previously discussed format. The camera will output a running Timecode along with the video stream as it records the video to the XQD memory card.
- **On (with HDMI output):** You will need to use one of the following Atomos external video recorder series types: Shogun, Ninja, or Sumo. When you connect an external Atomos video recorder to your Z6, the camera will output a running Timecode value that will be included with the video stream and recorded by the external recorder. Go to **www.Atomos.com** to examine the previously mentioned recorders. I currently use an Atomos Ninja V.
- **Off:** No Timecode will be output with the video stream from the camera.

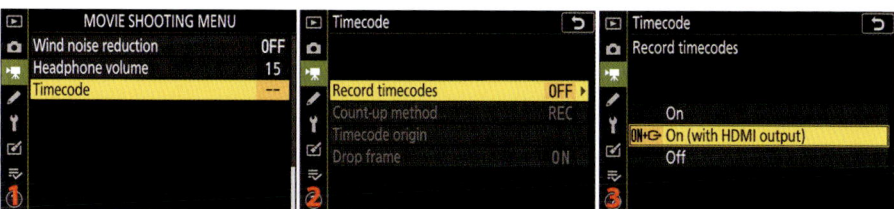

Figure 8.28A: Recording timecodes

Use the following steps to enable the Timecode system on your camera:

1. Follow the screen flow shown in figure 8.28A, images 1 and 2 (*Timecode > Record timecodes*) until you arrive at the third screen in the series.
2. Refer to the previous list and highlight one of the three settings. Press the OK button or tap your choice to lock in the value (figure 8.28A, image 3).

Count-Up Method

The Count-up method lets you choose how you want the Timecode output to run. Here are explanations of the two types:

- **Record run (REC):** Timecodes are incremented while the video is being recorded only.
- **Free run (FREE):** Timecodes are incremented continuously, even when the camera is turned off.

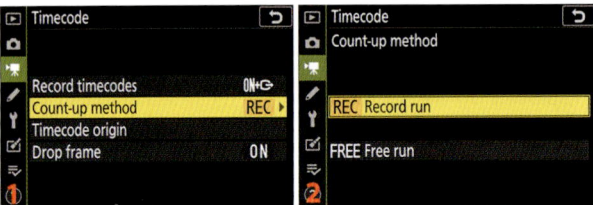

Figure 8.28B: Count-up method

Use the following steps to set a Count-up method:

1. Choose Count-up method from the Timecode menu and scroll to the right (figure 8.28B, image 1).
2. Refer to the previous list and highlight one of the two settings. Press the OK button or tap your choice to lock in the value (figure 8.28B, image 2).

Timecode Origin

The Timecode origin setting allows you to control how the Timecode receives its initial values in the 00:00:00.00 (HH:MM:SS.FF) positions. There are three methods available to input these values:

- **Reset:** The camera automatically resets the Timecode to 00:00:00.00.
- **Enter manually:** You will need to enter the HH:MM:SS.FF values manually.
- **Current time:** The Z6 gets the intial values directly from the camera's internal clock.

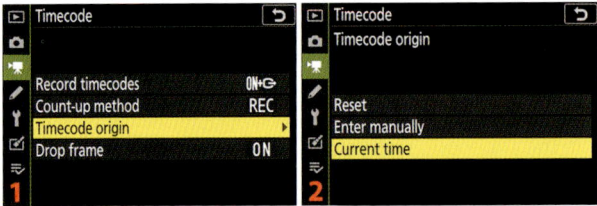

Figure 8.28C: Timecode origin

Use the following steps to set a Timecode origin:

1. Choose Timecode origin from the Timecode menu and scroll to the right (figure 8.28C, image 1).
2. Refer to the previous list and highlight one of the three settings. Press the OK button or tap your choice to lock in the value (figure 8.28C, image 2).

Drop Frame

The Drop frame method allows you to compensate for discrepancies between the frame count and the actual recording time when using frame rates of 30 and 60 fps. What does that mean?

Even though the camera lists the frame rates as 30 fps and 60 fps, the actual rate for 30 fps is 29.97 fps, and for 60 fps it's 59.94 fps. Since the camera can count video frames only in whole numbers, there ends up being a discrepancy between the frame count in the Timecode and the actual frame count recorded.

Using 30 fps as our example, the difference between the frames actually recorded and the count of those frames is 0.03 second per frame (30 − 29.97 = 0.03). In other words, for every second of recording time, 0.03 frames are unaccounted for—that's about 1.8 frames per minute.

The Drop frame method causes the camera to drop a whole frame count number when those 0.03-second discrepancies add up to a whole frame. The Z6 does not actually drop or remove a recorded video frame; it just drops a single frame count number to bring the counting sequence back to actual frames recorded. Here is a list of what each setting does:

- **On:** Uses the Drop frame method to compensate for the unaccounted frames, keeping the Timecode frame count accurate.
- **Off:** The Drop frame method is not used and the Timecode gradually becomes inaccurate compared to actual frames recorded.

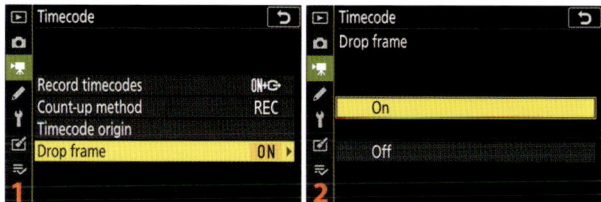

Figure 8.28D: Drop frame

Use the following steps to set a Timecode origin:

1. Choose Drop frame from the Timecode menu and scroll to the right (figure 8.28D, image 1).
2. Refer to the previous list and highlight one of the two settings. Press the OK button or tap your choice to lock in the value (figure 8.28D, image 2).

Settings Recommendation: If you are using your Z6 to record family videos for fun, you can safely ignore Timecode usage. Timecode is for advanced videographers who are capturing video using multiple devices, such as external sound recorders. I suggest doing a little internet research if you think you might use this type of functionality. Search for "video timecode" and you will find many sources to help you.

Author's Conclusion

The Nikon Z6's Movie Shooting Menu brings virtually all the video functions for your powerful camera together into one convenient menu system. This means no more searching among the other menus for video functions.

This shows how much progress the video subsystems have made in the last few years for our Nikon cameras. They are fully endowed with both video and still image capability. With so many video functions all together in one menu, it is even easier than ever before to create excellent videos with your camera.

The next chapter begins a discussion of the very large Custom Setting Menu, which is the core of the camera's configuration for various shooting styles. Be sure to have your camera in hand as we proceed through the deepest, most technical parts of Z6 customization, the Custom Setting Menu.

9 Custom Setting Menu

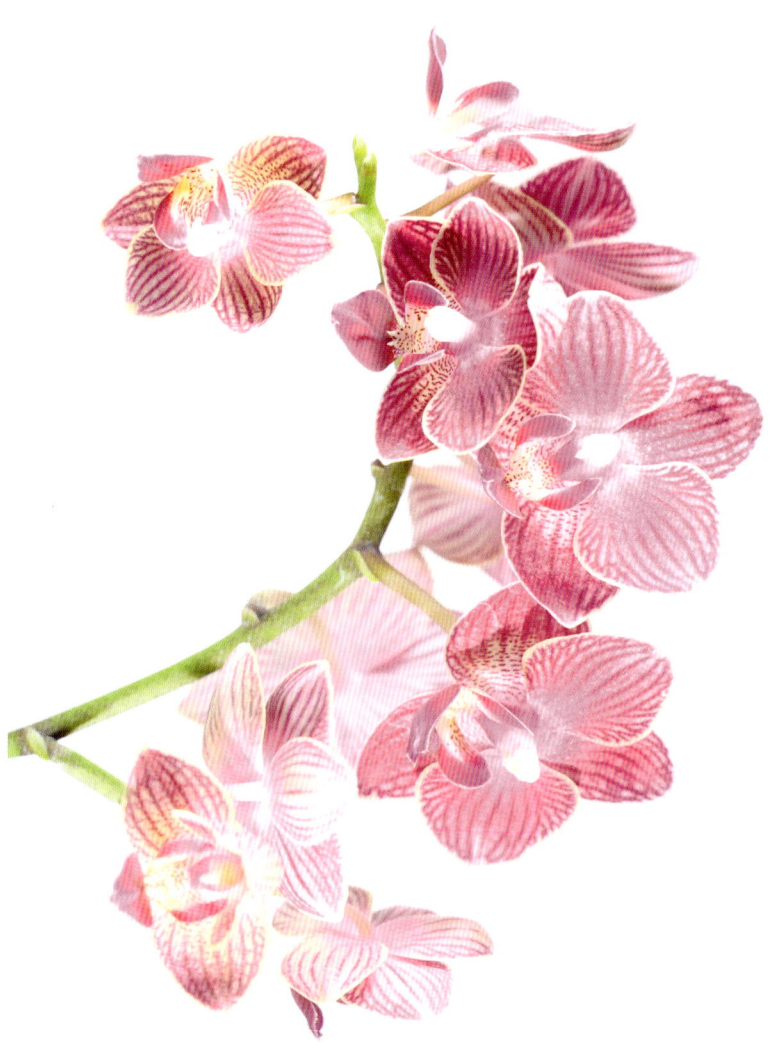

Miniature Orchid © 2019 Robert Rogers (*a4str*)

The Custom Setting Menu contains the core configuration of the Nikon Z6 camera. The three User settings on the Mode dial allow you to configure the Custom Setting Menu functions for multiple styles of photography. The Z6 has deep configurability, with many choices for you to learn about and adjust. Keep in mind that in this chapter we will be configuring only one of the three User settings (U1–U3). Once we have stepped through all of these functions and the settings within each function, we will have configured a single User setting. You have two additional User settings you can optionally configure if you want your camera to act as if it is three different cameras, for different purposes. Like a chameleon, the Z6 can change its colors to fit different situations.

I count no fewer than 51 Custom Settings in the Z6; therefore, we've got a lot of ground to cover, and we will, in great detail. When finished with this chapter, you'll have a much deeper knowledge of this camera's inner workings and capabilities.

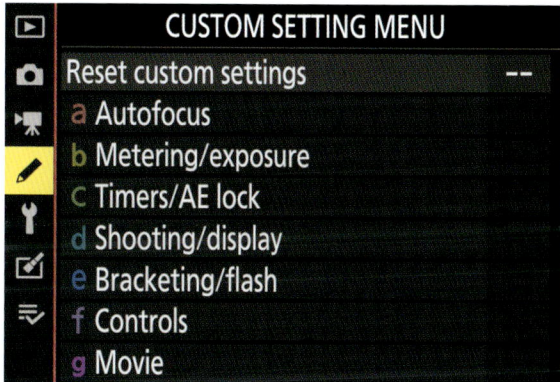

Figure 9.1: Location of the Custom Setting Menu

Without further ado, let's dive right into the settings and see what they do. First let's locate the Custom Setting Menu in the camera's menu system (figure 9.1). The Custom Setting Menu is the fourth menu down on the left side of the menu screen, with a pencil as its symbol. Select the pencil and scroll to the right.

Let's start by examining the method you can use any time you want to reset all the current Custom Setting Menu functions back to factory defaults.

Reset Custom Settings

If you want to start fresh with a factory default configuration of the Custom Setting Menu, Nikon makes it easy. Be careful, this function will return all the settings in the Custom Setting Menu back to their defaults, removing any changes you have made.

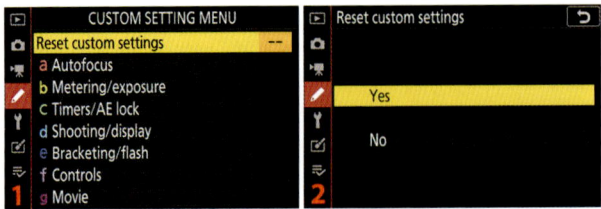

Figure 9.2: Resetting all Custom Setting Menu functions

Use the following steps to reset the Custom Setting Menu:

1. Choose Reset custom settings from the top of the Custom Setting Menu and scroll to the right (figure 9.2, image 1).
2. Highlight Yes and press the OK button or tap Yes to reset the menu (figure 9.2, image 2). There will be no warning screens. As soon as you select Yes, the reset will take place and the camera will return to the main Custom Setting Menu screen. Select No to cancel.

Settings Recommendation: I use this function whenever I purchase a pre-owned camera so that I can start fresh with my configuration.

SECTION ONE: a Autofocus

Custom Settings a1 to a13

You'll find 13 settings within the *a Autofocus* menu in the Z6.

- **a1:** AF-C priority selection
- **a2:** AF-S priority selection
- **a3:** Focus tracking with lock-on
- **a4:** Auto-area AF face detection
- **a5:** Focus points used
- **a6:** Store points by orientation
- **a7:** AF activation
- **a8:** Limit AF-area mode selection
- **a9:** Focus point wrap-around
- **a10:** Focus point options
- **a11:** Low-light AF
- **a12:** Built-in AF-assist illuminator
- **a13:** Manual focus ring in AF mode (this menu item appears only when a compatible lens is mounted)

Custom Settings a1–a13 allow you to configure the autofocus system in various ways. The whole process is rather complex—yet important for good photography.

I felt that autofocus and its related functions were important enough to include an entire chapter titled **Focus, AF-Area, and Release Modes** (page 75). It covers autofocus and its supporting functions in much deeper detail. Please be sure to read that chapter thoroughly.

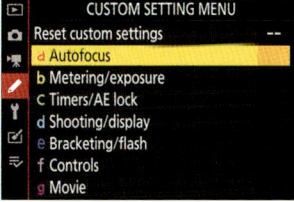

All thirteen "a" functions and their internal settings—discussed within the following sections—are found on the Custom Setting Menu under the *a Autofocus* menu item (figure 9.3).

Figure 9.3: *a Autofocus*

Custom Setting a1: AF-C Priority Selection

AF-C priority selection is designed to let you choose how the autofocus works when using Continuous-servo Focus mode (AF-C). Make sure you understand how this function works. If you configure this setting incorrectly for your style of shooting, it's possible that a number of your pictures will be out of focus. Why? Well, if you'll notice in figure 9.4 there are two specific selections:

- **Release:** This allows the shutter to fire every time you press the Shutter-release button, even if the image is not in focus. Releasing the shutter has "priority" over autofocus. If the image must be taken no matter what, you will need to set AF-C priority selection to Release. The camera will attempt to focus on your subject; however, it will still fire the shutter, even if it can't obtain focus. You must rely on your experience to make sure the subject is in focus by using techniques such as prefocusing or using depth of field to cover the subject. Release is the factory default setting.
- **Focus:** This setting is designed to prevent your camera from taking a picture when it cannot find focus. In other words, if the picture is not in focus, the shutter will not release. It does not mean that the camera will always focus on the correct subject. It simply means that your camera must focus on *something* before it will allow the shutter to release. Nikon cameras do a very good job with autofocus, so you can usually depend on the AF module to perform well. The Focus setting will drastically increase the chances that your image is in correct focus. While using a Continuous release mode, the camera will focus on every frame, which may cause pauses in the firing sequence when good focus is not available.

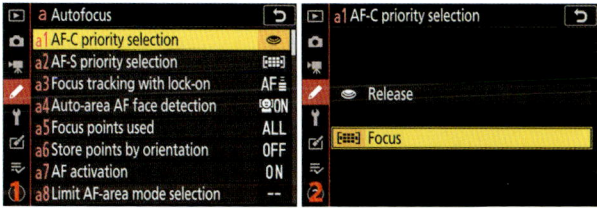

Figure 9.4: Choosing a shutter-release priority for AF-C mode

Here are the steps to select a shutter-release priority for AF-C mode:

1. Choose a1 AF-C priority selection from the a Autofocus menu and scroll to the right (figure 9.4, image 1).
2. Choose one of the settings from the menu, with full understanding of what may happen if you don't choose Focus (figure 9.4, image 2). If you have the experience to use depth of field to cover autofocus, in case of slight focusing errors, or if you use the AF-ON button instead of the Shutter-release button for initiating autofocus, you may do well with AF-C priority selection set to Release. Otherwise, select Focus. Press the OK button or tap the option to select your shutter-release priority.

Settings Recommendation: Since I'm not a sports or action shooter, I choose Focus. Even if I were an action shooter, I would choose Focus. I don't need a series of out-of-focus images.

However, if you are an action shooter and have enough experience to deal with a camera that will fire the shutter when you press the Shutter-release button even if it has not obtained good focus, or if you use the AF-ON button for back button focus, then the Release setting may work better for you. Certain types of high-speed photography may be best captured with AF-C priority set to Release. Use Release only if you have sufficient experience to know when you can safely use it instead of Focus.

Custom Setting a2: AF-S Priority Selection

AF-S priority selection is similar to AF-C priority selection. It too allows you to choose whether the camera will take a picture without something in focus. With this function, you set a shutter-release priority for Single-servo autofocus mode (AF-S). Set it wrong and many of your pictures may be out of focus. There are two modes to choose from (figure 9.5, image 3):

- **Release:** A photo can be taken at any time, even if there is nothing in focus. This can lead to images that are out of focus, unless you manually focus each time you take a picture, or you've dialed in sufficient depth of field (smaller aperture opening) to cover your subject. The camera's priority is releasing the shutter when you press the Shutter-release button.
- **Focus:** The image must be in focus or the shutter will not release. This means that the shutter won't release unless the camera is focused on something. This is the closest thing to a guarantee that your image will be in focus when you press the Shutter-release button. However, if you are focused on the wrong part of your subject, the camera will still fire. Focus is the factory default setting.

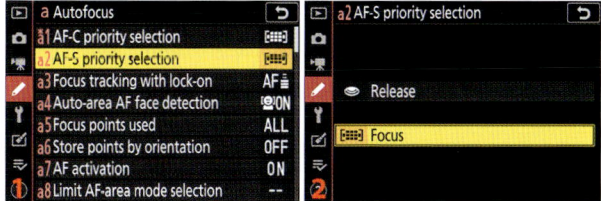

Figure 9.5: Choosing a shutter-release priority for AF-S mode

Here are the steps to select a shutter-release priority for AF-S mode:

1. Choose a2 AF-S priority selection from the a Autofocus menu and scroll to the right (figure 9.5, image 1).
2. Choose one of the settings from the menu, with full understanding of what may happen if you don't choose Focus (figure 9.5, image 2). If you have the experience to use depth of field to cover autofocus, in case of slight focusing errors, or if you use the AF-ON button instead of the Shutter-release button for initiating autofocus, you may do well with AF-S priority selection set to Release. Otherwise, select Focus. Press the OK button or tap the option to select your shutter-release priority.

Settings Recommendation: I set both a1 and a2 to Focus priority. I'm not a high-speed shooter, so I don't need my camera to take a picture "no matter what." What good are out-of-focus nature images or portraits? However, if you are a sports or action shooter, you'll probably want to experiment with the Release priority settings and with back button focus (initiating autofocus with the AF-ON button, instead of the Shutter-release button). We discussed this previously in the chapter titled **Focus, AF-Area, and Release Modes** (page 75).

Custom Setting a3: Focus Tracking with Lock-On

Focus tracking with lock-on allows you to select the length of time your camera will ignore an intruding object that blocks your subject.

Let's say you're focused on a bird flying past you. As you pan the camera with the bird's movement, the autofocus system tracks it and keeps it in good focus. A road sign briefly interrupts the focus tracking as the bird moves behind it and then reemerges. How would you feel if the bright, high-contrast road sign grabbed the camera's attention and you lost tracking on the bird? That would be quite aggravating, wouldn't it?

On the other hand, if you are an action photographer, photographing multiple subjects, you may want to be able to quickly switch to a different subject without the camera refusing to focus on the new subject for several seconds because it is locked onto a different subject.

The Blocked shot AF response setting prevents the Z6 from losing focus on your moving subject due to intruding objects (figure 9.6, image 2). Since the camera's focus is locked on to your subject, it tries to keep its focus on the subject even if something briefly comes between it and the camera. Without Focus tracking with lock-on, any bright object that gets between you and your subject may draw the camera's attention and cause you to lose focus on the subject. The Blocked shot AF response timeout period allows your camera to stay locked on the subject for a predetermined length of time when an obstacle interrupts its view of the subject. You can adjust the Blocked shot AF response timeout according to the delay time period that works best for you. Plan to experiment a bit so that you can determine what is best for your style of shooting.

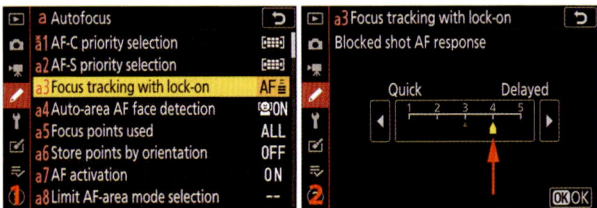

Figure 9.6: Focus tracking with lock-on

Following are the steps to configure Focus tracking with lock-on:

1. Choose a3 Focus tracking with lock-on from the a Autofocus menu and scroll to the right (figure 9.6, image 1).
2. Press left or right on the Multi selector pad or tap the left/right pointers to move the yellow indicator along the scale from 1 (Quick) to 5 (Delayed). Figure 9.6, image 2, shows the yellow indicator at the point of the red arrow. Move it toward the right (toward 5, or Delayed) to delay the camera's response to a new object blocking your current subject. The closer to the Delayed (5) setting you move the indicator, the longer the camera will wait before switching focus to the intruding object. Move the yellow indicator to the left (toward 1, or Quick) if you want the camera to switch focus to a new subject more quickly. Press or touch OK to lock in your choices.

Settings Recommendation: I leave Focus tracking with lock-on enabled at all times. When I'm tracking a moving subject, I don't want my camera to be distracted by every bright object that gets in between me and the subject. Nikon gives us variable focus lock timeouts so that we can change how long the camera will keep seeking the old subject when we switch to a new one.

I strongly suggest you play around with this function until you fully understand how it works. Watch how long the camera stays locked on one subject before an intruding object grabs its attention, and then adjust that timeout with the Blocked shot AF response setting. This function is a very useful and powerful addition to the subject tracking system in your Z6 camera.

Custom Setting a4: Auto-Area AF Face/Eye Detection

Your Nikon Z6's autofocus usually examines the scene for two things when using subject tracking mode: subject motion and subject color. However, you can also add human face recognition to the mix with *Auto-area AF face/eye detection.*

This function won't add anything useful if you're tracking subjects like wildlife or race cars, but it certainly will help you when photographing moving people, such as an ice skater moving quickly on the ice or a skier moving down the hill.

With this mode enabled, not only does the camera use the motion and color of a human subject, but it also uses the skin tones and shape of a human face to more accurately track a moving person.

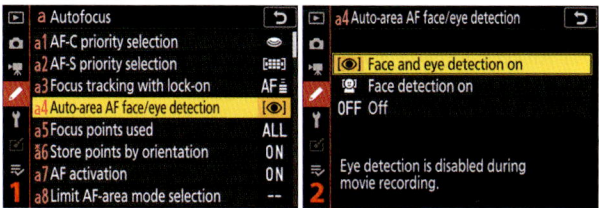

Figure 9.7: Using human face recognition while using Auto-area AF and AF-C

Use the following steps to choose one of two different types of human face detection when you are using *Auto-area AF* AF-area mode and *Continuous-servo AF* Focus mode (AF-C):

1. Choose Auto-area AF face detection from the a Autofocus menu and scroll to the right (figure 9.7, image 1).
2. If you have installed firmware version C2.00 (or greater, see page 561) you will have two choices in this menu: Face and eye detection on, or Face detection on (figure 9.7, image 2). Previous to firmware C2.00, no eye detection was available. Choosing Face and eye detection on adds face and eye detection to standard motion and color tracking, whereas choosing Face detection on lets the camera ignore the eyes and focus less precisely on just the face. Adding eye detection will allow the camera to better focus on people's faces—attempting to keep the eyes acceptably sharp—but may be a slightly slower (more precise) autofocus method. Press the OK button or tap the option to lock in your choice.

Settings Recommendation: This function can be very useful for those who regularly track moving people, such as a sports photographer. As a nature photographer, I leave it set to Off. I don't want my camera looking for human faces while tracking a bear, a flying bird, or a skunk waddling through camp (of course, skunk tracking may require face detection so that I can capture all the people running from the skunk). For those who need this functionality, it adds another layer of tracking capability, improving accuracy when tracking moving people.

Custom Setting a5: Focus Points Used

Focus points used allows you to adjust the distance the focus point (AF point) moves when you move it around the screen with the Multi selector pad or Sub-selector joystick. This function works only in Single-point AF, Dynamic-area AF, and Wide-area AF (S). It does not work in Pinpoint AF, Wide-area AF (L), or Auto-area AF (firmware C2.00).

If you move your AF point often, it might get tiring to scroll through all 273 of the available focus points. With so many available focus points to choose from, it could take longer than you want to scroll from one side of the viewfinder to the other. Nikon has given you a choice. If you'd rather not scroll through every AF point, you can skip every other point when scrolling (figure 9.8).

All 273 focus points are still active, you are merely skipping points to save time scrolling. When skipping points, you may not be able to precisely choose a specific point that falls in just the right place on your subject, forcing you to slightly recompose the image to get an AF point on the chosen area. Of course, with so many focus points, this won't often cause a problem.

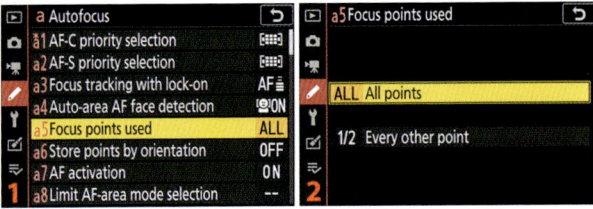

Figure 9.8: Focus points used

Here are the steps to select how to scroll across the 273 AF points:

1. Choose Focus points used from the a Autofocus menu and scroll to the right (figure 9.8, image 1).
2. Select All points (ALL) or Every other point (1/2) and press the OK button or tap the option to lock in your choice (figure 9.8, image 2).

Settings Recommendation: I usually leave my camera set to All points for nature work because I have time to scroll among the AF points in an unhurried fashion. The only time I'll change that is when I need to shoot very quickly at an event that moves at a rapid pace, like a graduation ceremony or wedding. At these events I may not have time to scroll through all 273 points to select an AF point on the edge of the Viewfinder, so I'll set Focus points used to Every other point (1/2). I also will set Custom Setting a9 Focus point wrap-around (page 376) to On.

Remember, setting this to 1/2 does not change how many AF points are actually used by the camera. It only affects how fast you can move among the AF points when you use the Multi selector pad or Sub-selector joystick to scroll around. Every other AF point is skipped during scrolling. You still get the benefit of all available points.

Custom Setting a6: Store Points by Orientation

Store points by orientation allows a photographer who changes the camera from horizontal (landscape) to vertical (portrait) orientation frequently to have separate control over the AF point in use for each orientation.

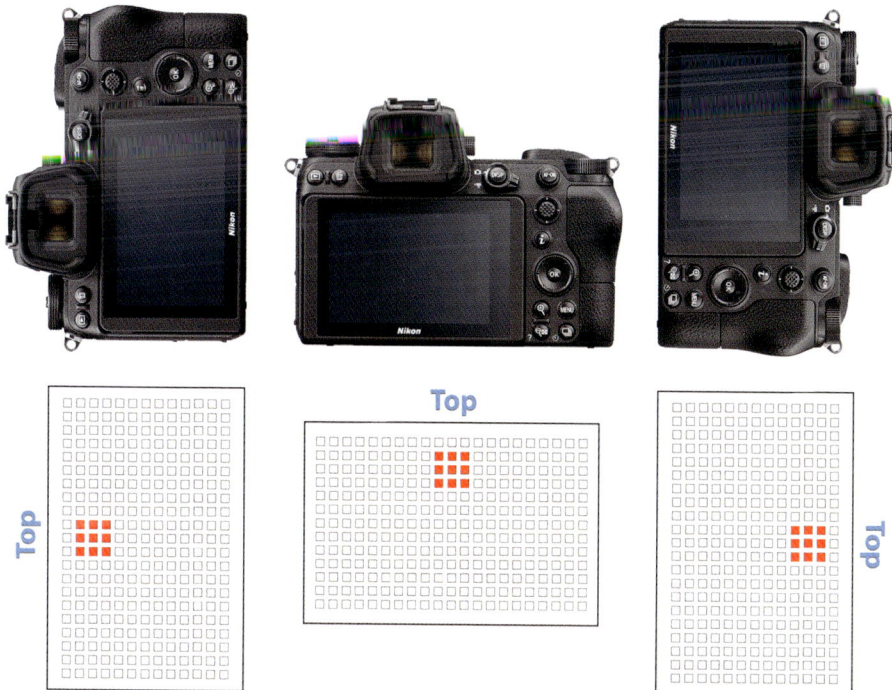

Figure 9.9A: Store by orientation in action

Figure 9.9A shows the three camera orientations related to the Store points by orientation function, using the Dynamic-area AF arrangement as an example.

Let's say you are shooting a wedding photo of a group. You moved the selected AF point to the top of the 273 points so that you can focus on faces with the camera in a horizontal orientation (figure 9.9A, middle). Afterward, the group leaves, but the bride and groom stay, and you decide to shoot with the camera in a vertical orientation for a nice, full-length portrait (figure 9.9A, left). If you have the Store by orientation function set to Focus Point, you can set the AF point to a completely different area of the 273 AF points for each orientation and the camera will remember the setting when you rotate the camera back to that orientation later (e.g., figure 9.9A, left and right). Let's examine how to do it.

Storing an AF Point Position

You must set the AF point position for all three available orientations or the camera will not automatically move the AF point when you change the orientation of the Z6. Instead, the AF point will stay directly in the middle of the 273 points. You must set each AF point position you want to use for a particular orientation (horizontal or one of the two vertical orientations).

In other words, after enabling Custom Setting a6, when you are shooting with the camera in the horizontal orientation, you will select the AF point position you want to use by simply scrolling there with the Multi selector pad or Sub-selector joystick. Afterward, you will switch to each of the vertical orientations and do the same thing—select the AF point you want to use while holding the camera in that orientation. No other action is required to set the AF point position for each camera orientation. Once set, the camera will automatically move the AF point to the correct position for the current camera orientation (figure 9.9A).

The camera will store the position of the AF point for one horizontal and two portrait orientations automatically, without you having to do anything other than select the AF point position for that orientation. You can have separate AF point positions for (1) horizontal (figure 9.9A, middle); (2) vertical with hand grip up (figure 9.9A, left); and (3) vertical with hand grip down (figure 9.9A, right). If you shoot with the camera upside down, it will use the AF point for the middle horizontal orientation; there is no separate upside-down orientation.

This function could save you significant time by preventing you from having to scroll the AF point constantly as you change camera orientations. Let's see how to enable the Store points by orientation function.

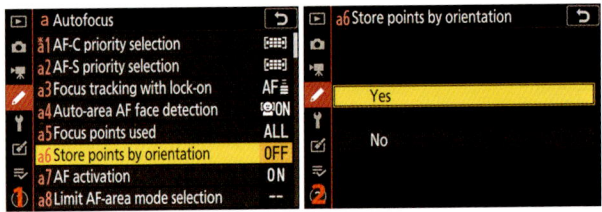

Figure 9.9B: Enabling or disabling Store points by orientation

Here are the steps to choose one of the Store points by orientation settings:

1. Choose Store points by orientation from the a Autofocus menu and scroll to the right (figure 9.9B, image 1).
2. Choose Yes to enable the storing of your AF positions by camera orientation or choose No to cancel (figure 9.9B, image 2). Press the OK button or tap the option in the setting.

Settings Recommendation: I leave this setting enabled because I want to store the location of the AF point arrangement for each orientation. I like having the AF point automatically pop to a certain position when I am creating vertical portraits or horizontal group shots. It saves me time!

Custom Setting a7: AF Activation

AF activation allows you to choose whether you want the Shutter-release button to cause the camera to autofocus. If you leave this setting at the factory default, the AF system will be activated when you press the Shutter-release button halfway down or when you press the AF-ON button. You can also select a setting that allows only the AF-ON button to initiate autofocus, but not the Shutter-release button.

The primary purpose of this function is to allow a very experienced photographer to separate shutter release and autofocus operations. Various styles of photography require the photographer to find a good autofocus point with the AF-ON button, and then fire many frames with the Shutter-release button with no danger of the camera changing the autofocus during shutter release. For example, sports photographers may want to autofocus the camera when they press the AF-ON button and not when they press the Shutter-release button. Here's a description of the two selections (figure 9.10):

- **Shutter/AF-ON:** Autofocus will be activated if you press the Shutter-release button halfway or if you press the AF-ON button.
- **AF-ON Only:** Autofocus works only when you press the AF-ON button. The Shutter-release button will not activate autofocus; it will only start metering and release the shutter. This setting has two subsettings, Enable and Disable, which allow you to set up a form of Release or Focus priority for the AF-ON button. Here's what each does:
  - **Enable:** With Enable selected, the camera will allow you to fire the shutter with the Shutter-release button, even if you have not used the AF-ON button to obtain focus on the subject (Release priority). Be careful when using back button focusing because Enable is the default setting.
  - **Disable:** With Disable selected, the camera will not allow you to fire the shutter with the Shutter-release button unless you have first obtained focus on something with the AF-ON button (Focus priority).

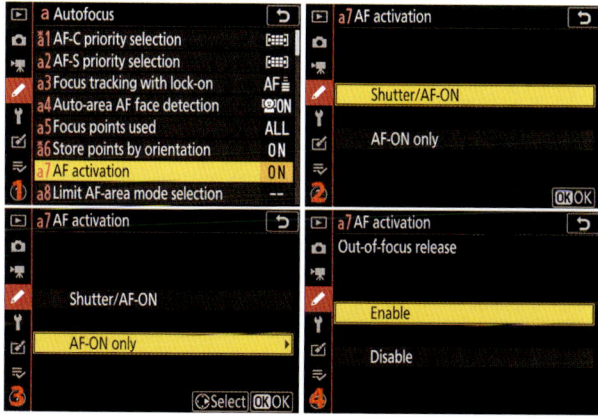

Figure 9.10: AF activation

Here are the steps used to configure AF activation:

1. Choose a7 AF activation from the a Autofocus menu and scroll to the right (figure 9.10, image 1).
2. Select one of the two choices from the menu (figure 9.10, image 2 or 3). Shutter/AF-ON allows *both* the Shutter-release button and AF-ON button to initiate autofocus. AF-ON only separates autofocus and shutter release into two separate functions: the Shutter-release button will release the shutter only and the AF-ON button will focus the camera only (called back button focus; see the sidebar on page 375). Choose the option you want to use and press or touch OK to lock it in. If you chose AF-ON only, then proceed to the next step.
3. Scroll to the right on the AF-ON only setting and you will find the AF-ON only subsettings: Enable and Disable (figure 9.10, image 4). Use Enable for Release priority and the shutter will fire even if nothing is in focus. Use Disable for Focus priority and the camera will refuse to fire the shutter unless something is in focus. Press the OK button or tap the option to lock in the settings.

Note: I have created a special document that discusses a technique called "trap focus" or "trap focusing." Trap focusing allows you to set up your camera to examine a certain area and when the camera detects something at that position, it will autofocus on the subject and fire the shutter.

Since the Nikon D3 era, many of Nikon's DSLRs have not supported trap focusing, even though Nikon's older film cameras did. However, with the Nikon Z6, you can once again do trap focusing. The document called **Trap Focusing with the Nikon Z6** is available on our downloadable resources web page:

http://rockynook.com/NikonZ6

Stop by **Nikonians.org** and let's discuss this method in the Nikon Z6 forum.

Settings Recommendation: I use Shutter/AF-ON most of the time because I'm primarily a nature shooter and don't often need to separate autofocus from shutter release. I don't have many fast-moving subjects, other than flying birds or leaping deer. And with those, it just feels more natural to me to autofocus and fire the shutter with one button.

However, when I am shooting a high-speed event and want to maximize my camera's firing speed (frame rate), I don't hesitate to set AF activation to AF-ON only, with its subsetting configured to Enable (Release priority). This lets me use my thumb to autofocus with the AF-ON button while my index finger is on the Shutter-release button firing bursts of images with the Continuous High frame rate. I use autofocus only when needed and can use depth of field to cover small focus variations. This allows me to get as many pictures into my camera as possible for later publication choices.

For additional information on using the AF-ON button for focusing, please see the sidebar **Back Button Focus**.

Back Button Focus

Configuring Custom setting a7 AF activation to AF-ON only allows you to use back button focus (a.k.a., back-button focus). Normally, pressing the Shutter-release button halfway down initiates autofocus, and then pressing it all the way down fires the shutter. However, when you set a7 to AF-ON only (figure 9.10, image 3), the Shutter-release button will not initiate autofocus, meaning that you will have to focus the camera with the AF-ON button (the infamous back button) instead. The Shutter-release button will release the shutter only.

If you want the Shutter-release button to fire the shutter only, and the AF-ON button to control autofocus only, then set Custom setting a7 AF activation to AF-ON only. The alternate setting, Shutter/AF-ON, defeats the back-button focusing concept because the focus on the subject will change every time you press the Shutter-release button or the AF-ON button. The camera defaults to Shutter/AF-ON, which means it does not use back-button focusing out of the box. Set a7 to **AF-ON only** for real back-button focusing.

Note: If you prefer, you can use other buttons for focusing instead of the AF-ON button. These other buttons will be discussed in the section **Custom Setting f2: Custom Control Assignment** in this chapter (page 423).

Custom Setting a8: Limit AF-Area Mode Selection

Limit AF-area mode selection allows you to choose which AF-area modes are available for selection on the camera screens. Once a mode is selected in this function, it will appear on the camera's screens as a choice in the *i* Menu. All six AF-area modes are selected by default. If you do not want one or more of the modes to appear on the camera's screens, you can simply uncheck the ones you do not want to use (except for Single-point AF).

AF-area modes are discussed in great detail in the chapter titled **Focus, AF-Area, and Release Modes** (page 89). AF-area modes affect the Focus area you see in the EVF or on the Monitor; they represent the area on the imaging sensor that the camera uses to determine the best autofocus for your subject.

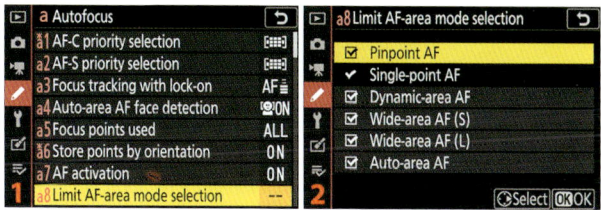

Figure 9.11: Providing AF-area mode selection choices

Use the following steps to select which AF-area modes you want to appear on camera screens as available options:

1. Choose a8 Limit AF-area mode selection from the a Autofocus menu and scroll to the right (figure 9.11, image 1).
2. Tap on the little box to the left of an AF-area mode name, or highlight an item and scroll to the right with the Multi selector pad, to check or uncheck the item (figure 9.11, image 2). Press or touch OK to lock in the list of AF-area modes you want to use later. The ones that are checked will appear on camera screens as available options. The ones you uncheck will not appear for selection.

Settings Recommendation: I have a use for all of the AF-area modes. Some I use more than others, but different styles of photography require each of these modes. Most of us will leave all of the AF-area modes checked and available for later use. If there is a mode or two you will never use, uncheck it and it will not appear on camera screens for selection or use.

Custom Setting a9: Focus Point Wrap-Around

Focus point wrap-around allows you to control how AF point scrolling in the EVF and on the Monitor works. When you are scrolling your selected AF point to the right or left, or up and down in the array of 273 available points, it will eventually come to the edge of the screen viewing area. What happens next is controlled by the settings in this function. Here is a description of the two settings:

- **Wrap:** This setting allows the selected AF point to scroll off of the edge of the screen and then reappear on the other side.
- **No wrap:** If you scroll the AF point to the edge of the screen, it stops there. You'll have to use the Multi selector pad or Sub-selector joystick to move the point in the opposite direction, back toward the middle.

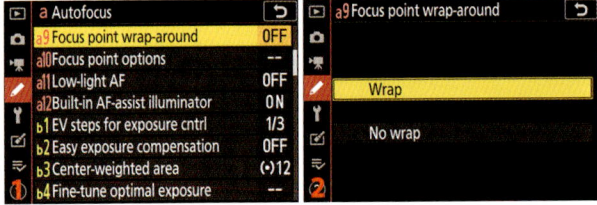

Figure 9.12: Focus point wrap-around

Here are the steps used to configure Focus point wrap-around:

1. Choose a9 Focus point wrap-around from the a Autofocus menu and scroll to the right (figure 9.12, image 1).
2. Choose one of the two choices from the menu: Wrap if you want to AF point to wrap around to the other side, or No wrap if you want the AF point to stop at the edges of the screen (figure 9.12, image 2). Press the OK button or tap an option to lock in the setting.

Settings Recommendation: Wrapping the AF point around from one side to the other used to drive me bonkers on DSLRs because they have really small autofocus areas and it took little time to scroll from one side to the other. However, using a camera with 273 AF points has made me rethink Focus point wrap-around. It may be faster, when close to the side of the screen, to simply scroll the shortest distance and let the AF point wrap around to the other side. Enable this feature and give it a try. Maybe this function, along with the previously considered Custom setting a5 Focus points used (page 370), will help you move your AF point frame around the screen more quickly.

Custom Setting a10: Focus Point Options

Focus point options allows you to choose how the AF points are presented to you on the camera's screens. Here is a brief summary of how each mode works:

- ***Manual focus mode:*** In Manual focus mode you can have a single AF point show in the Viewfinder, or no AF points at all. When set to On, the camera displays the AF point at all times. If set to Off, it shows the AF point only when you are moving it with the Sub-selector joystick or Multi selector pad. As soon as you stop moving the AF point, it disappears (figure 9.13A).
- ***Dynamic-area AF assist:*** When using Dynamic-area AF AF-area mode, a frame of eight dots surrounds the normal AF point square in the middle when this setting is set to On. If you change this setting to Off, only a single AF point square with no surrounding dots will be displayed. It will look identical to Single-point AF, except that the surrounding eight AF points are active, though invisible (figure 9.13D).

Now let's examine how to select each of these modes and take a closer look at the AF point square and dot arrangements so that you can choose your favorite style.

Manual Focus

The Manual focus mode can be set to show an AF point or not show it. Figure 9.13A, images 1 and 2, show how the Viewfinder will look in both conditions (Manual focus mode: On and Off).

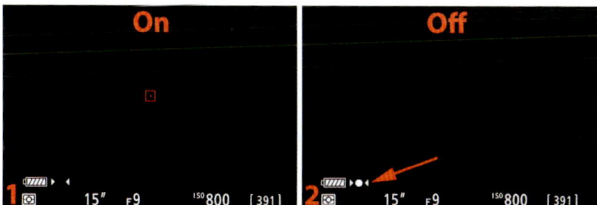

Figure 9.13A: AF point square in left image (On), and no AF point square in right image (Off)

If you are using focus Peaking for Manual focus mode, you may not want to use the AF point. However, the AF point is still useful in Manual focus mode because it turns green when the camera is in focus.

Note: This is discussed in much more detail, including several focus assist modes (e.g., Good-focus dot and pointers, focus Peaking, rangefinder, AF point color: see figure 9.13C), under **Manual Focus** in the chapter titled **Focus, AF-Area, and Release Modes** (page 85).

Let's see how to enable or disable the AF point during manual focus operations.

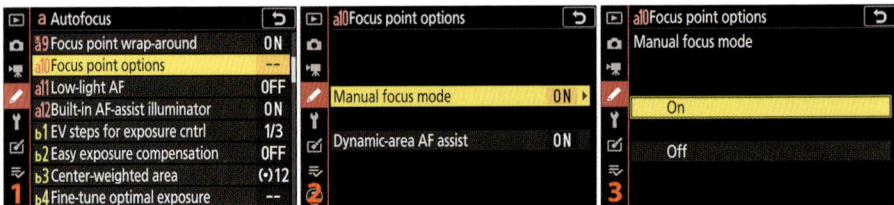

Figure 9.13B: Enabling or disabling the AF point square for Manual Focus mode

Use the following steps to enable or disable the AF point square in Manual focus mode:

1. Follow the screen flow shown in figure 9.13B, images 1–2 (*a Autofocus > a10 Focus point options > Manual focus mode*), until you arrive at the third screen in the series.
2. Choose either On or Off (figure 9.13B, image 3). Press the OK button or tap On or Off to lock in your choice.

Choosing On for Manual focus mode causes an AF point square to appear, allowing you to control manual focus very specifically by placing the AF point square over your subject with the Sub-selector joystick (figure 9.13C, top-right arrow). When the AF point is green it means the camera has achieved focus; red means the camera is not in focus.

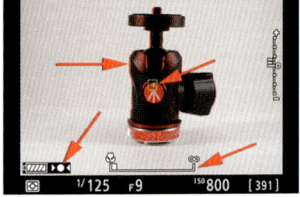

Figure 9.13C: Four focus assist aids

You can also use the good-focus indicator (a round dot in the bottom-left corner of the screen) to assist you (figure 9.13C, bottom-left arrow). The dot will appear when the lens detects good focus. Turn the focus ring in the direction the pointer indicates until the dot is displayed and the pointers disappear.

Choosing Off disables the AF point square and you must use eyesight or focus Peaking (figure 9.13C, top-left arrow) to determine correct focus. Peaking highlights (page 409), which is available in four colors, is extremely effective at helping you acquire the best focus.

The rangefinder (figure 9.13C, bottom-right arrow) gives you a general indication of focus range, from minimum focus distance to infinity (not very useful in this case).

Settings Recommendation: I have found that leaving the Manual focus mode set to On gives me the most utility for manual focusing. I can move the single AF point to whatever area of my subject I want to focus on and the camera will give me an accurate good-focus indication for the area under the AF point by displaying the good-focus indicator dot in the bottom-left corner of the screen and turning the AF point green. This works especially well for macro photography. I also enjoy focus Peaking (page 409) for its extremely accurate method of outlining the area that is in good focus with one of four colors (red, yellow, blue, or white).

Dynamic-Area AF Assist

Dynamic-area AF assist allows you to control the appearance of the pattern of nine AF points when using Dynamic-area AF AF-area mode.

Figure 9.13D, image 1, reflects the actual pattern you can move around the Viewfinder with the Multi selector pad or Sub-selector joystick. It shows how the Viewfinder will display that movable pattern if Dynamic-area AF assist is set to On. All the focus points inside the dotted square area are active, although the center square starts autofocus.

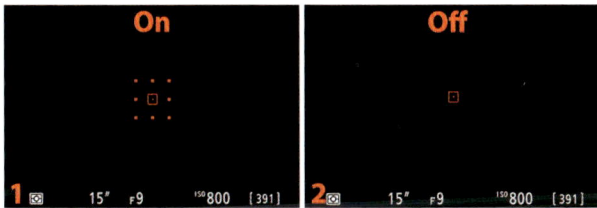

Figure 9.13D: Dynamic-area AF nine-point pattern. Image 1 shows actual AF points in use. Image 2 shows the AF point pattern with only the center AF point visible.

If you set Dynamic-area AF assist to Off, the camera will display only the middle AF point square and none of the surrounding AF points while you are using a Dynamic-area AF mode (figure 9.13D, image 2). However, the surrounding points are still active even though they are invisible.

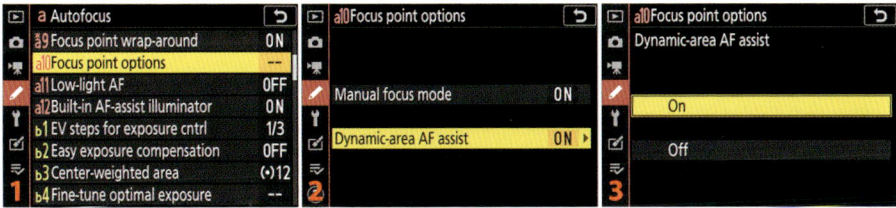

Figure 9.13E: Changing the appearance of the Dynamic-area AF mode focus frame

Use the following steps to choose a Dynamic-area AF pattern outline display:

1. Follow the screen flow shown in figure 9.13E, images 1–2 (*a Autofocus > a10 Focus point options > Dynamic-area AF assist*), until you arrive at the third screen in the series.
2. Choose either On or Off (figure 9.13E, image 3). On causes dots to appear around the area the actual AF points cover (figure 9.13D, image 1). If Off is selected, only a single AF point square from the middle of the pattern will appear (figures 9.13D, image 2). Press the OK button or tap On or Off to lock in your choice.

Settings Recommendation: When using Dynamic-area AF modes, I enjoy having the dots outlining the area with active focus points. That way, I know where my subject can move in the Viewfinder, or where I can move the pattern with the Multi selector pad or Sub-selector joystick and still have active AF points covering the subject. I leave Dynamic-area AF assist set to On at all times. If you choose to set it to Off, you will have only a single AF point in the Viewfinder and you will have to imagine the surrounding dots. On is best for most of us!

Custom Setting a11: Low-Light AF

The *Low-light AF* function lets you inform the camera that you will be shooting low-light photography. This asks the camera to strive for autofocusing accuracy at the expense of focus speed.

You can use this setting for still photography only when you have the Single-servo AF (AF-S) mode enabled. Low-light AF is not available unless you have the mode dial set to one of the P, S, A, or M modes (or U1–U3 with a P, S, A, or M mode programmed). Auto exposure mode (green camera icon) on the Mode dial disables Low-light AF.

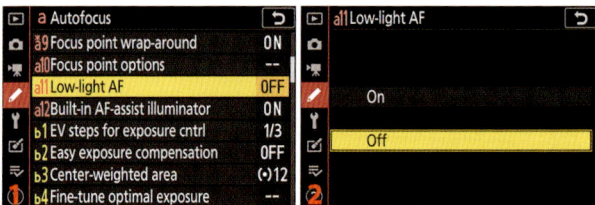

Figure 9.14: Enabling or disabling Low-light AF

Use the following steps to enable or disable Low-light AF:

1. Choose a11 Low-light AF from the a Autofocus menu and scroll to the right (figure 9.14, image 1).
2. Highlight On or Off and press the OK button or tap an option to lock in your choice (figure 9.14, image 2).

Custom Setting a12: Built-In AF-Assist Illuminator

You've seen the very bright little light on the front of the Z6, just below the Mode dial (figure 9.15A). Nikon calls this light the *Built-in AF-assist illuminator.* It lights up when the camera senses low-light conditions to assist with autofocus. The best range of the light is from 3 feet, 4 inches (1 meter), to about 9 feet, 10 inches (3 meters).

Custom setting a12 allows you to control when that pov on. There are two settings for the Built-in AF-assist illuminator:

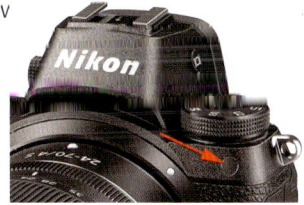

Figure 9.15A: Built-in AF-assist illuminator

- **On** (default). If the light level is low, the Built-in AF-assist illuminator lights up to help illuminate the subject enough for autofocus. This works with Single-servo AF (AF-S) Focus mode and any of the AF-area modes. When Continuous-servo AF (AF-C) Focus mode is selected the Built-in AF-assist illuminator becomes inactive.

- **Off:** The AF-assist illuminator will not light up to help you in low-light autofocus situations. The camera may not be able to autofocus in very low light.

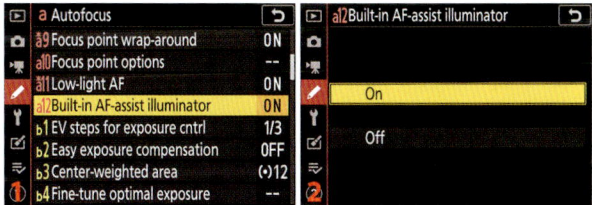

Figure 9.15B: Built-in AF-assist illuminator settings

Here are the steps to set the Built-in AF-assist illuminator to On or Off:

1. Highlight a12 Built-in AF-assist illuminator and scroll to the right (figure 9.15B, image 1).
2. Choose On or Off from the menu and press the OK button or tap On or Off to lock in the setting (figure 9.15B, image 2).

Settings Recommendation: I leave Built-in AF-assist illuminator set to On most of the time. It is activated only when the light is low enough to need it. However, let me qualify this for specific circumstances. If you are trying to take pictures without being noticed, such as from across the room with a zoom lens or while doing street photography, you certainly don't want this extremely bright little light drawing attention when you start autofocus.

Or, you may be shooting wildlife, such as a giant grizzly bear, and surely don't want to call attention to yourself by shining a bright light into the bear's eyes. Use this feature when you don't mind others noticing you—especially if they are eight feet tall with claws—because it will draw attention immediately.

Custom Setting a13: Manual Focus Ring in AF Mode

In order to see Custom setting a13 in your camera's menu system, you must have a lens that is compatible with this function. If an incompatible lens is mounted, the a13 Manual focus ring in AF mode menu item does not even appear under *Custom Setting Menu > a Autofocus*.

Manual focus ring in AF mode is a function that allows you to hold down the Shutter-release button halfway, while focusing the camera with the lens focus ring. It disables AF while you are holding down the Shutter-release button. To reenable AF, simply lift your finger from the Shutter-release button and press it down halfway again. You must have Enable selected in the menu if you want to use the function. Disable turns it off.

Unfortunately, none of the lenses I have will work with this function, so I cannot provide menu images. I contacted Nikon support and they could not tell me which lenses are compatible with this functionality.

SECTION TWO: b Metering/Exposure

Custom Settings b1 to b4

You'll find four settings within the *b Metering/exposure* menu in the Z6:

- **b1:** EV steps for exposure cntrl
- **b2:** Easy exposure compensation
- **b3:** Center-weighted area
- **b4:** Fine-tune optimal exposure

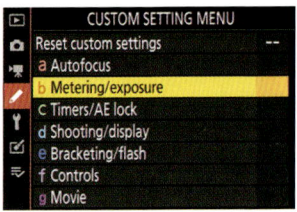

Let's examine how to use the b Metering/exposure functions.

All four "b" functions and their settings—discussed within the following sections—are found on the Custom Setting Menu under the *b Metering/exposure* menu item (figure 9.16).

Figure 9.16: *b Metering/exposure*

Custom Setting b1: EV Steps for Exposure Cntrl

EV steps for exposure cntrl refers to the number of exposure value (EV) steps in the shutter speed and aperture because those are your main exposure controls. It also encompasses the exposure and flash bracketing system. Basically, you can increment the EV steps in either 1/3 or 1/2 steps (see the sidebar: **What Is EV?**). This setting controls the EV step capability for the following settings:

- Shutter speed
- Aperture
- ISO sensitivity

- Exposure bracketing
- Flash bracketing
- Exposure compensation

Now, let's examine the concept in more detail. All *EV steps for exposure cntrl* really means is that when you are adjusting the shutter speed or aperture manually, each will work incrementally in the following steps.

Shutter and Exposure (starting at a random shutter speed or aperture)

- 1/3 step EV:
  Shutter: 1/100, 1/125, 1/160, 1/200, 1/250, 1/320, etc.
  Aperture: f/5.6, f/6.3, f/7.1, f/8, f/9, f/10, f/11, f/13, etc.

- 1/2 step EV:
  Shutter: 1/90, 1/125, 1/180, 1/250, 1/350, 1/500, etc.
  Aperture: f/5.6, f/6.7, f/8, f/9.5, f/11, f/13, f/16, f/19, etc.

Bracketing

- 1/3 step EV:
  Bracket: 0.3, 0.7, 1.0, 2.0. 3.0

- 1/2 step EV:
  Bracket: 0.5, 1.0, 2.0, 3.0

Nikon chose to lump shutter speed, aperture, and bracketing all under Custom setting b1. The factory default value for *EV steps for exposure cntrl* is 1/3 step. Let's see how to choose an EV step value.

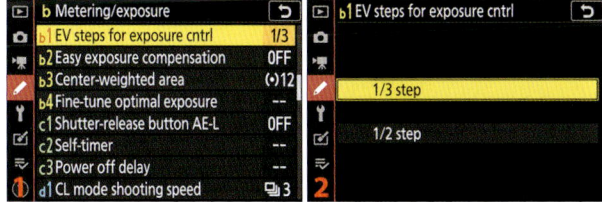

Figure 9.17: EV steps for exposure cntrl

Use the following steps to adjust *EV steps for exposure cntrl:*

1. Choose b1 EV steps for exposure cntrl from the b Metering/exposure menu and scroll to the right (figure 9.17, image 1).
2. Highlight either 1/3 step or 1/2 step on the menu and press the OK button or tap the option to lock in the setting (figure 9.17, image 2).

Settings Recommendation: Similar to *ISO sensitivity step value,* I keep *EV steps for exposure cntrl* set to 1/3 step. It's critical to control the EV steps with granularity, especially with exposure. It's also best to increment the EV in small steps for use with the histogram.

> **What Is EV?**
>
> EV simply means exposure value, which is an agreed-upon value of exposure metering. It is spoken of in full or partial EV steps, like 1/3, 1/2, or 1. It simply means different combinations of shutter speeds and apertures that give similar exposures. An EV step corresponds to a standard logarithmic "power-of-2" exposure step, commonly referred to as a *stop*. So, instead of saying 1 EV, you could substitute 1 stop. EV 0 (zero) corresponds to an exposure time of 1 second at an aperture of f/1.0 or 15 seconds at f/4. EV can be positive or negative. EV −6 equals 60 seconds at f/1.0. EV 10 equals 1/1000 seconds at f/1.0 or 1/60 seconds at f/4. The EV step system was invented in Germany back in the 1950s. Interesting, huh?

Custom Setting b2: Easy Exposure Compensation

Easy exposure compensation lets you set the camera's exposure compensation without using the +/− Exposure compensation button. Instead, you can use the Command dial of your choice to dial in exposure compensation.

There are three settings in Easy exposure compensation: On (Auto reset), On, and Off. If you set the camera to On (Auto reset) or On, you can use the Command dials to set exposure compensation instead of the +/− Exposure compensation button. Off means what it says—you will have to use the +/− Exposure compensation button.

Each exposure mode (P, S, A, M) reacts somewhat differently to Easy exposure compensation. Let's consider how the Program (P), Shutter-priority (S), and Aperture-priority (A) modes act when you use the three settings. The Manual (M) mode is not affected by Custom setting b2, although it does allow compensation with the normal +/− Exposure compensation button. Here are the values and how they work:

- ***On (Auto reset):*** Using the Sub-command dial in Program (P) or Shutter-priority (S) mode or the Main command dial in Aperture-priority (A) mode, you can dial in exposure compensation without using the normal +/− Exposure compensation button. The other Command dial will control the aperture or shutter speed, as it normally would. Once you allow the meter to go off, or turn the camera off, the compensation value you dialed in is reset back to 0. That's why it's called Auto reset. If you have already set a compensation value using the normal +/− Exposure compensation button, then the process of dialing in compensation with the Command dial simply adds or substracts compensation from the value you added with the normal +/− Exposure compensation button. When the meter resets, it returns back to the compensation value you added with the +/− Exposure compensation button and not to 0.
- ***On:*** This works the same way as On (Auto reset), except that the compensation you've dialed in does not reset; it stays in place even if the meter or camera is turned off.
- ***Off:*** Only the normal +/− Exposure compensation button applies exposure compensation.

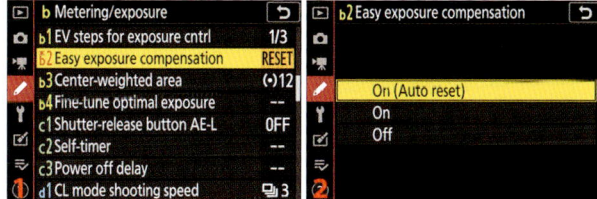

Figure 9.18: Easy exposure compensation

Here are the steps used to configure Easy exposure compensation:

1. Choose b2 Easy exposure compensation from the b Metering/exposure menu and scroll to the right (figure 9.18, image 1).
2. Choose one of the three items on the menu and press the OK button or tap the option to lock it in (figure 9.18, image 2).

Note: The granularity of Easy exposure compensation's EV step fine-tuning is affected by Custom setting b1, with 1/3 or 1/2 EV step settings. Also, the Command dials used to set compensation and change shutter speed and aperture can be swapped in *Custom Setting Menu > f5 Customize command dials > Change main/sub,* which we will consider later in this chapter.

When you adjust exposure compensation with either the normal +/− Exposure compensation button or with Easy exposure compensation, a +/− symbol will appear on the EVF and Monitor while exposure compensation is active.

Settings Recommendation: I really like this functionality because it allows me to set the shutter speed and aperture with one Command dial, and dial in exposure compensation with the other. It is very fast and allows me to watch the live histogram on my screen and dial it so that the bright side just touches the edge of the window (exposing for the highlights).

Why not experiment with this for a few minutes and see if you like dialing in compensation with the Command dials instead of, or in addition to, the +/− Exposure compensation button?

Custom Setting b3: Center-Weighted Area

Center-weighted area allows you to control the area of the EVF or Monitor that has the greatest weight in metering a subject when the camera is using Center-weighted metering mode (page 55).

The Center-weighted meter can be configured to use a central area of the screen to do most of its metering—with less attention paid to the subject outside of this area—or it can be set to simply average the entire frame.

The two Center-weighted area settings available (firmware C2.00) are 12 mm and Average (figure 9.19, images 3 and 4). If you select 12 mm, the Center-weighted meter assigns the greatest weight to the center of the Viewfinder frame, and everything outside the circle in the center is not as important. If you select the Average (Avg) setting, the entire Viewfinder frame is used to meter the scene. The camera takes an average of the entire frame by including all light and dark areas mixed together for an averaged exposure.

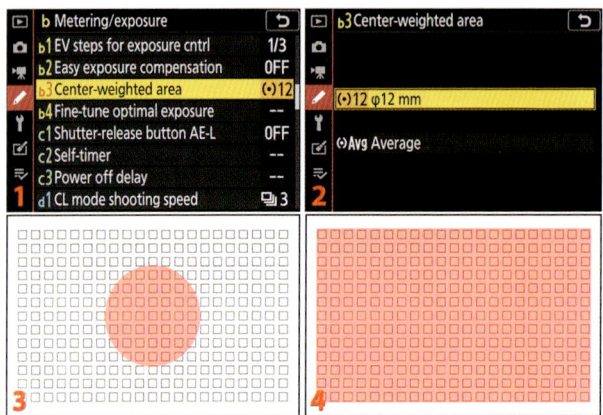

Figure 9.19: Choosing a Center-weighted metering mode area

Use these steps used to choose a Center-weighted metering mode area:

1. Choose b3 Center-weighted area from the b Metering/exposure menu and scroll to the right (figure 9.19, image 1).
2. Choose either 12 mm or Average from the menu (figure 9.19, image 2). The red circle shown in image 3 corresponds to the 12 mm setting, and the red rectangle in image 4 corresponds to the Average area. Once you have chosen your setting, press the OK button or tap the option to lock it in.

Please see the chapter titled **Metering, Exposure Modes, and Histogram** (page 53) for much deeper information on using the Z6's Metering modes.

Settings Recommendation: You will need to experiment and see whether the Center-weighted or Averaging metering method are most satisfactory to you. I leave mine set to the default of 12 mm and when I use it (rarely), it seems to work well. I use Matrix metering most of the time, along with the Spot meter when special metering is needed.

Custom Setting b4: Fine-Tune Optimal Exposure

Nikon has taken the stance that users should be allowed to fine-tune most major camera systems. The exposure system is no exception. *Fine-tune optimal exposure* allows you to fine-tune the Matrix, Center-weighted, Spot, and Highlight-weighted metering systems by +1/−1 EV in 1/6 EV steps, independently.

In other words, you can force each of the four metering systems to add or deduct a little exposure from what it normally would use to expose your subject.

This stays in effect with no further notice until you set it back to zero. It is indeed fine-tuning because the maximum 1 EV step up or down is divided into six parts (1/6 EV). If you feel that your camera is too conservative with the highlights, mildly underexposing, and you want to force it to add 1/2 step exposure, you simply add 3/6 EV to the compensation system for that metering system. (Remember basic fractions—where 1/2 equals 3/6?)

This works like the normal compensation system except it allows you only 1 EV of compensation. As image 2 of figure 9.20A shows, an ominous-looking warning appears telling you that your camera will not show a compensation icon (as it does with the normal +/− Exposure compensation button) when you use the Fine-tune optimal exposure system. This simply means that while you have this fine-tuning system dialed in for your light meter, the camera will not remind you that it is fine-tuned by showing you a compensation icon. If it did turn on the compensation icon (+/− on the Control panel and in the Viewfinder), how could it show you the same icon when you are using normal compensation at the same time as meter fine-tuning? Let's examine how to use the exposure fine-tuning system.

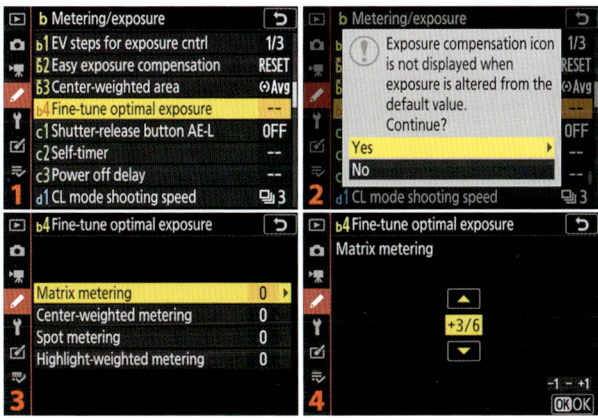

Figure 9.20A: Fine-tune optimal exposure

Use the following steps to fine tune any of the four metering systems:

1. Choose b4 Fine-tune optimal exposure from the b Metering/exposure menu and scroll to the right (figure 9.20A, image 1).

2. Select Yes from the popup question box that says: *Exposure compensation icon is not displayed when exposure is altered from the default value. Continue?* (figure 9.20A, image 2).

3. Select the metering system you want to adjust. In figure 9.20A, image 3, you can see that I selected Matrix metering. Now scroll to the right. All four of the meter fine-tuning operations work exactly the same way, and each meter can be adjusted independently of the other three. If you want to adjust a different meter besides Matrix metering, simply substitute one of the other meter types in this step (Center-weighted metering, Spot metering, or Highlight-weighted metering).

4. Scroll up or down with the Multi selector pad or touch the up/down pointers with your fingertip (figure 9.20A, image 4). This allows you to fine-tune the meter in 1/6 EV steps. I set +3/6, which is the equivalent of adding +1/2 EV of extra exposure to the Matrix metering system.

5. Press or touch OK to lock in the fine-tuning value for the metering system you selected in step 3 only. *You must fine-tune each metering system separately*.

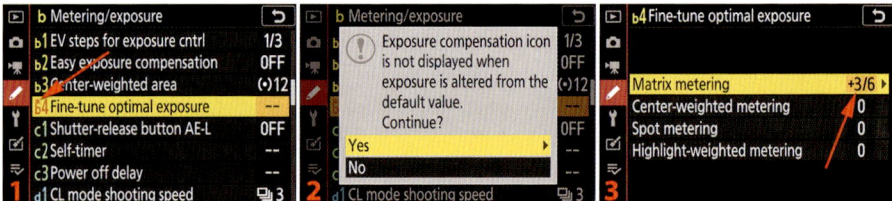

Figure 9.20B: The Matrix meter has been fine-tuned

6. The only way to know which of the meters has been fine-tuned is to open the screens shown in figure 9.20B, which displays the results of our Matrix meter fine-tuning operation. Your first clue that one or more of the meters has been fine-tuned is the small asterisk that appears above the b in b4 (image 1, red arrow). Next, select *b4 Fine-tune optimal exposure > Yes* and examine the screen shown in figure 9.20B, image 3, to see if any of the meters have been fine-tuned. Be sure to turn off fine-tuning for each meter if the circumstances that require fine-tuning change; otherwise, you could have under- or over-exposed images.

That's all there is to it! Just remember that you have Fine-tune optimal exposure turned on because the camera will not remind you (other than the small asterisk above the b of b4). Watch your histogram to make sure you're not regularly underexposing or overexposing images once you have the fine-tuning adjustment in place. If so, just go back in and adjust the fine-tuning up or down or turn it off.

Settings Recommendation: Unless you have a good reason to adjust this, most of us will leave it alone. It certainly won't hurt anything to make a fine-tuning adjustment, if you feel confident that you really need it. I used to run +3/6 on my Nikon D300 a few years back to force a brighter exposure. However, the Z6 has one of the most accurate light metering systems I have ever used; therefore, it may not be necessary to fine-tune any of the four metering types in your camera.

You have the ability to fine-tune your cameras to an amazing degree. Whether you need this now or not, you might later. Learn how it works and, as always, experiment with it to see if fine-tuning your light meter gives you better exposures. Learn to use the histogram (page 67) to help guide your exposure choices!

SECTION THREE: c Timers/AE Lock

Custom Settings c1 to c3

You'll find three settings within the *c Timers/AE lock* menu in the Z6:

- **c1:** Shutter-release button AE-L
- **c2:** Self-timer
- **c3:** Power off delay

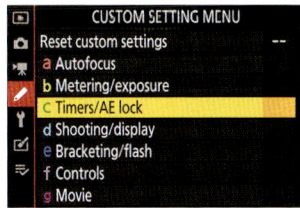

Let's examine each of them and learn how to control the various timers in the camera. We will also explore how to use auto-exposure lock (AE-L).

All three "c" functions and their settings—discussed within the following sections—are found on the Custom Setting Menu under the *c Timers/AE lock* menu item (figure 9.21).

Figure 9.21: *c Timers/AE lock*

Custom Setting c1: Shutter-Release Button AE-L

Shutter-release button AE-L is designed to allow you to lock your camera's exposure when you press the Shutter-release button halfway down. Normally, this type of exposure lock happens only when you press and hold a different control that has previously been assigned AE lock only (see **f2 Custom control assignment** on page 423).

However, when you have Shutter-release button AE-L set to On, your camera will lock out exposure changes each time you press the Shutter-release button halfway down or all the way down, per the setting you choose. When you release the Shutter-release button, the camera returns to normal exposure.

This function allows you to meter from one area of the scene and then recompose to another area without losing the meter reading from the first area, as long as you hold the Shutter-release button halfway down. Press the Shutter-release button the rest of the way down to capture the exposure. Here is a list of the three modes and what they do:

- **On (half press):** Allows you to lock exposure by pressing the Shutter-release button halfway down
- **On (burst mode):** Causes the camera to lock exposure when you hold the Shutter-release button all the way down (firing a burst of pictures)
- **Off:** Disables the function

Let's see how to select one of the settings.

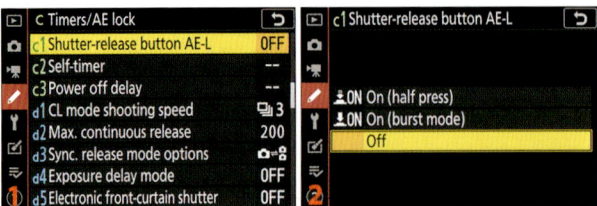

Figure 9.22: Shutter-release button AE-L

Here are the steps used to configure Shutter-release button AE-L:

1. Choose c1 Shutter-release button AE-L from the c Timers/AE lock menu and scroll to the right (figure 9.22, image 1).
2. Referring to the previous list, highlight one of the three items on the menu and press the OK button or tap the option to lock in the setting (figure 9.22, image 2).

Note: When you are shooting with the 12-fps, High-speed continuous (extended) burst mode with a camera firmware previous to version 2.0, the Z6 always locks the exposure on the first frame. However, with firmware version 2.0 Nikon introduced full-time AE metering during bursts, making this c1 function useful for 12-fps shooting.

If you are using the 5.5 fps High-speed continuous mode, the camera always meters for each frame, regardless of firmware version. If you set c1 Shutter-release button AE-L to On (burst mode), the Z6 will lock the exposure on the first frame.

Settings Recommendation: If you often use AE lock only, then you might want to consider using this function as a matter of convenience. If you rarely shoot with AE lock only, then you can safely ignore this function. If you do use this function, just make sure the exposure doesn't change on your subject while you are locking the auto exposure (AE) system, or you could end up with some bad exposures.

I regularly use On (half press) so that I can include the setting sun in my images without underexposing the picture (e.g., sunsets). I meter from an area of the sky with the sun slightly out of the frame, hold down the Shutter-release button halfway to lock the exposure, and then recompose with the sun in the frame.

Custom Setting c2: Self-Timer

The *Self-timer* setting allows you to take pictures remotely or without touching the camera except to start the Self-timer operation. Hands-off shooting on a tripod can reduce vibrations so that you have sharper pictures. Additionally, it gives you time to place yourself in group shots so there will be some pictures of you to look at later. Put yourself in front of the camera from time to time, or no one will remember what you look like! There are three settings in the c2 Self-timer function, as follows:

- **Self-timer delay:** This setting allows you to specify a delay before the shutter fires so you have time to position yourself for the shot or allow vibrations to settle down. The time delay ranges from 2 to 20 seconds. This setting can be used instead of a remote release, and you won't have cables to trip over.
- **Number of shots:** Use this setting to choose how many shots will be taken for each cycle of the Self-timer. You can choose from one to nine shots in a row.
- **Interval between shots:** If you are taking more than one shot during a Self-timer cycle, this setting allows you to choose a time interval between each shot, ranging from 0.5 second to 3 seconds. Having some time between shots allows vibrations from the previous shot to settle down.

To set the Self-timer, use the steps shown in the following three subsections. When you press the Shutter-release button, the Self-timer will start its timed countdown and will flash the small green Self-timer lamp (AF-assist illuminator) until just before the shutter fires, at which point the light will become continuous.

Self-Timer Delay

Here is a list of the four available Self-timer delay settings:

- **2 s:** 2 seconds
- **5 s:** 5 seconds
- **10 s:** 10 seconds (default)
- **20 s:** 20 seconds

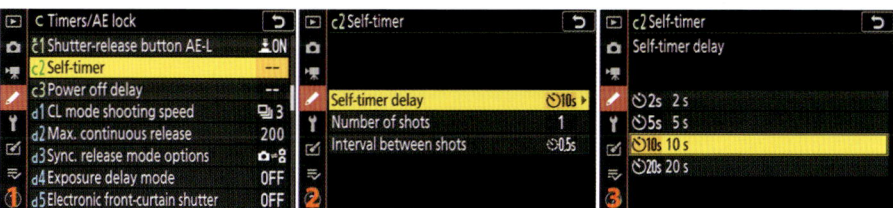

Figure 9.23A: Setting the Self-timer delay

Use the following steps to configure the Self-timer delay:

1. Follow the screen flow shown in figure 9.23A, images 1 and 2 (*c Timers/AE lock > c2 Self-timer > Self-timer delay*), until you arrive at the third screen in the series.
2. Choose one of the four options (2 s to 20 s) from the menu and press the OK button or tap the option to lock in the setting (figure 9.23A, image 3). When you press the Shutter-release button the camera will start the self-timer countdown based on this value.

Number of Shots

Next, let's examine how to configure the Number of shots for each Self-timer cycle.

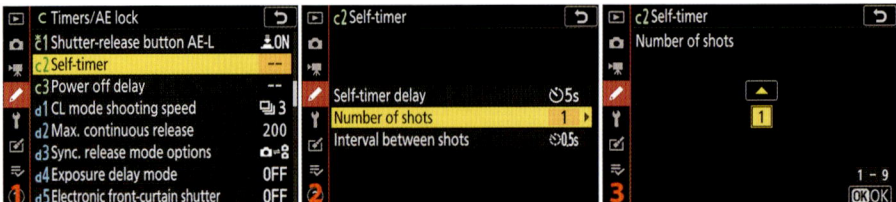

Figure 9.23B: Setting the Number of shots

Use the following steps to configure the Number of shots:

1. Follow the screen flow shown in figure 9.23B, images 1 and 2 (*c Timers/AE lock > c2 Self-timer > Number of shots*), until you arrive at the third screen in the series.
2. Choose the Number of shots, from 1 to 9, by scrolling up or down with the Multi selector pad or by tapping the up/down pointers (figure 9.23B, image 3). Press or touch OK to lock in the setting.

Settings Recommendation: When I'm taking a group shot, invariably someone will have their eyes closed or will be looking at something to the side. The only solution I've found for this problem is to instruct the group to "look at the camera and smile," and then take several shots, hoping at least one will be usable. The Z6 allows you to take up to nine shots with a short interval between each shot (next subsection). I take at least three shots each time.

Interval Between Shots

Finally, let's look at how to configure the Interval between shots for each Self-timer cycle. Here is a list of the four available Interval between shots settings:

- **0.5 s:** 1/2 second (default)
- **1 s:** 1 second
- **2 s:** 2 seconds
- **3 s:** 3 seconds

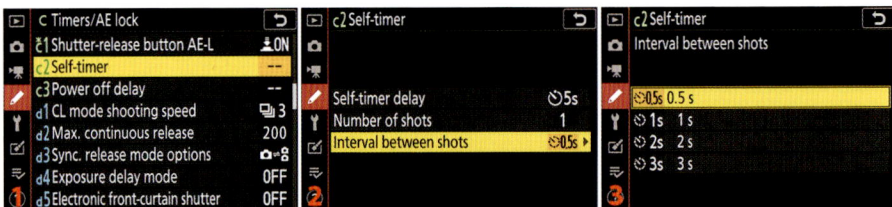

Figure 9.23C: Setting the Interval between shots

Use the following steps to configure the Interval between shots:

1. Follow the screen flow shown in figure 9.23C, images 1 and 2 (*c Timers/AE lock > c2 Self-timer > Interval between shots*), until you arrive at the third screen in the series.
2. Choose the Interval between shots, from 1/2 second (0.5 s) to 3 s, and press the OK button or tap the option to lock in your selection (figure 9.23C, image 3). The camera will now wait between shots for the Interval you specified.

The Self-timer is also available under the Release mode function of the *i* Menu, as seen in Figure 9.23D.

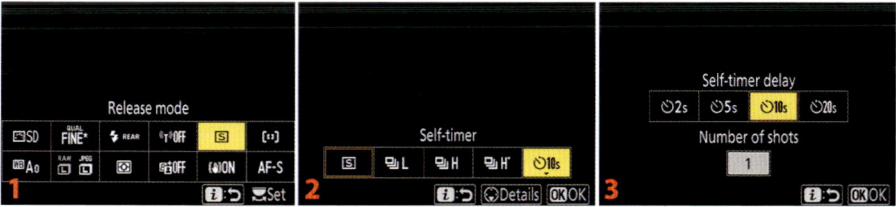

Figure 9.23D: Self-timer on the *i* Menu

Use the following steps to access the Self-timer on the *i* Menu:

1. Press the *i* Button on the camera's back to open the *i* Menu.
2. Tap the Release mode position on the *i* Menu or scroll there with the Multi selector pad and press the OK button (figure 9.23D, image 1).
3. Select the last Release mode on the right, which is the Self-timer position (figure 9.23D, image 2). Press or touch OK to select the default 10 second (10s) delay. If 10s is the delay you want to use, press or touch OK again to lock it in and skip the rest of these steps. If you would prefer to use a different delay, tap the Details control or scroll down with the Multi selector pad.
4. The final Self-timer screen allows you to control everything c2 Self-timer lets you control, except for the Interval between shots. Choose a Self-timer delay and the Number of shots, then press or touch OK to lock in your choices. The camera will use the default of 1/2 second (0.5s) as the Interval between shots, unless you have previously changed this setting, in which case the Z6 will use whatever the previous Interval between shots was set to (0.5s to 3s).

Settings Recommendation: Often, if I don't want to take the time to plug in a remote release cable, I just put my camera on a tripod and set the Self-timer delay to 2 or 5 seconds. This lets the Z6 make a hands-off exposure so I don't shake the camera or the tripod. If I must run to get into position for a group shot, I often increase the delay to at least 10 seconds to keep from looking like an idiot as I trip while running for position. I can also control how many shots to take each time I use the Self-timer and how long to delay between those shots to allow vibrations to go away.

Custom Setting c3: Power Off Delay

Power off delay lets you set a timeout for the various camera display screens and EVF. You can select a variable timing for four individual settings. The screens controlled by those settings will stay on until the timeout period expires. Here is a list of the individual settings:

- Playback
- Menus
- Image review
- Standby timer

We will review each of these settings to see how they work, after we see how to access them in the menu.

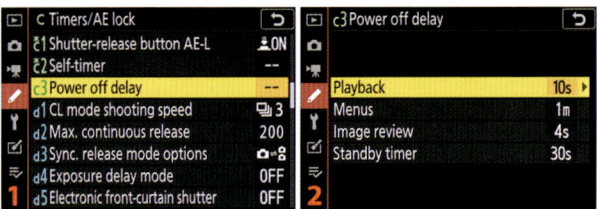

Figure 9.24A: Power off delay

Here are the steps to get to the screen for adjusting the timeouts. We'll consider each setting individually after these first steps:

1. Choose c3 Power off delay from the c Timers/AE lock menu and then scroll to the right (figure 9.24A, image 1).
2. Choose one of the four choices on the menu, as shown in figure 9.24A, image 2, and scroll to the right. You can set the Power off delay for each specific type. Let's examine each one.

Playback

First, let's look at setting a timeout for *Playback*. This is used when you are "playing back" images you have taken previously. This is not the Image review timeout, which is used when the camera displays a picture on the Monitor immediately after taking it. Playback is for when you are later looking at a series of images on the Monitor for your own enjoyment and quality verification or when you are showing images to another person. The available timeout is from 4 s to 10 min.

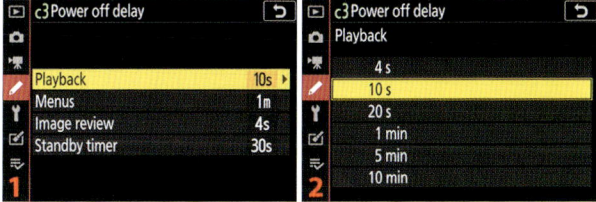

Figure 9.24B: Power off delay – Playback

Use the following steps to choose a Power off delay for viewing images on the Monitor after pressing the Playback button (figure 9.24B begins where figure 9.24A ends):

1. Select Playback from the c3 Power off delay screen and scroll to the right (figure 9.24B, image 1).
2. Choose from 4 seconds (4 s) to 10 minutes (10 min) delay time (figure 9.24B, image 2). Press the OK button or tap the option to lock it in.

Menus

Next, let's look at setting a timeout for the *Menus* when you make adjustments to camera settings. How long do you want the timeout to be before the screen shuts off (4 s to 10 min)?

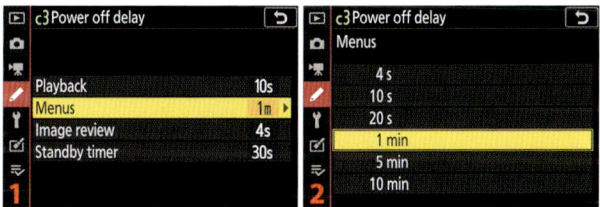

Figure 9.24C: Power off delay – Menus

Use the following steps to choose a Power off delay for viewing screens on the Monitor after pressing the Menu button (figure 9.24C begins where figure 9.24A ends):

1. Select Menus from the c3 Power off delay screen and scroll to the right (figure 9.24C, image 1).
2. Choose from 4 seconds (4 s) to 10 minutes (10 min) delay time (figure 9.24C, image 2). Press the OK button or tap the option to lock it in.

Image Review

Now let's look at setting a timeout for *Image review*. When you take a picture and have *Playback Menu > Image review* set to On, the camera will display a picture on the Monitor for a specific period of time, controlled by the Image review timeout (2 s to 10 min).

Please note that Image review is not the same as Playback, which is concerned with viewing a series of images sometime after they were taken. Image review sets the timeout for how long a single image appears on the Monitor immediately after you take it.

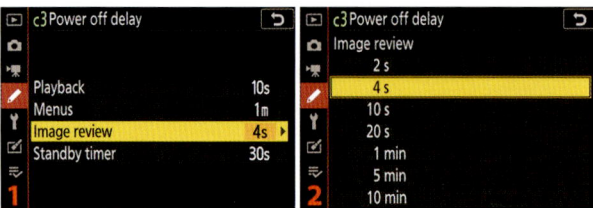

Figure 9.24D: Power off delay – Image review

Use the following steps to choose a Power off delay for viewing images immediately after taking them (figure 9.24D begins where figure 9.24A ends):

1. Select Image review from the c3 Power off delay screen and scroll to the right (figure 9.24D, image 1).
2. Choose from 2 seconds (2 s) to 10 minutes (10 min) delay time (figure 9.24D, image 2). Press the OK button or tap the option to lock the setting in.

Standby Timer

Finally, let's look at setting a timeout for *Standby timer*. This timeout is used when you are taking still pictures or videos with the Monitor or EVF and when you are examining settings on the top Control panel. The Standby timer delay affects how long these screens will stay active once you have stopped using the camera before they shut off to save battery. Choose shorter times to save battery life.

The camera defaults to turning off the displays 30 seconds after last use. The screens will dim for a few seconds just before shutting down. You can select delay timeouts from 10 seconds to No limit (no shutoff).

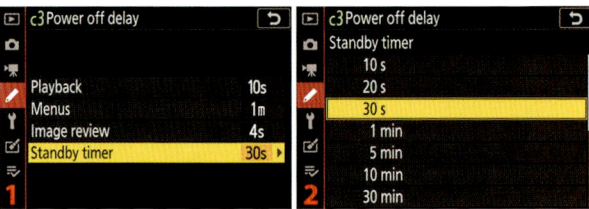

Figure 9.24E: Power off delay – Standby timer

Use the following steps to choose a Power off delay for Live view displays and the Control panel (figure 9.24E begins where figure 9.24A leaves off):

1. Select Standby timer from the c3 Power off delay screen and scroll to the right (figure 9.24E, image 1).
2. Choose from 10 seconds (10 s) to No limit delay time (figure 9.24E, image 2). Press the OK button or tap the option to lock it in.

Settings Recommendation: I set Power off delay to 1 min for Playback, Menus, and Image review on my Z6. I set the Standby timer to 30 seconds.

If you want to conserve battery power, leave the Power off delay set to a low value like 4 to 20 seconds. The longer the Z6's screens stay on, the shorter the battery life, so extend the screen time only if you really need it. Like a small notebook computer screen, the big, luxurious Monitor and EVF pull a lot of power. The Monitor and EVF backlights are probably the biggest power drains in the entire camera. However, you don't need to be overly concerned about this. With as much image review as I do, I can still shoot most of a day on one battery charge. With a mirrorless camera, it is best to carry at least two or three batteries for extended shooting times.

SECTION FOUR: d Shooting/Display

Custom Settings d1 to d11

Within the *d Shooting/display* menu, you'll find 11 settings in the Z6, as follows:

- **d1:** CL mode shooting speed
- **d2:** Max. continuous release
- **d3:** Sync. Release mode options
- **d4:** Exposure delay mode
- **d5:** Shutter type
- **d6:** Limit selectable image area
- **d7:** File number sequence
- **d8:** Apply settings to live view
- **d9:** Framing grid display
- **d10:** Peaking highlights
- **d11:** View all in continuous mode

Each of these functions has something to do with viewing images.

All eleven "d" functions and their settings—discussed within the following sections—are found on the Custom Setting Menu under the *d Shooting/display* menu item (figure 9.25).

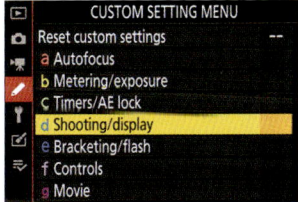

Figure 9.25: *d Shooting/display*

Custom Setting d1: CL Mode Shooting Speed

CL mode shooting speed (figure 9.26A) controls how many frames per second (fps) the camera can take when set to Continuous low speed (Continuous L or CL) under the Release mode function on the *i* Menu (from 1 fps to 5 fps). CL mode is for those who would like to use a more conservative fps rate than the 5.5- to 12-fps of the Continuous high speed modes (H or Extended).

Unless you are shooting race cars driving by at 200 mph, and unless you have large memory cards, you may not want a large number of frames of the same subject a few hundredths of a second apart. Therefore, Nikon has given you CL mode to rein in the number of images you will capture in a burst, while still giving you multiple-image capture capability.

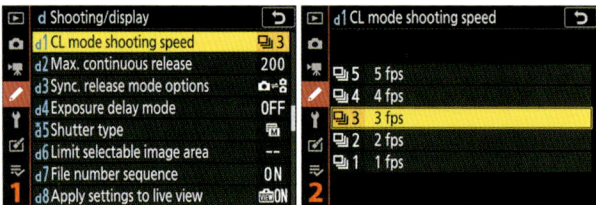

Figure 9.26A: CL mode shooting speed

Here are the steps used to configure CL mode shooting speed:

1. Choose d1 CL mode shooting speed from the d Shooting/display menu (figure 9.26A, image 1).
2. Choose one of the five choices (1 fps to 5 fps) from the menu and press the OK button or tap the option with your fingertip to lock in the setting (figure 9.26A, image 2).

As the screen in figure 9.26A, image 2, shows, you can adjust CL mode shooting speed so that your camera shoots at any frame rate from 1 to 5 fps. The default is 3 fps. Remember, you always have CH mode for when you want to blast off images like there's no end to your memory card(s), or when you want to impress bystanders with that extra-cool Nikon shutter-clicking sound.

CL mode shooting speed is also available under the Release mode function of the *i* Menu, as seen in figure 9.26B.

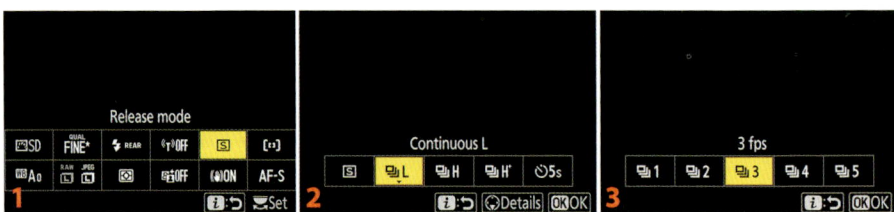

Figure 9.26B: CL mode shooting speed on the *i* Menu

Use the following steps to access the CL mode shooting speed on the *i* Menu:

1. Press the *i* Button on the camera's back to open the *i* Menu.
2. Tap the Release mode position on the *i* Menu or scroll there with the Multi selector pad and press the OK button (figure 9.26B, image 1).
3. Select the second Release mode on the left, which is the Continuous L (CL) position (figure 9.26B, image 2). Press or touch OK to select the CL mode along with whatever the current fps setting is (default is 3 fps) and skip the rest of these steps. If you want to change the setting to something other than the default 3 fps, touch the Details control or scroll down with the Multi selector pad.
4. The final screen allows you to choose a frames per second rate from 1 fps to 5 fps (figure 9.26B, image 3). Choose a new fps rate and then press or touch OK to lock in your choice.

Settings Recommendation: Use your favorite CL mode shooting speed, and grab a few, or many, frames with each press and hold of the Shutter-release button (or AF-ON button). I leave mine set at 3 fps because that is reasonably fast yet not wasteful of card space. If you'd like, you can slow it all the way down to 1 fps and take only one picture each second that you hold down the Shutter-release button. You'll need to play around with this setting and decide for yourself what speed you like.

Again, remember that you have both low (CL) and high (CH) speeds for the camera's shooting rate. This function is for the low-speed setting (CL) only.

Custom Setting d2: Max. Continuous Release

Max. continuous release sets the maximum number of images you can shoot in a single burst. It sounds like you can just start blasting away with your camera, shooting in a single burst until you have reached the number specified in figure 9.27, image 2, which is up to 200 images. However, due to internal memory buffer limitations, that may not be possible.

There's a list on page 234 of the new Z7/Z6 user's manual (for firmware C2.00) that specifies how large your camera's buffer is for each image type. Here is a summary of what the User's Manual reports:

- **NEF (RAW) files:** In FX mode (36×24 Image area), the memory buffer holds from 26 to 43 images. The amount may vary for other Image area settings.
- **TIFF files:** In FX mode (36×24 Image area), the memory buffer holds from 27 to 35 images, depending on the size of the TIFF file (Large, Medium, and Small). The amount may vary for other Image area settings.
- **JPEG files:** In FX mode (36×24 Image area) the camera will hold from 44 to 51 JPEG images in its internal buffer. The amount may vary for other image area settings.

Note: All the preceding figures are approximate and will vary with the complexity of the subject matter in the image. The maximum number of images stored in the buffer may drop to a lower number in the following situations:

- You are using JPEG images with a star (e.g., JPEG fine ★). A JPEG with a "★" is using Optimal quality compression, resulting in larger file sizes. For the buffer to be able to store from 44 to 51 JPEG images, the Z6 must use size-priority compression (no star, such as JPEG fine).
- Auto distortion control is On.

In reality it is very unlikely you will ever be able to shoot much more than maybe 40 JPEG fine images without filling up the buffer and dropping the frame rate to between 1 and 3 fps. Faster memory cards will make a difference, though. Therefore, maybe you should use the Max. continuous release function to reign in realistic numbers up to maybe 40 images, when you don't need to shoot the full amount.

On the other hand, if you are using a slow shutter speed, the write speed on a fast XQD card (e.g., Sony G series) may be enough to allow you to shoot a full 200 frames and bump up against the Max. continuous release limit. You may want to experiment with various shutter speeds to see if slower speeds will allow the camera time to buffer significantly more images.

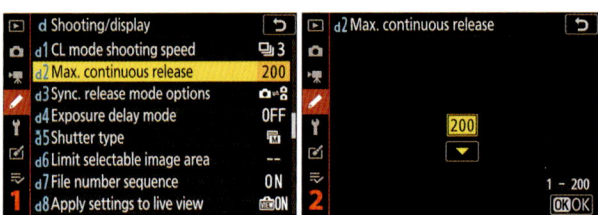

Figure 9.27: Max. continuous release

Here are the steps used to configure Max. continuous release:

1. Choose d2 Max. continuous release from the d Shooting/display menu and scroll to the right (figure 9.27, image 1).
2. Use the Multi selector pad to scroll up or down or tap the up/down pointers to set the maximum number of images you want in each burst (figure 9.27, image 2). Press or touch OK to lock in the setting.

Settings Recommendation: If you have a need to limit your camera to a maximum number of images in each shooting burst, simply change this number from its default of 200 images to whatever you feel works best for you. Personally, I want the buffer to hold as many images as it possibly can when I am blasting away in high-speed shooting modes, so I leave Max. continuous release set to 200.

However, you may want to artificially limit the camera to a maximum number of frames in one burst. If so, simply select the maximum number of images in figure 9.27, image 2, and the camera will stop when it reaches that number. This allows you to maintain some control over your enthusiastic high-speed shooting. Do you really need dozens and dozens (and dozens) of images of your child playing football?

Custom Setting d3: Sync. Release Mode Options

With the Nikon WR-1 Wireless Remote Controller, the more affordable Nikon WR-T10 Wireless Transmitter (from the WR-10 Wireless Remote Controller kit), or the very powerful professional Nikon WT-7A Wireless Transmitter, you can make your Nikon Z6 act as a "master camera" that controls "remote cameras" (see **Other Accessories** in the Z7/Z6 User's Manual on page 184).

When you use the wireless transmitters mentioned, *d3 Sync. release mode options* enables the Nikon Z6 to act as a master camera so that when it fires its shutter, all the remote cameras fire their shutters as well.

Affordable Nikon Transmitter and Receiver

A relatively inexpensive way to enable your Nikon Z6 to control compatible remote cameras is to use a new Nikon WR-10 Wireless Transmitter. You'll need to purchase the Nikon WR-10 Wireless Remote Controller kit, which contains the following:

- WR-T10 Transmitter
- WR-R10 Receiver
- WR-A10 10-pin Adapter (not needed for Z cameras, but included in kit)

You will also need an additional WR-R10 receiver for each compatible remote camera (Z7, Z6, D500, D850, or other Nikon cameras compatible with the WR-10 Wireless Remote Controller kit).

When you set the d3 Sync. release mode function to its Sync setting—having already "paired" all the cameras—and you press the release button on the WR-T10 transmitter, the remote cameras will fire their shutters at the same time the Nikon Z6 fires its shutter. Synchronized release!

Of course, configuring all these optional attachments is beyond the scope of this book; however, with the instructions that accompany the Nikon WR-10 Wireless Remote Controller kit, it is fairly easy to set up.

Synchronized Release Mode Configuration

Let's examine how to configure Custom setting d3 for synchronized shutter release.

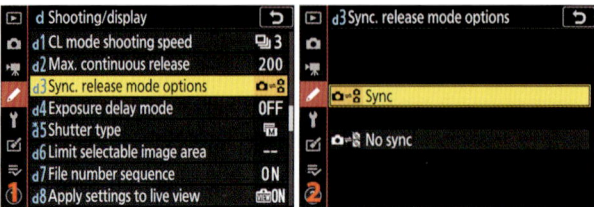

Figure 9.28: Enabling or disabling synchronized (master/remote) release of camera shutters

Use the following steps to enable or disable remote shutter synchronization:

1. Choose d3 Sync. release mode options from the d Shooting/display menu and scroll to the right (figure 9.28, image 1).
2. Choose either Sync or No sync and press the OK button or tap the option to lock in your setting (figure 9.28, image 3).

Settings Recommendation: If you want to shoot with multiple cameras and set up a master/remote relationship among them, your Z6 is ready to comply. Just pick up the radio controller equipment mentioned previously and you can set up your own series of synchronized cameras.

Custom Setting d4: Exposure Delay Mode

Exposure delay mode introduces a delay of 0.2 to 3 seconds after the Shutter-release button is pressed before the shutter is actually released. Hopefully, during the delay period, camera vibrations will die down and the image will be sharper.

The following settings are available in Exposure delay mode (figure 9.29):

- *0.2 s, 0.5 s, 1 s, 2 s,* or *3 s:* After you press the Shutter-release button, the camera waits from 0.2 to 3 seconds before firing the shutter, depending on the selection you choose, as shown in figure 9.29, image 2. This allows the vibrations from the mirror movement to dissipate before the shutter fires. Of course, this won't be useful at all for shooting anything moving or for any type of action shots. For shooting static scenes, this is a great feature.
- *Off:* The shutter has no delay when this setting is selected.

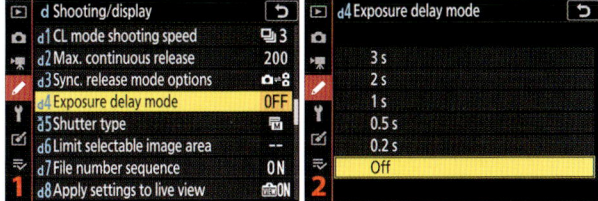

Figure 9.29: Exposure delay mode

Here are the steps used to configure Exposure delay mode:

1. Choose d4 Exposure delay mode from the d Shooting/display menu and scroll to the right (figure 9.29, image 1).
2. Choose Off or a time delay from 0.2 s to 3 s (figure 9.29, image 2). Press the OK button or tap the option to lock in your setting.

Settings Recommendation: Exposure delay mode is very important to me. As a nature shooter, I use it frequently for single shots. When I'm shooting handheld or especially on a tripod—and want a really sharp image—I use this mode to allow vibrations I might have caused when pressing the Shutter-release button to die down. I find that 1 s or 2 s works well for me on a tripod, or even handheld. If you shoot mostly static subjects and want sharper pictures, this will help.

Custom Setting d5: Shutter Type

Use Electronic front-curtain shutter (EFCS) under *d5 Shutter type* when you want to eliminate vibrations that are caused by the camera's physical shutter movement—called "shutter shock." Certain shutter speeds can be more prone to shutter shock than others. For instance, shutter speeds between 1/2 sec and 1/50 sec may suffer from this malady. Also, when using long telephoto lenses at shutter speeds below the reciprocal of the lens focal length (e.g., less than 1/200 sec for a 200mm lens, or 1/400 sec for a 400mm lens), shutter shock can sometimes cause less sharp images.

The Z6 has two mechanical curtains in its shutter assembly: a front curtain and a rear curtain. Normally, the camera uses both of these shutter curtains during an exposure with all Release modes (e.g., Single frame, Continuous High).

However, when you enable the EFCS, the camera withdraws the mechanical first curtain before the exposure starts. Exposure is then initiated by turning on the sensor to receive light, for whatever shutter speed time is selected, and then the sensor is turned off. At the end of the exposure, the rear curtain closes to block light from hitting the sensor, ending the exposure. Since no light is being recorded when the rear curtain closes, it does not cause shutter shock. Using the EFCS removes the vibration caused by the mechanical front curtain moving out of the way to start the exposure. However, there are some limitations when using the EFCS:

- The maximum shutter speed is reduced from 1/8000 second to 1/2000 second.
- The maximum ISO is reduced for Z6 cameras with a firmware previous to version 2.0. After firmware 2.0 or higher is installed there is no reduction in maximum ISO.

Neither of these limitations causes much trouble for normal shooting, so many photographers use the EFCS regularly. If you regularly need faster shutter speeds than 1/2000 second, you may not need the EFCS. Of course, at shutter speeds that fast, shutter shock is not much of a problem anyway.

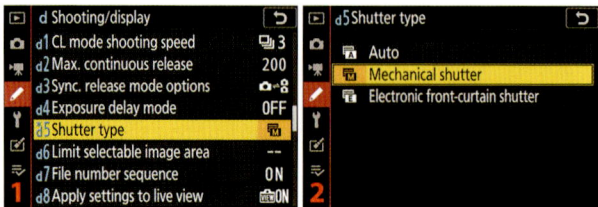

Figure 9.30: Enabling or disabling the Electronic front-curtain shutter setting

Here are the steps used to configure the Shutter type setting:

1. Choose d5 Shutter type from the d Shooting/display menu and scroll to the right (figure 9.30, image 1).
2. Choose Auto to let the camera decide which Shutter type to use, or select one of the two Shutter types manually. Your choices are: Mechanical shutter or Electronic front-curtain shutter (figure 9.30, image 2). Press the OK button or tap the option to lock in your setting.

Note: Previous to firmware 2.0 Auto and Mechanical shutter were not available within this d5 function and it was named *Electronic front-curtain shutter* instead of *Shutter type*.

Settings Recommendation: I use Electronic front-curtain shutter when I am in the Great Smoky Mountains taking lovely landscapes. I don't need fast shutter speeds or high ISO sensitivity in that environment. It works especially well for natural-light portraiture since somewhat longer lenses are often used at slower shutter speeds. If you are an action shooter and need very fast shutter speeds, maybe the EFCS is not for you. This is a mode that you should experiment with to see if it benefits your style of photography.

Custom Setting d6: Limit Selectable Image Area

When you assign the Choose image area function to one of the 12 available slots on the *i* Menu, or to a camera button (e.g. Fn1, Fn2), you can use *Limit selectable image area* to limit which Image area modes appear as selections.

Normally, you will have the five Image area modes listed in figure 9.31, image 2, available for selection from an assigned camera control. The camera will offer the checked

Image area modes in screens like the one shown in figure 9.31, image 3. The screen in image 3 is the result of my using Custom Setting f2 Custom control assignment (page 423) to assign Choose image area to the Fn1 button. When I press the Fn1 button and rotate either of the camera's Command dials, I can select from the displayed Image area modes.

If you uncheck any of the Image area modes listed in figure 9.31, image 2, the unchecked mode will not appear on screens like the Choose image area screen shown in image 3.

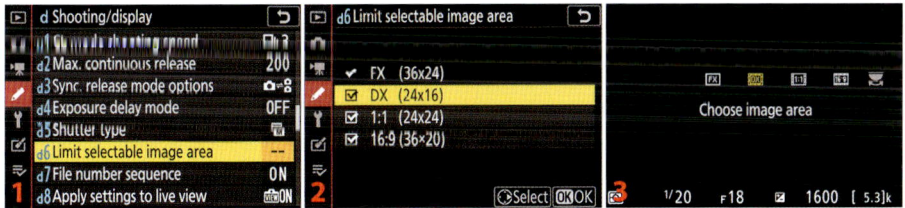

Figure 9.31: Limit the Image area mode selections for assignable controls

Use the following steps to limit the selection of Image area modes for assignable camera controls:

1. Choose d6 Limit selectable image area from the d Shooting/display menu and scroll to the right (figure 9.31, image 1).
2. Remove the check marks from the Image areas that you do not want to show up on an assignment to the *i* Menu or an assignable button/dial arrangement. To add or remove a check mark, tap the little box next to the option, or highlight the option [e.g., 1:1 (24.24)] and scroll to the right with the Multi selector pad. The FX (36×24) mode cannot be unchecked. When you have selected the Image area modes that you want to see on your camera screens for Assigned control/dial arrangements or an *i* Menu assignment—as seen in figure 9.31, image 3—press or touch OK to lock in the settings.

Settings Recommendation: I enjoy having all the camera's Image area modes available when I assign Choose image area to a button or the *i* Menu. However, there may be Image area modes that you will never use and would rather not have to scroll through. In that case, uncheck them and they will not appear. Most of us will leave this function set to factory default so as not to limit our choices.

Custom Setting d7: File Number Sequence

File number sequence allows your camera to keep count of the image file numbers for each picture you take, in a running sequence from 0001 to 9999. After 9999 pictures, it rolls back over to 0001. Or you can cause it to reset the image number to 0001 when you format or insert a new memory card. Here are the three settings, and an explanation of how each works:

- **On:** Image file numbers start at 0001 and continue running in a sequence until the image count exceeds 9999, at which point the camera creates a new folder and image numbers roll over to 0001 again. The File number sequence continues even if a new folder is created, a new memory card is inserted, or the current memory card is formatted. If you insert a different memory card that contains an image number in the current folder with a higher value than the previous memory card, the camera will adopt the new higher image number. In other words, file numbering continues from the last number used or the largest file number in the current folder, whichever is bigger, until 9999 images are reached, at which point the camera starts the numbering sequence over at 0001.
- **Off:** Whenever you format or insert a new a memory card, the number sequence starts over at 0001. If you exceed 5000 images in a single folder, the camera automatically creates a new folder and starts counting images at 0001 again (i.e., 5001 becomes 0001).
- **Reset:** This is similar to the On setting. However, it is not a true running total to 9999 because the image number is dependent on the folder in use. The camera simply takes the last number it finds in the current folder and adds 1 to it, up to 9999. If you switch to an empty folder, the numbering starts over at 0001. Each folder has its own number series and causes a File number sequence Reset.

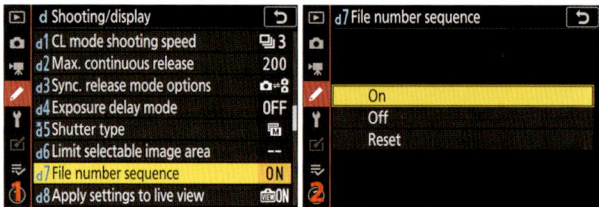

Figure 9.32: File number sequence

Here are the steps used to configure File number sequence:

1. Choose d7 File number sequence from the d Shooting/display menu and scroll to the right (figure 9.32, image 1).
2. Choose one of the three choices on the list (figure 9.32, image 2). On is the best choice for most of us. Press the OK button or tap the option to lock in your setting.

Note: A strange event could possibly occur with Nikon's image numbering system. If the current folder to which the camera is writing images is numbered 999 *and* it contains either 5000 pictures or a picture numbered 9999, the camera will disable its shutter and stop allowing pictures (or videos) to be taken. You will need to follow these two steps to reenable the camera's shutter:

1. Use the screens shown in figure 9.32 to set d7 File number sequence to Reset.
2. Insert a new memory card or format the current card (*Setup Menu > Format memory card*). Be sure you've backed up your images before formatting the card!

Settings Recommendation: I heartily recommend that you set File number sequence to On, if it has been turned off. After much experience with Nikon DSLR and now Z cameras, and many years of storing thousands of files, I've found that the fewer number of files with similar image numbers, the better. Why take a chance on accidentally overwriting the last shooting session when copying files on your computer just because they have the same image numbers?

Custom Setting d8: Apply Settings to Live View

One of the benefits of using a mirrorless camera with an EVF is the ability to immediately see changes to settings reflected in the image preview in the EVF or on the Monitor. In effect, the camera previews the final image before you take it. Add in the live histogram for precise exposure control and you have an especially powerful ability to create beautiful, well-exposed images.

When the *Apply settings to live view* function is enabled, changes to image settings such as exposure, Picture Controls, White balance, and depth of field are updated immediately on the "live view" EVF or Monitor screens. (See the sidebar **Previewing Depth of Field Accurately**.)

If you disable the Apply settings to live view function, the camera will use its EVF and Monitor to make sure you can see your subject well, regardless of the ambient light (unless too dark to use). The EVF and Monitor will not reflect how the final image will look. In other words, with the Apply settings to live view function disabled you will have no automatic image preview.

Let's examine how to enable or disable the Apply settings to live view function.

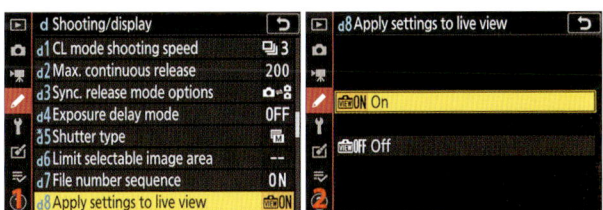

Figure 9.33: Enabling or disabling Apply settings to live view

1. Choose d8 Apply settings to live view from the d Shooting/display menu and scroll to the right (figure 9.33, image 1).
2. Select On to enable live image preview, or Off to use the live view screens merely to view the subject well (figure 9.33, image 2). On is the best choice for most of us. Press the OK button or tap the option to lock in your setting.

Settings Recommendation: I leave the Apply settings to live view function set to On at all times. I love the automatic image preview with setting change updates. It is one of the unique benefits of investing in mirrorless camera technology. It makes me feel confident that my final image will look exactly the way I want it to look before I release the shutter.

However, if you want the live view screens to simply show you your subject well, even in low light, without reflecting changes to important settings (such as exposure or white balance), then set this function to Off.

Previewing Depth of Field Accurately

Depth of field is automatically previewed in the EVF and on the Monitor, but down to f/5.6 only. Limitations to the autofocus system prevent the camera from focusing well with apertures set to values below f/5.6 (too dark). Therefore, the camera limits depth of field in automatic image preview to f/5.6 and larger apertures. Even if you are using f/16 or f/22, the depth of field seen on the EVF or Monitor is from an f/5.6 aperture setting. If you need full depth of field preview, you will have to assign the Preview function to an assignable button, such as Fn1 or Fn2. Then you can press the Assigned control to stop down the lens fully and see the actual depth of field at any aperture. See **Custom setting f2: Custom control assignment** (page 423) for information on assigning functions to camera buttons.

Custom Setting d9: Framing Grid Display

The *Framing grid display* function allows you to have a grid overlay on the EVF and Monitor in all Image area modes. The grid (figure 9.34, image 3) allows you to keep the horizon level and to align your camera with objects, such as doors, windows, and buildings. The grid overlay does not appear in the captured image or video. There are two settings in the Framing grid display function:

- **On:** Gridlines are displayed on the EVF and Monitor
- **Off:** No gridlines are displayed.

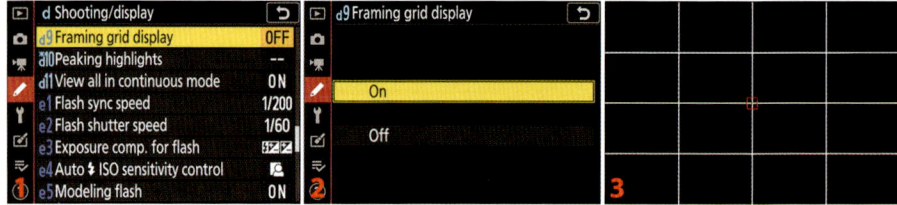

Figure 9.34: Framing grid display configuration

Here are the steps used to enable or disable the Framing grid display:

1. Choose d9 Framing grid display from the d Shooting/display menu and scroll to the right (figure 9.34, image 1).
2. Select On to enable the grid display, or Off to use normal screens, and press the OK button or tap the option to lock in your setting (figure 9.34, image 2).

Figure 9.34, image 3, shows the Framing grid display with the camera's lens cap on for maximum contrast.

Settings Recommendation: I use these gridlines to line up things as I shoot so that I won't have weird tilted horizons or buildings. Many of us tend to tilt the camera one way or another, and gridlines help us see that we've tilted the frame.

I especially enjoy shooting with gridlines enabled when I'm down at the beach. Who needs tilted ocean views? When you're shooting architecture, the gridlines are invaluable for making sure buildings, walls, and doors are correctly oriented with the edge of the frame.

Custom Setting d10: Peaking Highlights

Peaking highlights allows you to control the color of the fringe you'll see surrounding the areas of your subject that are in good focus (when Focus peaking is enabled). The camera offers four Peaking highlights colors so that you can adjust your camera to a color that contrasts with your subject and background.

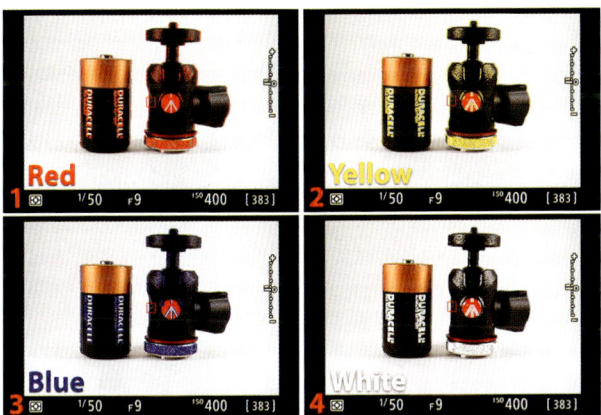

Figure 9.35A: Peaking highlights colors (Red, Yellow, Blue, and White)

Notice the four Peaking highlights colors in figure 9.35A, images 1–4. I focused manually on the Duracell words on the battery and the contour of the Manfrotto micro ball head. You can see clearly how the focus peaking color is highlighting the edges of the Duracell words and the contour of the micro ball head, signifying that the colored area is in good focus.

First let's see how to select a Peaking level (intensity of color fringe) and enable focus peaking, and then we will examine how to set the Peaking color.

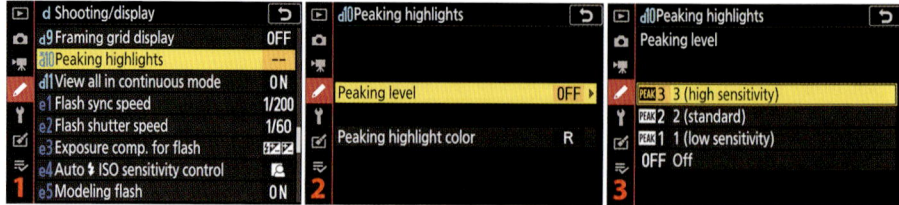

Figure 9.35B: Choosing a Peaking level (edge color intensity) and enabling focus peaking

Use the following steps to choose a Peaking level and enable focus peaking:

1. Choose a10 Peaking highlights from the d Shooting/display menu and scroll to the right (figure 9.35B, image 1).
2. Highlight Peaking level and scroll to the right (figure 9.35B, image 2).
3. Choose a Peaking level from PEAK 1 (low sensitivity) to PEAK 3 (high sensitivity) (figure 9.35B, image 3). Press the OK button or tap the option to lock in the sensitivity and intensity level. The larger the Peaking level number, the higher the sensitivity and larger the focus peaking highlight fringe will be. My camera is set to PEAK 3 (high sensitivity). The four color choices can be seen in figure 9.35A, images 1–4. When you choose a Peaking level (anything but Off), you have also enabled focus peaking for manual focusing in Live view. There is no way to enable or disable focus peaking other than selecting a Peaking level or setting it to Off.

Note: Once focus peaking is enabled (step 3), you can focus manually and see when particular areas of your subject are in focus as the color fringe becomes very prominent on color-change edges and rough contours (figure 9.35A).

Settings Recommendation: I set the camera to PEAK 3 so that it would be easy to see the focus peaking highlight fringe in the graphics. PEAK 3 may be a little overkill for most uses. I use PEAK 2 most of the time.

Next let's see how to select a highlight color.

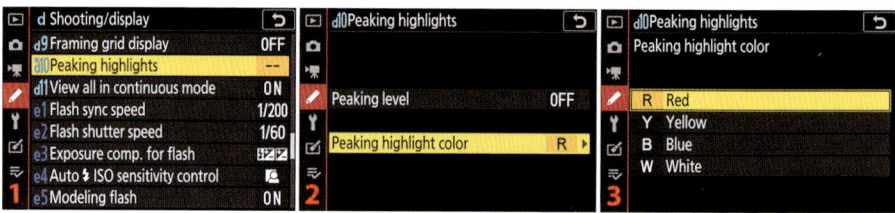

Figure 9.35C: Selecting a Peaking highlight color

Use the following steps to choose a Peaking highlights color:

1. Choose d10 Peaking highlights from the d Shooting/display menu and scroll to the right (figure 9.35C, image 1).
2. Select Peaking highlight color and scroll to the right (figure 9.35C, image 2).

3. Choose one of the highlight colors: Red, Yellow, Blue, or White (figure 9.35C, image 3). Press the OK button or tap the option to lock in your choice.

Settings Recommendation: I generally choose the Red setting for the Peaking highlight color because red seems to contrast well with most other colors. Of course, some subjects will do better with other colors; therefore, you have a choice of three more when needed.

Custom Setting d11: View All in Continuous Mode

The *View all in continuous mode* function allows you to control whether the camera's EVF and Monitor are active or disabled when you are burst shooting in one of the Continuous modes (CL or CH). If it is set to Off, both screens go dark during burst shooting and come back on afterward.

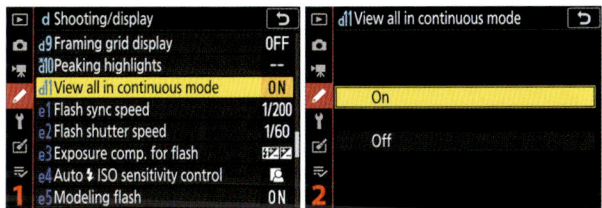

Figure 9.36: Enabling or disabling the camera's screens during burst shooting

Use the following steps to turn the Monitor and EVF on or off when using CL or CH mode:

1. Choose d11 View all in continuous mode from the d Shooting/display menu and scroll to the right (figure 9.36, image 1).
2. Select On to leave screens active during burst shooting, or Off to disable the screens during burst shooting. Press the OK button or tap an option to lock in your choice (figure 9.36, image 2).

Settings Recommendation: As a landscape photographer, I rarely use burst shooting and I cannot imagine a time when I would not want to see what my camera is capturing while shooting bursts of images. However, since Nikon gave us this function there must be reasons that some photographers will want the Monitor and EVF to turn off during burst shooting. Most of us will ignore this function.

SECTION FIVE: e Bracketing/Flash

Custom Settings e1 to e7

In the *e Bracketing/flash* section, there are seven functions to consider:

- **e1:** Flash sync speed
- **e2:** Flash shutter speed
- **e3:** Exposure comp. for flash
- **e4:** Auto [flash] ISO sensitivity control
- **e5:** Modeling flash
- **e6:** Auto bracketing (mode M)
- **e7:** Bracketing order

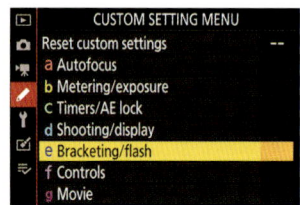

Figure 9.37: *e Bracketing/flash*

Each of these functions has something to do with bracketing or Speedlight flash use.

All seven "e" functions and their settings—discussed within the following sections—are found on the Custom Setting Menu under the *e Bracketing/flash* menu item (figure 9.37).

Custom Setting e1: Flash Sync Speed

Flash sync speed lets you select a basic flash synchronization speed from 1/200 s to 1/60 s (figure 9.38, image 2). Or, if you prefer, you can use the Auto FP mode in your camera—1/200 s (Auto FP).

Auto FP high-speed sync enables the use of fill flash even in bright daylight with wide aperture settings. It allows you to set your camera to the highest shutter speed available, up to 1/8000 s, and still use the external flash unit to fill in shadows. See the next section, **Auto FP High-Speed Sync Review** (page 413), where we discuss how this works.

The Auto FP mode is available only with certain external Nikon Speedlights. See the upcoming sidebar **Which Flash Units for Auto FP High-Speed Sync Mode?** (page 415) to see if your Nikon Speedlight(s) are compatible.

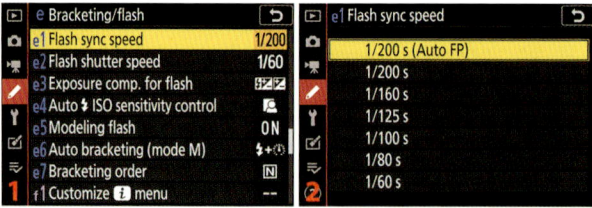

Figure 9.38: Flash sync speed

Here are the steps used to adjust your camera's Flash sync speed:

1. Choose e1 Flash sync speed from the e Bracketing/flash menu and scroll to the right (figure 9.38, image 1).
2. Choose one of the seven choices on the list—1/200 s (Auto FP) to 1/60 s. In figure 9.38, image 2, 1/200 s (Auto FP) is selected, which enables the Auto FP mode. Press the OK button or tap an option to lock in the setting.

When you're using Auto FP mode, the output of your flash is reduced but doesn't cut off the frame for exposures using a shutter speed higher than the normal flash sync speed (X Sync). Why? Let's review.

Auto FP High-Speed Sync Review

In a normal flash situation, with shutter speeds of 1/200 second and slower, the entire shutter is fully open and the flash can fire a single burst of light to expose the subject. It works like this: there are two shutter curtains in your camera. The first shutter curtain opens, exposing the sensor to your subject. The flash fires, providing correct exposure, and then the second shutter curtain closes. For a very brief period, the entire sensor is uncovered. The flash fires during the time when the sensor is fully uncovered.

However, when your camera's shutter speed is set above 1/200 second, the shutter curtains are never fully open for the flash to expose the entire subject in one burst of light. The reason is that at higher shutter speeds, the first shutter curtain starts opening and the second shutter curtain quickly starts following it. In effect, a slit of light is scanning across the surface of your sensor, exposing the subject. If the flash fired normally, a flash of light would expose the width of that slit between the shutter curtains, but the rest of the sensor would be blocked by the curtains. You would have a band of correctly exposed image, and everything else would be underexposed.

What happens to your external Nikon Speedlight to allow it to follow that slit of light moving across the sensor? It changes from a normal flash unit into a pulsing strobe unit. Have you ever danced under a strobe light? A strobe works by firing a series of light pulses. Similarly, when your camera's shutter speed is so high that the Speedlight cannot fire a single burst of light for correct exposure, it can use its Auto FP high-speed sync mode and fire a series of light bursts over and over as the shutter curtain slit travels in front of the image sensor. The Speedlight can fire thousands of bursts per second. To a photographer or subject, it still looks like one big flash of light, even though in reality it is hundreds or thousands of bursts of light, one right after the other.

When the camera is set to Auto FP mode, you'll see something like this on the Speedlight's LCD monitor:

- TTL FP
- TTL BL FP

The "FP" tells you that the camera and Speedlight are ready for you to use any shutter speed you'd like and still get a good exposure—even with wide-open apertures!

You can safely leave your camera set to 1/200 s (Auto FP) all the time because the high-speed sync mode does not kick in until you raise the shutter speed above the maximum setting of 1/200 s. Below that shutter speed, the flash works in normal mode and does not waste any power by pulsing the output.

This pulsing of light reduces the maximum output of your flash significantly but allows you to use any shutter speed you'd like while still firing your external Speedlight. The higher the shutter speed, the lower the flash output. In effect, your camera is depending on you to provide enough ambient light to offset the loss in power. I've found that even my powerful SB-5000 Speedlight can provide only enough power to light a subject out to about 8 feet (2.4 m) when using a 1/8000 s shutter speed. With shutter speeds that high, there needs to be enough ambient light to help the flash light the subject, unless you are very close to the subject.

However, now you can use wide apertures to isolate your subject in direct sunlight—which requires high shutter speeds. The flash will adjust and provide great fill light if you're using Auto FP high-speed sync mode.

Note: If your flash fires at full power in normal modes, it will blink the flash indicator in the Viewfinder to let you know that all available flash power has been used and that you need to check to see if the image is underexposed. When the camera is firing in Auto FP high-speed sync mode, that doesn't happen. You'll get no warning in the Viewfinder if the image does not have enough light. Check the camera's histogram often to validate your exposures when using Auto FP.

Special Shutter Speed Setting X + Flash Sync Speed

When using Manual (M) or Shutter-priority auto (S) exposure modes, there is still one more setting below 30 seconds, BULB, and TIME that you can use; it's named X + Flash sync speed. This special setting allows you to set the camera to a known shutter speed and shoot away. You will see "x 200" in the top Control panel and "x 1/200" on the Information display if *Custom Setting Menu > e1 Flash sync speed* is set to 1/200 s. Whatever Flash sync speed you select will show up after the X. If you select a Flash sync speed of 1/125 s, then X 125 will show up as the next setting below BULB. Selecting a Flash sync speed of 1/60 s means that X 60 will show up below BULB and TIME.

When you select this setting, the shutter speed will not vary from your chosen setting. The camera will adjust the aperture and flash when in Shutter-priority auto (S) mode, or you can adjust the aperture while the flash controls exposure in Manual (M) mode.

This special X-Sync mode is not available in Aperture-priority auto (A) or Programmed auto (P) mode because the camera controls the shutter speed in those two settings. Primarily, you'll use this setting when you are shooting in Manual or in Shutter-priority auto and want to use a known X-Sync speed.

Settings Recommendation: I leave my camera set to 1/200 s (Auto FP) as shown in figure 9.38, image 2, all the time. The camera causes the flash to work just as it normally would until one of its settings takes the shutter speed above 1/200 s, at which time the flash starts pulsing the light to match the shutter curtain travel.

Once again, you won't be able to detect this high-frequency strobe effect because it happens so fast it seems like a single burst of light. Just remember that the flash loses significant power (or reach) at higher shutter speeds because it is forced to work so hard.

Be sure you experiment with this to get the best results. You can use a big aperture opening like f/1.4 to have very shallow depth of field in direct bright sunlight because you can use very high shutter speeds. This will allow you to make images that many others simply cannot create. Learn to balance the flash and ambient light in Auto FP high-speed sync mode. All this technical talk will make sense when you see the results. Pretty cool stuff!

Which Flash Units for Auto FP High-Speed Sync Mode?

At the time this book was being written, the following external Speedlights allow you to use any shutter speed and, if the flash exceeds the sync speed, the Speedlight will adjust (pulse) to match lighting needs: SB-5000, SB-910, SB-900, SB-800, SB-700, SB-600, SB-500, and SB-R200. With the larger Speedlights, you'll need to learn how to balance ambient light with light from the flash when using shutter speeds higher than 1/200 s. Just remember that your flash unit's range will be seriously reduced at higher shutter speeds.

Custom Setting e2: Flash Shutter Speed

Flash shutter speed controls the minimum shutter speed your camera can use in various flash modes. You can select from 1/60 second (1/60 s) to 30 seconds (30 s). Whereas the previous function, Flash sync speed, controls the fastest shutter speed available, Flash shutter speed controls the slowest shutter speed available in specific modes. Let's consider each mode and its minimum shutter speed:

- ***Front-curtain sync, Rear-curtain sync,*** or ***Red-eye reduction:*** In Programmed auto (P) mode or Aperture-priority auto (A) mode, the slowest shutter speed can be selected from the range of 1/60 second (1/60 s) to 30 seconds (30 s) (figure 9.39). Shutter-priority (S) mode and Manual (M) mode cause the camera to ignore Flash shutter speed, and the slowest shutter speed can be as slow as 30 seconds (30 s) if the photographer chooses a speed that slow.
- ***Slow sync, Red-eye reduction with slow sync,*** or ***Slow rear-curtain sync:*** These three modes ignore Flash shutter speed, and the slowest shutter speed can be as slow as 30 seconds (30 s) if the camera or photographer chooses a shutter speed that slow.

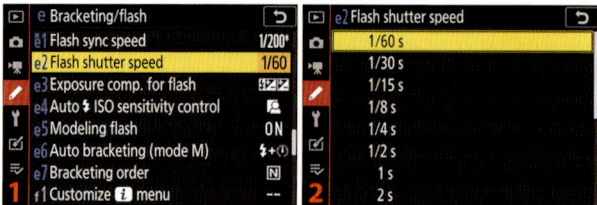

Figure 9.39: Flash shutter speed

Here are the steps to set the Flash shutter speed minimum:

1. Choose e2 Flash shutter speed from the e Bracketing/flash menu and scroll to the right (figure 9.39, image 1).
2. Choose one of the settings on the list—from 1/60 s to 30 s. In figure 9.39, image 2, 1/60 s has been selected. You will need to scroll down with the Multi selector pad, or by swiping with your fingertip to find the slower shutter speeds (e.g., 30 s). Remember that slower shutter speeds can cause subject ghosting when flash is used in high ambient light conditions. Press the OK button or tap the option to lock in the setting.

Note: Custom setting e2 is only partially used by the flash modes because the default is preset to as slow as 30 seconds in Shutter-priority and Manual modes.

Settings Recommendation: I normally use 1/60 s. Shutter speeds slower than 1/60 s can cause ghosting if the ambient light is too high. The subject can move after the flash fires but with the shutter still open and with enough ambient light to record a blurred ghost effect. You'll have a well-exposed picture of the subject with a ghost of your subject also showing in the image. Use slower shutter speeds only when you are sure that you'll be in dark conditions and the flash will provide the only lighting—unless you're shooting special effects, like a blurred aftereffect following your subject to imply movement.

Custom Setting e3: Exposure Comp. for Flash

The *Exposure comp. for flash* function allows you to treat the subject and background differently when you use flash. You can separate the normal exposure compensation function (for the background) and the flash compensation function (for the subject). Exposure compensation can be applied to the background only, or to the background and subject (the entire frame) with flash. There are two available settings:

- **Entire frame:** Both the flash and the exposure compensation work normally.
- **Background only:** The nonflash exposure compensation (that you adjust with the Exposure compensation button) and the flash compensation (that you apply with the Flash compensation button) are separate. Flash compensation applies to the subject only, and nonflash exposure compensation applies to the background only.

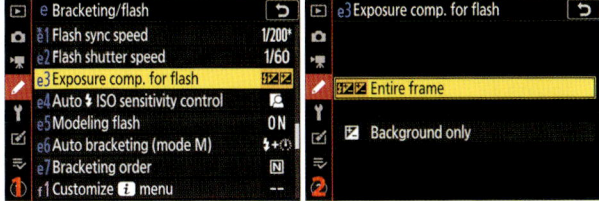

Figure 9.40: Exposure comp. for flash

Use the following steps to choose a flash and exposure compensation combination:

1. Choose e3 Exposure comp. for flash from the e Bracketing/flash menu and scroll to the right (figure 9.40, image 1).
2. Choose either Entire frame or Background only (figure 9.40, image 2). If you choose Background only, the nonflash and flash compensation functions are applied separately. Press the OK button or tap the option to lock in your choice.

Settings Recommendation: I leave my Z6 set to Entire frame for most shooting. If I need to change the light level relationship between the subject and the background, I set the camera to Background only and experiment until I find the best compensation for balance or to emphasize one or the other. Why not spend some time experimenting and learning how to use this technology?

Custom Setting e4: Auto [Flash] ISO Sensitivity Control

Auto [Flash] ISO sensitivity control allows you to select whether the subject (only) or the subject and background is used for automatically adjusting exposure when you are using the Auto ISO sensitivity control and flash. The camera can isolate the subject because it has focus (distance) information from the lens. There are two settings in this function:

- **Subject and background:** The camera examines both the subject and the background when you are using a flash unit and will adjust ISO sensitivity so that both are exposed well (if possible).
- **Subject only:** The Z6 examines only your subject and adjusts the ISO setting to make sure it is exposed well, regardless of the background's exposure.

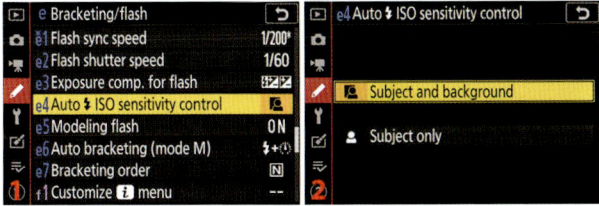

Figure 9.41: Choosing how flash works with ISO-AUTO

Use the following steps to configure how your flash unit works with ISO-AUTO:

1. Choose e4 Auto [flash] ISO sensitivity control from the e Bracketing/Flash menu and scroll to the right (figure 9.41, image 1).
2. Choose either Subject and background or Subject only and press the OK button or tap the option to lock in your choice (figure 9.41, image 2).

Settings Recommendation: To effectively use this function, you will have to decide whether the subject is more important than the background or whether they have equal importance. Normally, I leave my camera set to the default of Subject and background, which can at times lead to higher ISO values as the camera tries to adjust for a larger range of lighting conditions. However, if I am shooting family portraits, I tend to focus more on the subject and may use the Subject only setting, ignoring the background.

Custom Setting e5: Modeling Flash

Modeling flash lets you fire a pulse of flashes to help you see how the light is wrapping around your subject. It works like modeling lights on studio flash units except it pulses instead of shines.

You can press the button to which Preview (depth-of-field preview) has been assigned to see the effect (see **Custom setting f2 Custom control assignment,** page 423).

This function works with Nikon's better Speedlight flash units: SB-5000, SB-910, SB-900, SB-800, SB-700, SB-600, SB-500, and SB-R200. Here's what each of the settings for Modeling flash accomplishes:

- **On:** This setting allows you to see (somewhat) how your flash will light the subject. If you have this setting turned On, you can press the button to which Preview has been assigned to strobe an attached/controlled external Speedlight unit, in a series of rapid pulses. These pulses are continuous and simulate the lighting that the primary flash burst will give your subject. The Modeling flash can be used for only a few seconds at a time to keep from overheating the flash unit, so look quickly.
- **Off:** This means that no Modeling flash will pulse when you press the button to which Preview has been assigned.

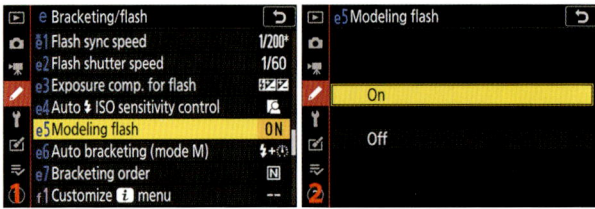

Figure 9.42: Modeling flash

Here are the steps used to configure Modeling flash:

1. Choose e5 Modeling flash from the e Bracketing/flash menu and scroll to the right (figure 9.42, image 1).
2. Choose On or Off and press the OK button or tap the option to lock in the setting (figure 9.42, image 2).

Settings Recommendation: I used to forget that Modeling flash was turned on and when I checked my actual depth of field on a product shot by pressing the Preview button, I would get the modeling light instead of depth of field. I didn't find this feature to be particularly useful, and it often startled me because of the buzzing noise the flash unit makes during the modeling flash cycle. I now leave it set to Off. However, you might like it if you do a lot of studio-style flash photography that requires a modeling light.

Custom Setting e6: Auto Bracketing (Mode M)

The *Auto bracketing (mode M)* function is a series of four settings that let you or the camera control the flash, shutter speed, and aperture in various ways during a bracketing operation, but only when the camera is set to Manual (M) exposure mode. This gives you a little finer control over manual camera settings while you are taking several exposures within a bracket of images.

Here is a list of the four settings under Auto bracketing (mode M) and what each does. The camera controls the selected setting when you are using Manual (M) exposure mode while bracketing. These functions are dependent on how *Photo Shooting Menu > Auto bracketing > Auto bracketing set* (page 271) is configured.

- **Flash/speed:** This setting allows you to control the aperture for best depth of field while still using bracketing. The camera will control the shutter speed. If *Photo Shooting Menu > Auto bracketing > Auto bracketing set* is configured to AE & flash bracketing, the camera will vary the shutter speed and flash level to expose the bracketed images while you control the aperture. If *Photo Shooting Menu > Auto bracketing > Auto bracketing set* is set to AE bracketing, the camera will vary only the shutter speed to get the exposures.
- **Flash/speed/aperture:** This setting is for those who want the camera to control the shutter speed, aperture, and flash while still using bracketing. If *Photo Shooting Menu > Auto bracketing > Auto bracketing set* is configured to AE & flash bracketing, the camera will vary the shutter speed, aperture, and flash level to expose the bracketed images. If *Photo Shooting Menu > Auto bracketing > Auto bracketing set* is set to AE bracketing, the camera will vary the shutter speed and aperture to get the exposures.
- **Flash/aperture:** This setting is for those who want to control the shutter speed for best action shots while still using bracketing. The camera will control the aperture and flash. If *Photo Shooting Menu > Auto bracketing > Auto bracketing set* is configured to AE & flash bracketing, the camera will vary the aperture and flash level to expose the bracketed

images. If *Photo Shooting Menu > Auto bracketing > Auto bracketing set* is set to AE bracketing, the camera will vary only the aperture to get the exposures.

• **Flash only:** This setting is for those who want to control only the flash while using
bracketing. The camera will vary the flash level only to get the bracketed exposures. AE
bracketing obviously does not apply with this setting.

Note: Flash bracketing is performed only with i-TTL or AA (auto aperture) flash control. If
any setting other than Flash only is selected and the flash is not used, the ISO sensitivity
will be fixed at the value for the first shot regardless of the setting selected for Auto ISO
sensitivity control.

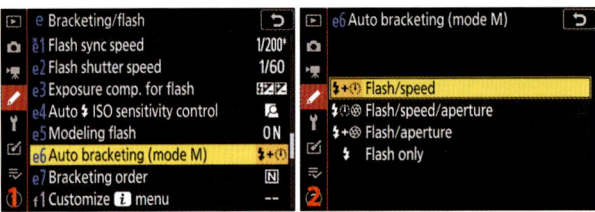

Figure 9.43: Auto bracketing (mode M)

Here are the steps used to configure Auto bracketing (mode M):

1. Choose e6 Auto bracketing (mode M) from the e Bracketing/flash menu and scroll to
   the right (figure 9.43, image 1).
2. Choose one of the four settings on the list and press the OK button or tap the option to
   lock in the setting (figure 9.43, image 2).

Settings Recommendation: Because I am mostly a nature shooter, I often leave my camera
set to Flash/speed so that the camera will control the shutter speed when I take a series of
bracketed images, but I'll control the aperture. That way I can choose how much depth of
field I want to allow in my images.

   If I were shooting important action shots and wanted to bracket, I'd select Flash/aper-
ture so that the camera would control the aperture and flash while I controlled the shutter
speed for action.

   If I were letting only my Speedlight flash control the exposure, as with indoor shots, I
might use Flash only during the bracket.

   Finally, if I wanted to let the camera alone decide how to get the best exposure during
the bracket, I might use Flash/speed/aperture. Then all I have to do is take pictures and let
the camera do the rest. This seems to me to be a small violation of the principle of manual
exposure, though.

Custom Setting e7: Bracketing Order

Bracketing order allows you to choose the order of your exposure settings (normal, over-exposed, and underexposed) during a bracketing operation. There are two bracketing orders available in the Z6. They allow you to control which images are taken first, second, and third in the bracketing series. Here are the three values in the bracket order and what they each mean:

- **MTR** = Metered value (normal exposure)
- **Under** = Underexposed
- **Over** = Overexposed

Next, let's see how these are used during bracketing:

- **MTR > under > over:** With this setting, the normal exposure (MTR) is taken first, followed by the underexposed image, and then the overexposed image. If you are taking a group of five images in your bracket, the camera will take the images like this: *normal exposure > most underexposed > least underexposed > least overexposed > most overexposed*. For WB bracketing, the pattern is *normal > amber > blue*. This does not apply to ADL bracketing.
- **Under > MTR > over:** Using this order for bracketing means that a five-image bracket will be exposed in the following manner: *most underexposed > least underexposed > normal exposure > least overexposed > most overexposed*. For WB bracketing, the pattern is *amber > normal > blue*. This does not apply to ADL bracketing.

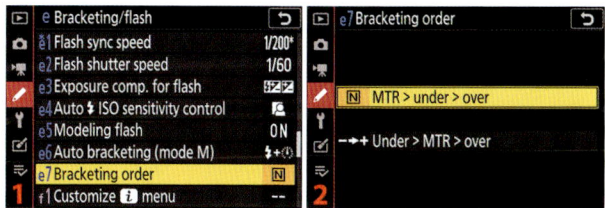

Figure 9.44: Bracketing order

Finally, let's look at the steps to actually configure the Bracketing order:

1. Choose e7 Bracketing order from the e Bracketing/Flash menu and scroll to the right (figure 9.44, image 1).
2. Choose one of the two bracketing orders on the list and press the OK button or tap the option to lock in the setting (figure 9.44, image 2).

Settings Recommendation: I leave Bracketing order set to *MTR > under > over,* so that when the images are displayed in series by the camera, I can see the normal exposure (MTR) first and then watch how it varies as I scroll through the bracketed images. It gets confusing to me if there are nine images in a bracket and I am trying to figure out which one is the MTR image, as I would with the other bracketing order.

If that doesn't suit you, change it to the other direction, *Under > MTR > over*. The normal exposure will be in the middle of the bracket instead of at the beginning. Some prefer the more natural flow of that bracketing order (under to over).

SECTION SIX: f Controls

Custom Settings f1 to f7

There are seven functions in the *f controls* section:

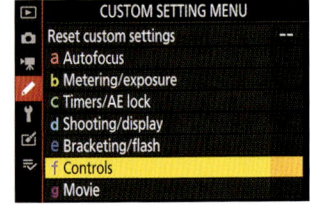

- **f1:** Customize *i* menu
- **f2:** Custom control assignment
- **f3:** OK button
- **f4:** Shutter spd & aperture lock
- **f5:** Customize command dials
- **f6:** Release button to use dial
- **f7:** Reverse indicators

Figure 9.45: *f controls*

Each of these allows you to configure how certain physical controls on your camera work.

All seven "f" functions and their settings—discussed within the following sections—are found on the Custom Setting Menu under the *f Controls* menu item (figure 9.45).

Custom Setting f1: Customize *i* Menu

The *i* Menu for still photography is a grouping of 12 camera functions that can be set from a single screen (figure 9.46A). The *i* Menu can be found by pressing the *i* button on the back of the camera, just below the Sub-selector joystick, while the Photo/movie selector switch is set to still photography mode (switch in top position). The *i* Menu defaults to the functions most commonly used by photographers.

The camera has a selection of 31 functions that can be assigned to those 12 function locations on the *i* Menu. Let's examine how to assign a function to one of the 12 available *i* Menu slots.

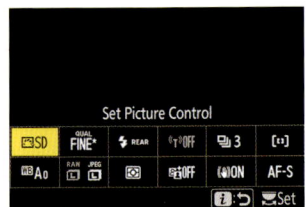

Figure 9.46A: The *i* Menu screen for still photography

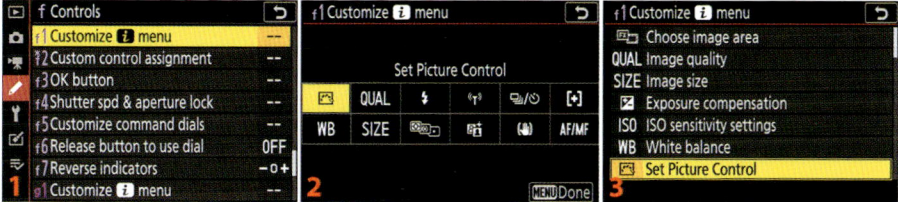

Figure 9.46B: Assigning a function to an *i* Menu location

Use the following steps to assign a function to an *i* Menu location:

1. Choose f1 Customize *i* menu from the f Controls menu and scroll to the right (figure 9.46B, image 1).
2. Highlight a location and press the OK button or tap the option to select it for assignment. The Set Picture Control location is selected for reassignment in figure 9.46B, image 2.
3. A scrollable list of 31 options will now appear (figure 9.46B, image 3). Scroll up or down in the list and highlight an option to replace Set Picture Control. Press the OK button or tap the option to assign it to the selected *i* Menu location, replacing Set Picture Control.
4. Repeat steps 2 and 3 for any other *i* Menu locations you want to change.

The *i* Menu is available for both still images and videos; however, it is separately configurable for the two. See **Custom setting g1 Customize *i* menu** (page 452) for information on customizing the *i* Menu for video.

In the downloadable resource document titled **Appendix A: *i* Menu Photo Functions** we examine each of the 31 assignable functions individually. Most of these functions are fully described in other parts of this book. Therefore, to prevent adding many extra pages (and more weight) to this already large book, we are providing a downloadable PDF document with details on each of the 31 functions. The downloadable resources are found at this web address:
http://rockynook.com/NikonZ6

Custom Setting f2: Custom Control Assignment

The Nikon Z6 has eight programmable controls for still photography, with 45 different functions that may be assigned to those controls. The *Custom control assignment* function presents a programming interface for all of the assignable controls on the camera body and a mounted Nikkor lens that has a programmable L-Fn button. Here is a list of the eight programmable controls (figure 9.47A, image 2):

- Fn1 button
- Fn2 button
- AF-ON button

- Sub-selector joystick directional movement
- Sub-selector joystick center press
- Movie record button
- Lens-Fn button (on a Nikkor lens that has an L-Fn button)
- Lens control ring (on a Nikkor lens that has a control ring—e.g., S lenses)

Some options can be assigned to most of the camera's programmable controls. However, not all options can be assigned to all controls. A few options can be assigned to particular controls only.

When programming the buttons for custom usage you can assign an option to a single button press (figure 9.47A, image 3: *Press* functions), or you can assign a different functionality to be executed when the button is held down while you turn a Command dial (figure 9.47A, image 4: *Press + command dials* functions).

Assigning a Function to a Control

In this subsection, we will consider the individual Nikon Z6 programmable controls and which functions can be assigned to each one (table 9.1). Then we will examine what each assignable function does.

Before we examine the list of functions that can be assigned to the camera's programmable controls, let's choose a sample control to work with. We'll use the Fn1 button.

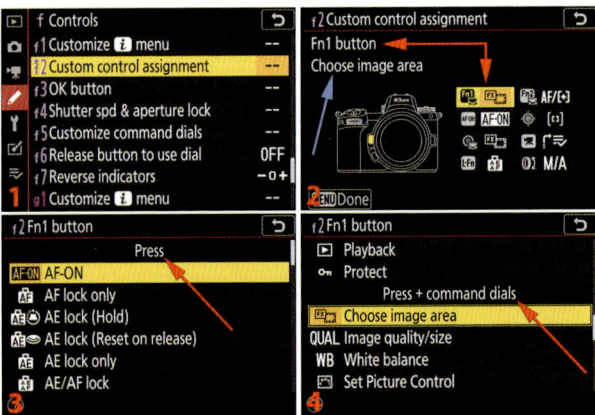

Figure 9.47A: Assigning a custom function to a camera control (sample: Fn1 button)

Use the following steps to assign a custom function to a camera control:

1. Choose f2 Custom control assignment from the f Controls menu and scroll to the right (figure 9.47A, image 1).
2. Highlight a control and press the OK button or tap the control to select it (figure 9.47A, image 2). Each control name is listed in the top-left area of the screen when the control is highlighted, in case you are unsure which control is selected (Fn1 button). Just below

the name of the control is the current function assignment for that control (Choose image area, blue arrow). As you scroll around the screen shown in figure 9.47A, image 2, you will see different control names (such as Fn1 highlighted in yellow) and function assignment names (e.g., Choose image area) appear in the top-left corner. Press the OK button or tap the highlighted yellow option to open the control assignment screen.

3. Figure 9.47A, image 3, shows a list of functions on the control assignment screen. You can choose one to activate when you press the Fn1 button (e.g., AF-ON, AF lock only). This list has an aptly titled heading: Press. If you scroll down on this same screen you will see another distinct list of functions under a new heading, Press + command dials (figure 9.47A, image 4). Each of the functions in this section (e.g., Choose image area, Image quality/size) requires you to hold down the button and turn either of the Command dials. Highlight the function you want to assign to the control and press the OK button or tap the highlighted function option to lock it in for use.

Note: A couple of the controls (i.e., AF-ON button and Lens control ring) have no Press + command dials function list available. The AF-ON button has only Press items, and the Lens control ring, not being a button, has no Press items or Press + command dials items. That wouldn't make sense for a control ring on a lens; therefore, there is just a simple list of items that you can assign to the Lens control ring.

Now let's consider a list of which functions can be assigned to which controls (table 9.1).

Control Assignment Options List

Table 9.1 contains a list of 45 available functions and shows which controls each function can be assigned to. A "✓" means that function is available for assignment to that particular control, whereas a blank cell means it is not available for that control.

The Function Name column in table 9.1 lists the same items that are partially visible in figure 9.47A, images 3 and 4. Each programmable control is listed across the top of the table, in the order in which the camera presents them, with a checkmark showing which functions can be used with that control.

The Lens ring has functions listed that can be used only with certain qualifications, as listed in the table caption (1 and 2).

Function Name	Fn1	Fn2	AF-ON	Joystick Directional	Joystick Center	Movie Record	L-Fn	Lens Ring
Access top item in MY MENU	✓	✓				✓	✓	
Active D-Lighting	✓	✓				✓		
AE/AF lock	✓	✓	✓		✓		✓	
AE lock (hold)	✓	✓	✓		✓	✓	✓	
AE lock only	✓	✓	✓		✓		✓	
AE lock (reset on release)	✓	✓	✓		✓	✓	✓	
AF lock only	✓	✓	✓		✓		✓	
AF-ON	✓	✓	✓		✓		✓	
Aperture								✓ [2]
Auto bracketing	✓	✓				✓		
Bracketing burst	✓	✓			✓		✓	
Center-weighted metering	✓	✓			✓		✓	
Choose image area	✓	✓			✓	✓		
Choose non-CPU lens number	✓	✓			✓	✓		
Exposure compensation								✓ [2]
Exposure delay mode	✓	✓				✓		
[Flash] Disable/ enable	✓	✓			✓		✓	
Flash mode/ Compensation	✓	✓				✓		
Focus (M/A)								✓ [1,2]
Focus mode/ AF-area mode	✓	✓				✓		
Focus point selection				✓				
Framing grid display	✓	✓			✓	✓	✓	
FV lock	✓	✓			✓		✓	
HDR (high dynamic range)	✓	✓				✓		
Highlight-weighted metering	✓	✓			✓		✓	
Image quality/size	✓	✓				✓		
Matrix metering	✓	✓			✓		✓	
Metering	✓	✓				✓		
Multiple exposure	✓	✓				✓		

Function Name	Fn1	Fn2	AF-ON	Joystick Directional	Joystick Center	Movie Record	L-Fn	Lens Ring
MY MENU	✓	✓				✓	✓	
+ NEF (RAW)	✓	✓			✓	✓	✓	
None	✓	✓	✓		✓	✓	✓	✓ 2
Peaking highlights	✓	✓						
Playback	✓	✓					✓	
Preview	✓	✓			✓	✓	✓	
Protect	✓	✓						
Rating	✓	✓						
Same as multi selector				✓				
Select center focus point			✓		✓			
Set Picture Control	✓	✓				✓		
Shutter spd & aperture lock	✓	✓				✓		
Spot metering	✓	✓			✓		✓	
Sync. release selection	✓	✓			✓		✓	
White balance	✓	✓				✓		
Zoom on/off	✓	✓	✓			✓	✓	

Table 9.1: Available functions and the controls to which they can be assigned, in alphabetical order (✓ = Yes; blank = No; 1 = Compatible lenses only; 2 = Regardless of options selected, in MF mode the control ring can be used to adjust focus only)

Assignable Functions Explained

In this subsection you will find a descriptive list of each assignable function mentioned in table 9.1. Since the various functions can be assigned to different controls, I used the words *Assigned control* (in italics) as a replacement for specific button names. When you see *Assigned control,* substitute the control name to which you are going to assign the particular function. The *Assignable Functions List* explains how each function works when you use it.

Assignable Functions List

- **Access top item in MY MENU:** You can use the *Assigned control* to jump directly to the top item in My Menu. This allows you to quickly modify a frequently used menu item.
- **Active D-Lighting** (figure 9.47B): Press and hold the *Assigned control* and rotate either of the Command

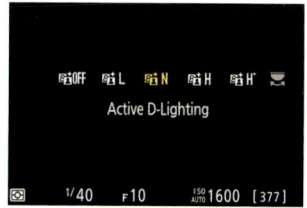

Figure 9.47B: Active D-Lighting

dials to adjust Active D-Lighting (ADL) to one of its six settings: Off (Off), Low (L), Normal (N), High (H), Extra high (H*), and Auto (A). You will see the symbols that represent the various settings—such as L and H—scroll by as you turn either of the Command dials.

- **AE/AF lock:** This allows you to lock AE (exposure) and AF (focus) on the last meter and autofocus system reading when you hold down the *Assigned control.*
- **AE lock (hold):** Enabling this function causes AE (exposure) to lock on the last meter reading when the *Assigned control* is pressed once. It stays locked until you press the *Assigned control* again. In other words, the *Assigned control* toggles AE lock. This is similar to AE lock (Reset on release) except that releasing the shutter does not reset the AE lock hold. You must press the *Assigned control* again to release AE lock.
- **AE lock only:** This allows you to lock AE (exposure) on the last meter reading when you hold down the *Assigned control.*
- **AE lock (reset on release):** Enabling this function causes AE (exposure) to lock on the last meter reading when the *Assigned control* is pressed once. It stays locked until you press the *Assigned control* again or release the shutter. If the light meter goes off, it will also reset this function.
- **AF lock only:** This allows you to lock AF (focus) on the last autofocus reading when you hold down the *Assigned control.*
- **AF-ON:** Pressing the *Assigned control* causes the camera to autofocus. In other words, when you press the *Assigned control* it's as if you had pressed the Shutter-release button halfway down or pressed the AF-ON button, starting autofocus only.
- **Aperture:** This function is assignable to the Lens ring only on a Nikkor lens that has one. When you rotate the Lens ring, the aperture changes. This works in a similar manner to the old days when we had aperture click-stop settings on a lens ring, except the Lens ring on S lenses does not have click stops but turns smoothly and silently.
- **Auto bracketing** (figure 9.47C): Press and hold the *Assigned control* and turn the rear Main command dial to select the number of shots in the bracketed series. Press the *Assigned control* and turn the front Sub-command dial to choose the exposure variation between each image. For more information on Auto bracketing and what the symbols on the screen mean, refer to the **Auto Bracketing** section in the **Photo Shooting Menu** chapter (page 269).

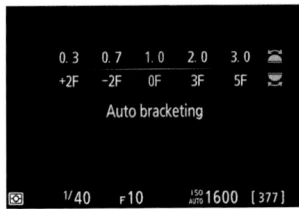

Figure 9.47C: Auto bracketing

- **Bracketing burst:** Normally, when you shoot a bracketing sequence, with the Release mode set to Single frame Release mode, you have to press the Shutter-release button (or AF-ON button) once for each image in the bracket. The only way to shoot all the images in the bracketed series without letting up on the Shutter-release button is to use Continuous L or H Release mode. If you assign Bracketing burst to a button, you can hold down the *Assigned control* while also holding down the Shutter-release button and the camera will take all the images in the bracket without letup. This seems a bit redundant to me. I think I'd rather just set the Release mode to Continuous L or Continuous H Release mode and shoot the bracketed burst. This applies to AE, Flash, and ADL bracketing, which each take one image for each shutter release. WB bracketing is mentioned in the manual, too, but because WB bracketing normally causes the camera to take the entire bracket in one shutter release, I don't see the point of using the Bracketing burst option. If you use this function for WB bracketing and hold down the Shutter-release button, you'll create multiple groups of bracketed images on your memory card. Be careful with this function when using WB bracketing.

- **Center-weighted metering:** If you do not use Center-weighted metering as your primary metering system but want to use it occasionally, you can turn on Center-weighted metering by holding down the *Assigned control*. When you release the button, the camera returns to your customary meter type, such as Spot, Matrix, or Highlight-weighted metering.

- **Choose image area** (figure 9.47D): You may press the *Assigned control* and rotate either of the Command dials to choose one of the camera's five Image area formats. As you turn a Command dial, you can select from the following choices: FX (36×24), DX (24×16), 1:1 (24×24), 16:9 (36×20). Refer to **Choose image area** under the **Photo Shooting Menu** (page 174) for more information.

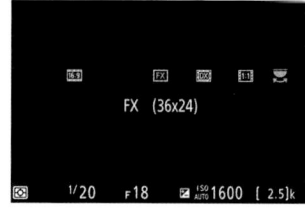

Figure 9.47D: Choose image area

- **Choose non-CPU lens number** (figure 9.47E): If you have registered non-CPU lenses under *Setup Menu > Non-CPU lens data,* you'll be able to hold down the *Assigned control* while rotating either Command dial to scroll through a list of up to 20 non-CPU lenses. As you rotate the Command dial, the screen will display the non-CPU lens focal length (200mm) and maximum aperture (F4), along with the number of the lens (No. 1 to No. 20). For example, when I mount my registered

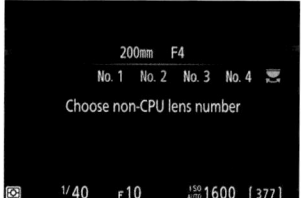

Figure 9.47E: Choose non-CPU lens number

AI Nikkor 200mm f/4 non-CPU lens on my Z6, I can press the *Assigned control,* rotate a Command dial, and watch the lenses scroll by until I see 200mm, F4, and No. 2. When you see the mounted lens appear on the camera displays, release the *Assigned control,* and the Z6 knows which non-CPU lens has been selected from the 20 available choices. Remember, you must have already registered at least one non-CPU lens in the camera for this function to be of benefit to you. See the **Non-CPU Lens Data** function in the **Setup Menu** (page 493) chapter for more information.

- **Exposure compensation:** This function is assignable only to the Lens ring on a Nikkor lens that has one. When you turn the Lens ring you will see the +/– Exposure compensation symbol appear on your screen and you will immediately see the results of the compensation on your subject. This works the same way as using the +/– Exposure compensation button, except that you get no EV step readout on the screen (e.g., +0.3, –0.7 +1.0); you just see the results reflected in the brightening and darkening of your subject. This function is especially useful when the Live histogram is on the screen since it lets you adjust the exposure and watch the histogram instantly respond. If you see the

+/– Exposure compensation symbol on your screen and have no idea what the actual value of the compensation is, just press the +/– Exposure compensation button to see a display of the EV compensation value (e.g., +0.3, +1.0)

- **Exposure delay mode** (figure 9.47F): Press the *Assigned control* and rotate either of the Command dials to choose an exposure delay of 1, 2, or 3 seconds. This is the same as setting an exposure delay with *Custom Setting Menu > d Shooting/display > d4 Exposure delay mode* (page 402). As you press the *Assigned control* and rotate a Command dial, the screen will show three characters signifying delay (DLY), and one of the following: Off, 0.2s, 0.5s, 1s, 2s, or 3s. For example, if

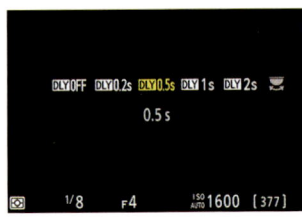

Figure 9.47F: Exposure delay mode

you select 3s, the camera will wait (delay) three seconds before it fires the shutter. This allows photographer-induced vibrations to die down, resulting in a sharper picture.

- **[Flash] Disable/enable:** If you have a flash unit mounted on the camera and it is currently turned off, the camera will use Front-curtain sync while you hold the *Assigned control* down. If the flash is turned on, it will not fire while you hold the *Assigned control* down.

- **Flash mode/compensation** (figure 9.47G): With this function you can press and hold the *Assigned control* and turn the front Sub-command dial to add or subtract flash exposure compensation (e.g., +0.3, –0.7), or the rear Main command dial to choose a Flash mode (e.g., fill flash, red-eye reduction). For more information on the various flash modes, see the **Flash Mode** heading in the **Photo Shooting Menu** chapter (page 256).

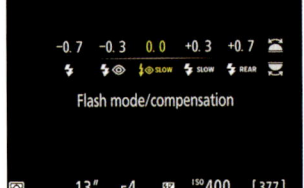

Figure 9.47G: Flash mode/ compensation

- **Focus (M/A):** This function can be assigned only to a Nikkor lens with a Lens ring. When you turn the Lens ring in manual focus (M) mode, you will have full control of focusing the camera. Be sure to enable focus Peaking (page 86) to help you obtain very accurate manual focus. When using autofocus (A), you can top off the focus by turning the Lens ring. If you have enabled focus Peaking and hold down the Shutter-release button halfway or press the AF-ON button while turning the Lens ring, focus Peaking will assist you with fine-tuning the camera's autofocus choice.

- **Focus mode/AF-area mode** (figure 9.47H): Hold down the *Assigned control* and turn the rear Main command dial to change the Focus mode (e.g. AF-S, AF-C), or the front Sub-command dial to change the AF-area mode (e.g., Pinpoint AF, Single-point AF).

- **Focus point selection:** This function is assignable only to the Sub-selector joystick directional movement (left, right, up, down, and diagonal) capability. This is the default setting for the joystick. It allows you to use

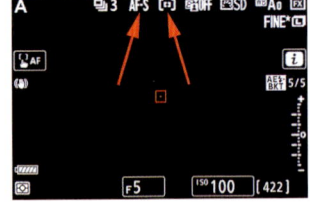

Figure 9.47H: Focus mode/AF-area mode

the joystick to move the AF point around in the grid of 273 AF points so that you can select the best AF point for your subject.

- **Framing grid display** (figure 9.47I): Press the *Assigned control* to toggle on and off a convenient Framing grid to assist with leveling horizons and alignment with architectural features.

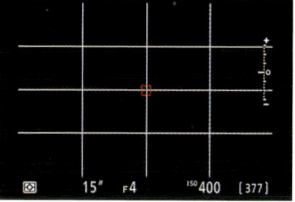

Figure 9.47I: Framing grid display

- **FV lock:** Pressing the *Assigned control* will cause the external Speedlight to emit a monitor preflash and lock the flash output to the level determined by the preflash. The flash output level will remain locked until you press the *Assigned control* a second time.

- **HDR (high dynamic range)** (figure 9.47J): Using this function is similar to using the *Photo Shooting Menu > HDR (high dynamic range)* function (page 283). Press the *Assigned control* and turn the rear Main command dial to select one of the following HDR modes: Off, On (single photo), or On (series). Press the *Assigned control* and turn the front Sub-command dial to select the Exposure differential: 1EV, 2EV, 3EV, and Auto. You cannot adjust the Smoothing (Low, Normal, or High)

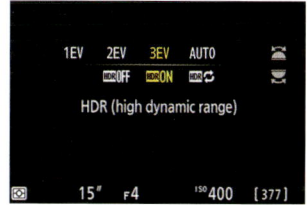

Figure 9.47J: HDR (high dynamic range)

subsetting (not shown) unless you use the *Photo Shooting Menu > HDR (high dynamic range)* function directly. However, this function does obey the current Smoothing setting in the HDR (high dynamic range) function (page 284).

- **Highlight-weighted metering:** If you do not use Highlight-weighted metering as your primary metering system but want to use it occasionally, you can turn on Highlight-weighted metering by holding down the *Assigned control*. When you release the button, the camera returns to your customary meter type, such as Center-weighted, Matrix, or Spot metering.

- **Image quality/size** (figure 9.47K): Press and hold the *Assigned control* while turning the front Sub-command dial to adjust the Image size (e.g., L, M, S), or the rear Main command dial to adjust the Image quality (e.g., RAW, FINE).

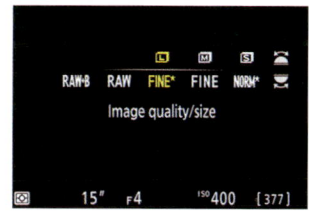

Figure 9.47K: Image quality/size

- **Matrix metering:** If you do not use Matrix metering as your primary metering system but want to use it occasionally, you can turn on Matrix metering by holding down the *Assigned control*. When you release the *Assigned control*, the camera returns to your customary meter type, such as Spot, Center-weighted, or Highlight-weighted metering.

- **Metering** (figure 9.47L): When you press and hold the *Assigned control* and turn either of the camera's Command dials, you can select from the following

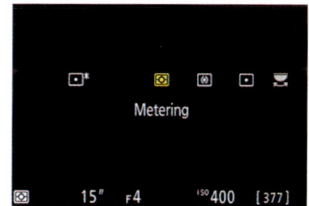

Figure 9.47L: Metering

Metering modes: Matrix metering, Center-weighted metering, Spot metering, and Highlight-weighted metering. The camera will remain in the chosen Metering mode until you change it. This function a shortcut method imitating the *Photo Shooting Menu > Metering* mode (page 235).

- **Multiple exposure** (figure 9.47M): Using this function is the same as using the *Photo Shooting Menu > Multiple exposure* function (page 277). Press the *Assigned control* and turn the rear Main command dial to select one of the following Multiple exposure modes: Off, On (single photo), On (series). Press the *Assigned control* and turn the front Sub-command dial to select the Number of shots (2 to 10). You cannot adjust the Over-

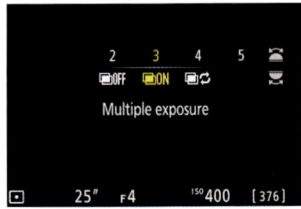

Figure 9.47M: Multiple exposure

lay mode, Keep all exposures, Overlay shooting, and Select first exposure (NEF) subsettings (not shown) without using the *Photo Shooting Menu > Multiple exposure* function directly. However, this function does obey the current Multiple exposure settings entered via the Photo Shooting Menu. See the Multiple exposure function on page 277 for more information.

- **MY MENU** (figure 9.47N): Pressing the *Assigned control* opens the MY MENU display with the first item highlighted. You can then access any of the other items on MY MENU by scrolling down or tapping the menu item with your fingertip. This is a quick way to get to your favorite menu items without digging around in the camera's regular menu system. There are only two items on my camera's MY MENU currently (Auto

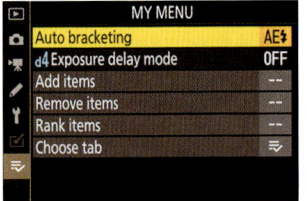

Figure 9.47N: MY MENU

bracketing and Exposure delay mode), but you can have as many as 20 items available.

- **+ NEF (RAW):** If you are a regular JPEG shooter and have any form of JPEG selected as the Image quality setting, you can press the *Assigned control* once (do not hold) to temporarily add a NEF (RAW) image to your JPEG capture. The camera will take a JPEG and a NEF (RAW) picture when you press the Shutter-release button. Once you take the JPEG + NEF (RAW) combo picture, the camera switches back to JPEG. If you decide not to take the NEF (RAW) picture before you press the Shutter-release button, just press the *Assigned control* again to return to JPEG mode. This function does not work with TIFF or NEF (RAW) Image quality modes, only JPEG mode.

- **None:** When this option is set, the *Assigned control* does nothing.

- **Peaking highlights** (figure 9.47O): Pressing and holding the *Assigned control* while turning the rear Main command dial to any setting besides Off, enables the Peaking highlights function. Choose from PEAK OFF, PEAK 1, PEAK 2, and PEAK 3. The higher numbers increase the sensitivity and saturation of Peaking. Pressing and holding the *Assigned control* while turning the front Sub-command dial allows you to select a

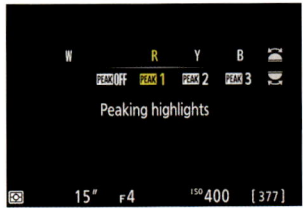

Figure 9.47O: Peaking highlights

Peaking highlights color: Red (R), Yellow (Y), Blue (B), or White (W). For more information on focus Peaking, see the **Custom Setting d10: Peaking Highlights** subheading earlier in this chapter (page 409).

- **Playback:** This option causes the *Assigned control* to act as if you had pressed the Playback button. Nikon included this so that you could play back images when using a big telephoto lens that requires two hands to use.

- **Preview:** The Z6 shows accurate depth of field for the live view of your subject in the EVF and on the Monitor, but only down to f/5.6. The camera would have difficulty autofocusing if allowed to stop down more than that, so the Z6 limits its smallest aperture with live image preview to f/5.6. To overcome this limitation, the Preview function is available for assignment to a convenient camera control. Pressing the *Assigned control* will activate Depth-of-field preview and stop the aperture all the way down to its actual setting (e.g., f/11, f/16, f/22), showing you the actual depth of field the current aperture offers.

- **Protect** (figure 9.47P): Display an important image you want to protect on the camera's Monitor (or EVF). To prevent accidental deletion, press the *Assigned control* and the image will be locked from deletion. Also, a protection key symbol will be displayed in the top-left corner of the image. As you scroll through your images, the protected pictures will have this symbol. Press the *Assigned control* again when an image with the symbol is displayed and the image protection—and symbol—will be removed.

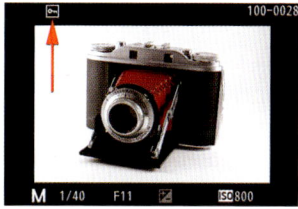

Figure 9.47P: Protect

- ★ **Rating** (figure 9.47Q): Display a picture to which you want to give a rating, then press and hold the *Assigned control*. The will camera present you with a 1–5 star rating scale (★ to ★★★★★) on the bottom-left corner of the screen (figure 9.47, bottom-left red arrow). Turn the rear Main command dial to add or subtract yellow stars. For example, if you rate an image as a four-star image, you will see four yellow stars in the

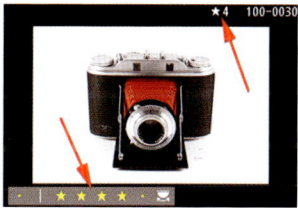

Figure 9.47Q: Rating

lower-left area of the screen. When you later view the picture you will see the symbol displayed in the upper-right area (★4, top-right arrow). This symbol is a reminder that the image was previously rated as 4 out of 5.

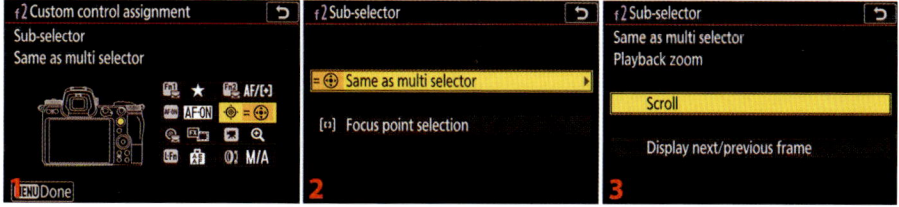

Figure 9.47R: Same as multi selector (scroll or display next/previous frame)

- **Same as multi selector** (figure 9.47R): Normally the Sub-selector joystick is set to Focus point selection, the factory default setting. However, the Sub-selector joystick's left, right, up, and down motions can be programmed to duplicate the Multi selector pad's motions by selecting Same as multi selector. This does not affect the Sub-selector's center press, which is a separately assignable control. Once you have selected Same as multi selector, you must choose what happens when a zoomed-in image is displayed on the screen. Choose Same as multi selector and scroll to the right (image 2). The following screen (image 3) gives you two choices that affect what happens when you have a zoomed-in image on the display. If you move the joystick with Scroll selected, the camera will scroll around within the zoomed-in image. If you move the joystick with Display next/previous frame selected, the camera will change images, according to which direction you press the joystick, instead of scrolling around within the zoomed-in image. The camera will stay zoomed in when it changes to a previous or next image. (**Settings Recommendation:** Since I normally zoom into an image to check it out well, I find that Scroll usually works best for me. However, if I want to quickly compare a certain point between two or three zoomed-in images, I can choose Display next/previous frame, and then scroll back and forth between the images with the joystick. Of course, remember that this assignment duplicates the functionality already present in the Multi selector, so you may just want to ignore this function.)
- **Select center focus point:** Pressing the *Assigned control* causes the camera to jump from whatever focus point (AF point) you were using to the center AF point instead.
- **Shutter spd & aperture lock** (figure 9.47S): Simply press the *Assigned control* and rotate the front Main command dial to lock the camera's shutter speed when you are using Shutter-priority (S) and Manual (M) modes. Or, press the *Assigned control* and turn the front Sub-command dial to lock the aperture setting when using Aperture-priority (A) and Manual (M) modes. A tiny "L" will appear next to the settings while they are locked (red arrows). Hold the *Assigned control* and turn the dial again to unlock a setting.

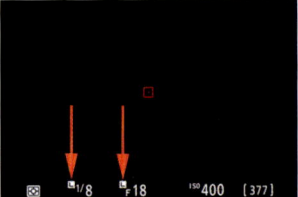

Figure 9.47S: Shutter spd & aperture lock

- **Set Picture Control** (figure 9.47T): Press the *Assigned control* and rotate the rear Main command dial to change which Picture Control (page 200) the camera uses for JPEG images.
- **Spot metering:** If you do not use Spot metering as your primary metering system but want to use it occasionally, you can turn on Spot metering by holding down the *Assigned control*. When you release the button, the camera returns to your customary meter type, such as Matrix, Center-weighted, or Highlight-weighted metering.

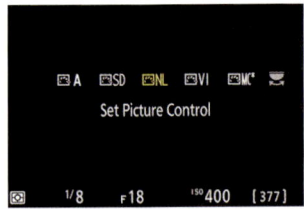

Figure 9.47T: Set Picture Control

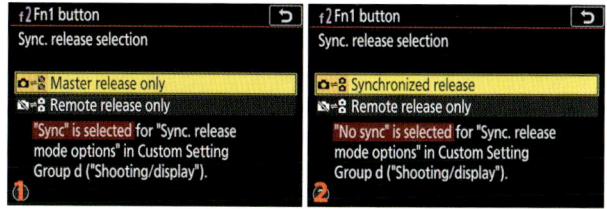

Figure 9.47U: Sync. release selection—you will see different choices depending on how *Custom setting d3 Sync. release mode options* is configured (page 401).

- **Sync. release selection** (figure 9.47U): When you are using a wireless transmitter such as the WR-T10 transmitter found in the Nikon WR-10 Wireless Remote Controller kit— to control multiple remote cameras (Master/Remote relationship) for synchronized shutter release, you can press the *Assigned control* to take synchronized pictures with multiple cameras in different ways, as described in paragraphs a and b below. This function depends on how *Custom Setting Menu > d Shooting/display > d3 Sync. release mode options* is configured (page 401). You will need to make a Sync. release selection immediately upon assigning this function to a control. After that you will press and hold the *Assigned control* while firing the shutter to execute your choice. To choose a different Sync. release selection you will need to reuse *Custom Setting Menu > f controls > f2 Custom control assignment > [Assigned control] > Sync. release selection* and choose a new release style. Here are the selections and how they work:
  - If you have chosen Sync in Custom setting d3, the following two items are available:
    a. **Master release only:** If you choose Master release only from the screen shown in figure 9.47U, image 1, you can keep the *Assigned control* pressed down to take pictures with the Master camera only.
    b. **Remote release only:** If you choose Remote release only from the screen found in figure 9.47U, image 1, you can keep the *Assigned control* pressed down to take pictures with the Remote camera(s) only.
  - If you have selected No sync in Custom setting d3, the following two items are available:
    a. **Synchronized release:** If you choose Synchronized release from the screen found in figure 9.47U, image 2, you can keep the *Assigned control* pressed down to synchronize the shutter releases on both the Master and Remote cameras.
    b. **Remote release:** If you choose Remote release only from the screen found in figure 9.47U, image 2, you can keep the *Assigned control* pressed down to take pictures with the Remote camera(s) only.
- **White balance** (figure 9.47V): Press and hold the *Assigned control* while turning the rear Main command dial to select a White balance type (e.g., Auto, Direct sunlight, Cloudy). While still pressing the *Assigned control,* you can turn the front Sub-command dial to select a sub-option if that White balance type has any sub-options (e.g., for Auto, a sub-option is A0 Keep

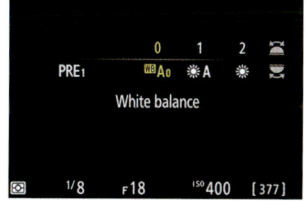

Figure 9.47V: White balance

white (reduce warm colors)). See **White balance** on page 116 for more information on options and sub-options.

- **Zoom on/off** (figure 9.47W): When you first assign this function to a control, you will be presented with a screen that asks you to choose a magnification level. Most of us will choose 1:1 (100%) because that is an accurate pixel-peeping level for viewing already taken images and for verifying focus or examining detail in a not-yet-captured subject. This function works for both. To use it, press the *Assigned control* and the image will immediately zoom in to the magnification level you assigned.

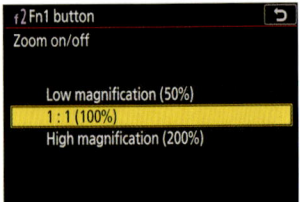

Figure 9.47W: Zoom on/off

Settings Recommendation: Here are the assignments I make for the controls on my camera:

- **Fn1:** Preview
- **Fn2:** Focus mode/AF area-mode
- **AF-ON:** AF-ON
- **Sub-selector joystick directional control:** Same as multi selector
- **Sub-selector joystick button press:** Select center focus point
- **Movie record button:** Zoom on/off (Movie mode has own settings)
- **Lens Fn (L-Fn) button:** AE lock only
- **Lens control ring:** Focus (M/A)

Of course, you may desire a completely different configuration that works better for your style of photography. You have a large number of options available!

Custom Setting f3: OK Button

The *OK button* setting determines how the button in the center of the Multi selector pad works in two different camera modes:

- **Shooting mode** is in force when you are actually using the camera to take pictures through the Viewfinder.
- **Playback mode** is in use when you are examining pictures you've already taken on the rear Monitor.

Let's examine each mode in detail.

Shooting Mode

Now we will examine the options available for the OK button (Multi selector center button) when you are actively taking pictures (Shooting mode), not viewing already taken pictures (Playback mode, see next subsection).

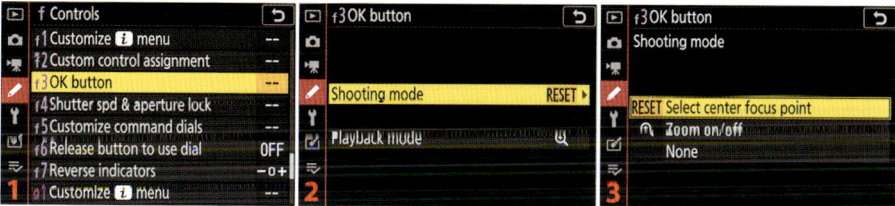

Figure 9.48A: OK button (Shooting mode)

Use these steps to begin configuration of the OK button for Shooting mode:

1. Follow the screen flow shown in figure 9.48A, images 1–2 (*f Controls* > *f3 OK button* > *Shooting mode*), until you arrive at the third screen in the series.
2. Choose one of the three choices, according to the upcoming descriptions of each selection (figure 9.48A, image 3). Press the OK button or tap the option to lock in the setting.

The three Shooting mode selections are as follows (figure 9.48A, image 3):

- **Select center focus point:** Often when shooting, you'll be using the Multi selector pad with your thumb to move the selected focus point (AF point) around the Viewfinder to focus on the most appropriate area of your subject. When you are done, you have to scroll the AF point back to the center. However, if Select center focus point is chosen, you can press the OK button to make the focus point pop back to the center point of the Viewfinder. This is the default action of the button.

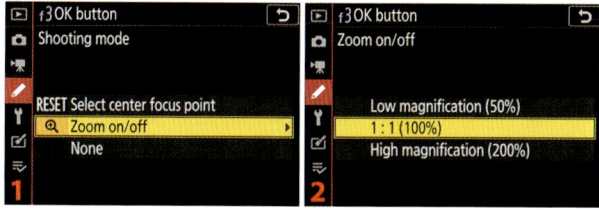

Figure 9.48B: OK button – Zoom on/off

- **Zoom on/off:** Figure 9.48B continues where figure 9.48A ends. If you choose Zoom on/off, you will need to select a magnification level (i.e., 50%, 100%, 200%), which will allow you to pixel-peep your subject for things like correct focus *before* taking the picture. You can preview your subject with the Monitor or EVF by pressing the OK button to zoom in to a magnified view and then pressing OK again to zoom back out to a normal view. While zoomed in, you can scroll around the screen with the Multi selector pad, make any adjustments (such as fine-tuning focus), and then zoom back out. You can take the picture while zoomed in or out.

- **None:** Nothing happens when you press the OK button in Shooting mode.

Playback Mode

Now let's examine how the OK button can be used in Playback mode. Playback mode is used when you are examining images on the camera's Monitor after you have taken them.

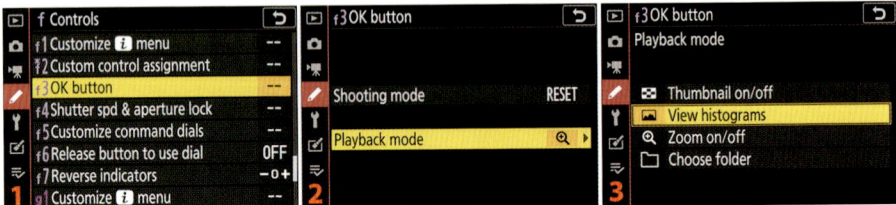

Figure 9.48C: OK button (Playback mode)

Use these steps to configure the OK button for Playback mode:

1. Follow the screen flow shown in figure 9.48C, images 1–2 (*f Controls > f3 OK button > Playback mode*), until you arrive at the third screen in the series.
2. Choose one of the four options on the list, according to the upcoming descriptions (figure 9.48C, image 3). If you choose Zoom on/off, you'll need to scroll to the right and select one of the three subsettings (use figure 9.48F in the upcoming subsection called **Zoom on/off**). If you select Choose folder, you'll also need to be aware of some additional screens your camera will present you with (use figure 9.48G in the upcoming subsection called **Choose folder**). Press the OK button or tap the option to lock in the setting.

There are four selections in Playback mode (figure 9.48C, image 3), which are described in the following subsections.

Thumbnail On/Off

This feature allows you to switch from viewing one image on your camera's Monitor to viewing multiple thumbnails instead. It's a toggle, so you can press the OK button to turn thumbnail view on and off. In figure 9.48D, image 1, Thumbnail on/off has been selected.

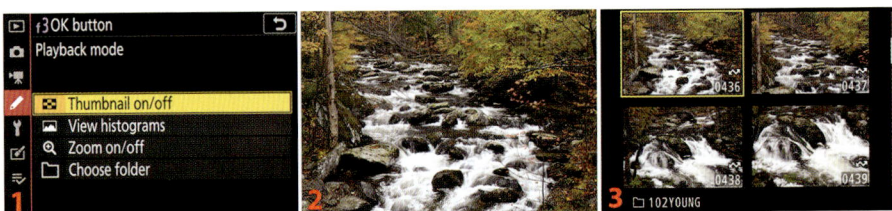

Figure 9.48D: OK button (Playback mode – Thumbnail on/off)

Use the following steps to configure and use Thumbnail on/off:

1. Figure 9.48D continues where figure 9.48C ends. Select Thumbnail on/off from the Playback mode menu and press the OK button or tap the option to select it (figure 9.48D, image 1).
2. Now when you press the Playback button and view a picture on the Monitor, like the river cascades picture in figure 9.48D, image 2, you can then press the OK button to get a thumbnail view of that image along with the three subsequent images (figure 9.48D, image 3). If you press the OK button repeatedly, the camera will toggle between normal view and thumbnail view with each button press.

View Histograms

I discovered the View histograms feature while I was writing a previous Nikon book, and now I immediately switch my new Nikons to this setting when I get one. Even though the Z6 has a live histogram and I use it, I still like to easily view the histogram after I've taken an image.

When the OK button function is set to View histograms, I can have an image open on my Monitor, and then press and hold the OK button to view a luminance histogram. This saves a lot of scrolling around through the data, RGB histograms, and information screens. It's a quick histogram view that disappears when the OK button is released. Great feature! Let's see how to configure and use it.

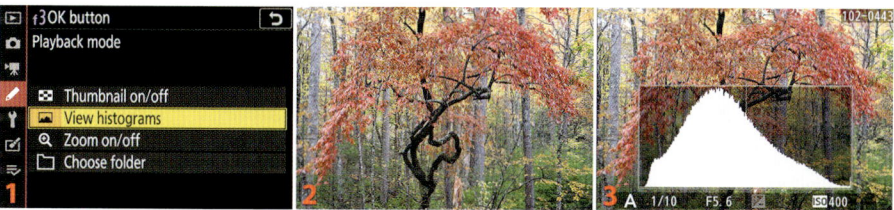

Figure 9.48E: OK button (Playback mode – View histograms)

Use the following steps to configure and use View histograms:

1. Figure 9.48E continues where figure 9.48C ends. Select View histograms from the Playback mode menu and press the OK button or tap the option to select it (figure 9.48E, image 1).
2. Now when you press the Playback button and view a picture on the Monitor, like this lovely tree in the Great Smoky Mountains (figure 9.48E, image 2), you can then press and hold the OK button to see a luminance histogram for that image (figure 9.48D, image 3). This is an extremely convenient setting for those who use the histogram regularly.

Zoom On/Off

If you want to zoom into your image on the Monitor without using the normal zoom in and out buttons, this is a good feature for you. If you have an image showing on the Monitor and Zoom on/off is selected, you can press the OK button to jump immediately to one of three levels of zoom. It works like a toggle switch—pressing the OK button a second time takes you back to a normal full-screen view.

Here is a description of the three levels of zoom available under this setting (Low to High):

- **Low magnification** seems to be the same as viewing the image at about 50 percent pixel-peeping level. Pressing the Zoom in button three times brings you to the same 50 percent level.
- **Medium magnification (1:1)** is for viewing the image at about 100 percent. This is like pressing the Zoom in button five times.
- **High magnification** is around the 200 percent viewing level. This is like pressing the Zoom in button six times.

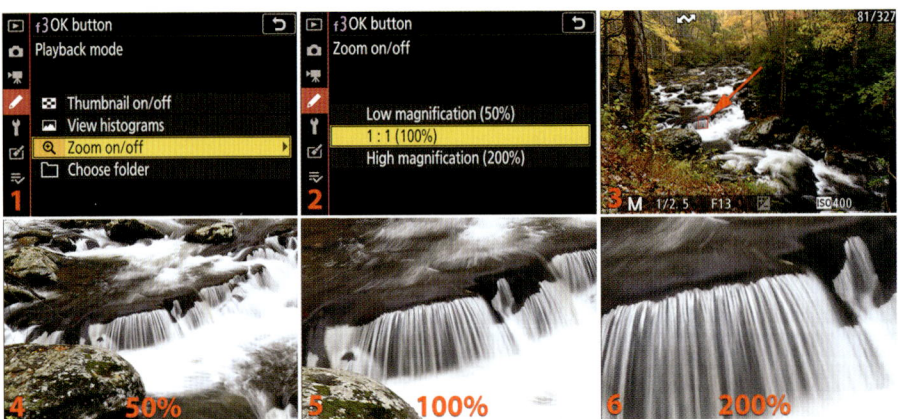

Figure 9.48F: OK button (Playback mode – Zoom on/off settings)

Use the following steps to configure and use Zoom on/off:

1. Figure 9.48F continues where figure 9.48C ends. Select Zoom on/off from the Playback mode menu and scroll to the right (figure 9.48F, image 1).
2. Select Low magnification (50%), 1:1 (100%), or High magnification (200%) from the Zoom on/off list and press the OK button or tap the option to select the setting (figure 9.48F, image 2).
3. Press the Playback button to display a picture on the Monitor (as shown in figure 9.48F, image 3, where you see cascades and a small waterfall in the Great Smoky Mountains).
4. Now press the OK button and the camera will immediately zoom in to view the picture on the Monitor (or EVF) at whatever magnification level you chose in step 2. The zoom display centers on the focus point used to take the image (figure 9.48F, image 3,

red arrow). Images 4, 5, and 6 in figure 9.48F match the zoom levels selectable in figure 9.48F, image 2: Low magnification (50%), 1:1 (100%), and High magnification (200%).

Note: If you are using Thumbnail view, you can select from a series of images on the Monitor. When you have one of the images selected, even though it is not full size, you can press the OK button and the image will be enlarged to whatever magnification level you previously selected. When you press the button again, the camera will switch back to Thumbnail view.

Choose Folder

When you select Choose folder, you will have a folder selection screen available while you are examining an image in Playback mode. To open the folder selection screen, press the OK button.

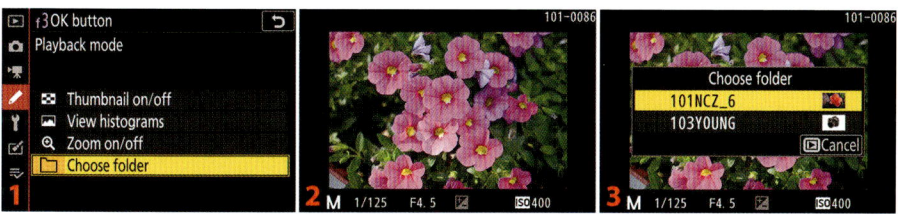

Figure 9.48G: OK button (Playback mode – Choose folder)

Use the following steps to configure and use Choose folder. (**Note:** The camera will now show images from the folder you have selected. If you have *Playback Menu > Playback folder* set to All or NCZ_6, the camera will switch folders, and even memory cards, when it gets to the end of the current folder):

1. Figure 9.48G continues where figure 9.48C ends. Select Choose folder from the Playback mode menu (figure 9.48G, image 1). Press the OK button or tap the option to select it.
2. Press the Playback button to display a picture on the Monitor (figure 9.48G, image 2). When you press the OK button, you will be presented with the screen shown in figure 9.48G, image 3. Highlight a folder name and press the OK button or tap the option to use that folder until you change to a different one later.

If *Playback Menu > Playback folder* is set to Current, the camera will show only the images in the current folder and will display no other images from any other folder or card.

    Settings Recommendation: I have my camera set so that when I press the OK button in Shooting mode, it jumps to the center AF point. This saves time because I don't have to scroll back manually.

    When I press the OK button in Playback mode, I have the camera show me a luminance histogram. I absolutely adore being able to see a histogram for an image I just took by pressing the OK button instead of scrolling to the histogram screen. This saves time by letting me see my camera's histogram when I need it most, right after taking the picture.

Custom Setting f4: Shutter Spd & Aperture Lock

Shutter spd & aperture lock is an interesting function that allows you to lock the shutter speed at the currently selected value when shooting in Shutter-priority (S) or Manual (M) mode. You can also lock the aperture at its current value when you are shooting in Aperture-priority (A) or Manual (M) mode. This function does not apply to and will not work when shooting in Programmed auto (P) mode.

You will need to choose a shutter speed or aperture before using this function. The camera will lock the currently selected shutter speed or aperture until you unlock it later.

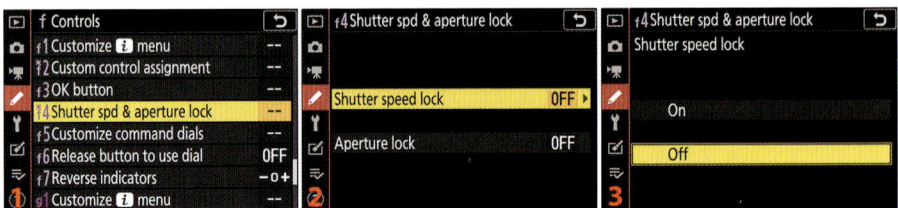

Figure 9.49: Selecting Shutter spd & aperture lock

Use the following steps to keep your shutter speed or aperture from changing, according to which exposure mode you are using:

1. Choose Shutter spd & aperture lock from the f Controls menu and scroll to the right (figure 9.49, image 1).
2. You will now see two selections, Shutter speed lock and Aperture lock (figure 9.49, image 2). When you are using Aperture-priority (A) mode, Shutter speed lock will be grayed out and unavailable. When you are using Shutter-priority (S) mode, Aperture lock will be grayed out and unavailable. If you have the camera set to Manual (M) mode, Shutter speed lock and Aperture lock are both available (figure 9.49, image 2). When the camera is set to Programmed-auto (P) mode, the entire Shutter spd & aperture lock function is grayed out and unavailable. If your shutter speed has already been chosen, select Shutter speed lock, or if an aperture has already been chosen, select Aperture lock (according to which exposure mode you are currently using) and scroll to the right.
3. Choose either On or Off from the list. In figure 9.49, image 3, Off has been chosen for Shutter speed lock. On locks the setting (Shutter speed or Aperture), whereas Off allows you to continue adjusting that setting. (The screens for Aperture lock are not shown in figure 9.49, but they work exactly the same way as Shutter speed lock.) Press the OK button or tap the option to select it.

Settings Recommendation: If I were shooting in a studio, under carefully controlled lighting, and wanted to lock the shutter speed or aperture to a value that would not change throughout the session, this function would do the job well. It can be a protection for when you do not want a value to change.

Custom Setting f5: Customize Command Dials

Customize command dials does exactly what it sounds like—it lets you change how the Command dials operate. There are several operations you can modify:

- Reverse rotation
- Change main/sub
- Menus and playback
- Sub-dial frame advance

Let's examine each of these items and the screens and steps used to change them.

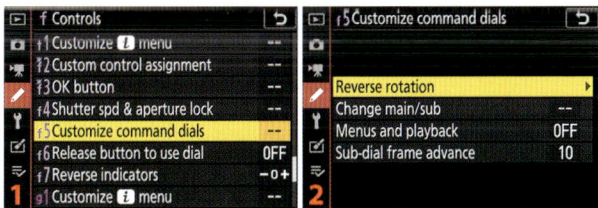

Figure 9.50A: Customize command dials

Use the following steps to change the functionality of the Command dials:

1. Choose f5 Customize command dials from the f Controls menu and scroll to the right (figure 9.50A, image 1).
2. Choose one of the four selections from the list (figure 9.50A, image 2). Use the screens and steps under each of the following sections to configure the four listed functions (figures 9.50B to 9.50G).

Reverse Rotation

Reverse rotation allows you to change what happens when you rotate the Command dials in a particular direction. You can reverse Command dial operations with this setting. There are two selections:

- **Exposure compensation:** When you press and hold the Exposure compensation button and turn the Sub-command dial clockwise, it increases the amount of compensation. If you place a check mark in this box and select Done, the camera will decrease the amount of compensation when you turn the Sub-command dial clockwise.
- **Shutter speed/aperture:** Normally, when the Z6 is set to Aperture-priority (A) or Manual (M) mode and you rotate the Sub-command dial clockwise, the aperture gets smaller. If you put a check mark next to Shutter speed/aperture, the aperture will instead get larger when you turn the Sub-command dial clockwise. The same goes for shutter speed in Shutter-priority (S) and Manual (M) modes. Normally, turning the rear Main

command dial clockwise slows down the shutter speed. If you put a check mark next to Shutter speed/aperture, the shutter speed will instead get faster when you turn the Main command dial clockwise. Finally, when you override the aperture setting in Programmed auto (P) mode by turning the Main command dial clockwise, instead of decreasing the size of the aperture, it increases it.

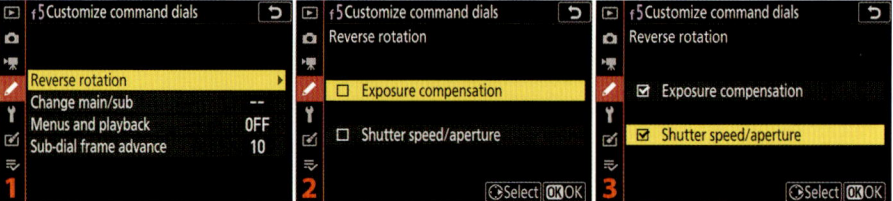

Figure 9.50B: Customize command dials (Reverse rotation)

Here are the steps to change the rotation direction of the Command dials:

1. Continuing from figure 9.50A, image 2, select Reverse rotation and scroll to the right (figure 9.50B, image 1).
2. Highlight Exposure compensation or Shutter speed/aperture and scroll to the right, or tap the option, to set a check mark in the corresponding small check box (figure 9.50B, images 2 and 3). In figure 9.50B, image 3, both selections have a check mark. Press or touch OK to lock in the setting.

Settings Recommendation: I leave the Command dials rotation set to factory default. I find life confusing enough without my camera working backward. Of course, if you come from a different camera brand than Nikon and are used to the dials working in the opposite direction, you may feel more comfortable reversing them on your Z6.

Change Main/Sub

Change main/sub allows you to swap the functionality of the two Command dials. The rear Main command dial will take on the functions of the front Sub-command dial, and vice versa.

You can configure the camera so that this reversal of the Main and Sub command dials applies to both the Exposure setting (aperture and shutter speed) and the Autofocus setting (Autofocus modes and AF-area modes).

Exposure Setting

The Exposure setting subfunction allows you to switch the Main and Sub functionality of the Command dials for changing the aperture and shutter speed. Normally, the aperture is controlled by the front Sub-command dial, and the shutter speed is controlled by the rear Main command dial. However, when switched, that is reversed.

Let's consider the three settings you can choose under this subfunction and see how each affects the actions of the Command dials. Here are the three setting variations:

- **On:** By selecting On, you reverse the functionality of the two Command dials so that the Sub-command dial controls shutter speed while the Main command dial controls aperture.
- **On (Mode A):** This special mode sets the camera so that the Main command dial controls the aperture when using Aperture-priority (A) mode only.
- **Off:** The functionality of the Command dials is set to the factory default. The Main command dial controls the shutter speed while the Sub-command dial controls the aperture.

Let's examine how to choose one of these settings.

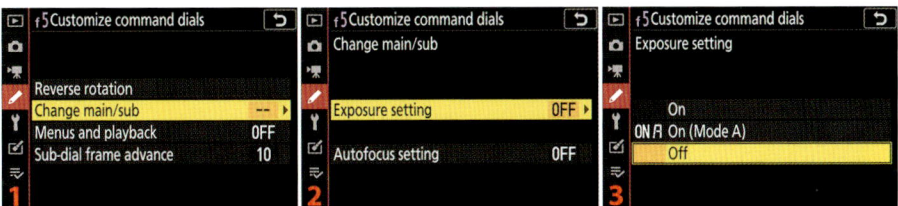

Figure 9.50C: Customize command dials (Change main/sub – Exposure setting)

Here are the steps to swap the functionality of the Command dials for the Exposure setting:

1. Continuing from figure 9.50A, image 2, select Change main/sub and scroll to the right (figure 9.50C, image 1).
2. Choose Exposure setting from the Change main/sub menu and scroll to the right (figure 9.50C, image 2).
3. Select one of the three settings: On, On (Mode A), or Off (figure 9.50C, image 3). Press the OK button or tap the option to lock in the setting.

Autofocus Setting

If you have *Focus mode/AF area-mode* assigned to one of the buttons (e.g., Fn2), and you adjust the Autofocus setting, you will hold in the *Assigned control* and turn one of the Command dials while watching the modes change on the Monitor or EVF. Normally, the rear Main command dial controls the Autofocus mode (i.e., AF-S, AF-C) and the front Sub-command dial controls the AF-area mode (e.g., Single-point AF, Dynamic-area AF). However, you can reverse that with the *Change main/sub > Autofocus setting* subfunction. Here is a list of the two settings within this subfunction and what each does:

- **On:** By selecting On, you reverse the functionality of the two Command dials so that the front Sub-command dial controls the Autofocus mode (i.e., AF-S, AF-C) and the rear Main command dial controls the AF-area mode (e.g., Single-point AF, Dynamic-area AF).

- **Off:** The functionality of the Command dials is set to the factory default. The front Sub-command dial controls the AF-area mode (e.g., Single-point AF, Dynamic-area AF) and the rear Main command dial controls the Autofocus mode (i.e., AF-S, AF-C).

Let's see how to choose one of these settings.

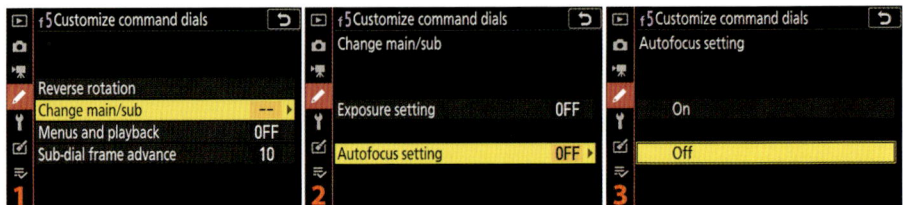

Figure 9.50D: Customize command dials (Change main/sub – Autofocus setting)

Here are the steps to swap the functionality of the Command dials for the Autofocus setting:

1. Continuing from figure 9.50A, image 2, select Change main/sub and scroll to the right (figure 9.50D, image 1).
2. Choose Autofocus setting from the Change main/sub menu and scroll to the right (figure 9.50D, image 2).
3. Select On or Off and press the OK button or tap the option to lock in the setting (figure 9.50D, image 3).

Settings Recommendation: I see no reason to reverse the functionality of the Command dials because I have trained my muscle memory over the last several years to work with the normal Main and Sub command dial functions. However, if you have recently come from a different camera brand over to the new Nikon Z6 and are used to the dials working in reverse, or you just prefer it that way, by all means reverse how the Command dials work.

Menus and Playback

Menus and playback is designed for those who do not like to use the Multi selector pad for viewing image Playback or Info screens. It also allows you to use the Command dials for scrolling though menus. There are two selections for how the menus and image playback work when you would rather not use the Multi selector pad:

- **On:** While viewing images during playback, turning the Main command dial to the left or right scrolls through the displayed images. Turning the Sub-command dial left or right scrolls through the data and histogram screens for each image. While viewing menus, turning the Main command dial left or right scrolls up or down in the screens. Turning the Sub-command dial left or right scrolls left or right in the menus. The Multi selector pad button works normally, even when this is set to On. This setting simply allows you two ways to view your images and menus instead of one. Also, when you are using thumbnail viewing of multiple images on the Monitor, turning the rear Main command dial moves left and right in the grid of thumbnail images, while the front Sub-command dial moves up and down in the grid of thumbnails.

- **On (image review excluded):** This works exactly the same as On, with one exception. When you use On alone (previous setting) and take a picture, the picture will show up on the Monitor and you can then use the Command dials to review images other than the one you just took. However, if you select On (image review excluded) instead of just On, you will not be able to scroll to other images with the Command dials when an image pops up for review after you take it. In other words, image review with the Command dials is excluded just after you take a picture. You can view only the picture you just took unless you use the Multi selector pad, not the Command dials, to scroll through the other images taken previously. You can still use the Command dials for Playback image review (after pressing the Playback button)—just not immediately after taking an image, when it first pops up on the Monitor.
- **Off:** This is the default action. The Multi selector pad or a finger swipe is used to scroll through images and menus.

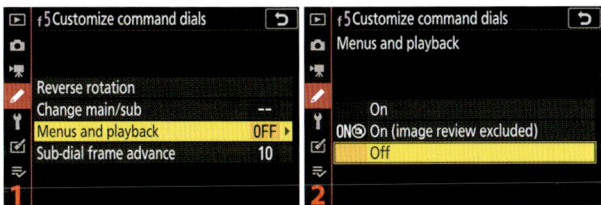

Figure 9.50E: Customize command dials (Menus and playback)

Here are the steps used to configure Menus and playback:

1. Continuing from figure 9.50A, image 2, select Menus and playback and scroll to the right (figure 9.50E, image 1).
2. Select one of the three settings from the list and press the OK button or tap the option to lock in the setting (figure 9.50E, image 2).

Settings Recommendation: I have my camera set to On for Menus and playback. I like the fact that I can use the Multi selector pad or the Command dials to move around in my camera's menus and images. Try this one out; you may like it, too!

Sub-Dial Frame Advance

With the huge memory cards available today, you may find yourself having hundreds or even thousands of images on a single memory card. Have you ever had to scroll through a large number of images to find an image you want to look at more closely? Nikon has come to our rescue with a function that lets you move around more efficiently within a large number of images, or even multiple folders, on a memory card.

After we examine how to select one of the seven available Sub-dial frame advance settings, we will explore what each setting does.

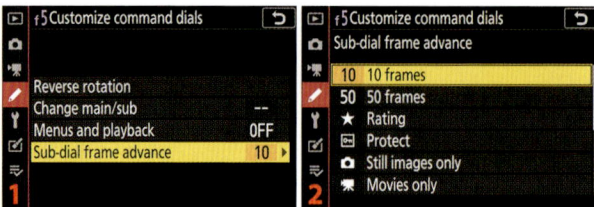

Figure 9.50F: Customize command dials (Sub-dial frame advance)

Use these steps to choose a Sub-dial frame advance setting:

1. Continuing from figure 9.50A, image 2, select Sub-dial frame advance and scroll to the right (figure 9.50F, image 1).
2. Select one of the six settings, referring to the upcoming list (figure 9.50F, image 2). Press the OK button or tap the option to lock in the setting.

Note: This function is closely tied to the previous function, Menus and playback. If you do not have On or On (image review excluded) set in Menus and playback (previous subheading), the camera will not respond to any settings in the Sub-dial frame advance function. When you rotate the front Sub-command dial during full-frame playback, nothing will happen.

Keeping in mind that each click of the rear Main command dial always moves forward or backward by only *one* image, here is a list examining what each click of the front Sub-command dial does, depending on how you have Sub-dial frame advance configured:

* **10 frames:** When you rotate the front Sub-command dial during full-frame playback, the camera will jump forward or backward 10 frames at a time, skipping over the frames in between.
* **50 frames:** When you rotate the front Sub-command dial during full-frame playback, the camera will jump forward or backward 50 frames at a time, skipping the frames in between.

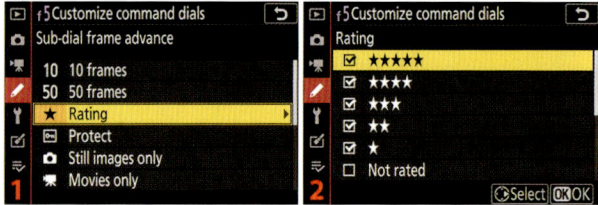

Figure 9.50G: Sub-dial frame advance (★ Rating)

* **★Rating** (figure 9.50G): When you rotate the front Sub-command dial the camera will immediately jump to the next or previous ★Rated image. You can control which rated images it will scroll among by checking or unchecking the boxes next to the star rating level(s) you want to see. To add or subtract check marks, tap the check boxes with your fingertip or highlight an item and scroll to the right.

- **Protect:** When you rotate the front Sub-command dial during full-frame playback, the camera will jump to the next or previous protected file (marked with the Protect key symbol).
- **Still images only:** When you rotate the front Sub-command dial during full-frame playback, the camera will jump to the next or previous still image (including protected images), skipping all movies.
- **Movies only:** When you rotate the front Sub-command dial during full-frame playback, the camera will jump to the next or previous video (movie), skipping all images.
- **Folder:** When you rotate the front Sub-command dial during full-frame playback, the camera will move between folders. If there is only one folder on the memory card, the Sub-command dial does nothing.

Settings Recommendation: I have my camera set to Folders because I often use different folders to separate the images on my camera's memory card. I currently shoot with 64GB Sony G-series cards and they will hold hundreds of RAW images and thousands of JPEGs. As memory cards increase in size and the larger ones become more affordable, I can foresee a time when this function will become even more important.

Custom Setting f6: Release Button to Use Dial

Release button to use dial provides a different method for those who don't like to or cannot hold down buttons and turn a Command dial at the same time. This function may be very useful to people with limited hand strength, allowing them to operate the camera more easily. The function works with the following buttons and functions: ISO button, Release mode/self-timer button, and the following functions assigned using *Custom setting f2 Custom control assignment* and *Custom setting g2 Custom control assignment*:

- Choose image area
- Image quality/size
- White balance
- Set Picture Controls
- Active D-Lighting
- Metering
- Flash mode/compensation
- Focus mode/AF-area mode

- Auto bracketing
- Multiple exposure
- HDR (high dynamic range)
- Exposure delay mode
- Shutter spd & aperture lock
- Peaking highlights
- Choose non-CPU lens number
- Microphone sensitivity

There are two settings under this function. Let's examine them and then look at the screens and steps to modify Release button to use dial:

- **Yes:** This setting changes a two-step operation into a three-step operation. Normally, you would press and hold down a button while rotating a Command dial. When you select Yes under Release button to use dial, the camera allows you to press and release a button, rotate the Command dial, then press and release the button again. The initial button press locks the button so that you do not have to hold your finger on it while turning the Command dial. Once you have changed whatever you are adjusting, you must press the button a second time to unlock it.

- **No:** This is the default setting. You must press and hold a button while rotating the Command dials in order to change camera functionality.

If the exposure meter turns off or you press the Shutter-release button halfway while the Yes operation is active, you must press the original button again to restart the action. You can set the exposure meter to No limit or a longer timeout in *Custom Setting Menu > c Timers/AE lock > c3 Power off delay > Standby timer* to prevent the exposure meter from turning off after a few seconds. This may make the function more useful if you have weak hands or must move slowly.

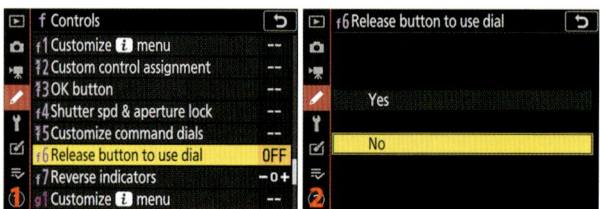

Figure 9.51: Release button to use dial

Here are the steps to configure Release button to use dial:

1. Choose f6 Release button to use dial from the f Controls menu and scroll to the right (figure 9.51, image 1).
2. Choose Yes or No from the list and press the OK button or tap the option to lock in the setting (figure 9.51, image 2).

Settings Recommendation: I haven't found this function useful for myself. However, a person with certain physical limitations may find this to be a very useful function.

Custom Setting f7: Reverse Indicators

Reverse indicators lets you change the direction of your camera's exposure displays. Normally, anytime you see the exposure indicators in your camera's Control panel, Viewfinder, or the Information display, the – is on the left and the + is on the right.

Figure 9.52A shows the Information display with the exposure indicator. The first image shows the normal (default) exposure indicator direction (underexposure on left). The second image shows the Information display with the exposure indicators reversed (overexposure on left).

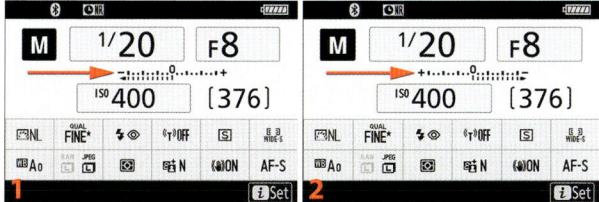

Figure 9.52A: Reversed indicators on the Information display (see red arrows)

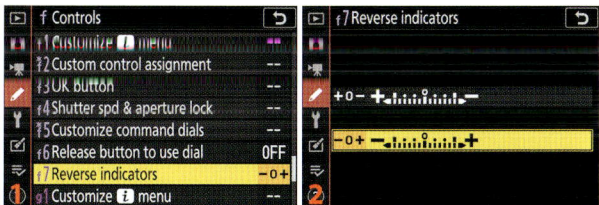

Figure 9.52B: Reverse indicators

Here are the steps to reverse the direction of all camera exposure indicators:

1. Choose f7 Reverse indicators from the f Controls menu and scroll to the right (figure 9.52B, image 1).
2. Choose one of the two selections from the list. In figure 9.52B, image 2, the normal exposure indicator direction is selected (default). Press the OK button or tap the option to lock in the setting.

Settings Recommendation: If you have been using an older Nikon SLR or DSLR, you may find the exposure indicator scale on your Z6 somewhat jarring at first. Newer Nikon cameras default to a reversed exposure indicator compared to older Nikons.

Having used Nikons since way back in 1980, I was quite used to my camera's exposure scale having the plus on the left and the minus on the right. When I first started using a Nikon that reversed this scale, it aggravated me to no end, and I changed it back to the "normal" +/– setting.

However, after thinking about it for a while, I realized that the histogram works in a –/+ direction, with dark on the left and bright on the right. I use the histogram frequently, so I changed the indicator direction back to the factory default of –/+. I have now used it this way for some time and it is beginning to make sense and feel more natural.

However, if you feel uncomfortable seeing the meter indicator working "backward," you may want to change the exposure indicator to the "correct" direction. If you do change it, you may also want to reverse the Exposure compensation direction with *Custom Setting Menu > f controls > f5 Customize command dials > Reverse rotation > Exposure compensation* (see the section **Custom Setting f5: Customize Command Dials** on page 443). Otherwise, you will notice that the Exposure compensation setting works backward from the reversed direction of the exposure indicator. It's a good thing we still have a choice about reversing things!

SECTION SEVEN: g Movie

Custom Settings g1 to f6

The final Custom settings group has a total of six custom settings:

- **g1:** Customize *i* menu
- **g2:** Custom control assignment
- **g3:** OK button
- **g4:** AF speed
- **g5:** AF tracking sensitivity
- **g6:** Highlight display

These functions are all related to capturing video with your Z6.

All six "g" functions and their settings—discussed within the following sections—are found on the Custom Setting Menu under the *g Movie* menu item (figure 9.53).

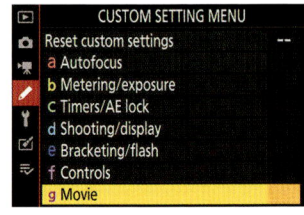

Figure 9.53: *g Movie*

Custom Setting g1: Customize *i* Menu

The *i* Menu for video capture is a grouping of 12 camera functions that can be set from a single screen (figure 9.54A). The *i* Menu can be found by pressing the *i* button on the camera's back, just below the Sub-selector joystick, while the Photo/movie selector switch is set to movie mode (switch at bottom position). The *i* Menu defaults to functions that are the most commonly used by videographers.

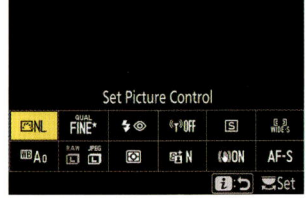

Figure 9.54A: The *i* Menu screen for video capture

This function works the same as *Custom setting f1 Customize i menu* for still photography. However, some of the available settings are different for video than for still photography. Nikon has given us a completely separate *i* Menu configuration for still photography and video capture, controlled by the position of the Photo/movie selector switch (to the left of the AF-ON button on the back of the camera).

The camera has a selection of 22 functions that can be assigned to one of the 12 function locations on the *i* Menu. Let's examine how to assign a function to one of the 12 available *i* Menu slots.

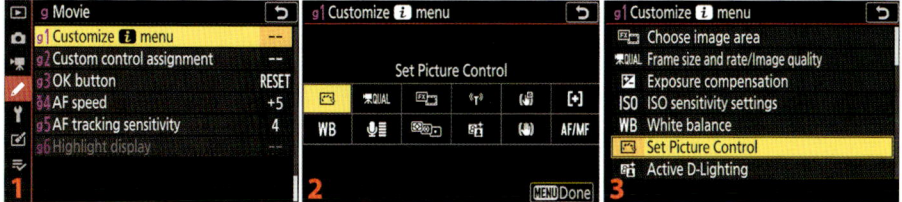

Figure 9.54B: Assigning a function to an *i* Menu location

Use the following steps to assign a function to an *i* Menu location:

1. Choose g1 Customize *i* menu from the g Movie menu and scroll to the right (figure 9.54B, image 1).
2. Highlight a location and press the OK button or tap the option with your fingertip to select it for assignment. The Set Picture Control location is selected for reassignment in figure 9.54B, image 2.
3. A scrollable list of 22 options will now appear (figure 9.54B, image 3). Scroll up or down in the list and highlight an option to replace Set Picture Control. Press the OK button or tap the option to assign it to the selected *i* Menu location.
4. Repeat steps 2 and 3 for any other *i* Menu locations you want to change.

As mentioned, the *i* Menu is available for both still images and videos; however, it is separately configurable for the two. See **Custom setting f1 Customize *i* menu** (page 422) for information on customizing the *i* Menu for still photography.

In the downloadable resource document titled **Appendix B: *i* Menu Video Functions** we examine each of the 22 assignable functions individually. Most of these functions are fully described in other parts of this book. Therefore, to prevent adding many extra pages (and more weight) to this already large book, we are providing this downloadable PDF. The downloadable resources are found at this web address:
http://rockynook.com/NikonZ6

Custom Setting g2: Custom Control Assignment

The Nikon Z6 has six programmable controls for video capture, with 28 different functions that may be assigned to those controls. This *Custom control assignment* function presents a programming interface for all the assignable controls on the camera body and a mounted Nikkor lens that has a programmable L-Fn button. Here is a list of the six programmable controls (figure 9.55A, image 2):

- Fn1 button
- Fn2 button
- AF-ON button
- Sub-selector joystick center press

- Shutter-release button
- Lens control ring (on a Nikkor lens that has one—e.g., S lenses)

Some options can be assigned to most of the camera's programmable controls. However, not all options can be assigned to all controls. A few options can be assigned to particular controls only.

When programming the buttons for custom usage you can assign an option to a single button press (figure 9.55A, image 3: *Press* functions), or you can assign a different functionality to be executed when the button is held down while you turn a Command dial (figure 9.55A, image 4: *Press + command dials* functions).

Assigning a Function to a Control

In this subsection, we will start by discussing how to make a function assignment to each programmable control. Then we will consider the individual Nikon Z6 programmable controls and which functions can be assigned to each control (table 9.2). And finally, we will examine what each assignable function does.

Let's see how to actually choose a custom function for a sample control. We will use the Fn1 button as our sample control.

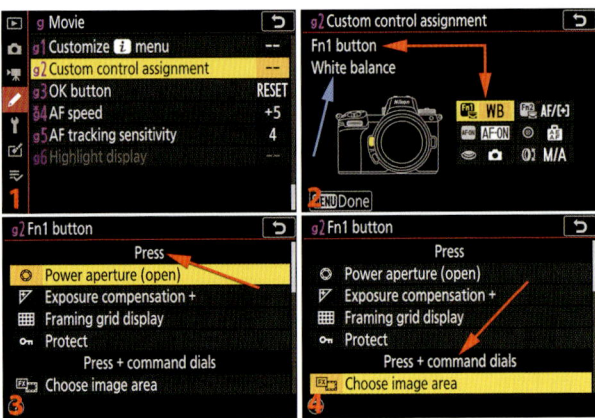

Figure 9.55A: Assigning a custom function to a camera control (sample: Fn1 button)

Use the following steps to assign a custom function to a camera control:

1. Choose g2 Custom control assignment from the g Movie menu and scroll to the right (figure 9.55A, image 1).
2. Highlight a control and press the OK button or tap the control with your fingertip (figure 9.55A, image 2). Each control name is listed in the top-left area of the screen when the control is highlighted, in case you are unsure which control is selected (Fn1 button). Just below the name of the control is the current function assignment for that control (White balance, at the blue arrow). As you scroll around the screen shown in

figure 9.55A, image 2, you will see different control names and function assignment names appear in the top-left corner. Press the OK button or tap the highlighted yellow option to open the control assignment screen.

3. Figure 9.55A, image 3, shows a list of functions on the control assignment screen. You can choose one to activate when you press the Fn1 button (e.g., Power aperture (open)). This list has an aptly titled heading: Press. If you scroll down on this same screen you will see another distinct list of functions under a new heading: Press + command dials (figure 9.55A, image 4). Each of the functions in this section (e.g., Choose image area) requires you to hold down the button and turn either of the Command dials. Highlight the function you want to assign to the control and press the OK button or tap the high-lighted function to lock in in for use.

Note: A couple of the controls (i.e., AF-ON button and Lens control ring) have no Press + command dials function list available. The AF-ON button has only Press items, and the Lens control ring (not being a button) has no Press or Press + command dials items. That wouldn't make sense for a control ring on a lens; therefore, there is just a simple list of items that you can assign to the Lens control ring.

Now let's consider a list of which function can be assigned to which control (table 9.2).

Control Assignment Functions List

Table 9.2 contains a list of 28 available functions and shows which controls the function can be assigned to. A "✓" means that function is available for assignment to that particular control, whereas a blank cell means it is not available for that control.

The Function Name column in table 9.2 lists the same items as partially seen in fig-ure 9.55A, images 3 and 4. Each programmable control is listed across the top of the table, in the order in which the camera presents them, with a check mark showing which func-tions can be used with that control.

The Lens ring has functions listed that can be used only with certain qualifications, as described in the table caption (1 and 2).

Function Name	Fn1 Button	Fn2 Button	AF-ON Button	Joystick Center	Shutter-Release Button	Lens Ring
Active D-Lighting	✓	✓				
AE/AF lock			✓	✓		
AE lock (Hold)			✓	✓		
AE lock only			✓	✓		
AF-ON			✓			
AF lock only			✓	✓		
Choose image area	✓	✓		✓		
Exposure compensation						✓ 2
Exposure compensation +	✓					

Function Name	Fn1 Button	Fn2 Button	AF-ON Button	Joystick Center	Shutter-Release Button	Lens Ring
Exposure compensation –		✓				
Focus (M/A)						✓ 1, 2
Focus mode/AF-area mode	✓	✓				
Framing Grid display	✓	✓		✓		
Metering	✓	✓				
Microphone sensitivity	✓	✓				
None	✓	✓	✓	✓		✓ 2
Peaking highlights	✓	✓				
Power aperture						✓ 2
Power aperture (close)		✓				
Power aperture (open)	✓					
Protect	✓	✓				
★ Rating	✓	✓				
Record movies			✓	✓	✓	
Select center focus point			✓	✓		
Set Picture Control	✓	✓				
Take photos					✓	
White balance	✓	✓				
Zoom on/off			✓			

Table 9.2: Available functions and the controls to which they can be assigned, in alphabetical order (✓ = Yes; blank = No; 1 = Compatible lenses only; 2 = Regardless of options selected, in MF mode the control ring can be used to adjust focus only)

Assignable Functions Explained

In table 9.2 you will find a list with each assignable function and what it does. Since the various functions can be assigned to different controls, I used the words *Assigned control* (in italics) as a replacement for specific control names. When you see *Assigned control,* substitute the name of the control to which you are going to assign the particular function. The *Assignable Functions List* explains how each function works.

Assignable Functions List

- **Active D-Lighting:** (figure 9.55B): Press and hold the *Assigned control* and rotate either of the Command dials to adjust Active D-Lighting (ADL) to one of its five settings: Off (Off), Low (L), Normal (N), High (H), and Extra high (H*). You will see the symbols that represent the various settings—such as L and H—scroll by as you turn either of the Command dials. Auto (A) Active D-Lighting is not available in Movie mode.

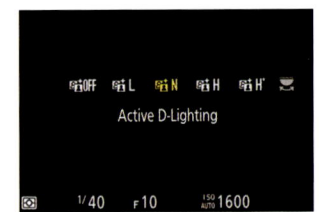

Figure 9.55B: Active D-Lighting

- **AE/AF lock:** This allows you to lock AE (exposure) and AF (focus) on the last meter and autofocus system readings when you hold down the *Assigned control*.
- **AE lock (Hold):** This function causes AE (exposure) to lock on the last meter reading when the *Assigned control* is pressed and released once. It stays locked until you press the *Assigned control* again or the exposure meter turns off.
- **AE lock only:** This allows you to lock AE (exposure) on the last meter reading when you hold down the *Assigned control*.
- **AF lock only:** This allows you to lock the AF (focus) system on the last autofocus reading when you hold down the *Assigned control*.
- **Choose image area** (figure 9.55C): When the camera is in Movie mode, you can press the *Assigned control* and rotate a Command dial to change the image area. Your image area choices are FX and DX. The live view will change on the Monitor to reflect the new image area. You cannot make this change while recording a movie.

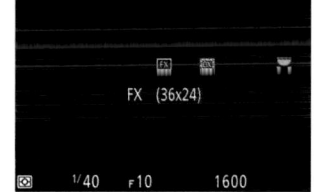

Figure 9.55C: Choose image area

- **Exposure compensation:** This function is assignable to the *Lens control ring* only. Turn the Lens control ring to visually add or subtract exposure from your video. When used in conjunction with the Live histogram, you have a very accurate method to fine-tune the exposure for your video. If you need to know how much actual exposure change you have made, press the +/– Exposure compensation button. Using the Lens control ring for Exposure compensation is a virtually silent method of fine-tuning exposure.
- **Exposure compensation +:** This function can be assigned to the *Fn1 button* only. By pressing the Fn1 button, you ask the camera to override the meter and add extra exposure (+) for each press of the button. When you enable the Exposure compensation + (plus) function for Fn1, the camera automatically selects the Exposure compensation – (minus) setting for the Fn2 button, and gives you an on-screen notice that says, *"Exposure compensation has been assigned to the Fn1 and Fn2 buttons."* At that point, the Fn1 and Fn2 buttons are paired, with Fn1 adding exposure (+) and Fn2 removing exposure (–). If you try to change the Fn1 button to another setting, breaking the pairing, the camera will display this message: *"Fn2 button exposure compensation assignment has been canceled,"* and the Fn2 button is set to None (Off).
- **Exposure compensation –:** This function can be assigned to the *Fn2 button* only. By pressing the Fn2 button, you ask the camera to override the meter and subtract exposure (–) for each press of the button. When you enable the Exposure compensation – (minus) function for Fn2, the camera automatically selects the Exposure compensation + (plus) setting for the Fn1 button, and gives you an on-screen notice that says, *"Exposure compensation has been assigned to the Fn1 and Fn2 buttons."* At that point, the Fn1 and Fn2 buttons are paired, with Fn1 adding exposure (+) and Fn2 removing exposure (–). If you try to change the Fn2 button to another setting, breaking the pairing, the camera will display this message: *"Fn1 button exposure compensation assignment has been canceled,"* and the Fn1 button is set to None (Off).

- **Focus (M/A):** This function can be assigned only to a Nikkor lens with a Lens ring. When you turn the Lens ring in manual focus (M) mode, you will have full control of focusing the camera. Be sure to enable focus Peaking (page 86) to help you obtain very accurate manual focus. When using autofocus (A), you can top off the focus by turning the Lens ring. If you have enabled focus Peaking and hold down the Shutter-release button halfway or press the AF-ON button while turning the Lens ring, focus Peaking will assist you with fine-tuning the camera's autofocus choice.

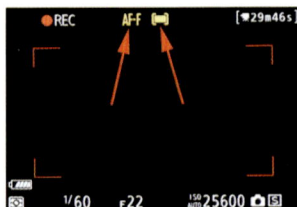

Figure 9.55D: Focus mode/AF-area mode

- **Focus mode/AF-area mode** (figure 9.55D): Hold down the *Assigned control* and turn the rear Main command dial to change the Focus mode (e.g., AF-S, AF-F), or turn the front Sub-command dial to change the AF-area mode (e.g., Single-point AF, Auto-area AF).

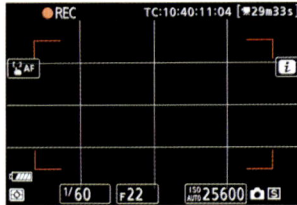

Figure 9.55E: Framing grid display

- **Framing grid display** (figure 9.55E): Press the *Assigned control* to toggle on and off a convenient Framing grid to assist with leveling horizons and alignment with architectural features.

- **Metering** (figure 9.55F): When you press and hold the *Assigned control* and turn either of the camera's Command dials, you can select from the following Metering modes: Matrix metering, Center-weighted metering, and Highlight-weighted metering. The camera will remain in the chosen Metering mode until you change it. This function a shortcut method imitating the *Movie Shooting Menu > Metering mode* (page 343).

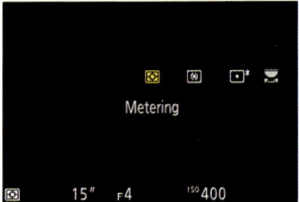

Figure 9.55F: Metering

- **Microphone sensitivity** (figure 9.55G): Press and hold the *Assigned control* and turn either of the Command dials to select a Microphone sensitivity level. Your choices are Auto, Off, and 1–20. This setting affects how sensitive to sound your favorite external mic or the built-in stereo mic is. You can let the camera control it automatically (Auto), disable the mic (Off), or manually control it yourself (1–20).

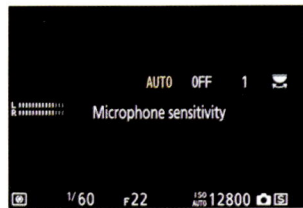

Figure 9.55G: Microphone sensitivity

- **None:** Pressing the *Assigned control* when using Movie mode does nothing.

- **Peaking highlights** (figure 9.55H): Pressing and holding the *Assigned control* while turning the rear Main command dial to any setting besides Off enables the Peaking highlights function. Choose from PEAK OFF, PEAK 1, PEAK 2, and PEAK 3. The higher numbers

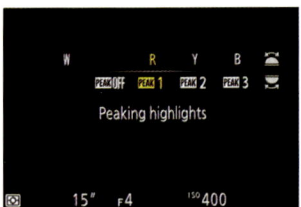

Figure 9.55H: Peaking highlights

increase the sensitivity and visibility of Peaking. Pressing and holding the *Assigned control* while turning the front Sub-command dial allows you to select a Peaking highlights color: Red (R), Yellow (Y), Blue (B), or White (W). For more information on focus Peaking, see the **Custom Setting d10: Peaking Highlights** subheading earlier in this chapter (page 409).

- **Power aperture:** This function is assignable to the *Lens control ring* only. Turn the Lens control ring to change the aperture. This works somewhat like the old aperture lens rings of old, without the click stops. As you turn the lens ring, you will see the aperture value change on the camera's display screens.

- **Power aperture (open):** This function may be assigned to the *Fn1 button* only. By selecting this function, you ask the camera to open the aperture to a larger opening when you press and hold the Fn1 button. This is accomplished automatically without you having to turn any dials; just pressing the Fn1 button opens the aperture smoothly and silently. When you set the camera to Power aperture (open) for the Fn1 button, the camera automatically selects the Power aperture (close) setting for the Fn2 button, and gives you an on-screen notice that says, *"Power aperture has been assigned to the Fn1 and Fn2 buttons."* At that point, the Fn1 and Fn2 buttons are paired. If you try to change the Fn1 button to another setting, the camera will give you a terse warning: *"Fn2 button power aperture assignment has been canceled,"* and the Fn2 button is set to None (Off). Power aperture assignments are available only in exposure modes A and M. When you press the Fn1 button, you will see the aperture number get larger (open up), and the results of that change (brightening of subject) are visible on the EVF or Monitor immediately.

- **Power aperture (close):** This function may be assigned to the *Fn2 button* only. By selecting this function, you ask the camera to close (stop down) the aperture to a smaller setting when you press and hold the Fn2 button. This is accomplished automatically without you having to turn any dials; just pressing the Fn2 button closes the aperture smoothly and silently. This function works in conjuction with the Power aperture (open) setting (Fn1). When Power aperture (close) is assigned to the Fn2 button, the camera automatically assigns Power aperture (open) to the Fn1 button. If you break that partnership by trying to assign another selection to the Fn2 button, the camera will give you the following message: *"Fn1 button power aperture assignment has been canceled,"* and the Fn1 button is set to None (Off). Power aperture assignments are available only in exposure modes A and M. When you press the Fn2 button, you will see the aperture number become smaller (stop down), and the results of that change (darkening of subject) will be visible on the EVF or Monitor immediately.

- **Protect** (figure 9.55I): Display an important video you want to protect on the camera's Monitor (or EVF). To prevent future accidental deletion, press the *Assigned control* and the image will be locked from deletion. As you scroll through your videos, the protected movies will have a protection key symbol in the top-left corner of the frame. Press the *Assigned control* again with a protected video displayed, and the protection and key symbol will be removed.

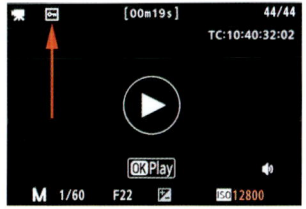

Figure 9.55I: Protect

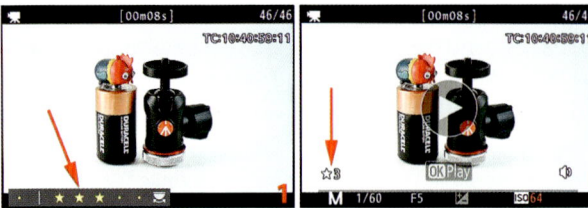

Figure 9.55J: Rating

- ★ **Rating** (figure 9.55J): Display a video to which you want to give a rating, and then press and hold the *Assigned control*. The camera will present you with a 1 to 5 star rating scale (★ to ★ ★ ★ ★ ★) in the bottom-left corner of the screen (figure 9.55J, image 1, red arrow). Turn the rear Main command dial to add or subtract yellow stars. For example, if you rate a video as a three-star movie, you will see three yellow stars in the lower-left area of the screen. When you press the Playback button and display the video, you will see the symbol (★3) displayed in the lower-left corner of the frame (figure 9.55J, image 2, red arrow). This symbol is a reminder that the image was previously rated as 3 out of 5 stars.

- **Record movies:** Press the *Assigned control* and the camera will immediately start recording a movie, just as if you had pressed the Movie record button. You can stop the recording by pressing the *Assigned control* again.

- **Select center focus point:** Pressing the *Assigned control* causes the camera to jump from whatever focus point (AF point) you were using to the center AF point instead.

- **Set Picture Control** (figure 9.55K): Press and hold the *Assigned control* while turning either Command dial to change which Picture Control (page 200) the camera uses for video recording.

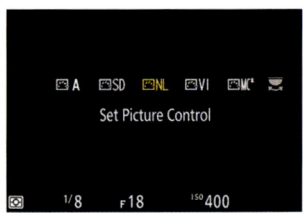

Figure 9.55K: Set Picture Control

- **Take photos:** This function can be assigned to the *Shutter-release button* only. If you are in the middle of recording a movie and you absolutely must have a still image immediately, you can acquire an image that matches the resolution of a single frame of the video by pressing the Shutter-release button all the way down. If your camera is currently recording video in 4K, the single image will be 8.29 MP in size (3840×2160). If recording 1080p (Full HD) video, the single image will be 2.07 MP in size (1920×1080). The camera will *continue recording* without interruption. Be careful not to shake the camera when you press the Shutter-release button to capture a frame while recording.

- **White balance** (figure 9.55L): Press and hold the *Assigned control* while turning the rear Main command dial to select a White balance type (e.g., Auto, Direct sunlight, Cloudy). While still pressing the *Assigned control,* you can turn the front Sub-command dial to select a sub-option, if that White balance type

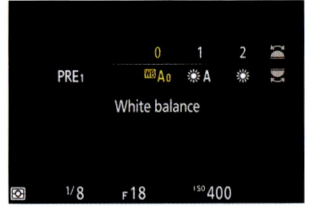

Figure 9.55L: White balance

has any sub-options (e.g., for Auto, a sub-option is A0 Keep white (reduce warm colors)). See **White balance** on page 108 for more information on options and sub-options.

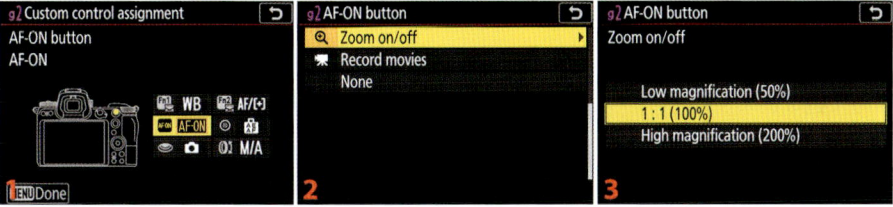

Figure 9.55M: Zoom on/off

- *Zoom on/off* (figure 9.55M): This function can be assigned only to the AF-ON button under *Custom setting g2: Custom control assignment;* however, you can also use *Custom setting g3: OK button* to select and use Zoom on/off (see next main heading). When you first assign this function to the AF-ON button, you will be presented with a screen that asks you to choose a magnification level (figure 9.55M, image 3). Most of us will choose 1:1 (100%) because that is an accurate pixel-peeping level for verifying focus or examining detail in a non-yet-videoed subject. This function is not available once you have started recording the video. To use it, press the AF-ON button and the camera will immediately zoom in to the magnification level you assigned.

Settings Recommendation: Here are the assignments I make for the controls on my camera:

- *Fn1:* White balance
- *Fn2:* Focus mode/AF area-mode
- *AF-ON:* AF-ON
- *Sub-selector joystick button press:* Select center focus point
- *Shutter-release button:* Take photos (still photography mode has own settings)
- *Lens control ring:* Focus (M/A)

Of course, you may desire a completely different configuration that works better for your style of videography. You have a sizable number of options available!

Custom Setting g3: OK Button

The *OK button* has a dual purpose in the Z6 when capturing video. There are three settings you can assign to the OK button, which we will discuss; however, anytime Movie mode is active, the OK button can be used to initiate focus tracking when Auto-area AF AF-area mode is selected. Let's examine the three settings you can choose to assign to the OK button:

- **Select center focus point:** If selected, pressing the OK button causes the AF point to jump to the middle of the screen.
- **Zoom on/off:** If selected, you can press the OK button to zoom in on your subject before you start recording a movie. This function will not work while video is being recorded.
- **Record movies:** If selected, you can press the OK button to stop or start recording video.

Now let's see how to assign a setting to the OK button for when you are recording videos.

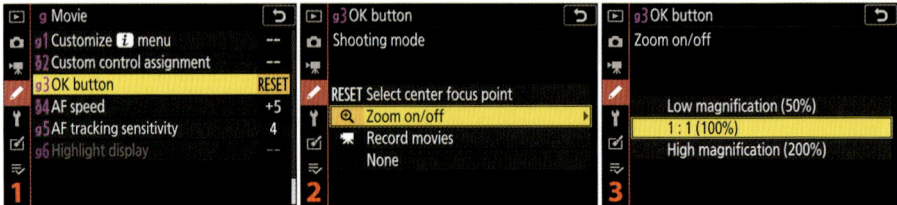

Figure 9.56A: Assigning a setting to the OK button for video

Use the following steps to assign a setting to the OK button for use while recording a movie:

1. Choose g3 OK button from the g Movie menu and scroll to the right (figure 9.56A, image 1).
2. Highlight one of the three available settings, referring to the previous list for a description of each option's functionality. If you choose Select center focus point or Record movies, press the OK button or tap the option to use it and then skip step 3 (figure 9.56A, image 2).

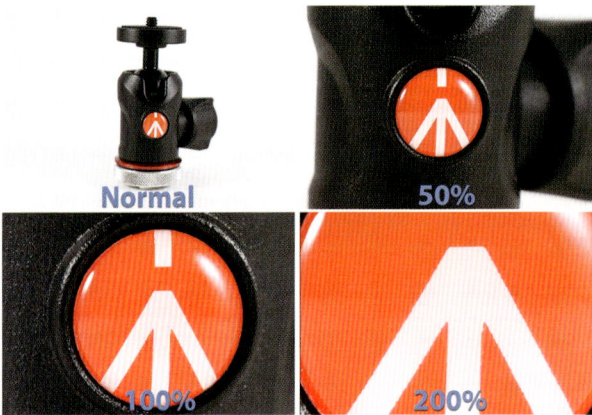

Figure 9.56B: Zoom magnification levels

3. If you select Zoom on/off you will need to choose a zoom magnification level. Sample zoom levels are shown in figure 9.56B—from Normal (no zoom) to 200%. This allows you to prepare the focus by examining a pixel-peeping closeup of your subject. To choose a zoom level, highlight it and press the OK button or tap the option with your fingertip.

Settings Recommendation: I set my camera to Zoom on/off at the 100% level. I have Select center focus point assigned to the Sub-selector joystick press function and prefer to use the joystick for all AF point movement in still photography and movie modes. I can then use the OK button to zoom in and make sure I have good focus set before I start the video recording session. The Zoom on/off setting will not work while a video is being recorded. Experiment with these three modes and see which works best for you.

Custom Setting g4: AF Speed

Use the AF speed function to choose how quickly the camera focuses on your subject when capturing a video and when not recording. Sometimes it can be jarring to have a subject snap into focus, such as when you are switching between two people in your video. You can control the speed with which the camera focuses on the new subject. Also, you can choose when the focus speed limitation applies:

- ***Always:*** The AF speed slider (−5 to +5) always controls how fast autofocus works during video recording and when not recording.
- ***Only while recording:*** The AF speed limitation works while you are recording a video only. When you are not recording a video the AF speed is equivalent to the +5 setting.

Let's see how to use the AF speed control.

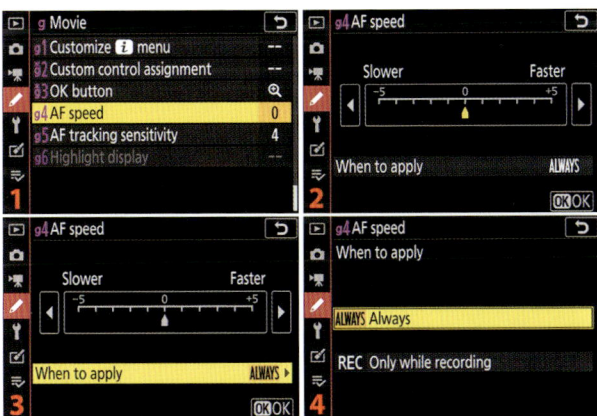

Figure 9.57: Using the AF speed control

Use the following steps to choose an AF speed and select when the AF speed limiter can control the AF speed:

1. Choose g4 AF speed from the g Movie menu and scroll to the right (figure 9.57, image 1).
2. Use the AF speed Slower/Faster slider control to set a focus speed (figure 9.57, image 2). Experiment with the speed (−5 to +5) and see which you like the best. Tap the little

pointer controls on either side of the slider scale to move the yellow pointer (red arrow) to the left toward –5 or to the right toward +5. Press or touch OK to lock in the setting.

3. If you want to limit when the AF speed control works, scroll down to When to apply and scroll to the right, or tap the When to apply setting with your fingertip (figure 9.57, image 3).

4. Highlight Always or Only while recording and press the OK button or tap the option to lock it in (figure 9.57, image 4). See the previous list to help with your decision.

Settings Recommendation: I don't shoot a lot of video where I need to control focus speed since I shoot mostly static nature videos. However, when working with people or multiple objects where I have to switch focus, I do prefer the less jarring look of a slower AF. This is very subjective and is governed by your needs. Experimentation is in order. I definitely use the *Only while recording* subsetting so that I can see faster AF results when I am setting up my video session initially. I leave the Slower/Faster slider set to 0 most of the time.

Custom Setting g5: AF Tracking Sensitivity

The *AF tracking sensitivity* function works in a similar manner to the **Custom setting a3: Focus Tracking with Lock-On** function (page 367) for still photography. The AF tracking sensitivity function controls how long the camera tries to maintain focus on your original subject when something passes between your camera and your subject. Let's see how it works.

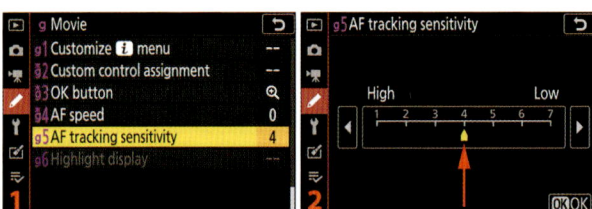

Figure 9.58: AF tracking sensitivity

Use the following steps to choose a time delay for changing focus away from your subject when an object comes between you and your subject:

1. Choose g5 AF tracking sensitivity from the g Movie menu and scroll to the right (figure 9.58, image 1).

2. You have seven settings on a sliding scale from 1 (High) to 7 (Low). The smaller numbers (High, or 1 to 3) force the camera to maintain its tracking focus on the subject for a *longer* period of time when something gets in the way. The larger numbers (Low, or 5 to 7) let the camera move focus to the intruding object more quickly, in a *shorter* period of time. Choose the setting you want by moving the yellow pointer (red arrow) toward High or Low by tapping the pointers at the ends of the scale (or scrolling with the Multi

selector pad). This scale feels a little backward to me. Just remember that the bigger numbers (Low) mean faster timeouts (lock-on to your subject for a shorter time) and the smaller numbers (High) mean slower timeouts (lock-on to your subject for a longer time). When you have made your choice, press or touch OK to lock in the value.

Settings Recommendation: It has been my experience that when tracking a moving subject, it is best to ask the camera to maintain the focus on your subject for a longer period of time (High, or 1 to 3). Otherwise, an object that temporarily gets in between you and your subject may pull the focus away from your subject. For my style of static nature video capture, I leave my camera set to High (1) most of the time. However, if you are videoing multiple people and want to switch to a subject closer to the camera, a Low (/) setting may allow you to do so more quickly. Experiment with this setting so that you will be prepared to use it well.

Custom Setting g6: Highlight Display

The *Highlight display* function allows you to control the look and sensitivity of the Highlight "zebra stripes" display. When enabled, the Highlight display allows your Nikon Z6 to use zebra stripes to warn you about overexposed areas while you are shooting a movie. You can also check for overexposure before the video recording starts by entering the Movie mode and pointing the camera at your subject. If zebra stripes appear anywhere on your subject before or during the recording, it is an indication that the striped area does not have detail (it is overexposed).

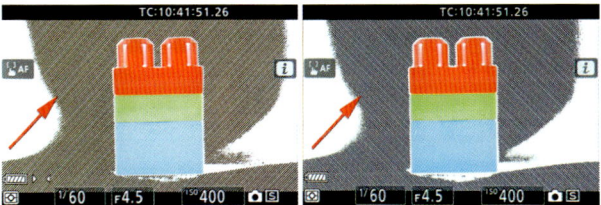

Figure 9.59A: Zebra stripes examples: Display Pattern 1 (left) and Display Pattern 2 (right).

You can see the Highlight display (zebra stripes) in the background of my camera's Live view screen in figure 9.59A. On the left is Pattern 1, which has zebra stripes that lean to the right. On the right is Pattern 2, which has strips that lean left.

If your camera's g6 Highlight display function is grayed out and unavailable, it likely means that you have enabled focus Peaking in **Custom Setting d10: Peaking Highlights** (page 409). Focus Peaking and Highlight display are mutually exclusive. One cannot be enabled unless the other is disabled (firmware version C2.00).

Let's examine how to choose one of the stripe patterns.

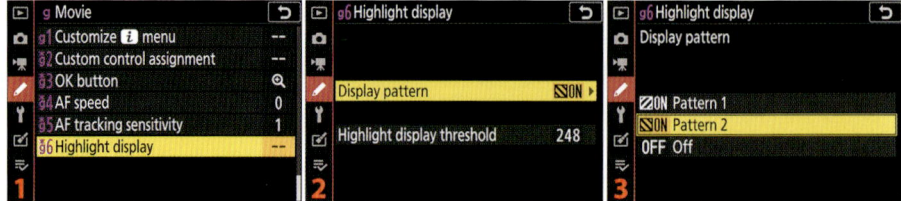

Figure 9.59B: Setting the Highlight display stripe pattern

Use the following steps to choose a Display pattern (direction in which the zebra stripes lean):

1. Choose g6 Highlight display from the g Movie menu and scroll to the right (figure 9.59B, image 1).
2. Select Display pattern and scroll to the right or tap the option to select it (figure 9.59B, image 2).
3. Highlight one of the two patterns (Pattern 1 or Pattern 2) or set it to Off (figure 9.59B, image 2). Refer to figure 9.59A to select the pattern you prefer. Press the OK button or tap the option to select the pattern.

Next, you can adjust the sensitivity of the Highlight display by selecting a Highlight display threshold in a range from 180 to 255. The lower the number, the more sensitive the Highlight display. Let's see how to set the Highlight display threshold and then we'll enable the Highlight display.

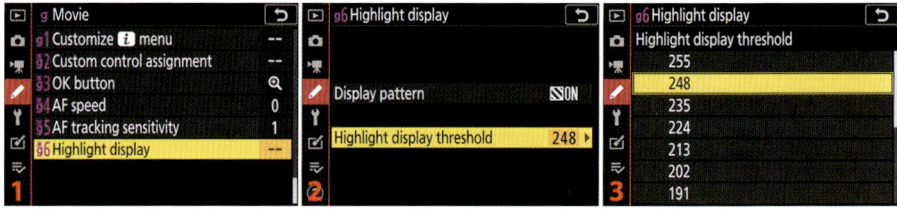

Figure 9.59C: Setting the Highlight display threshold

Use the following steps to set a Highlight display threshold:

1. Choose g6 Highlight display from the g Movie menu and scroll to the right (figure 9.59C, image 1).
2. Select Highlight display threshold and scroll to the right or tap the option with your fingertip (figure 9.59C, image 2).
3. Highlight one of the values on the list (figure 9.59C, image 3). You can choose from 180 to 255. The lower the Highlight display threshold number, the sooner the zebra stripes will appear. Basically, by setting 255, the camera will show zebra stripes only in areas that are fully blown out to pure white (no detail). A number lower than that will enable zebra stripes for less and less detail loss. The camera defaults to 248, which allows a zebra stripe warning to appear just before all detail is lost (at 255). To understand what

these numbers mean, study the histogram on page 69. Press the OK button or tap the option to lock in your Highlight display threshold number.

Settings Recommendation: I like the zebra stripes display. I generally set my camera to 248 or 235, just so that I can get a warning when I am approaching data loss due to overexposure (when light reaches 255, see histogram on page 70). This Highlight display is a great feature for videographers. Learn to use it!

Author's Conclusion

Your Z6 can change the way it shoots on the fly, in much less time than it takes to talk about it, by switching to a different User setting (U1, U2, or U3) on your camera's Mode dial. Now that you've read this chapter over and configured the camera for a particular style of photography, save the configuration to one of the User settings (page 474). Then reconfigure the camera and set up the other two User settings. Think of the ways you most often take pictures and configure your Z6 for each of those ways. Your camera will be customized to you!

Now let's move into the next menu system—the Setup Menu—and configure the camera's basic setup. The Setup Menu is very important for initial camera configuration, but only a few of its functions are used after initial setup.

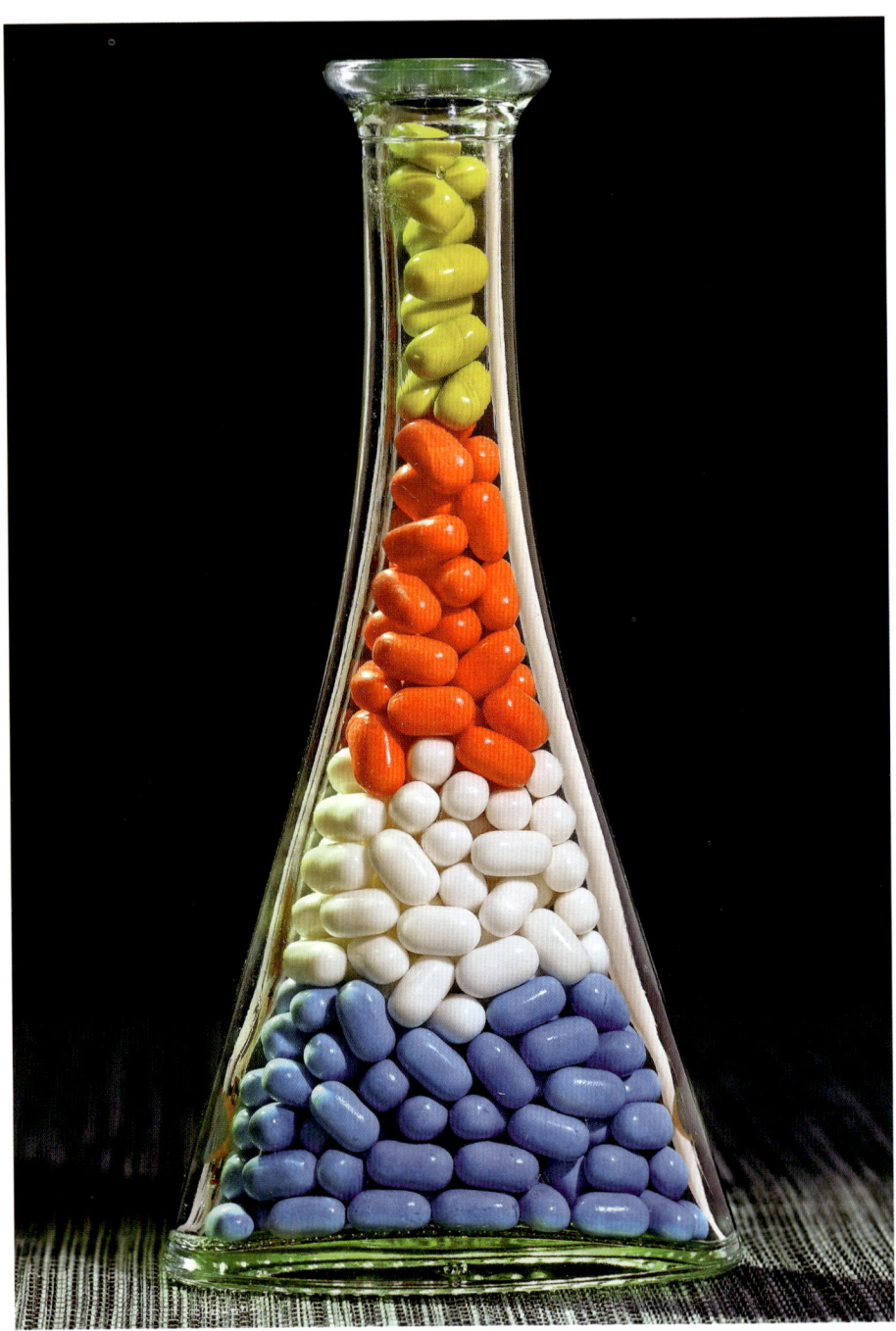

Tic Tacs in a Bottle © 2019 Dave Gould (*davegould68*)

The Setup Menu contains a series of settings for basic camera configuration that are not directly related to taking pictures. It covers things like Monitor brightness, battery information, firmware version, the default language, Wi-Fi, Bluetooth, smart device connectivity, and many other basic settings. Here is a look at the Setup Menu location (figure 10.1).

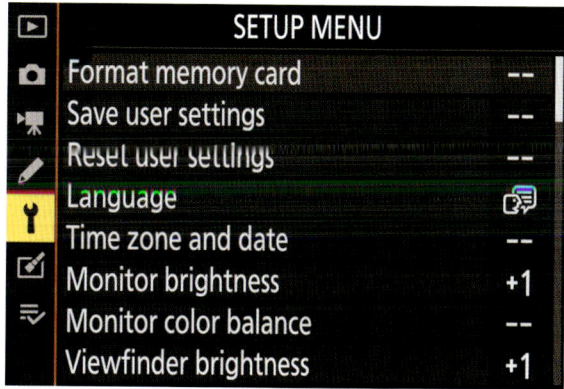

Figure 10.1: The Setup Menu

The settings in the Setup Menu are most likely the first ones you'll configure when you prepare your new Nikon Z6. You'll have to set the Time zone and date, Language, and Copyright information—for embedding in the metadata of your pictures—among many other things.

Following is a list of the 34 functions available in the Setup Menu:

- **Format memory card:** This function allows you to delete all images from your camera's memory card(s).
- **Save user settings:** You can configure the camera under the individual user settings U1, U2, and U3 on the Mode dial and save the settings to internal memory. The Z6 will remember the settings and reload them when you select U1, U2, or U3.
- **Reset user settings:** If you want to return one of your user settings (U1, U2, or U3) to the factory default, this function will do it for you.
- **Language:** Choose the language you would like your camera to use from a list of four languages (firmware C2.00). Menus and screens will be displayed in the chosen language.
- **Time zone and date:** Set the Time zone, Date and time, Date format, and Daylight saving time in your camera.
- **Monitor brightness:** Choose the brightness level for the Monitor on the back of your camera.
- **Monitor color balance:** Select the color balance of the Monitor. You can use a reference shot taken by the camera, such as a picture of a color chart, to calibrate the Monitor's color balance.
- **Viewfinder brightness:** Use this to set the brightness level for the Viewfinder (EVF).

- *Viewfinder color balance:* Select the color balance of the EVF. You can use a reference shot taken by the camera, such as a picture of a color chart, to calibrate the EVF color balance.
- *Control panel brightness:* Set the brightness level of the small, black-and-white, OLED Control panel on top of the camera.
- *Limit monitor mode selection:* You can choose from four different arrangements of EVF and Monitor usage, including: Automatic display switching (eye sensor will cause the camera to use the EVF when your eye is at the Viewfinder, and the rear Monitor when it is not), Viewfinder only, Monitor only, and Prioritize viewfinder.
- *Information display:* This allows you to control how the Information display screen (page 489) looks on the camera's Monitor. You can select Dark on light or Light on dark.
- *AF fine-tune:* You can fine-tune the autofocus for up to 30 of your current Nikkor lenses (e.g., S, AF-S). After you have fine-tuned and saved a lens, the camera will detect which lens you have mounted and correct for front or back focus according to your settings.
- *Non-CPU lens data:* This function lets you save the focal length and maximum aperture of 20 non-CPU lenses, such as AI and AI-S Nikkor lenses from the late 1970s to now. Each lens is registered within the camera with its own number so you can select it and use it later.
- *Clean image sensor:* This function allows you to initiate immediate cleaning of the imaging sensor to remove dust spots, or you can configure the camera to clean the sensor at shutdown.
- *Image Dust Off ref photo:* You can create a dust off reference photo to help remove a dust spot from images accidentally taken with some dust on the sensor. This requires the use of a program like Nikon Capture NX-D to actually remove the dust, with the reference photo as a guide.
- *Image comment:* Add a comment (up to 36 characters) that embeds itself in the internal metadata of each image. This can help you protect yourself from image theft or simply add pertinent personal or location information to each image.
- *Copyright information:* This function is designed for those who use their images commercially or for those who worry about image theft. It allows you to input Artist (36 characters) and Copyright (54 characters) information that will be embedded into your pictures' internal metadata.
- *Beep options:* Use this function to control the Volume and Pitch of the beep that occurs when the camera successfully autofocuses in Single-servo AF (AF-S) mode; while the self-timer is counting down; while you use the touch screen for keyboard entry; and while several other camera processes are at work. This function defaults to Off because many photographers do not like their cameras to beep at them.
- *Touch controls:* The Z6 allows you to use the Monitor as a touch screen, somewhat like a smartphone. This function allows you to enable or disable the touch control system as well as the gesture direction—the "flick" or swipe—used to move between images.
- *HDMI:* You can select various HDMI sync rates for interfacing with an HDTV or other external monitor.

- **Location data:** If you own a GPS that can be connected to the Nikon Z6—such as the Accessory shoe–mounted Nikon GP-1 or another GPS unit—this function allows you to record Latitude, Longitude, Altitude, Heading, and UTC (Coordinated Universal Time) into the metadata of each image.
- **Wireless remote (WR) options:** This function allows you to adjust the settings for optional WR-R10 Wireless Remote Controller units and for optional radio-controlled flash units.
- **Assign remote (WR) Fn button:** Use this function to assign one of several Button options to the Fn button on an optional wireless remote controller (if it has an Fn button, of course).
- **Airplane mode:** Use this to enable or disable the camera's internal Wi-Fi and Bluetooth capability. This function does not affect optional external wireless transmitters, which can be disabled only by removing them from the camera.
- **Connect to smart device:** This function allows you to adjust the settings, including a password, for connection to smart devices. You can also configure, pair, enable, and disable the cameras Bluetooth and Wi-Fi capability.
- **Connect to PC:** Allows the camera to participate in an ad hoc Wi-Fi network between the camera and a wireless computer (e.g., MacBook, Windows PC). You can wirelessly transfer files directly from from the camera to your computer.
- **Wireless transmitter (WT-7):** With a WT-7 wireless transmitter connected to your camera, you can connect to computers or FTP servers through a wireless or Ethernet network.
- **Conformity marking:** This allows you to view the symbols associated with the standards with which the camera has complied.
- **Battery info:** This function gives you information about the battery's current charge, the number of pictures taken with the battery on the current charge, and the useful life remaining in the battery (battery age) before you should dispose of it.
- **Slot empty release lock:** This function allows you to choose whether or not the camera can take a picture when there is no memory card in the camera. If enabled, the Monitor will display pictures you just took using "demo mode" when there is not a memory card inserted in the camera. However, with no memory cards inserted, the picture(s) will not be saved.
- **Save/load settings:** This function allows you to save the current menu configuration of most internal camera settings to the memory card in the primary slot for later backup on your computer. By backing up complex configurations, you can restore them to the camera when needed.
- **Reset all settings:** This function allows you to reset all internal menu settings, in all camera menus, back to factory default values. The only two settings in the entire menu system that are not reset are *Setup Menu > Language* and *Setup Menu > Time zone and date*. Consider this a full camera reset for when you decide to start fresh with menu configuration, or for when you are about to upgrade to a new Nikon and want to sell the Z6 to offset the cost.

- **Firmware version:** Discover the current firmware version installed in your camera. Firmware is the camera's operating system software that is embedded on in-camera memory chips. It can be upgraded when Nikon releases new firmware specific to your camera.

Let's examine each of these settings in detail.

Format Memory Card

Format memory card allows you to prepare the inserted memory card for use in your camera. Formatting is the best way to prepare a memory card, and it should be done in-camera before using a brand-new card and after images have been transferred. Let's see how to format a card.

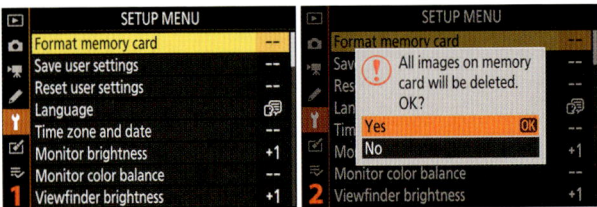

Figure 10.2: Format memory card with Setup Menu screens

Use the following steps to format a memory card:

1. Select Format memory card from the Setup Menu and scroll to the right (figure 10.2, image 1).
2. The next screen makes it very clear with an ominous-sounding message that you are about to delete all the images on the card you have selected for formatting (figure 10.2, image 2). The screen presents a big red exclamation point and the message *All images on memory card will be deleted. OK?* If you have decided not to format the card, just select No and press the OK button; otherwise, highlight Yes and press or touch OK to start the format. After you start the formatting operation, you'll see two popup messages in quick succession. The first will say *Formatting memory card.* A few seconds later—when the card has been successfully formatted—you'll briefly see a final message that says *Formatting complete.* The card is now formatted and you can take lots of pictures.

Settings Recommendation: It is likely best to format each new memory card in the camera before using it for the first time. Some people format their cards in their computers, but that may not be a good idea. Formatting from some computer operating systems may differ from the format used by the camera. Therefore, it is much safer to format the card in-camera only.

Memory Card Information, Error Prevention, and Recovery

Memory card types: The Z6 has one XQD memory card slot, which will soon be compatible with CFexpress memory cards (from a future camera firmware update) if Nikon follows through on its promise to update the camera. XQD and CFexpress cards use the same form factor. While XQD cards are blazingly fast, CFexpress cards are even faster—if the camera's internal hardware can make use of the extra speed, which is yet to be seen.

Accidental formatting: If you accidentally format a memory card that has unsaved images on it, all is not lost. Formatting doesn't actually remove any images from the card. Instead, it removes their entries in the memory card's file allocation table (FAT) so the pictures can no longer be seen or found by the camera. However, you can use card recovery software to rescue most of the pictures *if you do not write anything new to the card* after you format it. That's a good thing to remember in case you ever accidentally format a card with images you wanted to keep.

Recovering images from a failed card: In the case of errors and card failures, the manufacturer of your chosen memory card brand usually has a free image recovery utility you can download to your computer. For instance, Sony has recovery software called "Memory Card File Rescue Software" and Lexar provides "Lexar Image Rescue." Google your card's brand name followed by "memory card recovery software." Search YouTube for videos on how to use the software. There are also several aftermarket memory card recovery products available. However, you should do some research before downloading any old image recovery software you find; there are many scammers on the Internet. Stick with companies you know or get a recommendation from your fellow photographers on Nikonians.org!

Individual image deletion: It is not a good idea to delete individual images from your memory card after you have taken them. This can cause future images to become fragmented as the camera tries to make good use of card memory by overwriting old images. If a new larger image cannot fit into the space of a smaller deleted image, the camera will write part of the image to where the smaller image was located, and then write another part of the image elsewhere. If you have a card problem and the images are fragmented, it is much harder to recover the images with image recovery software. It is better to leave all the image files on the card until you transfer them to your computer and then delete the unwanted images there.

Overfilling a memory card: It may not be a good idea to regularly fill up a memory card to the point where the camera can no longer write an image. Memory cards need a little overhead for error provisioning. Most memory cards have some extra space already allocated for error provisioning; however, that space may be gradually used up as the card ages and sectors are marked as bad by the card manager chip. If you have been using a memory card for a while and you regularly fill it up, the card may suddenly fail with no warning because it has run out of room for error provisioning. This is rare, but why take a chance?

Memory card life span: Please remember that memory cards have a certain life span. This is even more important on Z cameras with a single card slot. While a memory card's lifespan may well be several years, as a card ages it becomes more prone to errors and failure. For important shoots, think carefully about using memory cards that are several years old. While you may get by with it for a while, one day you may have a card failure for the simple reason that the card has no more room for sector errors and subsequently self-destructs. I replace my memory cards at least every two years.

Save User Settings

Save user settings allows you to save up to three user settings. Later you can recall those settings by selecting U1, U2, or U3 from the Mode dial. Each user setting can save most configuration preferences in the Photo Shooting Menu, Movie Shooting Menu, and Custom Setting Menu, along with other specific camera settings. The following lists include items that can and cannot be saved:

Items that can be saved
- Adjustments to one exposure mode (e.g., P, S, A, M) per user setting, including aperture (modes A and M), shutter speed (modes S and M), and flexible program mode (mode P*)
- Exposure and flash compensation (+/− EV settings)
- Flash mode (e.g., Fill flash, Red-eye reduction, Slow sync)
- Focus point (currently active AF point position)
- Metering mode (e.g., Matrix meter, Spot meter)
- Autofocus modes (e.g., Single-servo AF, Continuous-servo AF)
- AF-area modes (e.g., Single-point AF, Dynamic-area AF, Auto-area AF) in both Viewfinder and Live view photography modes
- Bracketing (e.g., Exposure, Flash, White balance, Active D-Lighting)
- Photo Shooting Menu (26 of 33 settings can be saved; seven settings cannot be saved [see next list])
- Movie Shooting Menu (24 of 27 settings can be saved; three settings cannot be saved [see next list])
- Custom Setting Menu (all 51 custom settings a–g)

Items that cannot be saved
- Reset photo shooting, movie shooting, and custom setting menu functions
- Storage folder (100NCZ_6)
- Choose image area settings for still images or video (e.g., FX, DX)
- Manage Picture Control settings for still images or video
- Multiple exposure settings
- Interval timer shooting settings
- Time-lapse photography settings
- Settings on other menus (i.e., Playback Menu, Setup Menu, Retouch Menu, My Menu, or Recent Settings menu)

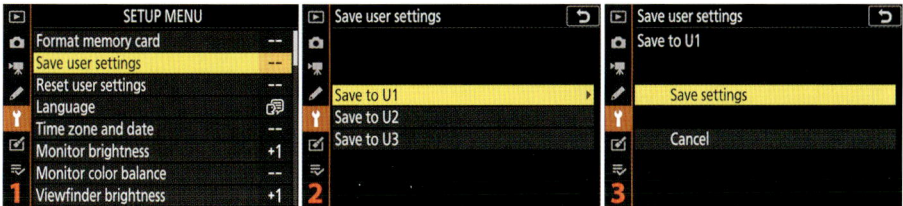

Figure 10.3: Saving a user setting (U1, U2, or U3)

Now let's examine how to save a user setting. Use the following steps to save one of the three user settings (U1, U2, or U3). This must be repeated for each of the settings.

1. Configure your camera's settings exactly how you want them to be saved for one user setting (U1, U2, or U3). Be sure to configure all the items in the *Items that can be saved* list that you want to save. When you are finished, set the Mode dial to whatever shooting mode you want to use for the user setting (such as P, S, A, M, Auto). Do *not* select U1, U2, or U3 on the Mode dial before you save the setting; instead, leave it set to one of the shooting modes.
2. Press the MENU button and scroll down to the Setup Menu. Select Save user settings and scroll to the right (figure 10.3, image 1).
3. Choose either Save to U1, Save to U2, or Save to U3 from the menu and scroll to the right (figure 10.3, image 2).
4. Select Save settings from the menu and press the OK button or tap the option to save the selected setting (figure 10.3, image 3).

Settings Recommendation: Anytime you make a modification to one of the two Shooting Menus or the Custom Setting Menu that you want to reuse, be sure to resave it under one of the user settings. If you are making a temporary change, it isn't important to save it. The user settings will not change unless you resave them. However, if you want to save a particular configuration for future reuse, just set the camera up the way you want to shoot and save the configuration under one of the user settings. Later, you can retrieve that configuration by simply selecting U1, U2 or U3 on the Mode dial.

Reset User Settings

Reset user settings allows you to reset one of the camera's user settings back to the factory defaults. The three user settings—U1, U2 and U3—are independent of each other and must be reset individually. If you have a preowned Z6, it is a good idea to reset all three user settings. That way, the user settings are fresh and ready to be configured for your styles of shooting.

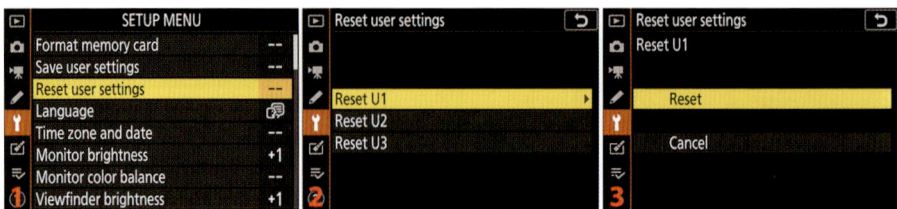

Figure 10.4: Resetting a user setting (U1, U2, or U3)

Here's how to reset one of your camera's user settings. Repeat these steps for each user setting:

1. Select Reset user settings from the Setup Menu and scroll to the right (figure 10.4, image 1).
2. Select Reset U1, Reset U2, or Reset U3 and scroll to the right (figure 10.4, image 2).
3. Choose Reset or Cancel and press the OK button or tap the option to lock in your setting (figure 10.4, image 3). If you chose Reset, the selected user setting will be reset immediately.

Settings Recommendation: If you bought a used Nikon Z6, why not reset the user settings? That way you can reconfigure the camera to your own styles of shooting. Anytime you want to start over with the Photo Shooting Menu, Movie Shooting Menu, or Custom Settings Menu, be sure to reset the user settings and resave after each reconfiguration.

Language

Language is a function that lets the camera know what language you prefer for the camera's menus, screens, and messages. The Z6 can display its screens and menus in four languages (firmware C2.00).

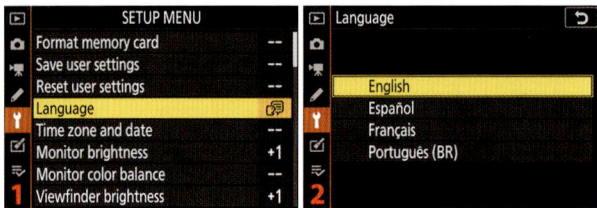

Figure 10.5: Language selection

Use the following steps to select your preferred Language:

1. Select Language from the Setup Menu and scroll to the right (figure 10.5, image 1).
2. Highlight your preferred Language and press the OK button or tap the option to lock in your choice (figure 10.5, image 2).

Settings Recommendation: The camera should come preconfigured for the main language that is spoken where you live. If you prefer a different one, use this setting to select it.

Time Zone and Date

Time zone and date allows you to configure the Time zone, Date and time, Date format, and Daylight saving time settings for your camera.

Let's examine how to set the various parts of Time zone and date. You may have already done this when you first received your camera. We discussed this briefly in the first chapter.

Time Zone

The *Time zone* screen for setting the local time zone displays a familiar world map from which you will select the area of the world where you live. Figure 10.6A shows the Time zone configuration screens. The camera displays some major city names and the coordinated universal time (UTC) below the Time zone map (image 3), in case you don't recognize your location.

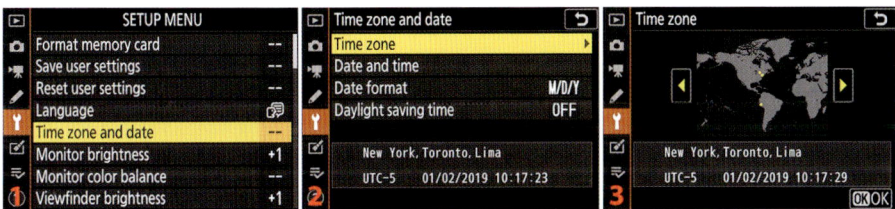

Figure 10.6A: Time zone settings

Use the following steps to set the Time zone:

1. Follow the screen flow shown in figure 10.6A, images 1 and 2 (*Time zone and date* > *Time zone*), until you arrive at the third screen in the series.
2. Use the Multi selector pad to scroll left or right, or tap the left and right yellow pointers on the screen, until your location or the nearest city is marked with a small yellow dot (figure 10.6A, image 3). Press or touch OK to lock in the Time zone.

Date and Time

Figure 10.6B shows the *Date and time* configuration screens. The final screen allows you to select the year, month, and day (Y, M, D), and the hour, minute, and second (H, M, S).

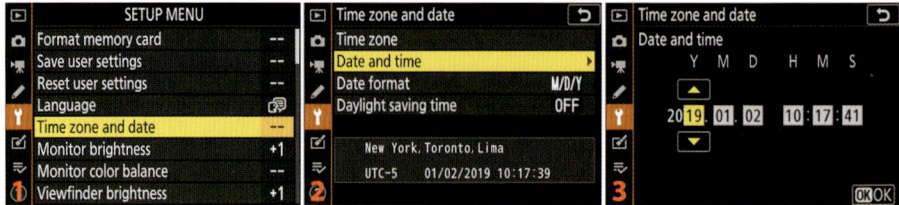

Figure 10.6B: Date and time settings

Use the following steps to set the Date and time:

1. Follow the screen flow shown in figure 10.6B, images 1 and 2 (*Time zone and date > Date and time*), until you arrive at the third screen in the series.
2. Use the Multi selector pad to scroll left or right until you've selected the value you want to change, or simply tap the option with your fingertip (figure 10.6B, image 3). The Y M D settings on the left are for the year, month, and day. The H M S settings on the right are for the hour, minute, and second. Scroll up or down, or tap the yellow arrows, to change each value. Press or touch OK to lock in the Date and time.

Note: The Z6 uses a 24-hour internal clock instead of the 12-hour clock most of us use. Therefore, to set the clock to 3:00 p.m., for example, you must set the H and M settings to 15:00.

If the clock has been reset due to a dead battery, you'll see a tiny flashing clock-face indicator on the camera's displays. It takes about two days of having a charged EN-EL15/a/b battery in the camera to fully charge the built-in clock battery. When the clock battery is fully charged, the clock will remain active without a main camera battery for up to one month.

Date Format

Date format gives you three different ways to format the camera's date, as follows:

- **Y/M/D:** Year/Month/Day (2019/12/31)
- **M/D/Y:** Month/Day/Year (12/31/2019)
- **D/M/Y:** Day/Month/Year (31/12/2019)

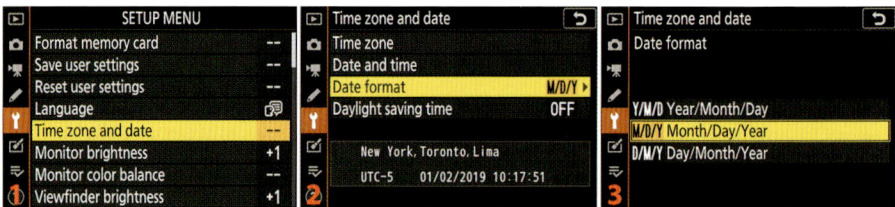

Figure 10.6C: Date format settings

Here are the steps to set the Date format:

1. Follow the screen flow shown in figure 10.6C, images 1 and 2 (*Time zone and date > Date format*), until you arrive at the third screen in the series.
2. Choose your favorite Date format from the menu (figure 10.6C, image 3). Press the OK button or tap the option to lock in the setting.

Daylight Saving Time

Some areas of the world observe daylight saving time. On a specified day in spring of each year, many people set their clocks forward by one hour. Then in the fall they set them back, leading to the clever saying "spring forward, fall back."

If you set *Daylight saving time* to On, the camera will move the time forward by one hour. In the fall, you will need to remember to change this setting to Off so that the camera will move the time back again. Otherwise, the time stamp on your images will be off by one hour for half the year.

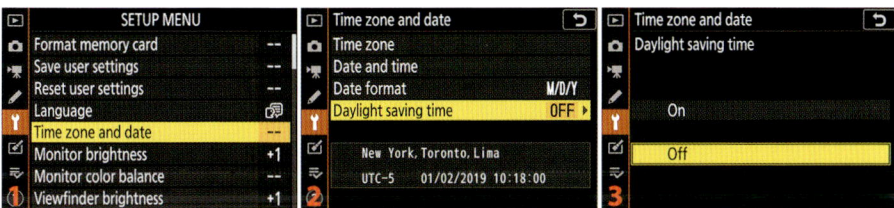

Figure 10.6D: Daylight saving time settings

Here are the steps to enable or disable Daylight saving time:

1. Follow the screen flow shown in figure 10.6D, images 1 and 2 (*Time zone and date > Daylight saving time*), until you arrive at the third screen in the series.
2. Figure 10.6D, image 3, shows you the two choices for Daylight saving time: On or Off. If you select On, your camera will move the time forward by one hour from its current setting. Select Off and the camera will move the time back by one hour. *This is not an automatic function.* You must remember to change this setting each time daylight saving time begins and ends if you are concerned with having a correct time stamp in your picture metadata. If you don't observe daylight saving time, just leave this set to Off and make sure the camera time matches your local time. Press the OK button or tap your selection to lock it in.

Settings Recommendation: This series includes the first settings you'll modify when you get a brand-new Z6 camera. It is important that all these items are set correctly because this information is written into the metadata of each image you make. Daylight saving time is optional, but if you use it, you must remember to change it in the fall and spring of each year so your camera's time will match the local time. I have a reminder set up on my smartphone so that I won't forget. When you are setting all of your clocks and watches for the semi-annual time change, just remember to set your camera's internal clock, too.

Monitor Brightness

Monitor brightness is more important than many people realize. If the Monitor is too dim, you'll have trouble seeing your images in bright light. If it is too bright, you might allow some images to be underexposed because they look fine on the Monitor. Even a seriously underexposed image may look okay on a screen that is too bright. The same goes for video capture.

Additionally, you may need to adjust the Monitor brightness when you are viewing menus or the Information display in bright sunlight or for night shooting. Keeping the Monitor at the right brightness level can be very useful.

The Z6 allows you to adjust the brightness of the Monitor manually. You can select from 10 levels of brightness, varying from –5 to +5.

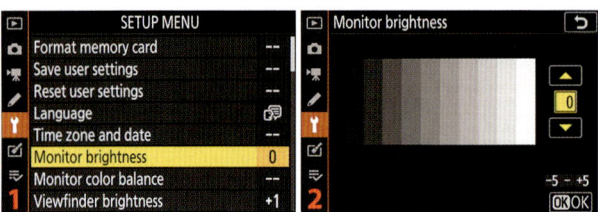

Figure 10.7: Monitor brightness level adjustment

Use the following steps to adjust the brightness of the camera Monitor:

1. Select Monitor brightness from the Setup Menu and scroll to the right (figure 10.7, image 1).
2. Use the Multi selector pad or tap the yellow up/down pointers with your fingertip to scroll through the values (–5 to +5). Scroll toward the negative values to dim the Monitor or toward the positive values to brighten it (figure 10.7, image 2). Use the gray-level bars (dark to light) as a guide and adjust the brightness until you can make a distinction between the last two dark bars on the left. That may be the best setting for your camera in the current ambient light. The brightness defaults to 0 (zero), which is right in the middle. Press or touch OK when you've found the value you like best.

Note: This function does not affect the exposure of the image. It applies only to the brightness of the Monitor. However, an overly bright or dim Monitor may cause you to adjust the exposure in a detrimental way. Be careful!

Settings Recommendation: I generally leave Monitor brightness set to the +1 setting to allow a tiny bit of extra light for my aging eyes. If you choose to set your camera to a level brighter or dimmer than 0, be sure to check the live histogram (page 68) to validate your exposures. Otherwise, you may find that you are mildly under- or overexposing images because they look fine on the Monitor due to the brightness changes. Learn to use the live histogram for the best pictures!

Monitor Color Balance

Monitor color balance is a function that allows you to control the tint of the camera's Monitor. If you feel the Monitor has, let's say, a greenish tint, you can add a little bit of a complementary color to change the color to one that is more acceptable to you.

The effect is not extremely strong, so you will not make your Monitor look garish with this function. However, the color tinting is strong enough that you can overcome any tint you perceive on the Monitor.

This effect does not change the color of your images in any way. It tints the color of the Monitor only, allowing you to balance it against other known color sources.

To balance the Monitor's color, you should have an image on the Monitor that best reflects your style of photography. That way, once you adjust the colors, you will see what pleases your eye for your main style of picture making.

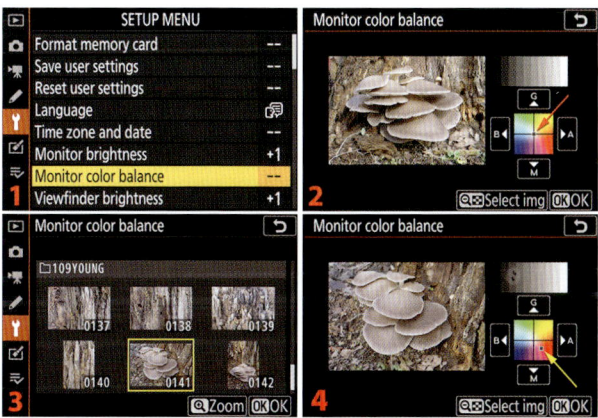

Figure 10.8: Choosing a sample image for color balancing the Monitor

Use the following steps to choose an appropriate sample picture and color balance your Monitor:

1. Choose Monitor color balance from the Setup Menu and scroll to the right (figure 10.8, image 1). The image you last took or viewed on the Monitor will be displayed (figure 10.8, image 2). If this image is acceptable, then you can proceed with color balancing the Monitor.
2. To choose a different picture, you can either: display it on the Monitor before selecting Monitor color balance from the Setup Menu, or press the Zoom out button or tap Select img at the bottom of the screen (figure 10.8, image 2), which will open up an image thumbnail view. From this thumbnail screen you can scroll around and select an appropriate picture for your needs (figure 10.8, image 3). Press or touch OK to select the picture you will use to balance the Monitor.

3. Now let's adjust the Monitor color balance. In figure 10.8, image 2, the red arrow is pointing at a small black square in the middle of a color box. The color box and the surrounding G, A, M, and B pointers provide four color axes you can use for color balance adjustment: green (G), amber (A), magenta (M), and blue (B). By moving the small black indicator toward a certain axis, you will add a tint for that color. You can blend the colors to arrive at nearly any tint you prefer by moving the indicator between axes. In figure 10.8, image 4, the yellow arrow is pointing at the small black square, which has been moved equally toward the amber (A) and magenta (M) axes of the color box, warming up the image slightly. To color balance the Monitor to your satisfaction, move the small black square toward certain colors (G, A, M, B) by tapping on the pointers or by scrolling with the Multi selector pad. Once you have arrived at an appropriate color balance, press or touch OK to save the new Monitor color balance. To reset it at any time, simply return the small black square to the middle of the color box.

Settings Recommendation: Since I do not often adjust images in-camera, I will not be influenced by the way the Monitor looks. I mostly use the Monitor to make composition choices and to check the histogram. I think the Monitor on my Z6 is excellent the way it is and have little need for this Monitor color balance function.

However, if I were shooting in a studio, with carefully controlled lighting, and needed to do careful color matching for a product shot, I might be more concerned about Monitor color balance.

Viewfinder Brightness

Similar to Monitor brightness, *Viewfinder* (EVF) *brightness* is important. If the EVF is too dim, you may accidentally overexpose your images. If it is too bright, you might allow some images to be underexposed because they look fine in the EVF. Even a seriously underexposed image may look okay on an EVF that is too bright. The same goes for video capture.

The Z6 allows you to adjust the brightness of the EVF manually. You can select from 10 levels of brightness, varying from –5 to +5. Or you can allow the camera to automatically adjust the brightness according to the ambient light level with the Auto mode.

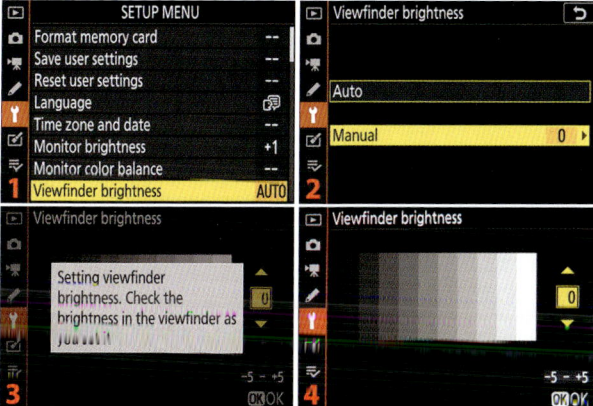

Figure 10.9: Adjusting the brightness of the EVF

Use the following steps to adjust the brightness of the EVF:

1. Select Viewfinder brightness from the Setup Menu and scroll to the right (figure 10.9, image 1).
2. Choose Auto to let the camera decide how bright the EVF needs to be, or select Manual and scroll to the right to adjust the brightness manually (figure 10.9, image 2).
3. If you do not have the camera up to your eye, it is impossible to adjust the Viewfinder brightness manually; therefore, the camera asks you to put your eye up to the Viewfinder to *Check the brightness in the viewfinder as you set it* (figure 10.9, image 3). Once you place your eye to the Viewfinder you will see the screen shown in figure10.9, image 4.
4. Use the Multi selector pad to scroll through the values (–5 to +5). Scroll toward the negative values to dim the EVF or toward the positive values to brighten it (figure 10.9, image 4). Use the gray-level bars (dark to light) as a guide and adjust the brightness until you can make a distinction between the last two dark bars on the left. That may be the best setting for your camera in the current ambient light. The brightness defaults to 0 (zero), which is right in the middle. Press the OK button when you've found the value you like best.

Note: This function *does not* affect the exposure of the image. It applies only to the brightness of the EVF. However, an overly bright or dim EVF may cause you to adjust the exposure in a detrimental way. Be careful!

Settings Recommendation: I set the Viewfinder brightness to +1 because the EVF seems a little too dark for me at 0. I like the little extra brightness that +1 gives me. You may not need it.

If you choose to set your EVF to a level brighter or dimmer than 0, be sure to check the live histogram (page 68) and validate your exposures. Otherwise, you may find that you are mildly under- or overexposing images because they look fine on the EVF due to the brightness changes. Learn to use the live histogram for the best pictures!

Viewfinder Color Balance

Viewfinder color balance is a function that allows you to control the tint of the camera's Viewfinder (EVF). If you feel the EVF has, let's say, a bluish tint, you can add a little bit of a complementary color to change the color to one that is more acceptable to you. The effect is not extremely strong, so you will not make your EVF look garish with this function. However, the color tinting is strong enough that you can overcome any tint you perceive in the EVF.

This effect does not change the color of your images in any way. It only tints the color of the EVF, allowing you to balance it against other known color sources.

To balance the EVF color, you should have an image on the EVF that best reflects your style of photography. That way, once you adjust the colors, you will see what pleases your eye for your main style of picture making.

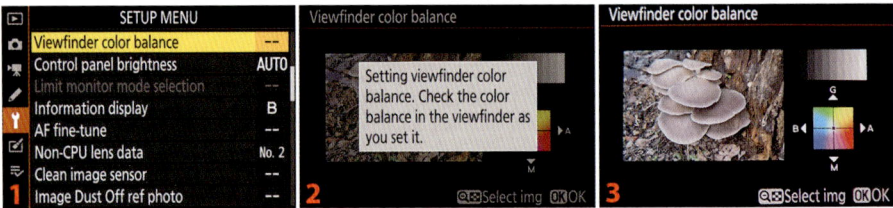

Figure 10.10: Color balancing the EVF

Use the following steps to color balance the camera's EVF:

1. Display a favorite image on the Monitor and press the MENU button. Choose Viewfinder color balance from the Setup Menu and scroll to the right (figure 10.10, image 1).
2. If you do not have the camera up to your eye, it is impossible to adjust the Viewfinder color balance manually; therefore, the camera asks you to put your eye up to the Viewfinder to *Check the color balance in the viewfinder as you set it* (figure 10.10, image 2). Once you place your eye to the Viewfinder you will see the screen shown in figure 10.9, image 3.
3. In figure 10.10, image 3, there is a small black indicator square in the middle of a color box. The color box and the surrounding G, A, M, and B pointers provide four color axes you can use for color balance adjustment: green (G), amber (A), magenta (M), and blue (B). By moving the small black indicator toward a certain axis with the Multi selector pad, you will add a tint for that color. You can blend the colors to arrive at nearly any tint you prefer by moving the indicator between axes. Once you have arrived at an appropriate color balance, press the OK button to save the new Viewfinder color balance. To reset it at any time, simply return the small black square to the middle of the color box.

Settings Recommendation: I mostly use the EVF to make composition choices, to preview the color and contrast of the subject, and to check the histogram for good exposure. I think the color balance of the EVF on my Z6 is excellent the way it is, and I have little need for this Viewfinder color balance function.

However, if I were shooting in a studio with carefully controlled lighting and needed to do careful color matching for a product shot, I might be more concerned about Viewfinder color balance.

Control Panel Brightness

The Control panel on top of the camera gives basic information about settings, including items such as shutter speed, aperture, battery charge, ISO sensitivity, Release mode, and remaining image capacity for the memory card.

The *Control panel brightness* function lets you control the brightness of this useful little OLED Control panel. Most of us will leave the brightness function set to Auto so that the camera can adjust the Control panel brightness according to ambient light conditions. However, the camera allows you to adjust the brightness manually if you'd like. You can select a brightness level in a range from 1 to 7, or even turn it Off. Let's see how to adjust the Control panel brightness.

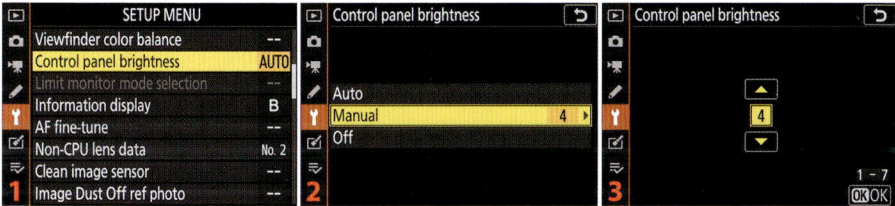

Figure 10.11: Setting the top Control panel brightness

Use the following steps to change the brightness settings for the Control panel on top of the camera:

1. Choose Control panel brightness from the Setup Menu and scroll to the right (figure 10.11, image 1).
2. If you are like most photographers, the Auto setting is likely the best choice, and it's the factory default setting (figure 10.11, image 2). Auto lets the camera decide which brightness is best, automatically dimming the Control panel in low light and brightening it in bright light. If Auto is fine with you, highlight it and press the OK button or tap the Auto option to lock it in, and then skip the following steps.
3. If you do not use the Control panel and would rather turn it off to save battery, you can do so on the screen shown in image 2 by selecting Off and pressing the OK button or tapping Off with your fingertip. However, if you need to manually control the brightness, you can do so by selecting Manual and scrolling to the right (figure 10.11, image 2).

4. The camera offers you an up/down menu with numbers ranging from 1 to 7 (figure 10.11, image 3). Smaller numbers dim the Control panel and higher numbers brighten it. Choose a number by scrolling up or down with the Multi selector pad or tapping on the yellow up/down arrows. Press or touch OK to lock in in the value.

Settings Recommendation: I leave the Control panel brightness set to Auto for my Z6. I don't use the Control panel on this camera nearly as much as I did with my Nikon DSLRs, but it still comes in handy for a quick look at or selection of important settings.

If you are doing night photography, would like to save battery power, or just don't need the Control panel, you can turn it off. If you need to make it very dim or very bright, then you can control the brightness manually.

Limit Monitor Mode Selection

Limit monitor mode selection allows you to choose which modes are available when you press the Monitor mode button on the side of the camera's Viewfinder (figure 10.12A, image 3, red arrow).

Here is a description of the four available modes, followed by how to enable or disable individual modes:

- **Automatic display switch:** When this mode is selected the camera will use its Eye sensor to detect when your eye is at the Viewfinder and switch the display output to the EVF. If nothing is near the Eye sensor, the camera uses the rear Monitor instead. (See the upcoming subsection, **Cautionary Note on Using the Eye Sensor**.)
- **Viewfinder only:** The camera uses the EVF only and leaves the Monitor turned off. Nothing will be displayed on the Monitor, even if you try to use a function that normally appears on the Monitor. The EVF is the camera's main display in this mode.
- **Monitor only:** The camera uses the Monitor only and leaves the EVF turned off. Nothing will be displayed on the EVF, even if you put your eye up to the Viewfinder. The Monitor is the camera's main display in this mode.
- **Prioritize viewfinder:** This mode makes the camera act more like a DSLR. The Monitor stays off until it needs to display a just-captured image or video—and your eye is not peering into the EVF. In effect, the EVF is prioritized, with the camera using the Monitor only when required by you, such as for image or video playback (i.e., you press the Playback button or the MENU button with your eye away from the Viewfinder).

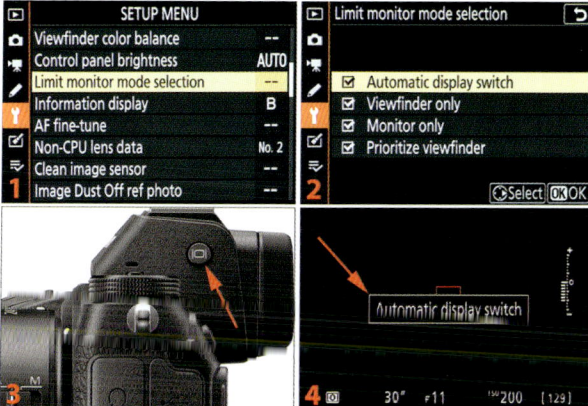

Figure 10.12A: Choosing which Monitor/EVF modes are available

Use the following steps to limit which Monitor modes your camera will offer you when you press the Monitor mode button:

1. Choose Limit monitor mode selection from the Setup Menu and scroll to the right (figure 10.12A, image 1).
2. To enable or disable one or more of the Monitor modes, you must check or uncheck each mode individually (figure 10.12A, image 2). Highlight one of the Monitor modes and scroll to the right to check or uncheck that mode. You can also tap a check box to add or remove a check mark. When you've checked only the modes you want to use, press or touch OK to lock in your choices.
3. Only modes that have check marks to the left of the name will be available when you press the Monitor mode button (figure 10.12A, image 3, red arrow). The camera will present a different mode on the Monitor or in the EVF with each press of the button—such as you see in figure 10.12A, image 4 (e.g., Automatic display switch). To select a Monitor mode, press the Monitor mode button (image 3) until the mode you desire to use shows on the Monitor or in the EVF.

Settings Recommendation: I normally leave the mode set to Automatic display switch for convenience. When I am out doing a walkabout, I may use Prioritize viewfinder, which makes the Monitor stay off except for displaying an image after I take it. I rarely use the Monitor only or Viewfinder only settings. However, I leave them available in case I need them.

Cautionary Note on Using the Eye Sensor

The Eye sensor is *very* sensitive. I was taking pictures on a rainy day in the mountains and a pinhead-sized rain droplet got on the sensor. The camera then refused to use the rear Monitor. I thought my new camera was ruined from being too wet, but then I noticed the tiny droplet, removed it, and all was well.

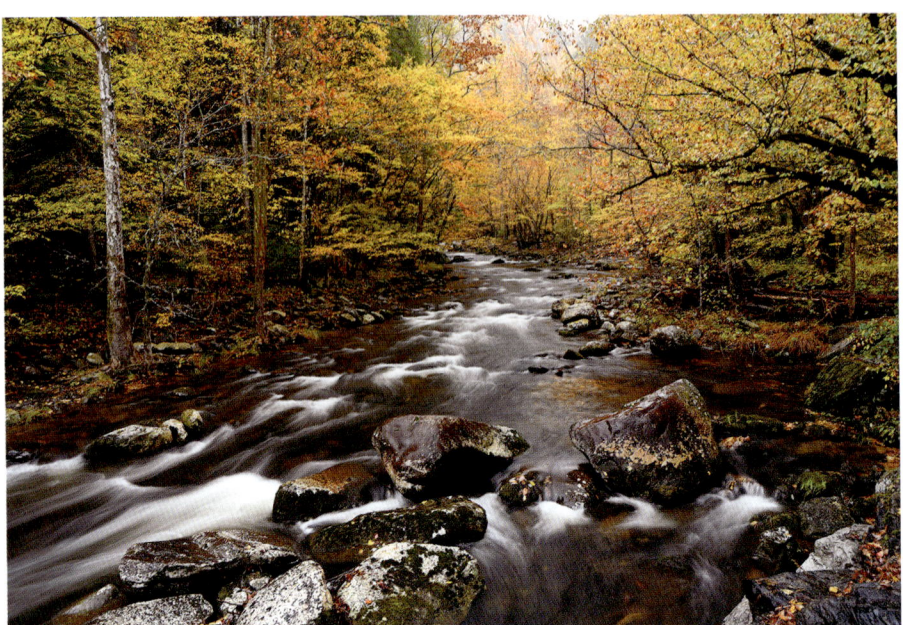

Figure 10.12B: Results from shooting all day in the rain in Great Smoky Mountains, Tennessee, USA.

I shot for several hours in a light rain, occasionally wiping the camera off with a lens cleaning cloth. The camera performed flawlessly (see figure 10.12B). Just keep dust and water droplets off the little dark rectangle at the top of the Viewfinder opening—that's the Eye sensor location.

Information Display

The *Information display* setting allows your camera to automatically sense how much ambient light there is in the area where you are shooting and adjust the color and brightness of the Information display screen accordingly. If the ambient light is bright, the color of the physical Information display screen will also be bright so that it can overcome the ambient light.

To open the Information display screen, press the DISP button multiple times until the Information display appears (figure 10.13A). Once you see the Information display, pressing the *i* button will bring up the *i* menu at the bottom of the screen, with the Information display at the top. The Information display screen shows the current shooting information: shutter speed, aperture, ISO, and frame count, plus the 12 items that are adjustable on the *i* menu.

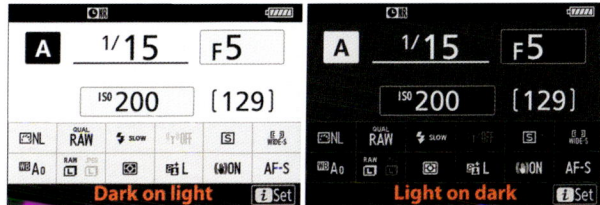

Figure 10.13A: Dark on light and Light on dark display screens

In the Light on dark screen shown in figure 10.13A, I brightened the screen's gray text considerably so that it is clear in the printed book. In real life it is dimmer than shown here to allow you to keep your night vision.

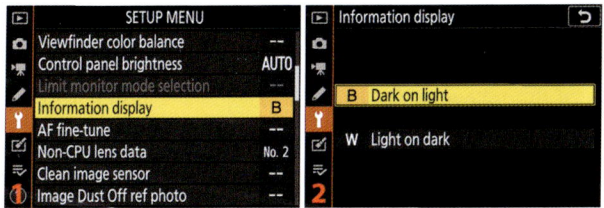

Figure 10.13B: Setting Information display to Auto

Use the following steps to configure the Information display:

1. Select Information display from the Setup Menu and scroll to the right (figure 10.13B, image 1).
2. Choose B Dark on light or W Light on dark and press the OK button or tap the option to lock in your setting (figure 10.13B, image 2).

Settings Recommendation: I leave Information display set to Dark on light for normal use. However, when I am doing night photography, the much dimmer Light on dark setting protects my night vision.

AF Fine-Tune

The *AF fine-tune* function allows you to *manually* adjust your camera to a particular lens so the lens focuses where you want it to focus.

Nikon has made provisions for keeping a table of up to 30 lenses fine-tuned for better focus. The idea behind fine-tuning is that you can push the focus forward or backward in small increments, with up to 20 increments in each direction (–20 to +20).

Once you have fine-tuned the autofocus system for a particular lens, the actual focus is moved from its default position forward or backward by the amount you've specified in the fine-tuning operation. If your lens has a consistent back focus problem and you move the focus a little forward, the problem is solved.

First let's see how to access the fine-tuning system, and then we will examine each of its four subsettings in detail (figure 10.14A, image 2).

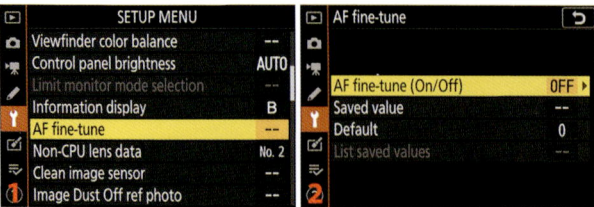

Figure 10.14A: Fine-tuning the focus of a lens

Use the following steps to start the process of fine-tuning a lens (figure 10.14A):

1. Choose *Setup Menu* > *AF fine-tune* (figure 10.14A, image 1).
2. The next four subsections show the screens used to configure AF fine-tune (figures 10.14B to 10.14E). Each of the following figures continues where figure 10.14A, image 2, ends.

AF Fine-Tune (On/Off)

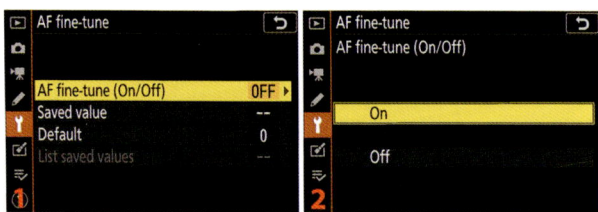

Figure 10.14B: Enabling or disabling AF fine-tune

Figure 10.14B shows the AF fine-tune (On/Off) screen and its selections. The two values you can select are as follows:

- **On:** This setting enables the AF fine-tune system. Set AF fine-tune (On/Off) to On if you are planning to fine-tune a lens now. Press the OK button or tap the option to save the value.
- **Off:** When AF fine-tune (On/Off) is set to Off, the camera focuses like a factory default Z6, with no fine-tuning applied.This default setting disables the AF fine-tune system.

Saved Value

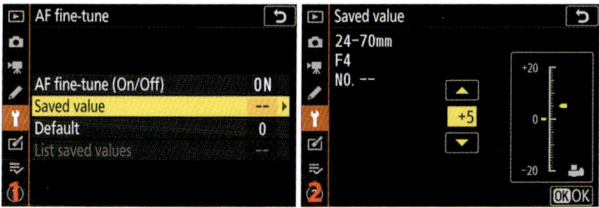

Figure 10.14C: Fine-tuning a lens with a Saved value

With an autofocus lens mounted, *Saved value* allows you to control the amount of front or back focus fine-tuning you would like to input for the listed lens. At the top left of figure 10.14C, image 2, just under the words Saved value, you'll see the focal length of the lens that is mounted on the camera, the aperture range (F4), and the number assigned to the lens. If you're configuring a lens for the first time, you'll see NO. ––. You can fine-tune a maximum of 30 lenses. After you save a lens configuration, a lens number will appear in place of the dashes (NO. 0 to NO. 99). We'll discuss how to assign a lens a certain number between 0 and 99 shortly.

To the right of the lens information is a scale that runs from +20 on the top to –20 on the bottom. The yellow pointer on the right starts out at 0. You can move this yellow pointer up or down to change the amount of focus fine-tuning you need for this lens. Moving the pointer up on the scale pushes the focal point away from the camera, and moving it down pulls the focal point toward the camera. I set my Nikkor Z 24–70mm F/4 S lens to +5 forward focus, as shown in figure 10.14C, image 2. When you set the fine-tuning amount you need, press or touch OK to save it.

Default

The *Default* configuration screen looks a lot like the Saved value screen, except no lens information is listed. This Default value will be applied to all AF lenses you mount on your camera. If you are convinced that your particular camera (not a lens) always has a back or front focus problem and you are not able or ready to ship it off to Nikon for repair, you can use the Default value to push the autofocus in one direction or the other until you are satisfied that your camera is focusing the way you'd like. *Again, this will affect all autofocus lenses you mount on your camera.*

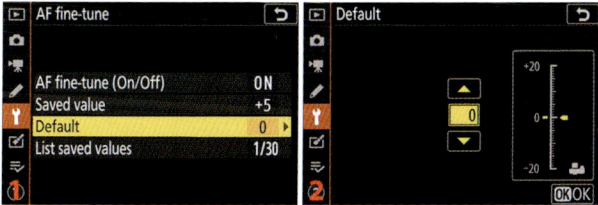

Figure 10.14D: Setting a Default fine-tune adjustment for all lenses

As shown in figure 10.14D, image 2, to set an *AF fine-tune > Default* value, use the scale that runs from +20 on the top to −20 on the bottom. The yellow pointer starts at 0. You can move this yellow pointer up or down to change the amount of focus fine-tuning you need for *every autofocus lens you will mount on the Z6,* if no value already exists in the Saved value for a particular lens (Saved value overrides Default).

Moving the pointer up on the scale pushes the focal point away from the camera (front focus), and moving it down pulls the focal point toward the camera (back focus). When you are done, press or touch OK. Be careful with this setting. Most people will not use it because it applies an AF fine-tune value to any AF lens mounted on the camera, whether that lens needs fine-tuning or not.

Note: You could use this Default value as a value for any of your AF lenses that do not have a Saved value. I tested this with a different lens (not shown) by setting a Saved value of +1 for my AF-S Nikkor 24–120mm lens. While the 24–120mm lens was still mounted, I set a value of −2 for the Default value. When I removed the 24–120mm lens and mounted an AF Nikkor 60mm micro lens, the +1 in the Saved value field disappeared, but the −2 in the Default field stayed put. So it appears that you can use the Default field either for all AF lenses that have no Saved value or for a currently mounted AF lens that you want to adjust but not save a value for.

List Saved Values

Notice in figure 10.14E that there are several screens used to configure the list of saved values. *List saved values* helps you remember which lenses you've fine-tuned. It allows you to set an identification number (00–99) for a particular lens out of the 20 lenses you can register.

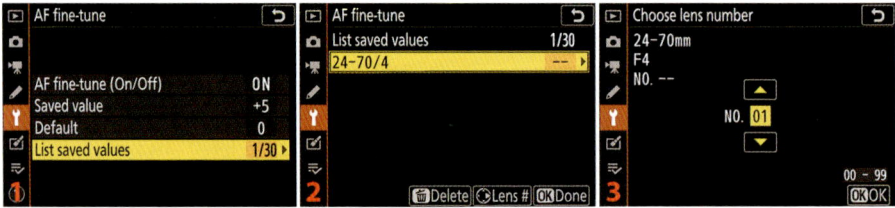

Figure 10.14E: Assigning an AF fine-tune lens number to one of your 20 lenses

In figure 10.14E, image 2, you can see my 24–70mm F/4 lens listed (24–70/4). This List saved values screen will show a list of all the lenses for which you have saved values—my camera just happens to have saved values for only one lens.

Some photographers use the last two digits of a lens's serial number as the Saved value identification number for that lens. Use the screen shown in figure 10.14E, image 3, to select any number from 00 to 99. Scroll up or down with the Multi selector pad or tap the up/down pointers on the screen to change the number in the yellow box.

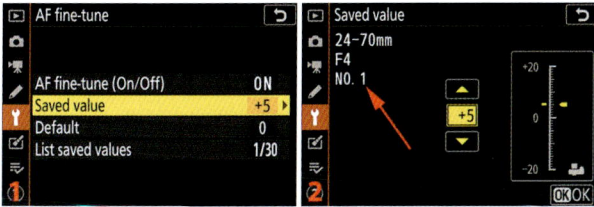

Figure 10.14F: NO. 1 set under Save value

You will see the results of this change when you examine the Saved value screen, as shown in figure 10.14F, image 2. Instead of NO. --, the screen in image 2 now reports NO. 1 (compare to figure 10.14C, image 2).

You can have up to 30 lenses listed on the List saved values screen (figure 10.14E, image 2), with each lens having a different number from 00 to 99.

Settings Recommendation: AF fine-tune is good to have. If I buy a new lens and it has focus problems, I don't keep it. Back it goes to the manufacturer for a replacement. However, if I buy a used lens or have had one long enough to go out of warranty and it later develops front or back focus problems, the camera allows me to fine-tune the autofocus for that lens.

Non-CPU Lens Data

Non-CPU lens data helps you use older non-CPU Nikkor lenses with your camera. Do you still have several older AI or AI-S Nikkor lenses? I do! The image quality from the older manual focus (MF) lenses is excellent.

Since the Z6 is positioned as an advanced enthusiast and pro camera, it must have the necessary controls to use both auto focus (AF) and manual focus (MF) lenses. Many photographers on a budget use the older MF lenses on a Nikon FTZ adapter to obtain professional-level image quality without having to break the bank on expensive lens purchases. You can buy excellent AI and AI-S Nikkor MF lenses on eBay for $100–$400, and with them you can achieve image quality that only the most expensive autofocus lenses can produce. Additionally, with all the aftermarket lens adapters currently available for the Z-camera line, MF lenses of all sorts and brands are available for photographers who like to experiment with non-Nikon lenses.

It's important to have a way to let the Z6 know something about the lens in use. This Non-CPU lens data function allows you to do exactly that. You can store information for up to 20 separate non-CPU lenses within this section of the Z6.

Here is an analysis of the Non-CPU lens data screen selections (figure 10.15A, image 2):

- **Lens number:** Using the Multi selector pad, you can scroll left or right to select one of your lenses. There are 20 lens records available. When you select a Lens number here, the focal length and maximum aperture of that lens will show up in the Focal length and Maximum aperture fields. If you haven't stored information for a particular Lens number, you'll see double dashes (– –) in the Focal length and Maximum aperture fields.

- **Focal length (mm):** This field contains the actual focal length in millimeters (mm) of the lens in use. You can select focal lengths from 6mm to 4000mm. Hmm, I didn't know they even made a 4000mm lens. I want one!
- **Maximum aperture:** This field is for the Maximum aperture of the lens. You can enter an f-stop number from F1.2 to F22. Remember, this is for the maximum aperture only (largest opening or f-stop).

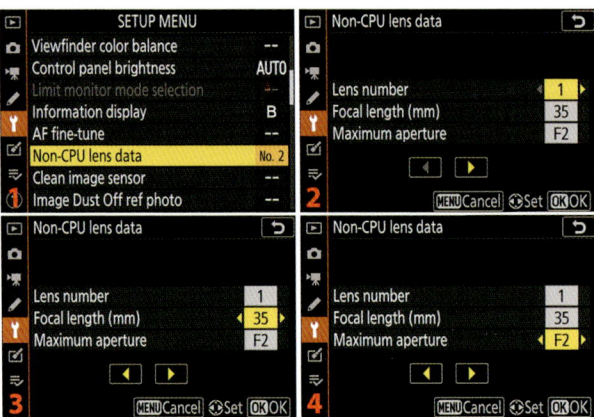

Figure 10.15A: Non-CPU lens data

Use the following steps to configure (save) each of your non-CPU lenses for use with your Z6:

1. Select Non-CPU lens data from the Setup Menu and scroll to the right (figure 10.15A, image 1).
2. Choose Lens number and scroll left or right until you find the number you want to use for this particular lens (figure 10.15A, image 2).
3. Scroll down to Focal length (mm) and scroll left or right to select the focal length of the lens (figure 10.15A, image 3). If you are configuring a non-CPU zoom lens, select the widest setting. This works because the meter will adjust for any light falloff that may occur as the lens is zoomed out.
4. Scroll down to Maximum aperture and scroll left or right to select the maximum aperture of the lens (figure 10.15A, image 4). If you are configuring a variable-aperture zoom lens, select the largest aperture the lens can use (e.g., f/2.8). This works because the meter will adjust for the variation in the aperture.
5. Press or touch OK to store the setting.

The screen shown in figure 10.15A, image 2, allows you to either select a lens or save changes to one or all 20 of your lenses. In other words, you can use the set of screens in figure 10.15A to both input and select a non-CPU lens.

When you have selected a lens for use, the *Setup Menu > Non-CPU lens data* selection will show the number of the lens you've selected. It will be in the format of No. 1 to No. 20. In figure 10.15A, image 1, you can see the lens selection (No. 1) at the end of the Non-CPU lens data line. That's my beloved AI Nikkor 35mm f/2 lens!

Selecting a Non-CPU Lens with External Camera Controls

As we discussed in the previous chapter, the Z6 allows you to customize several of its buttons and controls with various options, one of which allows you to select a non-CPU lens.

If you frequently use several manual focus non-CPU lenses, you can use the Custom Setting Menu to assign the setting called *Choose non-CPU lens number* to one of the camera's buttons (*Custom Setting Menu > f Controls > f2 Custom control assignment; page 423*). This will allow you to select Non-CPU lens data very quickly. You hold down the assigned button (e.g., Fn1, Fn2) and turn either of the Command dials to select one of the 20 non-CPU lenses you have registered with the camera.

To select a non-CPU lens using external camera controls (after making an assignment to one of the camera's buttons), hold down the button you've assigned (e.g., Movie record button) and turn either Command dial until the number of your lens is highlighted in yellow (No. 1 to No. 20; figure 10.15B), then release the button. Now your camera knows which lens is mounted. The focal length and maximum aperture (e.g., 200mm F4) of the selected non-CPU lens will appear at the top of the screen.

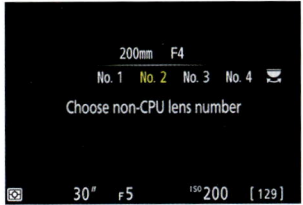

Figure 10.15B: Non-CPU lens data from assigned button

Using the FTZ Adapter with Non-CPU Lenses

Because the FTZ adapter does not have an aperture indexing prong and cannot manually connect to a lens, the Z6 has no way to know which aperture the camera is using with non-CPU lenses. If you examine the internal metadata of an image you have taken with a non-CPU lens, using the camera's Overview screen (page 148), you will notice that the camera registers only the maximum aperture of the non-CPU lens—the one you previously entered—and not the actual aperture you used to take the picture. This is because the camera has no idea which aperture you have selected. In fact, you will notice that the top Control panel, EVF, and Monitor will be flashing "F− −" the entire time you have a non-CPU lens mounted. The Z7/Z6 User's Manual lists this as an error (page 164); however, in this case it simply means the camera cannot determine which aperture is in use. Ignore the flashing "F− −" and use stop-down metering with assistance from the live histogram (page 68) to obtain an accurate exposure. If you have favorite non-CPU lenses that you want to use frequently, you can find a company that will add a CPU chip to a non-CPU lens so that it will pass aperture information. Using focus Peaking (page 409) with non-CPU lenses will help you achieve excellent manual focus.

Clean Image Sensor

Clean image sensor is Nikon's helpful answer to dust spots on your images that are due to a dirty imaging sensor. Dust is everywhere and will eventually get on your camera's sensor. The Z6 cleans the sensor by vibrating the entire sensor unit. These high-frequency vibrations will hopefully dislodge dust and make it fall off the filter so you won't see it as spots on your pictures.

The vibration cleaning method seems to work pretty well. Of course, if sticky pollen or other moist dust gets into the camera, the vibration system won't be able to remove it. Then it may be time for brush or wet cleaning.

Clean Now

Clean now allows you to clean the imaging sensor at any time. If you detect a dust spot, or just get nervous because you are in a dusty environment with your Z6, you can simply select Clean now and the camera will execute a sensor cleaning cycle.

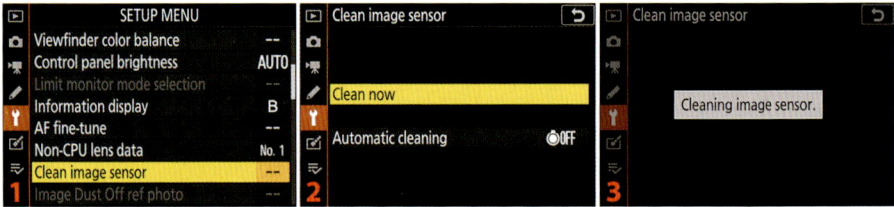

Figure 10.16A: Clean now screens

Use the following steps to clean the camera's sensor immediately:

1. Select Clean image sensor from the Setup Menu and scroll to the right (figure 10.16A, image 1).
2. Select Clean now from the menu and press the OK button or tap the option with your fingertip (figure 10.16A, image 2).
3. Step 2 starts the automatic cleaning process. A screen will appear that says *Cleaning image sensor* (figure 10.16A, image 3). When sensor cleaning is finished, a screen that says *Done* will briefly appear (not shown in figure). Then the camera switches back to the Setup Menu.

Now, let's examine how to select an active method for regular sensor cleaning.

Automatic Cleaning

For preventive dust control, some photographers set their cameras to clean the sensor at shutdown. There are two selections for Automatic cleaning:

- Clean at shutdown
- Cleaning off

These settings are self-explanatory. I find it interesting that I don't detect any shutdown delay when using Clean at shutdown mode. I can turn my camera on and immediately take a picture. The cleaning cycle seems to be very brief, or at least interruptible, in this mode.

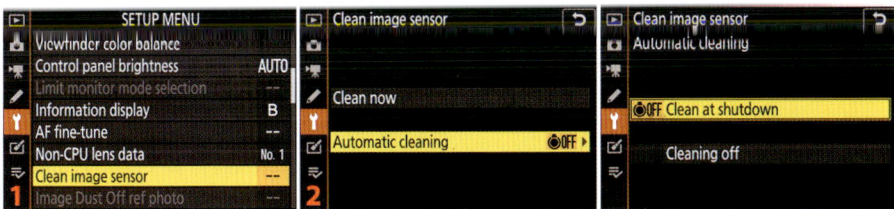

Figure 10.16B: Automatic cleaning screens

Use the following steps to enable or disable Automatic cleaning:

1. Select Clean image sensor from the Setup Menu and scroll to the right (figure 10.16B, image 1).
2. Choose Automatic cleaning from the menu and scroll to the right (figure 10.16B, image 2).
3. Select Clean at shutdown to enable Automatic cleaning, or select Off to disable it (figure 10.16B, image 3). Clean at shutdown seems to be the best choice for most photographers. Press the OK button or tap the option to lock in your choice.

Nikon suggests that you hold the camera at the same angle as when you are taking pictures (bottom down) when you use these modes to clean the sensor.

Settings Recommendation: I leave my camera set to Clean at shutdown. That way it will do a cleaning cycle every time I turn the camera off. It doesn't seem to slow down shooting; I can still turn on the camera and immediately begin taking photographs. A little sensor cleaning in this dusty world seems like a good idea to me.

Image Dust Off Ref Photo

You may go out and do an expensive shoot only to return and find that some dust spots have appeared in the worst possible places in your images. If you immediately create an *Image Dust Off ref photo,* you can use it to remove the dust spots from a series of images, and then you can clean the camera's sensor for your next shooting session.

When you use the following instructions to create the Image Dust Off ref photo, you'll be shooting a blank, unfocused picture of a pure white or gray background. The dust spots in the image will then be readily apparent to Nikon Capture NX-D software. Yes, you must use Nikon's free software to automatically batch-remove dust spots from a large number of images.

When you load the image(s) to be cleaned into Capture NX-D, along with the Image Dust Off ref photo, the software will use the Image Dust Off ref photo to automatically remove the dust spots in your pictures.

The position and amount of dust on the sensor may change. You should take Image Dust Off ref photos regularly and use one that was taken within one day of the photographs you wish to clean up.

Finding a Subject for the Dust-Off Reference Photo

First, you'll need to select a featureless subject to make a photograph for the Image Dust Off ref photo. The key is to use a material that has no graininess, such as a bright, well-lit white card. I tried using plain white sheets of paper held up to a bright window, but the resulting reference photo was unsatisfactory to Capture NX-D. It gave me a message that my reference photo was too dusty when I tried to use it.

After some experimentation, I finally settled on three different subjects that seem to work well:

- A slide-viewing light table with the light turned on
- A computer monitor with a blank white word processor document
- A plain white card under bright light

All of these were bright and featureless enough to satisfy both my camera and Capture NX-D. The key is to photograph something fairly bright, but not too bright. You may need to experiment with different subjects if you don't have a light table or computer.

Now, let's prepare the camera for the actual reference photo.

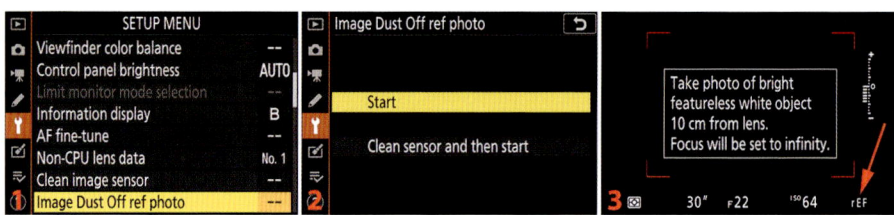

Figure 10.17A: Image Dust Off ref photo settings

Here are the steps you'll use to create an Image Dust Off ref photo:

1. Select Image Dust Off ref photo from the Setup Menu and scroll to the right (figure 10.17A, image 1).

2. Choose Start and press the OK button, or tap Start with your fingertip (figure 10.17A, image 2). (There is also a Clean sensor and then start selection. However, since I want to remove dust on current pictures, I won't use this setting. It might remove the dust bunny that is imprinted on the last 500 images I just shot! I'll clean my sensor after I get a good Image Dust Off ref photo. Choose Clean sensor and then start *only* if the Image Dust Off ref photo will not be used with existing images!)

3. Once you've selected Start, you'll see the characters rEF on the screen (figure 10.17A, image 3, red arrow). This simply means that the camera is ready to create the image. When the camera displays the screen in figure 10.17A, image 3, hold the lens about 4 inches (10 cm) away from a blank subject. The camera will not try to autofocus during the process, which is good because you want the lens at infinity. You are not trying to take a viewable picture; you're creating an image that shows where the dust is on the sensor. Focus is not important, and neither is minor camera shake.

4. If you try to take the picture and the subject is not bright enough, too bright, or too grainy (not feature-less), you will see the screen shown in figure 10.17B. If you are having problems with too much brightness, use a gray surface instead of white. Most of the time this error is caused by insufficient light. If you don't see the screen in figure 10.17B and the shutter fires, you have successfully created an Image Dust Off ref photo. You can double-check that you were successful by pressing the Playback button.

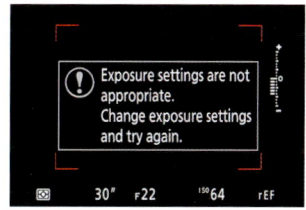

Figure 10.17B: Image Dust Off ref photo failure

5. If you see the image shown in figure 10.17C on your camera screen, the reference photo was captured. A file of approximately 16 MB is created on your camera's memory card with a filename extension of .NDF (an example file name is DSC_1234.NDF). This NDF file is basically a small database of the millions of clean pixels in your imaging sensor and a few dirty ones. You cannot display the Image Dust Off ref photo on your computer. It will not open in Nikon Capture NX-D or any other graphics program that I tried. It is used only as a reference by Capture NX-D when it's time to clean images.

Figure 10.17C: Successful Image Dust Off ref photo

Using Capture NX-D to Remove Dust Spots

To store the reference photo for later use in removing spots, copy the NDF file (figure 10.17C) from your camera's memory card to the computer folder containing the images that have dust spots on them, the ones for which you created this Image Dust Off ref photo. You can use the Image Dust Off function (figure 10.17D) in Nikon Capture NX-D to remove the dust spots from all of the images represented by the Image Dust Off ref photo.

In figure 10.17D, the red-rimmed cutout in the middle is an enlargement of the *Window > Edit > Camera and Lens Corrections* window in the control bar on the right side of Capture NX-D version 1.5.0.

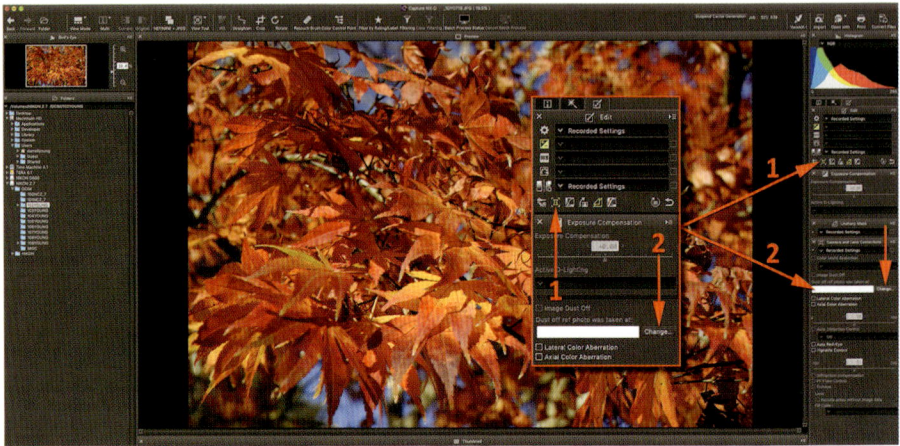

Figure 10.17D: Nikon Capture NX-D's Image Dust Off function

Here are the steps to use the Image Dust Off functions in Nikon Capture NX-D to remove dust from a group of images, using an Image Dust Off ref photo (figure 10.17D):

1. Copy your images into a folder on your computer, along with the Image Dust Off ref photo. It is best if they are in the same folder to make sure they represent the images you recently shot. You can browse to a different folder if you want to store the dust off photo elsewhere.
2. Now, open Capture NX-D and use the folder browser on the left side of the screen to browse to the folder that contains your images and the dust off photo.
3. Click on the Edit tab on the right side of the screen, and then click on the Camera and Lens Corrections icon (figure 10.17D, arrow 1).
4. Select the image you want to process and make sure it is shown large in the center section of Nikon Capture NX-D. Wait a moment—when the software detects a dust off ref photo in the folder, the Change button (figure 10.17D, arrow 2) will become available.
5. Click on the Change button and a query window will open with the following question: *Do you want to use a Dust off ref photo that is in the same folder as the active image?* Click the Yes button and Capture NX-D will process the images in the folder against the Image Dust Off ref photo, removing the dust spots from all the images in the folder. It will take some time to process the image, and the computer will show a wait indicator until the picture is processed. Capture NX-D does not inform you that it is done, but when the hourglass or other wait indicator goes away the process is complete.
6. In the text field next to the Change button, check to see the date-and-time stamp of the Image Dust Off ref photo used to correct the image. It will look like this: "2019/04/30 15:50:10."

Settings Recommendation: Nikon Capture NX-D is free, and it's a good form of insurance, even if you use it for nothing more than removing dust from your images. Whenever you find yourself out in nature or shooting in an environment that might be dusty, why not create an Image Dust Off ref photo as the last photo of the day? That dust off photo may save you a lot of dust removal work. Let Capture NX-D do it for you!

Additionally, Nikon has recently added the "color control points" back into the Capture software. Many of us used those powerful control points in Nikon Capture NX-2 to selectively post-process exact areas of the image. When Nikon stopped supporting Capture NX-2 and brought out NX-D instead, the color control points were missing. Well, with version 1.5.0 of Capture NX-D, the powerful color control points are back! Download the free Nikon Capture NX-D at the following website:

http://downloadcenter.nikonimglib.com/en/products/162/Capture_NX-D.html
If for some reason the URL doesn't work, just Google "Download Nikon Capture NX-D" and I'm sure you will find it.

White Card Tip

Remember, all your camera needs to create an Image Dust Off ref photo is a good look at its imaging sensor so it can map the dust spots into an NDF file (ref photo file). If you get the warning screen shown in figure 10.17B that says exposure settings are not appropriate, change the exposure settings and try again with a nice bright, clean, white surface. Put the lens very close to the surface, and make sure it is not in focus. Nikon recommends less than 4 inches (10 cm). You might even want to manually set the lens to infinity if you are having problems with this. When you've found your favorite white or gray surface for Image Dust Off ref photos, keep it safe and use it consistently.

Image Comment

Image comment is a useful setting that allows you to attach a 36-character comment to each image you shoot. The comment is embedded in the picture's internal metadata and does not show up on the image itself. I attach the comment "Photo by Darrell Young" to my images.

You could include your copyright here, even though the camera has a place to put Copyright information (see the next section), or you could insert a comment with some details about the picture series.

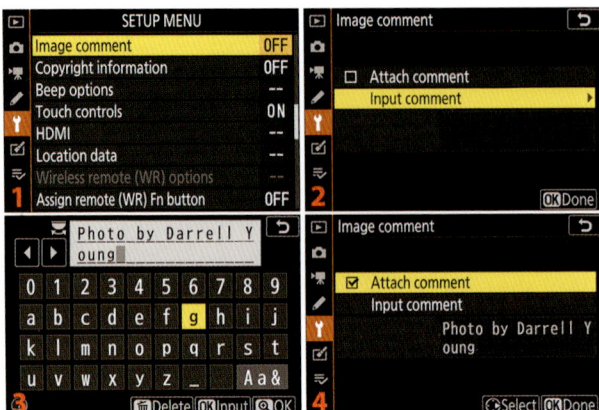

Figure 10.18: Attaching an Image comment

Use the following steps to create an Image comment:

1. Select Image comment from the Setup Menu and scroll to the right (figure 10.18, image 1).
2. Select Input comment from the menu and scroll to the right (figure 10.18, image 2).
3. The comment entry keyboard is shown in figure 10.18, image 3. You can insert an image comment by tapping the characters you want to use on the Monitor, and they will appear in the position marked with the dark-gray cursor in the comment field (Photo by Darrell Young). You can enter up to 36 characters. Use the left/right arrow tip touch controls in the top-left corner to move left and right in the comment field. To change from upper to lower case—or to access symbols, such as #—tap the Aa& control in the lower-right corner of the screen (just above the OK touch control). If you make a mistake, position the dark gray cursor over the error and tap the Delete control at the bottom of the screen. When you've finished entering the comment, press or touch OK to save it. You will see the word *Saved* appear briefly on the Monitor. (**Note:** If you would prefer not to use the touch-screen features, you can move the selection cursor with the Multi selector pad to highlight a character in the list below the comment field, then press the OK button to insert the character. To correct an error, turn the rear Main command dial to move back and forth along the field that contains the new comment, and press the Delete button to remove the error. Press the OK button when you are finished entering the comment.)
4. The camera will switch back to the Image comment screen (figure 10.18, image 4). Now you must put a check mark in the Attach comment check box so the comment will attach itself to each new image you take. To toggle a check mark on or off in the check box, highlight the Attach comment line and scroll to the right with the Multi selector pad, or tap the check box with your fingertip.
5. Press or touch OK (Done) to save the new comment.

Settings Recommendation: You can use this comment field for any text you want to add to the internal metadata of the image (up to 36 characters). There is another Setup Menu selection called **Copyright information** (see the next section) that allows you to add your personal copyright. I added basic "who took it" information here because I am worried about image theft. You may want to add other text—since the camera provides a specific Copyright information screen—such as information to identify the shoot. Remember, you are limited to 36 characters in the comment.

Copyright Information

Copyright information allows you to embed Artist and Copyright data into each image. Refer to figure 10.19 and use the following steps to add personal information to your camera. Your Artist name and Copyright information will then be written into the metadata of each of your images, but is not visible on the image itself.

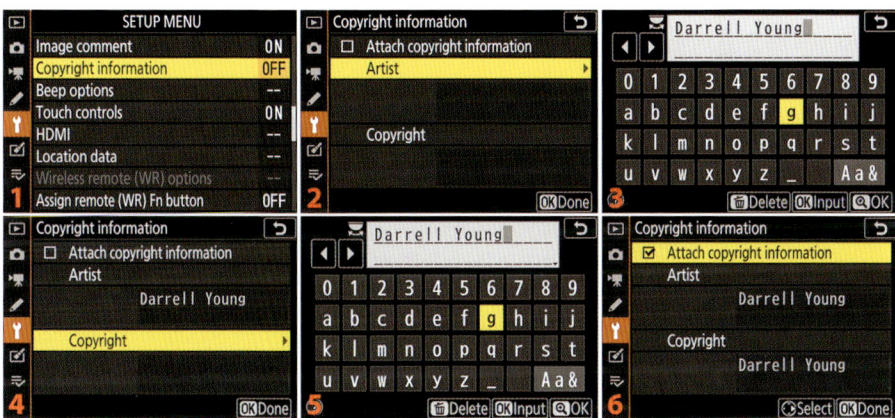

Figure 10.19: Copyright information settings

Here are the steps to enter your Artist and Copyright information:

1. Select Copyright information from the Setup Menu and scroll to the right (figure 10.19, image 1).
2. Scroll down to Artist and scroll to the right (figure 10.19, image 2).
3. The data entry keyboard is shown in figure 10.19, image 3. You can insert your name (or other information) by tapping the characters you want to use on the Monitor, and they will appear in the position marked with the dark-gray cursor in the data entry field (Darrell Young). You can enter up to 36 characters. Use the left/right arrow tip touch controls in the top-left corner to move left and right in the field. To change from upper to lower case—or to access symbols, such as #—tap the Aa& control in the lower-right corner of the screen (just above the OK touch control). If you make a mistake, position

the dark-gray cursor over the error and tap the Delete control at the bottom of the screen. When you have entered your information, press or touch OK to save it. (**Note:** If you would prefer not to use the touch-screen features, you can move the selection cursor with the Multi selector pad to highlight a character in the list below the data entry field, then press the OK button to insert the character. To correct an error, turn the rear Main command dial to move back and forth along the field that contains the new comment, and press the Delete button to remove the error. Press the OK button when you have finished entering your information.) Now scroll down to the Copyright line on the Copyright information screen and scroll to the right (figure 10.19, image 4).

4. Add your name using the method and controls described in step 3, and then press or touch OK to save the Copyright (figure 10.19, image 5).
5. Scroll up to the Attach copyright information line (figure 10.19, image 6). You must put a check mark in the Attach copyright information check box so the Artist and Copyright information will attach itself to each new image you take. Scroll to the right with the Multi selector pad, or tap the check box, and you'll see a tiny check mark appear in the box.
6. Press or touch OK to save your Artist and Copyright information.

Settings Recommendation: Be sure to add your name in both the Artist and Copyright sections of this function. With so much intellectual property theft going on these days, it's a good idea to identify each of your images as your own. Otherwise, you may post an image on Instagram or Facebook to share with friends and later find it on a billboard along the highway. With the Artist and Copyright information embedded in the image metadata, you will be able to prove that the image is yours and charge the infringer.

Embedding your personal information is not a foolproof way to identify your images because unscrupulous people may steal them and strip the metadata out of them. However, if you do find one of your images on the front page of a magazine or on someone's website, you can at least prove that you took the image and have some legal recourse under the Digital Millennium Copyright Act (DMCA). When you've taken a picture, you own the copyright to that image. You must be able to prove you took it. This is one convenient way.

You'll have even more power to protect yourself if you register your images with the U.S. Copyright Registry at the following web address:

https://copyright.gov/registration/

If you sell your camera, or loan it to someone, be sure to remove the Artist and Copyright information to prevent misuse of your name. You can either remove it manually or use *Setup Menu > Reset all settings,* which resets all camera settings back to their factory defaults.

Beep Options

The *Beep options* setting allows your camera to make a beeping sound (if enabled) to alert you during the following events:

- Focus lock while in Single-servo AF (AF-S) mode, if Focus is selected for Custom setting a2 (page 366)
- Countdown in Self-timer mode operations
- At the end of Time-lapse movie
- When the touch screen is used for keyboard entry

You can set the camera to beep with a high- or low-pitched tone, and you can adjust the volume of the beep—or you can turn the beep sound off. When Beep is active, you'll see a little musical note displayed in the Information display on the Monitor, and of course, you will hear the camera beeping when you do the things in the list.

First let's examine how to turn the Beep sound on or off. It defaults to Off in the Z6.

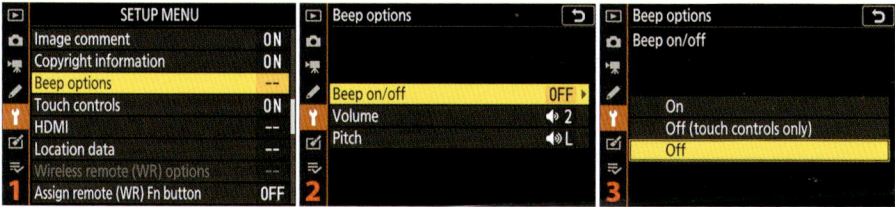

Figure 10.20A: Enabling or disabling the camera's Beep sound

Use the following steps to enable or disable the camera's beep sound:

1. Follow the screen flow in figure 10.20A, images 1 and 2 (*Beep Options > Beep on/off*), until you arrive at the third screen in the series.
2. Choose On if you want the camera to always beep when an event on the previous list occurs. Choose Off (touch controls only) if you prefer that the camera beep when an event in the previous list occurs, *except* for when you tap the Monitor touch controls. Select Off if you do not want the camera to beep under any circumstances. Press the OK button or tap the option to lock in your choice.

Next let's see how to change the volume of the beep, in case you need to use the beep sound.

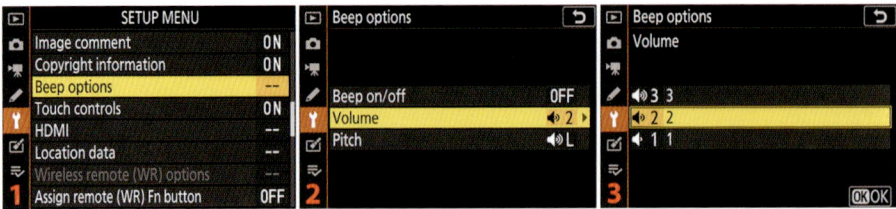

Figure 10.20B: Choosing a Volume level for the camera's Beep

Use the following steps to select one of the Beep Volume choices:

1. Follow the screen flow shown in figure 10.20B, images 1 and 2 (*Beep options > Volume*), until you arrive at the third screen in the series.
2. Choose one of the three options from the list (1, 2, or 3). In figure 10.20B, image 3, Volume level 2 is selected (factory default). If you have *Beep options > Beep on/off* set to On, you will hear a sample beep for each volume level as you choose it. The level 1 beep is rather quiet, so you may not hear it well unless you hold your ear close to the camera, whereas the level 3 beep is relatively loud. Press the OK button or tap the option to lock in the setting.

Next, let's consider the screens and steps to select a pitch for the beep.

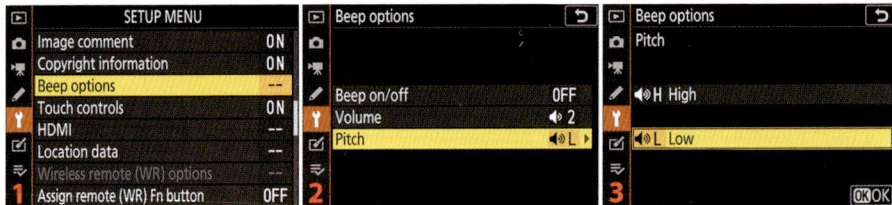

Figure 10.20C: Choosing a Pitch for the camera's Beep

Use the following steps to select a Beep Pitch:

1. Follow the screen flow shown in figure 10.20C, images 1 and 2 (*Beep options > Pitch*), until you arrive at the third screen in the series.
2. Choose one of the two options from the list (High or Low). In figure 10.20C, image 3, Low is selected. If you have *Beep options > Beep on/off* set to On, you will hear a sample beep in each pitch when you choose it. Press the OK button or tap the option to lock in the setting.

Settings Recommendation: I keep Beep turned Off on my Z6. If I were using my camera in a quiet area, why would I want it beeping and disturbing those around me? However, you might want the reassurance of hearing a beep when AF has been confirmed or when the Self-timer is counting down. If so, turn it on. The Self-timer lamp flashes during Self-timer operations, so I generally use that instead of Beep.

Touch Controls

The Nikon Z6 has a convenient touch-control capability that lets you use your fingertip to enter the names of various items, select touch controls on the Monitor, swipe from one picture or video to another when viewing them on the Monitor, and press Play on displayed videos.

The *Touch controls* function allows you to enable or disable the touch-control feature, as well as set the swipe (flick) direction for when you are viewing pictures. Let's examine how to configure the two parts of the Touch controls system.

Enabling or Disabling the Touch Controls System

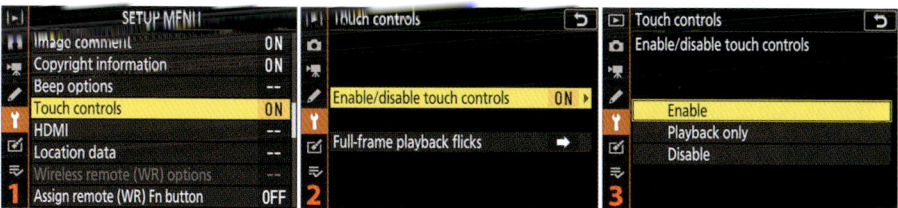

Figure 10.21A: Enabling or disabling the camera Touch controls system

Use the following steps to enable or disable the camera's Touch controls system:

1. Follow the screen flow shown in figure 10.21A, images 1 and 2 (*Touch controls > Enable/disable touch controls*), until you arrive at the third screen in the series.
2. Select Enable to use all available touch controls, Playback only if you want to use touch controls only when viewing images/videos on the Monitor (Playback), or Disable if you do not want to use touch controls at all (figure 10.21A, image 3). Press the OK button or tap the option to lock in the setting. The factory default is Enable.

Settings Recommendation: I have been using the Touch controls system quite often as I work through the many functions it supports. I find it quite convenient when entering data, compared to fiddling around with physical buttons and pads.

The only gripe I have is that I would prefer a QWERTY keyboard layout instead of an alphabetical series of letters, just because I'm used to using that layout on my smartphone (texting). Why couldn't Nikon make a keyboard that looks more like my iPhone's keyboard, including the touch button locations and functionality, so that I (and you) don't have to search for each character? Aren't we all used to using tiny smartphone keyboards by now? Why have an Aa& touch button instead of ⊠ and 123?

Otherwise, the Touch controls system works well and is easy to use. I think our smart cameras are finally joining the digital world, at least to some degree.

Changing Swipe (Flick) Direction for Viewing Images

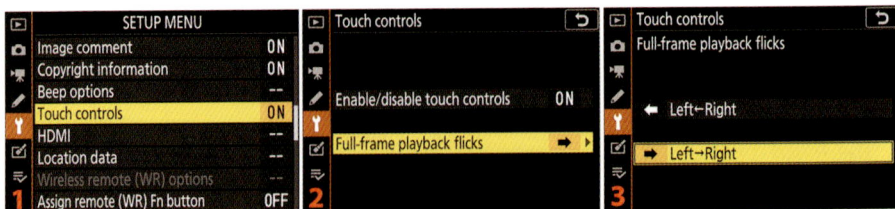

Figure 10.21B: Setting the direction of the finger swipe when viewing images on the Monitor

Use the following steps to change the direction of the swipe used to scroll through pictures:

1. Follow the screen flow shown in figure 10.21B, images 1 and 2 (*Touch controls > Full-frame playback flicks*), until you arrive at the third screen in the series.
2. Select either Left←Right or Left→Right from the menu (figure 10.21B, image 3). Press the OK button or tap the option to lock in the setting.

Settings Recommendation: I've been scratching my head trying to figure out why someone would want the swipe (flick) to work in the opposite direction of what smartphone users have trained their muscle memory to expect. When I am swiping on my camera's Monitor, I expect to see the next image by swiping from right to left, just like on my iPhone.

However, if you would prefer the swipe to work in the opposite direction, choosing Left→Right will fix you right up. Then, when you swipe right to left, the camera will display the previous picture instead of the next picture.

HDMI

HDMI (high-definition multimedia interface) allows you to display your images and videos on a high-definition television (HDTV), external video monitor, or computer monitor with an HDMI connection. You can also use the HDMI port to stream clean, 4K, 10-bit, 4:2:2, N-Log video to an external video recording device, such as one of the recorders found on **www.Atomos.com**.

You'll need an HDMI Type-A to HDMI Type-C cable, which is not included with the camera but is available from many electronics stores. This cable is also known as a mini-HDMI–to–HDMI A/V HD cable.

Figure 10.22A gives you a closeup look at both ends of the cable. The smaller end (mini-HDMI Type-C) goes into the HDMI port under the rubber flap on your camera, and the other end (HDMI Type-A) plugs into your HD device.

The HDMI setting has two options—Output resolution and Advanced—which we will discuss next.

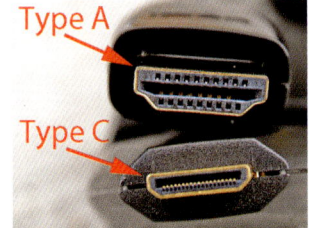

Figure 10.22A: HDMI cable ends

Output Resolution

You can select one of the following formats for output to your HDMI device, including external video recorders:

- **Auto:** This allows the camera to select the most appropriate format for displaying your image on the currently connected device.
- **2160p (progressive):** 3840 × 2160 progressive UHD format
- **1080p (progressive):** 1920 × 1080 progressive Full HD format
- **1080i (interlaced):** 1920 × 1080 interlaced Full HD format
- **720p (progressive):** 1280 × 720 progressive HD format
- **576p (progressive):** 720 × 576 progressive SD format
- **480p (progressive):** 640 × 480 progressive SD format

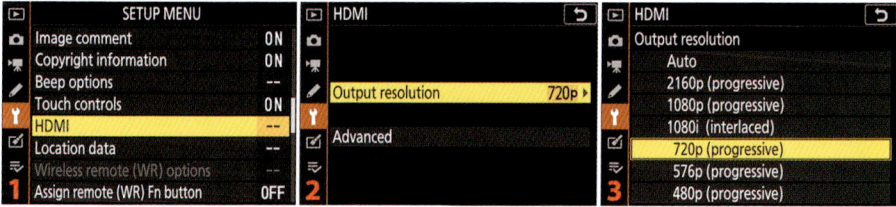

Figure 10.22B: Selecting an HDMI Output resolution

Use the following steps to select an Output resolution:

1. Follow the screen flow shown in figure 10.22B, images 1 and 2 (*HDMI > Output resolution*), until you arrive at the third screen in the series.
2. Select one of the six output resolutions or Auto (figure 10.22B, image 3). I chose 720p (progressive) as an example because it matches the output format of the external video capture device I use to capture images for this book. The camera offers resolutions from as low as old standard-definition television (SDTV) resolutions up to ultra-high definition 4K television (UHDTV), so it's quite flexible! You might want to try Auto at first to see if the camera and display device will interface by themselves. If not, read the user's manual for the display device to find out what output resolution works best with it, and set the camera accordingly. Press the OK button or tap the option to lock in your selection.

HDMI Output Resolution Setting – External versus Internal Video Recording
The Output resolution setting directly sets the HDMI output for an external recorder, such as a Ninja, Sumo, or Shogun by Atomos (**www.Atomos.com**). Older external Atomos video recorders, such as a Ninja-2, are limited to Full HD (1080p), whereas a newer Ninja V can record up to 4K UHD at 60 fps progressive (2160/60p). Currently, the Nikon Z6 is limited to 4K UHD at 30 fps progressive (2160/30p).

However, Output resolution *does not* affect the internal video recording capability of the camera, which ignores the HDMI Output resolution and instead relies on the resolution selected under *Movie Shooting Menu > Frame size/frame rate* or the *i* menu's *Frame size and rate/Image quality* setting, when your camera's Photo/movie selector switch is set to Movie.

Power Off Delay and the Standby Timer

The HDMI output you will use to send video to your external recorder has a default 30-second Power off delay to save battery charge, which means your camera will shut off after 30 seconds of recording, unless you extend the Power off delay. You should set the Standby timer (page 396) to a significantly longer timeout setting, such as 10 minutes, 30 minutes, or No limit.

Use the *Custom Setting Menu > c Timers/AE lock > c3 Power off delay > Standby timer* setting to lengthen the HDMI video stream timeout. Use a longer delay or No limit for the Standby timer setting.

Progressive versus Interlaced

What's the difference between progressive and interlaced? Technically speaking, progressive video output displays the video frame starting with the top line and then draws the other lines until the entire frame is shown. The camera displays 2160 lines progressively from the top of what the imaging sensor captured to the bottom (lines 1, 2, 3, 4 … 2160).

Interlaced video output displays every even line from top to bottom, then comes back to the top and displays every odd line (lines 2, 4, 6, 8 … 2160; then 1, 3, 5, 7 … 2159).

Progressive output provides a higher-quality image with less flicker and a more cinematic look. Most of the HDMI Output resolution settings are for progressive output; however, Nikon has provided 1080i (interlaced) in case we need to use an interlaced output later.

Advanced

With the large variety of display and external recording devices available, your camera has to deal with all sorts of video standards. Here is a brief list of the controls available for modifying the HDMI video output:

- *Output range:* Controls how color is displayed on the receiving device. You can limit the RGB video output to a Limited range of 16 to 235, or a Full range of 0 to 255. Or you can select Auto to let the camera decide for you.
- *External recording control:* If you are using an external HDMI video recorder that will support the Atomos Open Protocol—such as the Atomos Shogun, Ninja, or Sumo series—you can control the external recorder with on-camera controls.
- *Output data depth:* You can choose from 8-bit or 10-bit output. The 10-bit selection is available in 4K only when the camera is connected by HDMI to an external Atomos recorder (firmware C2.00). The 8-bit selection will work for recording 4K video either to

the internal memory card or an external recorder. The camera can use 10-bits when recording to the XQD card at 1080/30p or lower video resolutions only. This could change with a firmware update.

- **N-Log setting:** Tells the camera to output a lower-contrast, higher dynamic-range video signal that tends to preserve shadow and highlight detail. The contrast and color when using N-Log are even flatter than the Flat Picture Control. A videographer will need to "grade" (post-process) the video later, adjusting color saturation and contrast until an acceptable look has been set for the video.
- **View assist:** Provides a live preview of the N-Log affect on the video recording. The colors may differ slightly between the camera's Monitor and the actual video. However, this preview has no effect on the video recording. It is merely informational, allowing you to make adjustments if needed.

Let's examine each setting on the Advanced menu in more detail.

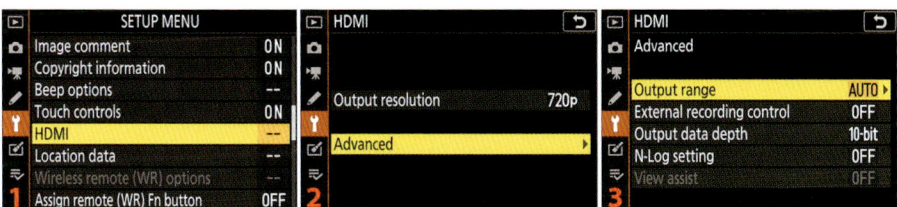

Figure 10.22C: Using Advanced HDMI settings

Use the following steps to open the Advanced menu (figure 10.22C):

1. Follow the screen flow shown in figure 10.22C, images 1 and 2 (*HDMI* > *Advanced*), until you arrive at the third screen in the series.
2. Select one of the five settings from the Advanced menu and scroll to the right (figure 10.22C, image 3).
3. Refer to figures 10.22D through 10.22K for details on the configuration of each Advanced item.

Output Range

Output range allows you to adjust the level of colors sent to a recording or display device. When you are outputting video to a device, such as an HDTV or recorder, the device may not accept normal *Full range* RGB with a color range of 0 to 255 correctly. Some devices accept only *Limited range* RGB input in the range of 16 to 235 color levels (YCbCr). If you try to send Full range RGB video output to a Limited range YCbCr device, you may end up with washed-out, grayish blacks and blown-out, featureless whites.

The solution is to match the correct output to the correct device type. If you see the problems just described when the camera is set to Full range (RGB), try the Limited range (YCbCr) setting instead. Or, you could try the Auto setting to see if the camera can detect what the display or recording device requires.

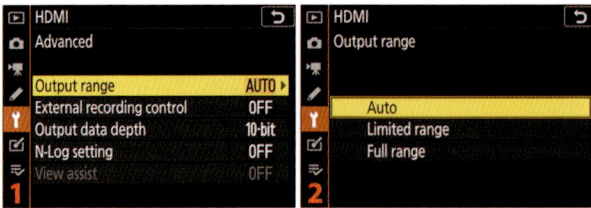

Figure 10.22D: Selecting an Output range

Use the following steps to select Full range or Limited range output (figure 10.22D continues from figure 10.22C):

1. Select Output range from the Advanced menu and scroll to the right (figure 10.22D, image 1).
2. Choose Auto, Limited range, or Full range from the Output range menu. Auto (factory default) is selected in figure 10.22D, image 2. Press the OK button or tap the option to select the Output range.

Settings Recommendation: Please spend some time familiarizing yourself with the features of this function. The Z6 camera has enhanced video output compared to its predecessors. Therefore, if you have not been fond of video with an HD-SLR in the past, you may want to reconsider now that you are using the mirrorless Nikon Z6. It's a portable home movie studio, with full UHD (4K) commercial capabilities!

External Recording Control

The *External recording control* setting allows you to control an Atomos external recorder (e.g., Ninja V) directly from your camera. You can start and stop recording on the external recorder by pressing the camera's Movie record button when the Z6 and recorder are connected by an HDMI cable.

Let's examine the Input tab on an Atomos Ninja V external recorder to see how to let the camera remotely control when the recorder starts and stops recording (figure 10.22E). We will need to set an HDMI Trigger.

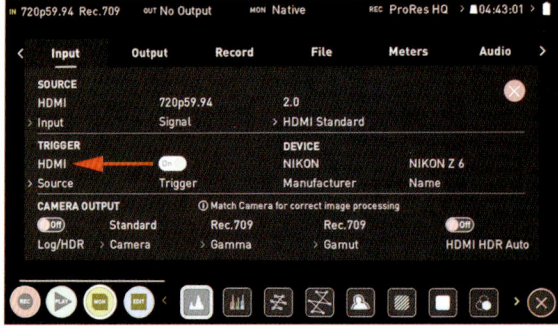

Figure 10.22E: Setting the Trigger to HDMI on an Atomos Ninja V external recorder

Figure 10.22E: You must set the Trigger under the Input tab of the Atomos external re-corder to HDMI. On the Atomos Ninja V external recorder screen shown in figure 10.22E, you will touch where the red arrow is pointing, multiple times, until HDMI appears. Make sure the little touch slider switch is set to On. Now, when you press the camera's Movie record button, the external recorder will automatically start receiving and recording the HDMI video output from your camera. Make sure you have selected an appropriate HDMI Source Output resolution so that the external recorder will record at the correct video resolution (e.g., 720p, 1080p, 2160p, see figure 10.22B on page 509).

Now that we have looked at a Ninja V screen, and configured the HDMI Trigger, let's discuss the screens you will see on your Z6 when you are using this feature.

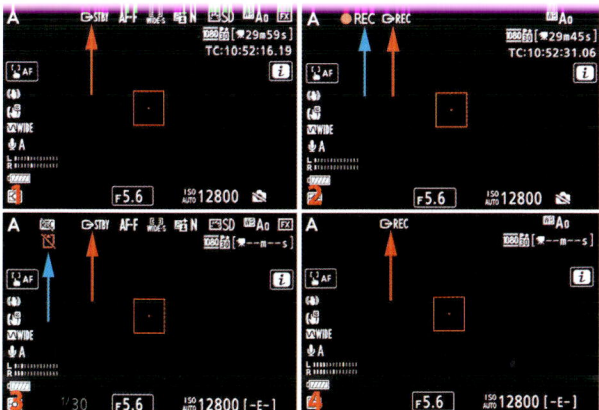

Figure 10.22F: External recording control symbols

The following paragraphs examine what the Movie recording symbols mean:

Figure 10.22F, image 1: There are several symbols you will see on your camera screen, according to how you are recording video. The Movie record screen will display a small standby (→STBY) symbol when the external recorder and camera are ready to start re-cording (figure 10.22E, image 1). Immediately to the left of the small →STBY symbol is a blank spot with no other symbols (compare to figure 10.22F, image 3, blue arrow). This is significant! The fact that there are no symbols, strangely enough, means that the camera is ready to send video to the external recorder *and* record video to the camera's memory card, at the same time. This will make more sense when we discuss figure 10.22F, image 3. When you press the Movie record button on the top of the camera, the external recorder *and* memory card will record video, and the next screen (image 2) will show. There are some limitations when recording to both devices as the same time, as discussed in the note below.

Note: In this and future discussions of recording video to both an external recorder and the internal XQD card at the same time, please remember the following information: The internal XQD card cannot accept 10-bit video at 4K UHD (2160p) resolution (using firmware C1.02); therefore, recording to both an external recorder and the internal XQD card at the same time requires using a video resolution of 1080/30p or below only. The *HDMI > Advanced > Output data depth setting* (next subsection) can be set to 8-bit or 10-bit, and then the external recorder and internal XQD card will receive video at the chosen resolution. In other words, recording in 4K resolution (2160p) to both the external recorder and the XQD card is not possible with camera firmware C2.00. That could change with a firmware update.

Figure 10.22F, image 2: When you have started recording video by pressing the Movie record button, the camera will display two symbols. First you will see the ●REC symbol (blue arrow). This ●REC symbol means the camera is recording video to its XQD memory card. To the right of the blue arrow's ●REC symbol, you will see a tiny recorder screen symbol with an arrow pointing at a smaller →REC symbol (red arrow). Where the blue arrow's ●REC symbol means the *camera* is recording video, the red arrow's →REC symbol means the *external video recorder* is now receiving video too, and should be recording it if the camera and the external recorder are connected properly.

Figure 10.22F, image 3: When you have the external recorder prepared to receive video, but have removed the camera's XQD memory card to prevent recording to it too, you will see the symbols shown at the blue arrow. The top symbol is a REC symbol with a slash through it and the lower symbol is a red memory card symbol with a slash through it (blue arrow). These two symbols signify that the camera will not record video internally, but will send the video stream to the external recorder only, when you press the Movie record button. The →STBY symbol (red arrow) means that the camera is awaiting your command to start sending video to the external recorder and that the external recorder is awaiting the Movie record button press to Trigger (see figure 10.22E) the recording.

Figure 10.22F, image 4: When you have pressed the Movie record button, and thereby triggered the external recorder, the →REC symbol shown at the red arrow means that the camera is sending a video stream to the external video recorder through the HDMI port. The lack of the ●REC symbol means the internal XQD memory card is *not* receiving video.

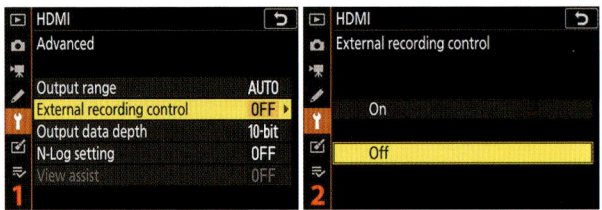

Figure 10.22G: Enabling or disabling External recording control

Use the following steps to enable or disable the External recording control (figure 10.22G continues from figure 10.22C):

1. Choose External recording control from the *HDMI > Advanced* menu and scroll to the right (figure 10.22G, image 1).

2. Highlight On or Off and press the OK button or tap the option to enable or disable the External recording control (figure 10.22G, image 2).

Settings Recommendation: If you own an Atomos external recorder, it is a good idea to turn the External recording control on. If you do not have an external recorder, you can leave it off and safely ignore this setting.

Output Data Depth

The *Output data depth* setting allows you to choose a bit depth for your video recordings. You can choose from 8-bit (16.7 million colors) or 10-bit (1.07 billion colors). The 10-bit 4K UHD (2160p) recording can be done with compatible external recorders only, such as the newer recorders in the Shogun, Ninja, or Sumo series by Atomos.

The camera's internal memory card can accept 8-bit video in all resolutions, including 4K, but can accept 10-bit video only at resolutions of Full HD (1080/30p) or below. None of the 1080/120p, 1080/100p, or slow-motion settings are available for 10-bit either. Again, this is based on firmware C2.00, and 10-bit 4K video (and the other settings mentioned) could become available for recording to the XQD card if Nikon decides to update the camera's firmware.

If you have 10-bit 4K selected, and you try to record to the XQD card when hooked up to an external recorder, the camera will disable video recording to the memory card. If you attempt to record 10-bit 4K directly to the XQD card alone, the Z6 will automatically switch to 8-bit recording, regardless of your having selected 10-bit.

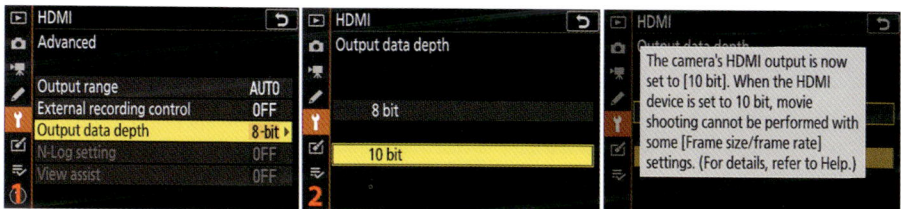

Figure 10.22H: Selecting 8-bit or 10-bit video recording

Use the following steps to select 8-bit or 10-bit video recording (figure 10.22H continues from figure 10.22C):

1. Choose Output data depth from the *HDMI > Advanced* menu and scroll to the right (figure 10.22H, image 1).
2. Highlight 8 bit (default) or 10 bit and press the OK button or tap the option with your fingertip (figure 10.22H, image 2). Whichever mode you select will change the HDMI video output to that bit level.
3. If you select 10 bit, an informational screen will pop up (figure 10.22H, image 3), informing you that only certain Frame size/frame rates can be used with 10 bit recording to the XQD card (as previously discussed).

N-Log Setting

N-Log setting causes the camera to output a low-contrast, high-dynamic-range HDMI video signal that preserves shadow and highlight detail. You will need to grade the video after the fact, making adjustments to color saturation and contrast in an app—such as Final Cut Pro or Adobe Premier Pro—until you are happy with how the video looks. Use N-Log only if you plan on grading the video later in a computer program. Otherwise, your video will appear washed out and will have pale colors.

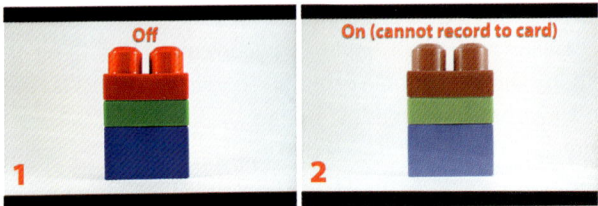

Figure 10.22I: N-Log setting: Off and On (cannot record to card)

In figure 10.22I you can see how the camera outputs a video signal with the Neutral Picture Control set (image 1), compared to using N-Log (image 2). These two screens were captured from the display of an Atomos Ninja V, with View assist (next subsection) enabled. Now let's consider how to enable and disable N-Log.

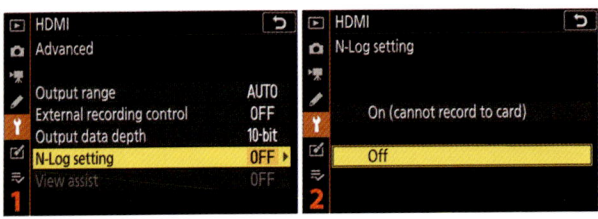

Figure 10.22J: Enabling or disabling N-Log output over HDMI

Use the following steps to enable or disable N-Log, with the understanding that N-Log cannot currently be recorded to the XQD memory card (firmware C2.00), and instead must be output through the HDMI port to an external recorder (figure 10.22J continues from figure 10.22C):

1. Choose N-Log setting from the *HDMI > Advanced* menu and scroll to the right (figure 10.22J, image 1).
2. Highlight Off or On (cannot record to card) and press the OK button or tap the option to select it. Select Off unless you plan to send video to an external HDMI recorder. The camera will not record video to the XQD memory card when N-Log setting is enabled! If you are prepared to record video on an external recorder and you will grade the video later in software, then select On (cannot record to card) instead.

View Assist

The *View assist* setting provides a live preview of how N-Log setting affects a recorded video. The colors may differ slightly between the camera's Monitor and the actual video. This is merely a preview and has no effect on the video recording. It is for informational purposes only, allowing you the opportunity to make adjustments.

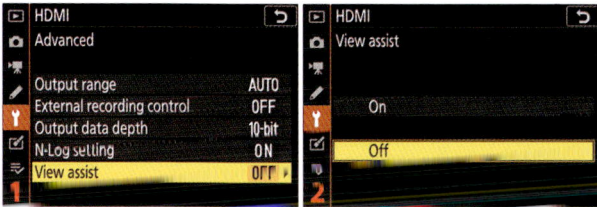

Figure 10.22K: Enabling or disabling the View assist setting

Use the following steps to enable or disable View assist for a live preview of N-Log video (figure 10.22K continues from figure 10.22C):

1. Choose View assist from the *HDMI > Advanced* menu and scroll to the right (figure 10.22K, image 1).
2. Highlight On or Off and press the OK button or tap the option to lock it in (figure 10.22K, image 2).

Settings Recommendation: I enjoy the live preview aspect of View assist and leave it on when I am sending N-Log video to my Ninja V external recorder. If you have no external recorder you can safely leave this setting at Off.

Location Data

The *Location data* function allows you to geotag your images with global positioning system (GPS) location data. It provides an easy-to-use interface for various GPS and smart devices.

Now when you shoot a spectacular travel image, you can rest assured that you'll be able to find that exact spot next year. With the Nikon GP-1 or GP-1A GPS units (or an aftermarket brand), or your smart device using SnapBridge, the Z6 will record some or all of the following GPS information into the metadata of each image:

- Latitude
- Longitude
- Altitude
- Heading (aftermarket only)
- UTC (time)

Using a Smart Device for GPS

The Nikon Z6 allows you to pull GPS data from your smart device (e.g., your smartphone) and automatically embed that location information in the metadata of your image(s). To use the SnapBridge app to transfer GPS data to your Z6, the following services must be enabled:

On the Smart Device

- **Bluetooth:** Enable Bluetooth under your smart device's settings menu.
- **Location services:** In order for your smartphone to use its built-in GPS system, you must have Location data enabled.
- **SnapBridge:** The Nikon Snapbridge app must be installed on your smartphone and already configured to communicate with your camera if you want to use Snapbridge to geotag your images. See the heading **Connect to Smart Device** later in this chapter (page 528).

On the Nikon Z6

- **Bluetooth:** Use the following function to enable Bluetooth on your camera: *Setup Menu > Connect to smart device > Pairing (Bluetooth) > Bluetooth connection*. See **Bluetooth Connection** under the heading **Connect to Smart Device** later in this chapter (page 534).
- **Location data:** Using the settings discussed in this chapter subsection, you must prepare Location data use, including SnapBridge's *Synchronize location data* (figure 10.23A). You will find the Location data timer at the following location: *Setup Menu > Location data > Standby timer*.

Let's examine how to enable Synchronize location data under SnapBridge so that you can embed location data in your images.

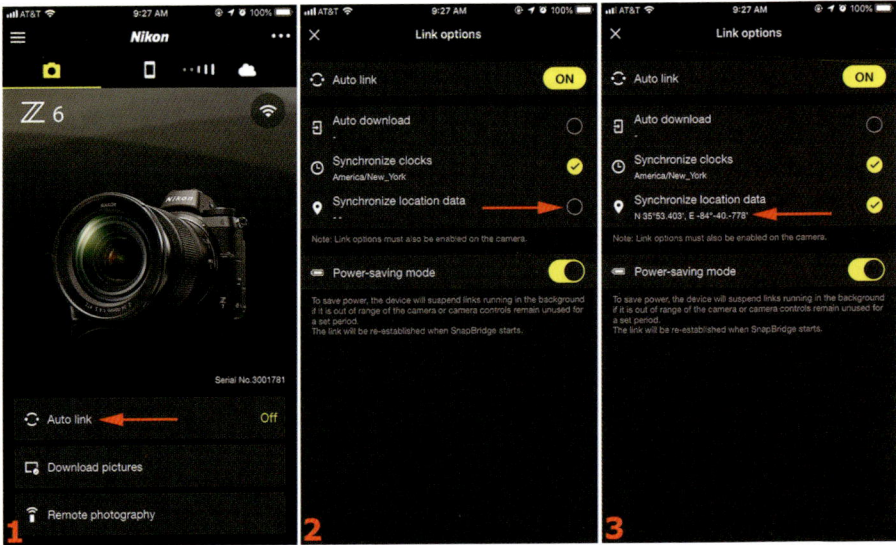

Figure 10.23A: Smartphone SnapBridge app screens for Synchronize location data

Use the following steps to enable location data synchronization between your smart device and the Z6:

1. Open your already connected SnapBridge app and touch the Auto link selection (figure 10.23A, image 1, red arrow). If your app and camera are not yet paired, see **Connect to Smart Device** on page 528 for information on pairing the camera and the SnapBridge app.
2. The Synchronize location data selection point is shown at the red arrow on right side of the SnapBridge screen (figure 10.23A, image 2, red arrow). Touch the little round circle, which will change the background color of the circle from black to yellow and add a check mark. You will see a popup screen letting you know that it may take a few minutes for your smart device to obtain valid GPS data (not shown).
3. When the SnapBridge app (your smart device) has synchronized with GPS satellites, you will see your current GPS location under the Synchronize location data label (figure 10.23A, image 3, red arrow). Once you enable Location data on your smart device, and it has valid GPS data, the data will automatically be fed to the camera—via Bluetooth—for embedding in your image metadata. The connection will automatically time out to save battery when the camera is not in range; when you set the camera to Airplane mode; or when you disable Bluetooth.

The Bluetooth connection with SnapBridge will use additional battery power, so it's a good idea to have extra batteries available when you're using SnapBridge for GPS. Also, your smart device will use up its battery charge more quickly.

Warning: Please be aware that others can determine the location of your shared pictures when Synchronize location data is enabled. If you are taking family pictures, especially of children, and you use geotagged pictures, those who download the pictures from social media sites (e.g., Facebook, Instagram) can examine the image metadata and will be able to determine exactly where the picture was taken. Maybe it's not a good idea to upload geotagged pictures of your kids, grandkids, or valuables if the pictures were taken at home.

Note: You may want to enable the Synchronize clocks setting (just above Synchronize location data on the SnapBridge screen shown in figure 10.23A, images 2 and 3). When the Synchronize clocks setting is enabled, the Z6 can embed time and date information received from the smart device for each picture taken.

Standby Timer

Figure 10.23B shows the screens used to set the camera to stay on the entire time an external GPS is connected, or shut down after the Standby timer expires.

The *Setup Menu > Location data* setting also has a subsetting named *Standby timer,* which can override the use of the *Standby timer* setting in *Custom Setting Menu > c Timers/ AE lock > c3 Power off delay*.

The Custom setting c3 *Standby timer* function is for all aspects of the camera. The Setup Menu's Location data *Standby timer* subsetting applies only to an attached GPS unit.

Enable or disable *Setup Menu > Location data > Standby timer* according to the information in the following list:

- **Enable** (default): The meter turns off after the *Custom Setting Menu > c Timers/AE lock > c3 Power off delay > Standby timer* delay expires (the default is 30 seconds). GPS data will be recorded only when the exposure meter is active, so allow some time for the external GPS unit, powered by the camera, to reacquire a satellite signal before taking a picture. This is hard to do when *Standby timer* is set to the default 30 seconds. You pretty much have to stand around with your finger on the Shutter-release button trying to keep the meter active. I suggest using Disable.
- **Disable:** The exposure meter stays on the entire time an external GPS unit is connected. As long as you have a good GPS signal, you will be able to record GPS data at any time. This is the preferred setting for using the GPS for continuous shooting. It does use extra battery life, so you may want to carry multiple batteries if you're going to shoot all day. Turn the camera off between locations.

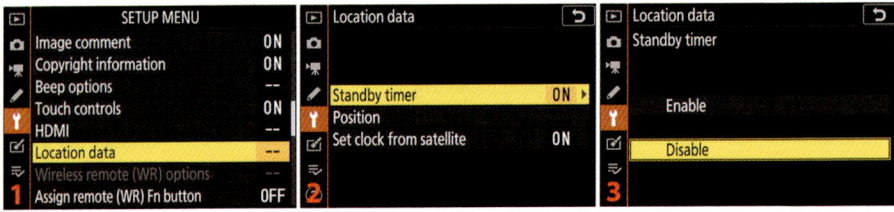

Figure 10.23B: Setting an Standby timer delay for GPS usage

Here are the steps to configure the Standby timer delay:

1. Follow the screen flow shown in figure 10.23B, images 1 and 2 (*Location data > Standby timer*), until you arrive at the third screen in the series.
2. Select Enable or Disable (figure 10.23B, image 3). Use Disable for more reliable GPS usage, with somewhat greater battery drain. It is a good idea to carry multiple batteries if you are shooting all day with a Nikon GP-1, GP-1A, or an aftermarket GPS unit attached. Even the SnapBridge Bluetooth connection will use up extra battery charge. Press the OK button or tap the option to lock in the setting.

Position

When an external GPS unit is attached to your Z6, or the SnapBridge app and your camera are paired, with Synchronize location data enabled, the *Position* screen shows the GPS location data being detected by the camera (figure 10.23C). If your GPS unit is not attached to your camera, or SnapBridge is not communicating, the Position selection will be grayed out.

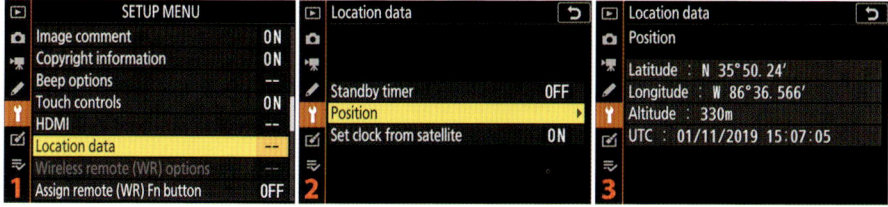

Figure 10.23C: GPS Position information screen

Use these steps to examine the Location data Position screen:

1. Follow the screen flow shown in figure 10.23C, images 1 and 2 (*Location data > Position*), until you arrive at the third screen in the series.
2. Examine the Position screen to see the four or five pieces of GPS satellite data (figure 10.23C, image 3). Notice that my SnapBridge/Z6 connection did not give me Heading information, nor would my Accessory shoe–mounted Nikon GP-1 GPS unit. Some aftermarket GPS units will give you Heading information, as discussed previously.

When the camera establishes communication with your GPS unit or SnapBridge, a couple of things will happen:

- Position information appears on the Position screen (figure 10.23C, image 3).
- An additional data information display screen will be displayed when you are using the Playback button to review images captured while the GPS was active (figure 10.23D). You can press up or down with the Multi selector pad to scroll through the image data screens on the Monitor. One of the data screens will be similar to the screen shown in figure 10.23D, which is a picture of the GPS position screen for a picture I took of a bare winter tree.

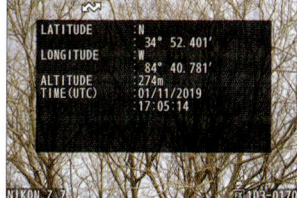

Figure 10.23D: Playback GPS position screen

Set Clock from Satellite

The *Set clock from satellite* function allows the Z6 to maintain accurate time by querying the GPS satellite to set the camera's clock. If you use GPS a lot, you might want to leave this on. The clock in the Nikon Z6 is not as accurate as a wristwatch, for instance, and tends to lose accuracy more quickly. It's a good idea to reset the camera's clock from time to time. This is an easy way to accomplish that for GPS users.

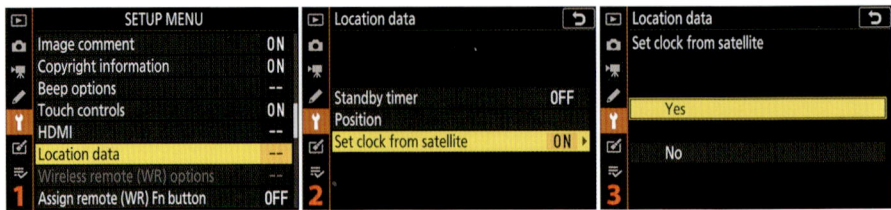

Figure 10.23E: Using GPS to set the camera's clock

Here are the steps to enable Set clock from satellite:

1. Follow the screen flow shown in figure 10.23E, images 1 and 2 (*Location data > Set clock from satellite*), until you arrive at the third screen in the series.
2. Choose Yes to enable the setting, and the GPS unit will be used to obtain a more accurate time setting, or choose No if you don't want to set the camera's clock from the GPS data (figure 10.23E, image 3). Press the OK button or tap the option to save the setting.

Using an External GPS Unit

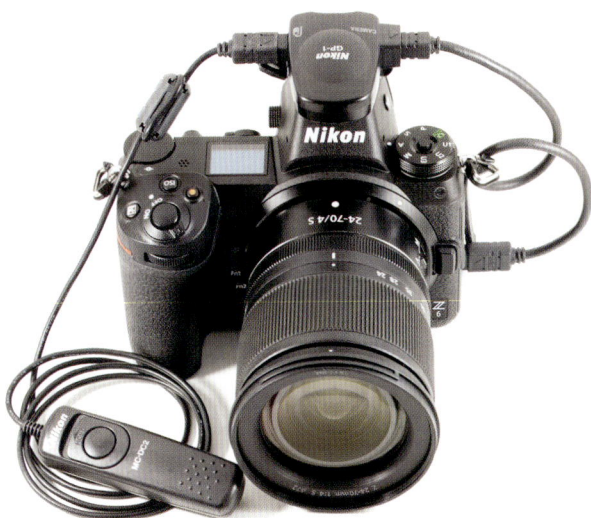

Figure 10.23F: Nikon Z6 with a Nikon GP-1 GPS unit (1), MC-DC2 remote release cable (2), and GP1-CA90 interface cable (3)

The GP1-CA10 cable will interface with Nikon cameras that have a 10-pin port on the body, including the following Nikon cameras: D200, D300, D300S, D500, D700, D800, D800E, D810, D850, D2X, D3, D3S, D3X, D4, D4S, and D5.

The GP-1 GPS unit also comes with a GP1-CA90 cable to interface with Nikon cameras, including the following models: D3*xxx*, D5*xxx*, D7*xxx*, D600, D610, D750, Df, Z7, and Z6. Therefore, it is a useful device for almost any of your Nikons.

You can also get an optional Nikon MC-DC2 remote release cable that plugs directly into the GP-1 GPS unit for hands-off, vibration-free photography. The MC-DC2 remote release cable can be used to fire the shutter on any Nikon DSLR that can interface with the GP-1 or GP-1A GPS unit. You can see the MC-DC2 remote release cable on the left side of the camera in figure 10.23F. It is plugged into the GP-1 GPS unit on the opposite side of where the GP1-CA90 cable plugs in. The mentioned cables are compatible with both the Nikon GP-1 and GP-1A GPS units.

Nikon GP-1 GPS satellite connection information: The rear LED light on the Nikon GP-1 GPS unit will blink red while the GPS is acquiring satellites; blink green when the GPS is locked onto two satellites; and shine solid green when the GPS is locked onto at least three satellites. Allow a few seconds for the GPS to acquire satellites when the camera has been turned off.

If you are a significant distance from where you last used the GP-1 GPS unit, it may require up to a minute or two to acquire a satellite lock. Once the GP-1 has a local satellite lock and you turn the camera off, the GPS unit will reacquire the signal in just a few seconds when the camera is turned back on.

Aftermarket GPS Unit Information: The Nikon GP-1 and GP-1A GPS units do not have a built-in digital compass, so they will not report heading information to the camera. Other GPS units do have the built-in compass and will report the heading. If that is important to you, please investigate the Geotagger GMAX GPS unit at **http://www.solmeta.com**.

Settings Recommendation: Get the Nikon GP-1 or GP-1A GPS unit from one of many vendors, or get the Solmeta GMAX-GD GPS from Amazon.com. Either unit is easy to use and has all the cables you need for interfacing with your camera.

If you choose one of the Nikon GPS units, the only other cable you'll need to buy is the optional MC-DC2 shutter-release cable (coiled on the left in figure 10.23F). I use the tiny Nikon GP-1 GPS unit constantly when I'm shooting nature images so that I can remember where to return in the future. After you start using a GPS unit, you'll find it hard to stop.

If you prefer to use a smart device for GPS, you will need to learn how to configure and use the SnapBridge app, which can be more battery intensive than using an external GPS unit. For occasional GPS use, the smartphone is fine, but for extensive GPS use, I would select an external GPS unit. An external GPS unit's physical connection may use less battery power than the SnapBridge/Z6 Bluetooth connection. Of course, you likely already have a smartphone and SnapBridge is free, so why not try it first and see if it works well for you.

Wireless Remote (WR) Options

The *Wireless remote (WR) options* function lets you adjust settings for optional WR-R10 Wireless Remote Controllers. The WR-R10 plugs into the Accessory port on the side of the camera and allows you to control multiple banks of remote (slave) flash units.

There are two settings in the Wireless remote (WR) options function:

- **LED Lamp:** The WR-R10 Wireless Remote Controller has two LED lamps on it that blink frequently as you use the device to control remote, radio-controlled, Speedlight flash units. In some instances, the blinking lights may be unwanted, so Nikon gives you the ability to turn them off and on as needed. The WR-R10 will work normally when the LEDs are turned off; it just won't signal you with blinking lights.
- **Link mode:** Remote devices controlled by a WR-R10 Wireless Remote Controller can be paired with the controller in two different ways. The default method requires you to press the Pairing button on the WR-R10 until a Link light is illuminated on the remote device. This method is somewhat insecure since anyone with a master WR-R10 can control any slave device configured to be controlled by a WR-R10. Therefore, Nikon has provided a secondary method for pairing a master WR-R10 with its remote slave units, which requires you to type in a PIN code on each slave device.

Let's examine how to configure each of these two settings.

LED Lamp

The LED lamps default to on, so they will blink regularly while the WR-R10 is in use. If you find this to be distracting, you can disable the LEDs. Let's see how.

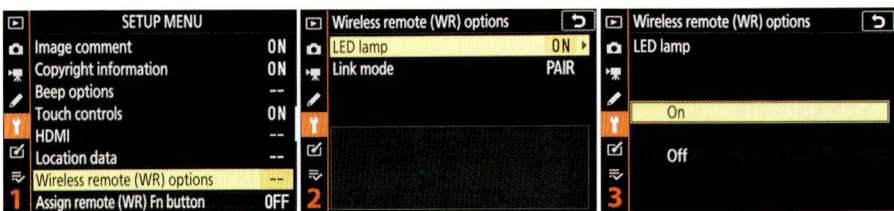

Figure 10.24A: Enable or disable the WR-R10 LED lamp

Use the following steps to enable or disable the WR-R10 LED lamps:

1. Follow the screen flow shown in figure 10.24A, images 1 and 2 (*Wireless remote (WR) options* > *LED lamp*), until you arrive at the third screen in the series.
2. Choose On or Off to control whether the LED lamps on the WR-R10 blink during use (figure 10.24A, image 3). Press the OK Button or tap the option to lock in the setting.

Settings Recommendation: When I am shooting in a studio environment and creating product shots, I do not mind if the lights blink on my WR-R10 Wireless Remote Controller. In fact, I find the blinking lights reassuring.

However, during a wedding, when I have a remote flash positioned for better lighting, I do not want blinking LED lights on my WR-R10 distracting the wedding party and proceedings, so I disable them. It is easy to turn them on and off, so do so when you need to for your style of photography.

Link Mode

If you are shooting in environments where there may be other photographers using WR-R10 units and you worry about one of them trying to take control of your remote slave units, you may want to use the PIN method to pair with your slave units.

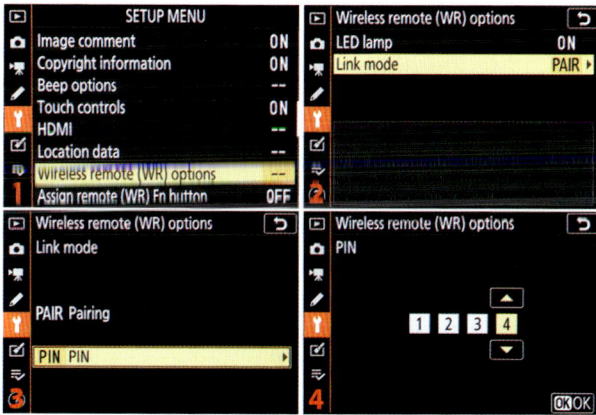

Figure 10.24B: Setting the style of Link mode pairing

Use the following steps to select the style of master/remote pairing you prefer when using your WR-R10 Wireless Remote Controller:

1. Follow the screen flow shown in figure 10.24B, images 1 and 2 (*Wireless remote (WR) options > Link mode*), until you arrive at the third screen in the series.
2. Choose one of the following link modes:
   a. ***Pairing:*** If you choose Pairing (figure 10.24B, image 3), highlight it and press the OK button or tap the option to lock in the setting. You will now need to set your slave units to use Pairing and then use the Pairing button on your WR-R10 to make a link. Refer to the instructions included with the WR-R10 and the remote flash units (e.g., SB-5000) to learn how to use the Pairing button(s) and remote Link lights.
   b. ***PIN:*** If you choose PIN (figure 10.24B, image 3), you will need to create a four-digit numerical pin number, from 0000 to 9999. Scroll to the right and tap the little yellow pointers on the screen or use the Multi selector pad to scroll up or down on each number selection box until you have created your PIN (figure 10.24B, image 4). Press the OK button to lock in the PIN setting. The PIN you entered will now appear on the Wireless remote (WR) options screen (figure 10.24C) so that you can access it easily in case you forget it.

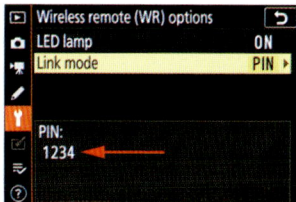

Figure 10.24C: PIN code available on camera screen

Settings Recommendation: I normally use the PAIR (Pairing) setting because I work by myself most of the time. In addition to configuring the WR-R10, you will need to configure each remote unit. Therefore, think carefully about how you will be working with your master/remote units. If you are shooting in an environment where there could be people who would like to aggravate you by taking over your remote units with their WR-R10, why not set up a PIN instead of using the Pairing button?

Assign Remote (WR) Fn Button

The *Assign remote (WR) Fn button* function allows you to program the camera to respond in various ways when you press the Fn button on an optional remote controller (one that has an Fn button, of course). You can assign 10 different functions to the controller's Fn button. First let's see an alphabetical list of the settings:

- AE/AF lock
- AE lock only
- AE lock (Reset on release)
- AF lock only
- AF-ON

- [Flash] Disable/enable
- FV lock
- + NEF (RAW)
- None
- Preview

Because this function is so similar to many other assignment functions we have already considered over the last few chapters, we will examine how to assign the Fn1 button, but will not discuss what each assignment function does.

If you do not know what a particular function does, please refer to the detailed list of functionality for each option under *Custom Setting Menu > f Controls > f2 Custom control assignment* (page 423).

Let's see how to assign a function to the Fn button on your remote controller.

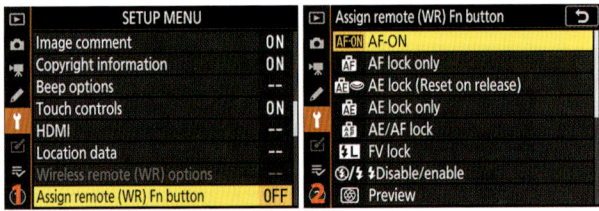

Figure 10.25: Assigning a function to the remote controller's Fn button

Use the following steps to select a function for an optional remote controller's Fn button:

1. Choose Assign remote (WR) Fn button from the Setup Menu and scroll to the right (figure 10.25, image 1).
2. Select one of the 10 available functions (figure 10.25, image 2) and press the OK button or tap the option to make the Fn button assignment.

Settings Recommendation: As a nature and event photographer, I have rarely used this Assign remote (WR) Fn button function. The camera defaults to +NEF (RAW) as the assignment for the remote Fn button. If you have a wireless remote and you think you might use this extra Fn button as part of its use, and +NEF (RAW) is not useful to you, then choose from the list of 10 functions the one you would most likely use.

Airplane Mode

Airplane mode in the Z6 works in a similar way to the airplane mode in your smart device. When you enable Airplane mode, the camera will turn off all radio transmissions of any type from within the camera body, including Wi-Fi and Bluetooth.

However, if you have a WR-R10 or another wireless controller plugged into the 10-pin port, it will continue sending and receiving radio signals. Unplug any external wireless controllers to have true radio silence.

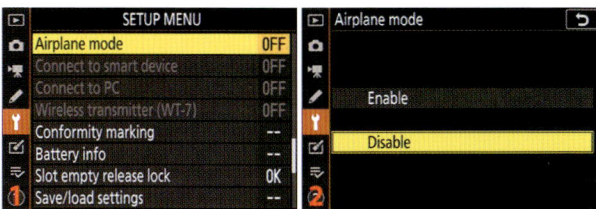

Figure 10.26: Enabling or disabling Airplane mode (no radio signals)

Use these steps to enable or disable Airplane mode in the Nikon Z6:

1. Choose Airplane mode from the Setup Menu and scroll to the right (figure 10.26, image 1).
2. Choose Enable to turn on Airplane mode and cause the camera to go into radio-silence mode, or Disable to turn Airplane mode off and allow the camera to send and receive radio signals (figure 10.26, image 2). Press the OK button or tap the option to lock in the setting.

Settings Recommendation: When I go out into the wild to shoot my nature images, I often set the camera to Airplane mode. In fact, I keep it as one of the options under My Menu (page 600) so that I can access it quickly. Sometimes, I need all the battery power I can get, and Airplane mode conserves battery.

Connect to Smart Device

The *Connect to smart device* function is the core function to enable Bluetooth and Wi-Fi connectivity with your Nikon SnapBridge app. This connection explanation is based on interfacing a Nikon Z6 with an iPhone 7 Plus smartphone, running the Apple iOS 12.1.2 operating system.

The SnapBridge app is available for both Android and iOS. The actual SnapBridge screens vary somewhat in appearance per smartphone operating system. However, they work in basically the same way. Whether using Android or iOS, you will find it fairly easy to make the camera and smart device connection.

Note: All SnapBridge and camera screens shown in this **Connect to Smart Device** section are from interfacing with my Z7. However, Nikon Z6 screens are the same.

Bluetooth versus Wi-Fi

The *Bluetooth* connection (page 534) allows your smart device to communicate directly with your Nikon Z6 using low-energy Bluetooth (BLE). Your Nikon Z6 and your smart device set up their own private Bluetooth network. Your smart device must be compatible with Bluetooth 4.0 and have BLE capability (most devices up to three or four years old work with BLE).

The *Wi-Fi* connection (page 537) sets up an "ad hoc" wireless network between the Nikon Z6 and the SnapBridge app on your smart device. The connection does not depend on any other Wi-Fi networks that may or may not be available in the area. It is a standalone, private connection between your camera and smart device.

The Nikon Z6 does not work with Nikon's older WMU app. The camera is designed to connect only with smart devices running the SnapBridge app.

Now let's discuss how to connect your Z6 to your smart device by using the SnapBridge app.

Pairing the Z6 with Your Smart Device

To make and use the connection (pairing) between your camera and smart device, you will need to use multiple radio-based services, including Bluetooth and Wi-Fi. Before you attempt to make the connection, you must enable Bluetooth and Wi-Fi on your smart device (e.g., iPhone). And if you want to use GPS location information (page 518), enable Location services.

The process of pairing the two devices is relatively easy. Let's step through the screens and steps used to make a connection between your Z6 and a smart device (SnapBridge app):

1. Download and install SnapBridge on your smart device. You will find SnapBridge in the Apple App Store for iOS and in the Google Play Store for Android. Once installed, do not open the app until instructed. First we need to get the camera ready to communicate with the SnapBridge app.

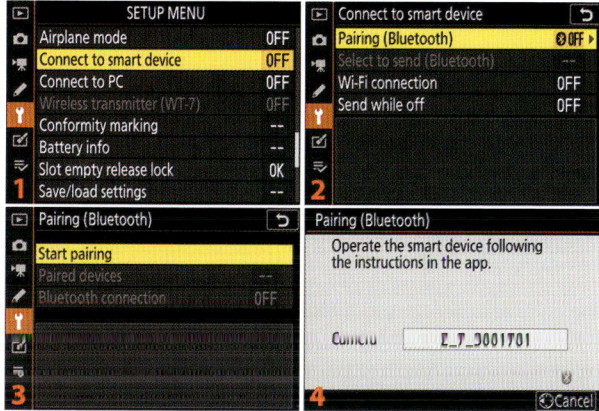

Figure 10.27A: Pairing your camera and smart device (initial steps on the camera)

2. Choose the Connect to smart device function from the Setup Menu and scroll to the right (figure 10.27A, image 1).
3. Select Pairing (Bluetooth) and scroll to the right (figure 10.27A, image 2).
4. Highlight Start pairing and press the OK button or tap the option with your fingertip (figure 10.27A, image 3).
5. The Pairing (Bluetooth) screen will be displayed with a special code for your Camera (e.g., Z_7_3001781). The code uses your camera's serial number as its last seven digits and is used as a Bluetooth connection name in your smart device. Once you have this screen (figure 10.27A, image 4) on the camera, it is time to open the SnapBridge app.

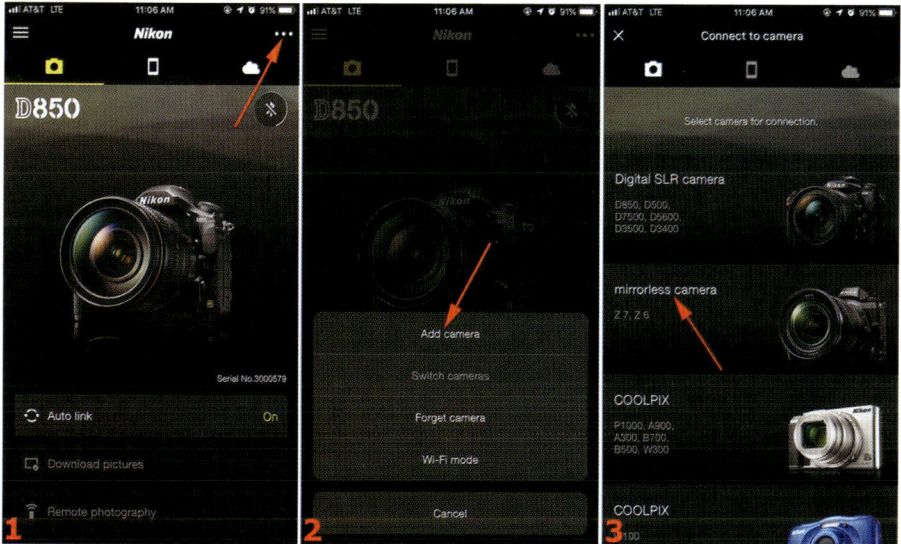

Figure 10.27B: Pairing the camera and smart device (initial steps on SnapBridge)

6. The initial SnapBridge screen in your smart device has a menu available under the three dots (figure 10.27B, image 1, red arrow). Tap on the dots and the menu will open.

7. Tap the Add camera selection on the SnapBridge menu (figure 10.27B, image 2). This will open the camera-type selection menu. (**Note:** If the SnapBridge app detects the camera immediately after you tap the Add camera button in image 2, it may skip the screens shown in figure 10.27B, image 3, and figure 10.27C, image 1, and go directly to the screen shown in figure 10.27C, image 2. If the Z6 skips these screens, continue with step 10; otherwise, move on to step 10.)

8. Select a camera type from the menu. In this case you will tap mirrorless camera (figure 10.27B, image 3).

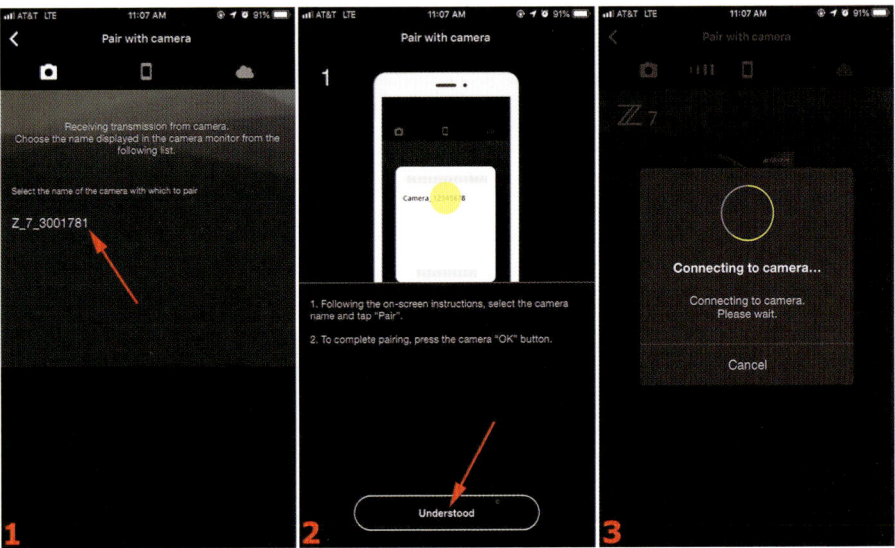

Figure 10.27C: Camera located, now let's connect

9. Once the SnapBridge app senses the camera, it will show a line similar to the one seen in figure 10.27C, image 1, red arrow. This line is the camera's name followed by the camera's serial number (e.g., Z7_3001781). Tap the camera name line to select it.

10. The SnapBridge app will provide instructions on proceeding with the connection and will wait for you to tap the Understood button at the bottom of the screen shown in figure 10.27C, image 2. When you are ready, tap the Understood button.

11. The SnapBridge app will now take a moment to connect to the camera via Bluetooth. You will see a screen that says *Connecting to camera* (figure 10.27C, image 3). Wait a moment until the SnapBridge app finds the camera. *Starting with step 13, the steps are time sensitive, so read them over carefully before proceeding.* Otherwise, while you are reading the steps the camera and SnapBridge app may time out in trying to communicate by Bluetooth, and you will have to start over. Once you start the process, if you do not complete it within about 10 seconds, the timeout will occur.

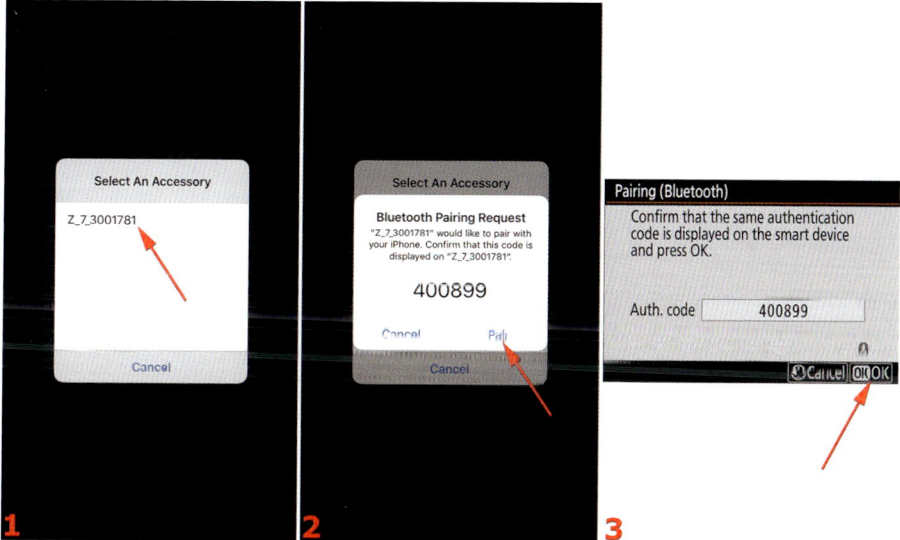

Figure 10.27D: Searching for the camera and listing it for connection

12. When you see the Select An Accessory screen in figure 10.27D, image 1, the app has located the camera and is reading its internal information. At first the list may be blank, with no camera listed. Be patient while the app and the camera communicate; it may take several seconds. When the app has read the camera's internal information, it will show you the camera name and serial number in the list (e.g., Z6_3001781). Tap the camera name line and wait a moment until both the camera and SnapBridge app display the following screens. *You must follow the next step quickly and in the exact order discussed.*

13. As figure 10.27D, images 2 (SnapBridge) and 3 (camera) show, the SnapBridge app and camera are displaying the same Auth. code number (e.g., 400899). *Complete the next two actions within a few seconds:* [**1**] Tap the Pair button on the SnapBridge app (figure 10.27D, image 2); [**2**] Tap the OK control on the camera Setup Menu screen (figure 10.27D, image 3). This causes the SnapBridge app and the camera to enter into the active pairing phase.

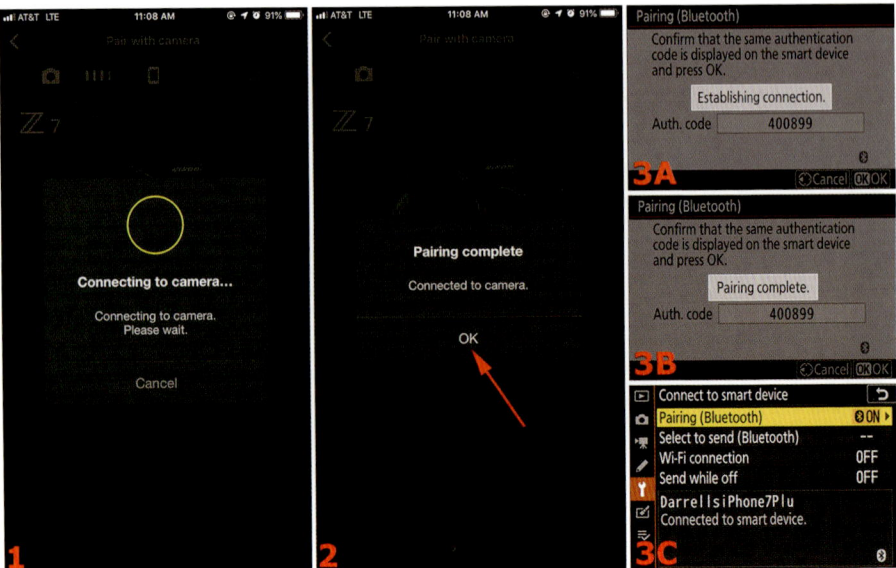

Figure 10.27E: Final handshaking and pairing complete

14. The camera and SnapBridge app will do some final handshaking while another *Connecting to camera* screen shows (figure 10.27E, image 1).

15. When the pairing is complete within the SnapBridge app, you will see the *Pairing complete* and *Connected to camera* screen (figure 10.27E, image 2).

16. In the meantime, the camera will rapidly display a series of screens (figure 10.27E, images 3A, 3B, and 3C). The first pairing screen will say *Establishing connection* (image 3A). The second pairing screen will say *Pairing complete* (image 3B). Then the camera will return to the Connect to smart device screen. This final screen will show the name of your smart device (e.g., DarrellsiPhone7Plu) and *Connected to smart device* (image 3C). At this point the camera and SnapBridge app are officially paired. Tap the OK button on the SnapBridge screen (figure 10.27E, image 2).

Congratulations! You got through the pairing process successfully. The camera and app are now ready to transfer images. If the pairing failed, try again by starting over with the following steps:

- Turn the camera off and back on to clear memory
- Shut down and restart the SnapBridge app
- Follow the previous 16 steps again

Above all, don't give up. Keep trying and you will be successful! (***Note:*** The SnapBridge app can connect to multiple Nikon cameras.)

Using or Deleting a Paired SnapBridge Connection

If you decide to delete a paired SnapBridge connection from your Z6, it is very easy to accomplish.

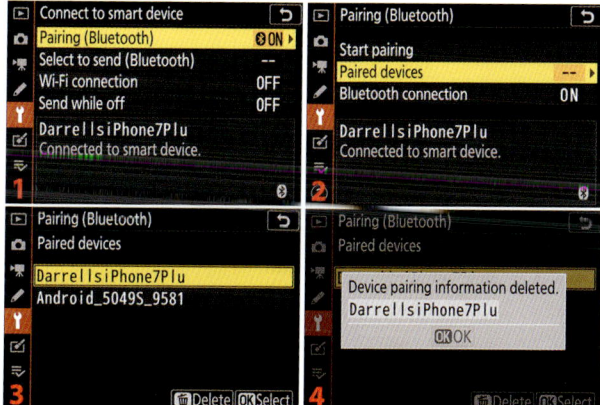

Figure 10.27F: Deleting a paired SnapBridge connection

Use the following steps to delete a paired SnapBridge connection:

1. Choose Pairing (Bluetooth) from the *Setup Menu > Connect to smart device* screen and scroll to the right (figure 10.27F, image 1).
2. Select Paired devices and scroll to the right (figure 10.27F, image 2).
3. You will see a list of Paired devices (figure 10.27F, image 3). My camera has both an iPhone and an Android device listed. If you want to use a listed smart device for image transfer or other purposes, simply select it and press or touch OK (Select).
4. If you want to delete a connection, highlight the smart device you want to disconnect (unpair) and press or touch Delete. A small window will pop up informing you that the connection has been broken. The screen will say, *Device pairing information deleted,* with the name of your smart device displayed. Press or touch OK to close the small window.

If you delete a paired connection from your camera, the connection still exists in Snap-Bridge and in your smart device's Bluetooth profile area. If you ever want to reconnect the device you just disconnected, you will need to remove the Bluetooth pairing information from SnapBridge and delete your camera's Bluetooth profile from your smart device first.

Figure 10.27B, image 2 (page 529), shows a menu with an item called *Forget camera.* Use this menu item to remove the camera from SnapBridge. Tap *Forget camera* and then touch the little minus (–) sign inside the small red circle next to the camera name to delete it (not shown).

Then you must remove the Bluetooth profile from your smart device. In an iPhone, it is under *Settings app > Bluetooth > My devices.* Tap the little "i" after the name (e.g., Z_7_3001781) and then touch Forget this device (not shown). In an Android it is found under the *Settings gear control* (swipe down from the top of the screen twice, and then tap the little gear). Find *Bluetooth* on the menu and tap it. Find your camera name (e.g., Z_7_3001781) under *Paired devices* and delete it (not shown).

Enabling or Disabling Bluetooth

You can enable or disable Bluetooth at any time to save battery. Disabling Bluetooth simply turns off the Bluetooth radio so that the camera can't communicate or waste battery when not needed; it does *not* remove the paired Bluetooth connection, thereby forcing you to pair the devices again.

You could also use Airplane mode to turn off all the camera's wireless connections. However, what if you want to use Wi-Fi but not Bluetooth right now? You can't do that if Airplane mode is enabled. Fortunately, you can disable just Bluetooth.

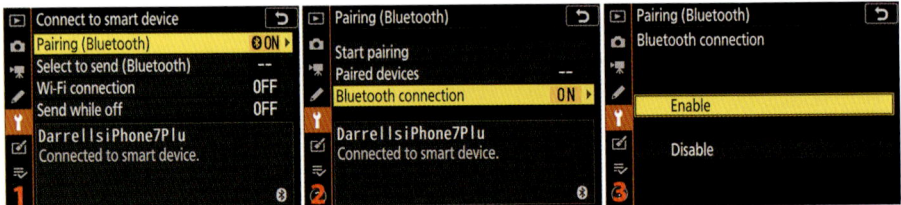

Figure 10.27G: Enabling or disabling Bluetooth (only)

Use the following steps to enable or disable Bluetooth temporarily:

1. Choose Pairing (Bluetooth) from the *Setup Menu > Connect to smart device* screen and scroll to the right (figure 10.27G, image 1).
2. Select Bluetooth connection and scroll to the right (figure 10.27G, image 2).
3. Highlight Enable or Disable and press the OK button or tap the option to lock in your choice.

Settings Recommendation: I leave my camera's Bluetooth enabled all the time. I find it easier to simply switch the camera into Airplane mode (page 527) when I want to save battery life.

Selecting Images to Send by Bluetooth

The camera gives you two ways to select images for transfer to your smart device. There is an automatic method, which will transfer all images you take from that point forward. There's also a manual method, which lets you send only selected images to your smart device. Additionally, you can deselect all images so they won't attempt to transfer.

If you want to automatically or manually transfer images, you must have *Auto download* (e.g., 2 megapixels) enabled under the *Auto link* menu selection on the main screen of the SnapBridge app.

Auto Select to Send

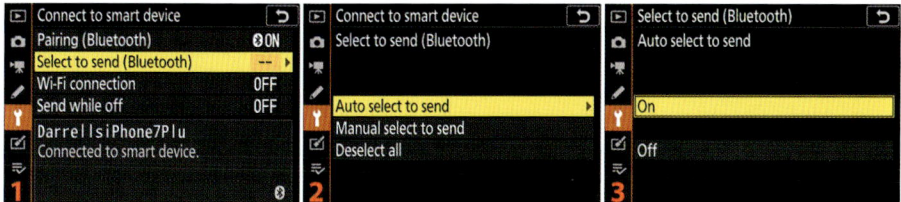

Figure 10.27H: Auto select to send (via Bluetooth)

Use the following steps to select images to send from your camera to your smart device:

1. Choose Select to send (Bluetooth) from the *Setup Menu > Connect to smart device* screen and scroll to the right (figure 10.27H, image 1).
2. If you want to automatically send all images you take to your smart device, choose the Auto select to send setting and scroll to the right (figure 10.27H, image 2).
3. Choose On to enable Auto select to send, or Off to disable it, and press the OK button, or tap the option to lock it in (figure 10.27H, image 3).

Once you have enabled Auto select to send, the SnapBridge app will automatically download any new images you take, as long as *Auto link > Auto download* is enabled under SnapBridge.

Manual Select to Send

If you would rather send selected images manually, you can choose individual images from a list of image thumbnails and mark them to send.

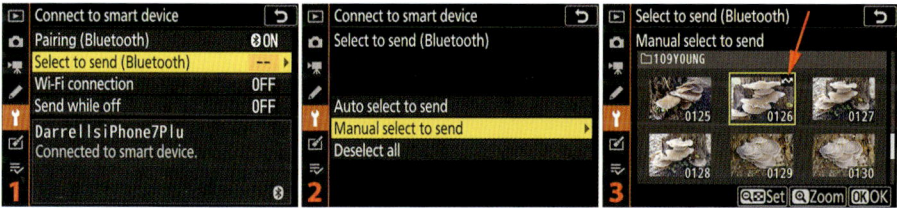

Figure 10.27I: Manual select to send (via Bluetooth)

Use the following steps to manually select images to send from your camera to your smart device:

1. Choose Select to send (Bluetooth) from the *Setup Menu > Connect to smart device* screen and scroll to the right (figure 10.27I, image 1).
2. Highlight Manual select to send and scroll to the right (figure 10.27I, image 2).
3. You will be presented with a screen of six image thumbnails (figure 10.27I, image 3). You can select or deselect an image by scrolling to it and pressing the Zoom out button, or you can simply tap the thumbnail. When selected, a small send-to-device symbol (like a sideways lightning bolt) will be displayed in the top-right corner of the thumbnail (red

arrow). You can zoom in to look at an image full screen by tapping the Zoom symbol or pressing the Zoom in button. Choose as many images as you would like and mark them for transfer. When you are finished, press or touch OK and the camera will briefly pop up a small window that says *Selection complete*. When the camera next connects to SnapBridge on your smart device, it will automatically transfer any marked images, as long as *Auto link > Auto download* is enabled under SnapBridge.

Settings Recommendation: I normally use Manual select to send when I want to send images to SnapBridge. I don't like filling up my smart device's limited storage with hundreds of images, even if they are only the "2 megapixels" versions that SnapBridge's *Auto link > Auto download* offers.

If you need to transfer all the images you take, why not use the **Connect to PC** function described in the next main chapter section (page 542). You can send your images directly to your laptop computer's much larger hard drive as you take them. The camera can use an existing local Wi-Fi network that both the camera and computer are members of (access-point Wi-Fi), or a one-to-one (ad hoc Wi-Fi) connection—directly between your Z6 and your computer—without using any outside wireless networks. The Z6 is a flexible little camera!

Deselect All

The *Deselect all* setting allows you to deselect all images marked for transfer. If you have been out shooting all day and accidentally have Auto select to send (page 535) selected, your camera is just itching to find SnapBridge so that it can send the 675 pictures you just took and fill up your smart device's storage.

To prevent this large image transfer from taking place, you can use the Deselect all setting to deselect all marked images. Later, you can transfer only the ones you want with Manual select to send (page 535).

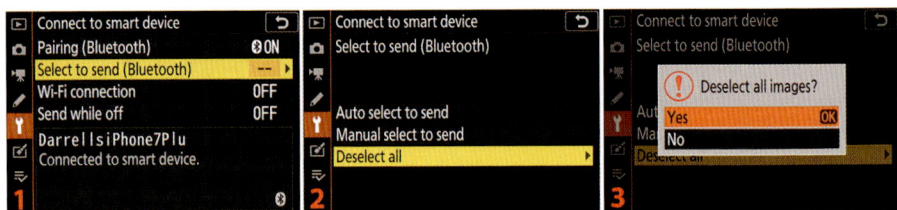

Figure 10.27J: Deselect all

Use the following steps to deselect all images and prevent their automatic transfer:

1. Choose Select to send (Bluetooth) from the *Setup Menu > Connect to smart device* screen and scroll to the right (figure 10.27J, image 1).
2. Highlight Deselect all and scroll to the right (figure 10.27J, image 2).
3. A popup window will appear with the warning question, *Deselect all images?* Highlight Yes and press or touch OK to remove the send markings from all images, or select No to cancel.

Wi-Fi Connection

Wi-Fi connection is best used when transferring large numbers of images and large items like videos to your smart device. You must make a Wi-Fi connection not entirely unlike when you connect a new smartphone or tablet to your home Wi-Fi.

Basically, the camera wants to be the Wi-Fi access point for your smartphone. While using the Wi-Fi connection, your smart device will not be able to access the internet. Instead the camera and smart device will be connected in a private (ad hoc) Wi-Fi network between the two devices only.

From the camera, it is quite easy to initiate the connection; however, you will need to know how to choose a Wi-Fi network from your smart device's settings app. Instead of choosing your normal home Wi-Fi network, you must choose the camera's Wi-Fi connection. Let's see how to initiate the Wi-Fi connection between the camera and your smart device.

Establish Wi-Fi Connection

There are two steps to establishing a Wi-Fi connection between your camera and a smartphone or tablet:

1. Enable Wi-Fi on the camera.
2. Connect to the camera's Wi-Fi connection from your smart device.

We will be considering how to enable Wi-Fi on the camera; however, it is beyond the scope of this book to describe (other than roughly) how to connect a smart device to the camera's Wi-Fi connection. There are simply too many smart devices out there, with slightly different ways to connect to a Wi-Fi network. Again, connecting to the camera's Wi-Fi is very similar to what you have surely done in the past when you connected your smart device to your home Wi-Fi. In other words, the Z6 becomes the source for your smart device's Wi-Fi connection instead of your home Wi-Fi.

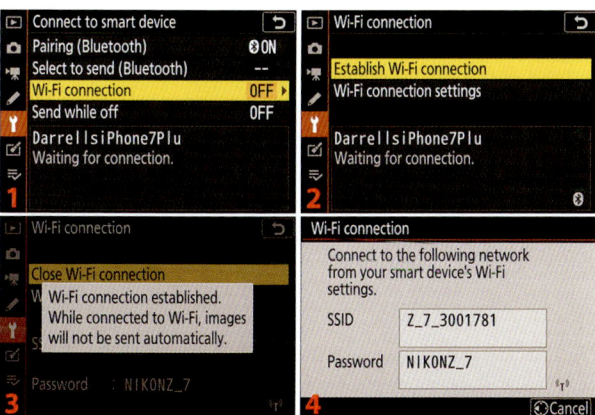

Figure 10.27K: Establishing an initial Wi-Fi connection

Use the following steps to enable the Wi-Fi connection in your camera so that you can connect your smart device to the camera's private Wi-Fi network:

1. Choose Wi-Fi connection from the *Setup Menu > Connect to smart device* screen and scroll to the right (figure 10.27K, image 1).
2. Highlight Establish Wi-Fi connection and press the OK button or tap the option with your fingertip (figure 10.27K, image 2).
3. The camera will briefly display a screen that tells you: *Wi-Fi connection established. While connected to Wi-Fi, images will not be sent automatically* (figure 10.27K, image 3), and then the final screen will display. Although this screen makes it seem that the camera is already connected to a smart device, it is not. The camera is merely broadcasting a Wi-Fi signal at this point and is waiting for you to connect your smart device to the camera's Wi-Fi by entering the SSID and Password provided into your smart device's Wi-Fi settings app (next step).
4. The Wi-Fi connection screen shown in figure 10.27K, image 4, gives you connection information that you can use to connect your smart device to the camera. You have three minutes to do so before the camera times out and shuts down its Wi-Fi. Therefore, using your smart device's settings app, choose the camera SSID (e.g., Z_7_3001781) and enter the Password (e.g., NIKONZ_7). Once the camera and smart device are connected you can then use the Wi-Fi features of the SnapBridge app to do things like transfer selected images and remotely control the camera.

Smart device connection info: Here is rough information on finding and establishing the Wi-Fi connection on smart devices:

* **iOS:** To connect to an iPhone or iPad, use the following path to enter a connection name (SSID) and password: *Setting app > Wi-Fi > Choose a network*. Choose the SSID (e.g., Z_7_3001781) and enter the password (e.g., NIKONZ_7), and when a check mark appears you are connected to the camera.
* **Android:** Swipe down from the top and look for the Wi-Fi symbol. Tap the symbol and look for the SSID (e.g., Z_7_3001781) and then enter the password (e.g., NIKONZ_7). The smart device will obtain an IP address and then will display "Connected, no internet" under the SSID name. The camera and Android are connected.
* **SnapBridge:** Try to use any feature in the SnapBridge app (e.g., Download pictures, Remote photography) and SnapBridge will ask you if you want to enable Wi-Fi. You will see this message: *Enable camera Wi-Fi, You must switch to Wi-Fi to use this feature. Note: Some time may be required to switch. Cancel/Ok.* Choose OK and SnapBridge will ask you: *SnapBridge wants to Join Wi-Fi network Z_7_3001781_SnapBridge?* Click Join.

Wi-Fi Connection Settings

The camera provides default Wi-Fi connection information, including an SSID of "Z_6_" followed by your camera's serial number (e.g., Z_6_1234567) and a password of NIKONZ_6. If you would prefer to use a more secure connection, in case an unauthorized person may try to connect to your camera over Wi-Fi, you can use the following steps to create a new

SSID and Password, along with other Wi-Fi settings. Let's examine how to configure a more secure Wi-Fi connection.

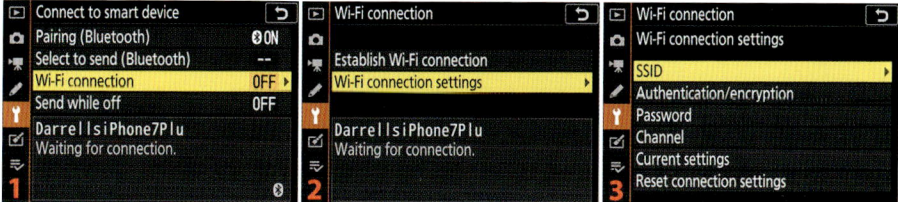

Figure 10.27L: Configuring secure Wi-Fi settings

Use the following steps to create a more secure Wi-Fi environment than the camera's default settings:

1. Choose Wi-Fi connection from the *Setup Menu > Connect to smart device* screen and scroll to the right (figure 10.27L, image 1).
2. Select Wi-Fi connection settings and scroll to the right (figure 10.27L, image 2).
3. The Wi-Fi connection settings menu gives you six settings that you can use to make the camera's Wi-Fi connection more secure (figure 10.27L, image 3). Let's consider each of these settings individually.

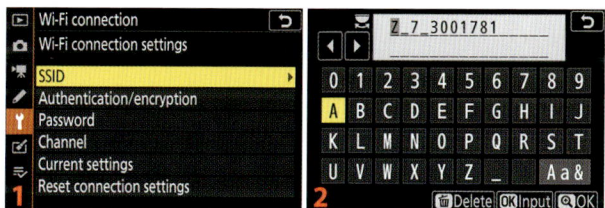

Figure 10.27M: Choosing an new SSID

4. Figure 10.27M continues where figure 10.27L ends. Choose SSID from the Wi-Fi connection settings menu and scroll to the right (figure 10.27M, image 1).
5. The SSID entry keyboard is shown in figure 10.27M, image 2. You can insert a new SSID by tapping the characters you want to use on the Monitor and they will appear in the position marked with the dark-gray cursor in the SSID field (Z_7_3001781). You can enter up to 36 characters. Use the left/right arrow-tip touch controls in the top-left corner to move left and right in the SSID field. To change from upper to lower case—or to access symbols, such as #—tap the Aa& control in the lower-right corner of the screen (just above the OK touch control). If you make a mistake, position the dark-gray cursor over the error and press or touch Delete. When you've finished entering the new SSID, press or touch OK to save it. (**Note:** If you would prefer not to use the touch-screen features, you can move the selection cursor with the Multi selector pad to highlight a character in the list below the SSID field, then press the OK button to insert the character. To correct an error, turn the rear Main command dial to move back and forth along

the field that contains the new SSID, and press the Delete button to remove the error. Press the OK button when you are finished entering the comment.)

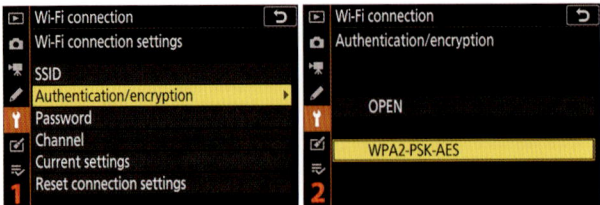

Figure 10.27N: Choosing an Authentication/encryption method

6. Choose Authentication/encryption from the Wi-Fi connection settings menu and scroll to the right (figure 10.27N, image 1).
7. Select OPEN if you do not want any security on your Wi-Fi connection. If you want to encrypt the Wi-Fi signal so that no one but you can access your camera's Wi-Fi, select the WPA2-PSK-AES setting.

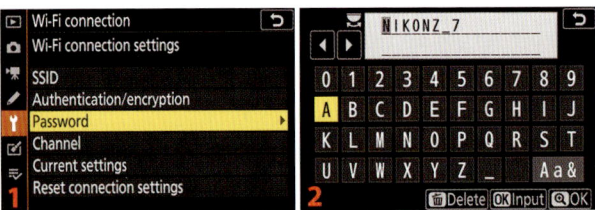

Figure 10.27O: Creating a new Wi-Fi password

8. Choose Password from the Wi-Fi connection settings menu and scroll to the right (figure 10.27O, image 1).
9. The Password entry keyboard is shown in figure 10.27O, image 2. You can insert a new password by tapping the characters you want to use on the Monitor and they will appear in the position marked with the dark-gray cursor in the password field (NIKONZ_7). You can enter up to 36 characters. Use the left/right arrow-tip touch controls in the top-left corner to move left and right in the Password field. To change from upper to lower case—or to access symbols, such as #—tap the Aa& control in the lower-right corner of the screen (just above the OK touch control). If you make a mistake, position the dark-gray cursor over the error and press or touch Delete. When you've finished entering the new password, press or touch OK to save it. (***Note:*** If you would prefer not to use the touch-screen features, you can move the selection cursor with the Multi selector pad to highlight a character in the list below the password field, then press the OK button to insert the character. To correct an error, turn the rear Main command dial to move back and forth along the field that contains the new Password, and press the Delete button to remove the error. Press the OK button when you are finished entering the comment.)

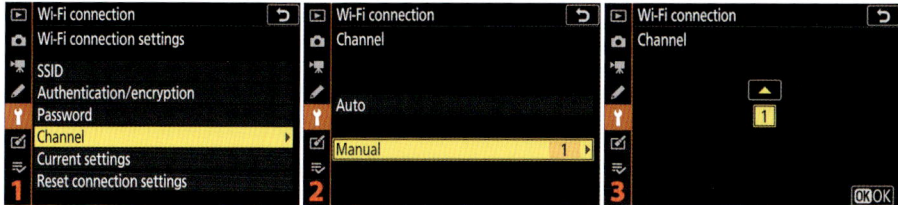

Figure 10.27P: Choosing a new Wi-Fi Channel setting

10. Choose Channel from the Wi-Fi connection settings menu and scroll to the right (figure 10.27P, image 1).

11. You have two choices: Auto and Manual (figure 10.27P, image 2). Most of us will choose Auto and let the camera figure out which is the best Channel to use. If you decide to use Manual, you will need to scroll to the right and select a Channel.

12. When using Manual, you can select Channels from 1 to 8. Press or touch OK to lock in your choice.

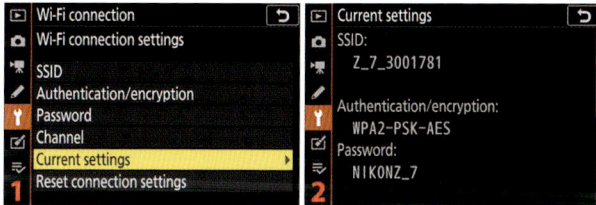

Figure 10.27Q: Examining the Current settings

13. Choose Current settings from the Wi-Fi connection settings menu and scroll to the right (figure 10.27Q, image 1).

14. The Current settings screen is an informational screen showing you a summary of the camera's current Wi-Fi connection settings so you don't have to scroll through a bunch of menus (figure 10.27Q, image 2). There are no adjustments to make on this screen.

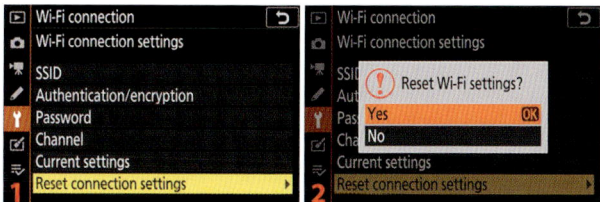

Figure 10.27R: Resetting the Wi-Fi connections back to factory defaults

15. Choose Reset connection settings from the Wi-Fi connection settings menu and scroll to the right (figure 10.27R, image 1).

16. A popup screen will display with the warning question: *Reset Wi-Fi settings? Yes/No.* Choose Yes and press or touch OK to reset the camera's Wi-Fi settings back to factory defaults, or select No to cancel.

Settings Recommendation: I change the SSID and Password to one I can remember easily, I always use authentication and encryption, and I leave the Channel set to Auto.

Send While Off

The *Send while off* setting is useful for those times when you have taken a large number of images and want to transfer them to your smart device without standing around waiting for the transfer to continue.

You can enable Send while off, start the transfer process, turn off your camera, and walk away. The camera will not shut down fully until all the images have transferred, and the smart device will usually shut itself off too.

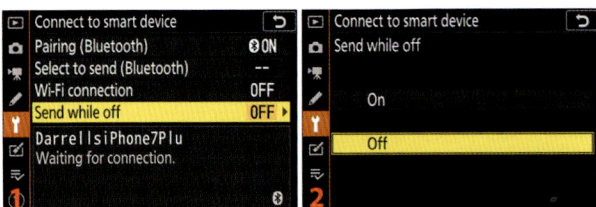

Figure 10.27S: Enabling or disabling Send while off

Use the following steps to enable or disable Send while off:

1. Choose Send while off from the Connect to smart device menu and scroll to the right (figure 10.27S, image 1).
2. Choose On to enable Send while off, or Off to disable it, and press the OK button or tap the option to lock it in (figure 10.27S, image 2).

Settings Recommendation: I generally don't use the Send while off feature because I like to monitor any image transfers for problems. Also, I worry about unnecessary battery drain. However, you may want to experiment with this setting to see if it is convenient for you.

Connect to PC

The *Connect to PC* function allows you to set up a connection for transferring images between your Z6 and a Mac or PC computer. You can connect to the computer on an existing home or business Wi-Fi network (Infrastructure mode), or by directly connecting the camera to a computer, using only the camera and computer's built-in Wi-Fi (Access-point mode).

Both styles of connection allow you to take a picture and have it transfer immediately to a designated folder on your computer. The camera has built-in Wi-Fi, so it is ready to connect by either style of Wi-Fi connection. Your computer must also have Wi-Fi capability to be used for receiving images (e.g., a laptop, or a desktop unit with a Wi-Fi dongle or card).

The Infrastructure mode is often used when you are at home or in the studio and you want to use your existing Wi-Fi network to connect the camera and computer for image transfer.

The Access-point mode is used when you are out in the field where there are no Wi-Fi networks available. The Z6 becomes a wireless access point and the computer connects to the camera's Wi-Fi directly.

You will need to download the Nikon Wireless Transmitter Utility for your Mac or PC. You will use the Connect to PC function to connect with the Wireless Transmitter Utility software. Download the software from Nikon at the following web address:

https://downloadcenter.nikonimglib.com/en/download/sw/128.html

If that address doesn't work, do a Google search for "download Nikon Wireless Transmitter Utility."

Before you proceed with the camera/computer pairing, be sure to have already installed the Nikon Wireless Transmitter Utility software on your computer so that it's ready to run.

Now let's see how to make the two types of Wi-Fi connections between your computer and camera. We will examine each type of connection individually.

Note: In this **Connect to PC** section, all computer screens are from a Mac computer. All camera screens are from a Nikon Z7. Windows PC and Nikon Z6 screens are the same.

Infrastructure Mode

The *Infrastructure mode* is just a cool-sounding way of saying that you will connect your camera to your PC or Mac by using an existing wireless home or business network.

You may use this mode to wirelessly transfer images to your PC or Mac across the same in-house wireless network you use to access printers, other computers, and the internet.

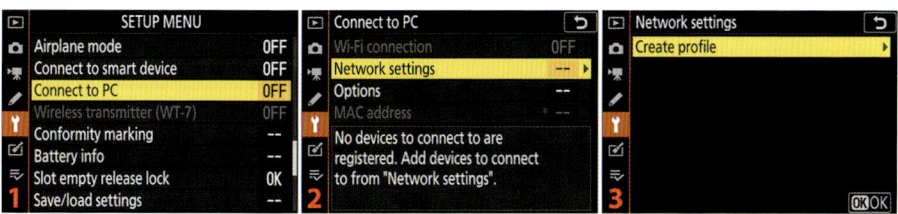

Figure 10.28A: Initial Wi-Fi network profile creation

Use the following steps to connect your camera to an existing Wi-Fi network:

1. Choose Connect to PC from the Setup Menu and scroll to the right (figure 10.28A, image 1).
2. Select Network settings from the Connect to PC menu and scroll to the right (figure 10.28A, image 2).
3. Highlight Create profile and scroll to the right (figure 10.28A, image 3).

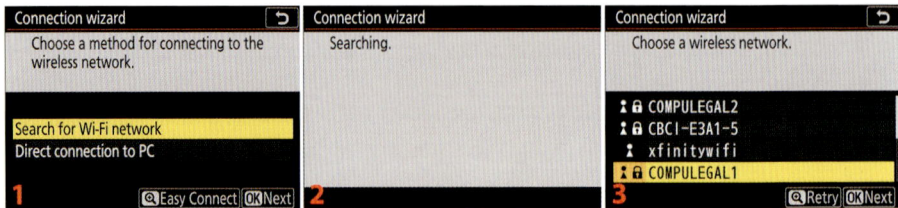

Figure 10.28B: Searching for an existing Wi-Fi network

4. Choose Search for Wi-Fi network from the Connection wizard screen and press or touch OK (Next) to start the search (figure 10.28B, image 1). (***Note:*** If your Wi-Fi network router can use Push-button WPS or Pin-entry WPS, you can tap the Easy Connect control at the bottom of the screen and bypass the rest of these pairing steps. See your Wi-Fi router's user's manual for information on how to use the WPS modes.)

5. The Connection wizard screen will display *Searching* while the camera looks for usable Wi-Fi networks (figure 10.28B, image 2). Discovering Wi-Fi sources may take several seconds, so be patient.

6. The Connection wizard screen will now display a list of available Wi-Fi network names (SSIDs). This works in a similar manner to how you have connected other devices to Wi-Fi networks in the past. The list will show your local Wi-Fi connection(s) and your neighbors' Wi-Fi connection(s). If a small lock symbol appears before the SSID name, it means the SSID requires a password to connect. If there is no lock symbol, the Wi-Fi source is "open" and does not require a password, nor is it secure. Choose your known and secure Wi-Fi SSID (mine is COMPULEGAL1) and press or touch OK (Next) to select the Wi-Fi network. Of course, your list of SSIDs will be different from my list of SSIDs.

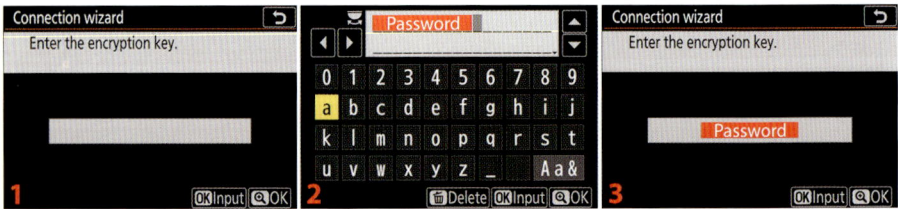

Figure 10.28C: Entering the password (encryption key) for your Wi-Fi network

7. The Connection wizard will now display a blank data input field for entering the password for the selected Wi-Fi network connection (figure 10.28C, image 1). Press or touch OK, or tap the data input field, and a password screen will open.

8. You can insert the Wi-Fi password by tapping the characters you want to use on the Monitor and they will appear in the position marked with the dark-gray cursor in the password field (Password). My actual Wi-Fi password is obscured by the red Password shown. You can enter up to 36 characters. Use the left/right arrow-tip touch controls in the top-left corner to move left and right in the Password field. To change from upper to lower case—or to access symbols, such as #—touch the Aa& control in the lower-right

corner of the screen (just above the OK touch control). If you make a mistake, position the dark-gray cursor over the error and press or touch Delete. When you've finished entering the new password, press or touch OK to save it. (**Note:** If you would prefer not to use the touch-screen features, you can move the selection cursor with the Multi selector pad to highlight a character in the list below the password field, then press the OK button to insert the character. To correct an error, turn the rear Main command dial to move back and forth along the field that contains the new Password, and press the Delete button to remove the error. Press the OK button when you are finished entering the comment.)

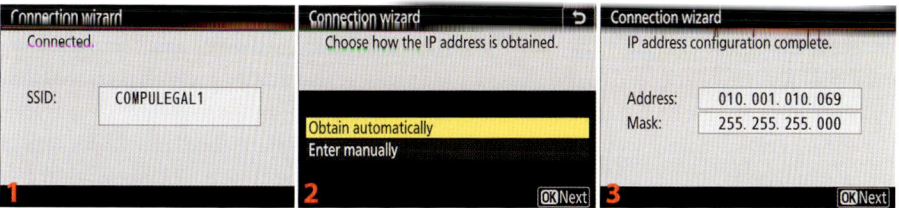

Figure 10.28D: Obtaining an IP address

9. The camera must now obtain an IP address (camera identifier) and sub-net Mask (host address range identifier) from the Wi-Fi network by using DHCP (Dynamic Host Configuration Protocol). Don't worry, you don't have to do anything except follow these screens; the camera and Wi-Fi network know how to communicate and handshake with each other. (**Geek Note:** if you are networking savvy and want to manually enter a static IP address and sub-net Mask after manually assigning a static IP and mask to your camera in your Wi-Fi router, the camera will allow you to do that with the Enter manually setting [figure 10.28D, image 2]. Most of us will ignore the Enter manually setting and use the Obtain automatically setting instead.) As seen in figure 10.28D, image 1, the Connection wizard will report *Connected* to your selected SSID (e.g., COMPULE-GAL1). In a moment it will automatically switch to the next screen.

10. As shown in figure 10.28D, image 2, the Connection wizard now requests that you choose how the IP address and Mask are obtained. To make things easy for yourself, choose Obtain automatically and press or touch OK.

11. The camera will handshake with the Wi-Fi network and automatically obtain an IP address (e.g., 010.001.010.069) and Mask (e.g., 255.255.255.000). When it is done, the camera will display the current connection information. Press or touch OK (Next) to continue. The camera is now connected to the local Wi-Fi network, but is not yet paired with your computer.

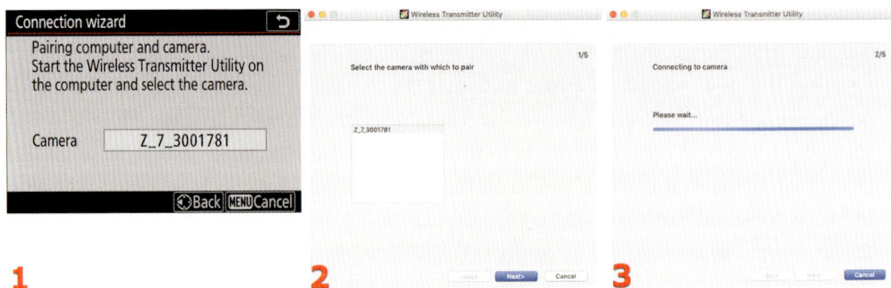

Figure 10.28E: Pairing the computer and camera – Camera selection

12. Now it's time to connect the camera to the computer. It is important that the computer also be connected to the same Wi-Fi network to which the camera is connected. Therefore, if it is not already connected, connect your computer to your Wi-Fi network (beyond the scope of this book). Your camera will be displaying the Connection wizard screen shown in figure 10.28E, image 1. Your camera name will be displayed in the Camera data field (e.g., Z_7_3001781). At this point you must run the Nikon Wireless Transmitter Utility.

13. When the Wireless Transmitter Utility first runs, and even before it displays a window on your computer, it seeks a Nikon camera on the local Wi-Fi network. If it finds your camera, the Wireless Transmitter Utility window will open and display a message that reads *Select the camera with which to pair,* with the name of your camera in a white box (figure 10.28E, image 2). Choose your camera name (e.g., Z_7_3001781) from the box and click the Next> button on the Wireless Transmitter Utility computer screen.

14. The Wireless Transmitter Utility will now display a window that says *Connecting to camera,* while a progress indicator moves across the window.

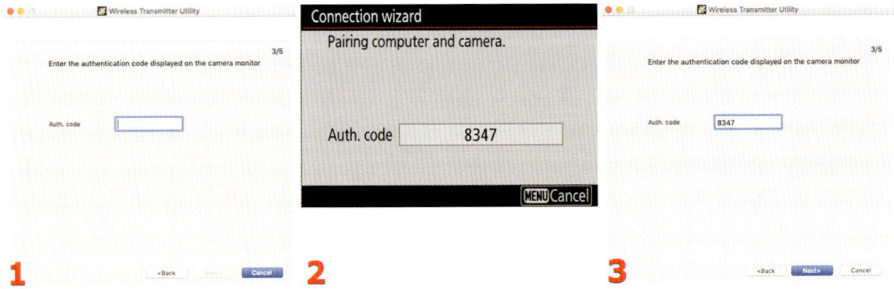

Figure 10.28F: Pairing the computer and camera – One-time pairing code entry

15. Once the Wireless Transmitter Utility locates your camera, the computer will display a window that says *Enter the authentication code displayed on the camera monitor,* with an Auth. code data entry box (figure 10.28F, image 1). It is awaiting your entry of an Auth. code (authorization code).

16. At the same time that your computer is displaying the window seen in figure 10.28F, image 1, the camera will display a *Pairing computer and camera* screen with an Auth. code (e.g., 8347), as seen in figure 10.28F, image 2.
17. Enter the Auth. code from your camera into the Auth. code data entry field on your computer. Click the Next> button (figure 10.28F, image 3).

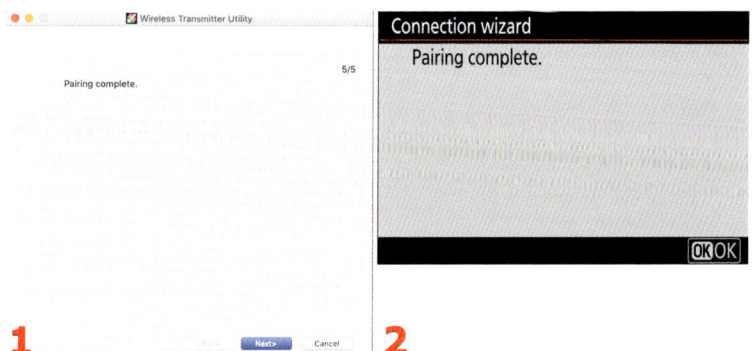

Figure 10.28G: Pairing the computer and camera – Pairing is complete!

18. Figure 10.28G, images 1 and 2, show the *Pairing complete* screens displayed by the computer and camera. Click the Next> button on the computer screen and press or touch OK on the camera to finalize the pairing.

Congratulations! The camera and computer are now connected through your local Wi-Fi network and you are ready to configure the computer to receive images. See the upcoming chapter subsection **Choosing a Picture Folder for Image Transfer** (page 550). But first, let's consider how to make a direct connection between your camera and a computer, with no external Wi-Fi network required.

Access-Point Mode

The *Access-point mode* is an impressive-sounding way of saying that you will connect your camera to your PC or Mac directly, on a wireless, ad hoc network between the camera and computer only. The camera will become a wireless access point with which the computer can connect.

You may use this mode to wirelessly transfer images to your PC or Mac on a private connection controlled by the camera. There is generally no Internet access on your computer while using this mode. You can use Access-point mode even when no Wi-Fi is normally available, such as when out shooting in nature or at a sports event.

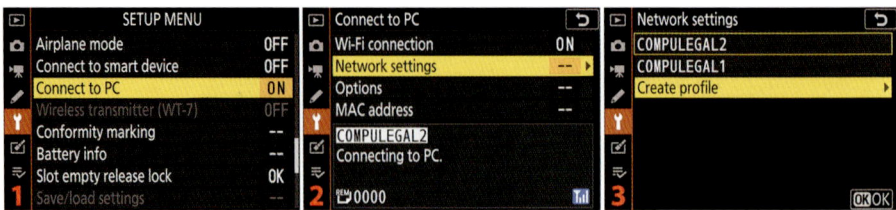

Figure 10.28H: Initial Access-point mode connection screens

Use the following steps to make a wireless connection between a single computer and your camera:

1. Choose Connect to PC from the Setup Menu and scroll to the right (figure 10.28H, image 1).
2. Make sure the Wi-Fi connection is enabled (On), using the Wi-Fi connection setting at the top of the menu in figure 10.28H, image 2. Now select Network settings and scroll to the right (figure 10.28H, image 2).
3. You will see a list of network connections if you have previously made any (e.g., COMPULEGAL1). At the bottom of the list is the Create profile setting (figure 10.28H, image 3). Select it and scroll to the right.

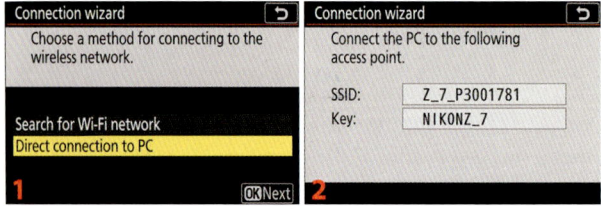

Figure 10.28I: Connect a computer directly to your camera

4. You now have two choices: Search for Wi-Fi network (see previous **Infrastructure Mode** subsection on page 543) and Direct connection to PC, which is what we will do in this Access-point mode subsection. Highlight Direct connection to PC and press or touch OK (Next) to proceed.
5. When you see the Connection wizard screen shown in figure 10.28I, image 2, the camera has started broadcasting a Wi-Fi signal. Its SSID and Key (password) are shown on the screen. The camera has become a wireless access point to which your computer can connect—using the Wireless Transmitter Utility. Now run the Wireless Transmitter Utility software on your computer so that it can connect to the camera.

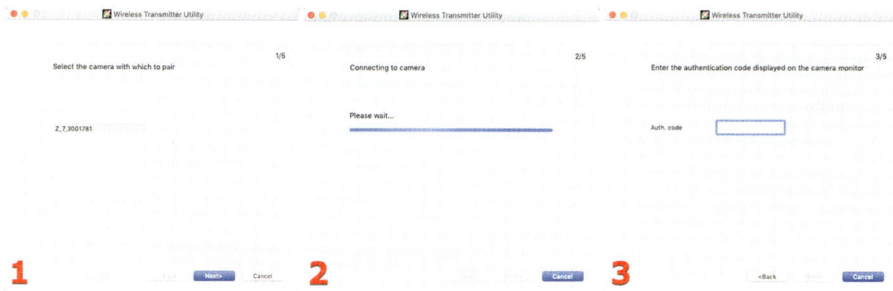

Figure 10.28J: Connecting the Wireless Transmitter Utility to the Camera

6. A Wireless Transmitter Utility software window will open with a screen that asks you to *Select the camera with which to pair* (figure 10.28J, image 1). Below the request is a box containing your camera name (e.g., Z_7_3001781). Select your camera name and press the Next> button.

7. The computer will now seek a connection with the camera (figure 10.28J, image 2). You will see the window that says *Connecting to camera, Please wait…* along with a progress indicator. Wait for several seconds while the camera and computer communicate.

8. After they are done communicating, another window will open on the computer, with the words *Enter the authentication code displayed on the camera monitor* (figure 10.28J, image 3). An Auth. code data entry field will await the entry of a code provided by the camera.

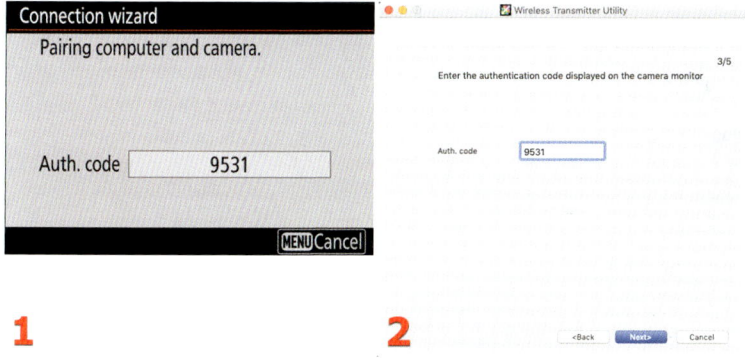

Figure 10.28K: Entering the authentication code

9. The camera will display an Auth. code on its Monitor (figure 10.28K, image 1). Enter the provided authentication code into the blank Auth. code field on the Wireless Transmitter Utility computer screen (e.g., 9531). Press the Next> button on the Wireless Transmitter Utility window.

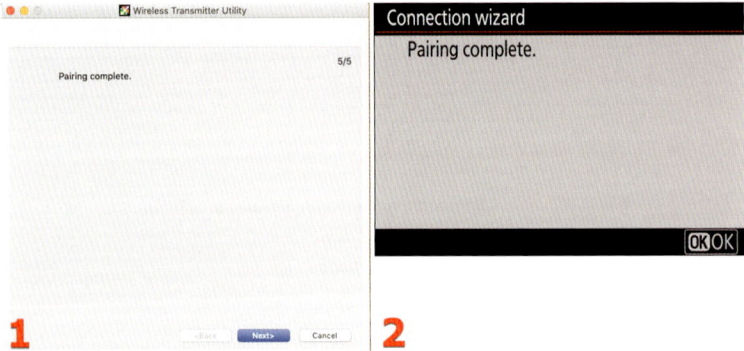

Figure 10.28L: The camera and computer are wirelessly paired with each other

10. A screen that says *Pairing complete* will be displayed on both the computer and camera (figure. 10.28L, images 1 and 2). The devices are now paired and ready to transfer images.

Congratulations! The camera and computer are now directly connected through an ad hoc Wi-Fi network that works between the camera and computer only. Now you should configure a picture folder to receive images on your computer. Let's see how to do that.

Choosing a Picture Folder for Image Transfer

Once you have made a connection between your camera and computer, using either Infrastructure mode (page 543) or Access-point mode (page 547), you must set up a folder to receive images. Afterward, you will use the Options menu (next subsection) to select how and when images will be transferred to your picture folder. Let's see how to create a picture folder on your computer.

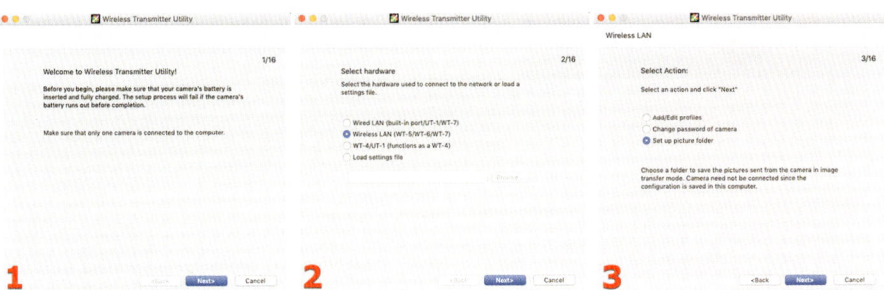

Figure 10.28M: Initial steps in creating a picture folder to receive images wirelessly

Use the following steps to create a picture folder to wirelessly receive images from your camera:

1. Run the Wireless Transmitter Utility on your computer. A Welcome to Wireless Trans-mitter Utility! window will open (figure 10.28M, image 1). It will give you two items of information: [**1**] *Before you begin, please make sure that your camera's battery is inserted and fully charged. The setup process will fail if the camera's battery runs out before comple-tion.* [**2**] *Make sure that only one camera is connected to the computer.* Click the Next> button to continue.

2. A Select hardware window will open next (figure 10.28M, image 2). It has the message: *Select the hardware used to connect to the network or load a settings file.* You have a choice of four items. Click the second item on the list: Wireless LAN (WT-5/WT-6/WT-7), and then click the Next> button.

3. A Select Action screen will appear next (figure 10.28M, image 3), with the message: *Select an action and click "Next".* There are three selections available and you should choose the last item: Set up picture folder. Click the Next> button to continue.

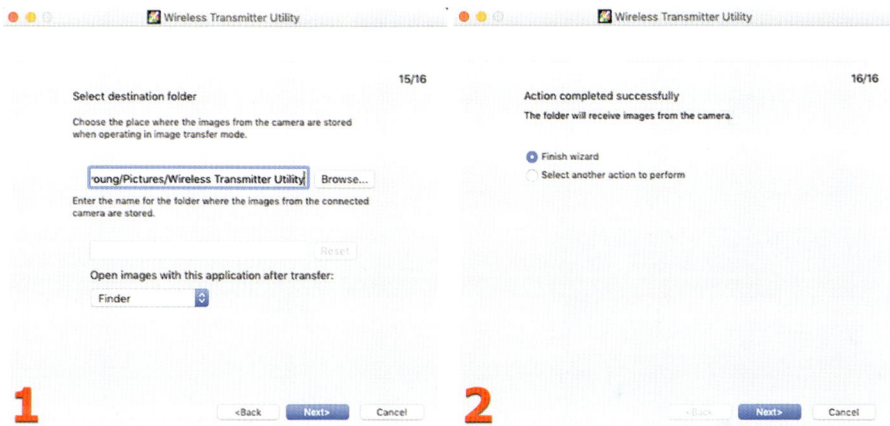

Figure 10.28N: Final steps in creating a picture folder

4. A Select destination folder window will open (figure 10.28N, image 1). It asks you to *Choose the place where the images from the camera are stored when operating in image transfer mode.* Below the request message is a data entry field with a Browse… button. Click the Browse… button and choose a folder for receiving images. Once you have chosen your picture folder, click the Next> button to continue.

5. The final window will now open with the heading Action completed successfully, and a message stating: *The folder will receive images from the camera.* There are two selections on this window. Click the first one, Finish wizard, and then press the Next> button to finish.

You have completed the configuration of your computer's picture folder. Your camera is ready to send images, and the computer is ready to receive images and save them to the picture folder. Now you need to make a choice as to how and when images will transfer to the computer.

Options (for Image Transfer)

The camera gives you four *Options* for sending images to your computer. Here is a list of the Options and what each does:

- **Auto send:** Once you have taken a picture and it has been written to the memory card, the camera will send it to your computer. Pictures taken during a video recording, and the video recording itself, are not automatically sent to the computer. You must manually send them afterward.
- **Delete after send:** Once you have taken a picture and it has been saved to the memory card, it will then transfer to your computer. When the image has successfully transferred to the computer, the camera will delete the image from its memory card. In all cases, sequential image numbering is used, regardless of the settings for Custom setting d7 File number sequence (page 405).
- **Send file as:** When you are taking pictures in one of the NEF (RAW) + JPEG modes, you can use this setting to select whether to send the JPEG image only or both the NEF (RAW) and JPEG images.
- **Deselect all?:** Use this setting to unmark all images marked for sending to the computer (or SnapBridge). If the camera is actively sending images, it will stop immediately.

Now let's see how to select one of these image transfer options.

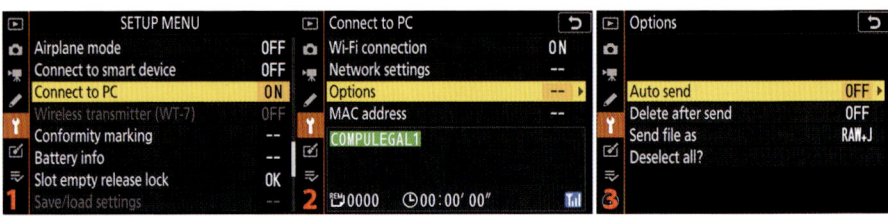

Figure 10.28O: Four image transfer Options

Use the following steps to send copies of your images to your computer:

1. Choose Connect to PC from the Setup Menu and scroll to the right (figure 10.28O, image 1).
2. Select Options and scroll to the right (figure 10.28O, image 2).
3. You are presented with four choices, as described in the previous list (figure 10.28O, image 3). Let's examine how to choose each option.

Auto Send

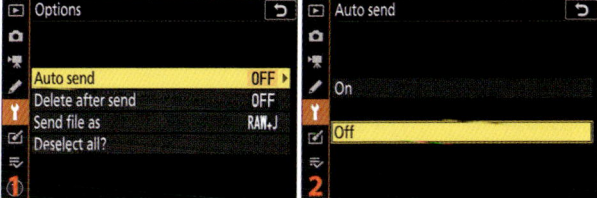

Figure 10.28P: Auto send

Use the following steps to Auto send copies of your images to your computer:

1. Figure 10.28P begins where figure 10.28O ends. Choose Auto send from the Options menu and scroll to the right (figure 10.28P, image 1).
2. Referring to the previous list, choose On to enable or Off to disable Auto send (figure 10.28P, image 2). Press the OK button or tap the option to select it.

Delete After Send

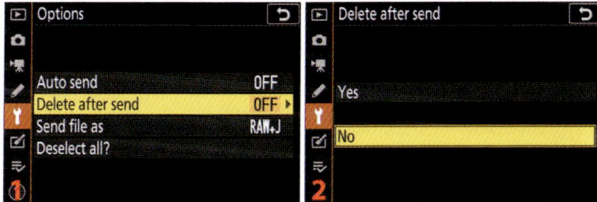

Figure 10.28Q: Delete after send

Use the following steps to delete the images from your camera's memory card after they are sent to your computer:

1. Figure 10.28Q begins where figure 10.28O ends. Choose Delete after send from the Options menu and scroll to the right (figure 10.28Q, image 1).
2. Referring to the previous list, choose Yes to enable or No to disable Delete after send (figure 10.28Q, image 2). Press the OK button or tap the option to select it.

Send File As

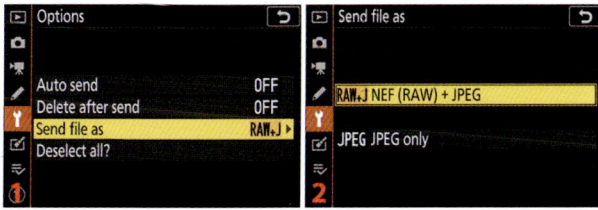

Figure 10.28R: Send file as

Use the following steps to send JPEG only or NEF (RAW) + JPEG copies of your images to your computer:

1. Figure 10.28R begins where figure 10.28O ends. Choose Send file as from the Options menu and scroll to the right (figure 10.28R, image 1).
2. Referring to the previous list, choose NEF (RAW) + JPEG to enable RAW and JPEG sending, or JPEG only to only send JPEGs (figure 10.28R, image 2). Press the OK button or tap the option to select it.

Deselect All?

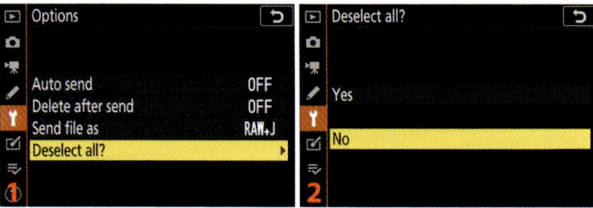

Figure 10.28S: Deselect all

Use the following steps to deselect all images marked for sending to your computer or smart device:

1. Figure 10.28S begins where figure 10.28O ends. Choose Deselect all? from the Options menu and scroll to the right (figure 10.28S, image 1).
2. Choose Yes to deselect all marked images or No to leave marked images selected for transfer (figure 10.28S, image 2). Press the OK button or tap the option to select it.

Image Sending Screen

In figure 10.28T you can see the screen shown when images are transferring. The file name of the image currently being transferred is shown in dark blue (e.g., _1DY0180.NEF), followed by *Now sending*.

At the bottom of the sending area, you will see the number of remaining images (e.g., REM 0001), the approximate time remaining (e.g., 00:01' 20") and the Wi-Fi signal strength in light blue on the bottom right (mine shows three bars, or full strength).

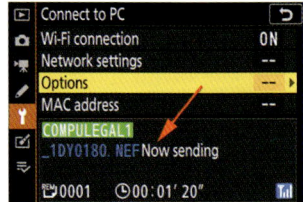

Figure 10.28T: Image(s) sending from camera to computer

MAC Address

For those who need to use their camera to connect to and use various network resources, it is imperative to have the *MAC address* of the camera available. Use this function to view the MAC address, which never changes.

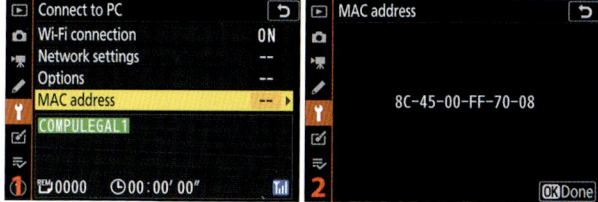

Figure 10.28U: Viewing the camera's MAC address

Use the following steps to view the MAC address of your Z6:

1. Choose MAC address from the Connect to PC menu and scroll to the right (figure 10.28U, image 1).
2. The MAC address is displayed (figure 10.28U, image 2).

Note: The MAC (Media Access Control) address has nothing to do with an Apple Mac computer. It is a unique series of characters assigned to each device with networking capabilities to help identify the device as a unique entity on a network.

Wireless Transmitter (WT-7)

With a Nikon WT-7 or WT-7a wireless transmitter attached to the Nikon Z6, the camera will be able to link with a computer or an FTP server by using a wireless or Ethernet network. The camera already has this functionality to some degree using less expensive tools and functions, such as SnapBridge (page 528), Connect to PC (page 542), and the WR-R10 wireless transmitter (page 523) along with the camera's built-in Wi-Fi and Bluetooth. While connected to a WT-7/a you will have the following settings under your control:

- Wireless transmitter
- Choose hardware
- Network settings
- Options

The primary benefit you will receive by using the rather expensive WT-7a transmitter is a more robust radio signal and greater range compared to the other wireless solutions mentioned earlier. It is unlikely that most of us will need the power of this high-end transmitter. If you have that need, you will already know it. If you are not sure, please do some research to see how the WT-7/a might benefit you.

The use of a WT-7/a transmitter is beyond the scope of this book. Please refer to the user's manual included with your Nikon WT-7 or WT-7a transmitter for details on using it to replace the camera's built in functionality and less expensive solutions.

Conformity Marking

Conformity marking is a simple function that lets you see the symbols for the various industry standards with which your camera conforms. These standards have symbols that you can research if you so desire.

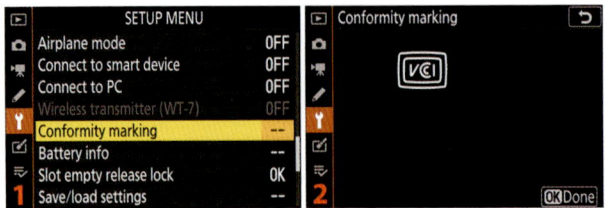

Figure 10.29: Viewing the symbols for the Nikon Z6's standards conformity

Use the following steps to view the camera's conformity standards:

1. Choose Conformity marking from the Setup Menu and scroll to the right (figure 10.29, image 1).
2. Figure 10.29, image 2, shows the Conformity marking screen with the symbols of conformity. Press or touch OK (Done) when you are finished viewing the symbol(s).

Battery Info

The *Battery info* screen (figure 10.30, image 2) will let you know how much battery charge has been used (Charge), how many images have been taken with this battery since the last charge (No. of shots), and how much life the battery has before it will no longer hold a good charge (Battery age).

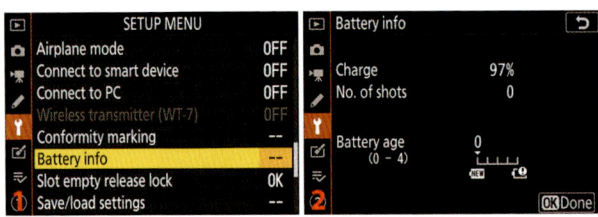

Figure 10.30: Battery info screen

Here are the steps to examine the Battery info:

1. Select Battery info from the Setup Menu and scroll to the right (figure 10.30, image 1).

2. The next screen is the Battery info screen (figure 10.30, image 2). It is just for informa-tion, so there's nothing to set. When you've finished examining your camera's Battery info, press or touch OK (Done) to exit.

The Z6 goes a step further than most cameras. Not only does it inform you of the amount of charge left in your battery, it also lets you know how much life is left. After some time, all batteries weaken and won't hold a full charge. The Battery age meter will tell you when the battery needs to be completely replaced. It shows five stages of battery life, from 0 to 4, so you'll be prepared to replace the battery before it gets too old to take many shots.

Settings Recommendation: It's important to use Nikon brand batteries in your Z6 so they will work properly with the camera. Aftermarket batteries may not charge correctly in the Z6 battery charger. In addition, they may not report correct Battery age information. There may be an aftermarket brand that works correctly, but I haven't found it. Instead, I use the batteries designed by Nikon to work with this camera. I am a bit afraid to trust a camera that costs this much to a cheap aftermarket battery of unknown origin.

Slot Empty Release Lock

Slot empty release lock defaults to locking the shutter when you try to take an image with-out a memory card inserted in the camera. By enabling it, you can take pictures without a memory card but cannot save them later.

This function exists so that when you have your camera tethered to your computer us-ing Nikon Camera Control Pro 2 software (not included), you can send pictures directly to the computer, bypassing the memory card.

You can allow the camera to take pictures with no card inserted when you select the OK Enable release setting. Here is a description of both settings:

- **LOCK Release locked:** When you choose this setting, your camera will refuse to release the shutter when there is no memory card present.
- **OK Enable release:** Use this setting if you want to use the optional Camera Control Pro 2 software to send images directly to a computer. If the camera is not tethered to a computer, it uses "Demo mode," which will display an image on the camera's Monitor, but you will have no way to save the image.

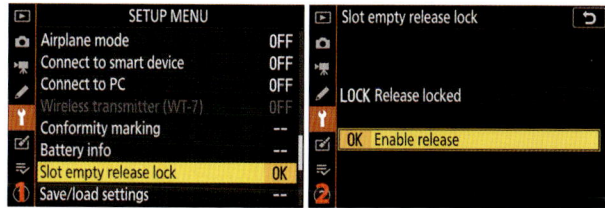

Figure 10.31: Slot empty release lock

Here are the steps used to configure Slot empty release lock:

1. Select Slot empty release lock from the Setup Menu and scroll to the right (figure 10.31, image 1).
2. Choose one of the two settings from the list (figure 10.31, image 2). Press the OK button or tap the option to lock in the setting.

Settings Recommendation: I tried using the OK Enable release setting as an experiment. I found that there is no real reason to use this setting other than when the camera is tethered to a computer. You cannot save the images in the memory buffer to a memory card later.

Save/Load Settings

Do you have your Z6 set up exactly the way you like it? Have you spent hours and hours reading this book and the Z7/Z6 User's Manual, or simply exploring menus, and finally you finally have all the settings in place? Are you worried that you might accidentally reset your camera or that it could lose its settings in one way or another? Well, worry no more! *Save/load settings* writes configuration settings to the memory card, allowing you to back up camera settings to your computer.

When you have your camera configured to your liking, or at any time during the process, simply use the Save/load settings function to save the camera configuration to your memory card. It creates a small file whose name begins with NCSET followed by three numbers that vary by camera (e.g., 001), and ending in .BIN, into the root directory of your Z6's memory card (e.g., NCSET001.BIN). You can then save that file to your computer's hard drive and have a backup of your camera settings.

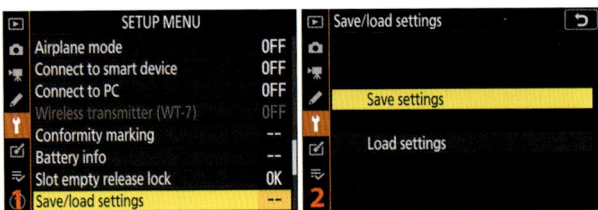

Figure 10.32: Save/load settings

Here are the steps to save or load the camera's settings:

1. Choose Save/load settings from the Setup Menu and scroll to the right (figure 10.32, image 1).
2. Select Save settings or Load settings from the Save/load settings menu, and then follow one of these two easy procedures (figure 10.32, images 2):

- **Save settings:** Select Save settings and press the OK button or tap Save settings with your fingertip (figure 10.32, image 2). Your most important camera settings will be saved to the root directory of your memory card. Afterward, copy the .BIN settings file (e.g., NCSET001.BIN) to your computer for safekeeping. **Warning:** You may notice that on the Save/load settings screen the Load settings selection is grayed out on your camera. If Load settings is not grayed out when you get ready to save the settings, be careful—you are about to overwrite previously saved settings that are currently on the memory card. The only time you'll see Load settings not grayed out is when a .BIN file already exists on the memory card.
- **Load settings:** Insert a memory card with a previously saved .BIN file (e.g., NCSET001. BIN) in the card's root directory, select Load settings, and press the OK button or tap Load settings with your fingertip (figure 10.32, image 2). The settings you previously saved will be reloaded into the Z6 and will overwrite your current settings without prompting you for permission, so be sure that you are ready to have the settings overwritten. If you change the name of the .BIN file, the Z6 will not be able to reload your settings.

Here is a list of settings that are saved or loaded when you make use of one of these functions. It doesn't save or load every setting in the Z6, only the ones listed here:

Playback Menu (5 settings)
- Playback display options
- Image review
- After delete
- After burst, show
- Rotate tall

Photo Shooting Menu (all four banks included, 25 settings)
- File naming
- Choose image area
- Image quality
- Image size
- NEF (RAW) recording
- ISO sensitivity settings
- White balance (includes fine-tuning adjustments and presets d–1 to d–6)
- Set Picture Control (Custom Picture Controls are saved as Auto)
- Color space
- Active D-Lighting
- Long exposure NR
- High ISO NR
- Vignette control
- Diffraction compensation
- Auto distortion control
- Flicker reduction shooting
- Metering
- Flash control
- Flash mode
- Flash compensation
- Focus mode
- AF-area mode
- Vibration reduction (settings may vary by lens mounted)
- Auto bracketing
- Silent photography

Movie Shooting Menu (25 settings)
- File naming
- Choose Image area
- Frame size/frame rate
- Movie quality
- Movie file type
- ISO sensitivity settings

- White balance
- Set Picture Control (Custom Picture Controls are saved as Auto)
- Active D-Lighting
- High ISO NR
- Vignette control
- Diffraction compensation
- Auto distortion control
- Flicker reduction
- Metering
- Focus mode

- AF-area mode
- Vibration reduction (settings vary by lens mounted)
- Electronic VR
- Microphone sensitivity
- Attenuator
- Frequency response
- Wind noise reduction
- Headphone volume
- Timecode (except for Timecode origin)

Custom Settings (50 settings)
- All Custom Settings except *Custom setting d3: Sync. release mode options*

Setup Menu (15 settings)
- Language
- Time zone and date (except for *Date and time*)
- Limit monitor mode selection
- Information display
- Non-CPU lens data
- Clean image sensor
- Image comment

- Copyright information
- Beep options
- Touch controls
- HDMI
- Location data (except for Position)
- Wireless remote (WR) options
- Assign remote (WR) Fn button
- Slot empty release lock

Settings Recommendation: This function is a great idea. After using my camera for a few days and getting it set up just right, I save the settings file to my computer for safekeeping. Later, if I change things extensively for some reason and then want to reload my original settings, I just put the backed-up settings file on a memory card, pop it into the camera, select Load settings, and I'm back in business.

Reset All Settings

The *Reset all settings* function allows you to do exactly what it says: reset all the settings within the Nikon Z6. At some point in the future, you may want to sell your camera to offset the cost of a new Nikon purchase, or you may just want to start over with fresh settings. This function allows you to do so.

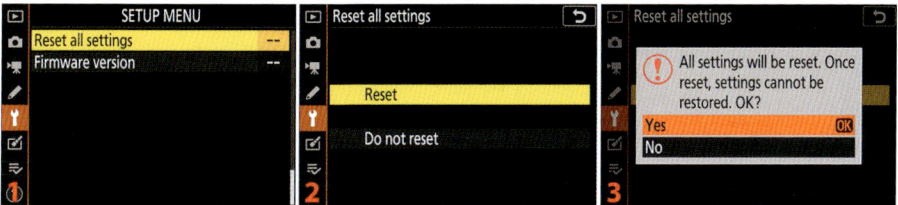

Figure 10.33: Reset all settings in the Nikon Z6

Use the following steps to reset your Z6's menu settings for a fresh start with menu configuration:

1. Select Reset all settings from the Setup Menu and scroll to the right (figure 10.33, image 1).
2. If you want to reset the camera's settings, highlight Reset and scroll to the right (figure 10.33, image 2). Choose Do not reset to cancel.
3. Choose Yes from the popup box that asks *All settings will be reset. Once reset, settings cannot be restored. OK?* (figure 10.33, image 3). Press or touch OK and the camera will execute a settings reset. Choose No to cancel.

Firmware Version

Firmware version is a simple informational screen, like the Battery info screen. It shows you which version of the camera's operating system (firmware) the Z6 is running. My camera is currently running version C2.00 and LF 1.00 (figure 10.34, image 2).

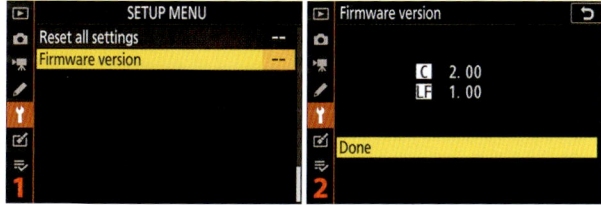

Figure 10.34: Viewing the camera's Firmware version

Here are the steps to see the Firmware version of your camera:

1. Choose Firmware version from the Setup Menu and scroll to the right (figure 10.34, image 1).
2. Examine the Firmware version (figure 10.34, image 2). Select Done and press the OK button.

When it's time to do a firmware update, you will use this same Firmware version menu to update the camera. An extra "Update" menu item will appear below the Done selection (not shown), allowing you to update the firmware. Follow the instructions provided on Nikon's website for each firmware update.

Author's Conclusion

Whew! The Z6 may seem like a complicated little beast, but that's what you get when you fold pro-level functionality into a relatively small DSLM body. For as complex as it is, I'm certainly delighted with it.

Next, we'll consider how to use the camera's Retouch Menu to adjust images without using a computer. If you are in the field shooting RAW files and you need a quick JPEG, black-and-white version of a file, or red-eye reduction, the Retouch Menu has you covered.

You can even do things like image distortion and perspective control, color balance changes, filtration, cropping, and image resizing—all without touching a computer. Let's see how!

11 Retouch Menu

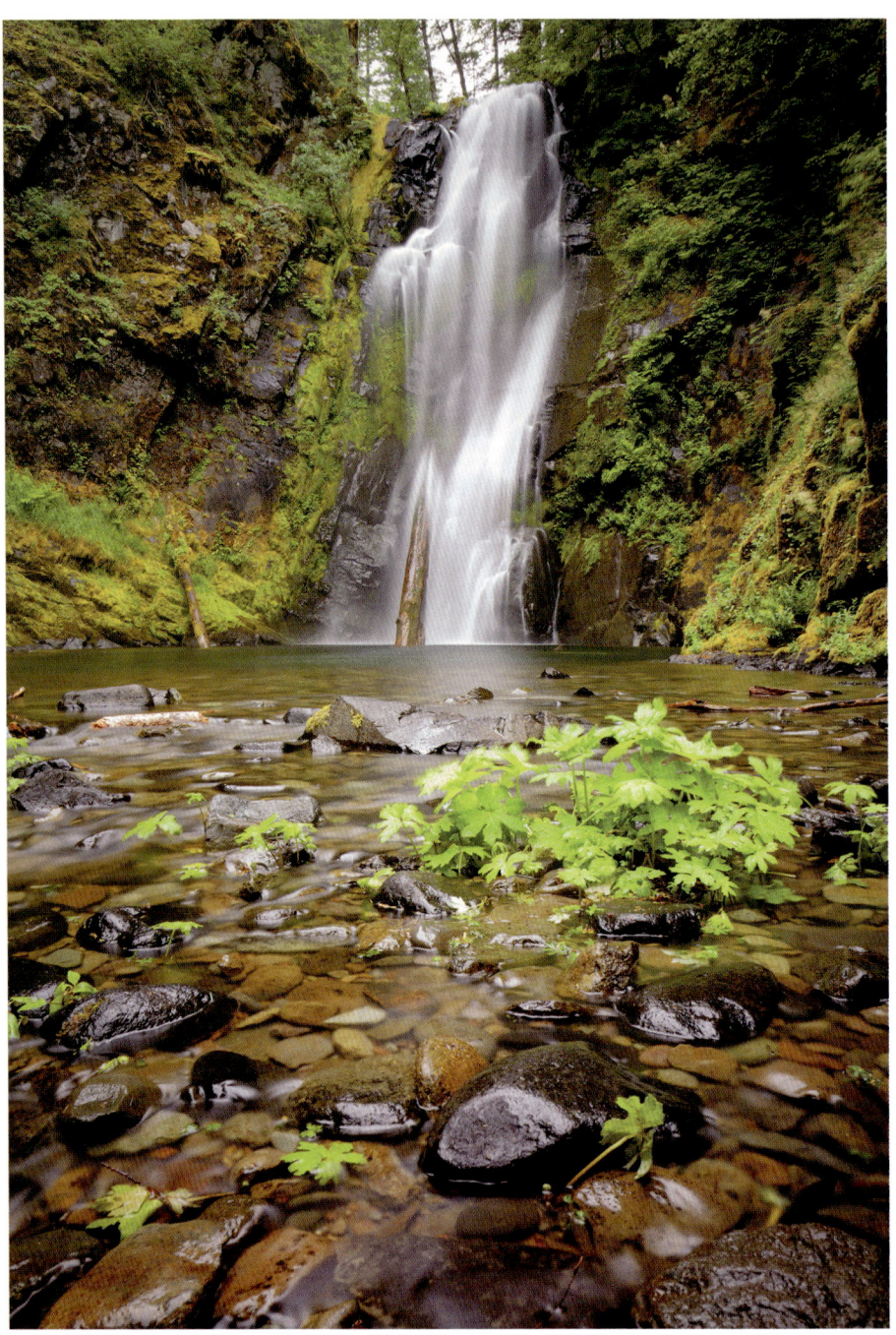

Waterfall in the Wilderness © 2019 John Miner (*D850fan*)

Retouching allows you to modify your images in-camera. If you like to do digital photography but don't particularly like to adjust images on a computer, these functions are for you! Obviously, the camera's Monitor is not large enough to allow you to make heavily creative changes to an image—as you could do within Nikon Capture NX-D, Lightroom, or Photoshop—but it's surprising what you can accomplish with the Retouch Menu.

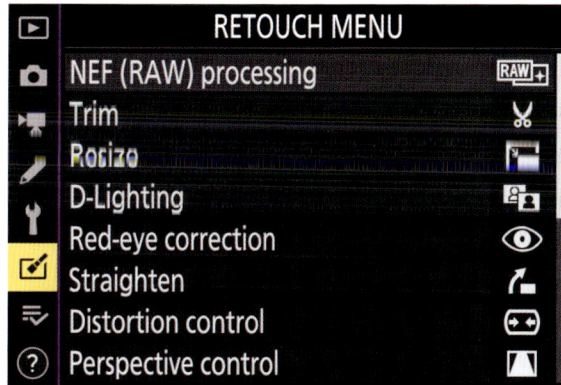

Figure 11.0: The Retouch Menu

The Retouch Menu is the sixth menu down the menu selection bar, just below the Setup Menu (figure 11.0). Its icon resembles a palette and paintbrush. If there aren't any images on either of the camera's memory cards, the Retouch Menu is grayed out and unavailable, for obvious reasons. No images, no retouching! The following is a list of each Retouch Menu function and what it does:

- **NEF (RAW) processing:** You can create highly specialized JPEG images from your NEF (RAW) files without using your computer.
- **Trim:** This feature creates a trimmed (cropped) copy of a selected photograph. You can crop the image according to several aspect ratios, including 1:1, 3:2, 4:3, 5:4, and 16:9.
- **Resize:** You can take a full-size image and convert it into a smaller size. This is useful if you would like to send an image via email or if you need a smaller image for other reasons.
- **D-Lighting:** This feature opens up detail in the shadows and tends to protect highlight details from blowing out. This is similar to the *Photo Shooting Menu > Active D-Lighting* function, but it's applied *after* the image is taken.
- **Red-eye correction:** This removes the unwanted red-eye effect caused by light from a flash reflecting back from the eyes of your subjects.
- **Straighten:** You can straighten an image with crooked horizons by rotating it in-camera. The camera will trim (crop) the edges of the image to create a normal image perspective without the tilt.
- **Distortion control:** You can remove barrel and pincushion distortion that affects the edges of the image. You can cause the camera to make automatic adjustments or you can do it manually. The camera automatically trims (crops) the edges of the image after adjustment.

- **Perspective control:** This is a useful control that helps correct perspective distortion in an image. It's useful for pictures of things like buildings, which sometimes look as though they're falling over backward when shot with a wide-angle lens. The camera automatically crops the edges of the image to allow the distortion to be removed.
- **Image overlay:** This creates a new image by overlaying two existing NEF (RAW) files. Basically, you can combine two RAW images to create special effects—such as adding an image of the moon into a separate landscape picture.
- **Trim movie:** You can shorten a movie by cropping out a small section from a large movie file.
- **Side-by-side comparison:** You can compare a retouched image—created via the Retouch Menu—with the original image. The images are presented side by side so you can see before and after effects. This function is not available from the main Retouch Menu. You'll find it on the Playback Retouch Menu only, which you access by pressing the *i* button when a picture is displayed on the Monitor.

Retouched Image File Numbering

When you use Retouch Menu items, the Z6 does not overwrite your original file. It always creates a JPEG file with the next available image number. The retouched image will be numbered as the last image on the memory card. If you have 100 images on your card and you are retouching image number DSC_0047, the new JPEG image will be numbered DSC_0101 (it will be the 101st image).

Accessing the Retouch Functions—Two Methods

There are two methods for accessing the Retouch Menu, as follows:

- Use the main Retouch Menu (figure 11.0) to choose an image to work with.
- Open the Playback Retouch Menu (figure 11.1) by displaying an image on the Monitor in Playback mode, and then pressing the *i* button and selecting Retouch from the menu that is displayed.

The two methods work basically the same, except the Playback Retouch Menu leaves out the step of choosing the image (since there is already an image on the screen), and it has fewer retouch selections. The most comprehensive retouch selections are available directly under the Retouch Menu.

Since both the Playback Retouch Menu and regular Retouch Menu methods have the same functions, we'll discuss them as if you were using the main Retouch Menu. However, in case you decide to use the Playback method, let's discuss it briefly.

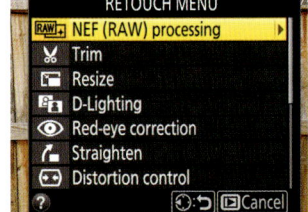

Figure 11.1: Playback Retouch Menu

Limitations on Previously Retouched Images

Sometimes there are limitations imposed when you are working on an image that has already been retouched or for other reasons. You may not be able to retouch a previously retouched image with another Retouch Menu function.

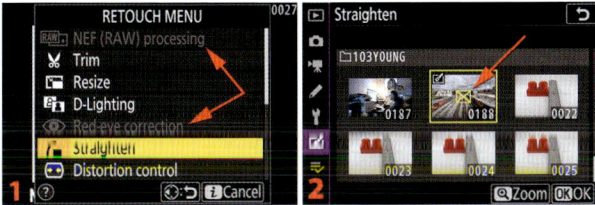

Figure 11.2: Cannot be retouched

When using the Playback Retouch Menu, certain menu items will be grayed out because they cannot be applied to an already retouched image. In figure 11.2, image 1, NEF (RAW) processing is grayed out because the selected image is a JPEG image, not a NEF (RAW) file; and Red-eye correction is grayed out because no flash was used when the picture was taken.

If you use the main Retouch Menu, any images that are overlaid with a box containing a yellow X cannot be retouched again with the current retouch function (figure 11.2, image 2).

Now let's consider each of the available Retouch Menu functions.

NEF (RAW) Processing

NEF (RAW) processing is a function that allows you to convert a RAW image into a new, separate JPEG picture inside the camera, without modifying the original RAW file. If you normally shoot in RAW but need a JPEG quickly, this is a great function.

The Nikon Z6 allows you to batch process groups of RAW files without using a computer. You can process individual RAW files or RAW files by specific dates.

There is quite a comprehensive catalog of things you can do to an image during NEF (RAW) processing. A RAW file is not yet an image, so the camera settings you used when you took the picture are not permanently applied. In effect, when you use NEF (RAW) processing, you are applying camera settings to the JPEG image after the fact, and you can change the settings you used when you originally took the picture.

Following is a list of post-shooting adjustments you can make with NEF (RAW) processing and basic explanations of each function. Keep in mind that, although the following functions discuss conversion of a single RAW file into a single JPEG file, the more powerful NEF (RAW) processing capability of the Z6 extends to batch-processing groups of files.

I've also included page number references for where you can find more detailed explanations of each function, when appropriate:

- **EXE:** This simply means execute. When you select this and press the OK button, all your new settings will be applied to a new JPEG, and the JPEG file will be saved to the memory card with a separate file name.
- **Image quality** (page 175): With NEF (RAW) processing, you are converting a RAW file to a JPEG file, so the camera gives you a choice of FINE★, NORM★, BASIC★, FINE, NORM, or BASIC. The starred versions have less compression and somewhat greater quality. These are equivalent to the *Photo Shooting Menu > Image quality* settings called JPEG fine★, JPEG normal★, JPEG basic★, JPEG fine, JPEG normal, and JPEG basic.
- **Image size** (page 180): This lets you select how large the JPEG file will be. Your choices are L, M, or S, which are equivalent to the Large (45.4 megapixels), Medium (25.6 megapixels), and Small (11.4 megapixels) *Photo Shooting Menu > Image size* settings.
- **White balance** (page 197): This lets you change the White balance of the image after you have already taken the image. You can select from a series of symbols that represent various types of White balance color temperatures. As you scroll up or down in the list of symbols, notice that the name of the corresponding White balance type appears just above the small picture on the Monitor. You can see the effect of each setting as it is applied.
- **Exposure compensation** (page 44): This function allows you to brighten or darken the image by applying −/+ Exposure compensation to it. You can apply compensation up to 2 EV in either direction (−2.0 to +2.0 EV).
- **Picture control** (page 200): With this setting you can apply a different Picture Control than the one with which you took the image. The camera offers a small camera symbol labeled Original, which represents the original Picture Control you used to take the image, plus abbreviations for each Nikon Picture Control (A, SD, NL, VI, MC, PT, LS, or FL), 20 Creative Picture Controls (01–20), and any Custom Picture Controls you might have created with the designations of C-1, C-2, C-3, etc. You will see a change in the picture on the Monitor as you select each Picture Control.
- **High ISO NR** (page 227): You can change the amount of High ISO noise reduction applied to the image. The camera offers you the Original High ISO NR setting you used to take the image, along with H, N, L, and Off settings, which are equivalent to the *Photo Shooting Menu > High ISO NR* settings called High, Normal, Low, and Off.
- **Color space** (page 221): You can change which Color space is applied to the image. You can choose from the camera's two Color space settings, sRGB or Adobe RGB. Adobe RGB is abbreviated as AdobeRGB in this setting. This is equivalent to the *Photo Shooting Menu > Color space* setting.
- **Vignette control** (page 230): This allows you to reduce the light falloff on the corners and edges of the frame, common when using a full-frame sensor with certain lenses. You have five choices: Original, High (H), Normal (N), Low (L), and Off.
- **Active D-Lighting** (page 223): This lets you manage the level of contrast in the image by brightening the shadows and protecting the highlights. You have five choices: Original,

High 2 (H2), High 1 (H1), High (H), Normal (N), Low (L), and Off. This function is similar to the *Photo Shooting Menu > Active D-Lighting* function, except it is applied after you have taken the image.

- **Diffraction compensation** (page 231): When you are using a small aperture (e.g., f/11, f/16), the light can hit the edges of the aperture blades as it flows through the small aperture opening. The causes the light to change its path slightly and can lead to less sharpness in the image. This light deflection is called diffraction. The camera attempts to compensate for diffraction at small apertures, leading to the amazingly sharp images for which Z-cameras are well known. You can leave Diffraction compensation set to Original, or choose On or Off.

Now let's examine the three methods you can use to choose images for conversion: Select image(s), Select date, and Select all images. All three of these methods serve as an entry point to the same NEF (RAW) processing system—they simply offer you a choice as to how you feed images into the conversion system.

Select Image(s)

Select image(s) allows you to choose one or several images from thumbnail screens by placing check marks on each image you want to convert from RAW to JPEG.

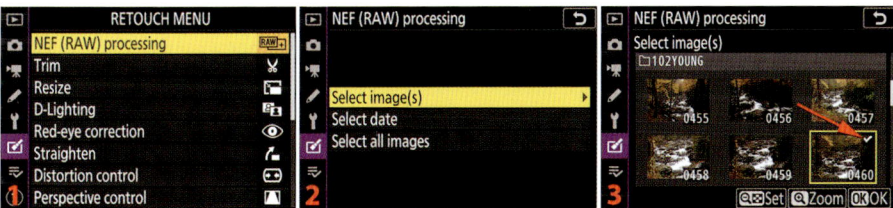

Figure 11.3A: Using Select image(s) to choose images for NEF (RAW) processing

Use the following steps to select individual images to feed into the RAW to JPEG conversion system:

1. Highlight NEF (RAW) processing on the Retouch Menu and scroll to the right (figure 11.3A, image 1).
2. Choose Select image(s) from the NEF (RAW) processing menu and scroll to the right (figure 11.3A, image 2).
3. Select one or more images for RAW to JPEG conversion by highlighting an image thumbnail and tapping the Zoom out (Set) control on the bottom of the screen or pressing the physical Zoom out button. A small check mark will appear in the upper-right corner of the image(s) you select for conversion (figure 11.3A, image 3). If you need to examine the image more closely before selecting it, press the Zoom in button or tap the Zoom control at the bottom of the screen. When you have scrolled around the thumbnail screen(s) and selected all the images you want to convert, press or touch OK to enter the NEF (RAW) processing system. Only the first image selected will show in

the NEF (RAW) conversion screens, but all of the selected images will be converted from RAW to JPEG and saved under new file names. The original RAW files remain untouched.

Select Date

Select date allows you to select all RAW images taken on certain dates for batch-processing into JPEG files. The camera offers you a list of dates and you can choose one or several dates. All RAW images on the chosen date(s) will be converted to JPEG with the settings you choose from the main NEF (RAW) conversion screens.

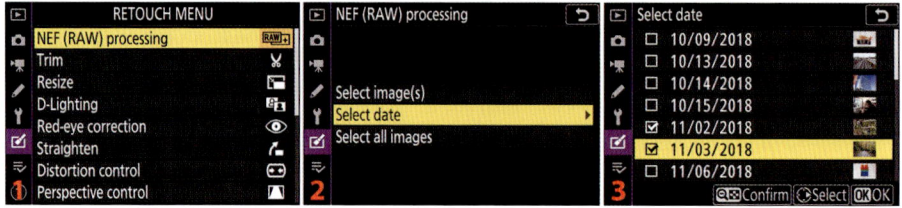

Figure 11.3B: Using Select date to choose images for NEF (RAW) processing

Use the following steps to select images for RAW to JPEG conversion according to date:

1. Highlight NEF (RAW) processing on the Retouch Menu and scroll to the right (figure 11.3B, image 1).
2. Choose Select date from the NEF (RAW) processing menu and scroll to the right (figure 11.3B, image 2).
3. Place a check mark next to one or more dates by tapping the date(s) with your fingertip, or by highlighting a date and scrolling to the right with the Multi selector pad (figure 11.3B, image 3). You can examine the images from a certain date by highlighting the date and tapping the Zoom out (Confirm) control or by pressing the Zoom out button. Press or touch OK to enter the NEF (RAW) processing system with your date(s) selected. All RAW files shot on the selected date(s) will be converted to JPEG files and saved under new file names, leaving the original RAW files unchanged. A thumbnail of the first image in the batch will show in the NEF (RAW) conversion screens during conversion.

Select All Images

Select all images allows you to select all RAW images found on a particular memory card (in all folders) for batch-processing into JPEG files. All RAW images on the card will be converted to JPEG with the settings you choose from the main NEF (RAW) conversion screens.

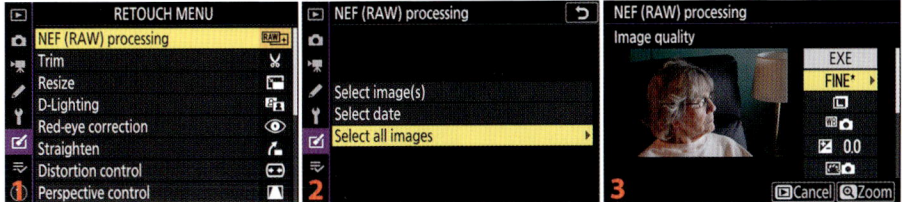

Figure 11.3C: Using Select all images to choose images for NEF (RAW) processing

Use the following steps to select all images on a particular memory card to feed into the RAW to JPEG conversion system:

1. Highlight NEF (RAW) processing on the Retouch Menu and scroll to the right (figure 11.3C, image 1).
2. Choose Select all images from the NEF (RAW) processing menu and scroll to the right (figure 11.3C, image 2).
3. The camera will immediately enter the NEF (RAW) processing system with all RAW images on that card selected (figure 11.3C, image 3). The RAW images will be batch-converted to JPEG files and saved under new file names, leaving the original RAW files unchanged. A thumbnail of the first image in the batch will show in the NEF (RAW) conversion screens during conversion. (***Note:*** The Z6 obeys the *Playback Menu > Playback folder* (page 141) and *Photo Shooting Menu > Storage folder* (page 168) settings as to which NEF (RAW) images are chosen for conversion when Select all images is used.)

Now let's examine the actual NEF (RAW) processing system and see how you can use original camera settings during RAW to JPEG conversion or change settings on individual files or an entire batch of files, before converting them to JPEG.

Using the NEF (RAW) Processing System

You will need to have first selected and configured one of the three previously discussed methods (Select image(s), Select date, or Select all images) for sending RAW files to the NEF (RAW) processing system. Once you have selected the RAW image(s) you want to process into JPEG files, the NEF (RAW) Processing system will open.

All screens in this section are continuations of one of the three previously discussed methods for feeding images into the conversion system. There are up to nine adjustments you can make to your images before the final RAW to JPEG conversion. Use the following steps:

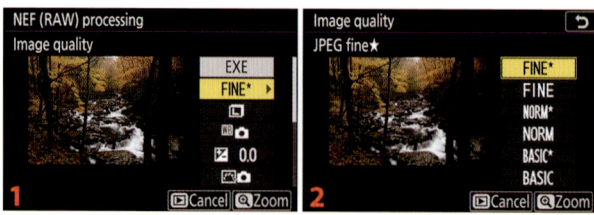

Figure 11.3D: NEF (RAW) processing – Image quality

4. Figure 11.3D, image 1, begins where figure 11.3A, 11.3B, or 11.3C ends. Choose the Image quality selection (see setting name above picture) from the NEF (RAW) processing system menu and scroll to the right. (**Note:** You will not use the first item (EXE) in the menu until the end of the configuration process, unless you want to use only the original camera settings for each converted image. If so, skip the rest of the steps in this section, select EXE, and press the OK button to start the conversion process immediately—using original image settings. If you intend to change any setting for all converted images, use this and the following steps to make changes to the conversion settings. Then you will select EXE last and start the conversion after making image configuration changes that apply to all images being converted from RAW to JPEG.)

5. Select one of the Image quality settings—FINE★, FINE★, NORM★, NORM, BASIC★, or BASIC—from the Image quality menu (figure 11.3D, image 2). FINE★ gives you the best possible quality in a JPEG image. You can cancel the operation by tapping Cancel or by pressing the Playback button. You can also zoom in to check the image quality by tapping Zoom or by pressing the Zoom in button. Press the OK button or tap the Image quality option to save the setting and return to the main NEF (RAW) processing configuration screen.

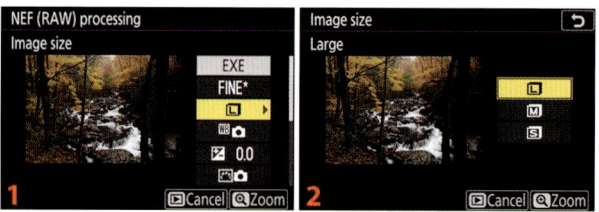

Figure 11.3E: NEF (RAW) processing – Image size

6. Highlight the Image size selection on the NEF (RAW) processing menu and scroll to the right (figure 11.3E, image 1).

7. Select one of the Image size settings from the Image size menu (figure 11.3B, image 2):
   - L – Large (8256×5504; 45.4 MP)
   - M – Medium (6192×4128; 25.6 MP)
   - S – Small (4128×2752; 11.4 MP)

   When you've selected a setting, press the OK button or tap the option with your fingertip to return to the main NEF (RAW) processing configuration screen.

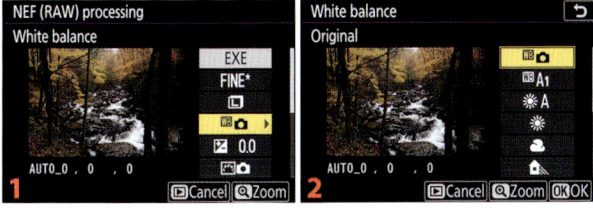

Figure 11.3F: NEF (RAW) Processing – White balance

8. Highlight the White balance position on the NEF (RAW) processing menu and scroll to the right (figure 11.3F, image 1).

9. Select one of the White balance settings for your new JPEG(s) (figure 11.3F, image 2). You can choose from Original (small camera icon), Auto (A0–A2), Natural light auto (A), Direct sunlight, Cloudy, Shade, Incandescent, Fluorescent, Flash, Choose color temperature (K), or Preset manual (PRE). After highlighting the one you want to use, press or touch OK to choose the selected White balance value for all the images in the conversion. Original is selected in figure 11.3F, image 2. Please review the chapter titled **White Balance** (page 107) for detailed information on each of these selections. The Auto, Fluorescent, K, and PRE settings have an additional screen with choices you must select. We won't consider how to select each individual White balance setting because they work basically the same. However, because Auto, Fluorescent, K, and PRE are different and have extra screens, we will examine each of those settings individually.

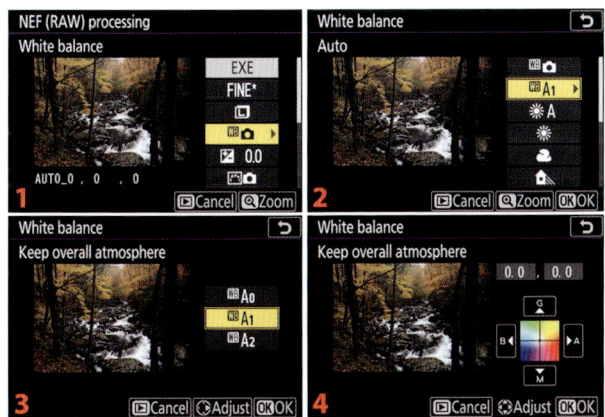

Figure 11.3G: NEF (RAW) processing – Auto White balance

a. **Auto:** Highlight the White balance position and scroll to the right (figure 11.3G, image 1). Select the Auto menu position and scroll to the right (figure 11.3G, image 2). Choose one of the three Auto types (figure 11.3G, image 3): A0 Keep white (reduce warm colors), A1 Keep overall atmosphere, or A2 Keep warm lighting colors (somewhat warmer pictures). If you don't want to fine-tune the selected White balance, press or touch OK to lock it in. To fine-tune the White balance, scroll to the right with the Multi selector pad to move to the fine-tuning screen, where you can adjust the color tint of the image by moving the black dot in the color box (figure 11.3G, image 4). Press or touch OK to save the setting or press the Playback button to cancel.

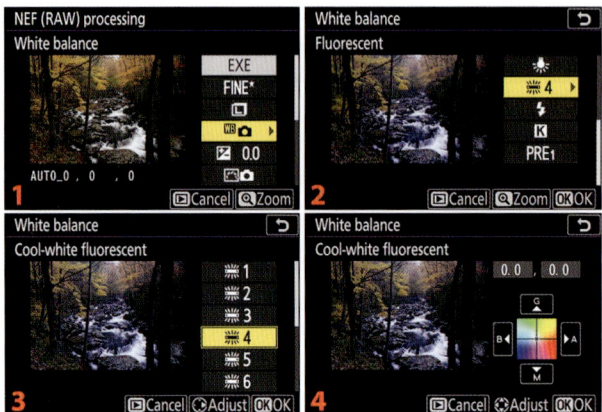

Figure 11.3H: NEF (RAW) processing – Fluorescent White balance

b. **Fluorescent:** Highlight the White balance position and scroll to the right (figure 11.3H, image 1). Choose Fluorescent and scroll to the right (figure 11.3H, image 2). There are seven choices in the menu, with names (above the picture) like Sodium-vapor lamps, Warm-white fluorescent, Cool-white fluorescent, etc. Each choice has a number assigned to it. Figure 11.3H, image 3, shows Cool-white fluorescent, which is number 4 on the list. If you don't want to fine-tune the selected White balance, press or touch OK to lock it in. To fine-tune the White balance, scroll to the right with the Multi selector pad to move to the fine-tuning screen, where you can adjust the color tint of the image by moving the black dot in the color box (figure 11.3H, image 4). Press or touch OK to save the setting or press the Playback button to cancel.

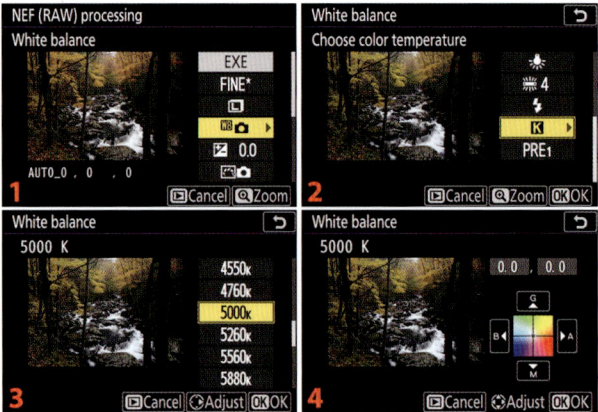

Figure 11.3I: NEF (RAW) processing – Choose color temp. (K) White balance

c. ***Choose color temp. (K):*** Highlight the White balance position and scroll to the right (figure 11.3I, image 1). Scroll down to near the bottom of the menu and select the K setting, then scroll to the right (figure 11.3I, image 2). You can now choose a color temperature from the list shown in figure 11.3I, image 3. Remember that color temperatures change how the image color looks by warming it (reddish) or cooling it (bluish). The list ranges from 2500K (cool) to 10000K (warm). After selecting a K value (e.g., 5000K) you can scroll to the right and use the fine-tuning screen to modify the color's base, if you'd like (figure 11.3I, image 4). If not, press or touch OK to save the setting or press the Playback button to cancel. (***Note:*** Camera White balance works backward from the "black body radiation" formula we learned in school because it is an additive process, adding colors [not radiating colors] that are needed to balance the color in the image.)

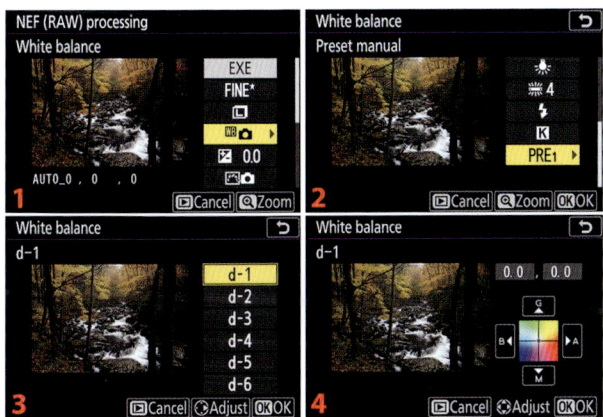

Figure 11.3J: NEF (RAW) processing – PRE White balance

d. ***Preset manual (PRE):*** Highlight the White balance position and scroll to the right (figure 11.3J, image 1). Scroll down to the last item on the menu and select the PRE setting (figure 11.3J, image 2). With this setting you can choose an already-saved White balance that you previously obtained while letting the camera measure the ambient light reflected from a gray or white card (the PRE method). See the chapter titled **White Balance** (page 120) for information on creating and storing ambient light (PRE) readings. Scroll to the right with the PRE setting highlighted, and on the next screen you can choose from up to six previous PRE readings that are stored in memory locations d–1 to d–6 (figure 11.3J, image 3). As you scroll through the list of PRE settings, you'll be able to see the color temperature of the image change. If you do not want to fine-tune the White balance setting, select the setting you want to use and press or touch OK to return to the main NEF (RAW) processing configuration screen. If you do want to fine-tune the White balance, scroll to the right with your choice of PRE value selected (e.g., d–1). On the following screen, you can fine-tune the colors of the individual PRE White balance by using the settings shown in figure 11.3J, image 4. You'll see your fine-tuning adjustment change the color temperature of the image. Press or touch OK to save the setting, or press the Playback button to cancel.

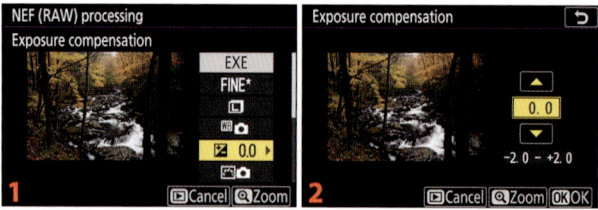

Figure 11.3K: NEF (RAW) processing – Exposure compensation

10. Highlight the Exposure compensation selection and scroll to the right (figure 11.3K, image 1).
11. Now you have an opportunity to lighten or darken the image by selecting an Exposure compensation value of up to –/+ 2.0 EV steps (figure 11.3K, image 2). Scroll up to add exposure and down to reduce exposure (or tap the yellow up/down pointers). When your image looks just right, press or touch OK to save the setting and return to the main NEF (RAW) processing configuration screen. You can cancel the operation with the Playback button.

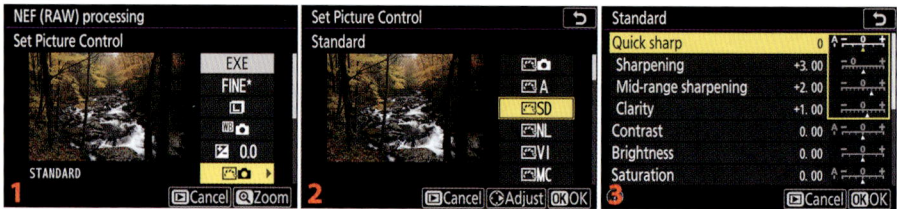

Figure 11.3L: NEF (RAW) processing – Set Picture Control

12. Highlight the Set Picture Control selection and scroll to the right (figure 11.3L, image 1).
13. You can apply a Nikon Picture Control or one of your own Custom Picture Controls, if you have created any (figure 11.3L, image 2). Choose the Picture Control you want to use from the following choices: Original (camera icon), Auto (A), Standard (SD), Neutral (NL), Vivid (VI), Monochrome (NC), Portrait (PT), Landscape (LS), Flat (FL), one of 20 Creative Picture Controls (01–20), or any of your custom controls (C–1 to C–9) that appear farther down the list than this screen shot shows (figure 11.3L, image 2). If you do not want to fine-tune the selected Picture Control, press or touch OK to lock it in, and skip step 11. If you do want to fine-tune any of the Picture Controls other than Original, highlight the control and scroll to the right.
14. Scroll up or down to select the settings you want to change (e.g., Sharpening, Clarity, Contrast) and then scroll left or right (–/+) to modify the selected setting (figure 11.3L, image 3). If you make a mistake and want to start over, press the Playback button or

tap Cancel. The Monochrome (MC) Picture Control not only lets you adjust things like Sharpening, Contrast, and Brightness in the fine-tuning screen, but it also gives you toning (tint) controls like the *Photo Shooting Menu* > *Set Picture Control* function (page 200). When the image looks just right, press or touch OK to save the setting and return to the main NEF (RAW) processing configuration screen. You can cancel the operation with the Playback button.

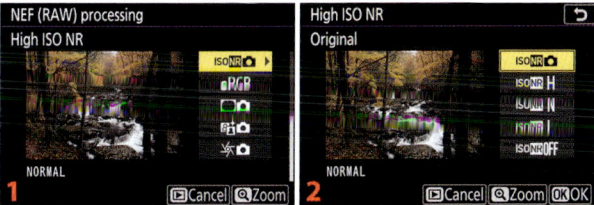

Figure 11.3M: NEF (RAW) processing – High ISO NR

15. Highlight the High ISO NR selection and scroll to the right (figure 11.3M, image 1).
16. If the image needs high ISO noise reduction, you can apply it now. You have a choice of five settings: Original (camera icon), High (H), Normal (N), Low (L), or Off (figure 11.3M, image 2). Choose one and press or touch OK to save the setting and return to the main NEF (RAW) processing configuration screen. You can cancel the operation with the Playback button.

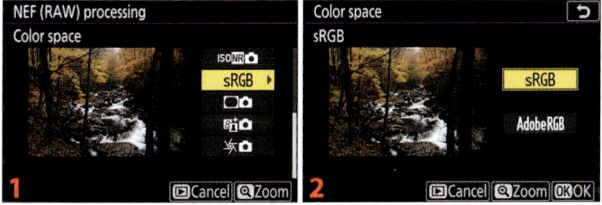

Figure 11.3N: NEF (RAW) processing – Color space

17. Highlight the Color space selection and scroll to the right (figure 11.3N, image 1).
18. The Color space function lets you choose one of the camera's two color space settings, sRGB or AdobeRGB (figure 11.3N, image 2). Choose one and press or touch OK to save the setting and return to the main NEF (RAW) processing configuration screen. You can cancel the operation with the Playback button. As a comparative test, why not look carefully at your picture while you switch back and forth between sRGB and AdobeRGB? You will find that AdobeRGB has a smoother look, if not quite as saturated, due to additional color range, when your subject actually has a good range of colors. AdobeRGB has a wider color gamut and is best for commercial printing, whereas sRGB may do better with computer and Internet display and home printing on basic inkjet printers.

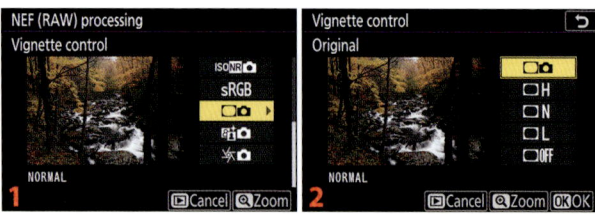

Figure 11.3O: NEF (RAW) processing – Vignette control

19. Highlight the Vignette control selection and scroll to the right (figure 11.3O, image 1).
20. Vignette control lets you choose a level for edge and corner light falloff correction (figure 11.3O, image 2), as is sometimes needed on an imaging sensor with certain lenses. You have a choice of five settings: Original (camera icon), High (H), Normal (N), Low (L), or Off. Choose one and press or touch OK to save the setting and return to the main NEF (RAW) processing configuration screen. You can cancel the operation with the Playback button.

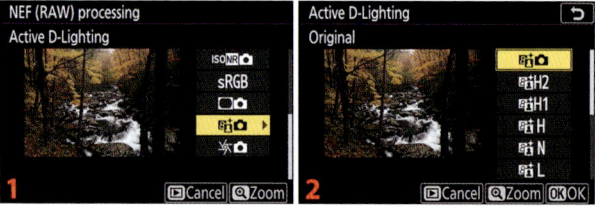

Figure 11.3P: NEF (RAW) processing – Active D-Lighting

21. Highlight the Active D-Lighting selection and scroll to the right (figure 11.3P, image 1).
22. Active D-Lighting is very similar to the *Shooting Menu > Active D-Lighting* setting in that it restores shadow detail and protects highlights in your images. Normal Active D-Lighting is applied at the time the image is taken; however, this version of Active D-Lighting is applied after the fact. Otherwise, they are basically the same thing. You can select from Original (camera icon), Extra High 2 (H2), Extra High 1 (H1), High (H), Normal (N), Low (L), or Off (figure 11.3P, image 2). Press or touch OK to set the Active D-Lighting level or press the Playback button to cancel.

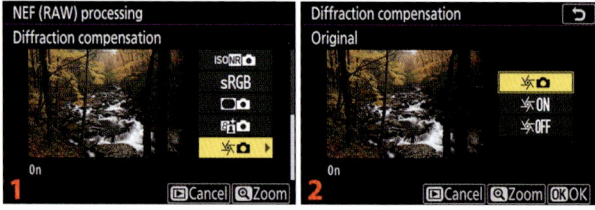

Figure 11.3Q: NEF (RAW) processing – Diffraction compensation

23. Highlight the Diffraction compensation selection and scroll to the right (figure 11.3Q, image 1).

24. Choose Original, On, or Off. This setting will help reduce diffraction in your image. Choosing Original lets you keep the Diffraction compensation setting you originally used when you first took the picture. Just in case you failed to use Diffraction compensation originally, you can use it now by selecting On. If you do not want to use Diffraction compensation, choose Off. Press or touch OK to lock in the value. Press the Playback button to cancel.

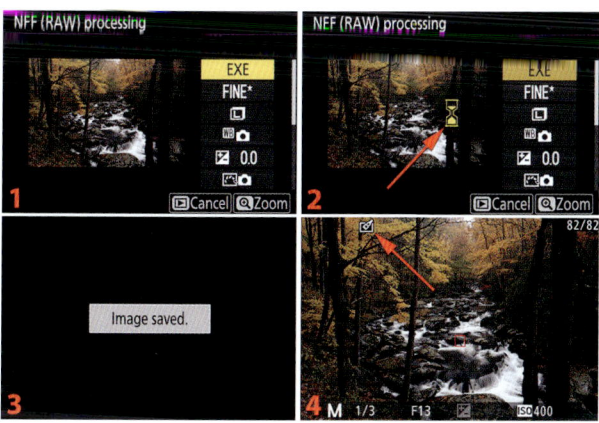

Figure 11.3R: NEF (RAW) processing – EXE, processing a single image

25. When you are finished with the configuration of the NEF (RAW) processing system *for a single image,* and you are ready to convert the image, scroll up to the EXE (execute) selection and press the OK button or tap EXE (figure 11.3R, image 1). Figure 11.3R shows the screens the camera displays when you are converting a single image (see upcoming figure 11.3S for the batch conversion of multiple images).

26. An hourglass symbol will appear on the screen while the conversion of a single file is taking place (figure 11.3R, image 2, red arrow).

27. An *Image saved* screen will appear briefly (figure 11.3R, image 3), indicating that the new JPEG has been saved on the memory card with a new file name.

28. The converted image will be displayed on the Monitor (figure 11.3R, image 4). You can cancel the operation with the Playback button. The retouch icon will appear in the top-left area of the new JPEG picture, as seen in image 4 (red arrow). Next, let's see how the camera screens are more complex when a batch conversion takes place (figure 11.3S). If you are processing a single image, you will not see the following screens.

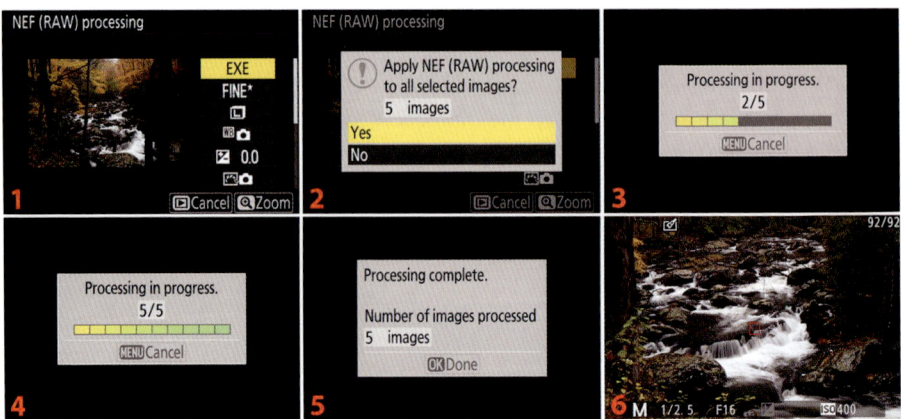

Figure 11.3S: NEF (RAW) processing – EXE, processing multiple images

29. When you are finished with the configuration of the NEF (RAW) processing system *for multiple images,* and you are ready to batch-convert the images, scroll up to the EXE (execute) selection and press the OK button or tap EXE (figure 11.3S, image 1).

30. Since you are processing more than one image, the camera asks you to validate the fact that you are doing a batch RAW-to-JPEG conversion of multiple images. Figure 11.3S, image 2, asks you *Apply NEF (RAW) processing to all selected images?,* and then shows you the number of images in the batch conversion (e.g., *5 images*). Highlight Yes and press the OK button or tap Yes.

31. The camera will now show you a progress screen that informs you of how the conversion process is proceeding. The example screens in figure 11.3S, images 3 and 4, show the progress bar as the conversion progresses. If you are converting many images, the process will take a while.

32. When the conversion is done, the camera informs you with a screen that says: *Processing complete. Number of images processed 5 images* (or whatever number of images you selected for conversion). Press or touch OK (Done) to finish the conversion (figure 11.3S, image 5).

33. The final image in the batch will be displayed on the Monitor (figure 11.3S, image 6). You can scroll through the converted images by swiping with your fingertip on the Monitor or by scrolling with the Multi selector pad.

This is a nice way to create specialized JPEG images from NEF (RAW) files without using a computer. How much longer will it be until our cameras come with keyboard, monitor, and mouse ports? They are powerful graphics-processing computers after all!

Settings Recommendation: NEF (RAW) processing is a complex, multistep process because you're doing a major conversion from NEF (RAW) to JPEG in-camera, without using your computer. You're in complete control of each level of the conversion and can even replace the camera settings you originally used when you took the picture.

If you want to simply convert the image without going through all these steps, just choose the EXE selection first and press the OK button. That will convert the image(s) immediately with the "Original" camera settings you used to take the picture.

Trim

The *Trim* function allows you to crop an image in-camera, change its aspect ratio, and save the file as a new image. Your original image is not modified. This is a useful function if you need to remove distracting elements from the background.

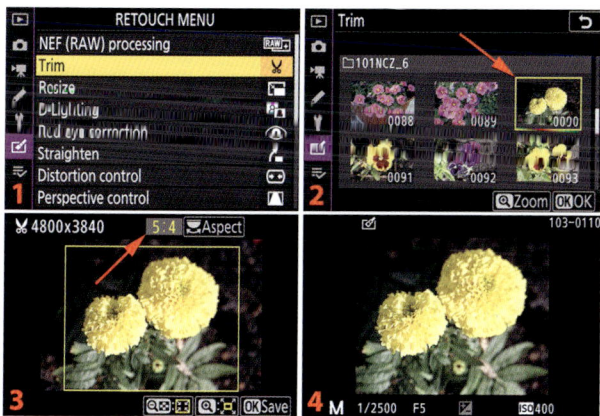

Figure 11.4: Trim function

Use the following steps to Trim an image in-camera:

1. Select the Trim function from the Retouch Menu and scroll to the right (figure 11.4, image 1).
2. Select the image you want to modify from the thumbnail screen and press or touch OK to open it (figure 11.4, image 2).
3. You'll see a screen that has an area of the image outlined in yellow (figure 11.4, image 3). Use the checkered Zoom out button to make the size of the yellow crop outline smaller or the Zoom in button to enlarge the outline (or use the on-screen zoom touch controls at the bottom of the screen). Use the Multi selector pad to move the yellow selection rectangle in any direction (or drag it with your finger) within the frame until you find the best crop. Select the aspect ratio of the cropped image by rotating the rear Main command dial or by tapping the Aspect touch control. Your choices are 3:2, 4:3, 5:4, 1:1 (square), or 16:9. Figure 11.4, image 3 (red arrow), shows that the 5:4 aspect ratio is selected. The pixel ratio of the new image will show in the top left corner of the screen (e.g., 4800×3840). When you have the cropped area correctly sized and the aspect ratio set, press or touch OK (Save) to save the image with a new file name (figure 11.4, image 4).

Settings Recommendation: This is a very useful function for cropping images without a computer. The fact that you have multiple aspect ratios available is just icing on the cake. The Z6 has some useful aspect ratios, including a square (1:1) and an HD format (16:9).

Resize

The *Resize* function allows you to convert an image from a full-size 24.5M (6048×4024) picture to a smaller one, with four available megapixel sizes. This function seems to be designed so you can create images that can easily be emailed or used on a website or blog. There are two selections:

• **Select image:** This selection allows you to choose one or more images for in-camera resizing.

• **Choose size:** You can choose from four image sizes (M = megapixels):
   3.5 M or 2304×1536
   2.5 M or 1920×1280
   1.1 M or 1280×856
   0.6 M or 960×640

Unless you want to use the default size of 2.5 M, you should choose the size of the image before you select the image to resize. Let's examine how to do it in that order.

Choose Size

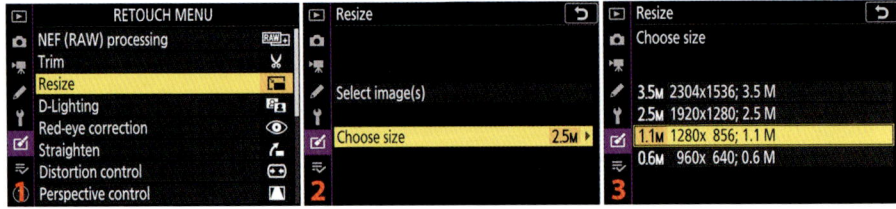

Figure 11.5A: Resize – Choose size

Use the following steps to choose a size for image reduction:

1. Choose Resize from the Retouch Menu and scroll to the right (figure 11.5A, image 1).
2. Select Choose size and scroll to the right (figure 11.5A, image 2).
3. You will see four sizes, from 3.5 M to 0.6 M (figure 11.5A, image 3). These are the actual megapixel sizes the image(s) will become after you save them. The old, full-size image is not affected. A resized copy of the old image will be created, with a new image file number. Select a size and press the OK button or tap the option to select it.

Now let's see how to select one or more images for resizing.

Select Image(s)

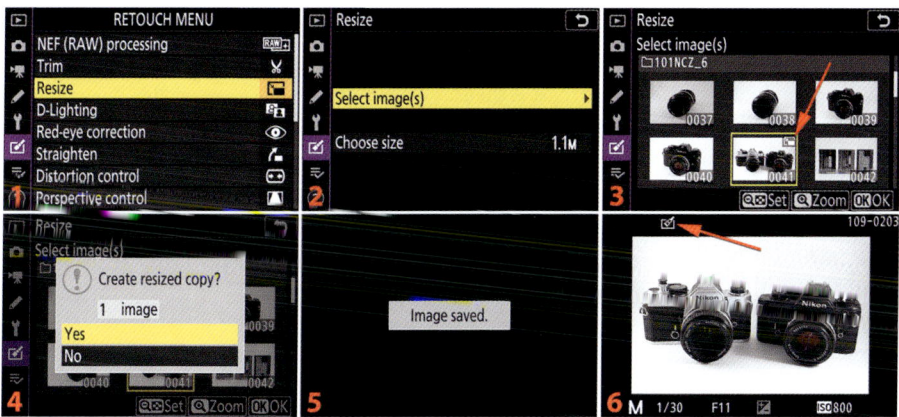

Figure 11.5B: Resize – Select image

1. Choose Resize from the Retouch Menu and scroll to the right (figure 11.5B, image 1).
2. Highlight Select image(s) and scroll to the right (figure 11.5B, image 2). You'll see six image thumbnails. Use the Multi selector pad to scroll around in this group of thumbnails
   and press the OK button to select an image you want to resize—or touch an image
   thumbnail and tap the Set touch control. You can select as many images as you'd like,
   and each of them will be resized. A tiny resize symbol will appear in the top-right corner
   of each thumbnail you select (figure 11.5B, image 3, red arrow).
3. When you have selected the images, press or touch OK. A screen will appear with a
   message asking, *Create resized copy?* (figure 11.5B, image 4). Select Yes and press the
   OK button or tap Yes to create the resized images. An hourglass will be displayed on
   the Monitor while the images are resized, and then an *Image saved* message will briefly
   appear (figure 11.5B, image 5). The last image in the group of resized images will appear
   on the Monitor (figure 11.5B, image 6). The resized images will look just like the originals
   except they'll each have a retouch icon in the top-left area of the image and they will
   have the new smaller size.

Settings Recommendation: I use this function when I'm in the field and want to make
a small image to send via email. The full-size JPEG file is too large to send through some
email systems. It's nice to have a way to reduce image size without having to find a computer. Please notice that this function does not reduce the image size by cropping, like
the Trim function we studied earlier. Instead, it simply reduces the image size in the same
aspect ratio as the original, except it has fewer megapixels.

D-Lighting

D-Lighting allows you to reduce the shadows in an image and maybe even rein in the highlights a bit, lowering the overall image contrast. It works like Active D-Lighting except that it is applied to the image after it is taken.

Remember that Retouch Menu effects are applied to a copy of the image, so your original picture is safe and untouched. In figure 11.6, you can see that I retouched a snapshot of my daughter and grandson, which was about one stop underexposed. I used High D-Lighting and brought out the shadow detail.

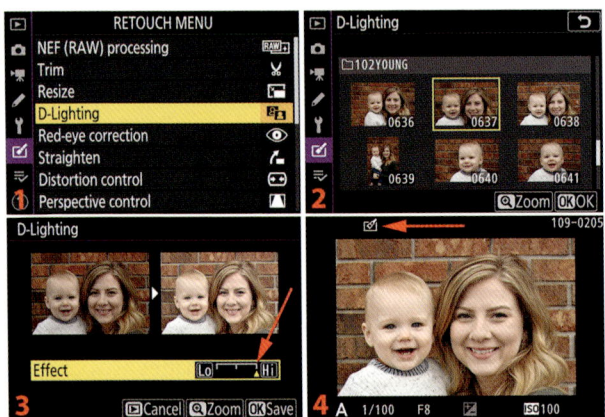

Figure 11.6: D-Lighting

Use the following steps to apply D-Lighting to an image:

1. Select D-Lighting from the Retouch Menu and scroll to the right (figure 11.6, image 1).
2. Choose the image you want to modify and press or touch OK (figure 11.6, image 2).
3. Select the level of D-Lighting you want to apply to the chosen image by moving the small yellow pointer left or right (figure 11.6, image 3, red arrow). You'll choose from low (Lo), medium (middle position on slider), and high (Hi) D-Lighting. The small picture on the left is the picture *before* adjustment and the picture on the right is the picture *after* adjustment. When the image on the right looks the way you want it to, press or touch OK (Save) to save the new file. I selected the Hi setting to bring out shadow detail in the mildly underexposed image of my daughter and tiny grandson.
4. The Z6 will display a brief *Image saved* notice between screens 3 and 4, and then display the new file on the Monitor. The retouched image will have a small palette-and-paintbrush icon to show that it has been retouched (figure 11.6, image 4, red arrow). The original image is still available for future retouching.

Settings Recommendation: There is no one setting that is correct for all images. I might use the middle setting between Lo and Hi to see if an image needs more or less D-Lighting, and then change to Hi or Lo if needed. Remember that any amount of D-Lighting has the potential to introduce noise in the darker areas of the image, so the less D-Lighting you use, the better.

Red-Eye Correction

Red-eye correction attempts to change bright-red pupils—caused by flash exposure reflection—back to their normal dark color. Red-eye makes a person look like one of those aliens with glowing eyes from a science fiction show.

If you've used flash to create a picture, the Red-eye correction function will work on the image if it can detect any red eye. If it can't detect red-eye in the image, you will briefly see a screen that says *Unable to detect red-eye in selected image*.

The camera will not let you select an image that was not taken with flash. Each image not taken with flash will have a box with a yellow X, signifying that the image cannot be selected for this function.

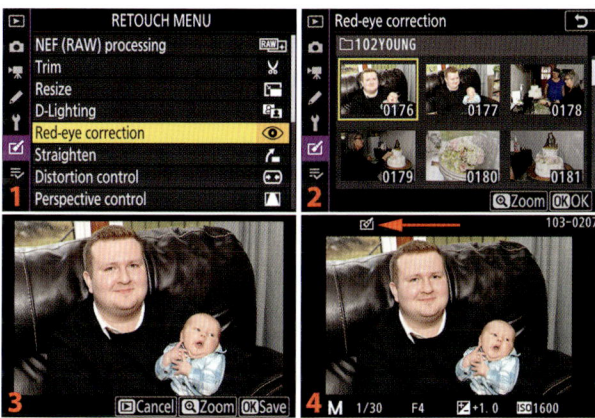

Figure 11.7: Red-eye correction

Use the following steps to execute the Red-eye correction function:

1. Select Red-eye correction from the Retouch Menu and scroll to the right (figure 11.7, image 1).
2. Choose the image you want to modify and touch or press OK (figure 11.7, image 2).
3. You'll see an hourglass on the Monitor while the camera detects and removes red eye, which may take several seconds, and then a screen appears that allows you to examine the results (figure 11.7, image 3). Press the Zoom in button or tap the Zoom control to enlarge the image and see how well the function worked. Press or touch OK (Save) to save the retouched image with a new file number, or press the Playback button to cancel.

4. The camera will then present you with the retouched image, which is marked with the retouch icon (figure 11.7, image 4, red arrow).

Settings Recommendation: I've found that the Red-eye correction function works pretty well as long as the subject is fairly large in the frame. I have tried Red-eye correction on smaller subjects, such as in larger groups of people, and sometimes it works and other times it doesn't. When the subject is smaller, the eyes are much smaller, too. The camera may struggle to find red eye in very tiny subjects. I would rate this function as quite helpful, but not always completely effective. It's a good function to have for quick red-eye correction on critical images you need to use immediately.

Straighten

Straighten is another excellent and useful function. Often, I'll be shooting a landscape or ocean view handheld, and in my excitement I'll forget to level the horizon. Or maybe I am doing some architectural photography and I accidentally let a building or doorway lean a bit to the side. With Straighten I can adjust the image to level before anyone else sees it.

You can rotate an image up to 5 degrees clockwise or counterclockwise, using the Multi selector pad to scroll right or left along a graduated scale line. Each increment on the line is equal to about 0.25 degrees. As you rotate the image, the camera will automatically trim the edges so that the picture looks normal. Of course, this means you are throwing away some of the image and making it smaller. However, it's better for the image to be a little smaller and have a nice level horizon or straight lines, don't you think?

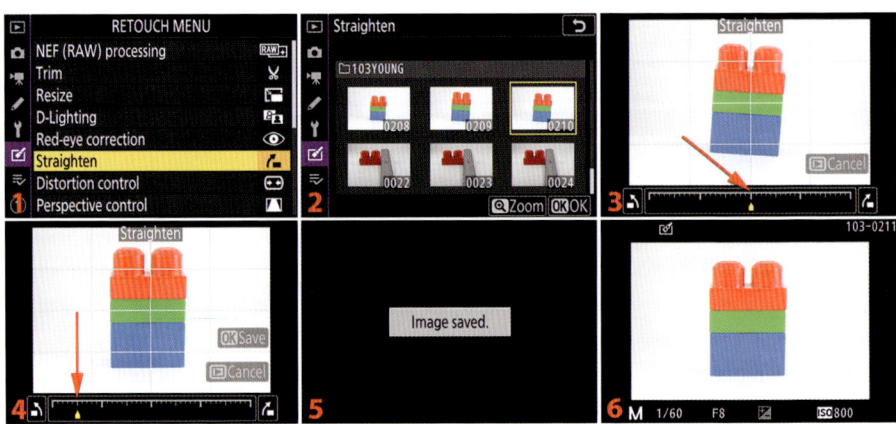

Figure 11.8: Straighten an image

Here are the steps to straighten an image:

1. Select Straighten from the Retouch Menu and scroll to the right (figure 11.8, image 1).

2. You'll see thumbnails of the images on your memory card(s). Use the Multi selector pad to scroll to the one you want to straighten—or tap an image thumbnail—and then press or touch OK to select it (figure 11.8, image 2).
3. Now, rotate the image to the left (counterclockwise) or right (clockwise) in 0.25 degree increments by scrolling left or right with the Multi selector pad, by sliding the yellow pointer with your finger, or by tapping the little arrow controls at either end of scale (figure 11.8, screens 3 and 4, red arrows).
4. When you are happy with the new image, press or touch OK (Save) to save it, and a screen that says *Image saved* will appear briefly (figure 11.8, image 5). Or you can press the Playback button to cancel.
5. The newly straightened image will appear on the Monitor (figure 11.8, image 6).

Settings Recommendation: This is a handy function to level an image—as long as it is not tilted more than 5 degrees—without using a computer. Some of us tend to tilt our cameras just a little when we take pictures. Use this function to save embarrassment later.

Distortion Control

The *Distortion control* function is a companion to the Straighten function. Whereas the Straighten function is concerned with leveling the image left to right, the Distortion control function is concerned with barrel and pincushion distortion. Barrel distortion causes the edges and center of a subject to bow outward, like a barrel. Pincushion distortion is the opposite: the edges and center bow inward, like an hourglass.

Using this control will remove some of the edge of the image as distortion compensation takes place. There are two settings in the Distortion control function: Auto and Manual. Let's consider both.

Auto Distortion Control

This setting asks the camera to automatically correct pincushion and barrel distortion in individually selected images you took with certain Nikkor lenses. You can also fine-tune the camera's distortion adjustment.

If you took the image with *Photo Shooting Menu > Auto distortion control* enabled, you cannot later use the fine-tuning tools provided with this Auto Distortion control. Images that cannot be fine-tuned will have a yellow box with an X in the middle of the thumbnail.

Select Auto when you want the camera to automatically make distortion corrections. Then you can fine-tune the adjustments yourself if you think the new image needs it (and the camera will allow it).

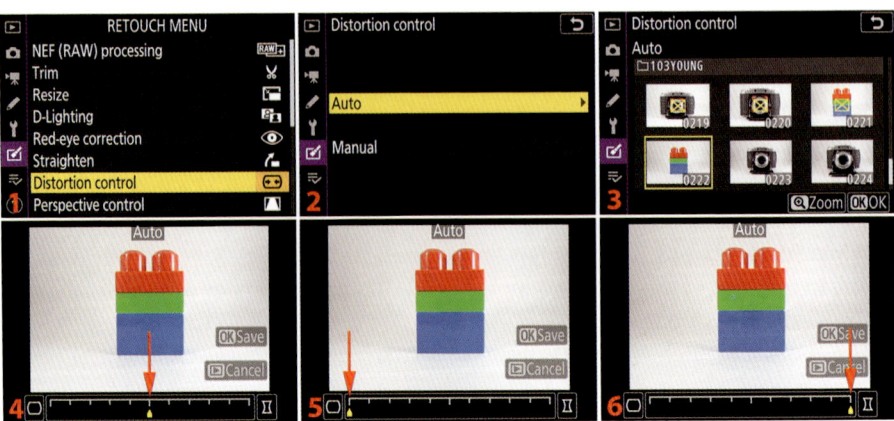

Figure 11.9A: Auto Distortion control

Following are the steps to let the camera automatically adjust for distortion and then fine-tune the Auto Distortion choice the camera made:

1. Follow the screen flow shown in figure 11.9A, images 1 and 2 (*Distortion control > Auto*), until you arrive at the third screen in the series.
2. Next you'll see the images on your memory card. Select the one you want to fix and press or touch OK (figure 11.9A, image 3). If there is a yellow box with an X in the center of the thumbnail, you cannot fine-tune that image.
3. The camera will automatically make its best adjustment and then display the adjusted image (figure 11.9A, image 4). The red arrow in image 4 points to the yellow adjustment pointer, which will be centered. If you are not satisfied with the camera's Auto adjustment, use the Multi selector pad or your fingertip to move the yellow pointer along the scale to the left to remove pincushion distortion (add barrel) or to the right to remove barrel distortion (add pincushion). Screens 5 and 6 in figure 11.9A show the maximum settings (red arrows).
4. When you are happy with the appearance of the image, press or touch OK (Save) to save it, or press the Playback button to cancel (not shown).

The effect is not easy to see in these small images or on the Monitor of the camera. However, if you look closely at figure 11.9A, image 5, and compare it to image 6, you can see a slight difference. Greater adjustments should be made on a computer with full-size images.

Manual distortion adjustments work the same way, except the camera does not make an Auto adjustment before displaying an image that you can manually adjust.

Manual Distortion Control

You are in control of this operation. You can adjust the image until you think it looks good, without interference from the camera. This setting makes no initial distortion adjustment.

I was able to use any Nikkor lens I own (e.g., AI, D, G, E, S) to take a picture that the camera later allowed me to adjust (no yellow box with an X).

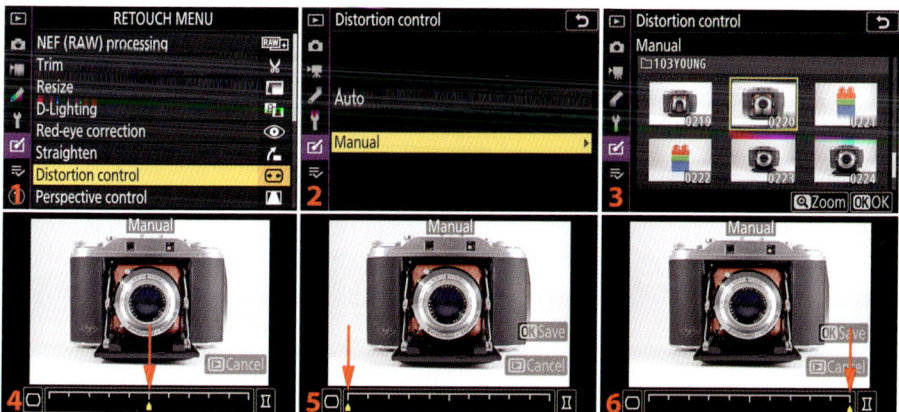

Figure 11.9B: Manual Distortion control

Here are the steps to manually correct distortion:

1. Follow the screen flow shown in figure 11.9B, images 1 and 2 (*Distortion control > Manual*), until you arrive at the third screen in the series.
2. You'll see thumbnails of the images on your memory card. Select the one you want to adjust and press or touch OK (figure 11.9B, image 3).
3. The image will be displayed with the yellow pointer centered under the scale (figure 11.9B, image 4, red arrow). No adjustment has been made at this point. Move the yellow pointer along the scale to the left to remove pincushion distortion (add barrel) or to the right to remove barrel distortion (add pincushion). Full barrel distortion correction is applied in figure 11.9B, image 5 (red arrow), and full pincushion distortion correction is applied in image 6 (red arrow). As with the Auto distortion adjustment, the Manual distortion adjustment is rather minor.
4. When you are happy with the appearance of the image, press or touch OK (Save) to save it, or press the Playback button to cancel. You'll see the new adjusted image on the Monitor.

Settings Recommendation: This function is only somewhat useful because it does not allow for larger corrections. However, it does allow minor distortion correction for images with just a little distortion. If you have no computer available and need to use an image that has a touch of distortion, this function may be helpful.

Perspective Control

When you use a wide-angle lens to take a picture from the base of a tall object, like a building, the object will look like it is falling over backward. You can correct the problem with a large-format, film-based, view camera by using its rise, fall, shift, tilt, and swing controls. Nikon makes perspective-control lenses that perform some of the functions of a view camera, namely tilt and shift—for a significant investment, of course.

Nikon has also given Z6 users some image correction capability with the Straighten, Distortion control, and *Perspective control* functions. We discussed the first two earlier in this chapter. Now let's see how to use Perspective control.

Perspective control allows you to stretch the left, right, top, or bottom of an image in a way that tends to twist leaning objects so they appear straighter in the corrected image. Figure 11.10A, image 3, shows yellow pointers and their indicators (identified by the red arrows). You can move these pointers to change the perspective of the image by tilting the top toward or away from you or rotating the image to the left or right. This is a powerful control because it can help give certain images a much better perspective.

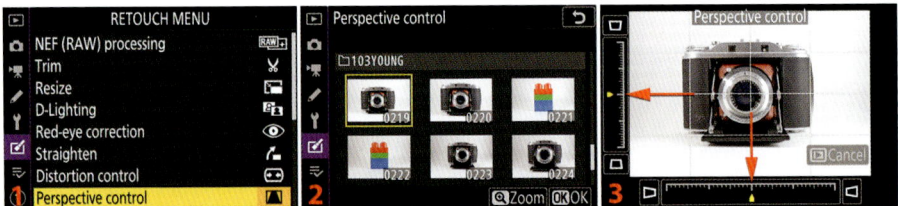

Figure 11.10A: Adjusting an image with Perspective control

Use the following steps to configure Perspective control:

1. Select Perspective control from the Retouch Menu and scroll to the right (figure 11.10A, image 1).
2. Choose an image from the list of thumbnails and press or touch OK to open it (figure 11.10A, image 2).
3. You will see gridlines for edge comparison and two slider controls that are operated by the Multi selector pad or your fingertip (figure 11.10A, image 3). Move the yellow pointer on the vertical scale up or down to tilt the top of the image toward you or away from you. Slide the yellow pointer on the horizontal scale to the left or right to turn the left or right edge toward you or away from you.
4. When the image looks the way you want it to, press or touch OK (Save) to save the image, or press the Playback button to cancel (figures 11.10B and C).

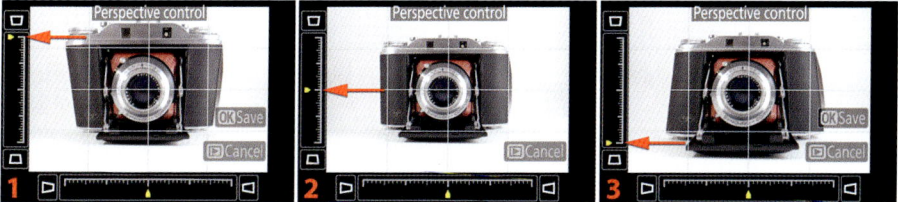

Figure 11.10B: Tilting the image

Figure 11.10B shows what happens to the image when you use the vertical slider on the left side. Notice how the top of the subject tilts either toward you or away from you (forward-to-backward leaning) according to how the vertical slider is positioned.

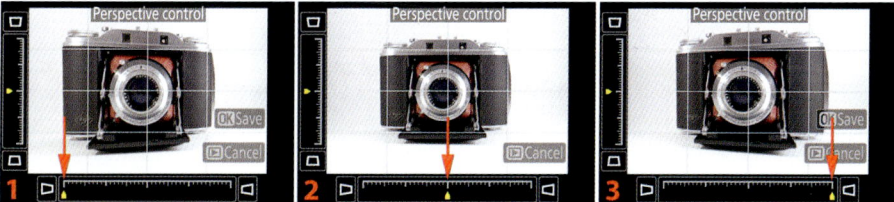

Figure 11.10C: Swinging the image

Figure 11.10C shows how the image swings to the left or right as you move the horizontal slider on the bottom. Can you see how powerful this functionality is to control perspective? The camera automatically crops off the top and bottom of the stretched ends to keep the image looking like a normal rectangle, so the final image will be smaller.

Settings Recommendation: Learn to use this rather powerful function! You now have excellent Perspective control, with no additional lens purchases! Add Straighten for leveling horizons (rotating the image), Distortion control for removing barrel and pincushion distortion, and finally Perspective control to remove angle distortion, and you have the basics of a graphics software program built right into the camera.

Image Overlay

The *Image overlay* function is a nice way to combine two RAW images as if they were taken as a multiple exposure. Basically, you can select a couple of NEF (RAW) shots and combine them into a new overlaid image.

The results can be a lot like what you get when using *Photo Shooting Menu > Multiple exposure,* but Image overlay gives you a visual way to overlay two separate images instead of shooting multiple exposures on one picture.

The results can be high quality because the overlay is done using RAW image data. You can vary the density of each image, with a review display (Overlay) showing how the combined image will appear, before you make the final combination of the two images.

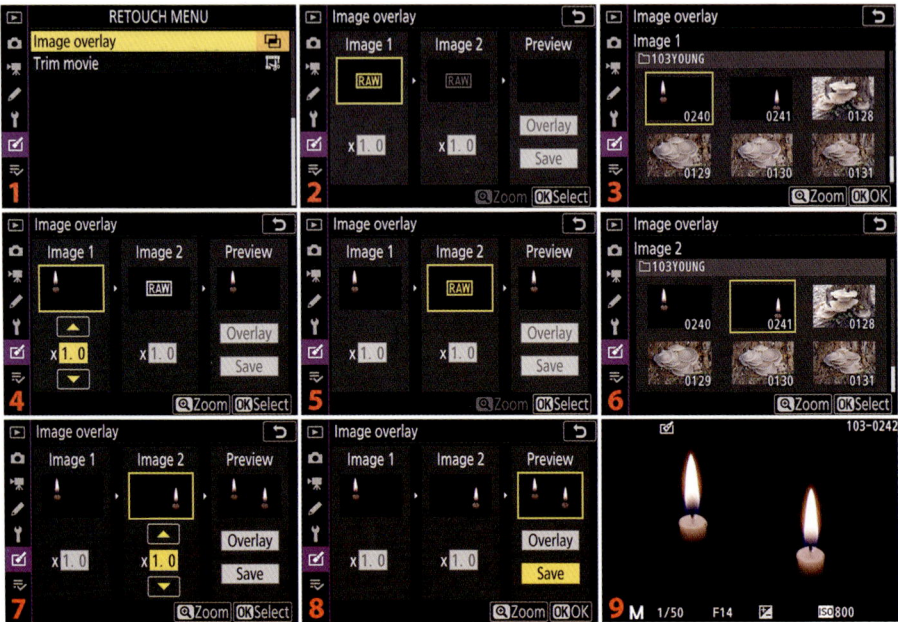

Figure 11.11: Image overlay settings

Use the following steps to do an Image overlay:

1. Select Image overlay from the Retouch Menu and scroll to the right (figure 11.11, image 1).
2. Select the RAW Image 1 box (outlined in yellow in figure 11.11, image 2) from the combination screen and press or touch OK (Select) to open the selection screen.
3. Select an image from the selection screen (figure 11.11, image 3). Press or touch OK again to return to the combination screen with an image selected in the Image 1 position (figure 11.11, image 4). You can vary the gain of the first image by using the Multi selector pad or tapping on the yellow up/down pointers to scroll up or down in the X1.0 field (figure 11.11, image 4). The X1.0 setting is variable from X0.1 to X2.0. It lets you control how bright or dark (dense) an image is so it can more closely match the density of the other image in the overlay. X1.0 is normal image density, as shown.
4. Use the Multi selector pad or tap the RAW symbol under Image 2 to move the yellow box to the RAW Image 2 position (figure 11.11, image 5). Press or touch OK (Select) to open the image selection screen for the second picture.
5. Highlight the second image (figure 11.11, image 6) and press or touch OK (Select) to insert the image into the Image 2 position (figure 11.11, image 7). As mentioned in step 3,

you can use the X1.0 field to vary the density of an image, in this case the second image in the overlay (figure 11.11, image 7). Try to match the density of Image 1 as much as possible to provide a realistic overlay.

6. Use the Multi selector pad or tap the Preview symbol to move the yellow box to the Preview area. You will see two selections below it: Overlay and Save (figure 11.11, image 8). Choose Overlay or Save and press or touch OK to achieve the following results:

   a. If you select Overlay, the Z6 will temporarily combine the images and you will see another screen that displays a larger view of the new image (not shown). You can press or touch OK (Save) to save the image with a new file name, or you can press the checkered Zoom out button to return to the previous screen.

   b. If you choose Save instead of Overlay and press or touch OK, the Z6 immediately combines the two images and saves the image with a new file name without letting you review the image first (figure 11.11, image 9). Basically, the Save selection saves now, and Overlay gives you a preview of the combination so you can modify or save it.

Settings Recommendation: This is an easy way to overlay images without a computer. There are some drawbacks, though. One image may have a strong background that is impossible to remove no matter how much you adjust the gain or image density (X0.1 to X2.0). This is a situation in which a computer excels because you can use software tools like masking in Photoshop to remove parts of the background and make a more realistic overlay. However, if you must combine two images in the field, you have a way to do it in-camera.

Trim Movie

Trim movie gives you a two-step process to cut a section out of the middle of a movie created with your Z6, or you can remove a beginning or ending segment. In addition, you can save an individual frame as a still image from anywhere in the movie.

There are two individual parts to the process of trimming a movie—choosing a start point and choosing an end point. You can use one or the other, or both. When you finalize one of the Start point and/or End point selections, the camera saves the file as a new movie with a new file name. This tends to create a bunch of smaller movies on your memory card that you'll need to delete, taking care that you don't delete the wrong one. There are two parts to Trim movie:

- **Choose start/end point:** This allows you to delete frames from the beginning or the end of your movie and choose a new starting or ending point.
- **Save current frame:** You can take a low-resolution 16:9 ratio JPEG snapshot of any frame in the movie.

Choose Start/End Point

You can start this entire process directly from the Retouch Menu, or you can select Trim movie from the *i* Menu when a video is showing on the Monitor (press the *i* button). The steps are basically the same except that you choose a movie from a list of movies in the Retouch Menu instead of starting with a movie on the Monitor, from the *i* Menu.

We will use the Retouch Menu method since we are in the Retouch Menu chapter. Just remember that these steps apply also to the Trim movie function under Retouch on the *i* Menu.

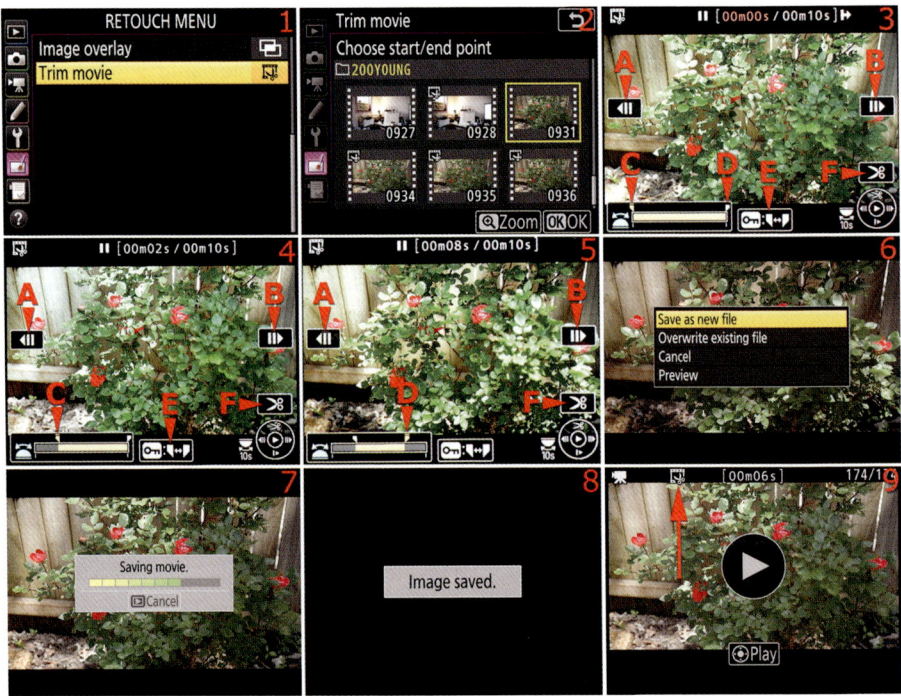

Figure 11.12A: Edit movie directly from the Retouch Menu

Following are the steps to choose a new start and end point for a movie directly from the Retouch Menu:

1. Highlight Trim Movie on the Retouch Menu and scroll to the right (figure 11.12A, image 1).
2. Choose a movie from the list of movies and press or touch OK to select it. You can briefly zoom in on the movie to make sure it is the one you want to edit by pressing and holding the Zoom in button or tapping the Zoom control (figure 11.12A, image 2).
3. In figure 11.12A, image 3, you will see several important controls labeled in red letters, A–F. The A and B touch buttons (top) control the positioning (trimming) of the yellow beginning- and end-of-movie trim tabs C and D (bottom). To trim the movie, you must

select either the beginning-of-movie trim tab C or the end-of-movie trim tab D. You can toggle between the C and D trim tabs by touching the trim tab change button E. The active trim tab (C or D) has a tiny yellow line just above the tab, as seen in image 3 at the tip of the C label. Scissors button F allows you to save the trimmed movie, as long as you have trimmed at least 5 seconds from the video length.

4. As seen in figure 11.12A, image 4, the beginning-of-movie trim tab has been moved to the right, signifying that frames have been removed from the start of the video. To move this tab (trimming frames), you will press the A or B touch buttons and watch the movie as it scrolls, until you find the position where you want the video to begin. If you don't want to trim anything from the end, you can save the movie immediately by tapping the scissors touch button (F), skipping the next step (step 5), and moving directly to step 6.

5. You can trim footage from the end of the movie by tapping the trim tab change button E. The emphasis will immediately switch from the beginning-of-movie trim tab C to the end-of-movie trim tab D (notice the tiny yellow line moving above the active tab; figure 11.12A, image 5). Now when you tap the A or B touch buttons, you will move the end-of-movie trim tab until you find your new end-of-movie position, dropping frames from the end of the video. When you have found the best movie ending position, tap the scissors touch button F to decide what to do with the new shortened movie. (**Note:** You can touch and drag either of the movie trim tabs C and D with your finger for high-speed movement through a long movie. Use the A and B touch buttons to fine-tune the trim position. A trim tab has to be active before you can drag it directly. Tap touch button E to toggle between the tabs.)

6. As shown in figure 11.12A, image 6, the camera is now ready to Save, Overwrite, Cancel, or Preview. Here is a list of what each option on the menu does:
   a. **Save as new file:** If you choose Save as new file, the camera will both retain the old, longer movie and create the new, shorter movie with its own new file name.
   b. **Overwrite existing file:** If you choose Overwrite existing file (be careful), the camera will overwrite the older, long movie with the new, shorter one.
   c. **Cancel:** If you choose Cancel, the camera returns to the location shown in figure 11.12A, image 4 or 5, and awaits further input from you.
   d. **Preview:** If you select Preview, the camera will play the movie from and/or to the position of the new cut point. In other words, it plays what would become the new, shorter movie if you save it. When the Preview movie is finished playing, the camera will return to the menu shown in figure 11.12A, image 6, and await further input.

7. Once you have chosen to save the file, the progress bar shown in figure 11.12A, image 7, will appear as the file is being saved to a brand-new, shorter movie file. When the save is complete, the screen shown in figure 11.12A, image 8, will appear briefly, informing you: *Image saved*.

8. Finally, the screen shown in figure 11.12A, image 9, will appear. The final screen is the new, shorter movie, saved under a new file name—as shown by the frame and scissors symbol at the red arrow.

Note: Your movie must be at least 1 second long when you're done or the camera will re-fuse to cut any more frames and will give you this terse message: *Movies cannot be edited to a length of less than 1 s.*

Save Current Frame

You can save an individual low-resolution frame from anywhere in the movie. The still im-age frame size is based on the format of the movie (2160p or 1080p), which is set in *Movie Shooting Menu > Frame size/frame rate:*

- A still image created from a 3840×2160 (4K or UHD) movie is a little larger than 8 megapixels.
- A still image created from a 1920×1080 (Full HD) movie is a little larger than 2 megapixels.

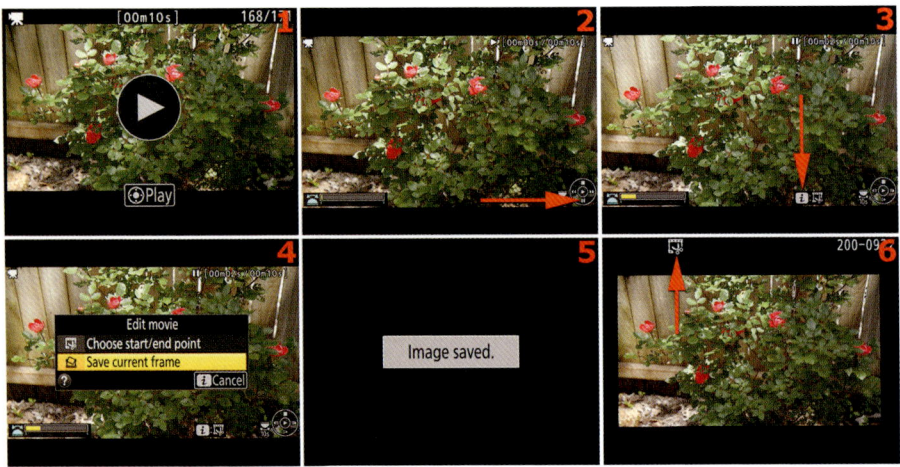

Figure 11.12B: Save an individual frame from a movie

Use these steps to save a single frame from the movie as a still image (using the Playback Retouch Menu):

1. Press the Playback button and scroll to the movie that contains the frame you want to save (figure 11.12B, image 1). Press the OK button or tap Play to play the movie.
2. Let the movie play until you reach the approximate point where you want to grab the frame from the movie, and then press down on the Multi selector pad to pause the movie (figure 11.12B, image 2).
3. The screen shown in figure 11.12B, image 3, will now appear. You can scroll left or right with the Multi selector pad to move one frame at a time while the movie is paused. You can also turn the rear Main command dial to jump forward or backward by 10 seconds in the movie. Once you've found the frame you want to save, press the *i* button to open the Edit movie menu.

4. Highlight Save current frame and press the OK button (figure 11.12B, image 4).
5. The Z6 will now cut out the frame you selected and save it under a new file name. A screen that says *Image saved* will appear briefly (figure 11.12B, image 5), and the new low-res image will appear on the Monitor (figure 11.12B, image 6).

Settings Recommendation: The Trim movie and Save current frame functions provide some editing functionality for those who do not like using a computer. Trimming a movie is better done in software like Apple Final Cut Pro or Adobe Premier Pro. Plus, the Z6 has the ability to capture a frame from a movie while it is being recorded, simply by pressing down on the Shutter-release button.

Side-by-Side Comparison

Side-by-side comparison allows you to compare an image you've retouched with its original source image. Interestingly, this function is not available from the main Retouch Menu. You'll find it on the Playback Retouch Menu only, which you access by pressing the *i* button when a picture is displayed on the Monitor.

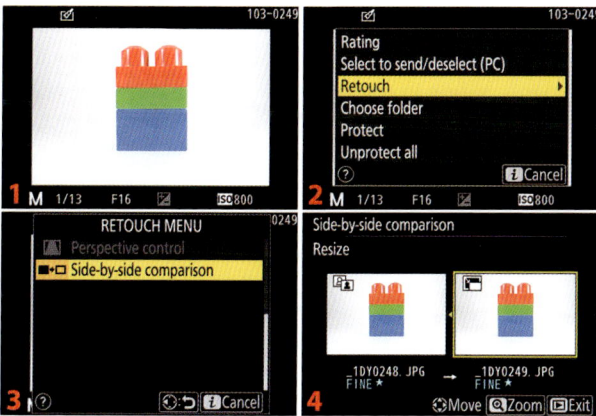

Figure 11.13: Side-by-side comparison

Here are the steps to compare an original and retouched image side by side on the camera's Monitor:

1. Press the Playback button and find the image you want to compare to its retouched versions (figure 11.13, image 1).
2. Press the *i* button to access the *i* Menu, select Retouch, and scroll to the right (figure 11.13, image 2).
3. Scroll all the way down to the bottom of the Retouch Menu, select Side-by-side comparison, and scroll to the right (figure 11.13, image 3). The original image will appear on the left, and one of the retouched versions will appear on the right (figure 11.13, image 4).

4. When you have performed multiple Retouch operations on an image, look for tiny yellow pointers on top, bottom, or sides. Scroll in the direction of those pointers to see all the operations performed on the original image. The two images showing reflect that the original image had a D-Lighting session applied (left) and was trimmed to a smaller size.

Settings Recommendation: This function is very convenient because you can choose the original image or one of the retouched images, and the camera is smart enough to place them in the proper position in the Side-by-side comparison. You can tell an image has been retouched by looking for the retouch icon in the upper-left corner of the image when it's displayed on the Monitor.

Author's Conclusion

Nikon has given camera users who dislike computers many ways to work with their images in-camera. Although the Retouch Menu is not as fully featured as a computer graphics program, it does allow you to do quick one-off conversions for convenience.

I didn't think this group of Retouch Menu functions would be all that useful to me when I first read about them. However, in the field I find myself using them more than I expected. Whether or not you use them often, it's good to know you have them for emergency use.

Next, we'll move into the final menu system in the camera. It's called My Menu, and it may become very valuable to you as you learn how it works. It's a place to put your often-used, favorite settings so you can get to them very quickly. Let's see how My Menu and its cousin, Recent Settings, work in the next chapter.

12 My Menu and Recent Settings

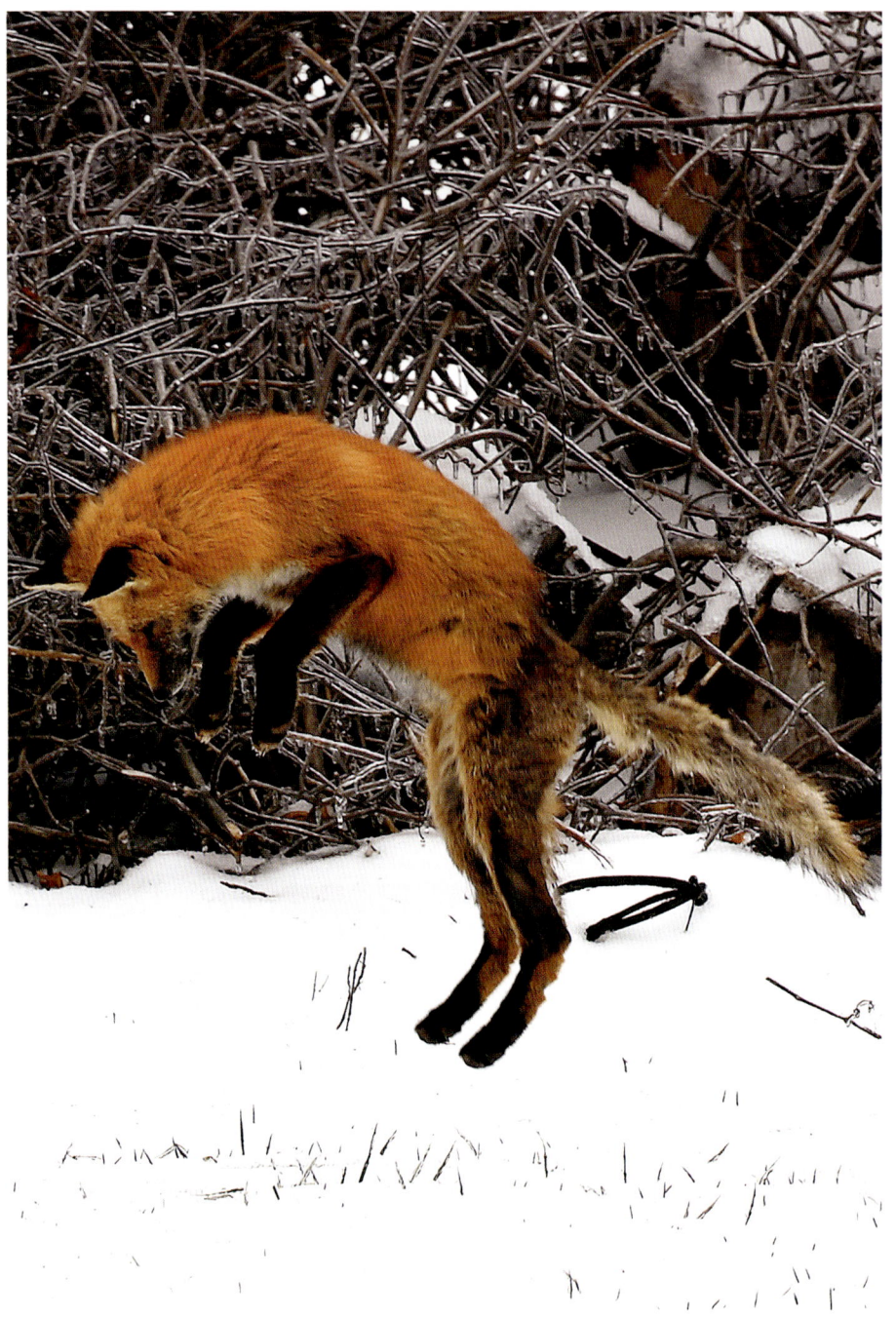

Backyard Passerby © 2019 Peter Mandzuk (*Petzuk*)

As you have read through this book and experimented with your camera, you've surely noticed that the Z6 has a large number of menus, screens, functions, and settings. When I took pictures of the camera's menus and screens for this book, I ended up with hundreds of images. That many screens can be complex to navigate. We need a shortcut menu for our most-used settings—a place to keep the functions we're constantly changing.

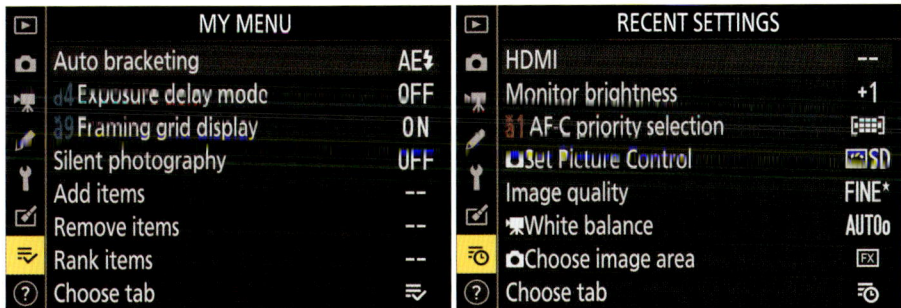

Figure 12.0: My Menu and Recent Settings

Nikon has given us two specialty menus in the Z6: My Menu and Recent Settings (figure 12.0). These are both designed to give us exactly what we need—a menu that we can customize with only our most-used functions, and a menu of recent changes to functions.

For instance, I often turn Custom Setting d4 Exposure delay mode on and off. Instead of having to search through all the Custom settings, trying to remember exactly where Exposure delay mode lives, I simply added that Custom setting to My Menu. Now, whenever I want to enable Exposure delay mode, I can just go to My Menu and select it. I can do it quickly and without searching.

I rarely use Recent Settings. I prefer the control I get with my own personally customizable menu—My Menu. The Recent Settings menu has very little flexibility because it's an automatically updated, camera-controlled menu system. On the other hand, My Menu is a personal collection of links to my most-used settings. It is completely configurable.

We'll consider both menus in this chapter, with an emphasis on configuring My Menu.

What's the Difference between My Menu and Recent Settings?

You can *manually* add up to 20 settings from the other menus in the camera to *My Menu*. The *Recent Settings Menu* will *automatically* show the last 20 settings you've modified in the other menus, but it's not configurable. The two menus are mutually exclusive and cannot appear on the Z6 at the same time. One takes the place of the other when you select the Choose tab setting at the end of each menu. The most important difference between the two menus is the level of control you have over what appears on them. My Menu is completely customizable and does not change unless you change it, and as mentioned previously, Recent Settings simply shows the last 20 changes you've made to your camera's settings. Recent Settings will change every time you change a setting in your camera. However, because it shows the last 20 changes, you ought to be able to find the ones you change most often somewhere in the list.

My Menu

My Menu is *my* menu! I can add, remove, or rank (position on menu) virtually any camera setting found on one of the primary menus. When I use My Menu, I don't have to spend time looking for the function buried in the main menu system. Because I often place my most used functions on My Menu, I'm glad to have it immediately available.

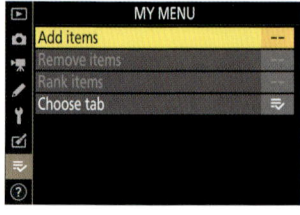

Figure 12.1: My Menu

My Menu is the last selection on the Z6's menu system (figure 12.1). Its icon looks like a list with a check mark on it.

When you first look at My Menu, you'll see nothing but the following menu options:

- Add items
- Remove items
- Rank items
- Choose tab

Let's examine each of these menu choices in detail.

Add Items

To add an item to My Menu, you'll need to locate the item first. Search through the menus until you find the setting you want to add, and then make note of where it's located. You could do this from within the Add items menu, but I find that it's harder to locate what I'm looking for if I haven't already confirmed where it lives. Is it under the Custom Setting Menu or one of the Shooting Menus, or maybe the Setup Menu? Make a note of where items you want to add to My Menu are located before you start adding them, or it may take longer than necessary.

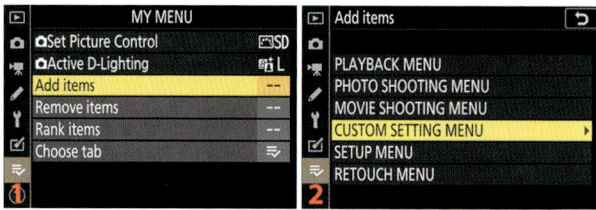

Figure 12.2: Adding items to My Menu

After you've found the item you want to add and made note of its location, use the following steps:

1. Select Add items from My Menu and scroll to the right. Notice that I've already added Set Picture Control and Active D-Lighting to My Menu (figure 12.2, image 1). I want to add something else.
2. The Add items screen shows all the primary menus available in the Z6 except My Menu and Recent Settings (figure 12.2, image 2). Let's add one of my favorite functions, Exposure delay mode.

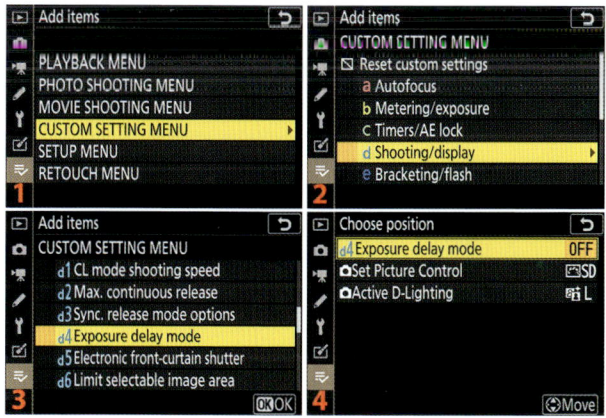

Figure 12.3: Adding Exposure delay mode to My Menu

3. Figure 12.3 starts where figure 12.2 ends. We already know that Exposure delay mode is under the Custom Setting Menu, so let's scroll down to it and then scroll to the right (figure 12.3, image 1).
4. We now see the Custom Setting Menu and Custom settings a through e (figure 12.3, image 2). Scroll down to d Shooting/display and then scroll to the right. ***Note:*** There are more Custom settings than appear on image 2. If you scroll down, you will also find Custom settings f and g.
5. Figure 12.3, image 3, shows the d4 Exposure delay mode function that we want to add. All we have to do is highlight it and press or touch OK. Once that is done, the Z6 switches to the Choose position (Rank) screen (figure 12.3, image 4).

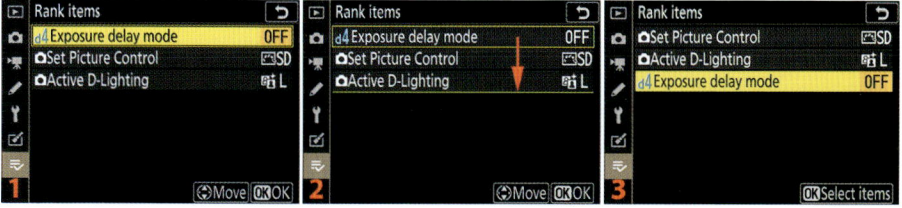

Figure 12.4: Choosing a position for Custom setting d4 Exposure delay mode on My Menu

6. Figure 12.4 begins where figure 12.3 ends. Since I've already added a couple of other items to My Menu, I now have to decide the order in which I want them to be presented. The new d4 Exposure delay mode setting is on top because it is the newest entry (figure 12.4, image 1). I think I'll move it down two rows and leave Set Picture Control in the top position.

7. To move the position of the selected item, simply scroll down. The d4 Exposure delay mode setting has a yellow box around it (figure 12.4, image 2). As you scroll down, a yellow underline moves down the list (red arrow). This yellow underline represents the place to which I want to move d4 Exposure delay mode. When I've decided on the position and have the yellow underline in place, I just press or touch OK. The screen pops back to the first My Menu screen, with everything arranged the way I want it (figure 12.4, image 3). Notice that d4 Exposure delay mode is now at the bottom of the list.

Remove Items

Now that we have discussed how to Add items, let's examine how to Remove items. The Z6 allows me to open the Set Picture Control menu by pressing the *i* button and choosing it from the *i* Menu. I think I'd rather use the Set Picture Control function on the *i* Menu than access it via My Menu, so I'll remove it from My Menu and save one of the 20 slots for something else.

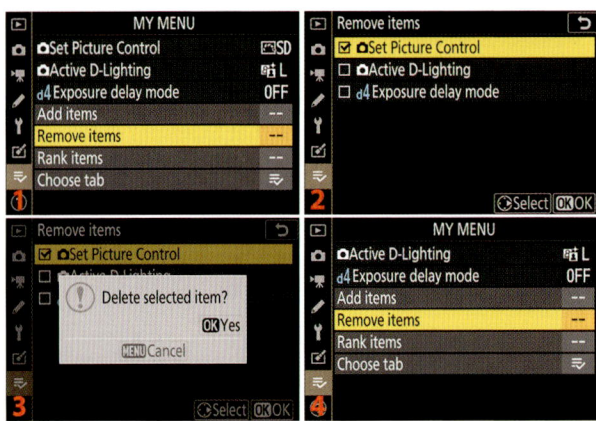

Figure 12.5: Removing an item from My Menu

Use the following steps to Remove items from My Menu:

1. Select Remove items from My Menu and scroll to the right (figure 12.5, image 1).

2. The Remove items screen presents a series of selections with check boxes (figure 12.5, image 2). Whichever boxes you check will be deleted when you press or touch OK. You can check the boxes by highlighting the line item you want to delete and scrolling right with the Multi selector pad. Pressing right on the Multi selector pad acts like a toggle and will check or uncheck a line item. You can also touch the check box with your fingertip to toggle a check mark on and off.

3. When you've checked the settings you want to remove, press or touch OK. A small white box pops up and asks, *Delete selected item?* (figure 12.5, image 3).
4. Pressing or touching OK (Yes) gives your approval and removes the Set Picture Control setting from My Menu. A screen displaying *Done* shows briefly, and then the Z6 switches back to the My Menu screen. You can press the MENU button to cancel if you decide you don't want to remove an item. You will notice in image 4 that Set Picture Control is now gone.

Rank Items

Ranking items is similar to positioning new additions in My Menu. All the Rank items selection does is move an item up or down in My Menu. You can switch your most-used My Menu items to the top of the list.

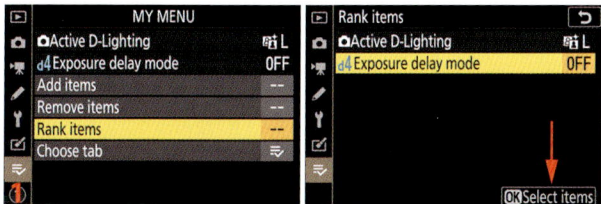

Figure 12.6: Ranking items in My Menu

Use the following steps to Rank items:

1. Select Rank items from My Menu and scroll to the right (figure 12.6, image 1).
2. Now you'll see the Rank items screen and all the current My Menu items (figure 12.6, image 2). I've decided that I use d4 Exposure delay mode more than Active D-Lighting, so I'll move it to the top. Highlight the item you want to move and press the OK button or tap OK Select items (image 2, red arrow). Continue with figure 12.7.

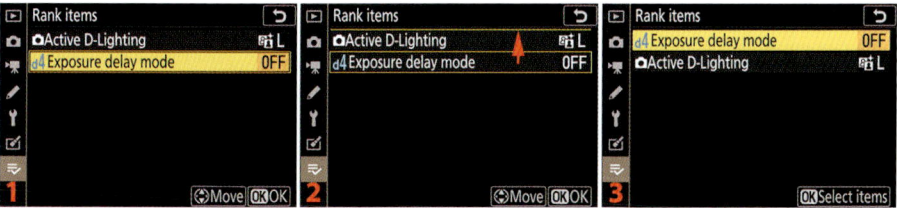

Figure 12.7: Ranking items in My Menu (continued)

3. A yellow box will surround your selected item (e.g., d4 Exposure delay mode). Press up on the Multi selector pad or tap the Move control (figure 12.7, image 1).
4. This action moves the yellow positioning underline to the top of the list (figure 12.7, image 2, red arrow). Press or touch OK to select the new position, and d4 Exposure delay mode will move to the top of the list (figure 12.7, image 3).

Choose Tab

Choose tab allows you to switch between My Menu and Recent Settings. Both menus have the Choose tab selection as their last menu choice.

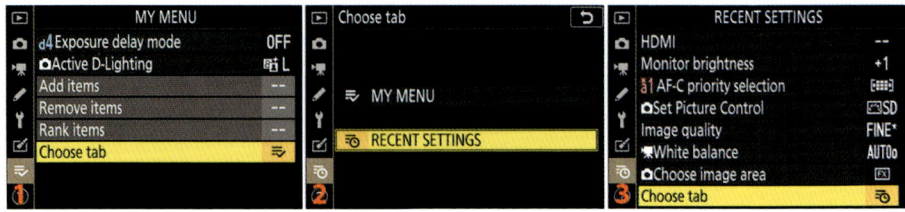

Figure 12.8: Selecting My Menu or Recent Settings (Choose tab)

Use the following steps to switch between My Menu and Recent Settings:

1. At the bottom of My Menu, select Choose tab and scroll to the right (figure 12.8, image 1).
2. You'll now have a choice between My Menu and Recent Settings. Choose Recent Settings and press the OK button, or tap Recent Settings to select it (figure 12.8, image 2).
3. The Recent Settings screen will now appear, completely replacing My Menu on the main menu screen (figure 12.8, image 3). Notice that it has a Choose tab selection at the bottom, just as My Menu does. The items you see on the Recent Settings menu are items I have recently adjusted. Your camera will display a different list of items. The last 20 items adjusted will be displayed when you scroll up or down on the Recent Settings menu. If you have never used the Recent Settings menu, the Choose tab selection is all you will see. As you make adjustments to other menu items, they will appear on the Recent Settings menu.
4. Select Choose tab and press the OK button to return to My Menu.

Clearly, this is a circular action. You can use the Choose tab selection as a toggle between the two menus. When you do, one menu replaces the other as the last selection on the camera's main menu screen.

Settings Recommendation: You can see how My Menu gives you nice control over a customized menu that is entirely yours. Configure it however you want by choosing from selections in the primary menus. My Menu will save you significant time when you look for your 20 most-used selections.

If you're inclined to use Recent Settings, just remember that after you pass 20 camera setting adjustments, the next setting you use will jump to the top of the list, moving everything down by one position. The last item on the list will simply disappear.

Now, let's take a look at Recent Settings in a little more detail.

Recent Settings

Recent Settings is very simple. This menu remembers the last 20 changes you've made to your Z6 camera. Each menu selection that was modified is stored in a temporary place called Recent Settings.

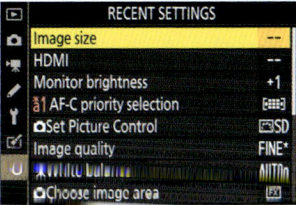

If you change something in your camera that's not already on the Recent Settings menu (figure 12.9), it will be added to the menu, replacing the oldest change with your new one—at the top of the list—if there is no room left at the bottom (i.e., you've exceeded 20 items).

This can be a convenient way to find something you've changed recently but whose location you have trouble remembering on the main menu systems.

Figure 12.9: Recent Settings Menu

Settings Recommendation: If you want a more permanent menu for your favorite changes to the Z6, you'll need to enable the My Menu system instead of the Recent Settings Menu. The Recent Settings Menu is fine, but I want to directly control what settings I have quick access to without searching. My Menu is my choice!

Afterword

Check the book's downloadable resources section from time to time because I intend to keep on adding material to supplement *Mastering the Nikon Z6*. The downloadable resources are found at this web addresses:

http://rockynook.com/NikonZ6

Stay in touch with me by using the following points of contact:

- ***Website:*** www.MasterYourNikon.com
- ***Facebook:*** www.facebook.com/groups/MasterYourNikon/
- ***Instagram:*** www.instagram.com/masteryournikon/
- ***Twitter:*** https://twitter.com/YourNikon
- ***Flickr:*** www.flickr.com/photos/masteryournikon/
- ***Pinterest:*** www.pinterest.com/MasterYourNikon/

If you will follow me, I will follow you on social media. Let's share our images and photographic experiences with each other. I hope to talk with you soon!

Thank You!

I'd like to express my personal appreciation to you for buying this book and for sticking with me all the way to the end of it. I sincerely hope that it has been useful to you and that you'll recommend my books to your Nikon-using friends.

Keep on capturing time…

Credits for Chapter Opening Images

Chapter 1: *Ready for Her Chicks* © **2019 Fred Crowden** (freqflyerfred)
Nikkor 28–300mm f/3.5–5.6 lens at 300mm (on FTZ adapter), 1/1000 sec at f/5.6, ISO 3600
I took this photo at the Hummingbird Aviary in the Arizona-Sonora Desert Museum, located west of Tucson and surrounded by Saguaro National Park. I was using a birds-in-flight camera setup to capture the quick movements of the hummingbirds. My wife called me over to grab a quick shot of this mother nesting. The docents bring in nesting materials (such as poodle fur!) from home and from the desert, which are cleaned and then hung in a netted bag for the birds to use. I realized when I got home that this was the most charming shot of the day. The auto ISO gave me a great exposure and negligible noise.

Chapter 2: *Grand Canyon at Sunset* © **2019 Francine Dollinger** (Francine)
Nikkor Z 24–70mm f/4 S lens at 24mm, 1/13 sec at f/10, ISO 100
This is a combined stacked image from five RAW images. I just started using focus stacking and fell in love with doing it. There is nothing like a sunset at the Grand Canyon.

Chapter 3: *Indecisive Princess Amirah* © **2018 Donald E. Jose** (donaldejose)
Nikkor Z 35mm f/1.8 S prime lens, 1/160 sec at f/1.8, ISO 640 (using LED constant lighting)
Nine-year-old granddaughter Amirah was going to Disneyworld. Her grandmother purchased a number of princess outfits so Amirah could feel like a Disney princess when she was there. I photographed Amirah in many of these outfits and asked her to visually respond to different words so I could obtain different facial expressions and body poses from her. This expression and pose was her response to the word "indecisive." I shot this image to test LED constant light shooting with the Z6's EVF and ISO. Amirah was lit with two octagonal softboxes, and the colorful fantasy background was created by placing gels over two LED lights. It was nice to be able to work with constant lighting and an EVF (instead of with flash and an OVF) so I could balance the brightness of the four constant LED lights through the viewfinder prior to the exposure. One of the great advantages of the Z6 (and Z7) is the ability to do this, especially when fine-tuning lighting ratios on the subject and also brightness between the subject and the background.

Chapter 4: *Pastel Blossom* © **2019 Don L. Williams** (donlwilliams1966)
Nikkor Z 24–70mm f/4 S lens at 70mm, 1/200 sec at f/5, ISO 400
I took this image in the early morning at a local botanical garden. The blossom was just beginning to open, showing the beautiful pastel colors of green, pink, and a hint of purple. This was one of the first pictures I took with my new Z6.

Chapter 5: *Mono Lake Tufas in Snow* © **2019 Eric Bowles** (ericbowles)
Nikkor Z 24–70 f/4 S lens at 24mm, 1/200 sec at f/11, ISO 100
Mono Lake is an ancient, high-elevation lake in the Eastern Sierra of California. The tufa spires of calcium carbonate were formed many years ago by the interaction of fresh water

and the alkaline water of the lake. During winter, the high elevation leads to lots of snow—making it a great photo destination if you don't mind walking through snow for half a mile. Throughout the year, this remote lake is great for photography, but the snow on the tufa spires is something special and why I was scouting it for the Nikonians ANPAT in 2020. I used base ISO 100 to maximize dynamic range of the bright scene. The EVF of the Z6 made it easy to check the histogram and virtual horizon to confirm the exposure and make sure the camera was level before making the image.

Chapter 6: *JS, the Cosplay Pirate* © **2019 Wen Wu** *(wwp512)*
AF Nikkor 80–200mm f/2.8D ED (on FTZ adapter) at 145mm, 1/2000 sec at f/2.8, ISO 320
I participated in a local "street-meet" event. This creative cosplayer got into the duck pond with his homemade raft. It soon sank and people were not getting the pictures they anticipated. I, however, waited a few moments longer and captured this image as he maintained his character and stared into my lens. Of interest is the realization that my 1980s zoom lens will not autofocus with the Z6 (first time out with this combo). The EVF plus manual focus assist came to the rescue and I was able to continue my shoot with this legendary F-mounted lens.

Chapter 7: *Tenmuki in Xidi Village* © **2019 Wen Wu** *(wwp512)*
Nikkor 85mm f/1.8 lens (on FTZ adapter), 1/500 sec at f/2.8, ISO 140
I was walking the Ancient Xidi Village in China, looking for one of those alley shots. A local gentleman saw me with my Z6 and started a conversation. He ended up showing me his favorite location. I had my daughter walk to me, adding human interest. The light rain added the mood and the reflection on the ground.

Chapter 8: *Societies Masterclass Model Shoot* © **2019 Garrett Hayes** *(Garrett Hayes)*
Nikkor Z 24–70mm f/4 S lens at 58mm, 1/200 sec at f/9, ISO 100
I was in London in January 2019 attending the Societies Photographic Convention at the Novotel Hotel. The event was a portrait-lighting master class with Panikos Hajistilly and we were given freedom to direct and photograph the models ourselves.

Chapter 9: *Miniature Orchid* © **2019 Robert Rogers** *(a4str)*
Nikkor Z 24–70mm f/4 S lens at 70mm, 0.2 sec at f/8, ISO 100
It was a dreary, cold, snowy, April day in Wisconsin and I desperately wanted to make an image with my new Nikon Z6—preferably something that would cheer me up. I spied my wife's miniature orchid on the plant stand and an idea for an image formed. I set the potted orchid on a table two feet in front of a white Bristol board. I placed two floor lamps with daylight bulbs on either side of the orchid to give even light on the orchid with no shadows on the white background. The Z6 was on a tripod. My aim was to create an image that had a soft, somewhat ethereal look. I edited the raw image in Capture One with slight modifications to color, but no increase in sharpness and a slight decrease in clarity. The resulting image picked my spirits up and reminded me that spring was just around the corner.

Chapter 10: *Tic Tacs in a Bottle* © 2019 Dave Gould *(davegould68)*
AF-S Micro Nikkor 105mm f/2.8G ED VR lens (on FTZ adapter), 1/200 sec at f/8, ISO 100
I am restricted to home these days, so a little table-top photography helps to pass the time, and I find it quite challenging. My granddaughter contributed a couple of boxes of Tic Tacs to use in a bottle that normally stores olive oil. I used BBF with the AF-S Mode and Pin-point Focusing here. The camera was mounted on a Manfrotto Tripod with an X-PRO head. I was using an SB-800 (in commander mode, with off-camera cord) and two SB-910 speedlights with gels. Post-processing in Nikon NX-D and Photoshop CC with a little NIK thrown in for good measure.

Chapter 11: *Waterfall in the Wilderness* © 2019 John Miner *(D850fan)*
Nikkor Z 24–70mm f/4 S lens at 24mm, 30 sec at f/11, ISO 100 (ND6 filter)
I took this image in the Gifford Pinchot National Forest in Southwest Washington, with me and my tripod standing in six inches of very cold water, early on an overcast June morning. The forests of the Pacific Northwest are filled with waterfalls and I like nothing better than hiking with my Nikon Z6 to photograph these beautiful places.

Chapter 12: *Backyard Passerby* © 2019 Peter Mandzuk *(Petzuk)*
Nikkor 28–300 f/3.5–5.6 lens at 300mm (on FTZ adapter), 1/320 sec at f/5.6, ISO 200
This image was taken in my backyard just before sunset. The fox was trying to catch a small, unseen critter. The fox repeatedly jumped and burrowed its nose into the snow while unsuccessfully trying to catch it. This gave me the time to get my camera equipment together. The critter eventually scurried between the fox's legs and into the brush.

Rear Cover © 2019 Jacques Grilli (grillij)
Nikkor Z 24–70mm f/4 S at 70mm, 1/750 sec at f/8, ISO 100
I took this picture on May 5, 2019, in Morin Heights, Quebec, in the early morning. The sun was still low, facing the horse, while the horse was running freely, almost showing off for the photographer. This shot shows the quality of the Z6 combination with the new Nikkor Z 24–70mm f/4 S lens.

Index

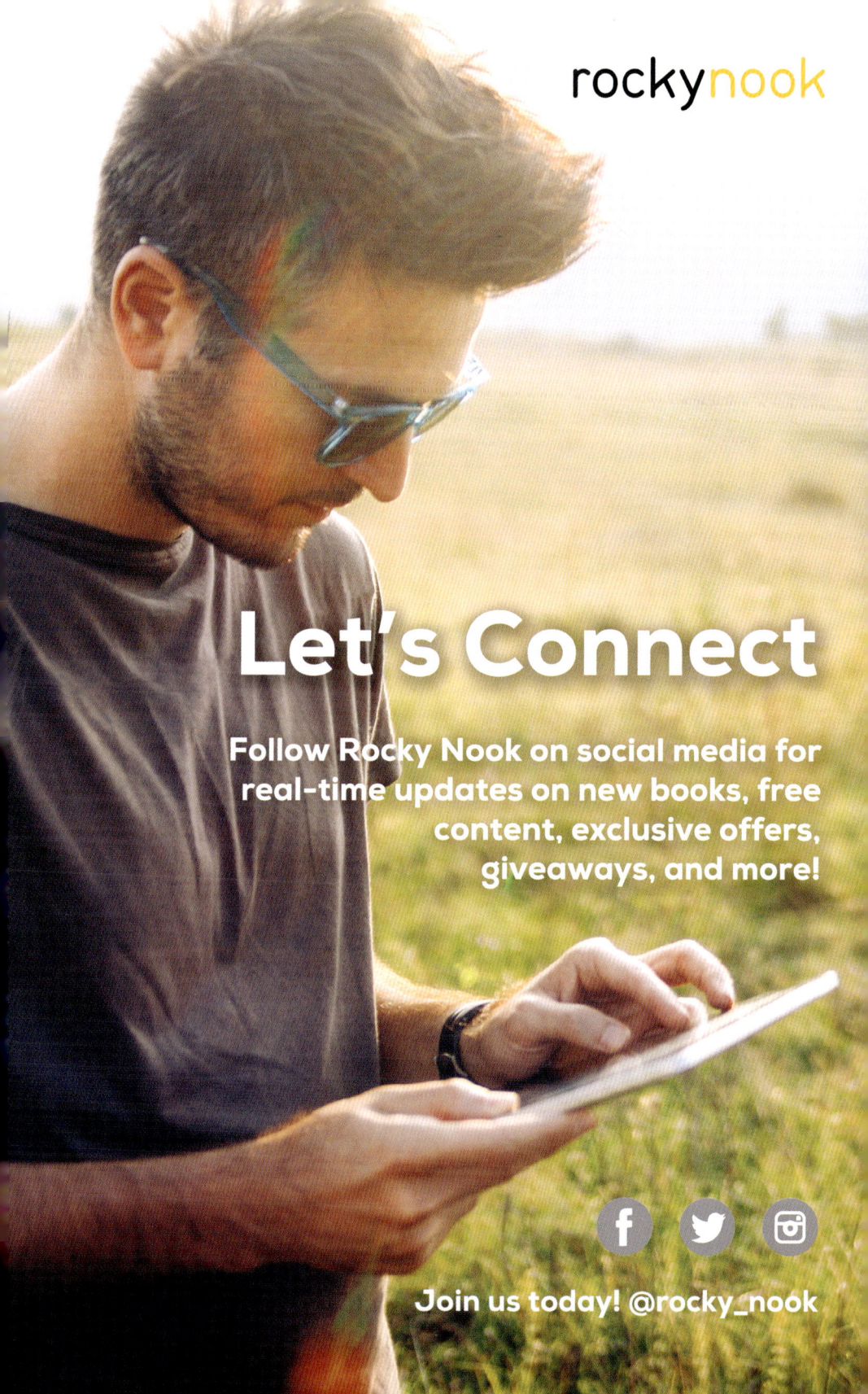

Don't close the book on us yet!

 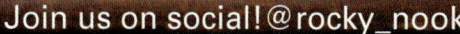 Join us on social! @rocky_nook

rockynook